Applied Industrial / Organizational Psychology

Applied Industrial / Organizational Psychology

Michael G. Aamodt
Radford University

Wadsworth Publishing Company
Belmont, California
A Division of Wadsworth, Inc.

Psychology Editor: Kenneth King
Editorial Assistant: Michelle Palacio
Production Editor: Deborah Cogan
Managing Designer: James Chadwick
Print Buyer: Martha Branch
Art Editor: Harry Voigt
Text and Cover Designer: Harry Voigt
Copy Editor: Steven Bailey
Photo Researcher: Sarah Bendersky
Compositor: Bi-Comp, Inc.
Cover Photographer: Eric Meola/The Image Bank
Signing Representative: Tom Orsi

Printed in the United States of America   85
1 2 3 4 5 6 7 8 9 10—95 94 93 92 91

Library of Congress Cataloging-in-Publication Data

Aamodt, Michael G.
    Applied industrial/organizational psychology / Michael G. Aamodt.
        p.   cm.
    Includes bibliographical references and index.
    ISBN 0-534-13770-9
    1. Psychology, Industrial.   I. Title.
HF5548.8.A17   1990
158.7—dc20   90-12395
                                                          CIP

Contents

4

Employee Selection: Recruiting and Interviewing / 134

5

Employee Selection: References and Testing / 174

6

Evaluating Employee Performance / 220

7

Designing and Evaluating Training Systems / 266

8

Leadership / 304

9

Group Behavior and Conflict / 340

10

Employee Motivation and Satisfaction / 374

11

Communication / 408

12

Working Conditions and Absenteeism / 442

Preface

I am convinced that Industrial/Organizational Psychology can enhance the quality of a person's life more than almost any other field. This opinion is based on the fact that most of us spend more of our waking hours at work than we do at any other activity in our lives. Support for this opinion can be found by listening to people talk. When people we know are unhappy, they often describe the "terrible problems" with their jobs. When people are happy, they often brag about their jobs and the organizations for which they work. Thus, a person who is happy and productive in his or her job will have a higher quality life than a person who is mismatched with his or her job.

The process of selecting and maintaining happy and productive employees is a complicated one and there are many different opinions about how this process is best accomplished. From this text, the reader will learn about the different approaches and, I hope, will come away with the knowledge to contribute to a high quality of work life.

I chose to write an I/O psychology text because the other texts that are currently available are not as applied as the field itself. Several of the current texts spend most of their time describing the details of studies and listing complicated statistical formulae. While this approach may be appropriate for some students at some universities, it tends to cause most undergraduates to remain unexcited about I/O psychology. Other texts focus on theories without helping the reader understand how to apply the theories.

This text was written for a student audience that is primarily undergraduate and whose members are probably not planning on becoming I/O psychologists but will nonetheless be involved in selecting, training, evaluating, and motivating employees. With such an audience in mind, it is essential that the material be presented in an applied fashion.

The applied nature of my approach is perhaps best demonstrated by *I/O Psychology in Action*, the workbook that accompanies this text. This supplement allows the student a chance to actually use the material that is presented in the text. The student will be able to conduct the critical incident technique, determine the utility of a test, take a personality test, write a job description, write a résumé, and develop a theory of leadership. The workbook also contains practice tests to help the student prepare for exams.

In the text itself, evidence of the applied approach can be found by looking at the topics that are covered. For example, in addition to covering the traditional selection areas, the text instructs the reader about how to survive an interview, how to write a résumé, and how to write a rejection letter. The applied nature of the text can also be seen in the number of meta-analyses that have been included. Most texts describe the details of an assortment of studies that often leave the reader confused. When possible, I have tried to use the "bottom line" that can be provided by a solid meta-analysis.

Another unique feature of this text is the inclusion of "Employment Profiles" in all but the first chapter. These profiles feature active I/O professionals describing their work and are designed to give students an idea of the variety of careers available in the I/O field.

When possible, I have tried to make the text more interesting by including examples, stories, and some humor. Even for people who are not one of us I/O fanatics, I/O psychology should be fun.

This book could not have been written without the work of the excellent staff at Wadsworth Publishing. In particular, I would like to thank my editor Ken King as well as Debbie Cogan, Peggy Meehan, Stacey Pollard, James Chadwick, and Michelle Palacio, and free-lancers Steve Bailey and Harry Voigt.

The quality of the book was greatly enhanced by the I/O psychologists who served as reviewers for the book. The text would not have been of such a high quality had it not been for the comments of Elizabeth S. Erffmeyer, Western Kentucky University; Dean E. Frost, Portland State University; David C. Gilmore and William Siegfried, University of North Carolina at Charlotte; Paul John Hanges, University of Maryland at College Park; Charles E. Lance, University of Georgia; and Paul R. Nail, Southwestern Oklahoma State University.

Finally, I would like to thank my wife, Krista, who provided many of the banking examples found in this text. Her patience during the years this book was being written can neither be measured nor appreciated enough.

Applied Industrial / Organizational Psychology

1

Laimute E. Druskis/Jeroboam

Introduction to Industrial/Organizational Psychology

Wouldn't it be great if all employees loved their jobs so much that they couldn't wait to get to work and were so well suited and trained for the jobs that their performances were outstanding? Well, such a situation would be great, and ultimately is the goal of industrial psychology. Unfortunately, not every employee will enjoy his or her job, and not every employee will do well on a job. The purpose of this book, however, is to provide the reader with the techniques developed by industrial/organizational (I/O) psychologists that will at least show the way toward the goal of a happy and productive work force.

Before we can talk about these techniques, however, several areas must be discussed in this first chapter that will help you better understand the rest of the book. In this chapter, you will find three distinct sections. The first section provides a brief overview of the field of I/O psychology, the second section discusses the research methods that will be mentioned throughout the text, and the third section explains the laws under which I/O psychologists must operate. At the end of this chapter then, you will have the basics needed to understand the rest of the book.

The Field of I/O Psychology

Differences Between I/O and Business Programs

Perhaps the best place to begin a textbook on I/O psychology would be to look at the field itself. **Industrial/organizational psychology** is a branch of psychology that applies the principles of psychology to the workplace. The application of psychological principles is what best distinguishes I/O psychology from related fields typically taught in business colleges. Although many of the topics covered in this text are similar to those found in a text on personnel management or organizational behavior, the techniques that are used and the reasons behind the techniques are quite different. For example, many personnel texts advocate the interview as an excellent solution to the problem of how best to select employees. I/O psychologists consider the interview to be of much less value and instead suggest the use of alternatives such as psychological tests, weighted application blanks, and assessment centers (Thayer, 1988).

A second difference between I/O psychology and business fields is that I/O psychology examines factors that affect the *people* involved in an organization as opposed to the broader aspects of running an organization

Typical I/O Coursework	Typical MBA Coursework
Statistics	Statistics
Experimental Methodology	Business Research
Psychometric Theory	Organizational Behavior
Employee Selection and Placement	Administrative Policy
Organizational Psychology	Managerial Economics
Employee Training and Development	Financial Management
Performance Appraisal	Marketing Management
Job Analysis	Managerial Accounting

**Table 1.1
Comparison of MBA
and I/O Master's
Degree Coursework**

such as marketing channels, transportation networks, and cost accounting (Feldman, 1986). As you can see from the typical graduate courses listed in Table 1.1, business programs examine areas such as accounting, marketing, and transportation, while I/O programs focus almost exclusively on human resource issues (Peggans, Chandra, & McAlarnis, 1986).

I/O psychology differs also from the clinical and counseling fields of psychology. I/O psychology relies extensively on research, quantitative methods, and testing techniques. I/O psychologists believe firmly in using empirical data and statistics rather than intuition or feelings to make decisions. I/O psychologists are not clinical psychologists who happen to be in industry, and they do not conduct therapy for workers.

One reason that I/O psychology continually increases in popularity is that, perhaps more than any other field, professionals in the field have the chance to have a positive impact on the lives of other people. To support this last statement, let us look at a typical day in the life of a typical person:

Work	8 hours
Commute to work	1 hour
Watching T.V.	3 hours
Sleep	8 hours
Meals	2 hours
Other	2 hours

With the possible exception of sleeping, a person spends more time at his job than at any other activity in life. Thus, it makes sense that a person who is happy with and productive at his job will lead a more fulfilling life than will a person unhappy with his job. If a person is unhappy, not only is it for eight hours a day, but also the residual effects of this unhappiness will affect the quality of that person's family and leisure life.

From a societal perspective, I/O psychologists also can improve the quality of life by increasing employee effectiveness, which in turn reduces the cost of goods sold by improving product quality, which in turn reduces repair and replacement costs by improving organizational efficiency, which can result in decreases in activities such as waiting in line.

Thus, I/O psychology can improve the quality of life at levels equal to, and often exceeding, those of fields such as counseling psychology and medicine. So, even though I/O psychologists make a good salary, the real benefits to the field involve the positive impacts on the lives of others.

Major Fields of I/O Psychology

Personnel Psychology

I/O psychologists who are involved in **personnel psychology** study and practice in areas such as employee-selection techniques, job analysis, employment tests, evaluation of employee performance, absenteeism, and job evaluation. Professionals working in these areas choose existing tests or create new tests that can be used to select and promote employees. These tests are then constantly evaluated to ensure that they are both fair and valid.

Personnel psychologists also analyze jobs to obtain a complete picture of what each employee does, often assigning monetary values to each position. After obtaining complete job descriptions, professionals in personnel psychology construct performance-appraisal instruments and then use these instruments to evaluate employee performance.

To do all of these things, personnel psychologists are heavily involved with research and statistical analysis. A survey conducted by Rassenfoss and Kraut (1988) indicated that the most common activities of personnel researchers are:

1. Developing, administering, and analyzing employee attitude surveys
2. Constructing performance appraisal instruments
3. Validating tests
4. Developing employee-selection tests
5. Conducting job analyses

Organizational Psychology

Psychologists involved in **organizational psychology** study and practice leadership, job satisfaction, employee motivation, organizational communication, conflict management, and group processes within an organization. Organizational psychologists often conduct surveys of employee attitudes to get ideas about what employees believe are an organization's strengths and weaknesses. Usually serving in the role of a consultant, an organizational psychologist will then make recommendations as to ways in which problem areas can be improved. For example, low job satisfaction might be improved by allowing employees to participate in making certain company decisions, and poor communication might be improved by utilizing an employee suggestion system.

Training and Development

Psychologists interested in training and development examine various methods that can be used to train both new and existing employees. People within this subfield usually work in a training department of an organization and are involved in activities such as identifying the training needs of an organization, and developing training systems and evaluating their success. Practitioners in training also operate as consultants and provide workshops on many topics.

Human Factors

Psychologists in the area of **human factors** concentrate on factors such as workplace design, man–machine interaction, and physical fatigue and stress. Sample activities in this subfield have included designing the optimal way to draw a map, designing the most comfortable chair, and investigating the optimal work schedule.

Brief History of I/O Psychology

Considering that the field of psychology itself has only been around for some 110 years (since 1879), it is not surprising that I/O psychology has a relatively short history. Although various experts disagree about the exact starting date of I/O psychology (Table 1.2), it is generally thought to be either in 1903 when Walter Dill Scott wrote *The Theory of Advertising,* in which psychology was first applied to business, or in 1913 when Hugo Munsterberg wrote *Psychology and Industrial Efficiency.* Regardless of the official starting date, I/O psychology was born in the early 1900s.

Year	Event
	Table 1.2
	Important Events in I/O Psychology
1903	Walter Dill Scott publishes *The Theory of Advertising*
1913	Hugo Munsterberg publishes *Psychology and Industrial Efficiency*
1918	World War I provides I/O psychologists with first opportunity for large-scale employee testing and selection
1921	First Ph.D. in I/O psychology awarded to Bruce Moore
1939	Hawthorne studies published
1945	Society for Industrial Psychology Established
1963	Equal Pay Act passed
1964	Civil Rights Act passed
1973	Division 14 of American Psychological Association changes name from Society for Industrial Psychology to Society for Industrial and Organizational Psychology
1989	Supreme Court sets conservative trend

I/O psychology made its first big impact during World War I. Because of the large number of soldiers who had to be assigned to various units within the armed forces, I/O psychologists were employed to test recruits and then place then into appropriate positions. The testing was mainly accomplished through the **Army Alpha** and **Army Beta** tests of mental ability. The more intelligent recruits were assigned to officer training, the less intelligent to the infantry.

In the 1930s, I/O psychology greatly expanded its scope. Until then, it had been primarily involved in personnel issues such as the selection and placement of employees. In the 1930s, however, spearheaded by the famous **Hawthorne studies,** psychologists became more involved in the quality of the working environment as well as in the attitudes of employees.

The 1960s were characterized by the passage of several major pieces of civil rights legislation that will be discussed in the last section of this chapter. These laws focused the attention of human resource professionals on developing fair selection techniques. As a result, the need for I/O psychologists greatly increased.

The 1970s brought great strides in the understanding of many organizational psychology issues that involved employee satisfaction and motivation. The decade also saw the development of many theories about employee behavior in organizations.

The 1980s brought three major changes to I/O psychology. The first involved an increased use of fairly sophisticated statistical techniques and methods of analysis. This change is evident if one compares journal arti-

	Highest Degree (percent)	
Employment Setting	M.A.	Ph.D.
Education	11.1	32.6
Industry	66.7	25.3
Government	13.9	6.9
Consulting	8.3	25.6
Other	0.0	9.6

**Table 1.3
Employment Settings
of I/O Psychologists**

cles written in the 1960s with those written in the 1980s. This reliance on statistics explains why the typical student enrolled in an I/O psychology doctoral program will take at least five statistics courses as part of her education.

A second change concerned a new interest in the application of cognitive psychology to industry. For example, articles written about performance appraisal in the 1970s primarily described and tested new methods for evaluating employee performance. In the 1980s, however, many articles approached the performance appraisal issue by examining the thought process used by managers when they conduct performance appraisals.

The final change in the 1980s was that I/O psychologists took a more aggressive approach in developing methods to select employees. In the 1960s and 1970s, the courts were still interpreting the major civil rights acts of the early 1960s, which resulted in I/O psychologists taking cautious approaches in selecting employees. By the mid-1980s, however, the courts became less strict, and a wider variety of selection instruments was developed and used.

Employment of I/O Psychologists

Throughout the text, you will find several "Employment Profiles" that look at the jobs done by people with degrees in I/O psychology; however, it might still be useful to examine some of the broad areas in which I/O psychologists work. As indicated in Table 1.3, the greatest number of Ph.D. I/O psychologists work at universities, followed by consulting firms and private industry (Schmitt & DeGregorio, 1986). Also, as shown in the table, Master's level I/O graduates have a different employment profile, with most Master's level graduates working in industry (Frizzell, 1989).

I/O professionals who work in industrial settings are involved in a wide range of activities such as training, research, work conditions, performance appraisal, productivity enhancement, test construction, test validation, job analysis, employee motivation, recruiting, and personnel selection (Cederbloom, Pence, & Johnson, 1984). Those employed by state and local governments are usually involved in job analysis and test construction but also perform other human resources–related functions.

At least a Master's degree is usually required to work in the field of I/O psychology. As of 1989, starting salaries for these Master's level positions were approximately $27,000, with average salaries reaching $42,000 after several years of experience (Frizzell, 1989). Starting salaries for Ph.D.s in nonacademic environments are some $5,000–$10,000 higher than for Master's level employees. Virtually no unemployment is seen in I/O psychology.

Educational Requirements

To obtain reasonable employment in I/O psychology, a Master's degree is required for most jobs and a Ph.D. for some. Obtaining a Master's takes between one and two years after the completion of the Bachelor's degree. Admissions requirements vary greatly from school to school, but an undergraduate grade-point average (G.P.A.) of at least 3.0 and a score of 1,000 on the **Graduate Record Exam (G.R.E.)** (the graduate school version of the Scholastic Aptitude Test, or SAT, that you took after high school) are not uncommon. Advice for getting into graduate school can be found in Box 1.1.

Types of Graduate Programs

Master's degree programs come in two varieties. Schools with **terminal Master's degree programs** do not have Ph.D. programs. Thus, a Master's degree is the highest that can be earned at such a school. Schools with doctoral programs have both the Master's degree and the Ph.D. Terminal programs usually have less-stringent entrance requirements and provide more financial aid and individual attention to Master's students than do Ph.D. programs. Doctoral programs, on the other hand, usually have more well-known faculty members as well as better facilities and research funding.

Most Master's programs require thirty to forty hours of graduate coursework to complete. Although fifteen to eighteen hours is considered to be a full undergraduate semester load, nine hours is considered a full graduate load. In addition to coursework, many programs require a student to complete a thesis, which is usually an original research work created and conducted by the student. The thesis is completed in the second year of graduate school.

**Table 1.4
I/O Programs with
Most Faculty
Publications in
*Journal of Applied
Psychology,*
1988–1989**

School	Program Type	Number of Publications
Michigan State University	Ph.D.	7.5
University of South Florida	Ph.D.	5.5
Bowling Green State University	Ph.D.	5.5
Colorado State University	Ph.D.	5.5
University of Minnesota	Ph.D.	5.0
University of Illinois, Urbana–Champaign	Ph.D.	4.5
University of Houston	Ph.D.	4.0
Rice University	Ph.D.	3.0
Georgia Tech	Ph.D.	2.5
Ohio State University	Ph.D.	2.5
UCLA	Ph.D.	2.0
Lafayette College	M.A.	2.0
Stevens Institute of Technology	M.A.	2.0
I.U.P.U.I.	M.A.	2.0
Purdue University	Ph.D.	2.0
University of Iowa	Ph.D.	2.0
University of Notre Dame	Ph.D.	2.0
Wayne State University	Ph.D.	2.0
University of Connecticut	Ph.D.	2.0
SUNY–Buffalo	Ph.D.	2.0
Baruch College	Ph.D.	2.0

Note: These figures only include articles by authors in psychology departments. For articles published by authors from more than one university, each university was awarded .5 of an article.

Most programs also allow the student to complete an **internship** or **practicum** with a local organization. These internship requirements vary by program. For example, at Radford University in Virginia, the student works ten hours per week at an organization during her last semester of graduate school. At East Carolina University, the student takes a semester off to work full-time with a company.

Finally, most programs require a student to pass a comprehensive oral or written examination or both before graduation. These exams usually are taken during the final semester and cover material from all of the courses taken during the graduate program. As you can see, completing a Master's degree program in I/O psychology is tough but will lead to excellent employment and professional benefits.

School	Degree Type	Year						Total	Rank
		1983	1984	1985	1986	1987	1988		
Bowling Green State University	Ph.D.	5	2	6	5	17	15	50	1
Radford University	M.A.	0	4	4	9	9	13	39	2
Old Dominion University	Ph.D.	5	7	7	5	9	2	35	3
Ohio State University	Ph.D.	3	4	9	7	2	8	33	4
University of Illinois–Chicago	Ph.D.	7	0	2	2	5	0	16	5
Wayne State University	Ph.D.	10	4	0	0	0	1	15	6
Kansas State University	Ph.D.	4	2	1	6	0	0	13	7
University of Nebraska–Omaha	Ph.D.	7	3	0	0	3	0	13	7
University of Illinois–Urbana	Ph.D.	10	0	0	2	0	1	13	7
Illinois Institute of Technology	Ph.D.	7	1	3	0	0	2	13	7
New York University	Ph.D.	5	3	0	2	1	2	13	7
University of Akron	Ph.D.	1	2	3	1	3	2	12	12
Northwestern University	Ph.D.	9	1	0	0	0	2	12	12
University of Missouri–St. Louis	Ph.D.	0	1	2	4	1	4	12	12
University of Minnesota	Ph.D.	0	0	1	8	2	0	11	15
University of Georgia	Ph.D.	0	5	2	0	1	2	10	16
Purdue University	Ph.D.	2	1	2	1	0	4	10	16
Michigan State University	Ph.D.	3	0	2	3	1	0	9	18
Brigham Young University	Ph.D.	0	0	7	1	0	0	8	19
Tulane University	Ph.D.	1	4	0	0	1	2	8	19
University of Tennessee	Ph.D.	0	0	0	0	7	1	8	19
Emporia State University	M.A.	5	0	1	1	0	0	7	22
University of Maryland	Ph.D.	0	2	1	3	0	1	7	22

Source: Surrette, 1989.

Note: Presentations made at Annual Graduate School Conference in Industrial/Organizational Psychology and Organizational Behavior.

Table 1.5
Number of Graduate Student Research Presentations, 1983–1988

Obtaining a Ph.D. is more difficult than obtaining a Master's, with the typical doctoral program taking five years to complete. Common entrance requirements are a 3.5 G.P.A. and G.R.E. score of 1,200.

The first two years of a doctoral program involve taking a wide variety of courses in psychology. In most programs, the student does not concentrate on I/O courses until the third and fourth years. In addition to a thesis, a student working toward a Ph.D. must complete a **dissertation**. No formal definition distinguishes a thesis from a dissertation, but the major differences are that the dissertation involves answering a series of questions, is evaluated more critically, and requires more original and independent effort than does the thesis. Doctoral programs also involve a

**Table 1.6
Programs with
Highest Average
G.R.E. Scores**

School	G.R.E. Score	Rank
Ph.D. Programs		
University of Illinois, Urbana–Champaign	1,361	1
Michigan State University	1,335	2
Ohio State University	1,323	3
Rice University	1,307	4
Pennsylvania State University	1,300	5
University of Maryland	1,300	5
University of Michigan	1,300	5
University of Illinois–Chicago	1,294	8
University of Houston	1,290	9
Colorado State University	1,275	10
Terminal Master's Programs		
University of Colorado	1,150	1
Lamar University	1,080	2
San Francisco State University	1,070	3
Western Kentucky University	1,050	4
University of New Haven	1,050	5
University of Wisconsin–Oshkosh	1,000	6
East Carolina University	988	7
Appalachian State University	975	8
University of West Florida	974	9
Radford University	910	10

Source: Society for Industrial and Organizational Psychology (1989). *Graduate training programs in I/O psychology and organizational behavior.* College Park, MD: Author.

Note: All scores are self-reported and the top scores of those universities who participated in the survey and chose to report scores.

series of comprehensive exams that are similar to, but more extensive than, the exams taken in a Master's program.

Although there is no "official" ranking of I/O graduate schools, programs have been compared on the basis of variables such as faculty research as measured by publications (Table 1.4), student research presentations (Table 1.5), entrance requirements as measured by G.R.E. scores (Table 1.6), and number of degrees granted (Table 1.7). Recognized I/O programs are listed in Table 1.8 (Master's) and Table 1.9 (Ph.D).

School	Number of Degrees	Rank
Ph.D. Programs		
Old Dominion University	12	1
University of South Florida	7	2
Hofstra University	7	2
Bowling Green State University	6	4
Illinois Institute of Technology	6	4
University of Minnesota	5	6
Rice University	4	7
University of Houston	4	7
University of Tulsa	4	7
Georgia Institute of Technology	4	7
University of Akron	4	7
University of Illinois–Chicago	4	7
Columbia University	4	7
New York University	4	7
Terminal Master's Programs		
University of New Haven	30	1
New York University	19	2
George Mason University	17	3
CSU–Long Beach	15	4
Radford University	13	5
University of West Florida	11	6
San Francisco State University	10	7
East Carolina University	9	8
Appalachian State University	8	9
Lamar University	5	10

**Table 1.7
Programs Awarding
Most I/O Degrees,
1983–1984**

Source: Society for Industrial and Organizational Psychology (1989). *Graduate training programs in I/O psychology and organizational behavior.* College Park, MD: Author.

Research in I/O Psychology

Now that you have a good idea about the field of I/O psychology, it is time to learn the essentials of one of the foundations of the upcoming chapters: research. This section will not provide the reader with an in-depth discussion of research, but it will provide enough information so that when a study is mentioned during the course of the text, you will understand the method that was used.

Table 1.8
Schools with I/O Psychology Terminal Master's Degree Programs

Alabama
  Jacksonville State University
  University of Alabama

California
  CSU–Chico
  CSU–Hayward
  CSU–Long Beach
  CSU–Los Angeles
  CSU–Northridge
  CSU–Sacramento
  CSU–San Bernardino
  St. Mary's College
  San Diego State University
  San Francisco State University
  San Jose State University

Colorado
  University Colorado–Denver

Connecticut
  University of Bridgeport
  University of Hartford
  University of New Haven

Florida
  University of Central Florida
  University of West Florida

Georgia
  Valdosta State College
  West Georgia College

Illinois
  Illinois State University
  Roosevelt University
  Southern Illinois University at Edwards-
    ville
  University of Chicago

Indiana
  Ball State University
  Indiana University/Purdue University–
    Indianapolis

Kansas
  Emporia State University
  University of Kansas

Kentucky
  Western Kentucky University

Maryland
  University of Baltimore

As mentioned earlier in the chapter, one of the characteristics of I/O psychology is its extensive use of research and statistics. Although there are many reasons for this reliance on research, the most important is that research ultimately saves an organization money. To many of you, this last statement may seem a bit insensitive. Keep in mind, however, that for most organizations, the most important thing is the bottom line. If an I/O psychologist is not able to save the company considerably more money than it pays for his salary and expenses, he will be without a job.

These monetary savings can result from many factors, including increased employee satisfaction, increased productivity, and fewer accidents. Perhaps an excellent example of how research can save a company money involves the employment interview. For years, many organizations relied on the employment interview as the main method for selecting employees (most still do). But research has shown that the employment interview is not the best predictor of future behavior on the job (Hunter & Hunter, 1984). Thus, without research, an organization might still be

Table 1.8
Continued

Massachusetts	Pennsylvania
Northeastern University	Villanova University
Springfield College	West Chester University
Michigan	South Carolina
Western Michigan University	Clemson University
New Jersey	Tennessee
Fairleigh Dickinson University	Austin Peay State University
Kean College	Middle Tennessee State University
Montclair State College	Tennessee State University
New York	University of Tennessee–Chattanooga
CUNY–Brooklyn	Texas
Rensselaer Polytechnic Institute	Lamar University
North Carolina	Saint Mary's University
Appalachian State University	Stephen F. Austin State University
East Carolina University	Virginia
University of North Carolina– Charlotte	George Mason University
	Radford University
Ohio	Washington
Wright State University	University of Central Washington
Xavier University	Wisconsin
	University of Wisconsin–Oshkosh

spending money on a method that actually lowers its profits rather than raising them.

Research Decisions

When conducting research, many decisions must be made to get the best results. The first, of course, is *what to research*. It is true that some psychologists have "great theoretical and research minds," but it is probably more true that most research ideas stem from a person starting a sentence with "I wonder." For example, a manager might say "I wonder why some of my employees can't get to work on time," an employee might say "I wonder if I could assemble more parts if my chair were higher," or a supervisor might ask "I wonder which of my employees is the best to promote." All three seem to be ordinary questions, but each is just as valid and important in research as those asked by a professor in a university. Thus, everyone is a researcher at heart, and conducting some form

**Table 1.9
Schools with I/O
Psychology Ph.D.
Programs**

Alabama
  Auburn University

California
  California School of Professional Psychology
  Claremont Colleges/Graduate School
  Stanford University
  UC Berkeley
  UC Irvine

Colorado
  Colorado State University

Connecticut
  University of Connecticut

Delaware
  University of Delaware

Florida
  University of South Florida

Georgia
  Georgia Institute of Technology
  Georgia State University
  University of Georgia

Illinois
  DePaul University
  Illinois Institute of Technology
  University of Illinois–Chicago

University of Illinois, Urbana–Champaign

Indiana
  Purdue University
  University of Notre Dame

Iowa
  Iowa State University

Kansas
  Kansas State University

Louisiana
  Louisiana State University
  Tulane University

Maryland
  University of Maryland

Michigan
  Central Michigan University
  Michigan State University
  University of Michigan
  Wayne State University

Minnesota
  University of Minnesota

Mississippi
  Mississippi State University
  University of Mississippi
  University of Southern Mississippi

of research to answer a question will undoubtedly lead to a better answer than could be obtained by guesswork alone.

Location of Research

A second decision that must be made involves the location where research will be conducted. There are two main areas, the laboratory and the field.

Laboratory Research

Often when one hears the word *research,* the first thing that comes to mind is an experimenter in a white coat running subjects in a basement

**Table 1.9
Continued**

Missouri
    University of Missouri–St. Louis
    Washington University

Nebraska
    University of Nebraska–Omaha

New Jersey
    Stevens Institute of Technology

New York
    Baruch College
    City University of New York
    Columbia University
    Fordham University
    Hofstra University
    New York University
    SUNY–Albany
    SUNY–Buffalo

North Carolina
    North Carolina State University

Ohio
    Bowling Green State University
    Ohio State University
    Ohio University
    University of Akron
    University of Cincinnati

Oklahoma
    University of Tulsa

Oregon
    Portland State University

Pennsylvania
    Carnegie-Mellon University
    Pennsylvania State University

Tennessee
    Memphis State University
    University of Tennessee–Knoxville

Texas
    Rice University
    Texas A&M University
    Texas Tech University
    University of Houston
    University of North Texas
    University of Texas

Utah
    Brigham Young University

Virginia
    George Mason University (Psy.D.)
    George Washington University
    Old Dominion University
    Virginia Institute of Technology

Washington
    University of Washington

laboratory in some building. Few experimenters actually wear white coats, but much I/O psychology research *is* conducted in a laboratory situation. Usually, this is done at a university, but it also can be conducted by researchers in special divisions of organizations such as AT&T and IBM.

One disadvantage of laboratory research concerns the problem of **external validity.** That is, will the results of laboratory research *generalize* to organizations in the "real world"? An example of this issue involves research about employee-selection methods. It is not uncommon in such research for subjects to view a résumé or a videotape of an interview and make a judgment about a hypothetical applicant. The problem: Is the situation similar enough to actual employment decisions made in the real world or is the laboratory environment so controlled and hypothetical that the results will not generalize? Although the answers to these questions still have not been resolved, research often is conducted in laboratories because they allow a researcher to control many variables that are not of interest to the researchers.

Field Research

Another location for research is away from the laboratory and out in the "field," which could be the assembly line of an automotive plant, the secretarial pool of a large insurance company, or the interviewing room at a personnel agency. **Field research** has the opposite problem to that of laboratory research. What field research obviously gains in external validity it loses in control of extraneous variables that are not of interest to the researcher.

Research Method

After a decision has been made regarding the location for the interview, the specific type of research method that will be used must be determined.

Experimental Method

As you might recall from your general psychology class, the experimental method is the most powerful of all research methods because it is the only method that can determine **cause-and-effect** relationships. Thus, if it is important to know whether one variable produces or causes another variable to change, then the **experiment** is the only method that should be used. What makes a research study an experiment? The key word is **manipulation.** For a research study to be an experiment, the researcher must actually manipulate a variable, which is called the **independent variable.** It is important to understand that the word *experiment* only refers to a study in which the independent variable has been manipulated by a researcher. Any study not involving such a manipulation cannot technically be called an experiment; instead, it is called a study, a survey, or an investigation.

Perhaps an example would make the point more clearly. Suppose we were interested in finding out whether wearing a three-piece suit to an interview is better than wearing a coat and slacks. We could study this issue by observing job applicants at a specific company and comparing the interview scores of people with three-piece suits with those of people wearing coats and slacks. We might find that the better dressed applicants received higher scores, but we could not conclude that the wearing of a three-piece suit *caused* the higher scores; something other than the suit may be at work. For example, perhaps applicants who own three-piece suits are more assertive than other applicants; it then might have been assertiveness and not dress style that led to the higher interview scores.

If we wanted to be more sure that dress style affects interview scores, we would have to manipulate the variable of interest and hold all other variables as constant as possible. How could we turn this into an experiment? Let us take one hundred people and give fifty of them three-piece suits to wear and the other fifty outfits of sports coats and nice pairs of slacks. Each subject would then go through an interview with a personnel director. Afterward, we would compare the interview scores of our two groups. The variable that we expect to change as a result of our manipulating the independent variable is called the **dependent variable.** In this case, the dependent variable would be the interview score.

Even though this particular research design has some problems (see if you can spot them), the fact that we manipulated the applicant's dress style gives us greater confidence that dress style would cause higher interview scores. Even though the results of experiments provide more confidence regarding cause and effect relationships, ethical and practical considerations do not always make experimental designs possible.

For example, we wish to study the effect of loud noise on worker performance. To make this an experimental design, we could have fifty subjects work on an assembly line while being subjected to very loud noise and fifty subjects work on an assembly line with no noise. Two months later we compare the productivity of the two groups. But what is wrong with this study? In addition to having lower productivity, the high-noise group now has poorer hearing. Not a very ethical experiment.

Nonexperimental Methods

Even though researchers would always like to use the experimental method, it is not always possible. Nonexperimental designs are then used. As an example, let us go back to our noise study.

Because we cannot manipulate the level of noise, we will instead test the noise level of one hundred manufacturing plants and compare the average productivity of plants with lower noise levels with that of plants with higher noise levels. As you can easily see, this is not as good a research design as the unethical experiment that we created earlier. There are too many variables other than noise that could account for any differences found in productivity; however, given the circumstances, it still provides us with more information than we had before the study.

Nonexperimental methods are often used to evaluate the results of a new program implemented by an organization. For example, an organization that had instituted a child care center wanted to see whether the center had any effect on employee absenteeism. To find the answer, the organization compared absenteeism levels from the year before the center was introduced with the absenteeism levels for the year following the implementation; the organization found that both absenteeism and turnover had decreased.

Although it would be tempting to conclude that the child care center was a success, such a conclusion would not be prudent: Many other variables might have caused the reduction. As shown in Table 1.10, the organization implemented several other progressive programs during the same period. Thus, the decrease in absenteeism and turnover could have been the result of other programs or some combination of programs. Furthermore, the economy changed so that jobs became more difficult to obtain: Workers may have reduced their absentee rates out of fear of being fired and turnover may have been reduced because employees realized that there were few jobs available. In addition, the weather improved in the second year, which meant workers were rarely unable to get to work.

Taken by itself, we would certainly not want to bet the mortgage on the results of our nonexperimental study. But, if ten other researchers use different nonexperimental designs to study the same question and find similar results, we might feel confident enough to make changes or reach conclusions based on the available research evidence.

Archival Research

Another research method that is commonly used in I/O psychology is that of **archival research.** Archival research involves using previously collected data or records ("going into the archives") to answer a research question. For example, if we wanted to know what distinguishes good workers from poor workers, we could look in the personnel files to see whether the backgrounds of good workers have common characteristics that are not shared by poor workers. Archival research has many nice features such as not being obtrusive and being relatively inexpensive, but it also has severe drawbacks. Records in files are not always accurate and they are not always kept.

Date (month/year)	Absenteeism (%)	External Factor	Internal Factor
1/85	2.8		
2/85	3.1		
3/85	4.7	Local unemployment rate at 4.1%	
4/85	4.7		
5/85	4.8		
6/85	6.7	Main highway closed	
7/85	6.5		
8/85	4.9	Highway reopens	
9/85	4.5		
10/85	4.4		
11/85	8.7	Terrible snow storm	
12/85	5.3		
1/86	5.3		Child care center started
2/86	5.4		
3/86	5.1		Flextime program started
4/86	2.1	Local unemployment rate hits 9.3%	
5/86	2.1		
7/86	1.8		Wellness program started
8/86	1.8		
9/86	2.0		New attendance policy
10/86	2.3		
11/86	4.0	Mild weather	
12/86	4.2	Mild weather	

Table 1.10
Why Nonexperimental Studies Are Difficult to Interpret: The Child Care Center

Note: Absenteeism rate in 1985 prior to day care center = 5.09%; rate in 1986 after day care center = 3.01%.

As an undergraduate, this author was involved with an archival study designed to determine why some students in a very special Master's of business administration (M.B.A.) program dropped out while others completed their coursework. What was supposed to be an easy job of getting records from a few files turned into a nightmare as the records of more than three hundred students were scattered in storage rooms in three locations in southern California and were not filed in any order; furthermore, almost every student had at least one important item missing from his or her file. Needless to say, these problems kept the results of the study from being as accurate as desired.

Introduction to
Industrial/Organizational
Psychology

Meta-Analysis

Perhaps the newest research method, **meta-analysis** is a statistical method of reaching conclusions based on previous research. Prior to meta-analysis, a researcher interested in reviewing the literature on a topic would read all of the available research, and then make a rather subjective conclusion based on the articles. With meta-analysis, the researcher goes through each article, determines the **effect size** for each article, and then finds a statistical average of effect sizes across all articles. Thus, meta-analysis will result in one number, called the **mean effect size** ($\bar{d}$), that indicates the effectiveness of some variable.

To make this process more clear, let us go through a hypothetical meta-analysis. If we were interested in determining whether child care centers are effective ways of reducing absenteeism, we would start our meta-analysis by searching for articles on child care. After a thorough search, we find sixty such articles. Only ten of the articles, however, represent actual empirical research. Thus, our meta-analysis would concentrate on only those ten empirical articles.

The next step in meta-analysis would be to compute an effect size for each article. This can be done in several ways. The most desirable way is to use the following formula:

$$\text{effect size} = \frac{\bar{X}e - \bar{X}c}{sd}$$

where $\bar{X}e$ is the **mean** of the experimental group, $\bar{X}c$ is the mean of the control group, and sd is the overall **standard deviation.** In the first article, suppose that we find that during the year before the child care center's establishment the average employee missed six days per year, and that in the following year the average employee missed three days per year; and the standard deviation was three. Our effect size for this study would be:

$$\frac{3 - 6}{3} = \frac{-3}{3} = -1.0$$

We would then compute effect sizes for each study until we had an effect size for all ten studies. The next step is to multiply each effect size by the number of people in each study, add these products, and then divide by the total number of subjects in all ten studies. The resulting number is our mean effect size. An example of this process is shown in Table 1.11.

Table 1.11
Example of
Meta-Analysis

Study	Performance Rating		sd	d	n	d·n
	Training	**No Training**				
Grace	6.3	4.1	2.2	1.00	52	52.00
Sandburg	5.1	4.8	1.4	.21	44	9.24
Dunston	8.2	6.3	3.5	.54	100	54.00
Law	7.3	7.1	1.6	.13	200	26.00
Berryhill	6.9	7.4	2.9	−.17	30	−5.17
Total					426	143.07
Mean				.34		

Note: *sd* = standard deviation; *d* = effect size; *n* = number of subjects in sample.

Several other steps would then be taken, but a complete discussion of meta-analysis is beyond the scope of this book and probably beyond the reader's interest as well. It is important, however, that you be able to interpret the outcomes of meta-analyses because they not only will be used in this text, but also appear to be the "wave of the future" in reviewing previous research.

So the question remains regarding how effect sizes should be interpreted. Effect sizes less than .40 are considered to be small, those between .40 and .80 are moderate, and those higher than .80 are considered to be large (Cohen, 1977). The average effect size for an organizational intervention is .44 (Guzzo, Jette, & Katzell, 1985). Another way to interpret an effect size is that it is roughly twice the size of a correlation. Thus an effect size of .40 is approximately equivalent to a correlation coefficient of .20.

Sample

Decisions also must be made regarding the size, composition, and method of selecting the subjects who will serve as the sample in an experiment. Although it is nice to have a large sample for any research study, a large sample size is not necessary if the experimenter can choose a random sample and control for many of the extraneous variables. But unless the study will be conducted in a laboratory using the experimental method, it is doubtful that a small sample size will be sufficient.

The method of selecting the sample is certainly dependent on the nature of the organization. A small organization will probably be forced to use all of its employees, which means that the sample will be small but highly representative of the intended population. For economical and practical reasons, a large organization will select only certain employees to participate in a study rather than use the entire work force. The problem then becomes one of which employees will participate.

If the study involves a questionnaire, it would be no problem to randomly select a desired number of employees and have them complete the survey. If, however, the study is more elaborate, such as investigating the effects of lighting on performance, it would be difficult to randomly select employees. That is, it would not be practical to have one employee work under high levels of light while the person next to her was uninvolved with the experiment. If we decide to have one plant work with high levels of light and another with lower levels, what we gain in practicality we loose in randomness and control. So we try to strike a balance between practicality and experimental rigor.

To increase experimental rigor and decrease the costs of conducting research, many studies are conducted at universities using students as subjects rather than employees. In fact, college students serve as subjects in 87% of all published I/O research (Gordon, Slade, & Schmitt, 1986). This use of students has led to considerable debate regarding the **generalizability** of university research: That is, do students behave in the same fashion as employees?

Research on this issue is mixed. Some researchers have found differences between student subjects and professional subjects, while others have not. For example, Landy and Bates (1973) found that students are more subject to contrast effects than are managers, but Hakel, Ohnesorge, and Dunnette (1970) had not found sample differences in an earlier study. In general, however, the preponderance of research indicates that college student samples behave differently than do real world or nonacademic samples (Barr & Hitt, 1986; Gordon, Slade, & Schmitt, 1986). Furthermore, some research suggests that results will differ based on the *major* of the the college sample. For example, both Staw and Ross (1984) and Forst (1987) found that business students rated managers differently than did psychology students. These findings suggest that in certain cases, research using students for subjects will not generalize to the real world.

A final important issue concerns the method used to recruit subjects. To obtain the best research results, it is essential a **random sample** be used so that the sample will be as representative as possible. This means that if a survey is randomly sent to one hundred employees, the research will be most accurate only if all employees return the survey. The problem is that researchers are unlikely to get a 100% return rate if study participation is voluntary.

But researchers are in something of a bind because the ethics of the American Psychological Association (APA) require voluntary participation, while accurate research often requires compulsory participation. How do researchers solve this dilemma? In some organizations on hiring, employees are required to sign a statement agreeing to participate in any organizational research studies. To underscore this agreement, research participation is listed in each employee's job description.

Proponents of this method argue that participation in research is still voluntary because the individual had the choice of either not taking the job or taking it with the advance knowledge of research requirements. Opponents argue that taking a job or not taking a job in order to make a living does not constitute a proper and completely free choice. Similarly, in some universities students have the option of participating in a few research studies or writing a term paper. Even though the students are given an alternative to research participation, some psychologists argue that the choice between writing a term paper that will take several days and participating in two or three experiments that will take a few hours is not a legitimate choice (Sieber & Saks, 1989).

Running the Study

Once all of the above decisions have been made, it is finally time to run the study and collect data. To ensure that data are collected in an unbiased fashion, it is important that all instructions to the subjects be stated in a standardized fashion and at a level that is understandable. Once the subject is finished with her participation, she should be **debriefed,** or told the purpose of the experiment and be given a chance to ask questions about her participation.

Statistics

After all data have been collected, the results are statistically analyzed. A discussion of statistics is beyond the scope of this book, but it is important to understand why statistics are used. Statistical analysis is used to determine how confident we are that our results are real and did not occur by chance alone. For example, if we conducted a "study" in your classroom in which we compared the average social security number of students on the left side of the room with that of students on the right side of the room, we would no doubt get a difference. That is, the average social security number of the students on the right would not be exactly the same as that for students on the left. If we did not conduct a statistical analysis of our data, we would conclude that people on the right side have higher social security numbers than people on the left side. Perhaps we could even develop a theory about our results!

Does this sound ridiculous? Of course it does. But it points out the idea that any set of numbers we collect will in all probability be different. The question is, are they *significantly different?* Statistical analysis provides the answer by determining the probability that our data were the result of chance. In psychology, we use the .05 level of significance, which means that if our analysis indicates that the probability that our data resulted from chance is 5% or less, we would consider our results to be statistically significant. This means that if someone were to replicate our research, we would be confident that other researchers would get results similar to ours 95% of the time. Although the .05 level of significance is the most commonly used, some researchers have suggested that we should be more flexible and use either more conservative or more liberal levels, depending upon the situation (Serlin & Lapsley, 1985).

At this point, a caution must be made about the interpretation of significance levels. Significance levels only indicate the level of confidence that we can place on a result being the product of chance. They say nothing about the strength of the results. Thus, a study finding results significant at the .01 level does not necessarily show a stronger effect than a study with results significant at the .05 level of confidence.

To determine the strength of a finding, we use the effect size discussed earlier in the section on meta-analysis. Significance levels tell us the "statistical significance" of a study, and effect sizes (combined with logic) tell us the "practical significance" of a study.

For example, suppose that we conduct a study comparing the SAT scores of male and female high school students. Based on a sample of five million students, we find that males average 490 and females 489. With such a huge sample size, we will probably find that the two means are statistically different. However, with only a one-point difference between the two groups on a test with a maximum score of 800, we would probably not place much practical significance in the difference.

Correlation

As mentioned earlier, a detailed discussion of statistics is beyond our scope. But it is necessary to discuss one particular statistic—**correlation**—because it is so widely used in I/O psychology and throughout this book.

Correlation is a statistical procedure that allows a researcher to determine the *relationship* between two variables: for example, the relationships found between an employment test and future employee performance, or job satisfaction and job attendance, or performance ratings made by workers and supervisors. It is important to understand that correlational analysis does not necessarily say anything about causality.

The result of correlational analysis is a number called a **correlation coefficient.** The values of this coefficient range from 0 to +1 and from 0 to −1. The further the coefficient is from zero, the greater the relationship between two variables. The + and − signs indicate the *direction* of the correlation. A positive (+) correlation means that as the values of one variable increase, so do the values of a second variable. For example, we might find a positive correlation between intelligence and scores on a classroom exam. This would mean that the more intelligent the student, the higher his score on the exam.

A negative (−) correlation means that as the values of one variable increase, the values of a second variable decrease. For example, we would probably find a negative correlation between the number of beers that you drink the night before a test and your score on that test. In I/O psychology, we find negative correlations between job satisfaction and absenteeism, age and reaction time, and nervousness and interview success.

Why does a correlation coefficient not indicate a cause and effect relationship? Because a third variable, an **intervening variable,** often accounts for the relationship between two variables (Mitchell, 1985). Take the example often used by psychologist David Schroeder. Suppose there is a correlation of +.80 between the number of ice cream cones sold in New York during August and the number of babies that die during August in India. Does eating ice cream kill babies in another nation? No, that would not make sense. Instead, we look for that third variable that would explain our high correlation. In this case, the answer is clearly the summer heat.

Another interesting example was provided by Mullins (1986) in a presentation about the incorrect interpretation of correlation coefficients. Mullins pointed out that data show a strong negative correlation between the number of cows per square mile and the crime rate. With his tongue firmly planted in his cheek, Mullins suggested that New York City could rid itself of crime by importing millions of head of cattle. Of course, the real interpretation for the negative correlation is that crime is greater in urban areas than in rural areas.

As demonstrated above, a good researcher should always be cautious about variables that seem related. A few years ago, *People* magazine reported on a minister who conducted a "study" of five hundred pregnant teenaged girls and found that rock music was being played when 450 of them became pregnant. The minister concluded that because the two are related (that is, they occurred at the same time), rock music must cause pregnancy. His solution? Outlaw rock music and teenage pregnancy would disappear. In my own "study" however, I found that in all five hundred cases of teenage pregnancy, a pillow also was present. To use the same logic as that used by the minister, the real solution would be to outlaw pillows, not rock music. Although both "solutions" are certainly strange, the point should be clear: Just because two events occur at the same time or seem to be related does not mean that one event or variable causes another (Brigham, 1989).

Legal Issues

The third section of this chapter discusses the legal issues with which I/O psychologists are concerned. This section was placed in the introductory chapter for the same reason as the research section; much of what I/O psychologists do is dictated by or limited by employment law. Thus, an understanding of the relevant laws is essential to understanding some of the concepts in later chapters.

Legal Process

To know whether a given employment practice is legal, it is important to understand the legal system as it relates to employment law. The first step in the legal system is for some legislative body such as the United States Congress or a state legislature to pass a law. If a law is passed at the federal level, states may pass laws that expand the rights granted in the federal law; they may not, however, pass laws that will diminish the rights granted in federal legislation. For example, if Congress passed a law that gave women six months of maternity leave, a state or local government could pass a law extending the leave to eight months but could not reduce the amount of maternity leave to less than the six months mandated by Congress. Thus, to be on legally firm ground, it is important to be aware of state and local laws as well as federal legislation.

Once a law has been passed, situations will always occur in which the intent of the law is not clear. For example, a law might be passed to protect handicapped employees. Two years later, an employee is denied promotion because he has high blood pressure. The employee may claim that high blood pressure is a handicap and that he can still work in spite of the handicap. The organization, on the other hand, might claim that high blood pressure is not a handicap and that even if it were, an employee with high blood pressure could not perform the job. In such situations, the employee often will file a charge against the employer.

As shown in Figure 1.1, this charge is usually filed with a government agency. A state agency is used if the alleged violation involves a state law, and a federal agency, usually the Equal Employment Opportunity Commission (EEOC), handles alleged violations of federal law. The governmental agency then will review the charge to determine whether it has merit; if it does, the agency will try to work out a solution without taking the case to court.

If an agreement cannot be reached, however, the case will go to either a state or a federal district court. When the court makes a decision, the decision becomes what is called **case law.** Case law is a judicial interpretation of a law and is important because it establishes a precedent for future cases. If one side does not like the decision rendered in a lower court, it may appeal to higher courts, perhaps eventually going to a state's supreme court or even to the U.S. Supreme Court. Obviously, a ruling by the Supreme Court carries more weight than rulings of district courts or state supreme courts.

Relevant Federal Laws

Fourth Amendment

The **Fourth Amendment** to the U.S. Constitution protects citizens against unreasonable search or seizure. Its importance to I/O psychology comes mostly in the area of drug testing and locker searches. Several courts have ruled that drug testing must be considered a "search," and therefore, to be legal, they must be reasonable and show cause. It is important to understand that the Fourth Amendment is limited to public agencies such as state and local governments. Private industry is not restricted by the Fourth Amendment, but drug testing and searches by a private organization must be conducted in "good faith and with fair dealing."

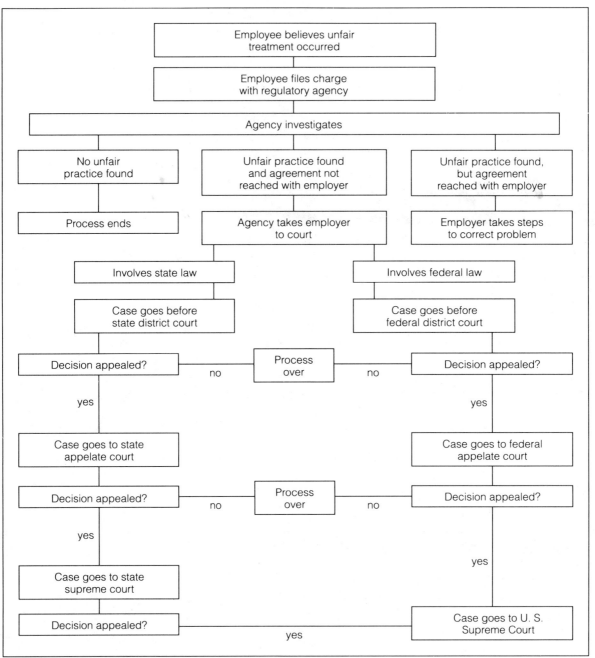

Figure 1.1
Legal Process in
Employment Law

Source: *Federal Register* (1988, April 11) *53*(69), p. 11970.

Type of Suspicion	Job	Finding	Case
No suspicion	Bus attendant	Illegal	*Jones* v. *McKenzie* (1987)
No suspicion	Teacher	Illegal	*Congress of Teachers* v. *Board of Education* (1987)
No suspicion	Bus driver	Illegal	*Amalgamated* v. *Sunline* (1987)
Accidents	Bus driver	Legal	*Amalgamated* v. *Suscy* (1976)
Accidents	Bus driver	Legal	*New Orleans* v. *Masaracchia* (1985)
No suspicion	Police officer	Illegal	*Lovorrn* v. *Chattanooga* (1986)
No suspicion	Police officer	Illegal	*Capua* v. *Plainfield* (1986)
No suspicion	Police officer	Illegal	*Fraternal Order of Police* v. *Newark* (1987)
No suspicion	Police officer	Illegal	*City of Palm Bay* v. *Bauman* (1985)
Anonymous tip	Police officer	Legal	*Turner* v. *Fraternal Order of Police* (1985)
Anonymous tip	Police cadets	Illegal	*Feliciano* v. *Cleveland* (1987)
No suspicion	Drug agents	Legal	*Treasury Union* v. *Von Raab* (1987)
No suspicion	Prison guards	Legal	*McDonnel* v. *Hunter* (1987)
No suspicion	Prison guards	Illegal	*Taylor* v. *O'Grady* (1987)
No suspicion	Aviation workers	Legal	*Government Employees* v. *Dole* (1987)
No suspicion	Aviation workers	Legal	*Mulholland* v. *Army* (1987)
No suspicion	Jockeys	Legal	*Shoemaker* v. *Handel* (1986)
Accidents	Railway workers	Illegal	*Burnley* v. *Railway* (1988)
Accidents	Power line workers	Legal	*Allen* v. *City of Marietta* (1985)
Observed use	Firefighter	Legal	*Everett* v. *Napper* (1987)

Table 1.12
Drug Testing Cases Involving Reasonable Cause

Drug Testing As shown in Table 1.12, drug testing conducted by a public agency must be based on "reasonable suspicion" and with "just cause." Based on prior cases, reasonable suspicion means that there is reason to suspect that employees are using drugs at work. Such suspicion can be produced from a variety of sources including "tips" that employees are using drugs (*Turner* v. *Fraternal Order of Police,* 1985), accidents or discipline problems (*Allen* v. *City of Marietta,* 1985), or actual observation of drug usage (*Everett* v. *Napper,* 1987).

Traditionally, just cause has been viewed by the courts to indicate the degree to which an employee's behavior affects the safety and trust of the public. For example, an air traffic controller has been deemed to be responsible for the safety of the public (*Government Employees* v. *Dole,* 1987), but a school bus attendant has not (*Jones* v. *McKenzie,* 1987).

Other factors involving drug testing that are taken into consideration by the courts include the accuracy of the drug tests and the care and privacy taken during the testing (*Triblo* v. *Quality Clinical Laboratories*, 1982; *Hester* v. *City of Milledgeville*, 1986). The issue of privacy is an especially interesting one because employees who use drugs often try to "cheat" on their drug tests. Attempts at cheating involve such behavior as bringing in "clean" urine that has been taken or purchased from a friend or diluting the urine sample with soap, toilet water, or other chemicals. To stop such attempts, some organizations have required employees to strip so that the employee cannot bring anything in to the test area; they also may require that the employee be observed while she provides the urine specimen. Testing conditions such as these would be allowed only under the most serious situations involving national security. The federal guidelines for collecting urine specimens are shown in Box 1.2.

Two other important issues are the appeal process (*Harvey* v. *Chicago Transit Authority* 1984), and the confidentiality of test results (*Ivy* v. *Damon Clinical Laboratory*, 1984). Employees must be given the opportunity to have their specimens retested and to explain why their tests were positive even though they may not have taken illegal drugs. Thus, for a drug testing program to be legal, the organization must have reason to suspect drug usage, the job must involve the safety or trust of the public, the testing process must be accurate and reasonably private, the results should be handled in a confidential manner, and employees who test positive must be given opportunities to appeal and undergo rehabilitation.

Office and Locker Searches Office and locker searches are allowed under the law as long as they are reasonable and with cause (*O'Conner* v. *Ortega*, 1987). Allowing employees to place their own locks on lockers, however, removes the right of the organization to search the locker.

Fourteenth Amendment

The "equal protection" clause of the **Fourteenth Amendment** mandates that no state may deny a person equal protection under the law. Basically, this implies that a government may not *intentionally* discriminate or allow intentional discrimination to take place. Because any suit filed under the Fourteenth Amendment must demonstrate intent, it is not often used.

Box 1.2

Federal Guidelines for Workplace Drug Testing

To ensure that drug testing of federal government employees be conducted properly, the National Institute on Drug Abuse developed the following guidelines. Although these guidelines were developed for use by the federal government, they provide an excellent model for other employers as well.

Integrity and Identity of Specimen Agencies shall take precautions to ensure that a urine specimen not be adulterated or diluted during the collection procedure and that information on the urine bottle and in the record book can identify the individual from whom the specimen was collected. The following minimum precautions shall be taken to ensure that unadulterated specimens are obtained and correctly identified.

1. To deter the dilution of specimens at the collection site, toilet bluing agents shall be placed in toilet tanks wherever possible, so the reservoir of water in the toilet bowl always remains blue. There shall be no other source of water (e.g., no shower or sink) in the enclosure where urination occurs.

2. When an individual arrives at the collection site, the collection site person shall request the individual to present photo identification. If the individual does not have proper photo identification, the collection site person shall contact the supervisor of the individual, the coordinator of the drug testing program, or any other agency official who can positively identify the individual. If the individual's identity cannot be established, the collection site person shall not proceed with the collection.

3. If the individual fails to arrive at the assigned time, the collection site person shall contact the appropriate authority to obtain guidance on the action to be taken.

4. The collection site person shall ask the individual to remove any unnecessary outer garments such as a coat or jacket that might conceal items or substances that could be used to tamper with or adulterate the individual's urine specimen. The collection site person shall ensure that all personal belongings such as a purse or briefcase remain with the outer garments. The individual may retain his or her wallet.

5. The individual shall be instructed to wash and dry his or her hands prior to urination.

6. After washing hands, the individual shall remain in the presence of the collection site person and shall not have access to any water fountain, faucet, soap dispenser, cleaning agent or any other materials which could be used to adulterate the specimen.

7. The individual may provide his or her specimen in the privacy of a stall or otherwise partitioned area that allows for individual privacy.

8. The collection site person shall note any unusual behavior or appearance in the permanent record book.

9. In the exceptional event that an agency-designated collection site is not accessible and there is an immediate requirement for specimen collection (e.g., an accident investigation), a public rest room may be used according to the following procedures: A collection site person of the same gender as the individual shall accompany the individual into the public rest room, which shall be made secure during the collection procedure. If possible, a toilet bluing agent shall be placed in the bowl and any accessible toilet tank. The collection site person shall remain in the rest room, but outside the stall, until the specimen is collected. If no bluing agent is available to deter specimen dilution,

Continued

Box 1.2 continued

the collection site person shall instruct the individual not to flush the toilet until the specimen is delivered to the collection site person. After the collection site person has possession of the specimen, the individual will be instructed to flush the toilet and to participate with the collection site person in completing the chain of custody procedures.

10. Upon receiving the specimen from the individual, the collection site person shall determine that it contains at least 60 milliliters of urine. If there is less than 60 milliliters of urine in the container, additional urine shall be collected in a separate container to reach a total of 60 milliliters. (The temperature of the partial specimen in each separate container shall be measured in accordance with paragraph (f)(12) of this section, and the partial specimens shall be combined in one container.) The individual may be given a reasonable amount of liquid to drink for this purpose (e.g., a glass of water). If the individual fails for any reason to provide 60 milliliters of urine, the collection site person shall contact the appropriate authority to obtain guidance on the action to be taken.

11. After the specimen has been provided and submitted to the collection site person, the individual shall be allowed to wash his or her hands.

12. Immediately after the specimen is collected, the collection site person shall measure the temperature of the specimen. The temperature measuring device used must accurately reflect the temperature of the specimen and not contaminate the specimen. The time from urination to temperature measurement is critical and in no case shall exceed 4 minutes.

13. If the temperature of a specimen is outside the range of 32.5°–37.7°C/90.5°–99.8°F, that is a reason to believe that the individual may have

altered or substituted the specimen, and another specimen shall be collected under direct observation of a same gender collection site person and both specimens shall be forwarded to the laboratory for testing. An individual may volunteer to have his or her oral temperature taken to provide evidence to counter the reason to believe the individual may have altered or substituted the specimen caused by the specimen's temperature falling outside the prescribed range.

14. Immediately after the specimen is collected, the collection site person shall also inspect the specimen to determine its color and look for any signs of contaminants. Any unusual findings shall be noted in the permanent record book.

15. All specimens suspected of being adulterated shall be forwarded to the laboratory for testing.

16. Whenever there is reason to believe that a particular individual may alter or substitute the specimen to be provided, a second specimen shall be obtained as soon as possible under the direct observation of a same gender collection site person.

17. Both the individual being tested and the collection site person shall keep the specimen in view at all times prior to its being sealed and labeled. If the specimen is transferred to a second bottle, the collection site person shall request the individual to observe the transfer of the specimen and the placement of the tamperproof seal over the bottle cap and down the sides of the bottle.

18. The collection site person and the individual shall be present at the same time during procedures outlined in paragraphs (f)(19)–(f)(22) of this section.

19. The collection site person shall place securely on the bottle an identification label which contains the date,

Continued

the individual's specimen number, and any other identifying information provided or required by the agency.

20. The individual shall initial the identification label on the specimen bottle for the purpose of certifying that it is the specimen collected from him or her.

21. The collection site person shall enter in the permanent record book all information identifying the specimen. The collection site person shall sign the permanent record book next to the identifying information.

22. The individual shall be asked to read and sign a statement in the permanent record book certifying that the specimen identified as having been collected from him or her is in fact that specimen he or she provided.

23. A higher level supervisor shall review and concur in advance with any decision by a collection site person to obtain a specimen under the direct observation of a same gender collection site person based on a reason to believe that the individual may alter or substitute the specimen to be provided.

24. The collection site person shall complete the chain or custody form.

25. The urine specimen and chain of custody form are now ready for shipment. If the specimen is not immediately prepared for shipment, it shall be appropriately safeguarded during temporary storage.

26. While any part of the above chain of custody procedures is being performed, it is essential that the urine specimen and custody documents be under the control of the involved collection site person. If the involved collection site person leaves his or her work station momentarily, the specimen and custody form shall be taken with him or her or shall be secured.

After the collection site person returns to the work station, the custody process will continue. If the collection site person is leaving for an extended period of time, the specimen shall be packaged for mailing before he or she leaves the site.

Collection Control To the maximum extent possible, collection site personnel shall keep the individual's specimen bottle within sight both before and after the individual has urinated. After the specimen is collected, it shall be properly sealed and labeled. An approved chain of custody form shall be used for maintaining control and accountability of each specimen from the point of collection to final disposition of the specimen. The date and purpose shall be documented on an approved chain of custody form each time a specimen is handled or transferred and every individual in the chain shall be identified. Every effort shall be made to minimize the number of persons handling specimens.

Transportation to Laboratory
Collection site personnel shall arrange to ship the collected specimens to the drug testing laboratory. The specimens shall be placed in containers designed to minimize the possibility of damage during shipment, for example, specimen boxes or padded mailers; and those containers shall be securely sealed to eliminate the possibility of undetected tampering. On the tape sealing the container, the collection site supervisor shall sign and enter the date specimens were sealed in the containers for shipment. The collection site personnel shall ensure that the chain of custody documentation is attached to each container sealed for shipment to the drug testing laboratory.

Source: *Federal Register* (1988, April 11) *53*(69), p. 11970.

Introduction to
Industrial/Organizational
Psychology

Civil Rights Act of 1964 (Title VII)

The Civil Rights Act of 1964 (known as Title VII) and its 1972 amendment extended the scope of the Fourteenth Amendment. Title VII makes it illegal for employers with more than fifteen employees, labor unions, employment agencies, state and local governmental agencies, and educational institutions to:

1. fail, refuse to hire, discharge any individual, or otherwise to discriminate against any individual with respect to his compensation, terms, conditions, or privileges of employment because of the individual's race, color, religion, sex, or national origin; or

2. to limit, segregate, or classify employees or applicants for employment in any way that would deprive, or tend to deprive, any individual of employment opportunities or otherwise adversely affect his stature as an employee because of such an individual's race, color, religion, sex, or national origin.

Unlike the Fourteenth Amendment, for an employment practice to be potentially illegal under Title VII, the discrimination does not have to be intentional (Arvey, 1979). Instead, proof of discrimination comes through statistical analysis of selection rates and is determined by the presence or absence of adverse impact, which will be discussed in detail later in this chapter.

In addition to employment decisions such as selection and promotion, Title VII also has been interpreted by the courts to cover the "atmosphere" of the organization, which includes such behavior as sexual harassment (*Broderick* v. *Ruder*, 1988; *Brundy* v. *Jackson*, 1971), age harassment (*Louis* v. *Federal Prison Industries*, 1986), and race harassment (*Hunter* v. *Allis-Chalmers*, 1986).

Equal Pay Act of 1963

The **Equal Pay Act** prohibits employers from paying employees of one sex at different rates than employees of the opposite sex for work that requires equal skill, effort, and responsibility and that is performed under similar working conditions. For jobs to be covered under this act, the work must be similar. The intent of the act was not to mandate "comparable worth," but rather to guarantee "equal pay for essentially equal work."

Age Discrimination in Employment Act

The **Age Discrimination in Employment Act (ADEA)** and its later amendments forbid an employer or union from discriminating against an individual who is over the age of forty. In part, this act was designed to protect older workers from employment practices aimed at reducing costs by firing older workers with higher salaries and replacing them with lower-paid younger workers. For an individual to file suit under this act, she must be able to demonstrate that she is in the appropriate age bracket and has been intentionally or unintentionally discriminated against due to her age (Faley, Kleiman, & Lengnick-Hall, 1984).

Vocational Rehabilitation Act of 1973

The **Vocational Rehabilitation Act** prohibits federal government contractors or subcontractors with contracts of more than $2,500 from discriminating against a physically or mentally handicapped individual for non–job-related reasons. For purposes of this act, a handicap is defined as something that restricts everyday life activities. In the 1987 case of *Nassau County* v. *Gene Arline*, the U.S. Supreme Court ruled that contagious diseases are considered handicaps. A year later, Congress approved the Civil Rights Restoration Act of 1988, a section of which confirms that contagious diseases are to be considered handicaps.

In *Vincent Chalk* v. *Orange County School Board* (1988), a district court ruled that a teacher could not be deprived of his job because he had Acquired Immune Deficiency Syndrome (AIDS). Essentially, the court ruled that AIDS was a contagious disease and therefore an afflicted person was protected from discrimination unless the handicap kept the person from properly performing his or her job.

Although the Vocational Rehabilitation Act protects handicapped individuals from discrimination, it does allow an employer the right to not hire a handicapped individual if the handicap prevents the individual from performing the job. The law, however, also provides for affirmative action in employing handicapped individuals and requires relevant employers to both make the workplace accessible to handicapped individuals and take reasonable steps to accommodate such individuals.

Vietnam-Era Veterans
Readjustment Act of 1974

The Vietnam-Era Veterans Readjustment Act mandates that any contractor or subcontractor with more than $10,000 in federal govern-

Table 1.13
Pregnancy Leave
Laws in Three States

	State		
	Connecticut	**Minnesota**	**Tennessee**
Who is covered	State employees	Employers with more than 21 employees	Employers with more than 100 employees
Employee requirements	Must sign statement that woman intends to return to work	Must have worked at least 20 hours per week for at least 12 months	Must be a female and give 3 months' notice
Conditions covered	Birth Adoption Sick child	Birth Adoption	Birth
Amount of leave	24 weeks	6 weeks	16 weeks

ment contracts must take affirmative action to employ and promote Vietnam-era veterans. This law is one reason that veterans applying for civil service jobs receive credit for their military service as well as for their qualifications.

Pregnancy Discrimination Act of 1978

The **Pregnancy Discrimination Act** states that "women affected by pregnancy, childbirth, or related medical conditions shall be treated the same for all employment related purposes, including receipt of benefit programs, as other persons not so affected but similar in their ability or inability to work." Simply put, this act requires pregnancy to be treated as any other disability. In the case of *California Federal Savings and Loan Association* v. *Guerra* (1987), the U.S. Supreme Court expanded the scope of the law. Pregnant women may receive better treatment than other persons with disabilities and cannot receive worse treatment.

Currently, several laws pending in Congress would stipulate minimum guidelines for pregnancy leave. Until these laws are passed, however, state laws will take or remain in effect. A sample of such laws for three states is shown in Table 1.13.

Case Law

As discussed earlier in this chapter, the above-mentioned laws are written in relatively general terms so that they can cover all conceivable situations. In writing laws at a general level, however, the legislative body does not specify everything that an employer can or cannot do. Thus, it is the job of the courts to determine how a law pertains to a particular situation and, if necessary, to provide an interpretation where a law is ambiguous.

Many employment-related cases have been taken to court, but the following are examples of case law that is important to I/O psychology.

Griggs v. Duke Power (1971)

In 1955, Duke Power (Charlotte, North Carolina) initiated a requirement that, with the exception of the labor department, any newly hired employee had to possess a high school diploma. Blacks were only allowed to apply for jobs in the labor department. In 1965, the company allowed blacks to apply for jobs in any department but required both a high school diploma and a passing score on two aptitude tests for hiring in other departments as well as for transfer from labor into other departments.

Because a much smaller percentage of blacks than whites was able to meet the employment and transfer requirements, a disparate number of blacks were forced to work in the lower-paying labor department. The case was taken to court and eventually reached the U.S. Supreme Court, which ruled against Duke Power, stating there was no demonstrated relationship between the employment and transfer requirements and job performance. Thus, even though the company had not intended to discriminate, the consequences of its policy were discriminatory. *Griggs* is considered to be important case law because it was the first time that the Supreme Court ruled that an employment test must be **job-related** to satisfy the requirements of the 1964 Civil Rights Act. In *Clara Watson* v. *Fort Worth Bank* (1988), the Court unanimously extended the protection described in *Griggs* to include subjective employment decisions such as promotions that do not result from formal employment testing.

Albemarle Paper Company v. Moody (1975)

After Albemarle underwent company reorganization, it used tests to hire and promote employees. Blacks scored significantly lower on the tests than did whites and thus were hired and promoted at rates lower than those for whites. The company claimed that the tests were legal because they had been "validated" as required in the 1964 Civil Rights Act. After reviewing the validation study, the U.S. Supreme Court ruled against

Albemarle on the grounds that the validation study was flawed. This case is important because it extended the findings of Griggs to state that strict standards would be used to determine job relatedness.

Washington v. Davis (1976)

On a test used by the District of Columbia's police department, 57% of black applicants failed but only 13% of white applicants. The police department was charged with violating the due process clause of the Fifth Amendment and was taken to court in a case that eventually reached the U.S. Supreme Court. This case is important because the Court ruled that (1) scores from training programs were considered to be legitimate criteria, and (2) cases filed under the Fifth Amendment must demonstrate intentional discrimination.

Uniform Guidelines

To help employers make legal employment decisions, the EEOC developed its "Uniform Guidelines on Employee Selection Decisions." The **Uniform Guidelines** were first published in 1970; following severe criticism, they were revised in 1978. The guidelines are not law, but are to be used by courts to determine whether the selection procedures used by employers are legal. At first, courts strictly adhered to the letter of the Uniform Guidelines, but in recent years they have become more practical and have made decisions based more on the spirit that motivated the guidelines' formation.

Affirmative Action

Affirmative action is one of the most misunderstood legal concepts concerning employment. Most affirmative action requirements are the result of presidential Executive Order 11246. This order, as well as sections of several laws, requires federal contractors and subcontractors with more than one hundred employees and federal contracts in excess of $100,000 to have formal affirmative action plans. These plans typically involve analyses of all major job categories that indicate which categories have underrepresentations of the protected classes as well as goals and plans for overcoming such underrepresentations.

In no way does affirmative action require an employer to hire an unqualified minority over a qualified white male. Instead, affirmative action requires employers to monitor their employment records to determine whether minority groups are underrepresented. If they are, affirmative action requires that an organization do the best it can to remedy the situation. For example, an organization might advertise in magazines primarily read by minorities or it might set up training programs designed to teach minorities the skills needed to obtain employment with the organization.

Affirmative action becomes controversial when an organization realizes that it has discriminated against a particular protected group. For example, police and fire departments have long been staffed by white males. In some cases, this composition has been accidental, in others it has been intentional. To remedy such situations, police and fire departments often set goals for minority hiring. These goals are objectives and are not to be confused with quotas, which *require* a certain percentage of minorities to be hired.

To help with affirmative action hiring, an organization usually keeps separate lists of qualified whites and qualified minorities. If the goal is to hire females for half of its work force, then the top male is hired from the male list and the top female is hired from the female list. This process continues until all openings have been filled. Although this process often results in members with lower test scores being hired over white males with higher test scores, the important point is that everyone who is hired has been determined to be qualified based on their test scores.

Should only a small number of minority applicants test highly enough to be considered qualified, the organization is under no obligation to hire unqualified applicants. In fact, if an organization hires unqualified minorities over qualified minorities, or if it sets unreasonable goals, it can be found guilty of reverse discrimination (Levin-Epstein, 1987). But if an organization makes a legitimate affirmative action effort, it will be allowed to keep its federal contracts.

As shown in the flow chart in Figure 1.2, the courts will use four criteria to determine the legality of an affirmative action plan. The first criterion examined is whether there has been a history of discrimination by a particular organization. If no discrimination has previously occurred, then an affirmative action plan is neither necessary nor legal.

The second criterion concerns the extent to which the plan benefits people who were not actual victims of discrimination. If the plan only benefits actual victims, it probably will be considered legal, but if it benefits people who were not directly discriminated against by the organization, other criteria will be considered.

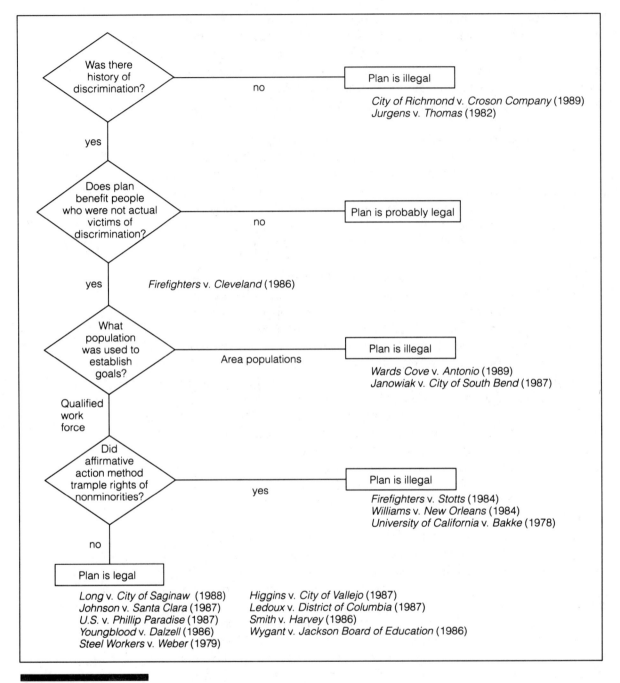

**Figure 1.2
Determining the
Legality of an
Affirmative Action
Plan**

The third criterion concerns which of two types of populations was used to statistically determine discrimination and to set affirmative action goals. With area populations, an organization compares the number of minorities in the general area with the number of minorities in each position in the organization. If a discrepancy occurs, the organization sets hiring goals to remedy the discrepancy. For example, if 80% of the area surrounding an organization is Hispanic but only 20% of the salaried workers in the organization are Hispanic, the organization might set hiring goals for Hispanics at 90% until the work force becomes 80% Hispanic.

Although the use of area population figures has been traditional, recent Supreme Court decisions have declared them inappropriate. Instead, the population that must be used in goal setting is that of the **qualified work force** in the area rather than the area population.

The fourth and final criteria used by the courts to determine the legality of an affirmative action program is whether the remedy designed to help minorities "unnecessarily trammels" the rights of nonminorities. That is, a plan that helps females cannot deny the rights of males. Preference can be given to a qualified minority over a qualified nonminority, but an unqualified minority can never be hired over a qualified nonminority.

Determining Employment Decision Legality

To determine whether a particular employment practice is illegal, several variables must be considered. As depicted in Figure 1.3, the first step determines whether the requirement directly refers to a member of a protected class. A **protected class** is any group of people for which protective legislation has been passed. Table 1.14 lists these protected classes and the legislation protecting them. Employment decisions based upon membership in a protected class (for example, "We will not hire females because they are not strong enough to do the job") are illegal unless the employer can demonstrate that the requirement is a **bona fide occupational qualification (BFOQ).**

If a job can only be performed by a person in a particular class, the requirement is considered a BFOQ. It might be possible to think of functions that could only be performed by a person of a particular gender; for instance, only a female could be a wet nurse. Few jobs in our society, however, involve the use of a protected class to define a BFOQ. Take, for example, a job that involves lifting 150-pound crates. Although it is true that, on average, males are stronger than females, a company could not set a male only requirement. The real BFOQ in this example is

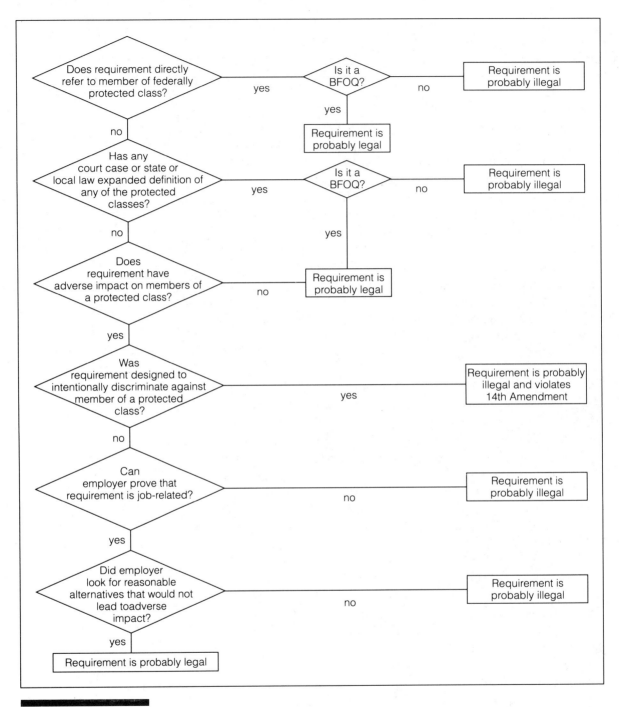

**Figure 1.3
Determining
Whether an
Employment
Practice Is Legal**

Protected Class	Federal Law
Age (over 40)	Age Discrimination in Employment Act
Handicap	Vocational Rehabilitation Act of 1973
National origin	Civil Rights Act of 1964 (Title VII)
Pregnancy	Pregnancy Discrimination Act of 1978
Race	Fourteenth Amendment (intentional)
	Civil Rights Act of 1964 (unintentional)
Religion	Civil Rights Act of 1964
Sex	Civil Rights Act of 1964
	Equal Pay Act of 1963
Vietnam veterans	Vietnam-Era Veterans Readjustment Act of 1974

Table 1.14
Federally Protected Classes

strength, not sex. Thus, restricting employment to males would be illegal.

If the employment practice does not directly refer to a member of a protected class, the next step is to determine whether the requirement adversely affects members of a protected class. **Adverse impact** means that a particular employment decision results in negative consequences more often for members of one protected group than for another. For example, an employee-selection requirement of a college degree would lead to a higher percentage of black applicants not being hired when compared to white applicants. Thus, even though such a requirement does not mention blacks (a protected class), it does adversely impact them.

Adverse impact is legally determined through the "four-fifths rule." That is, the percentage of blacks hired must be at least 80% of the percentage of whites who are hired. It is important to keep in mind that adverse impact refers to *percentages* rather than raw numbers. For example, if we hire twenty-five of fifty white applicants, the hiring percentage would be 50%. If we had ten black applicants, at least four would need to be hired to avoid adverse impact. Why four? Because the hiring percentage for blacks must be at least 80% of the white hiring percentage. Because our white hiring percentage was 50%, our hiring percentage for blacks must be at least four-fifths (80%) of 50%. Thus, $.50 \times .80 = .40$, indicating that we would need to hire at least 40% of all black applicants to avoid adverse impact and a potential charge of unfair discrimination. With ten applicants, this results in hiring at least four of the ten applicants.

If our employment requirement does not result in adverse impact, it is probably legal. If adverse impact does result, then the burden of proof shifts to the employer, who can offer one of the following defenses.

1. *Valid testing procedures.* An employment practice may still be legal even though it leads to adverse impact as long as the test is professionally developed, job-related (valid), and reasonable attempts have been made to find other tests that might be just as valid and yet not show adverse impact. For example, if an employer uses an intelligence test to select employees, there is a strong possibility that adverse impact will occur. If the employer can demonstrate, however, that the intelligence test predicts performance on the job and that no other available test will predict performance, the use of the test is probably justified. A more in-depth discussion of validity strategies can be found later in Chapter 3.

2. *Bona fide seniority system.* An organization that has had a long-standing policy of promoting employees with the greatest seniority or laying off employees with the least seniority can continue to do so even though adverse impact occurs. But if discrimination occurred earlier in the organization and was the reason that members of a protected class were lower on the seniority list, a court probably will discredit the seniority system, declaring that it is not bona fide (Twomey, 1986).

Chapter Summary

In this chapter, we discussed three separate topics: the field of I/O psychology, research methods used by I/O psychologists, and the legal system under which I/O psychologists must operate.

In the first section, you learned that the field of I/O psychology is relatively young and consists of four major subfields: personnel psychology, training, organizational psychology, and human factors. Industrial psychologists work in a variety of settings including industry, government, education, and consulting firms. At least a Master's degree is required to find employment in the field, and starting salaries are around $27,000 at the Master's level and $37,000 at the Ph.D. level.

In the second section, research was described as an important part of the I/O psychologist's job. Research decisions that must be made include what to research, the location of the research (laboratory or field), the research method that will be used (experimental method, nonexperimental method, archival research, meta-analysis), the sample that will be used, and the statistics that will be used to analyze the research data.

In the third section, the legal process was discussed. Here you learned that important laws include the Fourth Amendment, which has been extended to cover drug testing and employee locker searches; the Fourteenth Amendment, which covers intentional discrimination; the 1964 Civil Rights Act, which covers unintentional discrimination; the Equal Pay Act of 1963, which requires equal pay for equal work; the Age Discrimination in Employment Act, which prohibits discrimination against people over age forty; the Vocational Rehabilitation Act, which forbids discrimination against the handicapped; the Vietnam-Era Veterans Readjustment Act, which protects and helps Vietnam veterans; and the Pregnancy Discrimination Act, which prohibits discrimination against employees who become pregnant or plan to do so.

Glossary

Adverse impact The instance of an employment decision resulting in members of a protected class being negatively affected at a higher rate than members of the majority class

Affirmative action The process of ensuring proportional representation of employees based on variables such as race and sex

Age Discrimination in Employment Act (ADEA) A federal law that, with its amendments, forbids discrimination against an individual who is over the age of forty

Archival research Research that involves the use of previously collected data

Army Alpha An intelligence test developed during World War I and used by the army for soldiers who can read

Army Beta An intelligence test developed during World War I and used by the army for soldiers who cannot read

Bona fide occupational qualification (BFOQ) A selection requirement that is necessary for the performance of job-related duties and for which there is no substitute

Case law The interpretation of a law by a court through a verdict in a trial, setting precedent for subsequent court decisions

Cause-effect relationship The result of a well-controlled experiment about which the researcher can confidently state that the independent variable caused the change in the dependent variable

Correlation A statistical procedure used to measure the relationship between two variables

Correlation coefficient A statistic, resulting from performing a correlation, that indicates the magnitude and direction of a relationship

Debriefing Informing the subject in an experiment about the purpose of the study in which he or she was a participant, and providing any other relevant information

Dependent variable The measure of behavior that is expected to change as a result of changes in the independent variable

Dissertation A formal research paper required of most doctoral students in order to graduate

Effect size Used in meta-analysis, a statistic that indicates the amount of change caused by an experimental manipulation

Equal Pay Act A federal act passed in 1963 that prohibits employers from paying employees of one sex differently from employees of the opposite sex for work that requires equal skill, effort, and responsibility

Experiment A type of research study in which the independent variable is manipulated by the experimenter

External validity The extent to which research results can be expected to hold true outside the specific setting in which they were obtained

Field research Research conducted in a natural setting as opposed to a laboratory

Fourteenth Amendment The amendment to the U.S. Constitution that mandates that no state may deny a person equal protection under the law

Fourth Amendment The amendment to the U.S. Constitution that protects against unreasonable search or seizure; the amendment has been ruled to cover drug testing

Generalizability Like external validity, the extent to which research results hold true outside the specific setting in which they were obtained.

Graduate Record Exam (G.R.E) A standardized admission test required by most psychology graduate schools

Hawthorne studies A series of studies conducted at the Western Electric Plant in Hawthorne, Illinois, that have come to represent any change in behavior that occurs when people react to a change in the environment

Human factors A field of study concentrating on the interaction between humans and machines

Independent variable The manipulated variable in an experiment

Industrial/organizational psychology A branch of psychology that applies the principles of psychology to the workplace

Internship A situation in which a student works for an organization, either for pay or as a volunteer, in order to receive practical work experience

Intervening variable A third variable that can often explain the relationship between two other variables

Job-related The case in which requirements needed to score well on a selection test are the same as those needed to perform well on the job

Manipulation The alteration of a variable by an experimenter in expectation that that alteration will result in a change in the dependent variable

Mean The arithmetic average of a series of scores

Mean effect size Used in meta-analysis, a statistic that is the average of the effect sizes for all studies included in the analysis

Meta-analysis A statistical method for cumulating research results

Nonexperimental methods Research methods in which the experimenter does not manipulate the independent variable

Organizational psychology The field of study that investigates the behavior of employees within the context of an organization

Personnel psychology The field of study that concentrates on the selection and evaluation of employees

Practicum A paid or unpaid position with an organization that gives the student practical work experience

Pregnancy Discrimination Act A 1978 federal law protecting the rights of pregnant women

Protected class Any group of people for which protective legislation has been passed

Qualified work force The percentage of people in a given geographic area that have the qualifications (skills, education, etc.) to perform a certain job

Random sample A sample in which every member of the relevant population had an equal chance of being chosen to participate in the study

Standard deviation A statistic that indicates the variation of scores in a distribution

Terminal Master's degree programs Graduate programs that offer a Master's degree but not a doctoral degree

Uniform guidelines Federal guidelines that are used to guide an employer in establishing fair selection methods

Vietnam-Era Veterans Readjustment Act A 1974 federal law that mandates that federal government contractors and subcontractors take affirmative action to employ and promote Vietnam-era veterans

Vocational Rehabilitation Act Federal act passed in 1973 that prohibits federal government contractors or subcontractors from discriminating against the physically or mentally handicapped

2

Job Analysis and Job Evaluation

In 1585, fifteen English settlers landed at and established a colony on Roanoke Island near what is now the Outer Banks of the North Carolina coast. When John White arrived at Roanoke Island in 1590, he found no trace of the colony and only the word "Croatan" carved on a tree. To this day, it is not known what happened to the settlers of the Lost Colony of Roanoke.

Many theories have been put forth to explain the fate of the lost colony—killed by Indians, moved to another location, and so on. One theory, however, is that the members of the colony were not prepared to survive in the new continent; that is, the group consisted of politicians, soldiers, and sailors, and farmers and survival experts were not part of the group. Although worthy individuals were sent to the New World, few had the necessary training and skills to survive. In fact, the colony might have survived if settlers with more appropriate skills had been sent instead of traditional explorer types. Thus, a better match between job requirements and personnel might have saved the colony.

Does this sound farfetched? Perhaps so, but the story does underscore the importance of a process called **job analysis**—the breaking down of a job into its component activities and requirements (Levine, 1983).

Importance of Job Analysis

Legal Importance

From Chapter 1, you should recall that any employment decision must be based on job-related information. One legally acceptable way to directly determine job relatedness is by job analysis. No law actually and specifically requires a job analysis, but several important guidelines mandate job analysis for all practical purposes.

First, in the Uniform Guidelines that were discussed in Chapter 1, there are several direct references to the necessity of job analysis. Even though the Uniform Guidelines are not law, courts have granted them "great deference" (Levine, 1983).

Second, several court cases have discussed the concept of job relatedness. For example, in *Griggs* v. *Duke Power* (1971), employment decisions were based in part upon applicants' possession of high school diplomas. Because a higher percentage of blacks than whites did not meet this requirement, a smaller percentage of black applicants was hired. Thus, a suit was filed against the Duke Power Company charging that a high school diploma was not necessary to carry out the demands of the job. The court agreed with Griggs, the plaintiff, stating that the company had indeed not established the job relatedness of the high school diploma requirement.

Although not specifically mentioning the term *job analysis,* the decision in *Griggs* was the first real one that addressed the issue of job relatedness. Subsequent cases such as *Albemarle* v. *Moody* (1975) and *Chance* v. *Board of Examiners* (1971) further established the necessity of job relatedness and the link between it and job analysis.

Practical Importance

Even if job analysis were not legally required, it has so many uses that it should still be an integral part of an organization's human resource system. Potential uses for job analysis include job descriptions, employee selection, training, personpower planning, performance appraisal, job classification, job evaluation, job design, and organizational analysis (Ash & Levine, 1980).

Job Descriptions

Often confused with job analysis, *job descriptions* are brief, two-to-five-page summaries of the tasks and job requirements found in the job analysis. In other words, the job analysis is the *process* of determining the work activities and requirements, and the job description is the written *result* of the job analysis.

A complete discussion of writing job descriptions can be found later in this chapter. It is more essential now, however, to realize just how important job descriptions are. Job descriptions provide guidelines that can be followed by employees, which can lead to greater employee performance by making clear exactly what is expected of an employee in a particular job (Campbell, 1983).

Employee Selection

It is difficult to imagine how an employee can be selected unless there is a clear understanding of the job's requirements. By identifying such requirements, it is possible to select tests or interview questions that will determine whether a particular applicant possesses the necessary and proper knowledge, skills, and abilities to carry out the requirements of the job. Although this seems like common sense, the discussion of the employment interview in Chapter 4 demonstrates that many non–job-related variables are often used to select employees. Examples are height requirements for police officers, firm handshakes for most jobs, and physical attractiveness for airline flight attendants.

Training

Again, it is difficult to see how employees can be trained unless the requirements of a job are known. Job analyses yield lists of job activities that can be systematically used to create training programs.

Personpower Planning

One important but seldom utilized use of job analysis is to determine *worker mobility* within an organization. That is, if an individual is hired for a particular job, to what other jobs can he or she expect to eventually be promoted and become successful? Many organizations have a policy of promoting the person who performs the best in the job immediately below the one in question. Although this approach has its advantages, it also can result in the so-called **Peter Principle**—that is, promoting a person until he or she eventually reaches his or her highest level of incompetence (Peter & Hull, 1969). Consider an employee who is the best salesperson in the company. Even though this person is known to be excellent in sales, it is not known what type of supervisor he will be. Promotion solely on the basis of sales performance does not guarantee that the individual will do well as a supervisor. Suppose, however, that job-analysis results are used to compare all jobs in the company to the supervisor's job. Instead of promoting the person in the job immediately below the supervisor, we promote the best employee from the most similar job; that is, the one that already involves much of the same knowledge, skills, and abilities as the supervisor's job. With this approach, there is a better match between the person being promoted and the requirements of the job.

Performance Appraisal

Another important use of job analysis is the construction of a performance-appraisal instrument. As in employee selection, the evaluation of employee performance must be job-related. Employees are often evaluated by forms that use vague categories such as "dependability," "knowledge," and "initiative." The use of specific job-related categories leads to more accurate performance appraisals that are not only better accepted by employees, but also accepted more readily by the courts (Field & Holley, 1982). When properly administered and utilized, job-related performance appraisals can serve as an excellent source of employee training and counseling.

Job Classification

Job analysis allows a human resource professional to classify jobs into groups based on similarities in requirements and duties. Job classification is useful for determining pay levels, transfers, and promotions.

Job Evaluation

Job-analysis information also can be used to determine the *worth* of a job. Job evaluation will be discussed in greater detail later in this chapter.

Job Design

Job-analysis information can be used for better designing a job—in other words, to determine the optimal way in which a job should be performed. By analyzing a job, wasted motions can be eliminated, work stations moved closer together, or two jobs can be combined into one.

Organizational Analysis

During the collection of job-analysis information, the job analyst often becomes aware of certain problems within an organization. For example, during a job-analysis interview, an employee may indicate that she does not know how she is evaluated or to whom she is supposed to report. The discovery of such lapses in organizational communication can then be used to correct problems and help an organization function better. For example, while conducting job-analysis interviews of credit union positions, job analyst Deborah Peggans discovered that none of the workers knew how their job performances were evaluated. This let the organization know that it had not done an adequate job of communicating performance standards with its employees.

Pre–Job-Analysis Decisions

Before a job analysis is undertaken, several decisions must be made. The first concerns the level of specificity. That is, should the job analysis break a job down into every minute, specific behaviors (for example, "tilts arm at ninety-degree angle" or "moves foot forward three inches") or should the job be analyzed at a more general level ("makes financial decisions"; "speaks to clients"). Although most jobs are analyzed at levels somewhere between these two extremes, there are times when the extent of analysis will be closer to one level than another.

For some jobs that involve intricate work, extensive and expensive efforts have been undertaken to identify the optimal way in which they should be performed. For example, in a window manufacturing plant, job analysis determined that many more windows could be mounted in frames by lifting the glass just six inches and then sliding it into place rather than lifting the glass higher and then placing it in the frame. In such a situation, the work obviously must be performed in a specific manner for the greatest financial savings. Thus the job analysis is more effective at a more detailed level.

A second pre–job-analysis decision addresses the issue of formal versus informal requirements. Formal requirements for a secretary might include activities such as typing letters or filing memos. Informal requirements might include making coffee or picking up the boss's children from school. Including previously informal requirements has certain advantages such as identifying and eliminating duties that may be neither legal nor necessary. In addition, informal requirements such as picking up mail may need to be made more formal to reduce potential confusion regarding who is responsible for the task.

A third decision to be made involves *who will conduct* the job analysis. Typically, such analysis is conducted by a trained individual in the personnel department, but it also can be conducted by job incumbents, supervisors, and outside consultants. If job incumbents or supervisors are used, it is essential that they be thoroughly trained in job-analysis procedures.

The state of Virginia developed a system in which all employees were asked to follow set guidelines and write their own job descriptions. The system itself was well conceived, but employees were not given enough job-analysis training, the lack of which resulted in substantial confusion and the writing of job descriptions that may not have been as accurate as desired.

A fourth decision to be addressed is the *number of employees* who should participate in the job analysis. For organizations with relatively few people in each job, it is advisable to have all employees participate in the analysis. But in organizations in which there are many people performing the same job (for example, teachers at a university or seamstresses in a clothing factory), it is not necessary to use every person. Rouleau and Krain (1975) have designed a system for estimating the number of employees who should participate in a job analysis, and Green and Stutzman (1986) have indicated that the number should be greater than three. Unfortunately, no research is yet available to verify these estimates.

After the number of participants has been determined, a final decision needs to be made as to *which particular employees* will participate. If not every employee will participate, the same sampling rules that are used in research should be used in job analysis. That is, participants should be selected in as random and yet representative a way as practical. The reason for such careful sampling is that research has shown that employee differences in sex, race, job-performance level, and personality sometimes can result in slightly different job-analysis outcomes (Aamodt, Kimbrough, Keller, & Crawford, 1982; Machungwa & Schmitt, 1983; Mullins & Kimbrough, 1988; Schmitt & Cohen, 1989).

Job-Analysis Methods

Unstructured Methods

Interviews

Perhaps the most common method of conducting a job analysis is the **job-analysis interview** (Jones & DeCotiis, 1969). Job-analysis interviews differ greatly from employment interviews: The purpose of the job-analysis interview is to obtain information about the job itself rather than about the person doing the job. Job-analysis interviews come in two main forms, individual and group. In the individual interview, the **job analyst** interviews one employee at a time. In the group interview, a larger number of employees are interviewed together. Individual interviews are, of course, more costly and time-consuming than group interviews, but the greater cost can many times be justified by the increased openness during an individual interview because an employee is more confident that what he says will remain confidential.

Regardless of whether individual or group interviews are used, certain guidelines should be followed that will make the interview go more smoothly (McCormick, 1979).

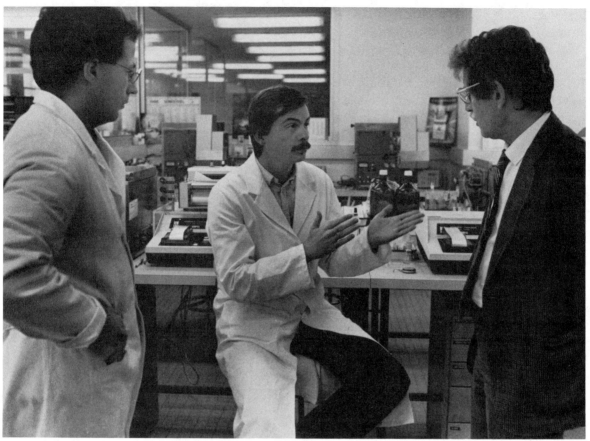

The job analyst obtains information for the job analysis by interviewing employees either individually or in groups.

1. *Prepare* for the interview by announcing the job analysis to employees well in advance of the interviews and by selecting a quiet and private interview location.
2. *Open* the interview by establishing rapport, putting the worker at ease, and explaining the purpose of the interview.
3. *Conduct* the interview by asking open-ended questions, using easy-to-understand vocabulary, and allowing sufficient time for the employee to talk and answer questions—and without being condescending.

Employment Profile

Robbie Estes, M.S.
Research Associate
Auburn University at
   Montgomery, Alabama

As a research associate, I constantly use both the job-analysis and job-evaluation knowledge discussed in this chapter. I work for the Center for Business and Economic Development (CBED) at Auburn University at Montgomery, Alabama. CBED is a part of the research division of Auburn University and is basically a consulting center that generates income for Auburn and its operations through contract and grant work. The center generated $950,000 in 1988.

Recently, I have been working on a classification and wage study for the finance department of the State of Alabama. The purpose of this project has been to develop a system that will allow the employees in this department to be paid fairly. I started the project by conducting background research on the occupational classes being studied to obtain information such as job descriptions, wage rates, and job-complexity levels. This initial information helped me to become familiar with every job in the department.

After this initial information had been obtained, we conducted individual site observations and interviews. We interviewed individuals in each job classification to get an idea of the activities they perform. These interviews were conducted in group sessions of five to twelve people each and resulted in the generation of the tasks and work behaviors that each employee performed as well as the knowledge, skills, and abilities needed to perform each of the jobs.

Next, based on information obtained from the interviews, we developed a classification questionnaire and a job-analysis questionnaire and then administered both questionnaires to all job incumbents. After the questionnaire data were obtained, they were entered into the computer, checked for accuracy, and then analyzed using a statistical program. The results from this statistical analysis allowed us to create a new classification system and to assign every employee into the proper wage classification.

In addition to projects such as the one described above, I perform a variety of duties for the Center such as rating incumbents in an assessment center, administering promotion exams, editing policy manuals and research reports, writing test-validation and job-analysis reports, consulting with governmental agencies about training and performance-appraisal projects, and conducting item-analysis sessions.

The successful completion of my job requires not only an extensive knowledge of job analysis and job evaluation, but also excellent written and oral communication skills. I enjoy my job very much and learn so much each day that it is like going to school again, but this time, I am getting paid!

Most workers are proud of their jobs and are very willing to talk about them. Once the initial apprehensions and jitters are over, most job-analysis interviews go well. A good way to start the actual interview is by asking the employee to describe what she does from the moment she first enters the parking lot at work to the moment she arrives back at her house. A question such as this provides some structure for the employee in recalling the various aspects of her job and also provides the interviewer with many follow-up questions and areas that will provide additional information.

A slightly more formal method for conducting group interviews is the technique described by Kosidiak (1987). With this technique, a committee of experts is gathered and asked to brainstorm the major duties that are involved in a job. Once this has been done, the committee is then asked to identify the tasks (work-related activities) that must be completed for each of the duties. The results of this procedure are then summarized in job descriptions or a job-analysis report. The employment profile of Robbie Estes shows a particular use for interview results.

Observations

Observations are useful job-analysis methods, especially when used in conjunction with other methods such as interviews. During a job-analysis observation, the job analyst observes incumbents as they do their jobs in the work setting. The greatest advantage of this method is that it provides the analyst with an opportunity to actually see the worker do her job and thus obtain information that the worker may have forgotten to mention during the interview. The method's greatest disadvantage is that it is very obtrusive: Observing someone without their knowing it is difficult. The best way to underscore this point is for the reader to think of the jobs at which he has worked. It is infrequent that there is anyplace from which an analyst could observe without being seen by employees. This is a problem, because once employees know they are being watched, their behavior changes, which keeps an analyst from obtaining an accurate picture of the way jobs are done.

Job Participation

A job also can be analyzed by actually performing it. The technique of **job participation** is especially nice because it is difficult to understand every aspect of a job until the analyst has done it herself. The technique is easily used when the analyst has previously performed the job. An excellent example would be a supervisor who has worked her way up through the ranks. As mentioned earlier, the problem with using nonanalyst supervisors or incumbents is their lack of training in job-analysis techniques.

A professional job analyst also can perform an unfamiliar job for a short period of time, although this is, of course, limited to certain occupations that involve quick training and minimal consequences from error. The job of brain surgeon probably would not be a good one to analyze by this method.

The analyst should spend enough time on the job to properly sample work behavior in addition to job difficulty. Yet spending long periods of time can be very expensive and still not guarantee that all aspects of behavior will be covered. Psychologist Wayman Mullins used job-participation techniques to analyze the job of a firefighter. Mullins spent two weeks living at the fire station and performing all the duties of a firefighter. The only problem during this two-week period? No fires. Thus, if Mullins had not already had a good idea of what a firefighter did, he would have concluded that the most important duties were sleeping, cleaning, cooking, and playing cards!

Semistructured Methods

Critical Incident Technique

The **Critical Incident Technique (CIT)** was first developed and used by John Flanagan and his students at the University of Pittsburgh in the late 1940s and early 1950s. The CIT is used to discover actual incidents of job behavior that make the difference between a job's successful and unsuccessful performance (Flanagan, 1954). This technique can be conducted in many ways, but the basic procedure is as follows.

1. Job incumbents each generate between one and five examples of both good and bad performance that they have seen on the job. These incidents can be obtained in many ways—log books, questionnaires, interviews, and so on. Research has shown that the method used makes little difference (Campion, Greener, & Wernli, 1973), although questionnaires are usually used because they are easiest. A convenient way to word requests for critical incidents is by asking incumbents to think of times they saw workers perform in an especially outstanding way and then to write down exactly what occurred. Incumbents are then asked to do the same for times they saw workers perform badly. This process is repeated as needed.

2. Job experts examine each incident and decide whether it is an example of good or bad behavior. This step is necessary because approximately 5% of incidents initially cited as bad examples by employees are actually good examples and vice versa (Aamodt, Reardon, & Kimbrough, 1986). In a recent job analysis of the position of university instructor, a few students described their worst teachers as those who lectured from material not included in their textbooks. A committee of faculty members and students who reviewed the incidents determined that lecturing from nontext material actually was good. Thus, the incidents were counted as examples of good rather than bad performance.

3. The incidents generated in the first stage are then given to three or four incumbents to sort into an unspecified number of categories. The incidents in each category are then read by the job analyst, who combines, names, and defines the categories.

Category	Good	Bad	Total
Interest in residents	31	19	50
Availability	14	27	41
Responsibility	12	20	32
Fairness	18	10	28
Self-adherence to the rules	0	28	28
Social skills	19	7	26
Programming	13	7	20
Self-confidence	12	8	20
Rule enforcement	4	14	18
Authoritarianism	1	16	17
Counseling skills	12	4	16
Self-control	5	2	7
Confidentiality	1	2	3

4. To verify the judgments made by the job analyst in step 3, three other incumbents are given the incidents and category names and asked to sort the incidents into the newly created categories. If two of the three incumbents sort an incident into the same category, the incident is considered part of that category. Any incident that is not agreed upon by two sorters is either thrown out or placed into a new category.

5. The numbers of both types of incidents sorted into each category are then tallied and used to create a table similar to Table 2.1. The categories provide the important dimensions of a job, and the numbers provide the relative importance of these dimensions.

The Critical Incident Technique is an excellent addition to a job analysis because the actual critical incidents can be used for future activities such as performance appraisal (Smith & Kendall, 1963) and training (Glickman & Vallance, 1958). The CIT's greatest drawback is that its stress on the difference between excellent and poor performance ignores routine duties. Thus, the CIT cannot be used as the sole method of job analysis.

Task Analysis

Another commonly used job-analysis technique is **task analysis.** Task analysis involves the gathering of a list of tasks that are thought to be involved with a job and then having job incumbents rate the task on several scales, such as frequency of occurrence and importance. The trick to this technique is in obtaining a list of tasks. Such a list typically is devel-

Table 2.2
Example of a Task
Inventory

Instructions:

Listed below are tasks that may be involved in your job. If you do not perform the task at all, circle 0. If you perform the task on occasion, circle 1. If you perform the task on at least a weekly basis, circle 2. If you perform the task at least daily, circle 3.

Task	Rating			
1. Patrol floors to ensure that building is secure and safe.	0	1	2	3
2. Write up residents who break rules.	0	1	2	3
3. Advise residents having problems with roommates.	0	1	2	3
4. Attend meetings of House Council.	0	1	2	3
5. Design bulletin boards and posters.	0	1	2	3
6. Issue keys to new residents.	0	1	2	3
7. Change hallway light bulbs that have burned out.	0	1	2	3

oped by reading old job descriptions, observing workers, and interviewing incumbents and supervisors (Gael, 1983).

Once the task list has been created (usually including some two hundred tasks), incumbents rate each task. Those that receive high ratings of importance, frequency, or both then are used to write job descriptions, develop training programs, and so on. Most **task inventories** are created with at least two scales. For example, consider the task "accurately shooting a gun." For a police officer, this task occurs infrequently, but when it does, its importance is paramount. If a frequency scale alone were used, shooting a gun might not be covered in training.

It also has been suggested that a few tasks that are not part of a job be placed into the task inventory, and incumbents who rate these irrelevant tasks as part of their job then can be removed from the job analysis due to their carelessness (Green & Stutzman, 1986). An example of a task inventory created for university-housing resident assistants is shown in Table 2.2.

Ammerman Technique

An excellent job-analysis technique for use with small organizations was developed by Ammerman (1965) and reported by Robinson (1981). The basic steps for the **Ammerman Technique** are:

1. Convene a panel of experts that includes representatives from all levels of the organization.
2. Have the panel identify the objectives and standards that are to be met by the ideal incumbent.
3. Have the panel list the specific behaviors that are necessary for each objective or standard to be attained.
4. Have the panel identify which of the behaviors from step 3 are "critical" to reaching the objective.
5. Have the panel rank order the objectives on the basis of importance.

The results of these procedures will yield a set of important objectives and the behaviors necessary to meet these objectives. These behaviors then can be used to create employee-selection tests, develop training programs, or evaluate the performance of current employees.

Job Elements

The **job-element approach** was developed by Ernest Primoff (1975) as a job-analysis system for use in the federal government. This technique basically involves a group interview in which six incumbents generate **job elements,** which are properties such as knowledge, skills, abilities, and interests that are important in a job's performance. The resulting job elements are then rated on four variables:

1. the extent to which barely acceptable workers have the element
2. the importance of the element in picking out superior workers
3. how much trouble is likely to occur if the element is not considered
4. the practicality of requiring applicants to possess the element

For each element, the ratings of these four variables are combined in a rather complicated fashion to provide a number that indicates each element's importance. These numerically weighted elements then can be used to design an employee-selection system.

Structured Methods

Position Analysis Questionnaire

The **Position Analysis Questionnaire (PAQ)** is a structured question-naire that was developed by McCormick, Jeanneret, and Mecham (1972). The PAQ contains 194 items that are organized into six main dimensions: information input, mental processes, work output, relationships with other persons, job context, and other job-related variables such as work sched-ule, pay, and responsibility. A sample PAQ page is shown in Figure 2.1.

The PAQ ofters many advantages. First, it is inexpensive and takes relatively little time to use (Levine, Ash, & Bennett, 1980). Second, it is one of the most standardized job-analysis methods, and its results for a particular position can be compared through computer analysis with thou-sands of other positions. Third, the PAQ was rated by experienced job analysts as being the most useful of the standardized techniques for job evaluation (Levine, Ash, Hall, & Sistrunk, 1983). Fourth, the PAQ is both reliable (Taylor, 1978) and robust (Jones, Main, Butler, & Johnson, 1982).

Although the PAQ has considerable support, research also has identi-fied large problems that, interesting enough, are caused by its strengths.

First, the PAQ's instructions suggest that incumbents using the ques-tionnaire have education levels between grades 10 and 12. Research has found, however, that the PAQ questions and directions are written at the college-graduate level (Ash & Edgell, 1975). Thus, many workers may not be able to understand the PAQ.

Second, the PAQ was designed to cover all jobs, but limited to 194 questions and six dimensions, the PAQ has not proven very sensitive. For example, a homemaker and a police officer have similar PAQ profiles (Arvey & Begalla, 1975). Similar profiles also are obtained regardless of whether an analyst actually observes the job or just looks at a job title (Smith & Hakel, 1979) or a job description (Friedman & Harvey, 1986; Jones, Main, Butler, & Johnson, 1982).

Third, having a large amount of information about a job yields the same results as having little information (Arvey, Davis, McGowen, & Dipboye, 1982; Surrette, 1988). Although these studies do speak favorably about the reliability of the PAQ, they also provide cause to worry because the PAQ appears to yield the same results regardless of how familiar the analyst is with a job. DeNisi, Cornelius, and Blencoe (1987), however, have suggested that even though job experts and nonexperts agree on whether or not a job involves a certain task, they disagree about the de-gree of the task's involvement.

Figure 2.1
Example of PAQ
Questions

RELATIONSHIPS WITH OTHER PERSONS

4 Relationships with Other Persons

This section deals with different aspects of interaction between people involved in various kinds of work.

Code Importance to This Job (I)
N Does not apply
1 Very minor
2 Low
3 Average
4 High
5 Extreme

4.1 Communications

Rate the following in terms of how important the activity is to the completion of the job. Some jobs may involve several or all of the items in this section.

4.1.1 Oral (communicating by speaking)

99 |I| Advising (dealing with individuals in order to counsel and/or guide them with regard to problems that may be resolved by legal, financial, scientific, technical, clinical, spiritual, and/or other professional principles)

100 |I| Negotiating (dealing with others in order to reach an agreement or solution, for example, labor bargaining, diplomatic relations, etc.)

101 |I| Persuading (dealing with others in order to influence them toward some action or point of view, for example, selling, political campaigning, etc.)

102 |I| Instructing (the teaching of knowledge or skills, in either an informal or a formal manner, to others, for example a public school teacher, a machinist teaching an apprentice, etc.)

103 |I| Interviewing (conducting interviews directed toward some specific objective, for example, interviewing job applicants, census taking, etc.)

104 |I| Routine information exchange: job related (the giving and/or receiving of job-related information of a routine nature, for example, ticket agent, taxicab dispatcher, receptionist, etc.)

105 |I| Nonroutine information exchange (the giving and/or receiving of job-related information of a nonroutine or unusual nature, for example, professional committee meetings, engineers discussing new product design, etc.)

106 |I| Public speaking (making speeches or formal presentations before relatively large audiences, for example, political addresses, radio/TV broadcasting, delivering a sermon, etc.)

4.1.2 Written (communicating by written/printed material)

107 |I| Writing (for example, writing or dictating letters, reports, etc., writing copy for ads, writing newspaper articles, etc.: do not include transcribing activities described in item 43, but only activities in which the incumbent creates the written material)

4.1.3 Other Communications

108 |I| Signaling (communicating by some type of signal, for example, hand signals, semaphore, whistles, horns, bells, lights, etc.)

109 |I| Code communications (telegraph, cryptography, etc.)

Source: E. J. McCormick, P. R. Jeannert, & R. C. Mecham, *Position Analysis Questionnaire,* copyright 1969 by Purdue Research Foundation, West Lafayette, Indiana 47907. Reprinted with permission of the publisher.

Use Visual Displays

Answer Questions from Others

Contact High Officials

Judge Distances

Treat the Sick or Injured

Work in a Cramped Space

**Figure 2.2
Sample Elements
from the Job
Element Inventory**

Job Structure Profile

A revised version of the PAQ was developed by Patrick and Moore (1985). The major changes in the revision, which is called the **Job Structure Profile (JSP),** included item content and style, new items to increase the discriminatory power of the intellectual and decision-making dimensions, and an emphasis on having a job analyst, rather than the incumbent, use the JSP. Research by JSP's developers has indicated that the instrument is reliable, but further research is needed before it is known whether the JSP is a legitimate improvement on the PAQ.

Job Element Inventory

A second instrument designed as an alternative to the PAQ is the **Job Element Inventory (JEI)** developed by Cornelius and Hakel (1978). The JEI contains 153 items and has a readability level appropriate for an employee with only a 10th-grade education (Cornelius, Hakel, & Sackett, 1979). Research comparing the JEI with the PAQ indicates that the scores from each method are very similar (Harvey, Friedman, Hakel, & Cornelius, 1988). Thus, the JEI may be a better replacement for the difficult-to-read PAQ. But as mentioned with the JSP, much more research is needed before conclusions can be confidently drawn. A list of sample elements from the JEI is shown in Figure 2.2.

Job Components Inventory

To take advantage of the PAQ's strengths while avoiding some of its problems, Banks, Jackson, Stafford, and Warr (1983) developed the **Job Components Inventory (JCI)** for use in England. The JCI consists of more than 400 questions covering five major categories: tools and equipment, perceptual and physical requirements, mathematical requirements,

Figure 2.3
JCI Questions

DO YOU OPERATE PRINTING
EQUIPMENT?

FOR EXAMPLE:

01   DUPLICATORS

02   SPIRIT DUPLICATORS

03   PHOTOCOPING MACHINES

04   ADDRESSOGRAPH MACHINES

05   SCREEN PRINTING

06   PRINTING STENCILS

07   COLLATING MACHINES

08   FOLDING MACHINES

ANY OTHERS?

WHAT FOR?

A22.

Source: Banks, M. H., Jackson, P. R., Stafford, E. M., & Warr, P. B. (1983). The Job
Components Inventory and the analysis of jobs requiring limited skill. *Personnel Psychology, 36,* 57–66. Reprinted with permission of the authors.

communication requirements, and decision making and responsibility. An
example of one JCI question is shown in Figure 2.3.

Because the JCI is fairly new, the published research on its use is not
abundant. But it does appear to be a promising technique, with research
indicating that it is reliable (Banks & Miller, 1984) and that it can differen-

Problem Solving		Table 2.3 Example of Threshold Traits Analysis
Job Functions Include	**Incumbent Must**	
Processing information to reach specific conclusions, answering problems, adapting and assessing ideas of others, and revising into workable form.	Analyze information and, by inductive reasoning, arrive at a specific conclusion or solution (trait also known as *convergent thinking, reasoning*).	

Level	Job Activities that Require Solving	Level	Incumbent Must Solve
0	Very minor problems with fairly simple solutions (running out of supplies or giving directions).	0	Very minor problems with fairly simple solutions.
1	Problems with known and limited variables (diagnosing mechanical disorders or customer complaints).	1	Problems with known and limited variables.
2	More complex problems with many known variables (programming or investment analysis).	2	Problems with many known and complex variables.
3	Very complex and abstract problems with many unknown variables (advanced systems design or research).	3	Very complex and abstract problems with many unknown variables.

Source: Adapted from Lopez, F. M., Kesselman, G. A., & Lopez, F. E. (1981). An empirical test of a trait-oriented job analysis technique. *Personnel Psychology, 34,* 479–502. Reprinted with permission of authors.

tiate between jobs (Banks, Jackson, Stafford, & Warr, 1983) and cluster jobs based on their similarity to one another (Stafford, Jackson, & Banks, 1984).

Threshold Traits Analysis

A structured approach similar to PAQ and JCI is **Threshold Traits Analysis (TTA),** which was developed by Lopez, Kesselman, and Lopez (1981). This method is only available commercially, but it will be discussed briefly here because of its unique style. The TTA questionnaire's 33 items identify the traits that are necessary for the successful performance of a job. The 33 items cover five trait categories: physical, mental, learned, motivational, and social. Examples of the items and their trait categories can be found in Tables 2.3 and 2.4. The TTA's uniqueness and

Area	Job Functions	Trait	Description: Can
Physical	Physical exertion	1 Strength	Lift, pull, or push objects
		2 Stamina	Expend physical energy for long periods
	Bodily activity	3 Agility	React quickly; has good coordination
	Sensory inputs	4 Vision	See details and color of objects
		5 Hearing	Recognize sound, tone, and pitch
Mental	Vigilance and attention	6 Perception	Observe and differentiate details
		7 Concentration	Attend to details and distractions
		8 Memory	Retain and recall ideas
	Information processing	9 Comprehension	Understand spoken and written ideas
		10 Problem solving	Reason and analyze abstract information
		11 Creativity	Produce new ideas and products
Learned	Quantitative computation	12 Numerical computation	Solve arithmetic and mathematical problems
	Communications	13 Oral expression	Speak clearly and effectively
		14 Written expression	Write clearly and effectively
	Action selection and projection	15 Planning	Project a course of action
		16 Decision making	Choose a course of action
	Application of information	17 Craft knowledge	Apply specialized information
		18 Craft skill	Perform a complex set of activities
Motivational	Working conditions		
	Unprogrammed	19 Adaptability—change	Adjust to interruptions and changes
	Cycled	20 Adaptability—repetition	Adjust to repetitive activities
	Stressful	21 Adaptability—pressure	Adjust to critical and demanding work
	Secluded	22 Adaptability—isolation	Work alone or with little personal contact
	Unpleasant	23 Adaptability—discomfort	Work in hot, cold, or noisy workplaces
	Dangerous	24 Adaptability—hazards	Work in dangerous situations
	Absence of direct supervision	25 Control—dependability	Work with minimum of supervision
	Presence of difficulties	26 Control—perseverance	Stick to a task until completed
	Unstructured conditions	27 Control—initiative	Act on own, take charge when needed
	Access to valuables	28 Control—integrity	Observe regular ethical and moral codes
	Limited mobility	29 Control—aspirations	Limit desire for promotion
Social	Interpersonal contact	30 Personal appearance	Meet appropriate standards of dress
		31 Tolerance	Deal with people in tense situations
		32 Influence	Get people to cooperate
		33 Cooperation	Work as member of a team

Source: Adapted from Lopez, F. M., Kesselman, G. A., & Lopez, F. E. (1981). An empirical test of a trait-oriented job analysis technique. *Personnel Psychology, 34,* 479–502. Reprinted with permission of authors.

Table 2.4
Threshold Traits
Analysis Categories

its greatest advantages are that it is short, reliable, and can correctly identify important traits (Lopez, Kesselman, & Lopez, 1981). TTA's greatest disadvantage is that it is only available commercially. Because the TTA also focuses on traits, its main uses would be in the development of an employee-selection system or a career plan (Lopez, Rockmore, & Kesselman, 1980).

Functional Job Analysis

Functional Job Analysis (FJA) was designed by Fine (1955) as a quick method that could be used by the federal government to analyze and compare thousands of jobs. All of the jobs listed in the **Dictionary of Occupational Titles (DOT)** were analyzed using FJA. Although rarely used in industry, FJA is important to understand for two reasons. First, it serves as the base for the DOT, and DOT codes must be used on many occasions when dealing with the federal government. Second, FJA is the job-analysis foundation upon which many government validity generalization programs using the **General Aptitude Test Battery (GATB)** are based.

Jobs analyzed by FJA are broken down into the percentage of time the incumbent spends on three functions—data (information and ideas), people (clients, customers, and co-workers), and things (machines, tools, and equipment). An analyst is given 100 points to allot to the three functions. The points are usually assigned in multiples of five, with each function receiving a minimum of five points. Once the points have been assigned, the highest level at which the job incumbent functions is then chosen from the chart shown in Figure 2.4 (Fine & Wiley, 1971).

AET

Developed in Germany by Rohmert and Landau (1983), AET is the acronym for "Arbeitswissenschaftliches Erhebungsverfahren zur Tatigkeitsanalyse" (try saying this three times!), which means "ergonomic job-analysis procedure." By "ergonomic," we mean that it is primarily concerned with the relationship between the worker and work objects. The **AET** is a 216-item standardized questionnaire that analyzes a job along the dimensions shown in Figure 2.5. Sample items from the AET can be found in Figure 2.6. Although the AET appears to be a promising method for obtaining certain types of job-analysis information, there has not been enough published research to draw any real conclusions.

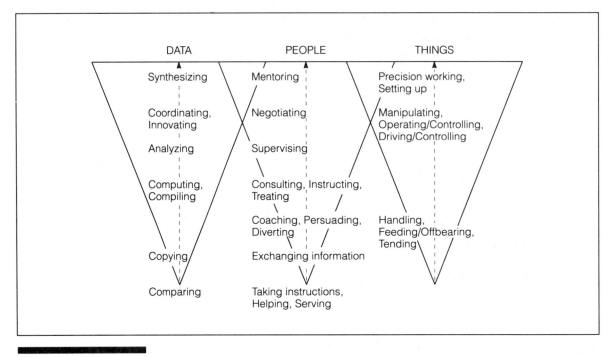

Figure 2.4
FJA Dimensions

Evaluation of Methods

In the previous pages, several job-analysis methods were presented. But the question left unanswered is, Which of the methods is best? Unfortunately, there is no cut-and-dried answer to this question. The best method to use in analyzing a job appears to be related to the end use of the job-analysis information. That is, different methods are best for different uses. As shown in Table 2.5, the *worker-oriented methods* such as CIT and TTA are best for uses such as employee selection and performance appraisal. *Job-oriented methods* such as task analysis and JCI are best for uses such as work design and writing job descriptions.

To get the most out of a job analysis, several techniques should be utilized (Rouleau & Krain, 1975). At least one of these methods should be worker-oriented and at least one job-oriented (Prien, 1977).

From a legal perspective, courts have ruled that job analysis is necessary (Ledvinka & Schoenfeldt, 1978) and that acceptable job analyses use several up-to-date sources, are conducted by experts, use a large number of job incumbents, and cover the entire range of worker activities and qualifications (Thompson & Thompson, 1982). Interviews and the CIT

Figure 2.5
AET Dimensions

Part A - Work System Analysis

1   Work objects
   1.1   material work objects (physical condition, special properties of the material, quality of surfaces, manipulation delicacy, form, size, weight, dangerousness)
   1.2   energy as work object
   1.3   information as work object
   1.4   man, animals, plants as work objects
2   Equipment
   2.1   working equipment
      2.1.1   equipment, tools, machinery to change the properties of work objects
      2.1.2   means of transport
      2.1.3   controls
   2.2   other equipment
      2.2.1   displays, measuring instruments
      2.2.2   technical aids to support human sense organs
      2.2.3   work chair, table, room
3   Work environment
   3.1   physical environment
      3.1.1   environmental influences
      3.1.2   dangerousness of work and risk of occupational diseases
   3.2   organizational and social environment
      3.2.1   temporal organization of work
      3.2.2   position in the organization of work sequence
      3.2.3   hierarchical position in the organization
      3.2.4   position in the communication system
   3.3   principles and methods of remuneration
      3.3.1   principles of remuneration
      3.3.2   methods of remuneration

Part B - Task Analysis

1   tasks relating to material work objects
2   tasks relating to abstract work objects
3   man-related tasks
4   number and repetitiveness of tasks

Part C - Job Demand Analysis

1   Demands on perception
   1.1   mode of perception
      1.1.1   visual
      1.1.2   auditory
      1.1.3   tactile
      1.1.4   olfactory
      1.1.5   proprioceptive
   1.2   absolute/relative evaluation of perceived information
   1.3   accuracy of perception
2   Demands for decision
   2.1   complexity of decision
   2.2   pressure of time
   2.3   required knowledge
3   Demands for response/activity
   3.1   body postures
   3.2   static work
   3.3   heavy muscular work
   3.4   light muscular work
   3.5   strenuousness and frequency of movements

Source: Rohmert, W., & Landau, K. (1983). *A new technique for job analysis.* New York: Taylor & Francis. Reprinted with permission of the publisher.

Figure 2.6
Sample AET Items

CNO	CC
1.1.7	Weight

Answer questions 22–24 indicating the individual proportions of *time* during which the incumbent performs tasks involving work materials of *different weights*.

22	D	*Low* weight

objects weighing up to 1 kg can normally be manipulated with fingers or hands

23	D	*Medium* weight

1–10 kg can normally be manipulated with hands

24		*Heavy* weight

more than 10 kg can partly be manipulated by one person without using additional auxiliaries, partly including the use of handling equipment and hoisting machines

1.1.8	Danger

Answer questions 25–30 indicating the individual proportions of *time* during which the incumbent performs tasks involving *dangerous work materials*.

25	D	Work materials that are *explosive*

e.g., explosives and igniting mixtures, ammunition, fireworks

26	D	Work materials that are *conducive to fire or inflammable*

e.g., petrol, technical oils, lacquers, and varnishes

27	D	Work materials that are *poisonous or caustic*

e.g., basic chemicals, chemical-technical materials, plant protectives, cleaning materials

28	D	Work materials that are *radioactive*

e.g., uranium concentrate, nuclear materials

29	D	Work materials *irritating skin or mucous membrane*

e.g., quartz, asbestos, Thomas meal, flax, raw cotton

30	D	Work materials *causing other health hazards*

If characteristic 1 is rated D = 5, continue with characteristic 34.

Source: Rohmert, W., & Landau, K. (1983). *A new technique for job analysis.* New York: Taylor & Francis. Reprinted with permission of the publisher.

seem to hold up well in court, while the job-elements approach does not (Kleiman & Faley, 1978; Thompson & Thompson, 1982).

Unfortunately, there has been no abundance of research directly comparing job-analysis methods. This lack of research is primarily because direct comparison of methods is virtually impossible: Each method yields

Job Analysis Method	Human Resource Function							
	A	B	C	D	E	F	G	H
Interview	+		+		−	−	−	
Observation		−		−	−	−	−	+
Participation	+			−	−	−		
Critical Incidents Technique	−	+	+	+	+	−	−	−
Task inventories	+		+	+				
Ammerman technique		+		+		−	−	−
Job Element Inventory	−	+		+		−	−	−
PAQ	−		−		−	+	+	−
Job Components Inventory					−			−
Threshold Traits Analysis	−	+		−	−		+	−
Functional Job Analysis			+	−	−			−
AET				−	−	+	+	

Note: A = job description; B = employee selection; C = training; D = personpower planning; E = performance appraisal; F = classification; G = job evaluation; H = job design.

Table 2.5
Ratings of Job Analysis Methods for Various Uses

results that differ in both the number and type of dimensions (Cornelius, Carron, & Collins, 1979). Thus, the comparative research that has been conducted has focused on opinions of job analysts.

Survey research by Levine, Ash, and their colleagues (Levine, Ash, Hall, & Sistrunk, 1983; Levine, Ash, & Bennett, 1980) has found the following:

1. The PAQ is seen as the most standardized technique and the CIT the least standardized.

2. The CIT takes the least amount of job-analyst training and task analysis the most.

3. The PAQ is the least costly method, CIT the most.

4. The PAQ takes the least amount of time to complete, task analysis the most.

5. Task analysis has the highest quality results, TTA the lowest.

6. Task analysis reports are longest, job elements shortest.

7. The CIT was rated at being the most useful, the PAQ the least.

8. Task analysis gave the best overall job picture, the PAQ the worst.

Keep in mind, however, that the above findings were based on users' opinions rather than actual empirical comparison.

Writing Job Descriptions

As mentioned earlier, one of the most useful results of a job analysis is the **job description**. A job description is a relatively short summary of a job and should be about two to five pages in length. This suggested length is not really typical of most job descriptions that are used in industry; they tend to be only one page. But for a job description to be of any real value, it must describe a job in enough detail that decisions about activities such as selection and training can be made. Such decisions probably cannot be made if the description is written in just one page.

Job descriptions can be written in many ways, but the following format is one that has been used successfully for many jobs, a combination used by many companies and suggested by several researchers. A job description should contain the following seven sections: job title, brief summary, work activities, tools and equipment used, work context, performance standards, and personal requirements.

Job Title

Including a job title is important for several reasons. First, a properly labeled title gives an indication of the nature of the job. When industrial psychologist David Faloona started a new job at Washington National Insurance in Chicago, his official title was Psychometric Technician. Unfortunately, none of the other workers knew what he did. To correct that problem, his title was changed to Personnel Assistant, and supervisors then began consulting with him on human resource–related problems.

An accurate title also aids in employee selection and recruitment. If the job title indicates the true nature of the job, people thinking of applying for it will have better ideas about the matches between their skills and experience and those required for the job in question.

When conducting a job analysis, it is not unusual for an analyst to find that some workers do not have job titles. In addition to the reasons cited above, job titles are beneficial in that they provide workers with some form of identity. Instead of just saying that she is a "worker at the foundry," a woman can say that she is a "welder" or a "machinist."

Brief Summary

The summary need only be a paragraph in length but briefly describe the nature and purpose of the job. This brief summary can be used in help wanted advertisements or company brochures.

Work Activities

The work activities section lists the tasks and activities in which the worker is involved. These tasks and activities should be organized into meaningful categories to make the job description easier to read and understand. The category labels are also convenient to use in the brief summary. Much has been written about the proper way to write a task statement (McCormick, 1979), but a job analyst should not get too bogged down worrying about format. Instead, the task statements in this section should be short and written at a level that can be read and understood by a person with the same reading ability as the typical job incumbent. It also has been suggested that for those activities that involve decision making, the level of authority should be indicated. This level lets the incumbent know which decisions he is allowed to make on his own and which decisions he needs approval from a higher level (Campbell, 1983).

Tools and Equipment Used

A section should be included that lists all the tools and equipment used to perform the work activities in the previous section. Even though tools and equipment may have been mentioned in the activities section, placing them in a separate section makes their identification simpler. Information in this section is primarily used for employee selection and training.

Work Context

A section should be included that describes the environment in which the employee works. Items that should be mentioned include stress level, work schedule, physical demands, level of responsibility, temperature, number of co-workers, degree of danger, and any other relevant information.

Performance Standards

The job description should outline standards of performance. This section contains a relatively brief description of how an employee's performance is evaluated and what work standards are expected of the employee.

Table 2.6
Use of Job Analysis Methods in Writing Job Descriptions

Job Analysis Method	Job Description Section						
	A	**B**	**C**	**D**	**E**	**F**	**G**
Interview	x	x	x	x	x	x	x
Observation		x	x	x	x		x
Participation	x	x	x	x	x	x	x
Critical Incidents Technique						x	x
Task inventories		x	x	x			x
Ammerman technique	x	x	x			x	x
Job Element Inventory							x
PAQ	x						x
Job Components Inventory	x		x	x			x
Threshold Traits Analysis							x
Functional Job Analysis	x	x					x
AET				x	x		

Note: A = job title; B = summary; C = work activities; D = tools; E = work context; F = performance; G = personal characteristics.

Personal Requirements

The personal requirements section contains what are commonly called **job specifications.** These are the knowledge, skills, abilities, and other (KSAOs) characteristics (interest, personality, training, and so on) that are necessary to be successful on the job. This section should be divided into two subsections. The first contains KSAOs that an employee must have at time of hiring. The second subsection contains the KSAOs that are an important part of the job but which can be obtained after being hired. The first set of KSAOs are used for employee selection and performance appraisal and the second for training purposes.

A sample job description for a credit union employee can be found in Box 2.1. An evaluation of which job-analysis techniques will yield information suitable for the seven sections of the job description is shown in Table 2.6.

Job Evaluation

Job evaluation is the process of determining a job's *worth*. Such evaluation is important because most workers want to be paid fairly—that is, they want to be paid an amount equal not only to the actual worth of their particular job, but also in amounts consistent with those paid to other workers in the same company (internal equity) as well as to workers in other organizations (external equity). Arriving at "fair and accurate" pay levels is difficult because most job-evaluation procedures determine the worth of a job based on the skill needed as well as on the demands that the job makes on the worker. But the results of job evaluations are often controversial because job-evaluation techniques do not take into account important factors that are not directly related to the job itself. These other factors include the status level of the job (physician versus hair stylist), intrinsic satisfaction of a job (teaching versus assembly-line work), local cost of living (California versus Arkansas), prevailing wage rates, and union agreements. With these limitations in mind, compensable job factors and the method of job evaluation—by ranking or by point— must be considered if the job evaluation is to be reasonable.

Compensable Job Factors

The first step in job evaluation is to decide what factors differentiate the relative worth of jobs. Possible **compensable job factors** include:

- level of responsibility
- physical demands
- mental demands
- education requirements
- training and experience requirements
- working conditions
- availability of workers in the work force

This is where the philosophical leanings of the person conducting the job evaluation come into play. Some analysts argue that the most important compensable factor is responsibility and that physical demands are not important. Others argue that education is most important. The choice of compensable factors thus is often more philosophical than empirical.

Choice of Methods

The second step in evaluating a job is to choose which method will be used. Just as there are many job-analysis techniques, there are many

Box 2.1

**Bookkeeper
Radford Pipe Shop Employee's
Federal Credit Union**

Job Summary Under the general supervision of the office manager, the Bookkeeper is responsible for all of the accounting duties of the office. Specifically, the Bookkeeper is responsible for: Keeping all financial records accurate and up-to-date; processing loans; and preparing and posting statements, reports, and bonds.

Work Activities The work activities of the Bookkeeper are divided into seven main functional areas:

Accounting Activities
- Prepares quarterly income statement
- Maintains and posts all transactions in general ledger book
- Pays credit union bills
- Prepares statistical reports
- Updates undivided earnings account
- Prepares and files tax returns and statements
- Completes IRA forms and reports in cooperation with CUNA
- Annually computes Cumis Bond
- Balances journal and cash records

Clerical Activities
- Looks up members' account information when requested
- Answers phone
- Makes copies of transactions for members
- Drafts statements of account to members
- Types Certificates of Deposit
- Makes copies of letters that are sent to members
- Picks up, sorts, and disperses credit union mail
- Folds monthly and quarterly statements and places into an envelope to be mailed to members

- Processes and mails savings and share draft statements
- Sorts checks or copies of checks in numerical order
- Orders supplies
- Types reports and minutes from board meetings
- Maintains and updates files for members
- Prepares, types, and files correspondence
- Enters change-of-address information into the computer

Teller Activities
- Enrolls new members and opens and closes accounts
- Reconciles accounts
- Issues money orders and traveler's checks
- Conducts history of accounts
- Processes and issues receipts for transactions
- Asks for identification if person making transaction is not known
- Daily enters transaction totals onto a list sent to the bank
- Orders new or replacement checks for members
- Prints and issues checks
- Makes proper referrals

Share Draft Activities
- Deducts fee from member's account when a share is returned
- Processes statements for share draft accounts
- Issues stop payments and sends copy of form to member
- Deducts fee in form of an overdraft when more than three transfers have occurred for any one member in a month
- Checks and records share drafts or additions from previous day
- Receives share draft totals for each member from CUNA data
- Decides on an individual basis whether overdrafts will be covered by credit union

Continued

- Determines if overdrafts on account have been paid
- Checks to see if share drafts have cleared
- Telephones Chase-Manhatten Bank when a member does not have enough money to cover a share draft

Collections Activities

- Holds money from member's check in order to meet loan payments
- Decides if a member who has a delinquent loan will be able to take money out of account
- Locates and communicates with members having delinquent loans
- Completes garnishee form to send to courts on delinquent loans
- Resubmits garnishee form once every three months until delinquent loan has been paid in full by member
- Makes collection on delinquent loans
- Checks on previous member's address and current job to see if loan payments can be made
- Determines number and length of time of delinquent loans
- Sends judgment form to court, which sends it to delinquent member
- If a member is delinquent, finds out if they are sick or on vacation

Payroll and Data-Processing Activities

- Checks and verifies payroll run for all necessary deductions
- Reads and interprets computer printouts
- Computes and subtracts deductions from payroll
- Sets up and changes deduction amounts for payroll savings plan
- Runs payroll on computer
- Annually sends out backup disk to outside vendor who transfers information to a magnetic tape that is sent to IRS
- Computes payroll

- Runs daily trial balances and transaction registers
- Loads paper into printer
- Makes backup copies of all daily computer transactions
- Runs quarterly and/or monthly statements on computer

Financial Operations Activities

- Scans business/financial environment to identify potential threats and opportunities
- Makes recommendations to the board regarding investments
- Invests all excess money into accounts that will earn interest
- Computes profits and amounts to be used for investments
- Prepares statements of financial condition and federal operating fee report
- Obtains enough funds for day-to-day operation of branch
- Notifies and makes available investment funds to the NCUA

Machines Used The Bookkeeper uses the following machines and equipment:

- Adding machine
- Typewriter
- Computer printer
- CRT
- Mainframe computer
- Credit history machine
- Motor vehicle
- Photocopy machine
- Folding machine
- Microfiche reader
- Safe
- Telephone
- Security check writer

Job Context The Bookkeeper spends the majority of time making entries in and balancing journals and ledgers. The work day is spent in a climate-controlled office with four co-workers. Physical demands are minimal and sitting is required for most of the day. Stress is moderate.

Continued

Work Performance To receive an excellent performance appraisal, the Bookkeeper should:
- Maintain neat and accurate records
- Meet all deadlines
- Maintain an orderly office
- Make sure all ledgers and journals balance
- Perform duties of other jobs when the need arises

Job Qualifications Upon hire, the Bookkeeper must:
- Have a basic knowledge of math and English

- Understand financial documents
- Be able to make limited financial decisions
- Have completed advanced course-work in accounting and finance
- Have had training in data processing

After hire, the Bookkeeper must:
- Learn general office procedures
- Learn credit union style accounting procedures and regulations
- Learn how to complete the various forms

methods of job evaluation. The method used is determined by such factors as the number of jobs to be evaluated, the expertise of the person conducting the job evaluation, and the philosophical leanings of the person conducting the job evaluation.

Ranking Method

The **ranking method** is the easiest and is often used in smaller organizations (Mann, 1965). Basically, jobs within an organization are rank ordered either on the basis of their perceived overall worth or on the basis of each of the compensable factors selected in the previous step. If the latter method is used, the rankings for each factor are then summed to form an overall ranking. Overall rankings are then compared to the actual salaries that are paid to workers in each position. In Table 2.7, for example, the receptionist job has been ranked higher than the gardener job. In such a case, the salary for the receptionist would be raised above the gardener's. Although this method is excellent for assigning **relative amounts** of compensation, it does not yield enough information to determine **absolute amounts** of compensation. Furthermore, it is difficult to find individuals to do the ranking who are familiar enough with all of the jobs in an organization.

A more complicated version of the ranking method is the assignment of differential weights to each factor by a job-evaluation committee (Yoder & Heneman, 1979). The average ranks for each factor are then multiplied

Job	Rank	Previous Salary ($)
Manager	1	30,000
Assistant manager	2	22,000
Salesperson	3	18,000
Secretary	4	15,000
Receptionist	5	10,000
Gardener	6	12,000
Janitor	7	9,000

Table 2.7
Example of Ranking Method of Job Evaluation

by the weight assigned to the factors. The products of these calculations are then summed to provide an overall rank order. Most of these calculations are done by computer programs purchased from consultants specializing in job evaluation. Typically, these computer programs already contain standard compensable factors and weights for each factor. Thus, the main job of the job-evaluation committee is to rank the jobs on each of the factors.

One version of this method, the **classification method**, is used by many governmental agencies including those of the federal government. In this version, jobs that are ranked near one another are grouped together to form several **grades**. Jobs within each grade level are considered to be of equal value and are paid at the same rate.

Point Method

The **point method** is the most commonly used method of job evaluation (Hills, 1987). To use this method, a five-step process is followed:

1. A job-evaluation committee determines the total number of points that will be distributed among the factors. Usually, the number is some multiple of 100 (for example, 100, 500, 1000) and is based upon the number of compensable factors. The greater the number of factors, the greater the number of points.

2. Each factor is weighted by assigning different numbers of points to the factors. The more important the factor, the greater the number that will be assigned.

3. Each factor is divided into degrees. For example, if one of the factors is education, the degrees might be
■ high school education or less
■ two-year college degree

Table 2.8
Example of the Point Method of Job Evaluation

Factors	Points
Education (200 points possible)	
No high school degree	0
High school degree	50
Two-year college degree	100
Four-year college degree	150
Master's degree	200
Responsibility (300 points possible)	
Makes no decisions	0
Makes decisions for self	100
Makes decisions for 1–5 employees	200
Makes decisions for more than 5 employees	300
Physical demands (100 points possible)	
Lifts no heavy objects	0
Lifts objects between 25 and 100 pounds	50
Lifts objects more than 100 pounds	100

- four-year college degree
- Master's degree
- doctorate

The number of points assigned to a factor is then divided into each of the degrees. If 100 points had been assigned to the factor of education then, 20 points (100 points/5 degrees) would be assigned to each degree. An example of this procedure is shown in Table 2.8.

4. The job-evaluation committee takes the job descriptions for each job and assigns points based on the factors and degrees created in the previous steps.

5. The total number of points for a job is compared with the salary currently being paid for the job. This comparison is typically graphed in a fashion similar to the **wage trend line** shown in Figure 2.7. Jobs whose point values fall below the line (as does job D's in Figure 2.5) are considered underpaid and are immediately assigned higher salary levels. Jobs with point values above the line (as with job H) are considered overpaid and the salary level is decreased once current jobholders leave.

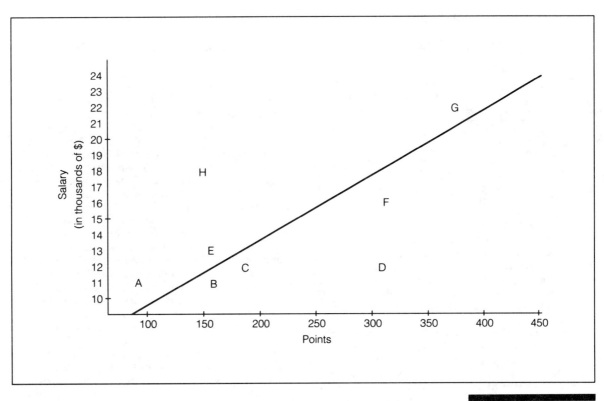

Figure 2.7
Example of a Wage
Trend Line

Other Methods

A few other methods can be used to evaluate jobs. The **factor-compari-son method** (Benge, Burk, & Hay, 1941), the job-components method, and **time span of discretion** (Jaques, 1961) are examples, but because they are both complex and not commonly used, they will not be discussed here. A description of the work performed by a compensation analyst can be found in the employment profile of Chris Davis.

Salary Surveys

The techniques described above are used to establish the **internal eq-uity** of an organization's compensation plan. To recruit and retain em-ployees, however, it is essential that an organization's compensation plan reflect **external equity.** In other words, it must be competitive with the compensation plans of other organizations. That is, a fast food restaurant that pays cooks $4.00 per hour will probably have trouble hiring and

Employment Profile

Chris Davis, M.S.
Compensation Manager
Dominion Bankshares

My job is a portion of the overall human resource (H.R.) function of a large multibank holding company. To explain my job, I'll start with the overall function of the H.R. group. The current organizational structure consists of several independently operating affiliate banks, each with its own management and separate H.R. department. In this environment, the corporate H.R. group develops, researches, and administers policy for the affiliates as well as provides consulting services in a variety of specialized content areas.

Base-salary administration is the specialized area of expertise that I provide for the corporation. Base-salary administration is that part of the compensation function that involves the fixed hourly, monthly, or annual rate at which a job should be paid and all the procedures that ensure that each employee is compensated equitably based on his or her contribution to corporate goals. Base-salary administration should not be confused with other ways in which an employee may be compensated such as benefits, merit pay, and performance bonuses.

My position supervises two employees. Together, we provide administrative, analytical, and consultative services for the corporation. Administratively, we review all payroll changes and salary increases and decreases before they are sent to payroll. In conjunction with this function, we develop annual salary budgets that determine the corporate expenditure for the year. Furthermore, we develop and publish the procedures for managers throughout the corporation to follow in administering salary to the employees they oversee.

Analytically, we do many things for the corporation. We provide methodology and training for all procedures required to describe and evaluate jobs throughout the corporation. Evaluations are simply the process of deciding what a job is worth based on its duties. These evaluations are completed by the affiliate H.R. managers and reviewed by my department. We also provide evaluation services for the corporate staff. These analytical services also include the collection and review of salary data from several sources.

Finally, and perhaps most important, we provide consultative services to the corporation. In the role of consultants, we provide a variety of advice and special project research services to address the many special situations that come up in the process of salary administration. For example, career-path planning, legal issues, recruiting, and retention all may present unique problems that require a special level of expertise in compensation.

My job specifically is to make sure that all these things are done either by doing them myself or by delegating them to my staff. Carrying out the duties of the job requires a great deal of analytical ability in conjunction with specific technical understanding of the principles of compensation. But perhaps most important to the job is the ability to communicate effectively with all areas of the organization. Communication is critical to the success of the salary-administration program because so much depends on the effective flow of relatively complex ideas both into and out of the salary-administration group.

keeping high-caliber employees if other fast food restaurants pay $4.50 per hour.

To determine external equity, organizations use **salary surveys.** Sent to other organizations, these surveys ask how much they pay their employees in various positions. An organization can either construct and send out its own survey or use the results of surveys conducted by trade groups, an option that many companies choose. A page from an actual salary survey is shown in Figure 2.8.

Job Title: Loan Interviewer	Total Number of Employees in this position: _____

Job Description:
The loan interviewer is responsible for servicing credit union members in reference to prospective loans by accepting loan applications, interviewing loan applicants, running credit reports, processing loan applications and communicating decision results to members. The factor that most differentiates a loan interviewer from a loan clerk is the amount of contact with the public.

Annual Salary Range for Position:

Minimum $ __ __, __ __ __   Maximum $__ __, __ __ __

Compensation Data for Each Employee in This Position:

Incumbent Number	Current Actual Annual Salary	Sex of Employee	Race of Employee	Years in Position	Education Level
01	$__ __, __ __ __	____	____	____	_____
02	$__ __, __ __ __	____	____	____	_____
03	$__ __, __ __ __	____	____	____	_____
04	$__ __, __ __ __	____	____	____	_____
05	$__ __, __ __ __	____	____	____	_____
06	$__ __, __ __ __	____	____	____	_____
07	$__ __, __ __ __	____	____	____	_____
08	$__ __, __ __ __	____	____	____	_____
09	$__ __, __ __ __	____	____	____	_____
10	$__ __, __ __ __	____	____	____	_____
11	$__ __, __ __ __	____	____	____	_____
12	$__ __, __ __ __	____	____	____	_____

**Figure 2.8
Example of a Salary Survey**

**Table 2.9
Salary Levels of
Women as Percent of
Men's Salaries, and
Women's Share of
Total Employment in
Selected
Occupations, 1981**

Occupation	Female–Male Pay Ratio[a]	Female Share of Total Employment
Professional		
Accountant	83	23
Auditor	86	22
Attorney	78	15
Chemist	75	14
Administrative		
Director of personnel	87	13
Job analyst	79	62
Buyer	80	20
Technical		
Engineering technician	85	8
Drafter	82	13
Computer operator	92	34
Photographer	80	7
Clerical		
Accounting clerk	82	92
Messenger	101	46
Purchasing assistant	74	85

Source: Sieling, M. S. (1984). Staffing patterns prominent in female–male earnings gap. *Monthly Labor Review, 107*(6), 29.

[a] Includes data only for workers identified by sex

Based on the results of these surveys, an organization can decide where it wants to be when compared with the compensation policies of other organizations. It may seem surprising that competing organizations would supply salary information to each other, but because every organization needs salary data from other organizations, compensation analysts tend to cooperate well with one another.

Comparable Worth

Comparable worth is an issue very much related to the discussion of job evaluation. Recently, comparable worth has been in the news as many groups claim that female workers are paid less than male workers. This feeling of pay inequity stems from the statistic that, on average, female workers in 1989 were paid only 70% of what male workers were paid (U.S. Department of Labor, 1989). But as Table 2.9 shows, this statistic is misleading. When males and females in the same jobs are compared, this percentage increases to around 80%. This figure also can be misleading because males have been in the work force longer, have a higher percentage of full-time jobs, and a higher percentage of college degrees (Mellor, 1984). As shown in Table 2.10, when males and females are compared on *identical* jobs with identical requirements, the percentage is approximately 95%. Thus, the issue of comparable worth is often less an issue of pay discrimination than one of vocational choice discrimination. To alleviate gender differences in pay, it is essential that young females be encouraged to enter historically male-dominated fields (assembly lines, management, police) and that young males be encouraged to enter historically female-dominated fields (nursing, clerical, elementary education).

Chapter Summary

The first section of this chapter discussed the job-analysis process. Even if job analysis were not legally required, it would still be useful for areas such as performance appraisal, employee selection, training, and job design. Before a job analysis is begun, decisions must be made about the type of information that will be obtained, who will conduct the job analysis, and who will participate in it. These are important decisions: Research indicates that different types of people and different types of information collected will result in different job-analysis outcomes.

The chapter also discussed 14 different methods of job analysis. Although no method is always better than others, each is best for certain purposes. For example, the PAQ is an excellent method for compensation uses, and the CIT is an excellent method for performance appraisal.

When a job analysis is completed, job descriptions can be written. A good job-description format includes a job title, a brief summary of the job, and information about work activities, tools and equipment, the work context, performance standards, and the personal requirements that are needed to perform the job.

The second section of the chapter discussed job evaluation—the process of assigning a monetary value to a job. This process can be accomplished by first choosing compensable factors and then using a method such as either the point method or the ranking method to determine the

Occupational Work Level	Average Monthly Salary[a]	Female–Male Pay Relationship[b]	Female Share of Total Employment		Occupational Work Level	Average Monthly Salary[a]	Female–Male Pay Relationship[b]	Female Share of Total Employment
Professional					**Technical**			
Accountant I	$1,372	99	46		Engineering technician I	1,137	97	24
Accountant II	1,679	98	34		Engineering technician II	1,307	98	17
Accountant III	1,962	96	19		Engineering technician III	1,527	97	9
Accountant IV	2,402	95	11		Drafter I	923	103	34
Accountant V	2,928	90	5		Drafter II	1,075	101	26
Auditor I	1,364	98	36		Drafter III	1,301	96	18
Auditor II	1,651	97	27		Drafter IV	1,611	94	8
Auditor III	2,033	92	21		Computer operator I	906	99	37
Auditor IV	2,456	90	8		Computer operator II	1,049	102	49
Attorney I	1,873	103	28		Computer operator III	1,220	97	35
Attorney II	2,338	99	24		Computer operator IV	1,475	97	24
Attorney III	3,031	95	13		Computer operator V	1,733	92	17
Attorney IV	3,738	94	9		Photographer II	1,425	96	6
Chemist I	1,508	96	38		Photographer III	1,704	106	5
Chemist II	1,757	94	29		**Clerical**			
Chemist III	2,120	93	15		Accounting clerk I	798	94	95
Chemist IV	2,567	92	10		Accounting clerk II	953	89	94
Administrative					Accounting clerk III	1,121	89	91
Buyer I	1,350	96	52		Accounting clerk IV	1,407	84	82
Buyer II	1,089	95	23		Purchasing assistant I	1,002	93	95
Buyer III	2,100	92	9		Purchasing assistant II	1,278	87	84
Director of personnel I	2,321	101	21		Messenger	783	101	46
Director of personnel II	2,933	94	10					
Director of personnel III	3,574	90	7					
Job analyst I	1,412	87	75					
Job analyst II	1,525	92	85					
Job analyst III	1,900	90	66					
Job analyst IV	2,393	94	29					

Source: Sieling, M. S. (1984). Staffing patterns prominent in female–male earnings gap. *Monthly Labor Review, 107*(6), 29.

[a]Includes data for workers not identified by sex

[b]Includes data only for workers identified by sex

Table 2.10
Salary Level by Sex and Occupational Level

relative worth of the job. Salary surveys are used to determine how competitive an organization's compensation plan is relative to other organizations.

Glossary

Absolute amounts The actual salary that is paid for a particular job

AET An ergonomic job analysis method developed in Germany

Ammerman Technique A job analysis method in which a group of job experts identifies the objectives and standards that are to be met by the ideal incumbent

Classification method A job evaluation system in which jobs of similar worth are placed into the same category and are paid at the same level

Comparable worth The idea that jobs requiring the same level of skill and responsibility should be paid the same regardless of supply and demand

Compensable job factors Factors, such as responsibility and education requirements, that differentiate the relative worth of jobs

Critical Incident Technique (CIT) The job analysis method developed by John Flanagan that utilizes written reports of good and bad employee behavior

Dictionary of Occupational Titles (DOT) A directory published by the federal government that supplies information for almost 30,000 jobs

External equity The extent to which employees within an organization are paid fairly compared to employees in other organizations

Factor-comparison method A job evaluation technique in which dollar amounts rather than point values are assigned to jobs

Functional Job Analysis (FJA) A job analysis method developed by Fine that involves rating the extent to which a job incumbent is involved with functions in the categories of data, people, and things

General Aptitude Test Battery (GATB) The most commonly used ability test used to select employees

Grade A cluster of jobs of similar worth

Internal equity The extent to which employees within an organization are paid fairly compared to other employees within the same organization

Job analysis The process of identifying the manner in which a job is performed as well as the requirements that it takes to perform the job

Job analysis interviews Obtaining information about a job by talking to the person performing the job

Job analyst The person conducting the job analysis

Job Components Inventory (JCI) A structured job analysis technique developed by Banks that concentrates on worker requirements for performing a job rather than on specific tasks

Job descriptions A written summary of the tasks performed in a job, the conditions under which the job is performed, and the requirements needed to perform the job

Job element approach A job analysis method developed by Primoff that involves the identification and rating of job elements

Job Element Inventory (JEI) A structured job analysis technique developed by Cornelius and Hakel that is similar to the PAQ but easier to read

Job elements Used in the job element approach, job elements are factors such as knowledge, skills, and abilities that are important to the performance of a job

Job evaluation The process of determining the monetary worth of a job

Job participation A job analysis method in which the job analyst actually performs the job being analyzed

Job specifications The knowledge, skills, and abilities needed to successfully perform a job

Job Structure Profile (JSP) A revised version of the PAQ designed to be used more by the job analyst than the job incumbent

KSAOs Acronym referring to knowledge, skills, and abilities, and other characteristics required to perform a job

Observation A job analysis method in which the job analyst watches job incumbents perform their jobs

Peter Principle The idea that organizations tend to promote good employees until they reach the level at which they are not competent—in other words, their highest level of incompetence

Point method A job evaluation system in which jobs are assigned points across several compensable factors to determine the worth of the job

Position Analysis Questionnaire (PAQ) A structured job analysis method developed by McCormick

Ranking method Job evaluation technique in which jobs in an organization are rank ordered based on their perceived worth

Relative amounts The relationship of one salary to another (for example, a secretary being paid more than a clerk)

Salary survey A questionnaire sent to other organizations to see how much they are paying their employees in positions similar to those in the organization sending the survey

Task analysis A job analysis method in which the job analyst identifies the tasks that are performed on the job

Task inventory A questionnaire containing a list of tasks for which the job incumbent rates each task on a series of scales such as importance and time spent

Threshold Traits Analysis (TTA) A 33-item questionnaire developed by Lopez that is designed to identify traits necessary to successfully perform a job

Time span of discretion A job evaluation technique in which the worth of a job is determined by the length of time an employee goes without receiving direction from a supervisor

Wage trend line A line that represents the ideal relationship between the number of points that a job has been assigned (using the point method of evaluation) and the salary range for that job

3

Frank Siteman/Stock Boston

Evaluating Selection
Techniques and Decisions

In Chapter 1, we learned that many laws and regulations affect the methods that can be used to select employees. In Chapters 4 and 5, we will discuss the best ways to recruit and select employees. But before we can discuss the various methods of selection that are available, we must first learn what determines whether a selection technique or decision is both fair and useful. That is the purpose of this chapter—to discuss how to evaluate the effectiveness, fairness, and usefulness of employee-selection techniques.

Characteristics of Effective Selection Devices

Reliability

To be of any value, the selection devices or techniques that will be discussed in Chapters 4 and 5 must be reliable. **Reliability** concerns the extent to which a score from a test is stable and free from error. If a test score is not stable or free from error, it is not useful in any way. For example, suppose that we are using a ruler to measure the lengths of boards that will be used to build a doghouse. We want each board to be four feet in length. Each time we measure a piece of wood, we get a different number. If the ruler does not yield the same number each time the same board is measured, the ruler cannot be considered reliable and thus is of no use.

The same is true of employment tests. If a person scores differently each time he takes a test, we are unsure of his actual score. Consequently, the scores from the tests are of little value. Therefore, the first characteristic of an effective test is that it must be reliable.

Characteristics Related to Test Reliability
Certain test characteristics affect the reliability of a test.

Test Length In general, the longer the test, the higher its **internal reliability** (Cureton, 1965). To illustrate this point, lets look at your final exam in this course. If the final were based on three chapters, would you want a test consisting of only three multiple-choice items? Probably not. When taking the test, if you make a careless mistake in marking your

Peter Menzel/Stock Boston

Employment tests must be reliably stable and free from error if they are to be useful.

answer or happened to have fallen asleep during part of the lecture from which a question was taken, your score will be low. But if the test has 100 items, one careless mistake or one missed part of a lecture will not severely affect the total score.

Homogeneity of Test Items A second factor that can affect the internal reliability of a test is **item homogeneity.** That is, do all of the items measure the same thing or do they measure different constructs? The more homogeneous the items, the higher the internal reliability. To illustrate this concept, let us again look at your final exam based on three chapters.

If we computed the reliability of the entire exam, it would probably be relatively low. Why? Because the test items are not homogeneous. They are measuring knowledge from three topic areas (three chapters), two sources (lecture and text), and two knowledge types (factual and conceptual). If we broke the test down by chapter, source, and item type, the reliability of the test would be higher because we are looking at groups of homogeneous items.

Homogeneity of the Sample A third factor that can affect test reliability is **sample homogeneity.** To obtain high reliability coefficients, it is important for the sample to have heterogeneous scores on the test. That is, some people must score low, some must score high, and others must score in the middle. If everyone scores the same, a low reliability coefficient will result.

Scorer Reliability A final factor that can affect a test's reliability coefficient is **scorer reliability.** A test can have homogeneous items and yield heterogeneous scores and still not be reliable if the person scoring the test makes mistakes. Scorer reliability is an issue especially in projective or subjective tests in which there is no one correct answer, but even tests that are scored with the use of keys suffer from scorer mistakes.

Determining the Reliability of a Test

There are three major ways to determine whether a test is reliable.

Test–Retest Reliability With the **test–retest reliability** method, several people each take the same test twice. The scores from the first administration of the test are correlated with scores from the second administration to determine whether the two sets of scores are similar. If the scores are similar, the test is said to have **temporal stability.** This means that the test scores are stable across time and not highly susceptible to random daily conditions such as illness, fatigue, stress, or uncomfortable testing conditions (Anastasi, 1982).

Subjects	Administration Order	
	First	Second
1–50	Form A	Form B
51–100	Form B	Form A

Table 3.1
Design for Typical
Parallel Forms
Reliability Study

There is no standard amount of time that should elapse between the two administrations of the test. The time interval should be long enough, however, that the specific test answers are not still in memory and yet not so long that the person actually changes.

For example, if three years elapsed between administrations of a personality test, we may find a very low correlation between the two sets of scores; but the low correlation may not be the result of low test reliability. Instead, the low correlation could be caused by changes in the personalities of the people in the sample over time. This is a problem especially when the sample used in the reliability study is composed of young people (Pinneau, 1961).

Likewise, if only 10 minutes separate the two administrations, a very high correlation between the two sets of scores might occur. This high correlation may only represent the fact that the person remembered how she answered the item the first time rather than what she actually believes. Typical time intervals between test administrations range from three days to three months. Usually, the longer the time interval, the lower the reliability coefficient (Anastasi, 1982).

Test–retest reliability is not appropriate for all kinds of tests. For example, it would make no sense to measure the test–retest reliability of a test designed to measure short-term moods or feelings. As an example, the *State–Trait Anxiety Inventory* measures two types of anxiety. *Trait anxiety* refers to the amount of anxiety that an individual normally has, while *state anxiety* refers to the amount of anxiety that an individual has at any given moment. For the test to be useful, it would be important for the measure of trait anxiety to have temporal stability, while the measure of state anxiety need not.

Parallel Forms Reliability With the **parallel-forms reliability** method, two forms of the same test are constructed. As shown in Table 3.1, a sample of 100 people are administered both forms of the test; one-half of the sample first receives Form A and the other half Form B. This **counterbalancing** of test-taking order is designed to eliminate any effects that first taking one form of the test may have on scores on the second form.

The scores on the two forms are then correlated to determine whether they are similar. If they are, the test is said to have **form stability.** Why would anyone use this method? More than one form of a test often is necessary. For example, if there is a high probability that people will take a test more than once, two forms are needed so that these individuals do not have an advantage the second time around. Such a situation might occur in police department examinations. To be promoted, most police departments require an officer to pass a promotion exam. If the officer fails the exam one year, she can retake the exam the next year. Thus, if only one form of the test were available, by the seventh time the officer took the test, she should remember many questions and thus probably score higher than an officer taking the test for the first time.

Multiple forms also might be used when a large number of people are taking a test and the test administrator is concerned about the possibility of cheating. Perhaps one of your professors has used more than one form of the same test to discourage cheating. The last time you took your written driver's test, multiple forms probably were used, just as they were when you took the SAT or ACT in order to be admitted to college. Thus, multiple forms of a test are not uncommon.

Recall that with test–retest reliability, the time interval between administrations usually ranges from three days to three months. With parallel forms reliability, however, the time interval should be as short as possible. If the two forms are administered three weeks apart and a low correlation results, the cause of the low reliability is difficult to determine. That is, it could be that the test lacks form stability or that the test lacks temporal stability. Thus, to determine the cause of the unreliability, the interval needs to be short.

In addition, a *t*-test should be conducted on the mean scores for each form to ensure that they truly are equivalent. The test in Table 3.2, for example, shows a perfect correlation between the two forms. People scoring well on Form A also scored well on Form B. But the average score on Form B is two points higher than on Form A. Thus, even though the perfect correlation shows that the scores on the two forms are parallel, the difference in mean scores indicates that the two forms are not equivalent. In such a case, either the forms must be revised or different standards (norms) must be used to interpret the results of the test.

Table 3.2
Example of Two
Parallel But
Nonequivalent
Forms

Subjects	Test Scores	
	Form A	Form B
1	12	14
2	18	20
3	11	13
4	6	8
5	24	26
6	19	21
7	17	19
8	12	14
9	21	23
10	9	11
Average score	14.9	16.9

Finally, we must understand what constitutes a different form of a test. Previously, it was stated that alternate forms usually consist of different questions. Research has shown, however, that administering a test on a computer rather than on paper can affect test scores (Lee, Moreno, & Sympson, 1986); so too can changing the order of item presentation. Consequently, any difference in the forms of a test should be examined to ensure that the forms *are* parallel and equivalent.

Internal Reliability One problem with using either the parallel forms or test–retest method is that in both cases, reliability can only be determined by giving two administrations of a test. Often this is neither possible nor practical. For example, if your instructor wanted to determine the reliability of his final exam, how could it be done? In the test–retest method, each student would take the exam at the end of the semester and then again during the next semester. Not only would few students want to retake a final exam, but much of the course knowledge would be lost.

In the parallel forms method, each student would have to take two final exams, which would not be popular. However, with internal reliability, the test need only be administered once and would measure **item stability.**

Internal reliability can be determined in many ways, but perhaps the easiest is to use the **split-half method.** With this method, the items on a test are split into two groups. Usually, all of the odd-numbered items constitute one group and the even-numbered items the second group.

103

The scores on the odd items are then correlated with the scores on the even items. Because the number of items in the test has been reduced, the **Spearman–Brown prophecy formula** is used to adjust the correlation. The Spearman–Brown formula is easy to use and takes the following form:

$$\text{corrected reliability} = \frac{2 \times \text{split-half correlation}}{1 + \text{split-half correlation}}$$

Thus, if the correlation between the two test halves is .60, the corrected reliability using the Spearman–Brown formula would be:

$$\frac{2 \times .60}{1 + .60} = \frac{1.20}{1.60} = .75$$

Cronbach's **coefficient alpha** (Cronbach, 1951) and the **Kuder–Richardson formula 20 (K–R 20)** (Kuder & Richardson, 1937) are more popular and accurate methods of determining internal reliability, although more complicated to use and thus calculated by computer program rather than by hand. Essentially, both the coefficient alpha and the K–R 20 represent the reliability coefficient that would be obtained from all possible combinations of split halves. The difference between the two is that the K–R 20 is used for tests containing dichotomous items (for example, "yes/no," "true/false"), while the coefficient alpha is used for tests containing interval and ratio items such as five-point rating scales.

Validity

Validity refers to the degree to which inferences from scores on tests or assessments are justified by the evidence. As with reliability, a test must be valid to be useful. But just because a test is reliable does not mean it is valid. For example, suppose that we want to use height requirements to hire typists. Our measure of height (a ruler) would certainly be reliable—most adults will get no taller and two people measuring an applicant's height will probably get very similar measurements. It is doubtful, however, that height is related to typing performance. Thus, height would be a reliable but not valid measure of typing performance.

Even though reliability and validity are not the same, they are related. The potential validity of a test is limited by its reliability. Thus, if a test has poor reliability, it cannot have high validity. But as we saw in the example above, a test's reliability does not imply validity. Instead, we think of reliability as having a *necessary but not sufficient relationship* with validity.

Methods for Determining Validity

Content Validity One way to determine a test's validity is to look at its degree of **content validity,** which refers to the extent to which tests or test items sample the content that they are supposed to measure. Again, let us use your final exam as an example. Your instructor tells you that the final exam will measure your knowledge of Chapters 8, 9, and 10. Each chapter is the same length, and your instructor spent three class periods on each chapter. The test will have 60 questions. For the test to be content-valid, the items must constitute a representative sample of the material contained in the three chapters; therefore, there should be some 20 questions from each chapter. If there are 30 questions each from Chapters 8 and 9, the test will not be content-valid because it left out Chapter 10. Likewise, if there are questions from Chapter 4, the test will not be content-valid because it requires knowledge that is outside of the appropriate domain.

In industry, the appropriate content for a test or test battery is determined by the job analysis. All of the important dimensions identified in the job analysis should be covered somewhere in the selection process. Anything that was not identified in the job analysis should be left out.

The readability of a test is a good example of how tricky content validity can be. Suppose we determine that independence is an important aspect of a job. We find a test that measures independence, and we are confident that our test is content-valid because it measures a dimension identified in the job analysis. But the "independence test" is very difficult to read and most of our applicants are only high school graduates. Is our test content-valid? No, because it requires a high level of reading ability, and reading ability was not identified as an important dimension for our job.

Criterion Validity Another measure of validity is **criterion validity,** which refers to the extent to which a test score is related to some measure of job performance called a **criterion** (criteria will be discussed more thoroughly in a later chapter). Criterion validity takes content validity a step further. Just because a test is reliable and has content validity does not necessarily mean that it will be related to job performance.

Criterion validity is established using one of two research designs: concurrent or predictive. With a **concurrent validity** design, a test is

Evaluating Selection
Techniques and
Decisions

given to a group of employees who are already on the job. The scores on the test are then correlated with a measure of their current performance.

With a **predictive validity** design, the test is administered to a group of job applicants who are going to be hired. The test scores are then compared to a measure of performance taken later. In the ideal predictive validity situation, every applicant is hired and the test scores are hidden from the people who will later make performance evaluations. By hiring every applicant, a wide range of both test scores and employee performance is likely to be found. Remember that the wider the range of scores, the higher the validity coefficient. But because it is rarely practical to hire every applicant, the ideal predictive design is not often used. Instead, most criterion validity studies use a concurrent design. Why is a concurrent design less strong than a predictive design? The answer lies in the homogeneity of performance scores. In a given employment situation, very few employees are at the extremes of a performance scale. Employees who would be at the bottom of the performance scale were either never hired or have since been terminated. Employees at the upper end of the performance scale often get promoted. Thus the **restricted range** of performance scores makes obtaining a significant validity coefficient more difficult.

A description of the criterion validation process is shown in the employment profile of Lisa Buchner on page 107.

Construct Validity Construct validity is the most theoretical of the validity types. Basically, **construct validity** is the extent to which a test actually measures the construct that it purports to measure. Construct validity is concerned with inferences about test scores in contrast to content validity, which is concerned with inferences about test construction (Cascio, 1987).

Perhaps a good example of the importance of construct validity is a situation this author encountered during graduate school. We had just completed a job analysis of the entry-level police officer position for a small town. One of the dimensions (constructs) that emerged as being important was honesty. Almost every officer insisted that a good police officer was honest, so we searched for tests that measured honesty and quickly discovered that there were many types of honesty. Some honesty tests measured theft, some cheating, while others measured moral judgment. None measured the construct implied by the police officers of not taking bribes and not letting friends get away with crimes. No test measured that particular construct even though all of the tests measured "honesty."

Employment Profile

Lisa Buchner, M.S.
Personnel Testing Specialist
Duke Power Company

As a personnel testing specialist, I work with a program within the human resources department called assessment services. I develop and implement personnel testing and selection programs that are designed to promote effective human resources management. What follows is a brief sample of some of my job duties and activities.

At Duke Power, employment tests are used for more than 100 different jobs. Therefore, much of my time is spent conducting test-validation studies. The use of valid selection tests helps to promote productivity by ensuring that the skills and abilities possessed by new workers match those required in their jobs. We use a criterion-oriented validation strategy in our studies. As discussed in this chapter, the purpose of this kind of validation is to demonstrate that a statistical relationship exists between how well workers do on specific aptitude tests and how well the workers perform in their jobs.

The first step in the validation process involves conducting a job analysis to determine the duties performed by incumbents and the knowledge, skills, and abilities required to perform these duties. The second step involves the development of tests that measure the abilities (for example, numerical or dexterity) required in each job or groups of jobs that have similar ability requirements. Third, the tests then are given to job incumbents while assessments of their job performance are obtained. Supervisors rate each incumbent's job performance in terms of the dimensions found to be critical to overall job effectiveness. Statistical analysis of the test and job performance data allows us to create test batteries using those tests with the highest validities.

In addition to paper-and-pencil tests, we have developed a telephone-simulation exercise for customer service–position applicants. One of the drawbacks of the previous test battery for the customer service representative jobs was that many of the critical skills and abilities

necessary for successful job performance were not being assessed. A customer service representative spends the majority of his or her time on the phone with customers giving information, solving problems, and handling requests or complaints. Through task surveys and several meetings with customer service supervisors, we determined the critical skills and abilities for the job. We then set out to create a test to measure abilities, such as stress tolerance, problem solving, and interpersonal communication, that were not being assessed by the previous battery of written tests.

The telephone simulation is a thirty-minute test in which each applicant plays the role of a customer service assistant and handles incoming calls from "customers" who are angry, requesting information, or needing assistance in some way. The customers are actually job-knowledge experts who have been trained how to rate applicants' performance in the exercise. Applicants study information about a hypothetical company for the first fifteen minutes of the exercise. This information includes product descriptions, troubleshooting guides, and tips on handling complaints. After studying this information, the applicants then are told that in the next fifteen minutes, they will receive four calls relating to the products and services of the company. Two assessors rate each applicant at the end of the exercise. If the applicant passes both the paper-and-pencil tests and the telephone simulation, he or she is recommended for an employment interview.

Although there are many things about my job that I am excited about and would love to discuss, I will mention only one additional responsibility, one that is not a task traditionally performed by people with I/O training. A significant portion of my time is spent providing psychological evaluations for all applicants, vendors, and employees who need unescorted access to our nuclear stations. To obtain unescorted access clearance, an individual must go through an extensive background check—part of which involves a psychological evaluation. At Duke Power, individuals are administered the MMPI. Should the profile indicate potential concerns about an applicant's psychological stability, the applicants are referred to a clinical psychologist for an interview so that we can gain more information.

Construct validity usually is determined by correlating scores on a test with scores from other tests. Some of the other tests measure the same construct, while others do not. For example, suppose we have a test that measures knowledge of psychology. One hundred people are administered our Knowledge of Psychology Test as well as another psychology knowledge test, a test of reading ability, and a test of general intelligence. If our test really measures the construct we say it measures—knowledge of psychology—it should correlate highly with the other test of psychology knowledge and not very highly with the other two tests. If our test correlates highest with the reading ability test, it could be that even though our test is content-valid (it contained psychology items), it is not construct-valid because scores on our test are based more on reading ability than on knowledge of psychology.

Face Validity Although face validity is not one of the three major methods of determining test validity, it still is important (Anastasi, 1982). **Face validity** refers to the extent to which a test looks as if it is valid. Face validity is important because if a test or its items do not appear valid, the test takers and administrators will not have confidence in the results. Likewise, if employes involved in a training session on interpersonal skills take a personality test and are given the results, they will not be motivated to change or to use the results of the test unless the personality profile given to them seems accurate.

But just because a test has face validity does not mean it is valid (Jackson, O'Dell, & Olson, 1982). A good example of this would be astrological forecasts. If you have ever read a personality description based on your astrological sign, you probably have found the description to be quite accurate. Does that mean that astrological forecasts are accurate? Not at all. If you also have read a personality description based on a different astrological sign, you probably found it to be as accurate as the one based on your own sign. Why is this? Because of something called **Barnum statements** (Dickson & Kelly, 1985).

Barnum statements are so general that they can be true of almost everyone. For example, if I described you as "sometimes being sad, sometimes being successful, and at times, not getting along with your best friend," I would probably be very accurate. The problem is that the same description would be accurate of almost anyone. So face validity by itself is not enough.

A technique created by Aamodt and Kimbrough (1982), however, allows a researcher to determine the face validity of a test while controlling for the effect of Barnum statements. In this technique, a test is administered to a group of individuals. Half of the individuals are then given a copy of the test interpretation that actually corresponds to their test scores, while the other half is given a test interpretation that corresponds to another person's test scores. Each subject then is asked to rate the extent to which the test interpretation is a good description of his or her behavior. If the ratings from the group receiving its own interpretation is significantly higher than the ratings from the group receiving others' interpretations, some support is established for the test's face validity. If the average ratings from the two groups are equal, the test interpretations can be said to suffer from Barnum statements.

Even though face validity may indicate that a test has potential value, more often than not face validity is meaningless. To highlight this point, Stagner (1958) conducted a study in which he found that personnel managers purchased a test just because it "looked like it was valid" even though the test itself was put together in a few minutes and actually measured nothing.

Known-Group Validity The second minor method of measuring validity is **known-group validity** (Hattie & Cooksey, 1984). This method is not a common one and should only be used when other methods are not practical. With known-group validity, a test is given to two groups of people who are "known" to be different on the trait in question.

For example, suppose we wanted to determine the validity of our new honesty test. The best approach might be a criterion validity study in which we correlate our employees' test scores with their dishonest behavior, such as stealing or lying. The problem is, how do we know who stole or who lied? We could ask them, but would dishonest people tell the truth? Probably not. Instead, we decide to validate our test by giving the test to a group known to be honest and to a group known to be dishonest. The two groups we pick are priests and criminals in state prison.

We administer the test to both groups and, sure enough, the priests score higher on honesty than do the convicts. Does this mean our test is valid? Not necessarily. It means that the test has known-group validity but not necessarily other types of validity. We do not know whether the test will predict employee theft (criterion validity), nor do we even know if the test is measuring honesty (construct validity). It is possible that the test actually is measuring another construct on which the two groups differ (for example, intelligence). Because of these problems, the best approach to take with known-group validity is that if the known groups do not differ on test scores, the test is probably not valid; and if they do differ, one still is not sure.

Even though known-group validity usually should not be used to establish test validity, it is important to understand because some test companies use known-group validity studies to sell their tests, claiming that they are valid. Personnel analyst Jeff Rodgers once was asked to evaluate a test that his company was considering for selecting bank tellers. The test literature sounded impressive, mentioning that the test was "backed by over 100 validity studies." Rodgers was suspicious and requested copies of the studies. After several months of "phone calls and teeth pulling," he obtained reports of the validity studies. Most of the studies used known-group methodology and compared the scores of groups such as monks and priests. Not one study involved a test of criterion validity to demonstrate that the test could actually predict bank teller performance. Thus, upon hearing that a test is valid, it is important to obtain copies of the research reports.

As we have seen, with at least five ways of measuring validity, one might logically ask which of the methods is the "best" to use. As with most questions in psychology, the answer is that "it depends." In this case, the answer depends on the situation as well as what the person conducting the validity study is trying to accomplish. If it is to decide whether the test will be a useful predictor of employee performance, then content validity would always be used and a criterion validity study also would be conducted if there were enough employees and a good measure of job performance was available.

If the person conducting the validity study is trying to create a test that can be used by a variety of organizations, then all five methods of establishing validity should be used. If only one of the five were to be used in this situation, most I/O psychologists would probably agree that construct validity would be the most desirable.

Finally, a test itself can never be valid. When we speak of validity, we are speaking about the validity of the *test scores* as they relate to a particular job. A test may be a valid predictor of tenure for counselors but not of performance for shoe salespeople. Thus, when we say that a test is valid, we mean that it is valid for a particular job and a particular criterion. No test will ever be valid for all jobs and all criteria.

Validity Generalization

A major issue concerning the validity of tests focuses on a concept known as validity generalization. **Validity generalization (VG)** refers to the extent to which a test found valid for a job in one location is valid for the same job in a different location. It was previously thought that the job of typist in one company was not the same as that in another company, the job of police officer in one small town was not the same as that in another small town, and that of retail store supervisor was not the same as supervisor in a fast food restaurant.

Recently, however, the work of Hunter and Hunter (1984), Schmidt, Hunter, Pearlman, and Hirsh (1985), and Schmidt, Gast-Rosenberg, and Hunter (1980) has indicated that a test valid for a job in one organization also is valid for the same job in another organization. Schmidt, Hunter, and their associates have tested hundreds of thousands of employees to arrive at their conclusions. They suggest that previous thinking resulted from studies with small sample sizes, and test validity in one location but not another was primarily the product of sampling error. With large sample sizes, a test found valid in one location probably will be valid in another—providing that the jobs actually are similar and not two separate jobs sharing the same job title.

The two building blocks for validity generalization are meta-analysis, which was discussed in Chapter 1, and job analysis, which was discussed in Chapter 2. Meta-analysis can be used to determine the average validity of specific types of tests for a variety of jobs.

For example, several studies have shown that cognitive ability is an excellent predictor of police performance. If we were to conduct a meta-analysis of all the studies looking at this relationship, we would be able to determine the average validity of cognitive ability in predicting police performance. If this validity coefficient is significant, then police departments similar to those used in the meta-analysis could adopt the test without conducting criterion validity studies of their own. This would be especially useful for small departments that have neither the number of officers necessary to properly conduct criterion validity studies nor the financial resources necessary to hire professionals to conduct such studies.

Validity generalization should only be used if a job analysis has been conducted and the results of the job analysis show that the job in question is similar to those used in the meta-analysis.

Finding Reliability and Validity Information

Over the previous pages, we have discussed different ways to measure reliability and validity. But even though most of you will eventually be involved with some form of employee testing, few of you actually will conduct a study on a test's reliability and validity. Thus, if you will use tests and understand that they must be reliable and valid, but you are not going to conduct a study yourself, how do you get this information?

Figure 3.1
Example of Entry in
Ninth Mental
Measurements
Yearbook

[537]

The IPAT Anxiety Scale Questionnaire. Ages 14 and over; 1957–76; ASQ; also called IPAT Anxiety Scale; title on test is Self Analysis Form, 1976 Edition; total score plus 7 optional scores (recommended only for experimental use): covert anxiety, overt anxiety, 5 component scores (apprehension, tension, low self-control, emotional instability, suspicion; reliability, validity, and norms data based on 1957 edition; no norms for part scores; 1 form ('76, 4 pages); handbook ('76, 106 pages); 1984 price data: $4.75 per 25 tests; $.85 per scoring stencil; $5.75 per handbook; $6.95 per specimen set; (5–10) minutes; Raymond B. Cattell, Samuel E. Krug (manual), and Ivan H. Scheier (manual); Institute for Personality and Ability Testing, Inc.*

    South African adaptation: Ages 15 and over; 1968; adaptation by Elizabeth M. Madge; Human Sciences Research Council [South Africa].*

See T3:1197 (48 references); for reviews by Richard I. Lanyon and Paul McReynolds, see 8:582 (85 references); see also T2:1225 (120 references) and ·P:116 (45 references); for a review by Jacob Cohen of the earlier edition, see 6:121 (23 references); for reviews by J. P. Guilford and E. Lowell Kelly and an excerpted review by Laurance F. Shaffer, see 5:70.

TEST REFERENCES

1. Cochrane, N., & Neilson, M. Depressive illness: The role of aggression further considered. PSYCHOLOGICAL MEDICINE, 1977, 7, 283–288.
2. Cox, R. J., & McGuinness, D. The effect of chronic anxiety level upon self control of heart rate. BIOLOGICAL PSYCHOLOGY, 1977, 5, 7–14.
3. Haskell, S. D. Desired family-size correlates for single undergraduates. PSYCHOLOGY OF WOMEN QUARTERLY, 1977, 2, 5–15.
4. Egeland, B. Preliminary results of a prospective study of the antecedents of child abuse. CHILD ABUSE & NEGLECT, 1979, 3, 269–278.
5. Lion, J. R. Benzodiazepines in the treatment of aggressive patients. THE JOURNAL OF CLINICAL PSYCHIATRY, 1979, 40, 70–71.
6. Hauri, P. Treating psychophysiologic insomnia with biofeedback. ARCHIVES OF GENERAL PSYCHIATRY, 1981, 38, 752–758.
7. Shirom, A., Eden, D., & Kellermann, J. J. Effects of population changes on psychological and physiological strain in kibbutz communities. AMERICAN JOURNAL OF COMMUNITY PSYCHOLOGY, 1981, 9, 27–43.
8. Dodez, O., Zelhart, P. F., & Markley, R. P. Compatibility of self-actualization and anxiety. JOURNAL OF CLINICAL PSYCHOLOGY, 1982, 38, 696–702.
9. Lapierre, Y. D., Tremblay, A., Gagnon, A., Monpremier, P., Berliss, H., & Oyewumi, L. K. A therapeutic and discontinuation study of clobazam and diazepam in anxiety neurosis. THE JOURNAL OF CLINICAL PSYCHIATRY, 1982, 43, 372–374.
10. Pecknold, J. C., McClure, D. J., Appeltauer, L., Allan, T., & Wrzesinski, L. Does tryptophan potentiate clomipramine in the treatment of agoraphobia and social phobic patients? BRITISH JOURNAL OF PSYCHIATRY, 1982, 140, 484–490.

Source: Mitchell, J. V. (1985). *The ninth mental measurements yearbook.* Lincoln, NE: University of Nebraska Press. Reprinted by permission of the publisher.

Figure 3.2
Example of Entry in
Tests

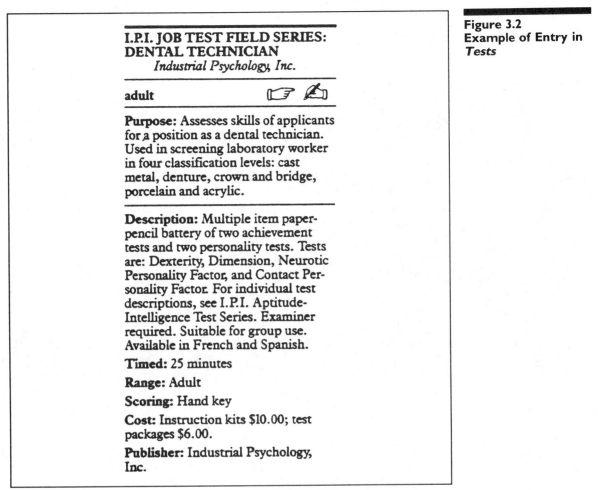

**I.P.I. JOB TEST FIELD SERIES:
DENTAL TECHNICIAN**
Industrial Psychology, Inc.

adult

Purpose: Assesses skills of applicants for a position as a dental technician. Used in screening laboratory worker in four classification levels: cast metal, denture, crown and bridge, porcelain and acrylic.

Description: Multiple item paper-pencil battery of two achievement tests and two personality tests. Tests are: Dexterity, Dimension, Neurotic Personality Factor, and Contact Personality Factor. For individual test descriptions, see I.P.I. Aptitude-Intelligence Test Series. Examiner required. Suitable for group use. Available in French and Spanish.

Timed: 25 minutes

Range: Adult

Scoring: Hand key

Cost: Instruction kits $10.00; test packages $6.00.

Publisher: Industrial Psychology, Inc.

Source: Sweetland, R. C., & Keyser, D. J. (1983). *Tests.* Kansas City, MO: Test Corporation of America. Reprinted by permission of the publisher.

Many excellent sources are available to find information about a test's reliability and validity. Most of these sources are found in the reference section of most university libraries.

Perhaps the most common source of information about tests is the *Tenth Mental Measurements Yearbook* (Conoley & Kramer, 1989). The **Mental Measurements Yearbook (MMY)** contains information about thousands of different psychological tests as well as reviews by test experts. One MMY test description is shown in Figure 3.1.

Another excellent source of information is a compendium titled *Tests* (Sweetland & Keyser, 1983), which contains information similar to the

MMY but without test reviews. A test description from *Tests* is shown in Figure 3.2. Box 3.1 lists other test compendia.

One problem with most test compendia is that to find information about a potential test for selection, we must know the name of the test. Unfortunately, sometimes we do not know which test we want. Instead, we conduct a job analysis, identify important dimensions, and then attempt to identify tests that measure the desired constructs. If only the test compendia are used, every page in each compendia must be examined to find which tests measure the appropriate construct.

To make this process easier, both the **Arkansas Index** (Aamodt & Kimbrough, 1983) and the Radford Index (Petro & Kelly, 1988) have been developed. Neither of these sources provides information about the reliability or validity of a test. Instead, they list hundreds of *dimensions* and the tests that measure the dimension. Traditional test compendia such as the MMY or *Tests* then can be used to find information about a particular test or tests. Using both the Arkansas Index and the Radford Index can reduce a two-week process to a 10-minute undertaking.

Box 3.1

Relevant Test Compendia

Bonjean, C. M., Hill, R. J., & McLemore, S. D. (1967). *Sociological Measurement: An inventory of scales and indices.*

Buros, O. K. (1975a). *Personality tests and reviews II.*

Buros, O. K. (1975b). *Vocational tests and reviews.*

Conoley, J. C., & Kramer, J. F. (1989). *The tenth mental measurements yearbook.*

Goldman, B. A., & Busch, J. C. (1978). *Directory of unpublished experimental measures—Volume II.*

Goldman, B. A., & Busch, J. C. (1982). *Directory of unpublished experimental measures—Volume III.*

Goldman, B. A., & Osborne, W. L. (1985). *Directory of unpublished experimental measures—Volume IV.*

Goldman, B. A., & Saunders, J. L. (1974). *Directory of unpublished experimental measures—Volume I.*

Mitchell, J. V. (1983). *Tests in print III.*

Robinson, J. P., Anthanasious, R., & Head, K. B. (1969). *Measurements of occupational attitudes and occupational characteristics.*

Sweetland, R. C., & Keyser, D. J. (1983). *Tests.*

Establishing the Usefulness of a Selection Device

Even though a test is both reliable and valid, it is not necessarily useful. At first, this may not make much sense, but imagine a test that has been shown to be valid for selecting employees for a fast food restaurant chain. Suppose there are 100 job openings and 100 jobseekers apply for those openings. Even though the test is valid, it would have no impact because the restaurant chain must hire every applicant.

As another example, imagine an organization that already has a test that does a good job of predicting performance. Even though a new test being considered may be valid, the old test may work so well that the current employees are all successful. Thus, a new test (even though it is valid) might not provide any improvement.

To determine how useful a test would be in any given situation, several formulas and tables have been designed; these will be discussed in the following pages. Each formula and table provides slightly different information to an employer. The Taylor–Russell tables provide an estimate of the percentage of total new hires who will be successful employees if a test is adopted (organizational success), both the Lawshe tables and expectancy charts provide a probability of success for a particular applicant based on his test scores (individual success), and the utility formula provides an estimate of the amount of money that an organization will save if it adopts a new testing procedure.

Taylor–Russell Tables

The **Taylor–Russell tables** (Taylor & Russell, 1939) are designed to estimate the percentage of future employees who will be successful on the job if an organization uses a particular test. To use the Taylor–Russell tables, three pieces of information must be obtained.

First needed is the test's *criterion validity coefficient*. There are two ways to obtain this coefficient. The best would be to actually conduct a criterion validity study with test scores correlated with some measure of job performance.

Often, however, an organization wants to know whether testing is useful before investing time and money in a criterion validity study. Here validity generalization comes into play. Based on findings by researchers such as Hunter and Hunter (1984) and Ghiselli (1973), we have a good idea of the typical validity coefficients that will result from various methods of selection. To estimate the validity coefficient that an organization

Selection Technique	Validity
Cognitive and psychomotor ability tests	.53
Job knowledge tests	.50
Biographical information blanks	.35
Structured interviews	.34
Assessment centers	.25
Personality tests	.24
Experience	.18
Interviews	.17
Reference checks	.13
College grades	.13
Vocational interests tests	.10
Amount of education	.10
Handwriting analysis	.00
Projective personality tests	.00
Age	.00

**Table 3.3
Typical Validity
Coefficients for
Selection**

Note: These coefficients result from combinations of various meta-analyses.

might obtain, one of the coefficients from Table 3.3 is used. The higher the validity coefficient, the greater possibility that the test will be useful.

The second piece of information that must be obtained is the **selection ratio,** which is simply the percentage of people that an organization must hire. The ratio is determined by the formula:

$$\text{selection ratio} = \frac{\text{number of openings}}{\text{number of applicants}}$$

The lower the selection ratio, the greater the potential usefulness of the test.

The final piece of information needed is the **base rate** of current performance, or the percentage of employees currently on the job who are considered successful. This figure usually is obtained in one of two ways. The first method is the most simple but the least accurate. Employees are split into two equal groups based on their scores on some criterion such as tenure or performance. The base rate using this method is always .50, because one-half of the employees are considered satisfactory.

The second and more meaningful method is to choose a criterion measure score above which all employees are considered successful. For example, at one real estate agency, any agent who sells more than

$150,000 in real estate makes a profit for the agency after training and operating expenses have been deducted. In this case, any agent selling more than $150,000 in property would be considered a success because he or she made money for the company. Any agent selling less than $150,000 in property would be considered a failure because he or she cost the company more money than was brought in.

In the above example, there is a clear point at which an employee can be considered a success. Most of the time, however, there is no such clear point. In these cases, a manager will subjectively choose a point on the criterion that she feels separates successful from unsuccessful employees.

After the validity, selection ratio, and base rate figures have been obtained, the Taylor–Russell tables are consulted (see Table 3.4). To understand how they are used, let us take the following example. Suppose we have a test validity of .40, a selection ratio of .30, and a base rate of .50. Locating the table corresponding to the .50 base rate, we look along the top of the chart until we find the .30 selection ratio. Next we locate the validity of .40 on the left side of the table. We then trace across the table until we locate the intersection of the selection ratio column and the validity row; we have found .69.

This number indicates that if the organization uses that particular test, 69% of future employees will be considered successful. This figure is compared with the previous base rate of .50, indicating a 19% increase in successful employees.

Expectancy Charts

Expectancy charts are easier to use but less accurate than the Taylor–Russell tables. These charts are easier because the only information that is needed are employee test scores and the criterion. The two scores from each employee are graphed on a chart similar to that in Figure 3.3. Lines are drawn from the point on the y-axis (criterion score) that represents a successful applicant and from the point on the x-axis that represents the lowest test score of a hired applicant. As you can see in Figure 3.3, these lines divide the scores into four quadrants. The points located in quadrant I represent employees who scored poorly on the test but performed well on the job. Points located in quadrant II represent employees who scored well on the test and were successful on the job. Points in quadrant III represent employees who scored high on the test yet did poorly on the job, and points in quadrant IV represent employees who scored low on the test and did poorly on the job.

Table 3.4
Taylor–Russell
Tables

Employees Considered Satisfactory	r	Selection Ratio										
		.05	.10	.20	.30	.40	.50	.60	.70	.80	.90	.95
10%	.00	.10	.10	.10	.10	.10	.10	.10	.10	.10	.10	.10
	.10	.14	.13	.13	.12	.12	.11	.11	.11	.11	.10	.10
	.20	.19	.17	.15	.14	.14	.13	.12	.12	.11	.11	.10
	.30	.25	.22	.19	.17	.15	.14	.13	.12	.12	.11	.10
	.40	.31	.27	.22	.19	.17	.16	.14	.13	.12	.11	.10
	.50	.39	.32	.26	.22	.19	.17	.15	.13	.12	.11	.11
	.60	.48	.39	.30	.25	.21	.18	.16	.14	.12	.11	.11
	.70	.58	.47	.35	.27	.22	.19	.16	.14	.12	.11	.11
	.80	.71	.56	.40	.30	.24	.20	.17	.14	.12	.11	.11
	.90	.86	.69	.46	.33	.25	.20	.17	.14	.12	.11	.11
20%	.00	.20	.20	.20	.20	.20	.20	.20	.20	.20	.20	.20
	.10	.26	.25	.24	.23	.23	.22	.22	.21	.21	.21	.20
	.20	.33	.31	.28	.27	.26	.25	.24	.23	.22	.21	.21
	.30	.41	.37	.33	.30	.28	.27	.25	.24	.23	.21	.21
	.40	.49	.44	.38	.34	.31	.29	.27	.25	.23	.22	.21
	.50	.59	.52	.44	.38	.35	.31	.29	.26	.24	.22	.21
	.60	.68	.60	.50	.43	.38	.34	.30	.27	.24	.22	.21
	.70	.79	.69	.56	.48	.41	.36	.31	.28	.25	.22	.21
	.80	.89	.79	.64	.53	.45	.38	.33	.28	.25	.22	.21
	.90	.98	.91	.75	.60	.48	.40	.33	.29	.25	.22	.21
30%	.00	.30	.30	.30	.30	.30	.30	.30	.30	.30	.30	.30
	.10	.38	.36	.35	.34	.33	.33	.32	.32	.31	.31	.30
	.20	.46	.43	.40	.38	.37	.36	.34	.33	.32	.31	.31
	.30	.54	.50	.46	.43	.40	.38	.37	.35	.33	.32	.31
	.40	.63	.58	.51	.47	.44	.41	.39	.37	.34	.32	.31
	.50	.72	.65	.58	.52	.48	.44	.41	.38	.35	.33	.31
	.60	.81	.74	.64	.58	.52	.47	.43	.40	.36	.33	.31
	.70	.89	.62	.72	.63	.57	.51	.46	.41	.37	.33	.32
	.80	.96	.90	.80	.70	.62	.54	.48	.42	.37	.33	.32
	.90	1.00	.98	.90	.79	.68	.58	.49	.43	.37	.33	.32
40%	.00	.40	.40	.40	.40	.40	.40	.40	.40	.40	.40	.40
	.10	.48	.47	.46	.45	.44	.43	.42	.42	.41	.41	.40
	.20	.57	.54	.51	.49	.48	.46	.45	.44	.43	.41	.41
	.30	.65	.61	.57	.54	.51	.49	.47	.46	.44	.42	.41
	.40	.73	.69	.63	.59	.56	.53	.50	.48	.45	.43	.41
	.50	.81	.76	.69	.64	.60	.56	.53	.49	.46	.43	.42
	.60	.89	.83	.75	.69	.64	.60	.55	.51	.48	.44	.42
	.70	.95	.90	.82	.76	.69	.64	.58	.53	.49	.44	.42
	.80	.99	.96	.89	.82	.75	.68	.61	.55	.49	.44	.42
	.90	1.00	1.00	.97	.91	.82	.74	.65	.57	.50	.44	.42
50%	.00	.50	.50	.50	.50	.50	.50	.50	.50	.50	.50	.50
	.10	.58	.57	.56	.55	.54	.53	.53	.52	.51	.51	.50
	.20	.67	.64	.61	.59	.58	.56	.55	.54	.53	.52	.51
	.30	.74	.71	.67	.64	.62	.60	.58	.56	.54	.52	.51
	.40	.82	.78	.73	.69	.66	.63	.61	.58	.56	.53	.52
	.50	.88	.84	.76	.74	.70	.67	.63	.60	.57	.54	.52
	.60	.94	.90	.84	.79	.75	.70	.66	.62	.59	.54	.52
	.70	.98	.95	.90	.85	.80	.75	.70	.65	.60	.55	.53
	.80	1.00	.99	.95	.90	.85	.80	.73	.67	.61	.55	.53
	.90	1.00	1.00	.99	.97	.92	.86	.78	.70	.62	.56	.53

Continued

Table 3.4
Continued

Employees Considered Satisfactory	r	Selection Ratio										
		.05	.10	.20	.30	.40	.50	.60	.70	.80	.90	.95
60%	.00	.60	.60	.60	.60	.60	.60	.60	.60	.60	.60	.60
	.10	.68	.67	.65	.64	.64	.63	.63	.62	.61	.61	.60
	.20	.75	.73	.71	.69	.67	.66	.65	.64	.63	.62	.61
	.30	.82	.79	.76	.73	.71	.69	.68	.66	.64	.62	.61
	.40	.88	.85	.81	.78	.75	.73	.70	.68	.66	.63	.62
	.50	.93	.90	.86	.82	.79	.76	.73	.70	.67	.64	.62
	.60	.96	.94	.90	.87	.83	.80	.76	.73	.69	.65	.63
	.70	.99	.97	.94	.91	.87	.84	.80	.75	.71	.66	.63
	.80	1.00	.99	.98	.95	.92	.88	.83	.78	.72	.66	.63
	.90	1.00	1.00	1.00	.99	.97	.94	.88	.82	.74	.67	.63
70%	.00	.70	.70	.70	.70	.70	.70	.70	.70	.70	.70	.70
	.10	.77	.76	.75	.74	.73	.73	.72	.72	.71	.71	.70
	.20	.83	.81	.79	.78	.77	.76	.75	.74	.73	.71	.71
	.30	.88	.86	.84	.82	.80	.78	.77	.75	.74	.72	.71
	.40	.93	.91	.88	.85	.83	.81	.79	.77	.75	.73	.72
	.50	.96	.94	.91	.89	.87	.84	.82	.80	.77	.74	.72
	.60	.98	.97	.95	.92	.90	.87	.85	.82	.79	.75	.73
	.70	1.00	.99	.97	.96	.93	.91	.88	.84	.80	.76	.73
	.80	1.00	1.00	.99	.98	.97	.94	.91	.87	.82	.77	.73
	.90	1.00	1.00	1.00	1.00	.99	.98	.95	.91	.85	.78	.74
80%	.00	.80	.80	.80	.80	.80	.80	.80	.80	.80	.80	.80
	.10	.85	.85	.84	.83	.83	.82	.82	.81	.81	.81	.80
	.20	.90	.89	.87	.86	.85	.84	.84	.83	.82	.81	.81
	.30	.94	.92	.90	.89	.88	.87	.86	.84	.83	.82	.81
	.40	.96	.95	.93	.92	.90	.89	.88	.86	.85	.83	.82
	.50	.98	.97	.96	.94	.93	.91	.90	.88	.86	.84	.82
	.60	.99	.99	.98	.96	.95	.94	.92	.90	.87	.84	.83
	.70	1.00	1.00	.99	.98	.97	.96	.94	.92	.89	.85	.83
	.80	1.00	1.00	1.00	1.00	.99	.98	.96	.94	.91	.87	.84
	.90	1.00	1.00	1.00	1.00	1.00	1.00	.99	.97	.94	.88	.84
90%	.00	.90	.90	.90	.90	.90	.90	.90	.90	.90	.90	.90
	.10	.93	.93	.92	.92	.92	.91	.91	.91	.91	.90	.90
	.20	.96	.95	.94	.94	.93	.93	.92	.92	.91	.91	.90
	.30	.98	.97	.96	.95	.95	.94	.94	.93	.92	.91	.91
	.40	.99	.98	.98	.97	.96	.96	.95	.94	.93	.92	.91
	.50	1.00	.99	.99	.98	.97	.97	.96	.95	.94	.92	.92
	.60	1.00	1.00	.99	.99	.99	.98	.97	.96	.95	.93	.92
	.70	1.00	1.00	1.00	1.00	.99	.99	.98	.97	.96	.94	.93
	.80	1.00	1.00	1.00	1.00	1.00	1.00	.99	.99	.97	.95	.93
	.90	1.00	1.00	1.00	1.00	1.00	1.00	1.00	1.00	.99	.97	.94
	r	.05	.10	.20	.30	.40	.50	.60	.70	.80	.90	.95

Source: Taylor, H. C., & Russell, J. T. (1939). The relationship of validity coefficients to the practical effectiveness of tests in selection: Discussion and tables. *Journal of Applied Psychology, 23,* 565–578.

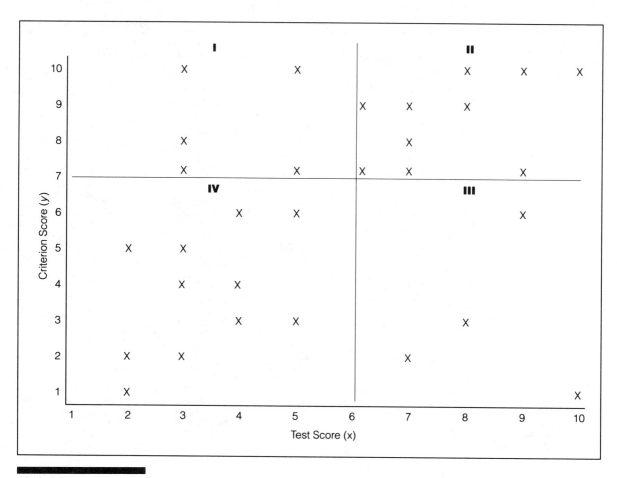

Figure 3.3
Example of an
Expectancy Chart

If a test is a good predictor of performance, there should be more points in quadrants II and IV because the points in the other two quadrants represent "predictive failures." That is, in quadrants I and III, no correspondence is seen between test scores and criterion scores.

To estimate the test's effectiveness, the number of points in each quadrant are totaled and the following formula used:

$$\frac{\text{points in quadrants II and IV}}{\text{total points in all quadrants}}$$

The resulting number represents the percentage of time that we expect to be accurate in making a selection decision in the future. To determine whether this is an improvement, we use the following formula:

points in quadrants I and II
——————————————————
total points in all quadrants

If the percentage from the first formula is higher than that from the second, our proposed test should increase selection accuracy. If not, it is probably better to stick with the selection method currently used.

As an example, look again at Figure 3.3. There are 5 data points in quadrant I, 10 in quadrant II, 4 in quadrant III, and 11 in quadrant IV. The percentage of time that we expect to be accurate in the future would be:

$$\frac{\text{II} + \text{IV}}{\text{I} + \text{II} + \text{III} + \text{IV}} = \frac{10 + 11}{5 + 10 + 4 + 11} = \frac{21}{30} = .70$$

To compare this figure to the test we were previously using to select employees, we compute the satisfactory performance baseline:

$$\frac{\text{I} + \text{II}}{\text{I} + \text{II} + \text{III} + \text{IV}} = \frac{5 + 10}{5 + 10 + 4 + 11} = \frac{15}{30} = .50$$

Using the new test thus would result in a 20% increase in selection accuracy (.70 − .50) over the selection method previously used.

Lawshe Tables

The Taylor–Russell tables were designed to determine the overall impact of a testing procedure. But often we need to know the probability that a *particular applicant* will be successful. The **Lawshe tables** (Lawshe, Bolda, Brune, & Auclair, 1958) were created to do just that. To use these tables, three pieces of information also are needed. The validity coefficient and the base rate are found in the same way as for the Taylor–Russell tables. The third piece of information is the applicant's test score. More specifically, did the person score in the top 20%, the next 20%, the middle 20%, the next lowest 20%, or the bottom 20%?

Once we have all three pieces of information, the Lawshe tables, as shown in Table 3.5, are examined. For our example, we have a base rate of .50, a validity of .40, and an applicant who scores third highest out of 10. First, we locate the table with the base rate of .50. Then we locate the appropriate category at the top of the chart. Our applicant scored

Table 3.5 Lawshe Individual Prediction Tables	Percent of Current Employees Considered Satisfactory	r	Applicant Scores on Selection Test				
			Top 20%	Next 20%	Middle 20%	Next 20%	Bottom 20%
	30%	.20	40	34	29	26	21
		.30	46	35	29	24	16
		.40	51	37	28	21	12
		.50	58	38	27	18	09
		.60	64	40	26	15	05
	40%	.20	51	45	40	35	30
		.30	57	46	40	33	24
		.40	63	48	39	31	19
		.50	69	50	39	28	14
		.60	75	53	38	24	10
	50%	.20	61	55	50	45	39
		.30	67	57	50	43	33
		.40	73	59	50	41	28
		.50	78	62	50	38	22
		.60	84	65	50	35	16
	60%	.20	71	63	60	56	48
		.30	76	66	61	54	44
		.40	81	69	61	52	37
		.50	86	72	62	47	25
		.60	90	76	62	47	25
	70%	.20	79	75	70	67	59
		.30	84	76	71	65	54
		.40	88	79	72	63	49
		.50	91	82	73	62	42
		.60	95	85	74	60	36

Source: Lawshe, C. H., Bolda, R. A., Brune, R. L., & Auclair, G. (1958). Expectancy charts II: Their theoretical development. *Personnel Psychology, 11*, 545–599.

Note: Percentages indicate probability that applicant with a particular score will be a successful employee.

third highest out of 10 applicants, so she would be in the second category, the next highest one-fifth or 20%. Using the validity of .40, we locate the intersection of the validity row and the test score column and find 59. This means that the applicant has a 59% chance of being a successful employee.

Utility

Another way to determine the value of a test in a given situation is by computing the amount of money that an organization would save if it used the test to select employees. Fortunately, Hunter and Schmidt (1983) devised a fairly simple **utility** formula to estimate the monetary savings to an organization. To use this formula, five items of information must be known.

1. *Number of employees hired per year (n).* This number is easy to determine: It is simply the number of employees who are hired for a given position in a year.

2. *Average tenure (t).* This is the average amount of time that employees in the position tend to stay with the company. The number is computed by using information from company records to identify the time that each employee in that position stayed with the company. The number of years of **tenure** for each employee is then summed and divided by the total number of employees.

3. *Test validity (v).* This figure is the criterion validity coefficient that was obtained through either a validity study or validity generalization (Cascio, 1987).

4. *Standard deviation of performance in dollars (sd$).* For many years, this number was difficult to compute. Research has shown, however, that a good estimate of the difference in performance between an average and a good worker (one standard deviation away in performance) is 40% of the employee's annual salary (Hunter & Schmidt, 1982). To obtain this, the total salaries of current employees in the position in question should be averaged.

5. *Mean standardized predictor score of selected applicants (m).* This number is obtained in one of two ways. The first method is to obtain the average score on the selection test for both the applicants who are hired and the applicants who are not hired. Then subtract the average test score of the nonhired applicants from the average test score of the hired applicants. Divide this difference by the standard deviation of all the test scores.

For example, we administer a test of mental ability to a group of 100 applicants and hire the 10 with the highest scores. The average score of the 10 hired applicants was 34.6, the average test score of the other 90 applicants was 28.4, and the standard deviation of all test scores was 8.3.

Table 3.6
Selection-Ratio
Conversion Table for
Utility Formula

Selection Ratio	m
100	0.00
90	0.20
80	0.35
70	0.50
60	0.64
50	0.80
40	0.97
30	1.17
20	1.40
10	1.76
5	2.08

The desired figure would be:

$$\frac{34.6 - 28.4}{8.3} = \frac{6.2}{8.3} = .747$$

The second way to find m is to compute the proportion of applicants who are hired and then use a conversion table such as that in Table 3.6 to convert the proportion into a standard score. This second method is used when an organization plans to use a test, knows the probable selection ratio based on previous hirings, but does not know the average test scores because the organization has never used the test. Using the above example, the proportion of applicants hired would be:

$$\frac{\text{number of applicants hired}}{\text{total number of applicants}} = \frac{10}{100} = .10$$

From Table 3.6, we see that the standard score associated with a selection ratio of .10 is 1.76.

To determine the savings to the company, we use the following formula:

$$\text{savings} = (n)\,(t)\,(v)\,(\text{sd\$})\,(m) - \text{cost of testing}$$

As an example, suppose that we will hire 10 auditors per year, the average person in this position stays two years, the validity coefficient is .40, and average annual salary for the position is \$30,000, and we have 50 applicants for 10 openings. Thus,

$n = 10$

$t = 2$

$v = .40$

sd$ = \$30,000 \times .40 = 12,000$

$m = 10/50 = .20 = 1.40$ (.20 is converted to 1.40 by using Figure 3.3)

cost of testing $= \$10$ per person

Using the above formula, we would have

(10) (2) (.40) (12,000) (1.40) $- \$500.00 = \$133,900$

This means that after accounting for the cost of testing, using this particular test instead of selecting employees by chance will save a company $133,900 over the two years that auditors typically stay with the organization. Of course, seldom does a company select employees by chance. Thus the same formula should be used with the validity of the test (interview, psychological test, references, and so on) that the company currently uses. The result of this computation should then be subtracted from the first.

This final figure, of course, is just an estimate. To be most accurate, it must be adjusted by such factors as variable costs, discounting, and corporate tax rates (Boudreau, 1983; Cascio, 1987).

Fairness of a Test

Once a test has been determined to be reliable, valid, and money-saving for an organization, the next step is to make sure that it is fair. Basically, fairness means that the test does not adversely impact any of the groups that are protected by law (see Chapter 1).

Adverse Impact

The first step in determining a test's fairness is finding out whether it will result in some **adverse impact.** There are two basic ways to determine this. The method that is best and most common is to find the percentage

Evaluating Selection
Techniques and
Decisions

of people in each Equal Employment Opportunity (EEO) group who are hired after taking the test. This procedure was discussed in Chapter 1.

If the selection rate for any of the protected groups is less than 80% of the selection rate for either white applicants or males, the test is considered to have adverse impact. Remember that a legal defense for adverse impact is job relatedness, and a valid test is a job-related test. Thus, even if the test has adverse impact, it *probably* will be considered a fair test.

But even though the test might be considered legally fair, an organization still might not want to use it for several reasons. First, if a test results in adverse impact, the organization probably will have to go to court to defend itself. Even though a valid test will probably allow the organization to win the case, going to court costs a lot of money. Thus, if the utility of the test is low, potential court costs will outweigh the minimal savings to the organization.

Second, a test with adverse impact will lead to poor public relations with minority communities, which could hurt the organization in other areas such as recruitment or marketing.

Using the 80% rule to determine a test's fairness means that an organization must wait until it has used the test to select employees, at which time damage already has been done. Thus, the second method of determining adverse impact might at times be better.

The second method compares the average scores of minority applicants with those of white and male applicants. This is most easily done by looking in the test manual to determine whether blacks and whites or males and females have significantly different test scores. If so, the test probably will have adverse impact and an alternative test can be sought.

Single-Group Validity

In addition to adverse impact, an organization must also determine whether a test has single-group validity. **Single-group validity** means that the test will significantly predict performance for one group and no others. For example, a test of reading ability might predict performance of white clerks but not for blacks.

To test for single-group validity, separate correlations are computed between the test and the criterion for each group. If both correlations are significant, the test does not exhibit single-group validity and passes this fairness hurdle. If, however, only one of the correlations is significant, the test is considered fair for only the one group.

Single-group validity is very rare (O'Connor, Wexley, & Alexander, 1975) and is usually the result of small sample sizes (Schmidt & Hunter, 1978). Where it occurs, an organization has three choices. It can disregard single-group validity because research indicates that it probably occurred by chance, it can stop using the test, or it can use it for only the one group and find another test to use for other groups.

The first option is probably the most appropriate given that most I/O psychologists believe that single-group validity occurs only by chance. As evidence of this, think of a logical reason why a test would predict differently for blacks than for whites or differently for males than for females. That is, why would a test of intelligence predict performance for males but not for females? Or, why would a personality test predict performance for blacks but not for whites? There may be many cultural reasons why two groups score differently on a test, but finding a logical reason why the test would predict differently for two groups is difficult.

If we do not believe that single-group validity is the result of chance, we must adopt one of the other two options. As you can see, even though the third option is legally and statistically correct, many public relations problems may result. For example, an applicant asks, "Why did I get one test and my friend another?" We could respond by saying, "Blacks get one test and whites get another." Such a response, however, is provocative and ultimately may be counterproductive for an organization.

Differential Validity

The last test of fairness that must be conducted involves differential validity. With **differential validity** a test is valid for two groups, but more valid for one than the other. Single-group validity and differential validity are easily confused, but there is a big difference between the two. Remember, with single-group validity, the test is valid only for one group. With differential validity, the test is valid for both groups, but it is more valid for one than for the other.

Like single-group validity, differential validity is rare (Schmidt & Hunter, 1981; Katzell & Dyer, 1977), but when it occurs, there are again two options. The first is to not use the test. Usually, however, this is not a good option: Finding a test that is valid and has utility is difficult; throwing away a good test would be a shame.

The second option is to use the test, but use separate regression equations for each group. Because applicants do not realize that the tests are scored differently, using separate regression equations does not present the public relations problems as using separate tests for single-group validity. Using separate equations is both legally and statistically defensible and acceptable.

If a test does not lead to adverse impact, does not have single-group validity, and does not have differential validity, it is considered to be fair. If the test fails to pass one of these three fairness hurdles, it may or may not be fair, depending on which model of fairness is followed (Arvey, 1979). But to be used with complete confidence, a test must be valid, have utility, and be fair.

Making the Hiring Decision

After valid and fair selection tests have been administered to a group of applicants, a final decision must be made as to which applicant or applicants to hire. At first, this may seem an easy decision to make—hire the applicants with the highest test scores. But the decision becomes more complicated as both the number and variety of tests increase.

Linear Approaches

Although it is most common to select those applicants with the highest scores, this approach can be used only when the relationship between the test score and the criterion is **linear.** That is, the higher an applicant scores on the test, the better she will do on the job. Usually, tests that are criterion-valid have linear relationships with criteria. Thus, if one test is used and is criterion-valid, selection decisions are usually based on the highest test scores.

If more than one criterion-valid test is used, the scores on the tests must be combined. Usually, this is done by a statistical procedure known as **multiple regression,** with each test score weighted according to how well it predicts the criterion. Research has shown, however, that converting test scores into standard scores, adding the standardized test scores, and then selecting applicants with the highest composite score is comparable to multiple regression (Aamodt & Kimbrough, 1985; Schmidt, 1971; and Wainer, 1976).

Nonlinear Approaches

Often tests that are used to select employees do not show a linear relationship between test scores and job performance. For example, suppose that the distance between the floor and the ceiling of an airplane cabin was six feet. Because the job of airline attendant would require that he stand while serving meals and assisting passengers, a content-valid requirement would be that the applicant must be shorter than six feet. Thus, as part of the selection testing process, we measure each applicant. Any applicant taller than six feet would be unable to perform the job regardless of other test scores. If we use a linear approach, however, a person five feet three inches tall would get more points than a person five feet eight inches tall. This would not make sense: Both applicants are able to satisfy the requirement of moving through the aisles of the airplane while standing. Being shorter would not give one person an advantage over another.

In such a situation, we would use a cutoff approach. With a **cutoff approach,** all nonlinear tests are scored on a pass/fail basis. Applicants are administered the complete battery of tests and must pass every nonlinear one. The regression, or standardized composite, method discussed earlier then is used to select applicants based on their scores on the linearly related tests.

An example may clarify this procedure. Suppose our job analysis finds that a good police officer is intelligent and confident, is in good health, can lift 100 pounds, is psychologically sound, and does not have a criminal record. Our validity study indicates that the relationship between both intelligence and confidence and job performance are linear—the smarter and more confident the officer, the better he or she performs.

The other tests have a nonlinear relationship with performance. To underscore this point, let us examine good health. Would an applicant with one cold in the last two years be a better officer than an applicant who has had two colds in the past two years? Probably not, but with a physically active job, we could be confident that an applicant with a bad back would not be able to handle the routine requirements of the job. Thus, physical health would be determined on a pass/fail basis—the applicant is either healthy enough to do the job or not.

Because we have more than one nonlinearly related test, we would adapt our procedure and use a multiple-cutoff approach combined with a linear approach as opposed to either a single-cutoff approach or a strictly linear approach. One problem with a multiple-cutoff approach is the cost. If an applicant passes only three out of four tests, he will not be hired, but the organization has paid for the applicant to take all four tests.

To reduce the costs associated with applicants failing one or more tests, **multiple-hurdle approaches** often are used. With a multiple-hurdle approach, the applicant is administered one test at a time, usually beginning with the least expensive. If the applicant fails a test, she is eliminated from further consideration and takes no more tests. If the applicant passes all of the tests, she then is administered the linearly related tests; the applicants with the top scores on these tests are hired.

To clarify the difference between a multiple-cutoff and multiple-hurdle approach, let us look at the following example. Suppose that we will use four pass/fail tests to select employees. The tests have the following costs and failure rates:

Test	Cost of Test ($)	Failure Rate (%)
Background check	$ 25	10
Psychological screen	$ 50	10
Medical checkup	$100	10
Strength	$ 5	10
Total per applicant:	$180	

With 100 applicants applying for a position, a multiple-cutoff approach would cost our organization $18,000 (100 applicants × $180 each) to administer the tests to all applicants. But with a multiple-hurdle approach, we can administer the cheapest test (the strength test) to all 100 applicants. Because 10% of the applicants will fail this test, we then can administer the next cheapest test to the remaining 90. This process continues until all tests have been administered; a savings of $3,900 results based on the following calculations:

Test	Test Cost ($)	Applicants	Total Cost ($)
Strength	5	100	500
Background check	25	90	2,250
Psychological screen	50	81	4,050
Medical checkup	100	73	7,300
Total cost			14,100

If a multiple-hurdle approach usually saves a company money, why is it not *always* used instead of a multiple-cutoff approach? For two reasons. First, many of the tests cited above take time to conduct or score. For example, it might take a few weeks to run a background check, or a few days to interpret a psychological screening. Therefore, the tests usually must be administered on several occasions and an applicant would have to miss several days of work to apply for a particular job. Because people often cannot or will not take more than one day off from one job to apply for another, many potentially excellent applicants are lost before testing begins.

Second, research has shown that in general the longer the time between submission of a job application and the hiring decision, the smaller the number of black applicants who will remain in the applicant pool because black populations have higher unemployment rates than whites' and people who are unemployed are more hurried to obtain employment than people with jobs. Thus, because the multiple-hurdle approach takes longer than multiple-cutoff, it may bring an unintended adverse impact and affirmative action goals may not be met.

Chapter Summary

In this chapter, we have learned that an organization should only choose selection techniques that are reliable, valid, fair, and useful. *Reliability* refers to the stability of scores and can be measured using (1) the test–retest method, which measures temporal stability; (2) the alternate forms method, which measures forms stability; and (3) the internal consistency method (split half, K–R 20, and coefficient alpha), which measures item homogeneity. *Validity* refers to the degree to which inferences from scores on tests or assessments are justified by the evidence. Validity can be assessed in one of three major ways: (1) content validity, which examines the extent to which the test items sample the appropriate domain; (2) criterion validity, or the extent to which a test score is related to some measure of job performance; and (3) construct validity, or the extent to which the test measures the construct that it purports to measure.

Once a test has been found both reliable and valid, its usefulness must be established. Taylor–Russell tables, Lawshe tables, expectancy charts, and utility formulas were discussed as ways to so establish the usefulness of a test.

The last step in evaluating a test's usefulness in selection is examining its fairness by testing for adverse impact, single-group validity, and differential validity. If the test is valid, fair, and useful, we can feel confident in its use.

Once a test has been selected and administered to a group of applicants, decisions have to be made about how to use the scores. If the relationship between test score and performance score is linear, hiring those applicants with the highest scores is acceptable. If there is no linear relationship, then the multiple-hurdle or multiple-cutoff approaches can be used.

Glossary

Adverse impact When the selection ratio for minority applicants is less than 80% of the selection ratio for nonminorities

Arkansas Index A source of information that indexes personality tests by dimension rather than by test name

Barnum statements Statements, such as those used in astrological forecasts, that are so general they can be true of almost anyone

Base rate Percentage of current employees who are considered successful employees

Coefficient alpha A statistic used to determine internal reliability of tests utilizing interval or ratio scales

Concurrent validity A form of criterion validity that compares test scores and measures of job performance for employees currently working for an organization

Construct validity The extent to which a test actually measures the construct that it purports to measure

Content validity The extent to which tests or test items sample the content that they are supposed to measure

Counter-balancing A method of controlling for order effects by giving half of a sample Test A first, followed by Test B, and giving the other half of the sample Test B first, followed by Test A

Criterion A measure of job performance, such as attendance, productivity, or a supervisor rating

Criterion validity The extent to which a test score is related to some measure of job performance

Cut-off approach A method of hiring in which an applicant must score higher than a particular score in order to be considered for employment

Differential validity The characteristic of a test that significantly predicts a criterion for two groups, such as both minorities and nonminorities, but predicts significantly better for one of the two groups

Expectancy charts Charts that indicate the probability of future success for an applicant with a particular test score

Face validity The extent to which a test looks like it is valid

Form stability The extent to which the scores on two forms of a test are similar

Internal reliability The extent to which responses to test items measuring the same construct are consistent

Item homogeneity The extent to which test items measure the same construct

Item stability The extent to which responses to the same test items are consistent

Known-group validity A form of validity in which test scores from two contrasting groups "known" to differ on a construct are compared

Kuder–Richardson Formula 20 (K–R 20) A statistic used to determine internal reliability of tests utilizing items with dichotomous answers (yes/no, true/false)

Lawshe tables Tables that use the base rate, test validity, and applicant percentile on a test to determine the probability of future success for that applicant

Linear A straight-line relationship between the test score and the criterion of measurement

Mental Measurements Yearbook (MMY) The name of a book containing information about the reliability and validity of various psychological tests

Multiple-hurdle approach When applicants are administered one test at a time and must pass that test before being allowed to take the next test

Multiple regression A statistical procedure in which the scores from more than one criterion-valid test are weighted according to how well each test score predicts the criterion

Parallel forms reliability The extent to which two forms of the same test are similar

Predictive validity A form of criterion validity in which test scores of applicants are compared at a later date with a measure of job performance

Radford Index A source of information that indexes tests used in industry by dimensions rather than by test names

Reliability The extent to which a score from a test is stable and free from error

Restricted range A narrow range of performance scores that makes it difficult to obtain a significant validity coefficient

Sample homogeneity The extent to which the sample of people taking the test have similar characteristics

Scorer reliability The extent to which two people scoring a test agree on the test score or the extent to which a test is scored correctly

Selection ratio The percentage of applicants that an organization must hire

Single-group validity The characteristic of a test that significantly predicts a criterion for one class of people but not for another

Spearman–Brown prophecy formula A formula that is used to correct reliability coefficients resulting from the split-half method

Split-half method A form of internal reliability in which the consistency of item responses is determined by comparing scores on half of the items with scores on the other half of the items

Taylor–Russell tables A series of tables based on the selection ratio, base rate, and test validity that yield informatiom about the percentage of future employees who will be successful if a particular test is used

Temporal stability The consistency of test scores across time

Tenure The length of time that an employee has been employed by an organization

Test length The number of items in a test

Test–retest reliability The extent to which repeated administration of the same test will achieve similar results

Tests The name of a book containing information about psychological tests

Utility The extent to which an organization will benefit from the use of a particular selection system

Validity The degree to which inferences from scores on tests or assessments are justified by the evidence

Validity generalization (VG) The extent to which inferences from test scores from one organization can be applied to another organization

4

Employee Selection:
Recruiting and Interviewing

In the motion picture *Dirty Harry*, actor Clint Eastwood played police detective Harry Callahan, who, upon learning that he had been transferred from homicide to personnel, replied, "Personnel—only idiots work in personnel!" Although this statement is a bit strong, it represents the attitude held by many people about the field of personnel. That is, if you can't do anything else, you can always work in personnel.

The image of the personnel field, however, has been greatly enhanced, for the most part, by its recent reliance on the use of modern scientific principles in employee selection as well as by industry's realization that properly designed employee-selection procedures can save companies a lot of money.

In this chapter, we will first explore ways to recruit employees and then discuss interviewing techniques as well as offer tips that the reader can use to obtain a desired job. In the next chapter, we will discuss non-interviewing techniques for selecting employees.

As shown in Figure 4.1, certain steps can be taken to successfully choose employees. Recruitment, test-selection, and rejection steps will be discussed in this and the following chapter, while other steps will be discussed in other chapters. Some of the steps are designed to attract excellent applicants to the company, others are designed to select the best applicants, and still others are designed to give applicants a good image of not only the company, but also the job-search process in general.

Keep in mind that for any job opening, many more people will apply than will be hired. Consider the number of people who are not hired and multiply that by the number of job openings each year; one can see that a lot of people will be in contact with a particular company. Those people who are not hired are potential customers with friends who also are potential customers. Leaving them with a positive image of the company should be a priority.

Job Analysis

As discussed in Chapter 2, job analysis is the cornerstone of personnel selection. Remember, unless a complete and accurate picture of a job is presented, it is virtually impossible to select excellent employees. Thus, during the job-analysis process, in addition to identifying the important tasks and duties, it is essential to identify the knowledges, skills, and abilities needed to perform the job. The methods thus, used to select

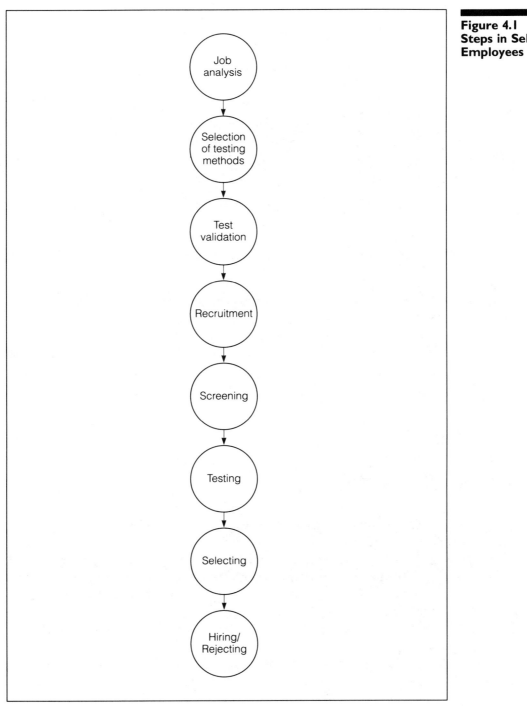

**Figure 4.1
Steps in Selecting
Employees**

	Method	
Table 4.1 **Common** **Recruitment Methods**	**Formal or Direct**	**Informal or Indirect**
	Advertisements	Employee referrals
	Newspapers	
	Journals	
	Television and radio	
	College Recruiters	Direct applications
	Employment agencies	Situation wanted ads
	Public	
	Private	
	In-store signs	
	Direct mail	
	Computer searches	
	Special events	

employees tie in directly with the results of job analysis. In other words, every essential knowledge, skill, and ability identified in the job analysis should be tested and every test must somehow relate back to the job analysis results. For example, if an analysis reveals that an office manager types correspondence and proofreads reports to ensure that they are grammatically correct, then selection tests perhaps will include a typing test and a grammar test.

Recruitment

An important step in selecting employees involves the process of **recruitment**—encouraging people who possess the job analysis–determined essential qualities to apply for the job. The first decision to be made is whether someone already with the organization should be promoted (**internal recruitment**) or whether someone outside the organization should be hired (**external recruitment**). Organizations such as AT&T and Norfolk and Southern Railroad first advertise employment openings to current employees for two weeks. If no qualified applicants are found, the organizations then advertise outside.

To enhance employee morale and motivation, it is often good to give current employees the advantage in obtaining new openings (Brumback, 1986). But if an organization always promotes employees from within, it

Author	Advice
Bucalo (1983)	Ads should be creative, written in language that is familiar to the applicant, and should emphasize the benefits of the position.
Fyock (1988)	Recruitment ads should be placed in other sections of the newspaper to attract more applicants.
	Recruitment advertisers should team with the company's marketing or advertising departments to create unique and distinctive ads.
Ilaw (1985)	Ads that use "attention-getting" words may be confusing and misleading to the applicant.
Mason and Belt (1986)	Ads that specify job qualifications screen out unqualified applicants.
Rawlinson (1988)	Recruitment ads should represent the image that the company wants.

**Table 4.2
Expert Advice on
Writing Help Wanted
Ads**

runs the risk of having a stale work force that is devoid of the many ideas that new employees bring with them. Thus, a balance between promoting current employees and hiring outside applicants is needed. This process can be seen in the employment profile of Jim Bodenmiller.

External Recruitment Methods

Media Advertisement

As shown in Table 4.1, an organization that chooses external recruitment of applicants has several methods it can use. The most obvious, of course, is running advertisements in local or national newspapers or in professional journals. In fact, in a survey of 188 organizations, personnel executives claimed newspaper advertising to be one of the most effective avenues of applicant recruitment (Mason & Belt, 1986).

Although little research is available on the best way to write recruitment advertisements, plenty of expert advice is available (see Table 4.2). Kaplan and Wilk (1989) tested expert advice by first determining the characteristics of help wanted ads and then comparing the design of actual help wanted ads in 10 newspapers with the quality and quantity of applicants who responded. After examining thousands of ads, Kaplan and Wilk identified 23 advertising characteristics (see Table 4.3). After comparing the presence or absence of the 23 characteristics with applicants' quantity and quality, the researchers found that ads that displayed the company emblem and used creative illustrations attracted the greatest *number* of

**Table 4.3
Important
Characteristics of
Help Wanted Ads**

Characteristic	Ads with Characteristic (%)
Ad design	
Company emblem included	21
Creative illustrations used	26
Creative wording	8
Size of ad	[a]
White space around ad	5
Job title enlarged or in boldface	74
Legal information	
Affirmative-action statement	38
EEO statement	41
Information about the job	
Benefit package listed	38
Job title mentioned	96
Salary description	36
Multiple jobs listed in same ad	75
Information about the company	
Company address listed	83
Company description included	63
Company name mentioned	59
Phone number listed	40
Applicant qualifications	
Education requirements	19
Personality traits desired	30
Previous experience requirements	64
Skills needed by applicants	50
Salary history requested	21

Source: Kaplan, A., & Wilk, D. (1989). Relationship between characteristics of recruitment advertisements and applicant pool quantity and quality. *Proceedings of the 10th annual graduate conference in I/O psychology and organizational behavior*, New Orleans, LA.

[a] Information not available.

applicants, while ads that included salary range and company phone number attracted the highest *quality* applicants.

In recent years, a new trend in help wanted advertising has been the use of creative ads such as those shown in Figure 4.2. By using innovative advertising, On-Line Software tripled the number of applicants who responded to its help wanted ad for secretarial positions. Hyundai's innovative ad cost only $5,000 and brought almost 2,000 applicants for com-

Figure 4.2
Creative Help
Wanted Ads

Source: Reprinted with permission of Ad Masters, Inc.

Continued

pany positions (Rawlinson, 1988). Thus, the use of the same techniques and imagination as in product advertising may increase the recruitment yield from help wanted ads. That is one reason why major advertising firms such as Bernard Hodes and Austin-Knight are increasingly involved in the development of recruitment ads and campaigns.

Recruitment advertisements are fairly common in newspapers, but aside from various armed forces commercials, they are not as common in the two other mass media areas—namely, television and radio. Perhaps the greatest use of television recruitment in the private sector has been by McDonald's, whose television commercials show McDonald's to be the

Figure 4.2
Continued

ideal place for retirees to work part-time. In addition to generating applicants, the commercials have been an excellent public relations vehicle.

An interesting twist in television recruiting was developed by Videosearch, a California-based employment agency. Videosearch's 30-minute program titled "Meet Your Next Employer" is paid for by organizations that advertise their job opportunities. The cost for this service is approxi-

Employment Profile

Jim Bodenmiller, M.S.
Director of Personnel
City of Springfield, Ohio

I am the director of personnel for a city in southwestern Ohio with a population of approximately 72,000. My responsibilities include test development, test validation, collective bargaining, labor and employee relations, organizational training and development, benefits administration, and employee recruitment and interviewing.

Quality recruitment and interviewing systems are an essential part of any successful organization in today's competitive work environment. Successful programs are needed to attract or promote quality employees. Often the reputation of a human resource professional within an organization is, in part, dependent upon his or her ability to bring in good people. Recruitment and interviewing techniques must complement each other, preferably with some additional type of selection test or tests, to achieve quality results.

Recruiting can be as simple or as complex as a particular position calls for. For example, in municipal government, many entry level and mid-level positions can be successfully recruited for by advertising in a local newspaper, or through internal job postings and promotions. More complex positions require some type of human resource planning based on past recruitment experience, availability of a quality work force, and attractiveness of the position itself. Although it goes without saying, a thorough job analysis is critical as an information base for recruitment efforts. Information gathered in the job analysis is reviewed in an attempt to identify the type of individual suitable for a particular position. One then must determine where those individuals are and actively recruit them. For upper level positions such as that of city manager, I would advertise in major newspapers as well as trade journals and magazines frequently used by city managers. Use of direct mail to similar and smaller-sized cities also would be of benefit. If necessary, it is often helpful to make direct phone contact with individuals identified as potential candidates. Enlisting the assistance of an executive search firm is also a common practice for upper-level positions.

A recruiting problem common to many cities throughout the country is that of attracting qualified minorities and females for police and fire positions. Springfield has enjoyed some successes in this area in terms of recruiting, although our successes can turn out to be disappointments because individuals who apply for positions often do not make it through the entire selection process. Many of the minority applicants have trouble with the physical or agility portions of the process. We are now in the process of redesigning our recruiting efforts to target a different market of female applicants, and we are working to develop a community group to assist in recruiting minorities.

One final note on recruiting: The issue of timing is crucial. Basically for a recruitment effort to be successful, the ideal candidate must be willing to consider a job change at the same time that you are looking to hire someone for a particular position. Fortunately for human resource professionals, there are generally many qualified applicants for any one position. Our job is to find them.

Following a successful recruiting effort, the issue of interviewing often comes into play. Like it or not, the interview is probably the most common selection method used by organizations today. Interviews in and of themselves are certainly not the best method of selecting quality employees; however, if done properly, they can be beneficial. A key to a successful interview is, again, a thorough job analysis. My favorite interview questions are situational, describing an event or situation and allowing applicants to respond as they see fit. Asking an applicant to describe past incidents in which he or she was involved gives the interviewer behavioral information to analyze.

mately $1,500 per minute for national exposure. A similar program called "CareerLine" is broadcast weekly on the Financial News Network. Although television advertising sounds promising, it is an area that needs more empirical investigation to determine its actual effectiveness.

Figure 4.3
Examples of
Situation Wanted
Ads

TOP SPEECHWRITER
Currently writing speeches for
Fortune 200 CEO. Background
in tech, multi-industry, Wall St.,
Wash. D.C.
Box EA-648, Wall Street Journal

AVAILABLE AUG. 15: Woman religious teacher.
College, seminary, adult education. Master's religious
ed, PhD, American Lit., Jour. Experience in men's,
women's, coed undergrad., grad., adult ed. Retreat
work, spir. dir., poet, writer. Interdisciplinary, incar-
nate person. Contact: Ad Random, Dept. D-166.

Situation Wanted Ads

Situation wanted ads are placed by applicants rather than by organizations. As shown in Figure 4.3, these ads take a variety of forms, with
some listing extensive qualifications, some giving applicants' names, and
some generally more creative than others. Willis and Miller (1987) investigated the effectiveness of situation wanted ads by contacting the people
who had placed then in a variety of daily and professional publications.
Much to their surprise, Willis and Miller found that 68% of the jobseekers
placing situation wanted ads were contacted as a result. But not all contacts were from employers; many were from employment agencies and
résumé-writing services, and one was even from someone trying to sell
the applicant an encyclopedia (how could the applicant afford an encyclopedia when he didn't even have a job?). Of the applicants who placed the
ads, 13% received actual job offers. Thus, situation wanted ads appear to
have some use in job searches. Given that they do not cost an organization money, they also may be a useful recruitment method.

Outside Recruiters

Another recruitment avenue is the use of outside sources such as private
and public employment agencies and executive search firms. Both private
employment agencies and executive search firms seek to profit from their

recruitment activities, but public agencies operated by state and local governments are strictly nonprofit.

Employment agencies operate in one of two ways. They either charge the company a percentage of the applicant's salary when she takes the job or charge the applicant a percentage of her salary. These latter fees usually range from 10% to 30% of the applicant's first-year salary.

From an organization's perspective, there are few risks in using an employment agency that charges the fee to the applicant. That is, if the employment agency cannot find an appropriate applicant, the organization has not wasted money. But if the employment agency is successful, the organization gets a qualified employee at no cost.

Employment agencies are especially useful if a personnel department is overloaded with work or an organization does not have an individual with the skills and experience needed to properly select employees. The disadvantage of employment agencies is that a company loses control over its recruitment process and may end up with undesirable applicants. Remember, most "counselors" at employment agencies are hired because of their skill in sales, not because of their solid background in personnel selection. In fact, one employment agency turned down one of its own job applicants because the applicant had a degree in personnel management. During the interview, the agency head told the applicant, "We are not really looking for a personnel professional. What we want is the type of person who could sell aluminum siding to the owner of a brick home."

The applicant seldom can go wrong using an employment agency. If the fee is charged to the company, then the applicant has a job at no cost. But even if the fee is charged to the applicant, it may still be a positive development. That is, suppose an applicant is having difficulty in finding a job, and an employment agency finds a good job paying $24,000 per year. Spending $2,000 for the job may be worthwhile because every month of unemployment costs the applicant $2,000 in lost income. The fee essentially is one month's salary that would not have been earned anyway without the job being taken.

Better known as "headhunters," **executive search firms** differ from employment agencies in several ways. First, the jobs they represent tend to be higher-paying, nonentry level, such as executives, engineers, and computer programmers. Second, reputable executive search firms always charge their fees to organizations rather than applicants. Third, executive search firm fees tend to be some 30% of an applicant's first-year salary.

A word of warning about both employment agencies and executive search firms. Because these firms make their money on the number of applicants they place, they tend to exert tremendous pressure on applicants to take the jobs that are offered. But an applicant is not obligated to take a job, and so should not be intimidated from turning down an unwanted job.

The third type of outside recruitment organization is the **state employment agency** (or local employment agency). Designed to help the unemployed find work, these agencies list job openings and often offer services such as career advisement and résumé preparation. From the organization's perspective, public employment agencies can be of great value in filling blue collar and clerical positions. Not only is there no cost involved in hiring the applicants, but also there are often government programs available that will help pay training costs. With the advent of standardized testing programs, which will be discussed in the next chapter, the quality of employees hired through public agencies also is much higher now than in the past.

Employee Referrals

A fourth area of recruitment is by **employee referral,** with current employees recommending family members and friends for specific job openings. Some organizations are so convinced of the attractiveness of this method that they provide financial incentives to employees who recommend applicants who are hired. For example, Washington National Insurance in Chicago gives its employees $500 for each applicant who is recommended and hired and who stays with the company for at least six months.

The average amount of such bonuses offered is $462, and the typical time period that a new employee must stay with a company before the referring employee is eligible for a bonus is three months (Ellenburg, Stewart, Hicks, & Kremen, 1989).

Surprisingly, Ellenburg and her colleagues found neither a significant relationship between the size of the bonus and the number of referrals nor that organizations offering referral bonuses received more referrals than organizations not offering bonuses. Thus, further research is needed to determine whether the popularity of employee-referral programs is justified. Surveys that have investigated this popularity indicate that approximately 40% of private organizations with more than 100 employees use them (Ellenburg et al., 1989; Bernard Hodes Advertising, 1985). Only 5% of public organizations such as state and city governments have such programs, and the few that do use them to encourage minority recruitment of police officers and firefighters (Daniel, 1989).

Although the idea of employee referrals sounds good, not all referrals are the same. Aamodt and Carr (1988) and Rupert (1989) compared the success of employees who had been referred by successful and unsuccessful employees and found that employees referred by successful employees had longer tenure than did employees who had been referred by unsuccessful employees. Thus, only those referrals made by successful employees should be considered.

The above finding, which is explained by social psychology research, indicates that our friends tend to be similar to us in characteristics such as personality, values, and interests. If a particular employee is a good employee, then the same characteristics that made her a good employee are probably shared by her friends and family. The same would be true of an unsuccessful employee. Thus, by hiring a friend of a successful employee, we essentially get a "clone" of that employee. By hiring a friend of an unsuccessful employee, we get a "clone" of the unsuccessful employee.

Even though referrals by successful employees are a good recruitment avenue, the similarity of friends also can pose some problems. The biggest is that our friends also tend to be the same sex, race, national origin, and religion as ourselves. Thus, if we use employee referrals and our organization consists predominantly of white male Protestants, we will never hire blacks or females. Thus, even though we do not intend to discriminate, the consequences of our recruitment policy have that very result.

Signs and Notices

A fifth method of recruitment is based on point-of-purchase advertising principles and involves the placement of **signs** in windows or notices on bulletin boards in the organization's facilities. For example, walking through a shopping mall, we see several stores with "Help Wanted" signs in their windows and "Help Wanted" signs at the teller windows of a bank. By law, public agencies such as city governments post their openings on bulletin boards. The greatest advantages of this method are its lack of expense and its targeting of people who frequent businesses. The greatest disadvantage is that only a limited number of people are exposed to such signs.

Because of the difficulty in obtaining employees, many fast food restaurants are taking unusual approaches in using in-store signs. McDonald's printed help wanted ads that included application blanks on its paper placemats, which are used by many customers; Wendy's printed the

Job fairs provide information in a personal fashion to many applicants.

Spencer Grant/Photo Researchers, Inc. (NYC)

words "Now hiring smiling faces" on its cash-register receipts; and Kentucky Fried Chicken took its signs outside, placing them on painted vans that drove around student-gathering places; applications and information about working for the company were then distributed.

Job Fairs

Job Fairs are designed to provide information in a personal fashion to as many applicants as possible. They typically are conducted in one of three ways. In the first, many different types of organizations have booths at the same location. Your college probably has one or two of these job fairs each year in which dozens of organizations send representatives to discuss employment opportunities with students and to collect résumés. In addition, company representatives usually hand out company literature and souvenirs such as T-shirts, yardsticks, and cups.

The second method is to have many organizations in the same field in one location. For example, a nursing job fair in New York City in 1988 had more than 100 medical organizations represented and attracted more than 1,500 potential nurses (Harper, 1988). The advantage of this type of job fair is that with a single employment field represented, each visitor is a potential applicant for every organization. The drawback, of course, is that each organization must compete directly with others at the fair.

The third approach is for an organization to hold a job fair by itself. Although this approach certainly is more expensive, it has the advantage of focusing the attention of applicants on only one company. Such an approach was taken by Compaq Computer Corporation. Because of a shortage of applicants with technical skills, Compaq created a traveling job fair called "Compaq, Texas." The fair traveled from city to city and was held in hotel ballrooms. Before the job fair arrived in each city, Compaq conducted a media blitz to tell prospective applicants about the fair. Upon arrival at the hotel, each prospective applicant was assigned a personal recruiter who would lead the applicant through "Compaq, Texas" with its product displays, videos, literature, and company representatives. The cost for each job fair was some $100,000. This amount seems high, but each job fair draws 1,000 or more applicants; with just five or more applicants being hired, the company saves money over the use of outside recruiters (Chauran, 1989).

Direct Mail

Because direct mailings have been successful in product advertising, several organizations have used the **direct mail** approach to recruit applicants. An employer typically obtains a mailing list and sends help wanted letters or brochures to people through the mail. One California branch of Allstate Insurance had been using newspaper advertisements and getting limited response. From a single mailing of 64,000 letters to current policy holders that explained the career opportunities available at Allstate, the company received more than 500 calls and was able to hire 20 new employees (Halcrow, 1989).

Figure 4.4
Example of Direct
Mail Recruitment
Advertisement

If You're Looking For:

- An OUTSIDE sales position with earnings between 40-50K and more for high performances, and a company car
- A TELEPHONE sales position with earnings between 30-40K and more for high performances
- A reputable, well accepted and needed product to sell
- Provided leads/Protected accounts
- An exceptional benefits package including health, dental, & 401K plan
- Five weeks paid comprehensive training
- Excellent opportunity for advancement
- A top notch work environment & management team
- A position that offers minimal travel

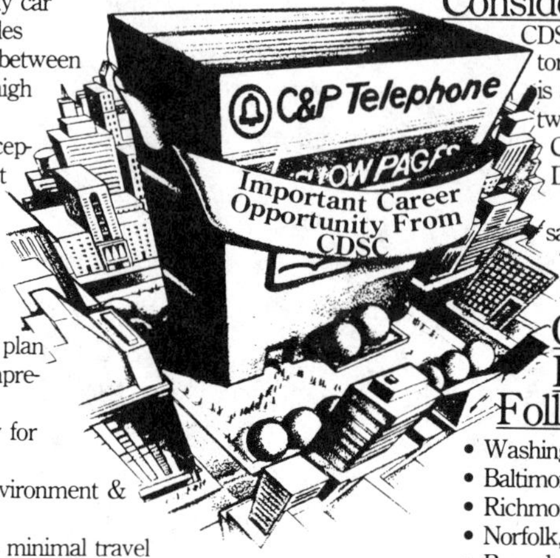

We're Looking For:

- Seasoned sales professionals with two years proven experience in commissioned outside or telephone sales to sell yellow page advertising space
- Individuals with strong professional selling skills

- Competitive, articulate and dedicated business men and women with integrity
- Team players

Consider CDSC.

CDSC, Chesapeake Directory Sales Company, is a new partnership between Bell Atlantic Corporation and GTE Directories Corporation and will be the official sales company for C&P Telephone Yellow Pages.

Opportunities Exist In The Following Areas:

- Washington, D.C. metro area
- Baltimore, MD metro area
- Richmond, VA
- Norfolk, VA
- Roanoke, VA
- Charleston, WV

If interested and for immediate consideration, please fill out and return the self-addressed Mini-Resume coupon by **JUNE 24.** We're hiring **NOW.**

CDSC is an equal opportunity employer.

C&P Telephone
YELLOW PAGES
Important Career Opportunity From CDSC

MINI-RESUME

Name _____

Address _____

City _____

State/Zip _____

Phone (h)_____ (w)_____

Degree/College _____

Current Employer _____

Current Position _____

Responsibilities _____

_____

_____

Other Related Experience _____

_____

_____

Position/City Interested In _____

_____

Source: Chesapeake Directory Sales Company. Used with permission.

Another company that successfully used direct mail recruitment was the Bank of America. To save money, the bank did something different than Allstate. Instead of sending a special recruitment mailing, Bank of America included recruitment literature in the regular monthly mailing of

Criterion	Recruitment Source		
	Advertisements	**Referrals**	**Walk-ins**
Number of applicants	40	30	20
Number qualified	10	15	5
Number hired	2	7	1
Number successful	0	4	1

Table 4.4
Evaluating the Effectiveness of Recruitment Strategies

bank statements to its customers. An example of direct mail recruiting is shown in Figure 4.4.

Evaluating Recruitment Strategies

Considering the number of potential recruitment sources, it is important to determine which source is the best to use. Such an evaluation can be conducted in several ways. As shown in Table 4.4, the first would be to examine the *number of applicants* that each recruitment source yields. That is, if a newspaper ad results in 100 applicants and an in-store sign results in 20 applicants, newspaper ads would be considered the better method.

But looking at only the number of applicants who apply does not take into account the cost of the recruitment campaign. Thus, a second method for evaluating the success of a recruitment campaign would be to consider the **cost per applicant,** which is determined by dividing the number of applicants by the amount spent for each strategy. Continuing with the example above, suppose our newspaper ad cost $200 and yielded 100 applicants and our in-store sign cost $5 and yielded 20 applicants. The cost per applicant for the newspaper ad would be $2, while the cost per applicant for the in-store sign would be just 25 cents.

Using this method of evaluation, the in-store sign would be better as long as it generated the number of applicants needed by the organization. That is, a method such as an in-store sign probably will not cost an organization much money. But if the organization needs to hire 10 new employees and only 5 applicants apply for jobs, the recruitment strategy by itself is not effective.

Although the cost-per-applicant evaluation method is an improvement on the applicant yield method, it also has a serious drawback. Even though an organization might receive a large number of applicants at a relatively low cost per applicant, as shown in the humorous example in

Employee Selection:
Recruiting and
Interviewing

**Figure 4.5
The Wording of Ads
Can Result in
Unintended
Consequences**

"confident self-starter"

"proven track record"

"polished professional"

"sales experience"

"team player"

"leadership potential"

"aggressive go-getter"

"hands-on experience"

IF THIS IS WHAT YOUR LAST WANT AD PULLED, CALL CORS.

WANT AD

"We are looking for a *confident self-starter* who has a *proven track record* successfully handling all types of people and accounts. Ideal candidate will be a *polished professional* with 3-5 years of consultative *sales experience*. This individual must be a *team player* who has the *leadership potential* to help us achieve our goals and objectives. Only *aggressive go-getters* who have the *hands-on experience* to make things happen need apply."

It seemed so easy when you placed that want ad. You described your ideal candidate, down to the last detail. Trouble is, it pulled practically everyone—except for the person you were looking for.

Next time you have a position to fill, start with something different—start with CORS. CORS is the largest recruitment research firm in the country, and has been serving the personnel community since 1974. In 5 days, for $2995 we'll find, screen and contact a minimum of 40 individuals who meet your specifications by job title and/or job description. These individuals come to you in a documented report that includes their objective accomplishments, not someone's subjective interpretation of your want ad.

For your **CORS** information packet plus a *free* "Want Ad Misfits" poster, call us toll free at **1-800-323-1352**, extension 146 (in Illinois, 312-250-8677).

CORS

Corporate Organizing and Research Services, Inc.
One Pierce Place, Suite 300 East
Itasca, IL 60143

CORS—Get what you're advertising for!

© CORS Inc. 1989   CIRCLE NO. 235

Source: Corporate Organizing and Research Services, Inc. © CORS Inc. 1989. Used with permission.

Figure 4.5, none may be qualified for a particular job. Therefore, the third and fourth strategies would be to look at either the **number of qualified applicants** or the **cost per qualified applicant.**

A final method for evaluating the effectiveness of various recruitment sources, and perhaps the best one, looks at the number of successful employees generated by each recruitment source. This is an effective method because, as shown in Table 4.4, not only will every applicant not be qualified, but also not every qualified applicant will eventually become a successful employee.

Research investigating the relationship between recruitment source and the success of future employees has been inconsistent. Some (Decker & Cornelius, 1979) has indicated that informal sources such as employee referrals lead to lower turnover than do formal sources such as advertisements. Other research (Swaroff, Bass, & Barclay, 1985), however, has found no differences in tenure or performance between applicants recruited through formal or informal sources. Other research has suggested that informal recruiting sources will lead to longer tenure for whites, and formal recruiting sources will lead to longer tenure for blacks (Caldwell & Spivey, 1983).

A meta-analysis by Aamodt and Carr (1988) found that employee referrals were the best method for finding employees who would stay with the organization (higher tenure), but that no method of employee referral resulted in better employee performance than another.

Even though employee referrals are superior when tenure alone is used as the criterion, several theories have been postulated about why referrals result in better employees. The first theory suggests that applicants who are referred by other employees receive more accurate information about the job than do employees recruited by other methods (Wanous, 1980). This theory has been supported in research by Breaugh and Mann (1984) and by Quaglieri (1982), who found that applicants referred by current employees received not only more information but also more accurate information about the jobs than did applicants who had been recruited through other channels.

The second theory postulates that differences in the effectiveness of recruitment sources is the result of different recruitment sources reaching and being used by different types of applicants (Schwab, 1982). Although some research has supported this theory (Breaugh & Mann, 1984; Ellis & Taylor, 1983; Swaroff, Bass, & Barclay, 1985; Taylor & Schmidt, 1983), other research has not (Aamodt & Carr, 1988; Breaugh, 1981). In fact, as shown in Table 4.5, more variables have been found to *not* relate than relate to the differential use of recruitment strategies.

**Table 4.5
Summary of
Relationship of
Personal Variables to
Various Recruitment
Sources**

Recruitment source	Research Finding	
	Related	Unrelated
Employment agencies	Low self-esteem	Age
Advertisements	Low self-esteem	Race
	Age (older)	Education
	Sex (males)	Sex
		Employment status
		Experience
		Ability
		Personality
		G.P.A.
		Financial standing
Employee referral	Age (young)	Self-esteem
		Race
		Sex
		Education
		Employment status
		Experience
		Ability
		G.P.A.
		Personality
		Financial standing
Direct application	Age (young)	Self-esteem
	Sex (female)	Sex
		Education
		Employment status
		Experience
		Ability
		Race
		G.P.A.
		Personality
		Financial standing

Furthermore, as shown in Table 4.6, the typical person looking for a job uses a wide variety of job search strategies. To underscore this point, think of the part-time jobs you have held. How did you find out about each one? Was it the same method each time? As you can see, it is unlikely that a certain type of person responds only to newspaper ads, while another type goes only to employment agencies.

A third theory might better explain the finding that employee referrals result in greater tenure than other recruitment strategies. This theory,

Position	Recruitment Source
Cook, Burger King	Newspaper ad
Clerk, K-Mart	Friend
Waiter, Big Sizzle	Sign in window
Camp counselor	State employment agency

Table 4.6
How Applicant Joe Smith was Recruited for Various Jobs

cited earlier in the discussion on employee-referral programs, has its roots in the interpersonal attraction literature, which indicates that people tend to be friends with those who are similar to themselves (Byrne, 1971). If true, and research strongly suggests that it is, then an employee recommending a friend for a job will more than likely recommend one who is similar to herself. Thus, it would make sense that a person who is happy with her job would recommend a person who, because of her similarity to the incumbent, should also be happy with the job. Likewise, an unhappy employee would recommend similar friends who would also be unhappy and thus probably have short tenure with the organization.

This theory has not been heavily researched, but it has been supported by two studies. As discussed earlier, both Aamodt and Carr (1988) and Rupert (1989) found that long-tenured employees referred applicants, who, after being hired, stayed on their jobs longer than applicants who were referred by short-tenured employees. No significant differences were formed when job performance was examined instead of tenure.

Regardless of the actual reason for the success of employee referrals, given that the effect size for employee tenure was small and that the effect size for employee performance was not significant, recruitment methods probably make a difference mostly in the number of applicants who are attracted per recruitment dollar spent rather than in the actual performance of future employees.

Realistic Job Previews

Because recruitment sources have only a slight effect on the tenure of future employees, other approaches used during the recruitment process may be helpful in recruiting applicants who will be successful. One such method is the **realistic job preview (RJP)**. RJPs involve giving an applicant "the truth" about a job. Instead of telling the applicant how much fun she will have working on the assembly line, the recruiter honestly tells the applicant that the work is often boring and that there is little chance for advancement.

The logic behind RJPs is that even though telling the truth may scare away many applicants, the ones who stay will not be surprised by the job. Because they know what they are getting into, informed applicants will tend to stay on the job longer than applicants who did not understand the true nature of the job.

In a meta-analysis of 21 RJP studies, Premack and Wanous (1985) found that RJPs have only a small effect on future employee tenure because the average effect size for tenure was only .12. The relationship between RJPs and performance was more complicated. RJPs given in either a written or oral fashion to an applicant had almost no effect at all; the mean effect size was −.04. But if the RJP was provided through audiovisual methods, the mean effect size was a respectable .32. Thus, RJPs may be a useful method that can be used during recruitment.

The Employment Interview

If the recruitment process is successful, an organization will have several applicants from which to choose employees. Many selection techniques can be used to pick the best person from this pool of applicants.

Undoubtedly the most commonly used method to select employees is the **employment interview.** In fact, if you remember all of the part-time and summer jobs for which you applied, you probably can recall the sweaty palms that went along with each interview. Because the interview is the most common method, it might logically follow that it must be the most effective. Unfortunately, most evidence suggests that the opposite is true—that is, the typical interview is almost useless in predicting future employee performance (Hunter & Hunter, 1984).

Perhaps the most critical look at the interview process was conducted by Meehl (1965), who examined the relative effectiveness of clinical versus statistical prediction. **Clinical prediction** in the employment setting looks at information about an applicant, combining that information in some *subjective* way (for example, using intuition, hunches, or experience) and then making a judgment about that person. On the other hand, **statistical prediction** uses numerical formulas that take the information gathered about an individual and mathematically determine a probability regarding that person's future behavior. If the interview is a good method for selecting employees, then clinical prediction should be better than statistical prediction. Such is not the case, however. In examining the results of 51 studies that investigated clinical versus statistical prediction, Meehl (1965) found that only one study concluded that clinical prediction was more accurate than statistical prediction. These results have been confirmed by others who more directly investigated the accuracy of the employment interview; they found a lack of both reliability and validity for the interview (Arvey & Campion, 1982; Mayfield, 1964; Ulrich & Trumbo, 1965).

Why does the interview *not* seem to predict future employee performance? Researchers have investigated this question for several years and have identified seven factors that have contributed to the poor reliability and validity of the interview process: lack of job relatedness, primary effects, contrast affects, negative information bias, interviewer–interviewee similarity, interviewee appearance, and nonverbal cues.

Lack of Job Relatedness

Articles by Martin (1979) and Hopkins (1980) have identified the most common questions asked by interviewers. As Box 4.1 shows, these questions are not related to any particular job. Furthermore, the proper answers to these questions have not been empirically determined. Research has shown which answers personnel managers prefer (Hopkins, 1980), but preference for an answer does not imply that it will actually predict future performance on the job. As discussed in this and earlier chapters, information that is used to select employees *must* be job-related if it is to have any chance of predicting future employee performance.

Box 4.1

Commonly Asked Employment Interview Questions

1. Why should I hire you?

2. What do you see yourself doing five years from now?

3. What do you consider your greatest strengths and weaknesses?

4. How would you describe yourself?

5. What college subjects did you like best? least?

6. What do you know about our company?

7. Why did you decide to seek a position with the company?

8. Why did you leave your last job?

9. What do you want to earn five years from now?

10. What do you really want to do in life?

Primacy Effects

Research indicates that information presented early in the interview (*primacy*) carries more weight than information presented later (Farr, 1973). Furthermore, interviewers may make up their minds about a candidate within five minutes of the start of a 15-minute interview (Dessler, 1984). In fact, of a group of personnel professionals, 74% said that they can make a decision within the first five minutes (Buckley & Eder, 1989).

Thus, the **primacy effect** may help to explain why research has shown no relationship between interview length and outcome (Huegli & Tschirgi, 1975). To reduce the primacy effect, interviewers are advised to make repeated judgments throughout the interview rather than one overall judgment at the end of the interview (Farr & York, 1975). That is, the interviewer might rate the applicant's response after each question or series of questions rather than waiting until the end of the interview to make a single rating or judgment.

Contrast Effects

The **contrast effects** variable concerns the idea that the interview performance of one applicant may affect the interview score given to the next applicant. Early research on this topic seemed to indicate that contrast effects do indeed occur (Carlson, 1970; Wexley, Sanders, & Yukl, 1973). If a terrible applicant precedes an average applicant, the interview score for the average applicant would be higher than if no applicant or a very qualified applicant preceded her. In other words, an applicant's performance is judged in relation to the performance(s) of previous interviewees. Thus, it may be advantageous to be interviewed immediately after someone who has done poorly.

Research by Wexley, Yukl, Kovacs, and Sanders (1972) found that interviewers who were trained to be aware of contrast effects were able to significantly reduce them. Other researchers (Aamodt, 1986; Landy & Bates, 1973), however, have questioned whether the contrast effect actually plays a significant role in the interview process.

Negative Information Bias

Negative information apparently is weighed more heavily than positive information (Rowe, 1989; Springbett, 1958) and positive information is underweighed (Hollman, 1972). **Negative information bias** seems to occur only when interviewers are not aware of job requirements

(Langdale & Weitz, 1973) and seems to support the observation that most job applicants are afraid of being honest in interviews out of fear that one negative response will cost them their job opportunities. Perhaps that is why interviewees often are not honest even earlier, during the application process itself (Goldstein, 1971).

This lack of honesty may be especially evident in the interview, where the face-to-face nature of the process increases the odds that an applicant will respond in such a way as to look better to the interviewer. In a study conducted to increase the honesty of applicants during the interview process, Martin and Nagao (1989) had applicants interview for a job under one of four conditions. In the first, applicants read written interview questions and then wrote their responses to the questions. In the second condition, applicants were "interviewed" by computer. In the third condition, applicants were interviewed face-to-face by an interviewer who behaved warmly; and in the fourth condition, applicants were interviewed by an interviewer who seemed cold.

As expected, Martin and Nagao (1989) found that applicants were more honest in reporting their G.P.A.s and SAT scores under the nonsocial conditions that involved paper and pencil and computer interviewing. Thus, one might increase the accuracy of information obtained in the interview by reducing social pressure and using written or computerized interviews.

Interviewer–Interviewee Similarity

If an interviewee's personality (Foster, 1986) and perhaps attitude (Frank & Hackman, 1975) are similar to that of the interviewer, the interviewee will receive a higher score. Available research, however, indicates that neither racial (Rand & Wexley, 1975) nor gender similarity (Rose & Andiappan, 1978) greatly affects interview ratings.

Interviewer–interviewee similarity affects interviews other than those for employment. Golightly, Huffman, and Byrne (1972) found that loan officers gave more money to loan applicants with attitudes similar to their own than they did to loan appicants whose attitudes were dissimilar.

Interviewee Appearance

The majority of evidence indicates that, in general, physically attractive applicants have an advantage over less attractive applicants (Dipboye, Fromkin, & Wilback, 1975; Gilmore, Beehr, & Love, 1986; Raza & Car-

Research suggests that a job applicant should dress conservatively.

penter, 1987). Interestingly enough, for women this relationship is moderated by the type of position for which they apply. Attractive females tend to get higher ratings for nonmanagerial jobs than unattractive females, but less attractive females get higher ratings than attractive females for managerial positions (Heilman & Saruwatari, 1979). Interviewee appearance, it seems, is a potent interview factor.

Along these same lines, Cash, Gillen, and Burns (1977) found that attractive males received the highest ratings for traditionally masculine jobs and attractive females received the highest ratings for traditionally feminine jobs. When the job was gender-neutral, attractive applicants in general received higher ratings than unattractive applicants.

Interviewers, however, are not as attuned to fashion or dress style as has been suggested in the popular press (see, for example, Molloy, 1978 and 1975). Still, research indicates that a job applicant should dress well and conservatively. That is, males should wear at least a coat and tie, and females should wear a skirt and blouse. For men, three-piece suits do not offer any more of an advantage than a two-piece suit (Aamodt, 1986). For women, a more masculine style of dress such as a suit may lead to higher interview scores (Forsythe, Drake, and Cox, 1985).

Strangely, Baron (1983) found that even something as trivial as wearing cologne or perfume can affect an interviewee's scores. Male interviewers gave lower scores to applicants who wore a pleasant scent, while female interviewers gave higher scores to applicants who wore perfume or cologne.

Nonverbal Cues

Perhaps the one interview variable that accounts most for high or low interview scores is nonverbal communication or **nonverbal cues.** Amalfitano and Kalt (1977) found that making eye contact led to higher interview scores. Aamodt (1986) found that making eye contact was the single best predictor of an applicant's interview score and that a firm handshake also led to a higher score. Young and Beier (1977) reported results that indicate 80% of the interview score variance can be accounted for by the presence or absence of eye contact, smiling, and head nodding.

Although many more studies and variables could be listed, the above discussion shows that the interview contains many sources of bias that are not job-related. Remember that one of the major purposes of the employment interview is to determine which applicant will be the most successful in performing a job. To determine this, decisions must be based on ability to do the job and not on variables such as physical attractiveness and eye contact.

Does this mean that the interview is useless as a predictor of employee performance? Not at all. It just means that care must be taken to ensure that interview questions and decisions are job-related. Even if the interview does not predict future employee success, it can still serve useful recruitment and orientation purposes by providing an opportunity for the interviewer to answer any questions that an applicant might have as well as to sell the organization to the applicant. Furthermore, most people do not feel comfortable hiring someone they have not seen. Fortunately, research has discovered techniques that will make the interview more job-related and valid.

Interviewer Training

As discussed earlier, Wexley and his associates (1972) have found that interviewers can be trained to avoid some of the more common types of interview bias. For example, simply being cautioned about the contrast effect led to a 20% reduction in its power. Going through a week-long workshop decreased the contrast effect by more than 90%. Success in training interviewers has also been found by Dougherty, Ebert, and Callender (1986), Mayfield, Brown, and Hamstra (1980), and Howard and Dailey (1979). Keenan (1978) found that training improved some aspects of interviewer behavior but not others. We hope that exposure to the interview biases discussed in this text will help minimize any errors that you might make as an interviewer.

Most interviewer-training programs have focused on avoiding errors in rating interviewee performance. Based on recent research, however, interviewers should be trained to perform the same type of nonverbal behaviors such as smiling and making eye contact that interviewees are trained to perform. Both Rynes and Miller (1983) and Gilmore (1989) found that applicants respond more positively and are more likely to accept a job when an interviewer is friendly and has good nonverbal communication skills.

Structured Interviews

Again returning to the idea that interviews must be job-related, the **structured interview** is perhaps the best way to ensure that interviewers base their decisions on relevant information. To create a structured interview, information about the job is obtained (job analysis) and questions are created to find the extent to which the applicant's skills and experiences match those that are needed to successfully perform the job. These questions are incorporated into an interview form that is used by all interviewers for all applicants. Examples of good and bad answers are located next to the questions to help an interviewer score the answers given by applicants. Research has shown that structured interviews are not only fairly reliable (Schwab & Heneman, 1969; Wiesner & Cronshaw, 1988) but also much more valid than the traditional unstructured interview (Campion, Pursell, & Brown, 1988; Pursell, Campion, & Gaylord, 1980; Reynolds, 1979; Wiesner & Cronshaw, 1988).

Situational Interviews

A special type of structured interview, the **situational interview,** was introduced a decade ago by Latham, Saari, Pursell, and Campion (1980). As shown in Box 4.2, the first step in creating a situational interview is to conduct a critical-incident job analysis, a technique we discussed in Chapter 2. These incidents are then given to job experts such as supervisors, who are asked to choose one or two incidents that typify each of the important job dimensions determined by the job analysis.

The incidents are then rewritten into questions to be used during the interview. Each job expert is asked to create three levels of answers for each question—excellent, mediocre, and terrible. These three answers serve as benchmarks for points 5, 3, and 1 on a 5-point scale. This process is shown in Box 4.3.

Box 4.2

Steps in Developing a Situational Interview

1. Collect critical incidents

2. Rewrite incidents into situations

3. Translate incidents into situational questions

4. Brainstorm several answers for each question

5. On a five-point scale, rate the level of performance represented by each answer

6. Choose the answers that most closely represent the five points on the scale

7. Conduct a validation study

The job-related questions then are asked during the employment interview. The answers given by the applicant are compared to the **benchmark answers** and each is given a score from one to five. At the end of the interview, the scores from the questions are summed and the resulting figure is the applicant's interview score, which has been arrived at without being affected by variables such as eye contact and the interviewee's attractiveness.

Following this procedure, Latham et al. (1980) were able to create interviews that were not only reliable but also correlated at .30 for supervisors and .46 for hourly workers. In other research:

1. Latham and Saari (1984) were able to obtain correlations between situational interview scores and performance of .39 by clerical workers and .14 for performance by utility workers.

2. Weekley and Geier (1987) also were successful in using a situational interview to predict success of sales clerks.

Box 4.3

Developing an Interview Question from Critical Incidents

The Incident A customer entered a bank and began yelling about how the bank had messed up his account. He became so angry that he began to swear, saying that he would not leave the bank until the problem was solved. Unfortunately, the information needed by the teller was not at this branch, so there was nothing she could do.

The Question You are working as a teller and have a long line of waiting customers. One customer runs to the front of the line and yells that he bounced a check and was charged $20, which caused other checks to bounce. He then swears at you and tells you that he will not leave until the problem is solved. You are unable to check on his account because the information is at another branch. What would you do?

The Benchmark Answers

Worst

1—I would tell him to get at the end of line and wait his turn.

3—I would explain to him that I cannot help him, try to calm him down, and ask him to come back tomorrow.

5—Because I do not have the information and the line is long, I would call my supervisor and have her talk to the customer in her office away from everyone else.

Best

Box 4.4

Successfully Surviving the Interview Process

Even though the employment interview has many problems, the odds are high that a person being considered for a job will be interviewed. Research and experience both indicate that an applicant can take several steps to increase his interview score.

Scheduling the Interview Contrary to advice given in popular magazines, neither day of week nor time of day affect interview scores. What will affect the score, however, is *when* the applicant arrives for the interview. If he arrives late, the score will be drastically lower. In fact, in a study done by Aamodt (1986), no applicant who arrived late was hired. No differences, however, have been found in interview scores based on whether an applicant arrives on time or 5 or 10 minutes early. Therefore, the interview can be scheduled for anytime of the day or week, but the applicant must not be late!

Before the Interview Learn about the company. Recall from Box 4.1 that one of the most commonly asked interview questions ("What do you know about our company?") is used to determine the applicant's knowledge of the organization. Not only does this advice make sense, but also research has found that an applicant's knowledge significantly correlated (.32) with the interview rating (Aamodt, 1986).

A former student tells the story about an interview for a managerial position that she had with Allstate Insurance Company. The night before the interview she read all the available information on Allstate at her local library. During the interview, she was asked why she wanted to work for Allstate. She replied that she was active in the community and was attracted to Allstate because of its "helping hands" community program—which she had read about the night before. The inter-

viewer was greatly impressed and spent the next 10 minutes describing the program and its importance. The interview was a success because the applicant had done her homework. (By the way, she was not offered the job, but as industrial psychologist Dan Johnson is known to say, "It still makes for a good story.")

The day of the interview, dress neatly. You might want to adjust your style to fit the situation, however. That is, if you are a male, enhance your attractiveness; if female, downplay your attractiveness if you are interviewing for a managerial position. Wear a scent only if the interviewer is female.

During the Interview Most suggestions about how best to behave in an interview take advantage of the interviewer biases that we have discussed in this chapter. Nonverbal behaviors should include a firm handshake, eye contact, smiling, and head nodding. Desired verbal behaviors include asking questions, subtly pointing out how you are similar to the interviewer, not asking about the salary, not speaking slowly, and not hesitating before answering questions. Keep in mind that first impressions are the most important. If you want to appear similar to the interviewer, look around the office. Kopitzke and Miller (1984) found that the contents of an interviewer's office are often related to his or her personality and interests.

After the Interview Immediately following the interview, write a brief letter thanking the interviewer for her time and reiterating why you believe that you are the perfect person for the job. Although research evidence supports all of the suggestions offered in this section, no research has been done on the effects of thank you letters. Still, this nice touch certainly cannot hurt.

3. Maurer and Fay (1988) found that situational interviews were evaluated more reliably than traditional interviews.

4. Lin, Petersen, and Manligas (1987) found that black, white, and Hispanic applicants scored equally well on a situational interview for custodians.

5. Buchner, Carr, and Manson (1988) found that increasing the number of benchmark answers from three to five increased the scoring reliability.

6. McShane (1990) found that nonverbal cues do not affect situational interview scores.

Overall, according to published research, situational interviews have an average validity of .38 and an average interrater reliability of .80.

The first situational interviews were designed for face-to-face use with an applicant, but recent years have brought several variations. In the public sector, these situations are commonly acted out and then shown on videotape to large numbers of applicants applying for positions such as police officers and prison guards. The applicants then write down what they would do in each situation, and the answers are later scored by a panel of experts. Even though videotaped situations appear more realistic and are more efficient than face-to-face interviews, none of the available research suggests that they are more valid or reliable.

An interesting variation in situational exercises was developed for the New York State Civil Service Commission by Kaiser and Brull (1987). Instead of presenting the situations face-to-face or through videotape, Kaiser and Brull placed the situations in booklets with series of possible answers. The applicant reads each situation and then uses a special latent ink pen to darken her response. The pen reveals a message telling the applicant, based on her answer, the page to turn to for the next situation. As innovative as the process may be, its validity is low ($r = .13$), and it needs further refinement if it is to be useful.

Résumés and Cover Letters

For many jobs, employers require applicants to send both **cover letters** and **résumés.** Basically, a résumé is a summary of an applicant's professional and educational background. Although research has pinpointed several factors that influence a personnel professional's judgments about résumés (see Box 4.5), little is known about their value in predicting future employee performance. Harrison (1986) used résumé data to successfully construct a weighted application blank (a concept to be discussed in the next chapter). Other studies have found that when an interviewer reads a résumé before interviewing an applicant, the validity of the employment interview may actually be *reduced*. (Dipboye, Stramler, & Fontennelle, 1984; Phillips & Dipboye, 1989). Beyond these studies, however, it is unclear how much predictive value, if any, that résumés have.

Résumés may not predict performance partly because they are intended to be advertisements for an applicant. Companies that specialize in résumé design openly brag about their ability to "make your strengths more obvious and your weaknesses hard to find." In fact, Janice Rulnick of Credential Check and Personnel Services in Michigan estimates that 30% of the resumes that her company investigates contain exaggerations. This figure of 30% is close to the 25% exaggeration figure estimated by LoPresto, Mitcham, and Ripley (1985) and by Broussard and Brannen (1986). Such attempts to enhance an applicant's chances of getting a job are compounded by résumé fraud.

Résumé Fraud

Résumé fraud is the intentional placement of untrue information on a résumé. Thomas Norton, president of Fidelifacts, a company specializing in the investigation of applicant information, has detailed six common types of résumé fraud, which are listed in Box 4.6.

Résumé fraud may not initially seem to be a great problem, but consider the following examples: Paul Crafton used 33 aliases to receive university teaching jobs; Abraham Asante, posing as a doctor, improperly gave anesthesia to a patient, who suffered brain damage; and a man on probation for a felony conviction posed as an electrical engineer and received a $95,000-a-year job by falsely claiming he spoke 13 languages. These stories are tragic and may not be typical of résumé fraud cases, but more than 80% of companies believe it to be enough of a problem to merit reference checks (Muchinsky, 1979).

Box 4.5

Writing Excellent Résumés

Contrary to popular belief, there is no one best way to write a résumé. Because people have such different backgrounds, no one format will make everyone look their best. Therefore, this section will provide only general advice about writing a résumé; the rest is up to you.

Physical Appearance The primary consideration here is to make the résumé attractive and easy to read. To do this, leave at least a one-inch margin on all sides, allow plenty of white space, and limit the length to one page if possible (Pibal, 1985). That is, do not "pack" information into the résumé. One undergraduate student had the "great idea" of typing his résumé on a legal-sized sheet of paper and then using a photocopy machine to reduce it to regular-sized paper with a one-inch margin. Although this technique may look nice, it is probably not advisable because information is still being packed into a small space, and personnel directors spend little time in reading résumés.

Another important point is to eliminate all spelling mistakes and grammatical errors (Pibal, 1985). Walter Pierce, Jr., a personnel officer for Norfolk–Southern Corporation, recalls that when he had his personnel internship with a large company, his supervisor received a résumé from an excellent applicant who was applying for a job as a computer programmer. Even though the applicant had outstanding credentials, the personnel director would not even offer him an interview—the applicant had misspelled two words on his résumé.

A similar story is told by Dick Williams, the general manager for N&W Credit Union. He once received two cover letters stapled together, both referring to a résumé that was not included. To make matters worse, four words were misspelled. There are many more horror stories, but the point is clear: Do not make careless mistakes!

In terms of paper type, research has shown that a résumé typed on white paper with a nice typewriter is best (Faloona, Henson, Jahn, & Snyder, 1985). Expensive typesetting is not necessary.

Information Layout A résumé can be written in many ways, but students are advised to use the format shown in Figure 4.6, which is based on the following psychological research and theory. The résumé should begin with a short summary of the applicant's strengths, taking advantage of the impression-formation principles of *priming* (preparing the reader for what is to come) and *primacy* (the importance of early impressions).

The statements in this section should be believable. That is, a statement about having "excellent sales ability" should be based on information presented later in the résumé. This is important; Knouse, Giacalone, and Pollard (1988) found that résumé readers often negatively react to attempts to manage their impressions of the applicant by using general and unsupported statements.

The next section should contain information about either education or experience. The stronger of the two should go first. The design of the education section is intended to provide an organizational framework that will make it easier for the reader to remember the contents. In this section, only the best activities and accomplishments should be listed. Do not list everything you may have done, because research by Spock and Stevens (1985) found that listing a few great things

Continued

Box 1.2 continued

Jane Doe
1111 Main Street
Smalltown, VA 22222
(703) 555-5555

PROFESSIONAL STRENGTHS
- Master's Degree in Counseling
- Three Years Counseling Experience
- Two Years Teaching Experience
- Supervisory and Leadership Experience
- Extensive Experience with Adolescents
- C.P.R. and Emergency First Aid Training

EDUCATION
M.S., Counseling Psychology (May, 1988)
College of Hard Knocks, Jonesville, Kentucky

B.A., Psychology and Sociology (May, 1985)
Iamsmart University, Bigtown, Virginia

Highlights:
- 4.00 Graduate G.P.A.
- 3.65 Undergraduate G.P.A.
- Nominated for Outstanding Graduate Student Award
- Participant in R.O.T.C.
- Earned Army Officers Commission
- Worked to Help Finance Education

RELEVANT EXPERIENCE
Instructor, Department of Psychology (1985–1987)
College of Hard Knocks, Jonesville, Kentucky
   Full responsibility for teaching eight sections of general psychology over a four-semester period. Activities included lecture writing, lecture presentation, test construction, and student counseling. Received excellent teaching ratings from both students and supervisor.

Counselor (August 1982 to August 1985)
Virginia Children's Home, Ambrose, Virginia
   Worked with six adolescents in a home for children with behavioral disturbances and/or family difficulties. Responsibilities included individual and group counseling; teaching interpersonal skills, goal setting, and social skills; organizing recreational activities; writing progress reports; and participating in staff meetings and reports.

**Figure 4.6
A Properly Written and Presented Résumé**

alone created a better impression than listing a few great things and many good things. This finding is based on Anderson's (1965) **averaging-versus-adding** model of impression formation, which implies that activity quality is more important than quantity. It is neither necessary nor desirable to list all coursework (Pibal, 1985).

   Finally, include a few personal details such as hobbies or interests. You may have heard that personal information should not be included in a résumé, but research on determinateness (Oliphant & Alexander, 1982) indicates that mentioning personal information of moderate value might be better than not mentioning it at all. The researchers found that where personal information is left off of a résumé, the reader often will "imagine the worst."

Résumé fraud takes many forms. Six of the most prominent are:

1. Misleading educational credits: In the typical educational fraud, the person usually did attend the school, but only for two years instead of the four years claimed. In many other educational fraud cases, one usually finds the job applicant took courses towards a degree, but did not complete them. You have to read the résumé carefully and question the applicant closely.

Caution: Many applicants will say that they majored in Business at Harvard (or other schools) for an MBA degree, but nowhere on the résumé do they actually claim to have been awarded a degree. Check carefully on Ph.D. degrees. Some applicants who claim them may be working toward a doctorate, but still have a long way to go—a thesis or orals.

2. Omitting a period of employment and/or stretching dates of
employment: An applicant may show the years he or she worked for another company, but not the number of months. Thus, if the applicant left ABC Co. in January 1980 and was hired by DEF Co. in November 1981, the applicant was really unemployed for almost two years. This gap is covered up if the applicant shows one job ending in 1980 and the next beginning in 1981—and the continuity of the years suggests continuous employment, which it was not.

3. Exaggerated or misleading claims of expertise and experience: Terms of achievement such as *supervised* (a department) . . . *managed* (an office) . . . *increased* (sales or profits) . . . *created* (a program or a campaign) frequently appear on applicants' résumés. They may be true, but can be misleading unless they are related to, and supported by, specific measures of accomplishment (the size

Continued

Chapter Summary

The beginning of the chapter discussed the first steps in the employee-selection process, starting with a job analysis. After the job analysis, the human resource professional recruits employees and then, based on the results of the job analysis, uses some formal means to determine whether the applicant will make a good employee.

Several methods for recruiting employees then were discussed. These included help wanted and situation wanted advertisements, employee referrals, employment agencies, signs, direct main, and job fairs. Research indicates that for longer employee tenure, employee referrals are the best method, especially when the referrals are made by a current employee who has a long tenure. In terms of future employee performance, recruitment methods appear to be equal.

of the department, or budget; the number of employees, the percentage of sales and profits, the scope of the program) which are brought to light through a probing interview and thorough background check.

4. The self-employment smokescreen: Always be alert to claims of self-employment. Many résumé fakers make this claim to cover periods of unemployment, or a job that they don't want uncovered for a variety of reasons. It is very difficult for an employer to confirm self-employment without actually going to the business address or examining court/county clerk records or interviewing people with whom the applicant did business when he or she was self-employed. As a result many employers (to their future regret) tend to skip checking out self-employment claims.

5. The consultant "con": Another favorite ploy is for an applicant to claim to have been a consultant out of a home address for five to six months. When you see such a claim, be sure to ask for the names of a few customers

and a bank reference—and then check them.

6. The out-of-business blind: It is not unusual for a résumé faker to claim employment with a company that is out of business, believing there is no way for you to check his or her record there. But many times, just by checking how long the firm was in business, one can prove that a résumé faker did not work during the period claimed. This investigative approach is one that is virtually impossible to work out by a mail check. One has to go to the address to check, or have the proper research tools with which to determine if, where, and for how long the alleged former employer was in business. In such a case, an investigative agency has the advantage in having the research material needed to determine if the company existed or, in many cases, to locate the former owners.

Source: Reprinted from Norton, T. W., *Personnel Marketplace*, P.O. Box 301, Huntington, NY 11743, (516) 427-3680. Reprinted with permission of the author.

The chapter also discussed the interview process in employee selection. In this discussion, factors such as contrast effects, negative information bias, nonverbal cues, interviewer–interviewee similarity, and primacy effects were cited as playing roles in the poor reliability and minimal validity of the interview. Traditional employment interviews apparently are not good at predicting employee performance, but new developments such as structured and situational interviews show promise as valid predictors of future employee success.

Glossary

Averaging-versus-adding model A model proposed by Anderson that postulates that our impressions are based more on the average value of each impression rather than the sum of the values for each impression

Benchmark answers Standard answers to interview questions, the quality of which have been agreed on by job experts

Clinical prediction When an individual looks at information about an applicant, combines that information in some subjective way, and then makes a judgment about that person

Contrast effect When the performance of one applicant affects the perception of the performance of the next applicant

Cost per applicant The amount of money spent on a recruitment campaign divided by the number of people that subsequently apply for jobs as a result of the recruitment campaign

Cost per qualified applicant The amount of money spent on a recruitment campaign divided by the number of qualified people that subsequently apply for jobs as a result of the recruitment campaign

Cover letter A letter that accompanies a résumé or job application

Direct mail A method of recruitment in which an organization sends out mass-mailings of information about job openings to potential applicants

Employee referral A method of recruitment in which a current employee refers a friend or family member for a job

Employment agency An organization that specializes in finding jobs for applicants and finding applicants for organizations looking for employees

Employment interview A method of selecting employees in which an interviewer asks questions of an applicant and then makes an employment decision based on the answers to the questions as well as the way in which the questions were answered

Executive search firms Employment agencies, often also called "headhunters," that specialize in placing applicants in high-paying jobs

External recruitment Recruiting employees from outside the organization

Internal recruitment Recruiting employees already employed by the organization

Job fairs A recruitment method in which several employers are available at one location so that many applicants can obtain information at one time

Media advertisements A recruitment method using newspapers, radio, and television

Negative information bias The fact that negative information receives more weight in an employment decision than does positive information

Nonverbal cues Factors such as eye contact and posture that are not associated with actual words spoken

Number of qualified applicants A method of evaluating the effectiveness of a recruitment program by looking at the number of qualified applicants that apply

Primacy effect The fact that information that is presented early in an interview carries more weight than information presented later

Realistic job preview (RJP) A method of recruitment in which job applicants are told both the positive and negative aspects of a job

Recruitment The process of attracting employees to an organization

Résumé A formal summary of an applicant's professional and educational background

Signs A method of recruitment based on point-of-purchase advertising principles in which help wanted signs are placed so that they can be viewed by people who visit the organization

Situational interviews A structured interview technique in which applicants are presented with a series of situations and asked how they would handle each one

Situation wanted ads Newspaper advertisements run by applicants looking for jobs rather than by organizations looking for applicants

State employment agency An employment service, operated by a state government, designed to match applicants with job openings

Statistical prediction The use of numerical formulas that take the information gathered about an applicant, and mathematically determine a probability regarding that applicant's future behavior

Structured interviews Interviews in which every applicant is asked the same questions and in which identical answers are given identical scores

5

Spencer Grant/Photo Researchers, Inc. (NYC)

Employee Selection: References and Testing

I n the last chapter, interviews and résumés were described as the most commonly used methods to select and screen employees. But even though they are the most commonly used, they are certainly not the best. In this chapter, we discuss several techniques that are preferred by industrial psychologists to select employees.

References and Letters of Recommendation

In psychology, it is commonly believed that the best predictor of future performance is past performance. Thus, if an organization wants to hire a salesperson, the best applicant might be one who has not only been a salesperson, but also was successful in sales jobs that were similar to the one for which she now applies.

Verifying previous employment is not difficult, but it can be difficult to verify the *quality* of previous performance. This author recently watched the National Football League's draft of college players on television and was envious of the fact that professional football teams could assess a player's previous performance by watching game films. That is, the scouts did not have to rely on the opinions of other coaches. Instead, they could watch literally every minute a player had spent on the field while in college.

Unfortunately, few applicants bring "game films" of their previous employment performances. Instead, an employer must obtain information about the quality of previous performance by asking an applicant to either supply names of references whom the employer can call or provide **letters of recommendation** from previous employers.

Problems

Even though references are commonly used to screen and select employees, they have not been successful in predicting future employee success (Muchinsky, 1979). In fact, the average validity coefficient for references and performance is only .13 (Browning, 1968; Mosel & Goheen, 1958). This low validity follows largely from four main problems with references and letters of recommendation: leniency, knowledge of the applicant, low reliability, and extraneous factors involved in writing and reading such letters.

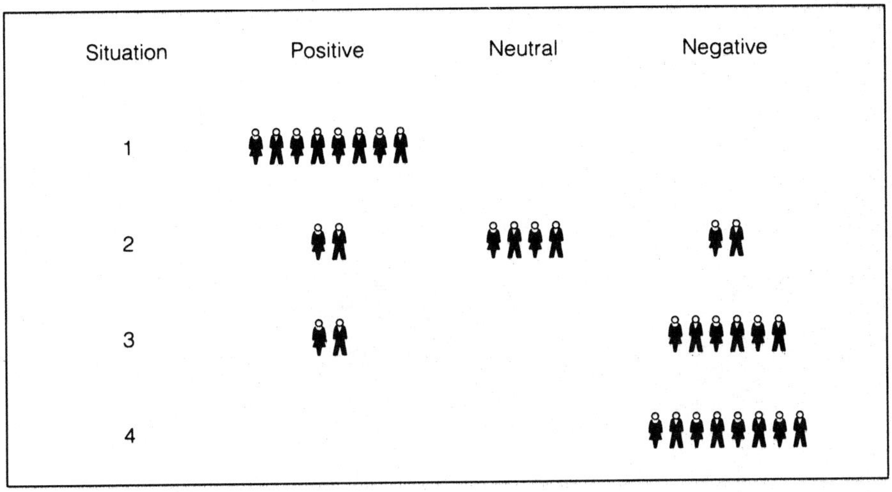

Figure 5.1
Co-Workers'
Attitudes Toward
Employee

Situation	Positive	Neutral	Negative
1	👥👥👥👥		
2	👥	👥👥	👥
3	👥		👥👥👥
4			👥👥👥👥

Leniency

Research is clear on the fact that most letters of recommendation are positive (Carroll & Nash, 1972; Myers & Errett, 1959; Whitcomb & Bryan, 1988; Yoder, 1962). Because we have all worked with terrible employees at some point in our lives, it would at first seem surprising that references typically are so positive. But keep in mind that *applicants choose their own references!* Even Nazi leader Adolph Hitler, serial killer Ted Bundy, or terrorist Abu Nidal would have been able to find three people who could provide them with favorable references.

To better understand this point, suppose a job applicant currently works in the nine-person office depicted in Figure 5.1. In the first situation, all of the applicant's eight co-workers have positive feelings about the applicant. Thus, if we ask for references from two co-workers, both would be positive *and* representative of the other six co-workers. In situation 2, most co-workers have neutral regard for the applicant, with two having positive feelings and two having negative feelings. In this situation, however, both references chosen by the applicant would be positive—and *more favorable* than most co-workers' attitudes.

In situation 3, only two of eight people like the applicant—yet the two reference letters will be the same as in the first and second situations even though most co-workers have negative feelings about our applicant. In situation 4, no one likes our applicant. In this case, our request for references either would keep the person from applying for our job or force the applicant to find references from somewhere else. But if we *require* work-related references, they probably, but not necessarily,

**Figure 5.2
A Typical Reference
Waiver**

Statement of Release

_____   _____
Name of person asked to write   Date
this recommendation

I request that you complete this recommendation form, which I understand will become a part of my file in the Radford University Graduate
College. I further understand:

　(1) that this recommendation statement from you will be a candid
　　　evaluation of my scholarship, work habits, and potential;

　(2) that the completed statement will be sent to the Radford Univer-
　　　sity Graduate College; and

　(3) that it will be held in confidence from me and the public by the
　　　Radford University Graduate Office.

_____   _____
Applicant's Name (print)   Applicant's Signature

---

would be negative because research has shown that co-workers _are_ willing to say negative things about unsatisfactory employees (Nash & Carroll, 1970).

　A second factor that influences the degree of leniency is the _confiden-
tiality of the reference_. By law, people have the right to see their reference letters. By signing a waiver such as that shown in Figure 5.2,
however, they can give up that right. This may be more beneficial for a
potential employer; research by Ceci and Peters (1984) and Shaffer and
Tomarelli (1981) indicates that people providing references tend to be
less lenient when an applicant waives her right to see a reference letter.
That is, when a person writing a reference letter knows that the applicant
is allowed to see the letter, the writer is more inclined to provide a favorable evaluation.

　Two other minor factors that affect the leniency of references are the
sex of the letter writer and the _race of the letter reader_. Carroll and Nash
(1972) found that female reference letter writers are more lenient when
referring female applicants, while Bryan (1989) found that black professionals are more lenient than white professionals in evaluating letter content. Thus, as shown in Figure 5.3, when an applicant can choose his
own references, retains his right to see reference letters, is referred by a
female co-worker, or is evaluated by a black professional, his references
are far more positive than if based solely on his actual performance.

```
Negative              Positive
     ┌─┬─┬─┬─┬─X─┬─┬─┬─┬─┐     Actual performance
     1 2 3 4 5 6 7 8 9 10

     ┌─┬─┬─┬─┬─┬─┬─X─┬─┬─┐     Choice of reference (Yoder, 1962)
     1 2 3 4 5 6 7 8 9 10

     ┌─┬─┬─┬─┬─┬─┬─┬─X─┬─┐     Retain rights to see file (Ceci & Peters, 1984)
     1 2 3 4 5 6 7 8 9 10

     ┌─┬─┬─┬─┬─┬─┬─┬─┬─X─┐     Female letter writer (Carroll & Nash, 1972)
     1 2 3 4 5 6 7 8 9 10

     ┌─┬─┬─┬─┬─┬─┬─┬─┬─┬─X     Black letter reader (Bryan, 1989)
     1 2 3 4 5 6 7 8 9 10
```

Knowledge of the Applicant

A second problem with letters of recommendation is that the person writing the letter often does not know the applicant well, has not observed all aspects of an applicant's behavior, or both. Professors often are asked to provide recommendations for students whom they know only from one or two classes. Such recommendations are not likely to be as accurate and complete as those provided by professors who have had students in several classes and perhaps worked with them outside the classroom setting.

Even in a work setting in which a supervisor supplies the recommendation, she often does not see all aspects of an employee's behavior (see Figure 5.4). Employees often act very differently around their supervisors than around co-workers and customers. Furthermore, as Figure 5.4 shows and as will be discussed in greater detail in a later chapter, those behaviors that a reference writer actually recalls are only a fraction of the behaviors actually occurring in the presence of the person writing the recommendation.

Reliability

The third problem with references and letters of recommendation involves the *lack of agreement* between two people who provide references for the same person. Research reveals that reference **reliability** is approximately only .40 (Baxter, Brock, Hill, & Rozelle, 1981; Mosel &

Because employees often act very differently around their supervisors than they do around co-workers and customers, the supervisor will see only some aspects of an employee's behavior.

Spencer Grant/Photo Researchers, Inc. (NYC)

Goheen, 1959; Mosel & Goheen, 1952). The reliability problem is so severe that Baxter and his colleagues (1981) found more agreement between recommendations written *by the same person* for two different applicants than between two people writing recommendations *for the same person*. Thus, letters of recommendation may say more about the person writing the letter than about the person for whom it is being written.

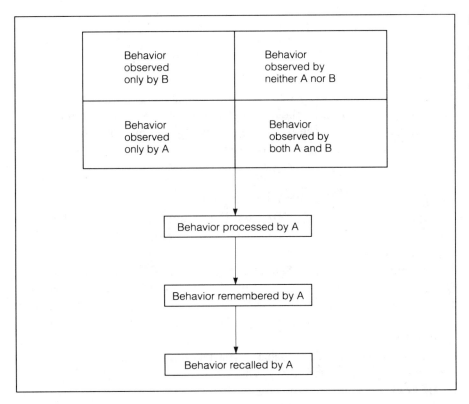

**Figure 5.4
A Reference Writer
Often Lacks
Complete Knowledge
of an Employee's
Behavior**

This low level of reliability probably results from the point cited earlier that a reference writer has not seen all aspects of an applicant's behavior. Thus, a reference provided by a professor who has seen an applicant in a classroom may not agree with a reference provided by a supervisor who has seen the same applicant in a work setting. But even though there may be good reasons for the low levels of reliability in reference letters, limiting their validity, research has yet to answer the question, If references do not agree, which one should be taken the most seriously?

Extraneous Factors

The fourth problem with letters of recommendation concerns extraneous factors that affect their writing. Research has indicated that the method used by the letter writer is often more important than the actual content. For example:

1. Knouse (1983) found that letters that contained specific examples were rated higher than letters that contained generalities.

2. Cowan and Kasen (1984) found that male and female writers use different titles when referring to applicants in their letters. Female writers refer to applicants as "Mr." or "Mrs.," while male writers refer to applicants by their first names.

3. Mehrabian (1965) and Weins, Jackson, Manaugh, and Matarazzo (1969) found that even though most letters of recommendation are positive, letters written by references who like applicants are longer than those written by references who do not.

Improving the Validity of References

To improve the validity of references, Peres and Garcia (1962) developed a unique way to make reference letters more useful by focusing on their relevant content rather than on their positiveness. As an example, see the two letters of recommendation in Figure 5.5. Although both describe the applicant in favorable terms, they differ greatly in the content words used to describe the applicant.

After examining thousands of letters of recommendation, Peres and Garcia (1962) found that the adjectives contained in such letters fall into one of five categories: dependability–reliability, consideration–cooperation, **mental agility, urbanity,** and **vigor.** A complete list of the trait words in each category is shown in Table 5.1.

Thus, to use letters of recommendation to accurately predict performance, an employer would use the following four-step process:

1. Determine the importance of each of these five categories to the performance of a particular job.

2. Read each letter of recommendation and underline the traits in each letter used to describe the applicant.

3. Use the list of words composed by Peres and Garcia (1962) and expanded by Whitcomb and Bryan (1988) to place each trait into one of the five categories.

4. Total the number of words for each of the five categories.

To demonstrate this process, Figure 5.6 shows the traits in the two letters first shown in Figure 5.5. The traits have been underlined and summed to provide a score for each of the five categories.

The only study to investigate the validity of the method developed by Peres and Garcia was conducted by Aamodt, Bryan, and Whitcomb (1989). These researchers found that the number of "mental agility" ad-

Figure 5.5
Two Letters of
Recommendation

Dear Personnel Director:

Mr. John Anderson asked that I write this letter in support of his application as an assistant manager and I am pleased to do so. I have known John for six years as he was my assistant in the accounting department.

John always had his work completed accurately and promptly. In his six years here, he never missed a deadline. He is very detailed oriented, alert in finding errors, and methodical in his problem solving approach. Interpersonally, John is a very friendly and helpful person.

I have great confidence in John's ability. If you desire more information, please let me know.

Dear Personnel Director:

Mr. John Anderson asked that I write this letter in support of his application as an assistant manager and I am pleased to do so. I have known John for six years as he was my assistant in the accounting department.

John was one of the most popular employees in our agency as he is a friendly, outgoing, sociable individual. He has a great sense of humor, is poised, and is very helpful. In completing his work, he is independent, energetic, and industrious.

I have great confidence in John's ability. If you desire more information, please let me know.

Table 5.1
Categories and Trait Words Found in Letters of Recommendation

Categories	Trait Words
Cooperation–Consideration	Accommodating
	Considerate
	Cooperative
	Courteous
	Friendly
	Helpful
	Nice
	Sincere
Dependability–Reliability	Critical
	Dependable
	Orderly
	Precise
	Prompt
	Reliable
	Responsible
	Trustworthy
Mental Agility	Bright
	Creative
	Intelligent
	Knowledgeable
	Logical
	Smart
	Thoughtful
	Wise
Urbanity	Bold
	Expressive
	Extroverted
	Gregarious
	Outgoing
	Poised
	Sociable
	Talkative
Vigor	Active
	Ambitious
	Eager
	Energetic
	Fast-paced
	Hustling
	Independent
	Speedy

Source: Peres, S. H., & Garcia, J. R. (1962). Validity and dimensions of descriptive adjectives used in reference letters for engineering applicants. *Personnel Psychology, 15,* 279–286.

**Figure 5.6
Identified Traits in
Letters of
Recommendation**

Dear Personnel Director:

Mr. John Anderson asked that I write this letter in support of his application as an assistant manager and I am pleased to do so. I have known John for six years as he was my assistant in the accounting department.

John was one of the most popular employees in our agency as he is a friendly, outgoing, sociable individual. He has a great sense of humor, is poised, and is very helpful. In completing his work, he is independent, energetic, and industrious.

I have great confidence in John's ability. If you desire more information, please let me know.

MA 0   CC 2   DR 0   U 4   V 3

Dear Personnel Director:

Mr. John Anderson asked that I write this letter in support of his application as an assistant manager and I am pleased to do so. I have known John for six years as he was my assistant in the accounting department.

John always had his work completed accurately and promptly. In his six years here, he never missed a deadline. He is very detailed oriented, alert in finding errors, and methodical in his problem solving approach. Interpersonally, John is a very friendly and helpful person.

I have great confidence in John's ability. If you desire more information, please let me know.

MA 0   CC 2   DR 6   U 0   V 0

jectives mentioned in a letter of recommendation correlated .34 with graduate grade point averages, and the number of traits in the "urbanity" category correlated .38 with teaching ratings received by general psychology instructors. Thus, the Peres and Garcia (1962) technique may indeed be a useful way to determine the validity of letters of recommendation.

Carroll and Nash (1972) developed another potentially useful method to improve on the validity of references. These researchers created a rating form, similar to that shown in Figure 5.7, containing 24 pairs of behavioral statements. Although the words in each pair had the same level of social desirability, only one of the two predicted success on the job. A reference writer was asked to complete the form, and the applicant's score was the number of "predictive" words that were chosen. This method was found to correlate at .22 with performance ratings of one group of clerical workers and at .47 with the performance ratings of a second clerical group.

As the above discussion shows, references and letters of recommendation often are unable to predict performance. But with further refinement and research, techniques such as those developed by Peres and Garcia (1962) and Carroll and Nash (1972) may increase the predictive abilities of such references.

Even if references and letters of recommendation do not predict performance in a linear fashion, they may still be useful in screening out applicants who are clearly undesirable. Remember from the discussion in the last chapter about résumé fraud that applicants often try to hide information from potential employers. This hidden or inaccurate information can range from the relatively harmless, such as the addition of a few weeks to the dates of employment for a job, to the serious, such as being fired from a job for violent behavior.

If an organization hires an applicant without checking her references and background, and she later commits a crime while in the employ of the organization, the organization may be found guilty of **negligent hiring.**

Negligent hiring cases typically are filed in court as common law cases, or torts. These cases are based on the premise that an employer has the duty to protect its employees and customers from harm caused by its employees or products. In determining negligent hiring, courts look at the nature of the job. Organizations that are involved with the safety of the public such as police departments and day care centers must conduct more thorough background and reference checks than organizations such as retail stores.

As an example, a child care center in California hired an employee without checking his references. A few months later, the employee mo-

Figure 5.7
Forced Choice
Reference Form

Instructions: In each set of traits, choose the one that most describes the applicant.

1. _____ friendly
   _____ responsible
   _____ creative

2. _____ detailed
   _____ outgoing
   _____ inventive

lested a child at the center. In fact, the employee had a criminal record of child abuse that would have been discovered with a simple call to his previous employer. As one would expect, the court found the employer guilty of negligent hiring because it had not taken "reasonable care" in ensuring the well-being of its customers.

In Virginia in 1989, an employee of a grocery store copied the address of a female customer from a check she had written to the store. The employee later went to the customer's home and raped her. In this example, a case for negligent hiring could not be made because the company had contacted the employee's previous employment references and had found no reason not to hire him. Because there was nothing to discover and because the store took reasonable care to check its employees, it was not guilty of negligent hiring.

Because an employer can be guilty of negligent hiring for not contacting references, a former employer also can be guilty if it does not provide relevant information to an organization that requests it. For example, if Dinero Bank fires John Smith for theft and fails to divulge that fact to a bank that is thinking of hiring Smith, Dinero Bank may be found liable if Smith steals money at his new bank.

This last example shows why providing references and recommendations can be so difficult. On the one hand, a former employer can be charged with slander or libel if it says something bad about an applicant that cannot be proven. On the other hand, an employer can be held liable if it does not provide information about a potentially dangerous applicant. Because of these competing responsibilities, many organizations will only confirm employment dates and salary information unless a former employee has been convicted of a criminal offense that resulted in her termination. Because of this, it is wise to have an applicant sign a waiver to protect the prospective employer as well as former employers from claims arising from reference checks (Morse, 1988).

Weighted Application Blanks

Because interviews and references generally have been found to be poor linear predictors of future employee success, industrial psychologists have developed many better prediction techniques. In the past few decades, of these many methods, one has clearly stood out as the single best predictor of future employee tenure: the weighted application blank based on biographical information (Ghiselli, 1966; Ellenburg, Kremen, Hicks, & Stewart, 1990).

Weighted application blanks (WAB) use statistical weighting techniques (mentioned in Chapter 4), which are superior to the clinical techniques used in the interview and résumé-evaluation processes. In a nutshell, the WAB is an application blank containing questions that research has shown measure the difference between successful and unsuccessful performers on a job. Each question receives a weight that indicates how well it differentiates poor from good performers. The better the differentiation, the higher the weight.

Validity

The WAB has several advantages. First, research has shown that it can predict work behavior in many jobs, including sales, management, clerical work, mental health counseling, hourly work in processing plants, grocery clerking, fast food work, and supervising. Furthermore, WABs have been able to predict criteria as varied as supervisor ratings, absenteeism, accidents, employee theft, loan defaults, sales, and tenure.

Second, WABs are easy to use, quickly administered, inexpensive, and not as subject to individual bias as interviews, references, and résumé evaluation. The major impediment to using a WAB is that despite its relative ease of design, it can be created properly only when data from a large number of employees (at least 150) are available.

**Figure 5.8
Biodata
Questionnaire**

1. Member of high school student government?
   ☐ No   ☐ Yes

2. Number of jobs in past 5 years?
   ☐ 1   ☐ 2   ☐ 3–5   ☐ More than 5

3. Length of time at present address?
   ☐ Less than 1 year   ☐ 1–3 years
   ☐ 4–5 years   ☐ More than 5 years

4. Transportation to work:
   ☐ Walk   ☐ Bike   ☐ Own car
   ☐ Bus   ☐ Ride with a friend   ☐ Other

5. Education:
   ☐ Some high school
   ☐ High school diploma or G.E.D.
   ☐ Some college
   ☐ Associate's degree
   ☐ Bachelor's degree
   ☐ Master's degree
   ☐ Doctoral degree

Development

With these considerations in mind, we now develop a typical weighted application blank. In the first step, we obtain information about employees. Information can be gathered in one of two ways.

First, we can use personnel files because they contain a lot of employee information for such areas as previous employment, education, interests, and family. As mentioned in the discussion of archival research in Chapter 1, the major disadvantage of the **file approach** is that information often is missing or incomplete.

Second, we can create a biographical questionnaire that is administered to all employees and applicants. An example is shown in Figure 5.8. The major drawback to the **questionnaire approach** is that information cannot be obtained from employees who have quit or been fired.

After the necessary information has been obtained, an appropriate criterion is chosen. As will be discussed in detail in Chapter 6, a **criterion** is a measure of work behavior such as quantity, absenteeism, or tenure. It is essential that a chosen criterion be relevant, reliable, and fairly ob-

A[a]		B[b]		C[c]	
Difference in Percentages	**Net Weight**	**Difference in Percentages**	**Net Weight**	**Difference in Percentages**	**Net Weight**
69	27	69	27	69	28
68	26	68	26	28	27
67	25	67	25	67	26
66	24	66	24	66	25
65	23	64–65	23	65	24
64	22	63	22	63–64	23
62–63	21	62	21	62	22
61	20	60–61	20	60–61	21
60	19	58–59	19	59	20
58–59	18	57	18	57–58	19
56–57	17	55–56	17	55–56	18
54–55	16	53–54	16	53–54	17
52–53	15	50–52	15	51–52	16
50–51	14	48–49	14	49–50	15
48–49	13	45–47	13	46–48	14
45–47	12	42–44	12	43–45	13
42–44	11	39–41	11	40–42	12
39–41	10	35–38	10	36–39	11
36–38	9	31–34	9	32–35	10
33–35	8	27–30	8	28–31	9
29–32	7	23–26	7	24–27	8
24–28	6	19–22	6	19–23	7
21–23	5	15–18	5	15–18	6
16–20	4	11–14	4	11–14	5
12–15	3	7–10	3	7–10	4
8–11	2	4– 6	2	4– 6	3
3– 7	1	2– 3	1	2– 3	2
0– 2	0	0– 1	0	1	1
				0	0

Source: Stead, W. H., & Shartle, C. L. (1940). *Occupational counseling techniques* (p. 255). New York: American Book Co.

[a] For use when both percentages are between 8 and 92.

[b] For use when one percentage is between 3 and 7 or 93 and 97.

[c] For use when one percentage is between 0 and 2 or 98 and 100.

Table 5.2
WAB Weighting Tables

Variable	Long Tenure (%)	Short Tenure (%)	Difference in Percentages	Weight
Martial status				
Single	40	80	40	−10
Married	59	15	44	+11
Divorced	1	5	4	−1

Table 5.3
WAB Weighting
Process

jective. This author was once asked to create a WAB to help reduce absenteeism in an organization by selecting applicants who had a high probability of superior future attendance. When initial data were gathered, it was realized that absenteeism was not an actual problem for this company. Less than one-half of the work force had missed more than one day in six months; but the company perceived a problem because a few key workers had missed many days of work. Thus, using a WAB (or any other selection device) to predict a nonrelevant criterion would not have been an accurate method.

Once a criterion has been chosen, employees are split into two **criterion groups** based on their criterion scores. For example, if tenure is selected as the criterion measure, employees who have worked for the company for at least one year might be placed into the "high tenure" group, while workers who quit or were fired in less than one year would be placed into the "low tenure" group.

After the employee data have been obtained and the criterion and criterion groups chosen, each piece of employee information is then compared with criterion-group membership. The purpose of this stage is to determine which pieces of information will distinguish the members of the high criterion group from those in the low criterion group. Traditionally, the **vertical percentage method** (England, 1971) has been used to do this. Percentages are calculated for each group on each item. The percentage of a particular response for the low group is subtracted from the percentage of the same response in the high group to obtain a weight for that item. To reduce the effect of sampling error, the differences in percentages are converted using a table such as the one shown in Table 5.2. An example of this weighting process is shown in Table 5.3.

Once weights have been assigned to the items, the information is weighted and then summed to form a **composite score** for each employee. Composite scores are then correlated with the criterion to determine whether the newly created WAB will significantly predict the criterion. Although this procedure sounds complicated, it actually is fairly easy.

Two items also must be mentioned about the construction of the WAB. First, the method has been used quite successfully for more than 20 years (England, 1971). Telenson, Alexander, and Barrett (1983) recently have proposed that a new method, **rare response scoring,** be used instead of the vertical percentage method. Basically, the rare response method assigns weights on the basis of how the typical employees respond to a specific item. That is, if a particular response to an item is given by few people, that response will receive the highest weight.

Such weighting is done because research from the fields of clinical psychology and social psychology tell us that the most revealing information about a person comes from unusual behavior. For example, if we find out that Bob enjoys eating pizza, we cannot make much of a judgment about Bob because almost everyone likes pizza (especially this author). However, if we are told that Bob is a vegetarian, we would probably give that information more weight because it tells us that Bob is different from most people.

But even though the rare response method sounds interesting, subsequent research (Aamodt & Pierce, 1987) has indicated that it has many problems; in its present state of development, it is not as good as the vertical percentage method. Future improvements, however, could lead to the rare response method being used more frequently.

The second item to be discussed concerns problems with **sample size.** To accurately create a WAB, it is desirable to have data from hundreds of employees. For most organizations, however, such large sample sizes are difficult if not impossible to obtain. In creating a WAB with a small sample, the risk increases of using items that do not really predict the criterion. This issue is important because most industrial psychologists advise that when a WAB is created, the employees should be split into two samples: One sample, the **derivation sample,** is used to form the weights; the other sample, the **hold-out sample,** is used to double-check the selected items and weights. Although this sample splitting sounds like a great idea, it is not practical when one is dealing with a small or moderate (less than 300) sample size.

Research by Schmitt, Coyle, and Rauschenberger (1977) suggests that there is less chance of error when a sample is not split. Discussion on whether to split samples is bound to continue in the years ahead, but because many personnel professionals will be dealing with relatively small numbers of employees, it might be best to create and validate a WAB without splitting employees into derivation and hold-out samples.

Criticisms

Even though WABs do a good job of predicting future employee behavior, they have been criticized on two major points. The first holds that the validity of WABs may not be stable—that is, their ability to predict employee behavior decreases with time. For example, Wernimont (1962) found that only three questions retained their predictive validity over the five-year period of 1954 to 1959. Similar results were reported by Hughes, Dunn, and Baxter (1956).

More recent research (Brown, 1978), however, suggests that declines in validity found in earlier studies may have resulted from small samples in the initial development of the WAB. Brown (1978) used data from more than 10,000 life insurance agents to develop his WAB, but data from only 85 agents were used to develop the WAB samples that were earlier criticized by Wernimont (1962). Brown compared the validity of his original sample (1933) with those from samples taken six years later (1939) and 38 years later (1971). The results indicated that the same items that significantly predicted the criterion in 1933 predicted at similar levels in 1971. Thus, WABs may be more stable across time than was earlier thought (Rothstein, Schmidt, Erwin, Owens, & Sparks, 1990).

The second criticism is that some WABs may not meet the legal requirements stated in the **Uniform Guidelines** (Pace & Schoenfeldt, 1977), the federal guidelines that establish fair hiring methods. Of greatest concern is that certain biodata items might lead to racial or sexual discrimination. For example, consider the selection item "distance from work." Applicants who live close to work might get more points than applicants who live farther away. The item may lead to racial discrimination if the organization is located in a predominantly white area. Removal of such discriminatory items, however, should eliminate most legal problems while still allowing for significant predictive validity (Reilly & Chao, 1982).

To make WAB use less disagreeable to critics, Gandy and Dye (1989) developed one containing items that had to meet four standards:

1. The item must deal with events under a person's control.

2. The item must be job-related.

3. The answer to the item must be identifiable.

4. The item must not invade an applicant's privacy.

193

Even though these four standards eliminated many potential items, Gandy and Dye (1989) still obtained a validity coefficient of .33. Just as impressive as the high validity coefficient was that the WAB showed good prediction for whites, blacks, and Hispanics.

Assessment Centers

An assessment center is a selection device characterized by the use of multiple assessment methods that allow multiple assessors to actually *observe* applicants perform job-related tasks. Its major advantages are that assessment methods are all job-related and multiple trained assessors help to guard against many (but not all) types of selection bias. For a selection procedure to be considered an assessment center, it must meet the following seven requirements (Ross, 1979):

1. Multiple assessment techniques, at least one of which must be a simulation, are used.
2. Multiple trained assessors are used.
3. The overall judgment regarding an applicant must be based on a combination of information from the multiple assessors and multiple techniques.
4. The overall evaluation of an applicant cannot be made until all assessment center tasks have been completed.
5. Simulation exercises that are reliable, objective, and job-related must be used.
6. All behaviors that are measured must be job-related.
7. All exercises must be designed to tap the job behaviors mentioned in requirement 6.

Development and Components

Although many different techniques may be used in assessment centers, the basic development and types of exercises are fairly standard. The first step in creating an assessment center is, of course, to do a job analysis. From this analysis, exercises are developed that measure different aspects of the job (Yager, 1980). Common exercises include the in-basket technique, simulations, leaderless group discussions, and business games.

The In-Basket Technique

The **in-basket technique** is designed to simulate the types of information that daily come across a manager's or employee's desk. The technique takes its name from the wire baskets that are typically seen on office desks. Usually these baskets have two levels, the "in" level, which holds paperwork that must be handled, and the "out" level, which contains completed paperwork.

During the assessment center, examples of job-related paperwork are placed into a basket and the job applicant is asked to go through the basket and respond to the paperwork as if she were actually on the job. Examples of such paperwork might include a phone message from an employee who cannot get her car started and does not know how to get to work, or a memo from the accounting department stating that an expense voucher is missing.

The applicant is observed by a group of assessors who score the applicant on several dimensions, which can include the quality of the decision, the manner in which the decision was carried out, and the order in which the applicant handled the paperwork—that is, did she start at the top of the pile or did she start with the most important papers?

Simulations

Simulation exercises are the real backbone of the assessment center because they allow assessors to see an applicant "in action." **Simulations,** which can include such diverse activities as role plays and work samples, are designed to place an applicant in a situation that is as similar as possible to that which will be encountered on the job (Kaman & Bentson, 1988). To be effective, simulations must be based on job-related behaviors and should be at least reasonably realistic.

A good example of a role-playing simulation can be found in an assessment center used by a large city to select emergency telephone operators. The applicant sits before a switchboard to handle a distressed caller describing an emergency situation. The applicant must properly answer the call, calm the caller, and obtain the necessary information in as little time as possible. Other examples include a police applicant writing a traffic citation for an angry citizen and an applicant for a resident assistant position breaking up an argument between two roommates.

To reduce the high costs associated with actual simulations, many public organizations such as the New York Civil Service Commission and the city of Fairfax, Virginia, have developed situational exercises shown on videotape. Organizations using video simulations administer them to a group of applicants who view the situations in the tape and then write down what they would do in each situation. The written responses are then scored by personnel analysts in a fashion similar to that used with situational interviews.

Usually, when a simulation does not involve a situational exercise, it is called a work sample (this will be discussed in more detail shortly). Examples of work samples might include an applicant for a position as mechanic repairing an automobile engine, a copy editor applicant editing a news story, or a secretarial applicant taking a typing test. Because the development of simulation exercises can be expensive, prepackaged exercises can be purchased at a much lower price (Cohen, 1980).

Leaderless Group Discussions

In this exercise, applicants meet in small groups and are given a job-related problem to solve or a job-related issue to discuss. No leader is appointed, hence the term **leaderless group discussion.** As the applicants discuss the problem or issue, they are individually rated on dimensions such as cooperativeness, leadership, and analytical skills.

Business Games

Business games are exercises that allow the applicant to demonstrate such attributes as creativity, decision making, and ability to work with others. A business game in one assessment center used a series of Tinker Toy models. Four individuals joined a group and were told that they were part of a company that manufactured goods. The goods ranged from Tinker Toy tables to Tinker Toy scuba divers, and the group's task was to buy the parts, manufacture the products, and then sell the products at the highest profit in an environment in which prices constantly changed.

The typical assessment center has 6 assessors, each of whom has been trained for an average of 3 to 5 days; has 4 to 7 exercises, which take an average of 2 to 5 days to complete; and evaluates 6 to 12 applicants at one time (Bender, 1973).

Evaluation of Assessment Centers

Research has indicated that the assessment center has been very successful in predicting a wide range of employee behavior (Gaugler, Rosenthal, Thornton, & Bentson, 1987; Mento, 1980). Klimoski and Strickland

(1977), however, have questioned the relative value of the assessment center by pointing out that many of the validation criteria (for example, salary and management level achieved) are measures of survival and adaptation rather than actual performance. Furthermore, other methods can predict the same criteria better and less expensively than assessment centers (Hunter & Hunter, 1984). Thus, even though an assessment center may be excellent in predicting certain aspects of employee behavior, other, less expensive methods may be as good if not better.

Work Samples

Work samples offer another method for selecting employees (Wernimont & Campbell, 1968). With a **work sample,** the applicant performs actual job-related tasks. For example, an applicant for a job as automotive mechanic might be asked to fix a torn fan belt, a secretarial applicant might be asked to type a letter, and a truck driving applicant might be asked to back a truck up to a loading dock.

Work samples are excellent selection tools for several reasons. First, because they are directly related to job tasks, they have excellent content validity. Second, scores from work samples tend to predict actual work performance and thus have excellent criterion validity (Asher & Sciarrino, 1974). Third, because job applicants are able to see the connection between the job sample and the work performed on the job, the samples have excellent face validity and thus are challenged less often in civil service appeals or in court cases (Whelchel, 1985). Finally, minorities tend to score better on work samples than on written exams (Cascio & Phillips, 1979; Schmidt, Greenthal, Hunter, Berner, & Seaton, 1977).

The main reason for not using work samples is that they can be expensive both to construct and administer. For this reason, work samples are best used for well-paying jobs for which many employees will be hired.

Psychological Testing

One of the most criticized and abused methods of employee selection is **psychological testing.** For several years, psychological tests were used by many organizations, mostly because it was in vogue. But in the 1960s and 1970s, the use of psychological testing declined sharply for several reasons. First, with the passage of the 1964 Civil Rights Act, many employers felt that psychological testing could lead to discrimination against minorities and females. Second, many personnel professionals questioned their usefulness in the selection process.

In recent years, however, psychological testing has again become popular, primarily because abundant and recent research has indicated that properly used psychological tests are excellent in predicting future employee performance (Hunter & Hunter, 1984). Furthermore, psychologists have realized that tests do not discriminate as much as once believed. Even though blacks and whites do score differently on many tests, these differences can be either overcome by using separate norms or justified by actual differences in work behavior (Donnoe, 1986).

Test Characteristics

Scoring

Tests can be scored in two primary ways: objectively and subjectively. Tests that are **objectively scored** typically involve the use of a scoring key so that an applicant's score will be the same, regardless of who does the scoring. Conversely, **subjective scoring** relies on the experience and knowledge of the scorer to interpret the meaning of the applicant's answers.

The **Rorschach Inkblot Test** is a good example of a subjectively (or projectively) scored test. In the Rorschach, an applicant is asked what pictures he sees in a series of inkblots. The answers are scored and then interpreted by a trained psychologist to reveal characteristics of the individual's personality.

Objectively scored tests are both more common and more accurate in employee selection than subjectively scored tests.

Administration

Tests can be administered either to individual applicants or groups of applicants. Certainly, group testing is usually less expensive and more efficient than individual testing, although important information may be lost in group testing. For example, one reason for administering an individual intelligence test is that the tester can observe the *way* in which a person solves a problem or answers a question. With group tests, only the answer can be scored.

A recent innovation in the administration of psychological tests involves the use of computers. An applicant takes a test at a computer terminal, the computer scores the test, and the test's results and interpretation are immediately available. Computer-assisted testing can lower testing costs, decrease feedback time, and yield results in which the test takers can have great confidence (Johnson & King, 1988). As with group testing, however, the testing process usually cannot be observed.

Speed versus Power Tests

The major differences between speed and power tests involve the amount of time given to an applicant to complete the test. With **speed tests,** applicants are given a large number of items with little time to complete them. High scorers correctly complete many items in the allowed period of time. With **power tests,** applicants are given as much time as necessary to answer the questions. Speed tests are primarily used to test applicants for jobs that require the rapid completion of relatively simple tasks such as typing, filing, and checking addresses. Power tests typically are used where quality is more important than quantity. Examples might be tests for supervisors and law enforcement officers.

Types of Psychological Tests

Mental Ability

Tests of mental ability are designed to measure the amount of knowledge an individual possesses. Note that the vast majority of the **mental** ability tests used by industrial psychologists (as opposed to clinical psychologists) measure how much an individual already knows rather than how much she is capable of knowing. The SAT or ACT tests that you probably took to get into college are good examples. One of the most widely used mental ability tests in industry is the **Wonderlic Personnel Inventory.** The short amount of time necessary to take the test (12 minutes) as well as the fact that it can be administered in a group setting make the test popular. Sample items from the Wonderlic are shown in Figure 5.9. Other popular mental ability tests are the Miller Analogies Test, Quick Test, and Raven Progressive Matrices (Anastasi, 1982).

Mental ability tests are excellent predictors of employee performance (Hunter & Hunter, 1984), but because they almost always result in adverse impact, they should be used with caution.

WONDERLIC

PERSONNEL TEST

FORM II

NAME .... Date ....
(Please Print)

READ THIS PAGE CAREFULLY. DO EXACTLY AS YOU ARE TOLD.
DO NOT TURN OVER THIS PAGE UNTIL YOU ARE
INSTRUCTED TO DO SO.

PROBLEMS MUST BE WORKED WITHOUT THE AID OF A CALCULATOR
OR OTHER PROBLEM-SOLVING DEVICE.

This is a test of problem solving ability. It contains various types of questions. Below is a sample question correctly filled in:

PLACE ANSWERS HERE

REAP is the opposite of
   1 obtain,   2 cheer,   3 continue,   4 exist,   5 <u>sow</u> .... [<u>5</u>]

The correct answer is "sow". (It is helpful to underline the correct word.) The correct word is numbered 5. Then write the figure 5 in the brackets <u>at the end of the line.</u>

Answer the next sample question yourself.

Paper sells for 23 cents per pad. What will 4 pads cost? .... [____]

The correct answer is 92¢. There is nothing to underline so just place "92¢" in the brackets.

Here is another example:

MINER   MINOR — Do these words
   1 have similar meanings,   2 have contradictory meanings,   3 mean neither the same nor opposite? [____]

The correct answer is "mean neither same nor opposite" which is number 3 so all you have to do is place a figure "3" in the brackets <u>at the end of the line.</u>

When the answer to a question is a letter or a number, put the letter or number in the brackets. All letters should be printed.

This test contains 50 questions. It is unlikely that you will finish all of them, but do your best. After the examiner tells you to begin, you will be given exactly 12 minutes to work as many as you can. Do not go so fast that you make mistakes since you must try to get as many right as possible. The questions become increasingly difficult, so do not skip about. Do not spend too much time on any one problem. The examiner will not answer any questions after the test begins.

Now, lay down your pencil and wait for the examiner to tell you to begin!

Do not turn the page until you are told to do so.

Source: E. F. Wonderlic Personnel Test, Inc., Northfield, IL. Reprinted by permission.

Interest Inventories

As the name implies, these tests are designed to tap vocational interests. The most commonly used **interest inventory** is the **Strong–Campbell**

Vocational Interest Blank (SCVIB), which asks individuals to indicate whether they like or dislike 325 items such as bargaining, repairing electrical wiring, or taking responsibility. The answers to these questions provide a profile that shows how similar a person is to people already employed in 89 occupations that have been classified into 23 basic interest scales and 6 general occupational themes. The theory behind these tests is that if an individual has interests that are similar to those of people in a particular field, she would be more likely to be satisfied in that field than she would in a field composed of people whose interests are not similar. Other popular interest inventories include the Minnesota Vocational Interest Inventory, the Kuder Occupational Interest Inventory, and the California Occupational Preference System.

Even though interest inventories have shown limited success in helping to select employees, they are useful in **vocational counseling**—that is, helping people find the careers for which they are best suited. Conducted properly, vocational counseling uses a battery of tests, which at minimum should include an interest inventory and a series of ability tests. The interest inventory scores suggest careers for which the individual's interests are compatible; the ability tests will tell her if she has the necessary abilities to enter into those careers. If interest scores are high in a particular occupational area, but ability scores are low, the individual is advised as to the type of training that would best prepare her for a career in that particular area.

Personality Tests

Personality tests have been roundly criticized in the personnel field, mostly because few personnel professionals have the knowledge to properly use the tests. Another problem with personality tests is that the thousands of available tests measure thousands of different types of personalities. The problem is less in the tests themselves, but with the theories behind the tests. For example, Raymond Cattell created a test called the 16-PF because his research indicated that only 16 major personality dimensions existed, while John Geier created the Personal Profile System because he believes (based on the work of Daniel Marston) that there are only four major personality dimensions.

As mentioned earlier, **personality tests** are of two main varieties. **Projective tests** provide the respondent with unstructured tasks such as describing inkblots and drawing pictures. Because projective tests are of questionable reliability and validity and are time-consuming and expen-

Figure 5.10
Types of Objective
Personality
Questions

True/False

I enjoy meeting new people	True	False
I am assertive	True	False

Forced Choice

Choose the adjective most like you and the adjective least like you.

	Most	Least
Assertive	____	____
Energetic	____	____
Playful	____	____

sive, they are rarely used in employee selection. One notable exception is the New York City Police Department's use of the House–Tree–Person test in which applicants are asked to draw pictures of a house, a tree, and a person. These drawings are then analyzed by trained clinical psychologists and are thought to reveal the psychological stability of potential police officers.

The **objective test** is the second variety of personality test. Objective tests are structured so that the respondent is limited to a few answers that will be scored by standardized keys. Samples of different question formats are shown in Figure 5.10. Examples of objective tests used in employee selection include the California Psychological Inventory, the Personal Profile System, the 16 PF, and the Edwards Personal Preference Schedule.

Aptitude Tests

Aptitude tests are designed to measure an applicant's abilities and talents and can be divided into one of two types, general and specific. A **specific aptitude test** measures an individual's ability in only one aptitude. For example, there are more than 400 specific aptitude tests that measure abilities such as mechanical aptitude, spatial aptitude, musical aptitude, and verbal aptitude (Donnoe, 1986). Although these tests are excellent in predicting future employee performance, the sheer number of specific aptitude tests leads to administrative problems because most jobs involve more than one type of aptitude. Therefore, several specific aptitude tests must be included in the test battery administered to applicants, which makes the battery both lengthy and costly.

Recall from the discussion of legal issues in Chapter 1 that any test used in industry must be job-related. One way in which the courts determine job relatedness is by asking whether test scores have been shown to correlate with some relevant aspect of job performance. With more than 400 specific aptitude tests, a tremendous amount of research time and money would have to be invested to validate the test scores for a particular type of job. Thus, specific aptitude tests are considered useful but not always practical tools for employee selection.

To overcome some of the problems with the use of specific aptitude tests, **general aptitude tests** were created; the most popular and widely used is the **General Aptitude Test Battery (GATB)**. Developed in the 1950s by the U.S. Department of Labor, the GATB has always been popular, but its use skyrocketed in the 1980s primarily because of validity generalization, which was discussed in Chapter 3.

As shown in Figure 5.11, the GATB consists of 12 speed tests that yield scores for eight aptitudes segmented into 3 dimensions. The cognitive dimension includes verbal, numerical, and general learning aptitudes; the perceptual dimension consists of spatial, form, and clerical perception aptitudes; and the psychomotor dimension contains motor coordination, finger dexterity, and manual dexterity aptitudes.

An applicant's scores on the aptitude tests can be compared to the requirements of thousands of jobs that have been analyzed through the Functional Job Analysis method discussed in Chapter 2. The state of Virginia, for example, is so sold on both the validity generalization concept and the GATB that all applicants seeking jobs through the Virginia Employment Commission are asked to take the GATB. Most other states and many municipalities have similar programs.

Honesty Tests

Honesty tests are designed to tell an employer the probability that an applicant would steal money or merchandise. Honesty tests are used mostly in the retail area and more than 3 million are sold each year. Such extensive use is due to the fact that 42% of retail employees, 62% of fast food employees, and 32% of hospital employees have admitted stealing from their employers (Jones & Terris, 1989).

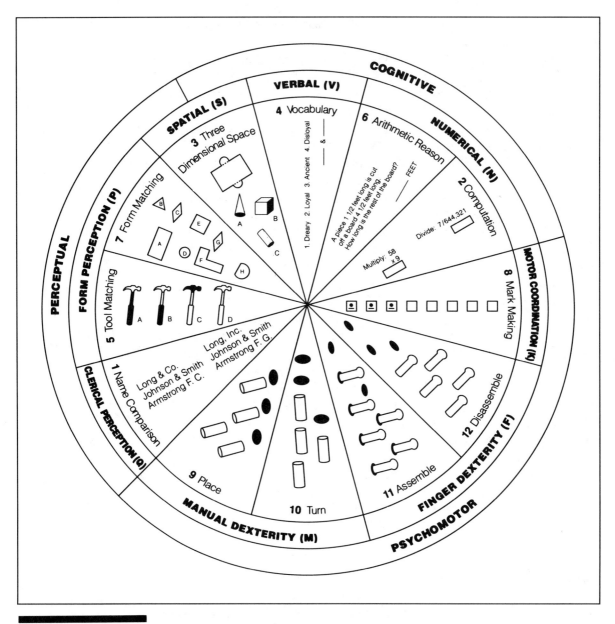

Figure 5.11
GATB Dimensions

Until recently, employers have used both electronic and paper-and-pencil honesty tests to screen applicants. In 1988, however, the U.S. Congress passed the Employee Polygraph Protection Act making general use of electronic honesty tests, such as the **polygraph** and the **voice**

204

Chapter 5

Test	Reliability	Overall Validity	Specific Criterion		
			Polygraph	Predictive	Theft Admission
Phase II	.91	.56	.89	.14	.64
P.O.S.	.76	.72	.72	—	—
P.S.I.	.67	.39	.47	.27	.55
Reid Report	.92	.42	.48	—	.29
Stanton	.91	.61	.79	—	.42
Milby Profile	—	.74	—	.74	—
T.A.S.	.95	.65	.65	—	—
Wilkerson	—	.69	.75	—	.63
P.E.A.Q.	—	.49	—	—	.49
Compu-Scan	.84	.45	.45	—	—
Total	.90	.58	.65	.38	.50

Table 5.4
Several Honesty Tests

Source: Snyman, 1990.

stress analyzer, illegal except in a few situations involving national security. The law did, however, allow the use of paper-and-pencil honesty tests.

Paper-and-pencil honesty tests are based on the premise that a person's attitudes about theft as well as his previous theft behavior will accurately predict his future honesty. Honesty tests measure attitudes by asking the test taker to estimate the frequency of theft in society, how harsh penalties against thieves should be, how easy it is to steal, how often he has personally been tempted to steal, how often his friends have stolen, and how often he personally has stolen.

Table 5.4 shows some of the many honesty tests on the market, several of which do a decent job of predicting either polygraph results or admissions of theft (Sackett, Burns, & Callahan, 1989; Snyman, 1990). Unfortunately, few studies have attempted to correlate test scores with actual theft. Of course, these would be difficult to conduct. Instead, the validity of honesty tests has been determined by comparing test scores with:

- polygraph test results
- self-admissions of theft
- shrinkage (the amount of goods lost by a store)

- known groups (for example, priests versus convicts)
- future theft

Unfortunately, all of these measures have problems. If polygraph results are used, the researcher is essentially comparing honesty test scores with the scores of a test—the polygraph—that has been made illegal partly because of questions about its accuracy. If self-admissions are used, the researcher is relying on dishonest people to be honest about their crime history. If **shrinkage** is used, the researcher does not know which of the employees is responsible for the theft or, for that matter, what percentage of the shrinkage can be attributed to employee theft as opposed to customer theft or incidental breakage. Even if actual employee theft is used, the test may only predict employees who *get caught* stealing as opposed to those who steal and do not get caught. The problems with known-group comparisons were discussed in great detail in Chapter 3.

Although paper-and-pencil honesty tests are inexpensive and may be useful in predicting theft, they also suffer serious drawbacks. The most important of these might be that males have higher failure rates than do females, and younger people have higher failure rates than do older people. Adverse impacts on these two groups pose little legal threat, but telling the parents of a 17-year-old boy that their son has just failed an honesty test is not the best way to foster good public relations. Failing an honesty test has a much greater psychological impact than failing a spatial relations test. For these reasons, some legal experts advise against letting applicants know that they were not hired because they failed honesty tests (Douglas, Feld, & Asquith, 1989).

Job-Knowledge Tests

Used primarily in the public sector, **job-knowledge tests** are designed to measure how much a person knows about a job. These tests are similar to the exams given several times a semester in a college class. They are typically given in multiple-choice fashion for ease of scoring, but they also can be written in essay format.

Job-knowledge tests have some of the same advantages as work samples. They have excellent content and criterion validity, and because of

their high face validity, they are accepted well by applicants (Robertson & Kandola, 1982). The major disadvantage to job-knowledge tests is that even though they do a good job of predicting performance (Ward, 1989), they often result in adverse impact (Schmidt et al., 1977).

The job of a testing professional is highlighted in the employment profile of Dave Faloona.

Physical Tests

Physical tests often are used for jobs that require physical strength and stamina such as police officer, firefighter, and lifeguard. These types of tests include climbing a ladder within a limited period of time, running 50 yards, or dragging a 150-pound dummy through 30 yards of water. Particular care must be exercised with physical tests because they often discriminate against female applicants (Arvey, 1979).

As with any test, physical tests must directly relate to job-analysis results. For example, if a job analysis indicates that a firefighter often must drag a 48-pound, 50-foot hose 75 feet across a street, then it would certainly be appropriate to have the applicant actually drag the hose 75 feet as part of her preemployment physical test. Asking the applicant to lift a 48-pound weight over her head would not be appropriate because it does not directly measure the *type* of ability necessary to perform the job.

The type of physical ability required is important because research has shown that seven different physical abilities are commonly found in very physical jobs (Daniel, 1987; Fleishman, 1979):

- dynamic strength (strength requiring repetitions)
- trunk strength (stooping or bending over)
- explosive strength (jumping or throwing objects)
- static strength (strength not requiring repetitions)
- dynamic flexibility (muscle flexibility)
- gross body equilibrium (balance)

An interesting example of the importance of physical ability testing was provided in a study by Padgett (1989), who was hired to determine vision requirements for a municipal fire department. Prior to Padgett's study, national vision standards for firefighters had been set without any empirical research and stipulated that firefighters needed a minimum uncorrected vision of 20/40 and could not wear contact lenses because they might be "blown out of their eyes."

After conducting his study of actual job-related duties, however, Padgett discovered that the minimum vision needed to perform firefighting tasks was 20/100 if the person wore glasses and that there was no minimum if the person wore contacts. The difference in requirements for contacts and glasses was because certain duties might result in a loss of glasses but that it was very unlikely a firefighter would lose contacts while performing a task requiring acute vision. As a result of this study, many qualified applicants who had been turned away because of the archaic vision requirements were now allowed the chance to become firefighters.

Drug Testing

Drug testing certainly is one of the most controversial testing methods used by personnel professionals. The reasons for its high usage is that personnel professionals believe that not only is drug use dangerous, but also that many employees are under the influence of drugs at work. Their beliefs are supported by research that indicates drug users are 16 times more likely to miss work, are 3 times as likely to be late, and have 4 times as many accidents on the job than non–drug users (Pendleton, 1986).

Because of such statistics, organizations are increasing their drug testing of applicants before they are hired. In fact, as of 1988, nearly half of the Fortune 500 companies were testing for drugs (Douglas, Feld, & Asquith, 1989).

Drug testing usually is done in two stages. In the first, an employee or applicant provides a urine sample that is subjected to an initial screening test. The most common initial drug screens are the **Enzyme Multiplied Immunoassay Technique (EMIT)** and **radioimmunoassay (RIA).** EMIT uses enzymes as reagents, while RIA uses radioactive tagging. Both cost approximately $10 per sample.

If the initial test for drugs is positive, then second-stage testing is done. The urine sample undergoes a more expensive confirmation test such as **thin layer chromatography** or **gas chromatography/mass spectometry analysis.** These tests can range anywhere from $30 to more than $100 per sample.

When both stages are used, testing is very accurate in detecting the presence of drugs. But drug tests are not able to determine whether an individual is impaired by drug use (Rosen, 1987). That is, an employee smoking marijuana on Saturday night will test positive for the drug on Monday, even though the effects of the drug have long since gone away. Most drugs can be detected two to three days after they have been used. The exceptions are the benzodiazepines, which can be detected for two weeks after use, and marijuana, which can be detected up to 5 days for the casual user and up to 30 days for the frequent user (Douglas, Feld, & Asquith, 1989).

Because positive drug tests have a certain degree of uncertainty, if an applicant fails a preemployment drug test, she can usually reapply six months later. With such a policy, there are few legal pitfalls.

In the public sector or in the union environment, however, drug testing becomes complicated when it occurs after employees are hired. Testing of current employees usually takes one of three forms:

1. All employees or randomly selected employees are tested at predetermined times.

2. All employees or randomly selected employees are tested at random times.

3. Employees who have been involved in an accident or disciplinary action are tested following the incident.

The second form is probably the most effective in terms of punishing or preventing drug usage, but the third form of testing is legally the most defensible (Veglahn, 1989).

Another important issue in the use of drug testing is the consequence facing an employee who fails a test. Most organizations allow such an employee to keep her job as long as she undergoes treatment for drug abuse and does not test positive again in the future. With such a policy, the organization is usually on better legal ground than if it fires any employee who tests positive.

Handwriting Analysis

An interesting method used to select employees by more than 3,000 American organizations and by 85% of all European organizations is **handwriting analysis,** or **graphology.** The idea behind handwriting analysis is that the way in which we write reveals our personality, which in turn should indicate work performance.

To analyze a person's writing, a graphologist looks at the size, slant, width, regularity, and pressure of a writing sample (Patterson, 1976). From these writing characteristics, information about temperament, mental traits, social traits, work traits, and moral traits is obtained (Currer-Briggs, 1971).

Research on graphology has revealed interesting findings. First, graphologists are consistent in their judgments about script features (Lockowandt, 1976) but not in their interpretation about what these features

Study	Year	Country	Sample	Criterion	Validity
Sonnemann & Kernan	1962	Germany	Executives	Supervisor ratings	.74
Keinan & Barak	1984	Israel	Military officers	Training success	.26
Ben-Shakhar et al.	1986	Israel	Bank tellers	Supervisor ratings	.25
Rafaeli & Klimoski	1983	U.S.A.	Salesmen	Sales performance	.04
Rafaeli & Klimoski	1983	U.S.A.	Salesmen	Supervisor ratings	.00
Zdep & Weaver	1967	U.S.A.	Salesmen	Sales commissions	−.05
Total					.21

Table 5.5
Handwriting Analysis Research

mean (Keinan & Barak, 1984; Rafaeli & Klimoski, 1983). Second, trained graphologists are no more accurate or reliable at interpreting handwriting samples than untrained undergraduates (Rafaeli & Klimoski, 1983) or psychologists (Ben-Shakhar, Bar-Hillel, Bilu, Ben-Abba, & Flug, 1986; Jansen, 1973). Finally, as shown in Table 5.5, handwriting analysis seems to predict performance in other countries but not in the United States. This mysterious finding might explain why graphology is used more in Europe than in the United States.

Comparison of Techniques

After reading this chapter, you are probably asking the same question that industrial psychologists have been asking for years: Which method of selecting employees is best? It is clear that the unstructured interview, education, and previous experience are not good predictors of future employee performance (Hunter & Hunter, 1984). It is also clear that ability (as measured by aptitude tests), work samples, biodata, and assessment centers do a fairly good job of predicting future employee performance (Hunter & Hunter, 1984; Schmitt, Gooding, Noe, & Kirsch, 1984). Personality tests predict some criteria fairly well (wages, performance ratings, sales) and others not so well (turnover, status change; Ghiselli, 1973). Furthermore, personality tests may predict an employee's performance after accounting for ability (Day & Silverman, 1989) or after he has been with the company a few years better than they predict performance immediately after hire (Helmreich, Sawin, & Carsrud, 1986).

As shown in Table 5.6, the issue of which method is best depends on the criteria being measured and the type of job involved. For example, Ghiselli (1973) found that personality tests best predicted sales success,

Technique	Criterion				
	Satisfaction	Tenure	Training	Promotion	Performance
Recruitment					
Realistic job previews[a]	.06	.06	—	—	.03
Written	—	—	—	—	−.02
Audiovisual	—	—	—	—	.15
Recruitment methods[b]					
Employee referral	—	.13	—	—	−.02
Media	—	−.20	—	—	.02
Employment agencies	—	−.18	—	—	.10
Selection					
Ability tests	—	—	—	—	.53
Assessment centers[c]	—	—	—	—	.25
Educational requirements	—	.27	—	—	.15
Experience	—	—	—	—	.37
Grade point average[d]	—	—	—	—	.18
Handwriting analysis	—	—	—	—	.21
United States	—	—	—	—	.00
Israel and Germany	—	—	—	—	.42
Interviews[e]					
Unstructured	—	.08	.19	.17	.17
Situational	—	.25	.27	.32	.39
Patterned behavior	—	—	—	—	.55
Job knowledge	—	—	—	—	.51
References					
Traditional	—	—	—	—	.13
Peres and Garcia method	—	—	—	—	.35
Personality tests					
Objective	—	—	—	—	.24
Projective	—	—	—	—	.00
Vocational interest	—	—	—	—	.10
Weighted application blanks[f]	—	.34	—	—	.36
Work samples	—	—	—	—	.21

[a] Premack and Wanous (1985)

[b] Aamodt and Carr (1988)

[c] Gaugler, Rosenthal, Thornton, and Bentson (1987)

[d] Bretz (1989)

[e] Wiesner and Cronshaw (1988)

[f] Ellenburg, Kremen, Hicks, and Stewart (1990)

Table 5.6
Typical Validity Coefficients for Recruitment and Selection

mental ability tests best predicted service occupation success, and mechanical aptitude tests best predicted success for machine operators. Schmitt et al. (1984) found biodata to be the best predictor of performance ratings, and mental ability to be the best predictor of achievement. Thus, different methods are best for different occupations and different criteria.

But even though some selection techniques are better than others, *all* are potentially useful methods for selecting employees. In fact, a properly constructed selection battery usually contains a variety of tests that tap different dimensions of a job. Take, for example, the job of police officer. We might use a physical ability test to make sure the applicant has the strength and speed necessary to chase suspects and defend herself, a situational interview to tap her decision-making ability, a personality test to ensure that she has the traits needed for the job, and a background check to determine whether she has a history of antisocial behavior.

Industrial psychologist Dan Johnson likens the selection process to a fishing trip. During our trip, we can try to catch one huge fish to make our meal or we can catch several small fish that, when cooked and placed on a plate, make the same size meal as one large fish. With selection tests, we try for one or two tests that will predict performance at a high level. But by combining several tests with smaller validities, we can predict performance just as well as with one test with a very high validity.

Rejection Letters

Once a decision has been made regarding which applicants will be hired, those who will not be hired must be notified. As mentioned earlier in the chapter, applicants who are rejected still should be treated well because they are potential customers and potential applicants for other positions that might become available in the company. With this in mind, what is the best way to reject an applicant? Even though specific rules of courtesy will be discussed, only one study has indicated what effect, if any, different kinds of **rejection letters** have on an applicant's attitude or behavior.

The best type of letter to use is not known, but it is believed that a few rules should be followed when rejecting an applicant. First, always respond to an application as quickly as possible. If you think back on your job-hunting experiences, nothing can be more irritating than to never hear from a company or to wait a long period of time before being notified.

Once it is known that certain applicants will not be hired, they should be notified so that they can continue their job hunting. Excuses about not having the funds to notify applicants are probably not justified when one considers the ill feelings that may result from not contacting an applicant.

Second, be as personable and as specific as possible in the letter. With the use of word processors, it is fairly easy to individually address each letter, express the company's appreciation for applying, and perhaps explain who was hired and what their qualifications were.

Aamodt and Peggans (1988) found that rejection letters differ to the extent that they do or do not contain the following types of responses:

- a personally addressed and signed letter
- the company's appreciation to the applicant for applying for a position with the company
- a compliment about the applicant's qualifications
- a comment about the high qualifications possessed by the other applicants
- information about the individual who was actually hired
- a wish of good luck in future endeavors
- a promise to keep the applicant's résumé on file

Furthermore, it was found that a statement about the individual who received the job actually increased applicant satisfaction with both the selection process and the organization.

Examples of good and bad rejection letters are shown in Figures 5.12 and 5.13. Notice that in the example of a bad letter, only two types of response—an appreciation for applying and a promise to keep the résumé on file—were included, while in the example of a good letter at least four types of response were included.

Perhaps the most important thing to consider when writing a letter of rejection is to be honest. Do not tell an applicant that his résumé will be kept on file if the files for each job opening will not be used. Adair and Pollen (1985) think that rejection letters treat job applicants like unwanted lovers; they either beat around the bush ("There were many qualified applicants") or stall for time ("We'll keep your résumé on file").

Dear Mr. Jones:

I am writing concerning your recent application for our position in sales. This has been a long and arduous process as we received more than 100 applications. We have finally chosen a new Sales Representative, Ms. Karen Anderson, who seemed to best fit our needs as she possesses a Bachelor's Degree in marketing as well as five years of sales experience.

We certainly appreciate your interest in our position, and thank you for your application. Your qualifications were outstanding, but as you can see from both the number of applications we received and the high quality of the person we selected, the competition was tough.

We wish you the best of luck in your efforts to obtain employment. We will keep your application on file for six months and should a position arise corresponding with your qualifications, we will keep you in mind.

**Figure 5.12
Example of a
Well-Designed
Rejection Letter**

Dear Applicant:

The sales position for which you applied has been filled and we appreciate your interest in the position. We will keep your application on file for six months should another opening arise.

**Figure 5.13
Example of a Poorly
Designed Rejection
Letter**

Chapter Summary

In this chapter, several employee-selection methods were discussed. References were seen as not being good linear predictors of performance, although they still are necessary because of negligent hiring concerns. Weighted application blanks, psychological tests, work samples, job-knowledge tests, and assessment centers were shown to be excellent potential predictors of employee performance. Physical ability tests were found to be good measures for some jobs, and paper-and-pencil honesty tests were found to be reasonably good predictors of employee theft. The chapter also pointed out that applicants should be treated professionally and that both recruitment techniques and rejection letters can be used to turn applicants who are not hired into friends of the organization.

Glossary

Aptitude test A test designed to measure an applicant's abilities and talents

Assessment center A method of selecting employees in which applicants participate in several job-related activities, at least one of which must be a simulation, and are rated by several trained evaluators

Business game An exercise, usually found in assessment centers, that is designed to simulate the business and marketing activities that take place in an organization

Composite score A single score that is the sum of the scores of several items or dimensions

Criterion A measure of work behavior such as quantity, quality, absenteeism, or tenure

Criterion groups Division of employees into groups based on high and low scores on a particular criterion

Derivation sample A group of employees that were used in creating the initial weights for a weighted application blank

Drug testing Tests that indicate if an applicant has recently used a drug

Enzyme Multiplied Immunoassay Technique (EMIT) A method of drug testing that utilizes enzymes to detect the presence of drugs

File approach The gathering of WAB data from employee files rather than by questionnaire

Gas chromatography/Mass spectometry Analysis A means of analyzing urine samples for the presence of drugs in which the urine sample is vaporized and then bombarded with electrons

General aptitude test A test battery that measures several different aptitudes

General Aptitude Test Battery (GATB) The most widely used general aptitude test

Graphology See Handwriting analysis

Handwriting analysis A method of measuring personality by looking at the way in which a person writes

Hold-out sample A group of employees that are not used in creating the initial weights for a weighted application blank but instead are used to double-check the accuracy of the initial weights

Honesty test A psychological test designed to predict an applicant's tendency to steal

In-basket technique An assessment-center exercise designed to simulate the types of information that daily come across a manager's or employee's desk in order to observe the applicant's responses to such information

Interest inventory A psychological test designed to identify vocational areas in which an individual might be interested

Job-knowledge test A test that measures the amount of job-related knowledge that an applicant possesses

Leaderless group discussion A selection technique, usually found in assessment centers, in which applicants meet in small groups and are given a problem to solve or an issue to discuss

Leniency An evaluation error in which an evaluator has a tendency to rate a person higher than that person should be rated

Letter of recommendation A letter written to an employer in support of an applicant's qualifications for a job

Mental ability tests Tests designed to measure the level of intelligence or the amount of knowledge possessed by an individual

Mental agility A category referring to intelligence, among the categories developed by Peres and Garcia for analyzing the adjectives used in letters of recommendation.

Negligent hiring The idea that an organization has the legal duty to protect its employees and customers from potential harm caused by its employees

Objective scoring A method of scoring psychological tests in which people scoring the test use keys or guides and have high scoring agreement

Objective tests A type of personality test that is structured to limit the respondent to a few answers that will be scored by standardized keys

Personality test A psychological test designed to measure various aspects of an applicant's personality

Physical tests Tests that measure an applicant's level of physical ability required for a job

Polygraph An electronic test that is intended to determine honesty by measuring an individual's physiological changes that occur after being asked questions

Power tests Tests in which an applicant is asked to correctly complete as many items as possible and is given an unlimited amount of time to complete the test

Projective tests A subjective test in which a subject is asked to perform relatively unstructured tasks, such as drawing pictures, and a psychologist analyzes his or her responses

Psychological testing A selection technique involving the use of paper-and-pencil tests, such as filling out a questionnaire, to determine an applicant's suitability for the job

Questionnaire approach The method of obtaining WAB data from questionnaires rather than from employee files

Radioimmunoassay (RIA) A method of drug testing that uses radioactive tagging to determine the presence of drugs

Rare response scoring A method of weighting WAB items in which unusual answers to an item get the most weight

Rejection letter A letter from an organization to an applicant informing the applicant that he or she will not receive a job offer

Reliability The extent to which a score from a test or from an evaluation is consistent and free from error

Rorschach Inkblot Test A projective personality test

Sample size The number of people that participate in a study

Shrinkage The amount of goods lost by an organization as a result of theft, breakage, or other loss

Simulation An exercise, usually found in assessment centers, that is designed to place an applicant in a situation that is similar to the one that will be encountered on the job

Specific aptitude test An aptitude test that measures an applicant's ability in only one kind of aptitude

Speed tests Tests in which an applicant is asked to correctly complete as many items as possible in a specific amount of time

Strong-Campbell Vocational Interest Blank (SCVIB) A popular interest inventory used to help people choose careers

Subjective scoring A method of scoring psychological tests in which people scoring the test rely on their own judgment more than on scoring guides and high scoring agreement is unlikely

Thin layer chromatography A method of analyzing urine specimens for drugs that is performed by hand and requires a great deal of analyst skill

Uniform guidelines Federal guidelines that are used to guide an employer in establishing fair selection methods

Urbanity A category referring to social skills and refinement, among the categories developed by Peres and Garcia for analyzing the adjectives used in letters of recommendation

Vertical percentage method The method for scoring weighted application blanks in which the percentage of unsuccessful employees responding in a particular way is subtracted from the percentage of successful employees responding in the same way

Vigor A category referring to energy, among the categories developed by Peres and Garcia for analyzing the adjectives used in letters of recommendation

Vocational counseling The process of helping an individual choose and prepare for the most suitable career

Voice stress analyzer An electronic test that is intended to determine honesty by measuring an individual's voice changes that occur after being asked questions

Weighted application blank (WAB) A method of selection involving application blanks that contain questions that research has shown will predict job performance

Wonderlic Personnel Inventory The mental ability test that is most commonly used in industry

Work sample A method of selecting employees in which an applicant is asked to perform samples of actual job-related tasks

6

Van Bucher/Photo Researchers, Inc. (NYC)

Evaluating Employee Performance

The Performance-Appraisal Process

Have you ever received a grade that you did not think was fair? Perhaps you had an 89.6 and the instructor would not "round up" to an A, or the test contained questions that had nothing to do with the class? If so, you probably were upset with the way in which your professor appraised your classroom performance. In this chapter, we will discuss the process of evaluating and appraising employee, rather than student, performance. The processes of evaluating a student's or an employee's performance, however, are similar.

The process can be broken down into several interrelated steps. The first step is to determine the reasons that an organization has for evaluating performance (Cleveland, Murphy, & Williams, 1989). This is important because the various performance-appraisal techniques are appropriate for some purposes but not others. For example, one of the methods that we will discuss—the forced choice scales—is excellent for evaluating performance to determine compensation but terrible for training purposes.

Once the uses of the performance evaluation have been established, the second step is to identify relevant criteria that can be used to evaluate employee performance. Criteria are ways of describing employee success. For example, it might be decided that attendance, quality of work, and safety are the three most important criteria for a successful employee.

After the relevant criteria are chosen, the third step is to choose and create methods for measuring the criteria. That is, how can we measure attendance, quality, and safety? Although this step is important, the choice of instruments is not as important as *how* the results of the evaluations are actually used (Hodap, 1986).

The fourth step in the process is to explain the system to both employees and supervisors and to elicit their suggestions and comments. At this point, a training program should be established for those supervisors who will be evaluating performance. At this point it is also imperative to provide supervisors with the necessary time and incentives to take the performance-appraisal process seriously. This can be accomplished in many ways, such as including performance-appraisal duties in supervisor job descriptions and making part of a supervisor's own performance evaluation dependent upon how well she evaluates her employees. For example, 20% of the performance evaluation scores for supervisors working for Salt Lake City are based on their efforts in evaluating employee performance. An example of this step can be seen in the employment profile of Donna Blankenship.

Employment Profile

Donna Blankenship, M.S.
Human Resources Manager
McEwen Lumber

As human resources manager for the Wood Products Distribution Division of International Paper Company, I manage the human resources function for two lumber and building materials distribution companies. My responsibilities include employment, compensation, safety management, training, benefits, affirmative action, employee relations, and coordination of the company's Quality Improvement Process. Combined, the companies in Wood Products Distribution have 29 branches and approximately 550 employees throughout the Southeast and Midwest.

One of the major challenges in my position is the extensive geographic spread of the distribution branches. Even the company headquarters present a problem because one is in North Carolina and the other is in Kansas. Limited contact with branch employees requires me to rely upon local managers to take a fairly large role in human resources issues. The physical characteristics of the companies also lead to greater reliance upon reporting and documentation for the communication of information concerning individual employees.

One way in which managers and supervisors provide valuable information is through performance appraisals. Performance appraisals are an important tool in many facets of human resources management. Performance improvement is the most obvious use of an appraisal instrument because problem identification and goal setting let an employee know what is expected of him or her in the job and how well those expectations are being met.

Performance appraisals also provide documentation of performance problems and an opportunity for the employee to correct those problems to avoid discipline or termination. Appraisals identify training needs, needed equipment, and technical improvements. The process also provides a vehicle for communicating and plays a role in employee relations by actively involving supervisors and employees in career planning and development.

The value of any appraisal instrument lies, of course, in its validity and reliability. If the written appraisal does not accurately and consistently reflect actual performance, it serves no purpose. Too often in evaluating work performance a supervisor simply chooses numbers on a scale in response to a list of characteristics. Typically, no training is provided for the rater and no significant information is provided to the employee or to other members of management.

Developing a sound appraisal instrument is crucial to a useful appraisal process. My work for a previous employer provides an example of the development of a performance-appraisal system. In response to complaints from supervisors and employees at a financial institution that the performance-appraisal process then in use was a dreaded and purposeless task, the company appointed a team of employees to evaluate and revise the written appraisal form as well as the appraisal process. The team first surveyed each employee to identify problems with the old procedures and generate ideas for the revision.

Employee suggestions led to the identification of seven major performance factors. Each of these factors then was listed on the new appraisal form. For each factor, the raters are required to note strengths, weaknesses, and examples that are to be taken into consideration in rating the factor on a five-point scale. Factors that are considered to be basic requirements for satisfactory performance such as attendance and cooperation are listed separately and rated as satisfactory or unsatisfactory.

Two supplemental forms add to the value of this process. An employee comment form is available to employees at any time and is required with each appraisal. It is designed to elicit general comments, suggestions for improvements of procedures or equipment, training needs, employee skills not being utilized, and career development interests. Performance observation forms are a tool to be used by supervisors and employees to record critical performance incidents throughout the review period. Maintaining a performance-observation file facilitates completion of the written appraisal and provides important concrete examples of both good and bad performance.

Support for the new performance-appraisal procedures was good at all levels of the organization. Allowing each person to have input into the revision encouraged a sense of ownership and greater acceptance. The form itself is easy to use and is tailored to fit the organization. With the appraisal tool in place, the basis of a sound performance-appraisal process had been formed. The key to continued accuracy and consistency lies in training the appraisers and providing visible managerial support of the process. The information provided then can be applied to numerous human resources functions.

Figure 6.1
Performance-Appraisal System Used by State of Wyoming

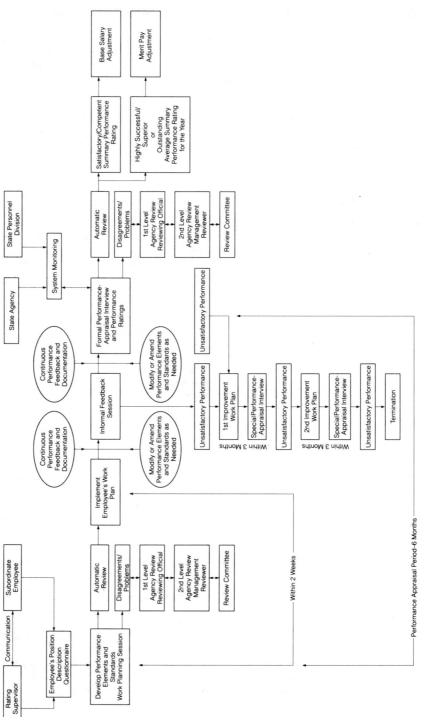

Source: Reprinted with permission of the Personnel Division, State of Wyoming.

The fifth step is the actual evaluation of employee performance using the instrument chosen and created in the second step. This step includes the observation and cognitive processing of behaviors, the recording or remembering of behaviors, and the actual evaluation of these behaviors. As we will see throughout this chapter, distortion and error frequently occur at this stage.

The final step is the **performance-appraisal review** itself, during which the supervisor formally communicates the results of the appraisal to the employee. Also during this time, the employee explains why her performance might have been poor, and the employee and supervisor discuss what steps will be taken to improve future performance. The performance-appraisal review will be discussed in greater depth toward the end of this chapter. An example of the performance-appraisal process used by the state of Wyoming is shown in Figure 6.1.

Reasons for Evaluating Employee Performance

Compensation

As mentioned in Chapter 2, a job's worth is determined by many factors, including the degree of responsibility and level of education required to perform the job. But the difference in compensation between two individuals within the same job is a function of both tenure and job performance. That is, it would not seem fair to pay a poor employee the same amount as an excellent employee. Thus, one important reason for evaluating employee performance is to provide a fair basis on which to determine an employee's salary.

Promotions

Another reason for evaluating performance is to determine which employees will be promoted. Although it would seem only fair to promote the best employee, this often does not occur. For example, the policy in some organizations is to promote employees with the most seniority. This is especially true of organizations whose employees belong to unions.

Even though promoting employees on the basis of performance or tenure seems fair, it may not always be smart. The best employee at one level is not always the best at the next level. Promoting the best or most senior employee often results in the so-called **Peter Principle**—that is, the promotion of an employee until he reaches his highest level of incompetence. Thus, if performance evaluations are used to promote employees, care should be taken to ensure that the employee is evaluated well on the job dimensions that are similar to the job dimensions of the new and open position.

For example, the five important job dimensions of a salesperson might be sales, communication skills, accuracy of paperwork, client rapport, and responsibility, and the four important job dimensions of sales manger would be communication skills, accuracy of paperwork, motivational ability, and employee rapport. The salesperson with the highest scores on the overlapping dimensions, which in this case are communication skills and accuracy of paperwork, should be the one promoted. Sales volume might not even be used as a factor in promotion.

Employee Training and Feedback

By far the most important use of performance evaluation is to improve performance by providing feedback to the employee about what she is doing both right and wrong. Even though employee training should be an ongoing process (see Chapter 7), the semiannual performance-appraisal review is an excellent time to meet with an employee and discuss her strengths and weaknesses. But more important, it is the time to determine how these weaknesses can be corrected. This process is thoroughly discussed later in the chapter.

Training-Needs Assessment

Another use of performance appraisal data is in training-needs analysis, which will be discussed in greater detail in Chapter 7. If many employees score poorly on a performance-appraisal dimension, an increase or change in training is probably necessary for all employees. If only a few employees have low scores, training at an individual level is indicated. Thus, performance appraisal can provide useful information about an organization's strengths and weaknesses.

Personnel Research

A final reason for evaluating employees is for personnel research. As discussed in previous chapters, employment tests must be validated, and one way this can be done is by correlating test scores with some measure of job performance. To do this, however, an accurate and reliable measure of job performance must be available.

The same is true in evaluating the effectiveness of training programs. To determine effectiveness, an accurate measure of performance must be available for use in determining whether performance increases as a result of training.

Although not the most important reason for evaluating employee performance, personnel research is still important, especially in organizations where union contracts forbid the use of performance evaluations in personnel decisions. In those situations, performance evaluations are still needed for effective personnel research.

Five Characteristics of Effective Criteria

Relevance

As we already know, criteria used to evaluate an employee must have **relevance**—that is, they must be job-related. To be job-related, a criterion must have been identified during the job analysis as an important part of a job. Criteria that involve traits rather than behaviors probably will not hold up in court (Field & Holley, 1982). For example, relevant criteria for a typist might include speed and accuracy of typing but probably not variables such as personal appearance or initiative. Likewise, cleanliness and accuracy of inventory might be relevant criteria for a janitor but tardiness and cooperation might not.

We may find it interesting that tardiness would not be a relevant criterion for a janitor. After all, shouldn't everyone be on time for work? True, being on time is good, but it is not always essential. With jobs in which customers or co-workers are dependent on an employee being prompt, tardiness is relevant, but in the case of a janitor, a few minutes being late would not greatly affect her performance. Because it would have little impact on performance, "nit-picking" about time might lead to lower rather than higher overall performance. We could, of course, argue that multiplying 5 minutes each day by 250 workdays would cost the organization 1,250 minutes or 20.8 hours per year in potential work. But we could also argue that the relevant criterion is clean rooms. Thus, if every room were cleaned by the end of the shift, the 5 minutes lost were not important. If, however, some rooms were left uncleaned, the janitor would receive lower marks for her work performance. Thus, a separate criterion for tardiness probably is not necessary.

Freedom from Contamination

The second characteristic of an effective criterion is its freedom from **contamination.** This means that the score on the criterion is determined by the actual work behavior of the employee rather than by some other factor. For example, two salespersons work in different locations. Bob Anderson sells an average of 120 air conditioners per month, while Fred Stone averages 93. Is this criterion free from contamination? Definitely not.

The number of sales are based not only on the skills of the salesperson, but also on factors such as the number of stores in the sales territory, the average temperature in the territory, and the relations between the previous salesperson and the store owners. Thus, if we used only the number of sales, Bob Anderson would be considered our top salesperson. But if we take account for the fact that sales are contaminated by the number of stores in the territory, we see that Bob Anderson sold 120 air conditioners in 50 possible stores, while Fred Stone sold 93 air conditioners in 10 stores. Thus, Bob Anderson sold an average of 2.4 air conditioners per store in an area with an average temperature of 93 degrees; Fred Stone sold an average of 9.3 air conditioners per store in an area with an average temperature of 80 degrees. By taking into account the potential areas of contamination, a different picture emerges of relative performance.

As the above example clearly shows, factors other than actual performance can affect criteria. Therefore, it is essential to identify as many sources of contamination as possible and to determine ways to adjust performance ratings to account for these contamination sources.

Discriminability

The third characteristic of an effective criterion is its **discriminability.** In other words, the criterion discriminates between individuals. When we use the word "discrimination" in this context, we do not mean racial or sexual discrimination. Instead, we mean that the scores on any particular criterion discriminate high performers from low performers. For example, an instructor could design a test for a class that is so easy that everyone scores 100 (in your dreams!) or a test so difficult that everyone scores zero. This would not be an effective criterion because every student scored the same. Thus, the criterion would provide no useful information.

Table 6.1
**Appropriateness of
Various Criteria for
Organizational Uses**

Criterion	Appropriateness			
	Research	**Promotions**	**Salary**	**Training**
Graphic rating scale	High	Moderate	Moderate	Moderate
Employee comparisons	High	High	Moderate	Low
Critical incidents	Low	Moderate	Moderate	High
Behaviorally Anchored Rating Scales (BARS)	High	Moderate	Moderate	High
Behavioral Observation Scales (BOS)	High	Moderate	Moderate	High
Mixed standard	High	Moderate	Moderate	High
Forced choice	High	Moderate	Moderate	Low
Quantity/quality	High	Low	High	Low
Attendance	High	Low	Moderate	Low
Safety	Moderate	Low	Low	Low

Reliability

The fourth characteristic of an effective criterion is that it must be reliable (this concept was discussed earlier, in Chapter 3). With **reliability,** we usually are most concerned about a criterion's similarity between two raters. That is, two people having observed the same person in similar contexts should probably rate the person at similar levels (remember alternate forms reliability in Chapter 3?).

In addition to interrater reliability, we are also concerned about the reliability of performance, the extent to which an employee performs her job over time (this is similar to test–retest reliability, which was discussed in Chapter 3).

Congruence

The fifth and final characteristic of an effective criterion is that it be **congruent** with the needs of the organization. If an organization uses criteria for promotion decisions, then the criteria should provide information that will place employees in some sort of rank order. In such a case, one overall rating or ranking or a **composite** of several ratings or rankings might be appropriate.

Similarly, if the criteria will be used to improve performance through training, they should produce specific feedback information for employees on their strengths and weaknesses. In such a case, one overall measure is not enough. Instead, **multiple criteria** measuring each aspect of the job are needed. Table 6.1 summarizes the appropriateness of certain criteria that will soon be discussed as well as their relationships with particular organizational needs.

Methods of Evaluating Employee Performance

As mentioned earlier in the chapter, the choice of the criteria and the methods used to determine the criteria are important. An excellent example of this importance comes from a study of the relationship between age and job performance. Using meta-analysis, Waldman and Avolio (1986) found a correlation of .27 between age and objective measures of job performance for 13 studies covering 40 separate samples. The correlation between age and supervisor ratings, however, was $-.14$. Thus, using the latter ratings would lead to the conclusion that older workers are not as good as younger workers. But using actual performance as the criterion leads to the opposite conclusion: Older workers performed better than younger workers.

We will now discuss a variety of methods in which employee performance can be evaluated. Industrial psychologists have spent considerable effort in developing different methods because each has its advantages and disadvantages. The human resource professional must choose the method that is most appropriate for her needs.

Objective Criteria

Objective criteria in performance appraisal are also called **hard criteria** because they are usually less subjective and based more on hard data than are **soft criteria** such as supervisor ratings. Common types of hard criteria are quantity of work, quality of work, attendance, and safety.

Quantity of Work

Evaluation of a worker's performance in terms of **quantity** is obtained by simply counting the number of relevant job behaviors that take place. For example, we might judge a salesperson's performance by the number of units he sells, an assembly-line worker's performance by the number of bumpers she welds, or a police officer's performance by the number of arrests he makes. Even Johnny Carson is evaluated on the number of viewers who watch his show.

Although quantity measures appear to be objective measures of performance, they often are misleading. From our previous discussion of contamination, it should be readily apparent that many factors determine quantity of work other than an employee's ability and performance. Furthermore, for many people's jobs it might not be practical or possible to measure quantity. Computer programmers, doctors, and firefighters are examples.

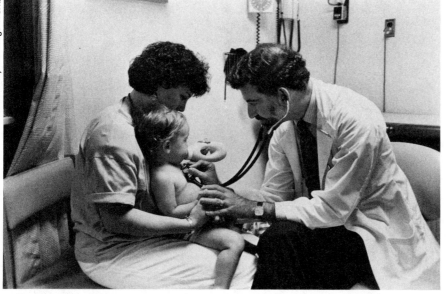

It is impossible to evaluate a doctor's performance in terms of quantity measurements.

Quality of Work

Another method to evaluate performance is by measuring the **quality** of the work that is done. Quality usually is measured in terms of **errors,** which are defined as deviations from a standard. Thus, to obtain a measure of quality, there must be a standard against which to compare an employee's work.

For example, a seamstress's work quality would be judged by how it compares to a "model" shirt; a secretary's work quality produced would be judged by the number of typos (the standards being correctly spelled words); and a cook's quality might be judged by how her food resembled a standard as measured by size, temperature, and ingredient amounts.

Kentucky Fried Chicken, for example, evaluates the quality of its franchises' food by undercover inspectors. These inspectors purchase food, drive down the road, and after parking, use a thermometer to see whether the food has been served at a standard acceptable temperature and also a scale to determine whether the weight of the mashed potatoes is within the acceptable range of the standard order.

Note that the definition of an error is *any* deviation from a standard. Thus, errors can even be work quality that is higher than a standard. Why is this an error? Suppose a company manufactures shirts that are sold for $10. To keep down the manufacturing costs of its shirts, the company probably uses cheaper material and has its workers spend less

A cook's work quality might be judged by how closely the prepared food matches standards of size, temperature, and amount of each ingredient.

Howard Dratch/The Image Works

time per shirt than does a company that manufactures $50 shirts (these are not the shirts I buy). Thus, if an employee sews a shirt with 15 stitches per inch instead of the standard 10, the company will lose money because of higher quality!

When this author was working his way through school, he held a summer job at an amusement park. The job involved wearing a pink and purple uniform and cooking prefabricated pizza. The standard for the large pepperoni pizza was 2 handfuls of cheese and 15 pieces of pepperoni. Now all pizza lovers recognize this to be a barren pizza. The cooks thus tried to increase the pizza quality by tripling the number of pepperoni pieces. The management quickly explained to the young "gourmet chefs" that exceeding the standards was considered poor work performance and that employees who did so would be fired.

A similar situation developed at a factory that produced parts for telephones. Most of the employees were older and took great pride in their work quality and in the fact that their parts had the lowest percentage of errors in the company. They were told, however, that their quality was too high and that the parts were lasting so long that the company was not getting much repeat business. Quality errors can occur in many strange ways!

Attendance

A common method for objectively measuring one aspect of an employee's performance is by looking at attendance. (This will be discussed in greater detail in Chapter 12.)

Attendance can be separated into three distinct criteria: absenteeism, tardiness, and tenure. Both absenteeism and tardiness have obvious implications for the performance-appraisal process. The weight that each has in the overall evaluation of the employee largely depends on the nature of the job.

Tenure as a criterion, however, is used mostly for research purposes when evaluating the success of selection decisions. For example, in a job such as cook at McDonald's, there is probably little difference in the quantity and quality of hamburger or french fries that are cooked. But an employee might be considered a "success" if she stays with the company for at least four months and "unsuccessful" if she leaves before that time. In fact, the importance of tenure can be demonstrated by noting that several major fast food restaurants and convenience stores have established bonus systems to reward long-tenure employees—that is, those who have worked for a company for at least six months. For each hour the

**Figure 6.2
A Graphic Rating
Scale**

Initiative	Poor	1	2	3	4	5	Excellent
Cooperation	Poor	1	2	3	4	5	Excellent
Dependability	Poor	1	2	3	4	5	Excellent

employee works, the company places a specified amount of money into an account that can be used by the employee to pay such education expenses as books and tuition.

Safety

Another method used to evaluate the success of an employee is safety. Obviously, employees who follow safety rules and who have no occupational accidents do not cost an organization as much money as those who break rules, equipment, and possibly their own bodies. As with tenure, safety usually is used for research purposes, but it also can be used for employment decisions such as promotions and bonuses.

Subjective Criteria

Supervisor Evaluations

By far the most common type of performance appraisal is the supervisor rating. In fact, Lacho, Stearns, and Villere (1979) estimated that 95% of all performance appraisals are conducted using supervisors' ratings of performance. The most common rating scale so used is called the **graphic rating scale.** An example is shown in Figure 6.2. As we can see, such scales are fairly simple, with five to seven points accompanied by words such as "good" and "poor" anchoring the ends of the scale.

The obvious advantage to graphic rating scales is their ease of construction and use, but they have been criticized because of their susceptibility to rating errors such as halo and leniency, which are discussed later in this chapter (Kingstrom & Bass, 1981). To minimize or prevent these problems, other rating methods have been devised.

Employee Comparison Methods

To reduce leniency, employees can be compared with one another instead of rated individually on a scale. The easiest and most common of these methods is the **rank order.** In this approach, employees are ranked in

	Dimension			
Employee	Knowledge	Dependability	Quality	Total
Bird	1	1	1	1.00
Johnson	2	3	2	2.33
McHale	3	2	3	2.67
Ainge	4	5	4	4.33
Parish	5	4	5	4.67

**Table 6.2
Ranking Method of
Evaluating
Performance**

order by their judged performance for each relevant dimension. As Table 6.2 shows, the ranks are then averaged across each dimension to yield an overall rank.

Rank orders are easily used when there are only a few employees to rank, but they become difficult to use with larger numbers. Ranking the top few and bottom few employees is relatively easy, but deciding which 2 of 50 employees should be placed at the 30th and 31st ranks is more difficult.

To make this process easier, **paired comparisons** can be used. This method involves comparing each possible pair of employees and choosing which one of each pair is the better employee. An example is shown in Figure 6.3. Even though comparing one pair of employees at a time is easier than simultaneously comparing a large number of employees, it does have its drawbacks. With large numbers of employees, the time necessary to make all of the comparisons becomes prohibitive. For example, to determine how many comparisons must be made, we can use the following formula:

$$\text{number of comparisons} = \frac{n(n-1)}{2}$$

where n = the number of employees. Thus, if we have 10 employees to compare:

$$\text{number of comparisons} = \frac{(10)(10-1)}{2} = \frac{(10)(9)}{2} = \frac{90}{2} = 45$$

Thus, we would need to make 45 comparisons for each performance dimension. Although this number is not too bad, evaluating 100 employees would result in 4,950 separate comparisons! And with 5 performance dimensions, some unfortunate supervisor would have to make almost

Figure 6.3
Example of Paired
Comparison Method

Employees

    Elway
    Marino
    Wilson
    Kosar
    Miller

Paired Comparisons: Circle the best employee in each pair.

(Elway)	Marino
(Elway)	Wilson
(Elway)	Kosar
(Elway)	Miller
(Marino)	Wilson
(Marino)	Kosar
(Marino)	Miller
Wilson	(Kosar)
(Wilson)	Miller
(Kosar)	Miller

Scoring

Employee	Number of Times Name Circled
Elway	4
Marino	3
Wilson	1
Kosar	2
Miller	0

25,000 separate comparisons! Obviously, the supervisor would not favor such a task.

The final type of employee comparison system is called the **forced distribution method.** With this method, a predetermined percentage of employees are placed into one of the five categories shown in Figure 6.4. This system is much easier to use than the other two employee comparison methods, but it also has a drawback. To use the method, one must assume that employee performance is normally distributed, that is, that

Figure 6.4
**Forced Distribution
Method of
Performance
Appraisal**

Jones	Wilhite Smith	Suhey Abercrombie Anderson James	Dickerson White	Payton
10% Terrible	20% Poor	40% Average	20% Good	10% Excellent

there are certain percentages of employees who are poor, average, and excellent. As we discussed in Chapter 5, employee performance probably is not normally distributed because of restriction of range. There probably are few terrible employees because they either were never hired or were quickly fired. Likewise, truly excellent employees probably have been promoted. Thus, employee performance is distributed in a nonnormal fashion.

Perhaps another way to look at this concept is by examining the grades given in a class. When students ask an instructor to "curve" a test, technically they are asking her to force their grades into a normal curve—that is, there will be approximately 10% A's and 10% F's. (Of course, what these students often really are asking for is extra points.)

Suppose that you are at the bottom of your class, yet you still have a 75% average on class exams. Do you deserve an F? What if you are the last person in the D category, and a student withdraws from the class with two weeks to go. To keep the distribution normal, you are given an F. Do you consider this fair?

Perhaps the greatest problem with all of the employee-comparison methods is that they do not provide information about how well an employee actually is doing. For example, even though every employee at a production plant might be doing an excellent job, someone has to be at the bottom. Thus, it might appear that one worker is doing a poor job (because he is last), when in fact he, and every other employee, is doing well.

Critical Incidents

Another approach that can be taken to appraise employee performance is to use **critical incidents.** (Remember the Critical Incident Technique from the discussion on job analysis in Chapter 2?) To use critical incidents to appraise employee performance, a supervisor maintains a log of all the

**Figure 6.5
Employee Critical
Behavior Record**

Dimension	Type of Performance	
	Poor	Good
Knowledge		
Employee relations		
Customer relations		
Accuracy of work		

critical behaviors that she observes her employees performing. These behaviors then are used during the performance-appraisal review process to assign a rating for each employee. The critical incidents refresh the supervisor's memory of her employees' performance and also provides justification for each performance rating.

The use of log books to record behaviors not only provides an excellent source of documentation, but also results in more accurate performance appraisals (Bernardin & Walter, 1977). This is especially true if the logs are organized by employee rather than maintained as only a random collection of incidents observed on the job (DeNisi, Robbins, & Cafferty, 1989).

A more formal method for using critical incidents in evaluating performance was developed by Flanagan and Burns (1955) for use by General Motors. Called the **Employee Performance Record,** this method consists of a two-color form similar to that shown in Figure 6.5. Half of the sheet is used to record examples of good behaviors, the other half to record examples of poor behaviors. On each side, there are columns for each of the relevant performance dimensions. Supervisors have a separate record for each employee and at the end of the day can record the observed behaviors.

The advantage of this format is that supervisors are only allowed to record job-relevant behaviors. At the end of the performance-appraisal period (every six months), the supervisor has a record of job-relevant behaviors recorded in an organized fashion.

The Employee Performance Record had several positive effects for General Motors. The number of disciplinary warnings declined, suggestions in the company suggestion box increased, and productivity increased.

When the use of critical incidents was first announced, supervisors at General Motors were opposed, thinking it would take too much time. The actual time per day spent on recording the incidents, however, was only 5 minutes.

Behaviorally Anchored Rating Scales

As promising as the use of critical incidents appears to be, one major problem exists: The rater must read the incidents and then arrive at a numerical rating. To make this process easier and more accurate, Smith and Kendall (1963) developed **Behaviorally Anchored Rating Scales (BARS).** Conceptually, BARS use critical incidents (samples of behavior) to formally provide meaning to the numbers on a rating scale. Although

BARS are time-consuming to construct, the process is not overly complicated. To construct a set of BARS, the following procedure is used.

Generation of Job Dimensions

In the first step in BARS construction, the number and nature of job-related dimensions are determined. If a job analysis already has been conducted, the dimensions can be obtained from the job-analysis report. If for some reason a job analysis has not been done, a panel of some 20 job experts—the employees—is formed. This panel determines the important dimensions on which an employee's performance should be evaluated. If 15 to 20 employees are not available, several supervisors can meet and develop the job dimensions as a group (Shapira & Shirom, 1980). Usually, 5 to 10 dimensions are generated (Schwab, Heneman, & DeCotiis, 1975).

Generation of Critical Incidents

Once the relevant job dimensions have been identified, employees are asked to generate examples of good, average, and bad behavior that they have seen for each dimension. Thus, if five dimensions have been identified, each employee is asked to generate 15 critical incidents—a good, an average, and a bad incident—for each of the 5 dimensions. If the organization is fairly small, employees may need to generate more than one example of the three types of behavior for each dimension.

Sorting Incidents

To make sure that the incidents written for each job dimension actually are examples of behavior for that dimension, three job experts independently sort the incidents into each of the job dimensions. The dimension into which each incident has been sorted by each of the three sorters then is examined. If at least two sorters placed an incident in the same dimension, the incident becomes part of that dimension. But each sorter has placed the incident in a different category, the incident is considered to be ambiguous and thus is discarded.

As discussed in Chapter 2, 3 sorters achieve results similar to those for 100 sorters. Many developers of BARS, however, use as many sorters as possible so that employees have a part in developing the scales. If many employees are involved, a 60% level of sorter agreement should be used to determine whether an incident is part of a dimension.

Rating Incidents

Another group of job experts is given the incidents and asked to rate each one on a scale that can have from five to nine points as to the level of job performance that it represents (Bernardin, LaShells, Smith, & Alveres, 1976). The ratings from each rater for all of the incidents are then used to determine the mean rating and **standard deviation** for each incident (typically by computer).

Choosing Incidents

The goal of this step is to find one incident to represent each of the points on the scale for each dimension. To do so, the incidents whose mean ratings come closest to each of the scale points and whose standard deviations are small are kept. This procedure usually results in the retention of less than 50% of the incidents (Green, Sauser, Fagg, & Champion, 1981).

Creating the Scale

The incidents chosen in the previous step are then placed on a vertical scale such as that shown in Figure 6.6. Because the mean for each incident is unlikely to fall exactly on one of the scale points, they are often placed between the points, thus serving as anchors for future raters.

Using the Scale

To use the scale when actually rating performance, the supervisor takes the incidents that she has recorded for each employee and compares them to the incidents on each scale. This can be done in one of two ways. The most accurate (and the most time-consuming) method compares each of the recorded incidents to the anchors and records the value of the incident on the scale that most closely resembles the recorded incident. This is done for each recorded incident. The value for each incident then is summed and divided by the total number of incidents recorded for that dimension; this yields an average incident value, which is the employee's rating for that particular job dimension.

In the second method (easier, but probably less accurate) all of the recorded incidents are read to obtain a general impression of each employee. This general impression then is compared to the incidents that anchor each scale point. The scale point next to the incident that most

**Figure 6.6
Example of
Behaviorally
Anchored Rating
Scale (BARS)**

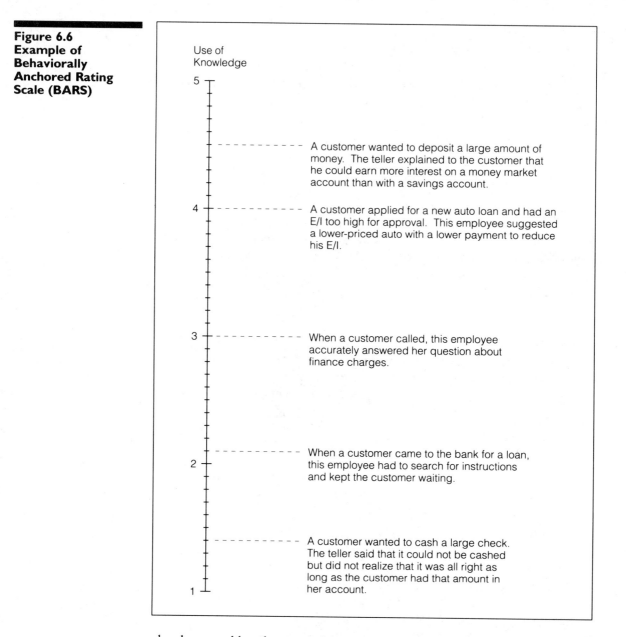

Use of
Knowledge

5 —

— — — — — — — — — A customer wanted to deposit a large amount of
money. The teller explained to the customer that
he could earn more interest on a money market
account than with a savings account.

4 — — — — — — — — — A customer applied for a new auto loan and had an
E/I too high for approval. This employee suggested
a lower-priced auto with a lower payment to reduce
his E/I.

3 — — — — — — — — When a customer called, this employee
accurately answered her question about
finance charges.

2 — — — — — — — — When a customer came to the bank for a loan,
this employee had to search for instructions
and kept the customer waiting.

— — — — — — — — A customer wanted to cash a large check.
The teller said that it could not be cashed
but did not realize that it was all right as
long as the customer had that amount in
1 — her account.

closely resembles the general impression gained from the incidents then becomes an employee's score for that dimension.

The third way to use BARS (and the least recommended) is to use the incidents contained in the BARS to arrive at a rating of the employee without recording actual incidents. Instead, the BARS are only used to provide meaning to the five scale points.

Figure 6.7
A Behavioral
Observation Scale
(BOS)

Job Knowledge

1. _____ Is aware of current interest rates?

2. _____ Offers suggestions to customers about how they can make the most interest?

3. _____ Knows various strategies for converting IRAs?

Employee Relations

1. _____ Offers to help other employees when own workload is down?

2. _____ Praises other employees when they do well?

Behavioral Observation Scales

Behavioral Observation Scales (BOS) are spinoffs of BARS that were designed by Latham and Wexley (1977) to make the rating process easier (see Figure 6.7). Even though BOS have no psychometric advantages over BARS (Bernardin & Kane, 1980), they are simpler to construct and easier to use (Latham, Fay, & Saari, 1979).

The development of BOS is relatively straightforward. The first few steps are the same as with BARS: Critical incidents and behaviors are obtained from employees, the incidents are placed into categories, and each incident is rated as to the level of job performance that it represents.

The behaviors then are listed. Supervisors read each behavior on the list and use the following scale to find the frequency for an employee performing that specific behavior:

1 = Employee engaged in behavior less than 65% of the time.

2 = Employee engaged in behavior 65–74% of the time.

3 = Employee engaged in behavior 75–84% of the time.

4 = Employee engaged in behavior 85–94% of the time.

5 = Employee engaged in behavior 95–100% of the time.

After each employee has been rated on each behavior, the scores from each item in each dimension are summed to give the dimension score. Dimension scores then are summed to yield an overall score. The greatest advantage to BOS is that a supervisor can show employees the *specific behaviors* that they currently do correctly and the specific behaviors that they should do to receive higher performance evaluations.

Because supervisors only conduct evaluations one every six months, BOS has been criticized for actually measuring only the *recall* of behaviors rather than measuring the actual *observation* of behaviors (Murphy, Martin, & Garcia, 1982). The importance of this distinction between recall and actual observation comes from research that has demonstrated that after some period of time, we cannot recall specific behaviors; instead, we "recall" behaviors that are consistent with sets of traits or **prototypes** that we attribute to employees (Feldman, 1981). That is, we assign certain traits or prototypes to employees, and then six months later, we recall behaviors that are consistent with those traits or prototypes. Furthermore, the closer an employee's behavior is to the prototype, the more accurate the performance evaluations (Mount & Thompson, 1987). Thus, as objective and behavioral as Behavioral Observation Scales appear, they may not be as accurate as initially believed because of cognitive processing distortions.

Forced Choice Rating Scales

One problem with BARS use is that supervisors often do not use the anchors when rating employees. Instead, they choose a point on the scale and then quickly glance to see which anchor is associated with the number. Because of this tendency, BARS often do not reduce leniency in ratings.

To overcome this problem, **forced choice rating scales** have been developed. These scales use critical incidents and relevant job behaviors as do BARS, but the scale points are hidden. An example of a forced choice scale is shown in Figure 6.8.

The development of forced choice scales is a long and complicated process, which partly explains why they are not commonly used. To create a forced choice scale, the first step is similar to that for BARS: Critical incidents and relevant job behaviors are generated. These incidents, of course, are only available when a job analysis has been conducted.

In the second step, employees rate all of the behaviors on the extent to which excellent employees perform them. After an approximately one-month interval, the employees again rate the items. This time, however, they rate the extent to which bad employees perform the behaviors. Finally, after another month, the employees again rate the behaviors for their **desirability.**

In the third step, the actual items for the rating scale are created. This is done by computing the value for each behavior. These values are computed by subtracting the average rating given to each behavior that de-

Figure 6.8
A Forced Choice
Rating Scale

Directions: In each of the following items, check
the one statement that is *most like* the teller being rated
and the one statement that is *least like* the
teller being rated.

	Most	Least	
1. a)	____	____	Teller is always on time (neutral).
b)	____	____	Teller is never short at end of day (bad).
c)	____	____	Teller smiles at each customer (good).
2. a)	____	____	Teller usually cross-sells (good).
b)	____	____	Teller keeps work area neat and orderly (bad).
c)	____	____	Teller is friendly to other employees (neutral).

scribes the bad employee from the average rating given to each behavior that describes the good employee. Behaviors with high positive values are considered to discriminate good from bad employees, items with high negative values are considered to discriminate bad from good employees, and behaviors with values near zero are considered neutral.

The next step in creating the items is to pick good, bad, and neutral behaviors that have similar desirability ratings. Thus, each rating item has three behaviors: One indicates good performance, one poor performance, and one indicates neither good nor bad performance. Furthermore, all of the behaviors for an item have the same level of desirability. This process is repeated until several items have been constructed for each of the relevant job dimensions.

In using the forced choice scale to evaluate employee performance, the supervisor chooses the behavior in each item that appears most typical of that performed by a given employee. The supervisor's choices then are scored by a member of the personnel department to yield the employee's rating on each dimension. The scores on each of the dimensions then can be summed to form an overall rating.

Although the development of a forced choice rating scale is long and complicated, it does have its advantages. For example, because the supervisor must choose behaviors without knowing "the key," common rating errors such as leniency and halo are less likely. Consequently, performance evaluations should be more accurate.

But the disadvantages of the forced choice scale probably outweigh its advantages. First, evaluations on forced choice scales can be "faked." A supervisor who wants to give an employee a high rating need only think

**Figure 6.9
A Mixed Standard
Scale**

Directions: Place a "+" after the statement if the typical behavior of the teller is usually better than that represented in the statement, a "0" if the typical behavior of the teller is about the same as that represented in the statement, and a "−" if the typical behavior of the teller is worse than that represented in the statement.

	Rating
1. Teller constantly argues with other employees (P).	_____
2. Teller smiles at customers (A).	_____
3. Teller asks customers how their families are doing (G).	_____
4. Teller helps other employees when possible (A).	_____
5. Teller is always friendly to and talks with (G) other employees.	_____
6. Teller asks customers what they want (P).	_____

Items 1, 4, and 5 are from the Employee Relations Dimension.
Items 2, 3, and 6 are from the Customer Relations Dimension.

---

about a good employee when evaluating the employee in question. Second, supervisors often object to forced choice scales because the key is secret. Not only does this secrecy deprive a supervisor of any control over the rating process, but also such secrecy can be seen by supervisors as a lack of trust in their abilities to evaluate their employees.

Most important, however, because the key must be kept secret, forced choice scales make feedback almost impossible. Thus, they should be used only when the major goal of the performance-appraisal system is accurate employee evaluation for purposes such as promotion and salary increases.

Mixed Standard Scales

To overcome some of the problems of forced choice scales, Blanz and Ghiselli (1972) developed **mixed standard scales,** an example of which is shown in Figure 6.9. Mixed standard scales are developed by having employees rate job behaviors and critical incidents on the extent to which they represent various levels of job performance. For each job dimension, a behavior or incident is chosen that represents excellent performance, average performance, and poor performance. These behaviors then are shuffled and the end results look similar to those shown in Figure 6.9.

To evaluate an employee, a supervisor reads each behavior and places a plus (+) next to it when a particular employee's behavior is usually

Table 6.3
Original Scoring
System for Mixed
Standard Scales

Statement Type			
Good	Average	Poor	Dimension Score
+	+	+	7
0	+	+	6
−	+	+	5
−	0	+	4
−	−	+	3
−	−	0	2
−	−	−	1

Source: Adapted from Blanz and Ghiselli (1972).

better than the behavior listed, a zero (0) if the employee's behavior is about the same as the behavior listed, or a minus (−) if the employee's behavior is usually worse than the behavior listed. To arrive at a score for each scale, the supervisor uses a chart like the one shown in Table 6.3. An overall score can be obtained by summing the scores from each of the scales.

Although mixed standard scales are less complicated than forced choice scales, they also have their drawbacks, the most important of which is that supervisors often make what are called "logical rating errors." For example, it would make no sense for a supervisor to rate an employee as better than the example of excellent performance or worse than the example of poor performance. Yet these types of errors are common. Logical rating errors still can be scored by using the revised scoring method developed by Saal (1979) (see Table 6.4), but their existence alone casts doubt on the accuracy of the entire performance appraisal.

Behaviorally Anchored Discipline Scales

A unique method for appraising discipline problems was recently developed by Kearney and Whitaker (1988). The **Behaviorally Anchored Discipline Scales (BADS)** that Kearney and Whitaker developed contain three scales: misconduct (fighting, absenteeism), repeat offense, and discipline. BADS are designed in similar fashion to those scales used by most state motor vehicle departments and private insurance companies. For example, each violation (speeding ticket, accident, and so on) is worth a certain number of points. Upon accumulation of a certain number of points, the driver loses her license.

The advantages to BADS are that they specify the types of unacceptable employee behaviors that must be dealt with as they occur; the scales

Table 6.4
Revised Scoring System for Mixed Standard Scales

Statement Type			
Good	Average	Poor	Dimension Score
+	+	+	7
0	+	+	6
+	+	0	6
+	0	+	6
−	+	+	5
+	+	−	5
+	0	0	5
+	−	+	5
0	+	0	5
0	0	+	5
−	+	+	5
−	0	+	4
+	0	−	4
+	−	0	4
0	+	−	4
0	0	0	4
0	−	+	4
−	+	0	4
−	−	+	3
+	−	−	3
0	0	−	3
0	−	0	3
−	+	−	3
−	−	+	3
−	0	0	3
−	−	0	2
0	−	−	2
−	0	−	2
−	−	−	1

Source: Adapted from Saal (1979).

thus serve as an objective way to provide specific consequences for unacceptable behaviors. The scales provided by Kearney and Whitaker are rather limited, but the idea appears to warrant further research and development.

Evaluation of Methods

In the previous pages, several methods for evaluating employee performance have been offered. Of course, we might now ask, "Is any one of these methods the best?" Probably not (Jacobs, Kafry, & Zedeck, 1980;

Kingstrom & Bass, 1981; Schwab et al., 1975). Research has shown that more complicated techniques such as BARS, forced choice scales, and mixed standard scales are only occasionally superior to the inexpensive and uncomplicated graphic rating scale (Giffin, 1989; Guion & Gibson, 1988). In fact, behavioral anchors sometimes bias supervisors' ratings by forcing them to concentrate on specific behaviors (Murphy & Constans, 1987). And yet graphic rating scales are seldom superior to these more complicated rating methods.

Although the more complicated techniques are only slightly more psychometrically sound, they still have some advantages over graphic rating scales. Because employees are directly involved in creating techniques such as BARS, they tend to see performance-evaluation results as being more fair. Furthermore, many supervisors who make such ratings prefer many of the more complicated behavioral approaches (Dickenson & Zellinger, 1980). Finally, feedback from BARS may lead to greater increases in future performance than feedback from graphic rating scales (Hom, DeNisi, Kinicki, & Bannister, 1982).

Alternative Rating Methods

Peer Rating

As discussed early in this chapter, only a small portion of an employee's behavior actually is observed by a supervisor. As depicted in Figure 6.10, the majority of behavior is performed either alone or in the presence of peers, subordinates, or customers. Thus, an accurate performance appraisal may need to include evaluations by significant others such as peers.

Research has shown that peer ratings are fairly reliable only when the peers who make the ratings are similar to and well acquainted with the employees being rated (Landy & Guion, 1970; Mumford, 1983). Most important, peer ratings have been successful in predicting the future success of promoted employees; they also tend to correlate highly with supervisor ratings (Cedarbloom, 1989). But even though peer ratings appear promising, few organizations use them (DeNisi, Randolph, & Blencoe, 1983; Lazer & Wikstrom, 1977).

Figure 6.10
Who Observes
Employee
Performance

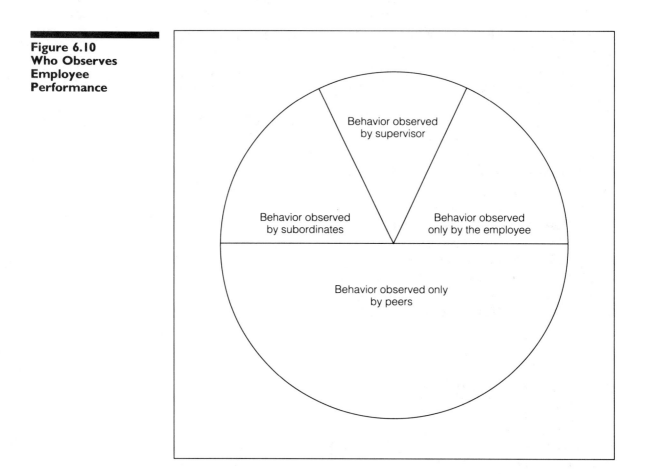

Self-Appraisal

Allowing an employee to evaluate her own behavior and performance is a performance-appraisal technique used by 12% of a sample of organizations (Lazer & Wikstrom, 1977). Research on self-appraisal, however, has found what we might expect to find: Employee self-appraisals tend to suffer from leniency (Holzbach, 1978; Meyer, 1980) and only moderately correlate (.29) with actual performance (Mabe & West, 1982).

Self-appraisals of performance appear to be most accurate when the purpose of the self-appraisal is for either research or use in performance-appraisal review interviews rather than for such administrative purposes as raises or promotions (Bassett & Meyer, 1968) and when the employee believes that an objective record of his performance is available with which the supervisor can compare the self-appraisal (Farh & Werbel, 1986).

Customer and Subordinate Ratings

A third alternative to supervisor ratings is performance evaluation by subordinates or customers. Informally, such evaluations are common in the forms of customer complaints and employee criticisms. But, with the exception of students rating teachers, formal methods are neither common nor well regarded by managers (McEvoy, 1988). Subordinate ratings may be more practical than customer ratings, but both probably provide insight into an employee's behavior that is not observed by peers or supervisors. Unfortunately, little research is available that indicates the reliability or accuracy of such ratings.

Problems in Evaluating Employees

Rating Errors

Distribution Errors

A common type of error in evaluating employee performance involves the distribution of ratings on a rating scale; such errors are known as **distribution errors.** One kind of distribution error is called **leniency error** because certain raters tend to rate every employee at the upper end of the scale, regardless of the actual performance of the employee.

A related error is **central tendency error,** which results in a supervisor rating every employee in the middle of the scale. Still another error, **strictness error,** rates every employee at the low end of the scale.

These types of errors pose problems for an organization because two employees doing equal work will receive different ratings if one employee is supervised by a lenient rater and another by a strict rater. This problem can be eliminated partly by having several people rate each employee (Kane & Lawler, 1979), although this is not often feasible, especially in small branch offices with only one manager or supervisor.

Halo Errors

A **halo error** occurs when a rater allows either a single attribute or an overall impression of an individual to affect the ratings that she makes on each relevant job dimension. For example, a teacher might think that a student is highly articulate. Because of that, the teacher might rate the student as being intelligent and industrious when, in fact, the student's student's articulateness to cloud her judgment of the student's other abilities. Halo effects occur especially when the rater has little knowledge of the job and is less familiar with the person being rated (Kozlowski, Kirsch, & Chao, 1986).

Usually, halo error is statistically determined by correlating the ratings for each dimension with those for the other dimensions. If they are highly correlated, halo error is often said to have occurred. But several industrial psychologists have argued that many times consistent ratings across several dimensions indicate not error but actual employee performance. Thus a teacher who is rated highly in classroom teaching, ability to work with students, knowledge, and fairness of grading actually may excel in those things. But proponents of the halo effect explanation would argue that the instructor is friendly and so well liked by her students that she receives high ratings on the other dimensions when, in fact, she may not have shown a high level of knowledge in her subject matter.

Halo errors may or may not be a serious problem, but they can be reduced by having supervisors rate each trait at separate times. That is, the supervisor might rate the employee on attendance one day and then rate him on dependability the next day (Cooper, 1981a, 1981b). Examples of halo, leniency, and strictness errors are shown in Figure 6.11.

Proximity Errors

Proximity errors occur when a rating made on one dimension affects the rating made on the dimension that immediately follows it on the rating scale. The difference between this error and halo error is in both the cause of the error and the number of dimensions that are affected. With halo error, all dimensions are affected by an overall impression of the employee. With proximity error, only the dimensions physically located nearest a particular dimension on the rating scale are affected; the reason for the effect, in fact, *is* the close physical proximity of the dimension rather than an overall impression.

Contrast Errors

As you'll remember we discussed the employment interview in Chapter 4. There we learned that the performance rating that one person receives can be influenced by the performance of a previously evaluated person. For example, a bank manager has six employees who are evaluated twice a year—on February 5 and again on August 5. The manager makes the evaluations in alphabetical order, starting with Joan Adams and then going

Figure 6.11
Examples of Rating Errors

Leniency Error

Norm Nixon						Walt Davis					
Cooperation	1	2	3	4	⑤	Cooperation	1	2	3	4	⑤
Knowledge	1	2	3	4	⑤	Knowledge	1	2	3	4	⑤
Leadership	1	2	3	4	⑤	Leadership	1	2	3	4	⑤

Earvin Johnson						John Lucas					
Cooperation	1	2	3	4	⑤	Cooperation	1	2	3	4	⑤
Knowledge	1	2	3	4	⑤	Knowledge	1	2	3	4	⑤
Leadership	1	2	3	4	⑤	Leadership	1	2	3	4	⑤

Strictness Error

Norm Nixon						Walt Davis					
Cooperation	①	2	3	4	5	Cooperation	①	2	3	4	5
Knowledge	①	2	3	4	5	Knowledge	①	2	3	4	5
Leadership	①	2	3	4	5	Leadership	①	2	3	4	5

Earvin Johnson						John Lucas					
Cooperation	①	2	3	4	5	Cooperation	①	2	3	4	5
Knowledge	①	2	3	4	5	Knowledge	①	2	3	4	5
Leadership	①	2	3	4	5	Leadership	①	2	3	4	5

Halo Error

Norm Nixon						Walt Davis					
Cooperation	1	2	3	4	⑤	Cooperation	1	2	③	4	5
Knowledge	1	2	3	4	⑤	Knowledge	1	2	③	4	5
Leadership	1	2	3	4	⑤	Leadership	1	2	③	4	5

Earvin Johnson						John Lucas					
Cooperation	1	2	3	4	⑤	Cooperation	①	2	3	4	5
Knowledge	1	2	3	4	⑤	Knowledge	①	2	3	4	5
Leadership	1	2	3	4	⑤	Leadership	①	2	3	4	5

to Frank Carr. Joan Adams is the best employee that the bank has ever had, and she receives the highest possible rating on each dimension. After evaluating Adams, the manager then evaluates Carr. When compared to Adams, Carr is not nearly as effective an employee. Thus, Carr receives lower ratings than he might normally receive simply because he has been evaluated immediately after Adams and his performance has been contrasted to Adams's performance rather than to some objective standard.

Such **contrast errors** also can occur between separate performance evaluations of the same person. That is, the ratings received on one performance appraisal will affect the ratings made on an appraisal six months later. For example, an employee's performance during the first six months of the year is "outstanding," and she receives outstanding performance ratings. For some reason, the employee's actual behavior in the next six months is only "good." What type of performance ratings will she receive? Based on the results of a study by Murphy, Gannett, Herr, and Chen (1986), the answer probably is that her ratings will be less than "good." In contrast to her initial excellent performance, the employee's subsequent performance (which may indeed have been "good") appeared to be lower than it actually was.

Smither, Reilly, and Buda (1988) found that contrast effects occur only when the person making the evaluation actually sees the employee perform during both rating periods. Even if a new supervisor reads that an employee's previous evaluations were excellent but she observes poor performance by the employee, she probably will continue to give excellent ratings—even though the employee's performance deteriorated. Smither and his colleagues call this rating error **assimilation.**

Training Raters to Reduce Errors

One way to reduce the number of rating errors is to train the people who will be making the performance evaluations (Spool, 1978). Research has indicated that training supervisors to become aware of the various rating errors and how to avoid them often increases accuracy (Smither, Barry, & Reilly, 1989), reduces leniency and halo errors (Bernardin & Buckley, 1981; Fay & Latham, 1982), increases the validity of tests validated against the ratings (Pursell, Dossett, & Latham, 1980), and increases employee satisfaction with the ratings (Ivancevich, 1982). This is especially true when the training technique uses discussion, practice in rating, and feedback about rating accuracy rather than lecture (Smith, 1986). These training effects, however, are short-lived unless additional training and feedback are provided, and they can even reduce the accuracy of ratings by substituting new errors (Bernardin & Pence, 1980).

The effectiveness of rater training also is a function of training format. Raters who receive frame-of-reference training make fewer rating errors and recall more training information than do untrained raters or raters only receiving information about job-related behaviors (Athey & McIntyre, 1987). **Frame-of-reference training** provides raters with job-related information, practice in rating, and examples of ratings made by experts as well as the rationale behind those expert ratings (Hauenstein & Foti, 1989; McIntyre, Smith & Hassett, 1984). Box 6.1 provides a good outline for a short rater training course that was developed by Sims, Veres, and Heninger (1987).

Sampling Problems

Recency Effect

Performance appraisals are typically conducted every six months, or biannually. The evaluation is designed to cover all of the behaviors that have taken place during the previous six months. Research has demonstrated, however, that recent behaviors are given more weight in the performance evaluation than behaviors that occurred during the first few months of the evaluation period. Such an effect penalizes workers who performed well during most of the period but tailed off toward the end, and it rewards workers who save their best work until just before the evaluation.

In baseball, the Los Angeles Dodgers had several poor seasons in which they lost many games early in the season, which eliminated them from pennant contention. But several players played well and produced great statistics during the final month of the season; the press called this

---

Box 6.1

Outline of a Short Performance-Appraisal Workshop

I. What is performance appraisal?
   A. Purpose
   B. Is this purpose contradictory?

II. How can performance appraisal improve performance?
   A. Necessary preconditions for effective performance
   B. Role of performance appraisal in achieving necessary preconditions

III. Why is performance appraisal so unpleasant?
   A. Negative feedback
   B. Lack of data
   C. Lack of communication

IV. How can performance-appraisal systems overcome unpleasantness?
   A. By focusing on task performance
   B. By demanding employee–supervisor interaction

V. Performance-appraisal documentation
   A. Back-up documentation for appraisals
   B. Notes
   C. Why document?

VI. Creating performance-appraisal documentation
   A. Task statements
   B. Writing performance standards

VII. Exercises
   A. Advantages to precise description
   B. Communication coaching
   C. Performance-appraisal interview
   D. Conclusions

VIII. Summary and wrap-up
   A. What do you do now that the workshop is over?
   B. Why bother?

Source: Sims, R. R., Veres, J. G., & Heninger, S. M. (1987). Training appraisers: An orientation program for improving supervisory performance ratings. *Public Personnel Management, 16,* 37–46. Reprinted with permission of the authors.

---

period the "salary drive" as opposed to the "pennant drive." This suggests that the players may have been aware of the **recency effect.** They hoped that high performance before contracts were renewed would bring better evaluations and thus higher salaries for the next year.

Infrequent Observation

As shown back in Figure 6.10, another problem that affects performance appraisals is that many managers or supervisors do not have the opportunity to observe a representative sample of employee behavior (Borman, 1978). **Infrequent observation** occurs for two reasons. First, managers are often so busy with their own work that they often have no time to "walk the floor" and observe their employees' behavior. Instead, they make inferences based on completed work or employee personality traits (Feldman, 1981). A good example involves a teacher who completes a reference form for a student. Reference forms commonly ask about characteristics such as the applicant's ability to cooperate or to get along with others. The teacher must base her evaluation on the term papers that she has seen and the student's test grades. Rarely does she have the opportunity to watch the student "get along with" or "cooperate with others." Instead, she surmises that because a group project was turned in on time and received an excellent grade, the student must have cooperated and gotten along well with other group members.

Employees often act differently around a supervisor than around other workers, which is the second reason why managers usually do not make candid observations. When the supervisor is absent, an employee may break rules, show up late, or work slowly. But when the boss is around, the employee becomes a model worker. In the eyes of the supervisor, the employee is doing an excellent job; the other workers, however, know better.

This problem can be alleviated somewhat by having several raters evaluate the employee. Other raters can be other supervisors, fellow workers (peer ratings), and even customers. A meta-analysis conducted by Harris and Schaubroeck (1988) indicated that supervisor ratings on the average correlate .62 with peer ratings. Thus, even though the two groups tend to agree with one another, the agreement is certainly not perfect.

Unfortunately, ratings from these sources often are subject to more errors than the uninformed ratings made by a supervisor. For example, customers may complain about a worker even though she is following policy; and a worker may provide low evaluations of her co-workers so that she will receive a higher raise. Even with these problems, multiple raters remain a good idea.

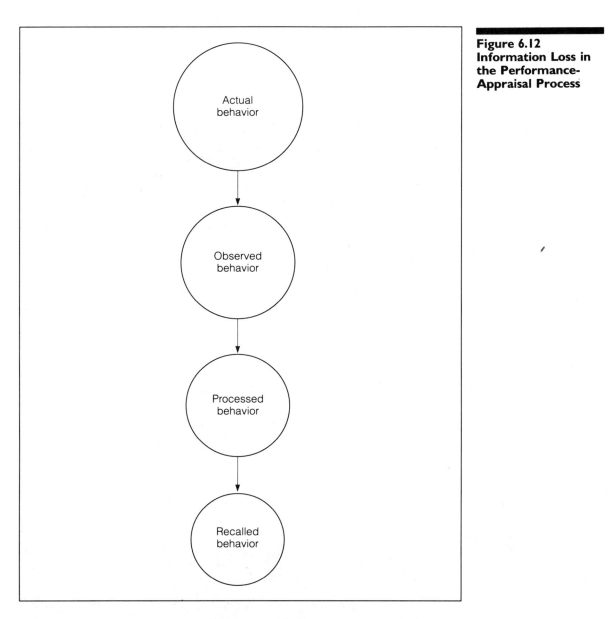

Figure 6.12
Information Loss in
the Performance-
Appraisal Process

Cognitive Processing of Observed Behavior

Observation of Behavior

As Figures 6.12 and 6.13 show, just because an employee's behavior is
observed does not guarantee that it will be properly remembered or recalled during the performance-appraisal review. In fact, research (Cooper,
1981a; Feldman, 1981) indicates that raters recall those behaviors that
are consistent with their general impression of an employee (a halo). And

257

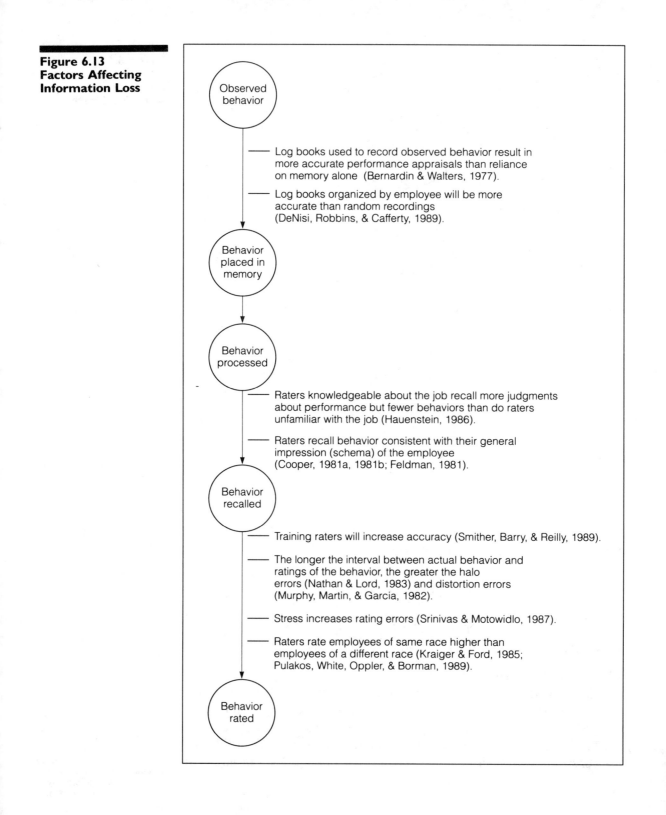

**Figure 6.13
Factors Affecting
Information Loss**

Observed behavior

—— Log books used to record observed behavior result in more accurate performance appraisals than reliance on memory alone (Bernardin & Walters, 1977).

—— Log books organized by employee will be more accurate than random recordings (DeNisi, Robbins, & Cafferty, 1989).

Behavior placed in memory

Behavior processed

—— Raters knowledgeable about the job recall more judgments about performance but fewer behaviors than do raters unfamiliar with the job (Hauenstein, 1986).

—— Raters recall behavior consistent with their general impression (schema) of the employee (Cooper, 1981a, 1981b; Feldman, 1981).

Behavior recalled

—— Training raters will increase accuracy (Smither, Barry, & Reilly, 1989).

—— The longer the interval between actual behavior and ratings of the behavior, the greater the halo errors (Nathan & Lord, 1983) and distortion errors (Murphy, Martin, & Garcia, 1982).

—— Stress increases rating errors (Srinivas & Motowidlo, 1987).

—— Raters rate employees of same race higher than employees of a different race (Kraiger & Ford, 1985; Pulakos, White, Oppler, & Borman, 1989).

Behavior rated

the greater the time interval between the actual behavior and the performance rating, the greater the probability that halo errors (Nathan & Lord, 1983) and distortion errors (Murphy, Martin, & Garcia, 1982) occur. Furthermore, raters who are familiar with the job being evaluated recall more judgments about performance but fewer behaviors than do raters who are unfamiliar with the job (Harriman & Kovach, 1987; Hauenstein, 1986).

But even though memory-based ratings lead to more distortion, in many circumstances they are more accurate than ratings made immediately after the behaviors occur (Murphy & Balzer, 1986). The reason for these increases in halo and accuracy is not yet clear. Supervisors perhaps realize that it will be a long interval between observation of employee behavior and the formal evaluation of that behavior and that they will not be able (without great effort or the use of log books) to remember specific behaviors. Thus, they form an overall impression of the employee and an overall impression of an ideal and a poor employee and evaluate the employee based on comparison with the ideal.

Problems in Rating Behavior

Stress The amount of **stress** under which a supervisor operates also affects her performance ratings. Srinivas and Motowidlo (1987) found that raters who were placed in a stressful situation produced ratings with more errors than did raters who were not under stress. This finding is important because performance evaluations are often conducted hurriedly as supervisors evaluate employee performance so that they can return to their "real" work. Methods for reducing this problem will be discussed later in this chapter.

Affect Raters who like the person being rated may be more lenient (Adams & DeLucca, 1987) and less accurate in rating employees than are raters who neither like nor dislike their employees (Cardy & Dobbins, 1986). But this does not mean that a person who is liked will always receive higher ratings than someone who is disliked. The rater may overcompensate in an effort to be "fair." The rater's feelings, or **affect,** toward an employee may interfere with the cognitive processing of actual performance information.

Racial Bias Research also has indicated that **racial bias** exists in performance evaluations. Kraiger and Ford (1985) conducted a meta-analysis of 74 studies and found that white raters gave higher performance ratings to white employees and that black raters gave higher ratings to black employees. Interestingly, this bias occurred only with studies involving real organizations. Laboratory research seldom reveals racial bias in rating.

The Performance-Appraisal Interview

The beginning of this chapter observed that perhaps the most important use of performance-evaluation data is in providing feedback to the employee and assessing his strengths and weaknesses so that further training can be implemented. Although this feedback and training should be an on-going process, the semiannual evaluation might be the best time to formally discuss employee performance. Furthermore, holding a formal review interview places the organization on better legal ground in the event of a lawsuit (Field & Holley, 1982).

The norm in most organizations is for a supervisor to spend a few minutes with an employee every six months to *tell* him about the scores he received during the most recent evaluation period. This process is probably the norm because most managers do not like to judge others; because of this dislike, they try to complete the evaluation process as quickly as possible (McGregor, 1957; Rapp, 1978).

Furthermore, seldom does evaluating employees benefit the supervisor (Rapp, 1978; Whisler, 1958). The best scenario is to hear no complaints and the worst scenario is a lawsuit. In fact, one study demonstrated that dissatisfaction and a decrease in organizational commitment occurs even when an employee receives an evaluation that is "satisfactory" but not "outstanding" (Pearce & Porter, 1986). Finally, in the "tell and sell" approach to performance-appraisal interviews, a supervisor "tells" an employee everything she has done poorly and then "sells" her on the ways in which she can improve. This method, however, accomplishes little.

Research suggests that certain techniques can be used to make the performance-appraisal interview more effective: time, scheduling, and preparation.

Allocating Time

Both the supervisor and the employee must have time to prepare for the review interview. Both should be allowed at least one hour to prepare before an interview and at least one hour for the interview itself.

Scheduling the Interview

The interview location should be in a neutral place that ensures privacy and allows the supervisor and employee to face one another without a desk between them as a communication barrier (King, 1984). Performance-appraisal review interviews should be scheduled at least once every six months for most employees and more often for new employees. Review interviews are commonly scheduled six months after an employee begins working for the organization. If this date comes at a bad time (such as during the Christmas season, a busy time for retail stores), the interview should be scheduled for a more convenient time.

Preparing for the Interview

While preparing for the interview, the supervisor should review the ratings she has assigned to the employee and the reasons for those ratings. This step is important because the quality of feedback given to employees will affect their satisfaction with the entire performance-appraisal process (Mount, 1983). Furthermore, employees perceive and react to the amount of time that a supervisor prepares for the interview (King, 1984).

Meanwhile, the employee should rate her own performance using the same format as the supervisor (Laumeyer & Beebe, 1988). The employee also should write down specific reasons and examples that support the ratings she gives herself.

During the Interview

At the outset of the interview, the supervisor should communicate: (1) the role of performance appraisal—that making decisions about salary increases and terminations is not its only purpose; (2) how the performance appraisal was conducted; and (3) how the evaluation process was accomplished. It is advisable that the supervisor also communicate her own feelings about the performance-appraisal process (Kelly, 1984).

The review process is probably best begun with the employee communicating her own ratings and her justification for those ratings (King, 1984). Research indicates that employees who are actively involved in the interview from the start will be more satisfied with the results (Burke, Weitzel, & Weir, 1978; Maier, 1976).

The supervisor then communicates her ratings and the reasons for them. The supervisor should limit this communication to statements about behavior and performance rather than traits that are or are not possessed by the employee (Ilgen, Mitchell, & Fredrickson, 1981). Of course, it would be nice to provide only positive feedback because employees then

261

Figure 6.14
Factors Affecting
Performance

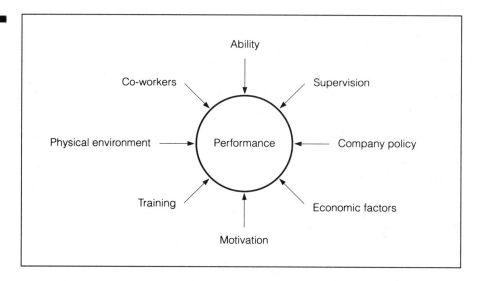

are more satisfied with their reviews (Dipboye & dePontbriad, 1981) and often develop negative attitudes toward management if feedback is negative (Gabris & Mitchell, 1988). But few employees are perfect, and some negative feedback is inevitable. Because of this, positive feedback generally should be given first (Stone, Gueutal, & McIntosh, 1984) because employees are likely to try avoiding negative feedback in order to maintain a positive self-image (Larson, 1989). Any major differences between the employee's self-ratings and those given by the supervisor should be discussed until both understand the differences.

The next step is perhaps the most important. Because few employees receive perfect evaluations, it is essential to discuss the reasons why an employee's performance is not considered to be perfect. The employee may lack some knowledge as to how to perform the job properly, may have been assigned too many duties, or may have outside problems that affect her work performance.

Acknowledging that there may be external reasons for an employee's poor performance can increase satisfaction with the review and allow the employee to perceive the feedback and evaluation as accurate and helpful and to understand and appreciate the supervisor's perceptions (Bannister, 1986; Baron, 1988).

Once the problems have been identified, the next and most difficult task is to find solutions to the problems (Nanry, 1988). What can the supervisor do to help? What can the organization do? What can the employee do? The idea here is that solutions to the problems result from joint effort. Too often, we attribute poor performance as being solely the fault of the employee, when, in fact, performance is affected by many factors (see Figure 6.14).

At the conclusion of the interview, goals should be set for future performance and behavior, and both supervisor and employee should understand how these goals will be met (Cedarbloom, 1982). Goals and goal setting will be thoroughly discussed in Chapter 9. For now, however, we should keep in mind that the goals should be concrete, reasonable (Brumback, 1988), and set by both employee and supervisor (Ivancevich, 1982).

Chapter Summary

This chapter has discussed the performance-appraisal process, which typically has five steps: (1) Determine the reasons for performance evaluation; (2) create an instrument to evaluate performance; (3) explain the system to those who will use it; (4) evaluate employee performance; and (5) review the results of the evaluation with the employee.

The reasons for evaluating employee performance are not limited to compensation and promotion decisions. Evaluations also can be used for training, needs assessment, and personnel research.

The criteria used to evaluate employee performance must be job-related (relevant), free from outside sources of contamination, and congruent with the organization's needs. If ratings are used, care must be taken to prevent common rating errors such as leniency, central tendency, strictness, halo, proximity, contrast, recency, and infrequent observation of behavior. Training raters to avoid these errors will have only short-term benefits unless the training is repeated.

Employees can be evaluated in many ways. Objective criteria include work quantity, work quality, attendance, and safety. Subjective criteria include: employee-comparison methods of ranking, paired comparisons, and forced distribution; critical incidents; and rating scales such as Behaviorally Anchored Rating Scales (BARS), Behavioral Observation Scales (BOS), forced choice scales, and mixed standard scales.

After employees have been evaluated, it is essential that the supervisor discuss the evaluations. Important factors in the success of this discussion include scheduling the review to eliminate or minimize interruptions, letting the employee discuss her feelings and thoughts, and setting goals for improvements in future performance.

Glossary

Affect Feelings or emotion

Assimilation A type of rating error in which raters base their rating of an employee during one rating period on the ratings that they gave the employee in a previous rating period

Behavioral Observation Scales (BOS) A method of performance appraisal in which supervisors rate how often they have observed an employee perform a series of specific behaviors

Behaviorally Anchored Discipline Scales (BADS) A standardized rating scale that can be used to evaluate employee misconduct

Behaviorally Anchored Rating Scales (BARS) A method of performance appraisal involving the placement of benchmark behaviors next to each point on a graphic rating scale

Central tendency error A type of rating error in which a rater consistently rates all employees in the middle of the scale regardless of their actual levels of performance

Composite The combining of several different criterion scores into one score

Congruent The quality of being consistent or in agreement

Contamination The condition in which a criterion score is affected by things other than those under the control of the employee

Contrast error A type of rating error in which the rating of the performance level of one employee affects the ratings given to the next employee being rated

Critical incidents A method of performance appraisal in which the supervisor records employee behaviors that were observed on the job and rates the employee based on that record

Desirability The extent to which a trait or behavior is valued as being good in society

Discriminability The extent to which there will be a wide variety of scores on a criterion measure

Distribution errors Rating errors in which a rater will use only a certain part of a rating scale when evaluating employee performance

Employee Performance Record A standardized use of the critical incident technique developed at General Motors

Errors Deviations from a standard of quality

Forced choice rating scales A method of performance appraisal in which a supervisor is given several behaviors and is forced to choose which of the behaviors is most typical of the employee

Forced distribution A performance-appraisal method in which a predetermined percentage of employees are placed into a number of performance categories

Frame-of-reference training A method of training raters in which the rater is provided with job-related information, a chance to practice ratings, examples of ratings made by experts, and the rationale behind the expert ratings

Graphic rating scale A method of performance appraisal that involves rating employee performance on an interval or ratio scale

Halo error A type of rating error that occurs when raters allow either a single attribute or an overall impression of an individual to affect the ratings that they make on each relevant job dimension

Hard criteria Measures of work performance such as quantity and quality that are thought to be reliable and objective

Infrequent observation The idea that supervisors do not see most of an employee's behavior

Leniency error A type of rating error in which a rater consistently gives all employees high ratings, regardless of their actual levels of performance

Mixed Standard Scale A method of performance appraisal in which a supervisor reads the description of a specific behavior and then decides if the behavior of the employee is better than, equal to, or poorer than the behavior described

Multiple criteria Two or more separate criteria that are used as part of the performance-appraisal system

Paired comparison A form of ranking in which a group of employees to be ranked are compared one pair at a time

Performance-appraisal review A meeting between a supervisor and a subordinate for the purpose of discussing performance appraisal results

Peter Principle The idea that organizations tend to promote good employees until they reach the level at which they are not competent—in other words, their highest level of incompetence

Prototype The overall image that a supervisor has of an employee

Proximity error A type of rating error in which a rating made on one dimension influences the rating made on the dimension that immediately follows it on the rating scale

Quality A type of objective criteria used to measure job performance by comparing a job behavior with a standard

Quantity A type of objective criteria used to measure job performance by counting the number of relevant job behaviors that occur

Racial bias The tendency to give members of a particular race lower evaluation ratings than are justified by their actual performance, or to give members of one race lower ratings than members of another race

Rank order A method of performance appraisal in which employees are ranked in order from best to worst

Recency effect The tendency for supervisors to recall and place more weight on recent behaviors when they evaluate performance

Relevance The extent to which a criterion is related to the job

Reliability The extent to which criterion scores are stable and free from error

Soft criteria Measures of work performance such as supervisor ratings that require subjective judgment on the part of the rater

Standard deviation A statistic that indicates the variation of scores in a distribution

Stress Perceived psychological pressure

Strictness error A type of rating error in which a rater consistently gives all employees low ratings, regardless of their actual levels of performance

Jacques Charles/Stock Boston

7

Designing and Evaluating
Training Systems

Employee performance can be improved in many ways. In Chapters 4 and 5, we learned that employee-selection procedures can bring higher employee performance. But as we also learned in Chapter 3, employee selection is not an effective way to improve productivity in situations in which only a few applicants compete for a large number of openings or when a job involves only easily learned tasks.

When these situations are encountered, *training* techniques rather than selection techniques must be emphasized (Kramm & Kramm, 1988). For example, this author once was involved in a project designed to develop a selection system for hiring intramural basketball officials. Although we were successful in finding a test that correlated significantly with referee performance, we ran into a problem with the selection ratio. The intramural department needed 35 referees each year, but only had 30 applicants. Thus, the selection test could not be used because the intramural department had to hire everyone who applied. The logical solution was to extensively train the referees who did apply.

This does not mean that training should be emphasized only when selection techniques are not appropriate. Instead, training should be used in conjunction with the selection systems discussed in Chapters 4 and 5 and with the motivational techniques that will be discussed in a later chapter.

Collectively, organizations realize the importance of training by spending more than $29 billion on it each year (Feuer, 1987a). Vice-presidents of training earn an average of $89,500 and executive-level training managers earn an average of more than $52,000 a year, while the average annual salary for a corporate trainer is more than $30,000 (Beatty, 1989; Feuer, 1987a; McMillan & Walters, 1988). The job of a trainer is depicted in the employment profile of Donna Lewis.

Needs Analysis

Conducting a **needs analysis** is the first step in developing a training system for employees (Schneier, Guthrie, & Olian, 1988). As its name implies, needs analysis is the process of determining the training needs for the organization. As shown in Figure 7.1, three types of needs analysis are typically conducted: organizational analysis, task analysis, and person analysis.

Employment Profile

Donna Lewis, M.S.
Training Representative
Radford Army Arsenal Plant

Presently, I am a training representative at a major propellant-manufacturing plant and have worked in this position for four years.

Our training department is service-oriented as we receive and respond to requests for training programs from various departments in the plant. Although most of our training classes are the result of a department request, some are mandated by the government, by law, or both. Our overall responsibility is to develop training material and then actually train each plant employee from the plant manager on down.

The duties of a training representative are varied and sometimes cover a wide range of activities. We are responsible for scheduling and coordinating classes with production and shift schedules. Other responsibilities include keeping training records, requesting duplicating services for our course materials, putting training manuals together, and corresponding with employees, supervisors, and outside training vendors. We also are required to attend classes and seminars on and off the plant site. Sometimes, I even make coffee.

For the last three years my assignment has been to design, develop, and implement training programs for a specific plant-modernization project. This project includes upgrading operations and constructing new facilities to automate the present manufacturing system. Because modernizing a plant involves many changes in the way in which work is performed, employees need to be retrained. This particular training program is targeted toward the operating and supervisory personnel. To achieve the best training results, I work closely on this project with another training representative and interact directly with the Project Manager, top production management, project engineers, procedure writers, and various other project personnel.

The process for developing training materials requires several preliminary research activities such as reviewing documents and technical manuals, interviewing on-plant topic experts, and touring appropriate production areas and operations. Once the research is complete, the unit of information is divided into lessons complete with evaluations as required. Sometimes, this also includes a hands-on oral examination. A lesson plan and course outline also are developed.

We decided to incorporate database management into the development of our training materials, and thus the computer has been the center of our materials development. Information about equipment and operations is gathered and then entered into a database using a software package designed to meet our needs. Using a database allows us to manipulate the data as needed.

Using this information and the plant-operating procedures, we write a technical manual for classroom use. Classes usually are conducted on the daylight shift and may last for five to ten days. These classes are conducted in the training building and at the job site.

Some of the training programs we have developed also incorporate interactive video by using a computerized system with a touch screen monitor and laser disc player. These programs are produced by the plant's media services department. We develop our own video scripts and shot descriptions. The video is taped on plant at the job site using plant personnel. Only the laser disc itself is produced off-plant. The trainees have been very receptive to these presentations, proving them to be a successful training tool. From a personal perspective, these programs are fun because the trainer acts as producer, writer, and director. Look out, Hollywood!

Working for the training department of a large manufacturing industry that also is government-owned has been an enlightening experience as well as hard work. When I came to work here, I soon discovered that in the actual workplace the theories discussed in texts such as this one only work part of the time. I had to learn to be flexible.

Inevitably, some stress occurs from demanding deadlines and conflicts between what may be wanted and what may be needed. The day-to-day contact with colleagues and trainees helps, but what really makes me feel good is when trainees say they enjoyed the course, learned a lot, and cannot wait to practice what they learned on the job. As with most jobs in the I/O area, mine requires excellent skills in both writing and public speaking.

Figure 7.1
The Needs-Analysis
Process

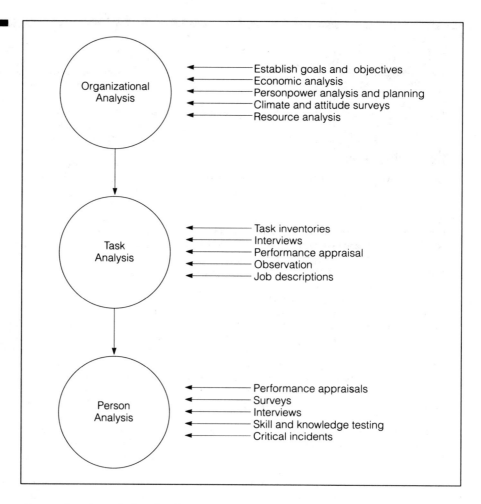

Organizational Analysis

The purpose of **organizational analysis** is to determine those organizational factors that either facilitate or inhibit training effectiveness. For example, an organization may view training as being important but may not have the money to properly fund its training programs. Or an organization may not wish to spend money on training because employees leave the organization after a short period of time. Thus, training will only be effective if the organization is willing to provide a supportive climate for training, if it can afford an effective program, and if the goals of a program are consistent with those of the organization.

Task	How Task Is Learned	
Answer customer questions about rates	Daily rate charts	**Table 7.1**
Process customer transactions	Basic teller training	**Comparing Task**
Calm irate customers		**Analysis Results with**
Check loan applications for accuracy	Loan-processing course	**Training Programs**
Ask customers to complete VISA applications		
Input customer transactions into computer	Basic teller training	
Answer customer questions about services	Basic teller training	

Task Analysis

If the results of the organizational analysis indicate that a positive organizational climate for training exists, the next step is to conduct a **task analysis.** A task analysis involves using the job analysis methods discussed in Chapter 2 to obtain information about the job itself as well as the overall performance of the employees who are responsible for each of the tasks (Sims, Veres, & Heninger, 1989).

Part of this process is determining whether there is a training program for each important task. For example, the hypothetical bank in Table 7.1 needs to develop training courses in both dealing with difficult customers and cross-selling.

Task analysis is important because training will only be effective if it addresses an area in which employees are weak. That is, if every employee in the organization already is proficient at using the computer system, providing training in computer use probably would not greatly enhance performance. Likewise, if the organization is not aware of a particular training need and thus does not provide training in that area, employee performance will be less than optimal (Gent & Dell'Omo, 1989).

To determine training needs from a job description, all tasks, knowledges, and task-required skills are evaluated to determine whether each is covered in some aspect of training or selection.

To illustrate, we will examine the job of a secretary. Obviously, tasks involving typing will be found throughout the job description. If we take just one of these tasks—typing internal memos—we can see that several knowledges and skills are involved: typing skills, knowledge of the word-processing package used by the company, knowledge of the computer used to do the word processing, and knowledge of the memo format used by the organization.

In all probability, the company will require a newly hired secretary to already possess typing skills; thus, learning how to type will not be a training need. Knowledge of the word-processing program may or may not be required at time of hire. If not required, then learning the program becomes a training need involving extensive training, while learning how to use a computer also becomes a training need (this training, however, should take only a short time). Finally, learning the memo format used by the organization is another training need but one with relatively little time required. With these needs in mind, the supervisor or the training officer must arrange for the new employee to receive training in the above areas.

Person Analysis

The third and final step in the needs-analysis process is determining which employees need training and in which areas (McGehee & Thayer, 1961). **Person analysis** is based on the recognition that not every employee needs further training for every task he performs. Thus, the purpose of person analysis is to use one or more of the following methods to determine the individual training needs for each employee: performance-appraisal scores, surveys, interviews, skill and knowledge tests, and critical incidents.

Performance-Appraisal Scores

Perhaps the easiest method of needs analysis is to use employees' **performance-appraisal scores.** Low ratings on a particular dimension for most employees may indicate that additional training in that dimension is needed. Conversely, if most employees score high on a particular dimension, relatively little training time is needed.

Table 7.2 provides an example of how performance-appraisal scores can be used. As can be seen, the employees as a whole need little training in loan processing or data entry, but they do need further training in cross-selling, customer relations, and keeping accurate teller drawers. But even though most employees can accurately process loans, Parish needs further training in this area; both Bird and Bagley probably can skip the training in teller drawer accuracy.

Although using performance-appraisal scores as a method of training-needs assessment appears fairly easy, two problems can interfere with their use. First, as discussed in the previous chapter, several types of rating errors can reduce the accuracy of performance-appraisal scores. The most relevant here are leniency errors and strictness errors. If the performance-appraisal scores are consistently high because of leniency

Performance Dimension	Employee					Average
	Bird	**McHale**	**Lewis**	**Parish**	**Bagley**	
Cross-selling	2	1	2	5	1	2.2
Loan processing	5	5	5	1	4	4.0
Data input accuracy	5	5	5	5	5	5.0
Customer relations	2	2	2	2	2	2.0
Teller drawer accuracy	5	3	1	2	5	3.2
Average	3.8	3.2	3.8	3.0	3.4	

**Table 7.2
Using Performance
Appraisal Scores for
Needs Analysis**

error, a human resource professional might make the erroneous conclusion that employees are proficient in a particular area and thus need no training. Likewise, consistently low scores might be interpreted as indicating a need for training when, in fact, the actual cause of the low scores is rater error.

The second problem involves the fact that situations in which all employees score either high or low on a dimension are rare. Instead, it is more common to find only a few employees scoring poorly. In this case, a person examining the average performance-appraisal scores might conclude that training in a particular dimension is unnecessary. But that conclusion would be only partially correct. True, not everyone needs training in that dimension, but concluding that training should not be conducted would be incorrect. The correct interpretation is that training should be conducted for the few employees who scored low for that dimension.

Surveys

The second common approach to determine training needs is by designing and administering a survey that asks employees what knowledges and skills they believe should be included in future training (Brinkerhoff, 1986). **Surveys** offer several advantages. First, they eliminate the problems of performance-rating errors that we discussed previously. Second, employees often know best their own strengths and weaknesses. Thus, to determine what an employee needs, ask him (Graham & Mihal, 1986). Finally, training needs can be determined with surveys even when the organization has not previously made an effort to design an effective performance-appraisal system or adequate job descriptions.

As with any type of survey, training-needs surveys can be conducted in many ways. The most common method is using a questionnaire that asks employees to list the areas in which they would like further training. Perhaps a better method was suggested by Graham and Mihal (1986): Provide a *list* of job-related tasks and knowledges and have the employees rate the need for training on each task and knowledge. The results of these ratings are given to supervisors, who then "validate" the results. This process is used both to determine whether the supervisors agree with their employees' perceptions and to prioritize training needs.

Interviews

The third method of needs analysis is the interview, which usually is done with a selected number of employees. Interviews are not used as extensively as surveys, but they can yield even more in-depth answers to questions about training needs (Donaldson & Scannell, 1986). The main advantage of interviews is that employee feelings and attitudes are revealed more clearly than with the survey approach. Their main disadvantage, of course, is that interview data are often difficult to quantify and analyze (Steadham, 1980).

Skill and Knowledge Tests

The fourth way to determine training needs is by administering a **skill test** or a **knowledge test.** Examples might include knowledge of lending laws for loan officers, knowledge of company policy for new employees, free-throw shooting for basketball players, or the dreaded mid-term exam for this course.

As with performance appraisals, if all employees score poorly on these tests, then training across the organization is indicated. If only a few employees score poorly, they are singled out for individual training. The greatest problem with testing as a needs-assessment method is that relatively few tests are available for this purpose. An organization that wants to use this method in all probability will have to construct its own tests— and proper test construction is time-consuming and expensive.

Critical Incidents

The fifth and final method for determining training needs is the Critical Incident Technique that was discussed in previous chapters. Although not a commonly used method, it will be discussed here because it is relatively easy to use, especially if a proper job analysis is available. To use this technique for needs assessment, the **critical incidents** are sorted into dimensions and separated into examples of good and poor performance as discussed in Chapter 2. Dimensions with many examples of poor performance are considered to be areas in which many employees are performing poorly and additional training is indicated (Glickman & Vallance, 1958).

Essentials of Adult Learning

Once training needs have been determined, the next step is deciding on which methods will be used to train the employees. But before methods are selected, we should understand the ways in which adults learn. We hope that much of this material will be familiar from a general psychology course.

Types of Learning

Operant Conditioning

Operant conditioning is one of the most important types of learning that is applied in employee training. Also called **behavior modification,** operant conditioning is based on the premise that humans learn to behave in ways that result in favorable outcomes, and not to behave in ways that result in unfavorable outcomes (Skinner, 1938; 1969).

Thus, if an employee is rewarded for certain types of behavior, the probability increases that he will continue to perform those behaviors. Likewise, if an employee is punished for certain types of behaviors, the probability decreases that he will perform those behaviors. Finally, if an employee is neither reinforced nor punished for a behavior, he will try other behaviors until he finds one that is reinforced.

Although the basic principles of operant conditioning are fairly simple, additional factors can modify the effectiveness of both reward and punishment.

Timing of the Consequence Research indicates that a *reinforcer* or a *punisher* is most effective if it occurs soon after the performance of the behavior. Unfortunately, if the **timing of the consequence** is too long, the effectiveness of operant conditioning in both training and other attempts to improve performance will be hindered. For example, if a restaurant employee is learning how to wait on tables, he performs many behaviors in the course of serving a customer. Not until the customers

When a waiter or waitress receives a tip, he or she cannot be sure which particular behavior during the course of the meal caused the customer to determine the size of the tip.

have left, however, does the waiter receive a tip. The size of the tip, of course, determines whether he has been rewarded or punished for his performance. If the tip is small, the employee is not sure which particular behavior caused the customers' displeasure. Likewise, if the tip is large, the employee is unsure which particular behavior or behaviors initiated the large tip.

Thus, for training involving operant conditioning to be most effective, the reward or punishment must be administered as closely after the behavior as possible. If it is not possible to immediately reward or punish a behavior, it should at least be made clear that the employee understands the behaviors that brought reward or punishment.

Contingency of Consequence To return to our example of the waiter, if he is told the reason for the size of his tip, he will better be able to change his behavior. Have you ever given a waiter or waitress a large tip even though the service was terrible? Most of us have. In so doing, however, the waiter or waitress is reinforced for poor performance and will have no incentive to improve unless poor performance has its own consequence. In a similar fashion, if the waiter had done an outstanding job but received a small tip, the probability of his repeating his outstanding performance is reduced.

The point of these examples is that reward and punishment must be made contingent upon performance; the **contingency of consequence** must be clear if learning is to occur. If the reward or punishment cannot be administered immediately, the employee must be told the purpose of the consequence so that the link between behavior and outcome is clear.

Type of Consequence The *type* of consequence is an important issue that we will also discuss in Chapter 10. It is obvious that different types of people like different types of rewards. For example, some employees value awards, others value praise, while still others most value money. Thus, for a reward to be effective, it must have value to an employee.

The same is true of punishment. Threatening an employee with a three-day suspension will only be effective if she needs the money or enjoys the work; yelling at an employee will only be effective if the employee does not like being yelled at; and threatening to not promote an employee will only be effective if the employee values promotions and perceives that she has a reasonable chance of being promoted.

Classical Conditioning

The second type of learning is **classical conditioning,** which was studied first by Pavlov. Classical conditioning's premise is that learning occurs through **association.** That is, when two events occur together in time, they are seen as belonging together.

An example of classical conditioning to which most people can relate involves the song on the car radio during a first date. For the next few months, every time the song is heard, the date is remembered. Another common example is the feeding of a dog or cat. When a can of pet food is opened with an electric opener, a pet often runs to where the can is being opened. The dog or cat has learned to associate the sound of the can opener with dinner.

In organizational training, however, classical conditioning probably is less important than operant conditioning. Still, classical conditioning does have a training role. Imagine a receptionist on his first day on the job. He has not yet mastered the phone system, and every time the phone rings and he must transfer a call, he becomes nervous and anxious. In the worst case, his anxiety will become associated with the ringing of the phone, and he may grow to dislike the phone enough to quit or to be rude to callers.

Modeling

Also called *social learning,* **modeling** is a vitally important method of learning for training in organizations. As the technique's name implies, employees learn by watching how other employees model a behavior. This is an important method of learning because it has such potential impact—both positive and negative.

For its positive effects, modeling is used in a specific training technique—behavior modeling—that will be described in more detail later in the chapter. Briefly here, the technique is used in a controlled setting, with employees observing proper work behavior and then practicing the behavior they observe. In less formal settings, employees observe good employees doing their jobs and then model that behavior.

Modeling as a learning technique is astoundingly pervasive. Think of how you first learned a sport such as baseball. You probably learned your batting stance by watching a favorite player. Why do you dress the way you do? You dress in your own way largely because you model the way your peers and idols dress.

As with other aspects of life, we are most likely to learn through modeling when we are unsure how to behave. For example, in our first days on a new job, we watch how others act. Do they take only the allotted time on breaks? Do they treat customers politely? Do they pay attention to their work? We learn how to behave at work by watching others so that we will fit in. A theory of job satisfaction that will be discussed in Chapter 10 hypothesizes that we even decide how satisfied we will be in our job by matching our level of job satisfaction with the levels exhibited by other employees.

As with operant conditioning, modeling is most effective under certain conditions. These conditions mainly involve characteristics of the employee whose behavior is being duplicated and the characteristics of the person attempting to model that performance.

Characteristics of the Model Of course, we do not model everyone else's behavior. Instead, we tend to model behavior of people who are *similar* to us, who are *successful,* and who have *status.* For example, if we are deciding what new clothes to purchase, who would we use as a model? If male, would we pick Farah Fawcett or Jimmy Carter? After all, both have status and have been successful. No, instead we would look for someone who is more similar to us both in gender and age.

Likewise, if we are going to model our batting stance after someone, who would it be? Almost certainly, we would choose someone in the major leagues because of their status and success. But which player would it be? It would not be one of the worst players in either league. Instead, we probably would choose someone such as Will Clark, Kirk Gibson, or another successful player. Finally, which successful player would it be? Probably the successful player who is most similar to us in terms of race, hair color, home town, position, and so on.

This raises an important point about models in industry. We tend to look for a model who is similar to us. For modeling to be effective, the appropriate role models for employees are similar to them in significant ways. That is why it is essential that a school faculty has both minority and female teachers, that a company has both minority and female managers, and that television shows portray all types of people in different occupational roles.

Characteristics of the Observer For an employee to model another's behavior, three conditions are necessary. First, the employee must pay *attention* to the behavior of other employees. All the role models in the world will be unable to effect a change in an employee's behavior if the employee pays no attention to the role model.

Second, the employee must be able to *retain* the information that is being modeled. Have you ever watched a person dance and then later tried the dance yourself? For most of us it is difficult to do if there are many steps to remember. Thus, even though we might have been paying close attention, there were too many behaviors to recall or retain. That is why training techniques that use modeling concentrate on only a few behaviors at a time.

Finally, the employee must have the ability or skill to *reproduce* the behavior that is seen. For example, I have watched the summer Olympics ever since I was a child. During the games, I have seen weightlifters lifting more than 400 pounds. But even though I have paid attention to their technique and can remember how they lift, I still cannot lift 400 pounds because I do not possess the strength to reproduce the behavior I have observed. Instead, I must content myself by watching the Olympics and performing 12-ounce Budweiser curls.

To use a work example, suppose that a new employee observes a veteran employee winding coils. If the new employee does not have the proper dexterity, technique alone will not allow the employee to be as successful as the veteran. Thus, it is important to limit the scope of the behaviors being modeled so that they are at a skill level that can be reproduced by the observing employee.

Other Essential Training Elements

In addition to those discussed above, other important elements in adult learning must be considered when creating a training program: transfer of training, massed versus distributed practice, incentives for learning, and feedback.

Transfer of Training

Research in learning has indicated that the more similar the training situation is to the actual job situation, the more effective training will be; in other words, the **transfer of training** will be greater. This principle is extremely important when a training program is being chosen or designed. For example, if a restaurant is training its employees how to wait on tables, the training will be more effective if the employees can practice in an environment that is similar to that encountered when they actually work. This realism might even include "customers" complaining and changing their orders.

Another example may be more meaningful if you have every competed in high school or college sports. During practice, teams try to simulate game conditions by performing in the same way they would expect to during a game. To enhance transfer of training, coaches have been known to have players wear the same colors as their opponents.

Another way to increase *positive* transfer of training is by having the trainee practice the desired behavior as much as possible. Such practice is especially important for tasks that will not be performed on a daily basis after training has been completed. For example, if a firefighter is learning to perform cardiopulmonary resuscitation (CPR), she must overlearn the task through constant practice. This **overlearning** is essential because it may be months before the firefighter will practice what she has learned.

In contrast, once our coil winder learns a task during training, it is time for him to move to another task. Overlearning is not necessary for the coil winder because he will perform the task every hour once training has been completed.

Chester Higgins, Jr./Photo Researchers, Inc. (NYC)

A firefighter, learning to give CPR, will overlearn the task through constant practice, as it may be months before he has a chance to put to use what he has learned.

The term "overlearning" as used above does not have the same meaning in training that it has on most college campuses. In training, overlearning means practicing a task even after it has been successfully learned. Many students, however, think of overlearning as the negative consequence of "studying too hard." Although it is commonly believed that one can study too hard and "overlearn" the material, research supports neither that this type of overlearning occurs nor that it would have negative consequences. Therefore, no one will be hurt by studying a little longer.

Finally, to further increase the transfer of training, practice in as many different situations as possible should be provided. For example, we might have our coil winder wind coils as fast as possible, wind them slowly, and wind them in various sizes. In this way, the employee will be better able to deal with any changes that occur in the job.

Massed Practice versus Distributed Practice

As alluded to earlier in the discussion of modeling, material learned in training should be presented in small, easily remembered chunks. If too much training occurs at one time, the employee probably will not be able to pay attention to all that is being taught or be able to remember that on which she did concentrate (Wexley & Latham, 1981).

Of course, the best example of this principle of **massed practice versus distributed practice** is studying for exams. If we *distribute* the reading over several days, the material is relatively easy to learn. But if we wait until the night before the test to read three chapters—that is, *mass* the reading—we will not retain much at all.

Incentives for Learning

One principle that is borrowed from operant conditioning is that no employee will be motivated to learn without some incentive to do so. That is, a coil winder who is taking a course in electronics probably will not study and learn unless he can see how the knowledge will improve his performance and how this improvement in performance will result in a desirable outcome such as a salary increase or chance of promotion.

One method of providing incentives to learn during training is **skill-based pay,** which is used by 5% to 8% of all U.S. organizations (Feuer, 1987b). With skill-based pay, an employee participates in a training program that is designed to increase a particular skill that will be needed for the employee to either be promoted or receive a pay raise. For example, an employee who is currently in the position of Printer III must learn to set his own type before he can be promoted to Printer II. The employee must demonstrate that he has mastered the newly trained skill rather than just having attended training sessions. Similarly, in situations where promotion is not possible, pay increases alone are given to employees who master new skills.

Skill-based pay not only provides incentives for employees to successfully complete training, but also results in increased savings for an organization. For example, a General Foods plant in Kansas found a 92% decrease in its quality reject rate and a 33% decrease in fixed overhead costs after introducing a skill-based pay program (Feuer, 1987b).

Feedback

Another essential aspect of training is **feedback.** While an employee learns a skill or specific knowledge, that learning is enhanced when feedback is provided on the employee's progress. With some tasks, feedback occurs naturally. For example, in baseball, a batter receives feedback on his swing by seeing how hard and far the ball travels.

For other tasks, however, judging the correctness of a behavior without additional feedback is difficult. For example, if you write a term paper

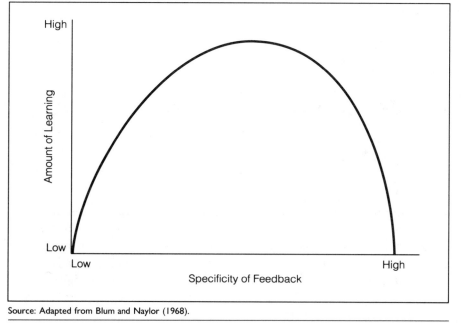

Source: Adapted from Blum and Naylor (1968).

Figure 7.2
Relationship between
Feedback Specificity
and Amount of
Learning

for this class and get a C, your next term paper probably will be no better unless your instructor has provided you with feedback about what was right and wrong with the previous paper.

The same is true for training in industry. Our coil winder needs feedback early in the training process to tell him if the winding is tight enough, if there is an easier way to wind the coil, or if the winding is equally distributed on the coil. A balance, however, must be maintained about the amount of feedback. As shown in Figure 7.2, if too little feedback is provided, the employee will not learn, and if too much or overly detailed feedback is given, the employee will become frustrated and will not learn at an optimal level (Blum & Naylor, 1968).

A final consideration for feedback concerns the type that is given. Research and common sense agree that if an employee correctly performs a task during training, then she should receive positive feedback that the task is being done correctly, and she should receive praise, which will provide an incentive for continuing correct behavior.

But if an employee is not performing a task correctly, should she receive **negative feedback?** Probably, even though negative feedback is more complicated than positive feedback. Negative feedback is most effective when it is provided by a supervisor or trainer who is regarded as trustworthy and knowledgeable and when correctly performing the task is considered important by the employee (Ilgen, Fisher, & Taylor, 1979).

Types of Training Methods

Organizations use many different types of training and training methods. The best programs use a variety of training methods so that employees will understand the reasons for doing a certain task, how it should be done, and in what situations it should be done (Sims, Veres, & Heninger, 1989). In the following pages, several of these methods will be discussed.

Classroom Instruction

Seminars

One of the most common training methods uses the lecture or **seminar** (Donaldson & Scannell, 1986). With this approach, either a member of the training staff or an outside consultant lectures to several or many employees at one time. A wide range of methods has developed over the years. At one extreme, a trainer can speak to hundreds of employees and provide training by giving a particular amount and type of information. At the other extreme, a consultant can work with a small number of employees to help them improve skills such as better communication and dealing with angry customers.

Of course, the method used will depend on the type of information that is to be learned. If the purpose of the training is to convey information about building locations and company policy to new employees, then a lecture conducted by a training staff member is appropriate. If the purpose of training, however, is to learn a complicated skill, the seminar should be conducted by an expert and the audience limited to relatively few employees. For example, at the AT&T plant in the New River Valley (Fairlawn, Virginia), seminars on problem solving are conducted by the training staff, communication-skills seminars by an outside consultant, and seminars on the principles of electronics by a local community college instructor. In many locations, employees can receive college credit for certain training programs (Forsyth & Galloway, 1988).

Tens of thousands of consultants around the country offer seminars to industry. In fact, almost 10,000 consultants annually use seminar materials provided by one company alone, Performax Systems International. Thus, many types of seminars are conducted by a wide variety of consultants. Needs analysis, however, must be used to determine whether such seminars are actually necessary. Sam Miller, personnel director for Roanoke Electric Steel Company (Roanoke, Virginia), has commented that he receives an average of two brochures each day advertising various seminars.

Even though a seminar may sound of interest, it should only be used if it directly relates to some aspect of the job or to the people doing the job. For example, a seminar on communication skills may sound interesting, but it probably would not improve a coil winder's performance. A seminar on electronics might. Likewise, a seminar on personal money management may not relate to the coil winder's job, but it might be useful if it solves outside problems that affect job performance or attendance.

As with college lectures, many activities can take place within a seminar, including lecture, the use of audiovisual aids such as slides and videotapes, discussion, and question-and-answer periods. Again, the choice of activities depends on the task or skill to be learned.

If the skill is complicated, such as learning to operate a machine or learning how to deal with an angry customer, lecture alone will not be enough. The seminar also should include some type of practice or role play. If the information is not complicated but involves visual material such as building locations, flow charts, or diagrams, visual aids such as slides should be added to the lecture. If the material covered is not comprehensive or if the feelings of the employees toward the material are important, then discussion should be included. Discussion not only helps to further learning, but also allows employees to feel that their opinions are important. As we will see in the discussion of quality circles, discussion often results in valuable ideas that can save a company money.

Another consideration is the use of films or videotapes in place of lectures. Eighty-one percent of all organizations with more than 50 employees use videotapes as part of their training programs (Gordon, 1986). Videos have a clear economic advantage over live lecture only when the lecture is to be repeated several times. A consultant-conducted seminar usually costs around $100 an hour plus expenses, while most videotapes can be purchased from $200 to $600. Thus, a two-hour videotape will pay for itself if used only two or three times.

Apparently, this economic advantage does not decrease training effectiveness—80% of research has found that videotapes are at least as effective as live lectures (Schramm, 1962). Perhaps one reason for their effectiveness is that videos ensure consistency in both the presentation of material and the control of the image received by the trainee (O'Grady & Matthews, 1987). That is, if a lecturer describes an object such as a graph or piece of machinery, each trainee develops his or her own image of the object. Thus, to describe objects or procedures, videotapes are appropriate substitutes for, or additions to, the lecture method (Storer, 1986).

One example of a popular training video used in industry is the *You Are . . . What You Were When* series created by psychologist Morris Massey. The tapes deal with the development of values and touch on topics such as why older workers value money and loyalty more than do younger workers. The six tapes in the series each cost approximately $450. The series is used by thousands of organizations each year to increase workers' understanding of themselves and other workers.

Listening to lectures and watching videos can indeed be boring, but research has indicated that lecture is still an effective training method (Goldstein, 1986; Miner, 1963). Many trainers, however, do not consider lecture to be an effective training technique (Carroll, Paine, & Ivancevich, 1972).

Programmed Instruction

One of the lecture method's disadvantages is that all employees must be taught at the same pace. This is unfortunate because some employees are brighter or more experienced than others and will be bored if a lecture moves too slowly. Other employees, however, will become frustrated if a lecture goes too quickly. Thus, to allow each employee to earn the material at her own pace, programmed instruction can be used.

Programmed instruction is effective because it takes advantage of several important learning principles (King, 1986). First, learning is self-paced—that is, each trainee proceeds at his own pace. You have probably been in classes in which the lecturer went too quickly and in others in which the lecturer went too slowly. When the presentation speed of the material does not parallel the comprehension speed of the learner, frustration occurs and the material will not be learned as well as it might.

Second, each trainee is actively involved in the learning. This contrasts sharply with the lecture method, where the employee might sit through two hours of lecture without being actively involved. Think of your favorite classes: The instructor probably allowed you to become involved and actually do things. (That is why some of the chapters in the text are so detailed. By making the text inclusive and complete, your instructor can spend class time on projects instead of straight lecture.)

Finally, programmed instruction presents information in small units or chunks because learning smaller amounts of material is easier than learning larger amounts. The use of small chunks is based on the principle of massed versus distributed practice, which was discussed earlier. To demonstrate this point, think of the exam for this class. Would your score on the test be higher if you read and reviewed one chapter each week or if you waited until the night before the test to read five chapters? (The answer is obvious, and hopefully you did not answer the question from experience!)

Programmed instruction can be delivered in one of three ways. In the oldest method, each employee is provided with a step-by-step booklet that provides the material to be learned as well as a series of exams that measure the employee's knowledge of the material. If the employee does not pass the test at the end of each unit, he must reread the material until he does succeed. In this way, the employee studies at his own pace, and the exams ensure that the employee understands the material.

The second method also uses booklets but has the answers printed in a special latent ink. With this special ink, the employee reads and answers a question and then uses a felt-tipped, latent-image developer pen to uncover "hidden" feedback about the correctness of the chosen answer. With this technique, not only does the employee receive immediate feedback, but also the trainer has a written record of the answers given and the progress made by each employee (Parsons, 1986).

The third method of programmed instruction uses computers. This is most commonly called **Computer-Assisted Instruction (CAI)** and is used by approximately 50% of all organizations (Gordon, 1986). CAI uses the same learning principles as programmed instruction; the only real difference is the manner in which the material and tests are delivered. With CAI, an employee studies at a computer terminal at his own pace. At the end of the material, the computer poses a series of questions to the employee. If the employee does not answer enough questions correctly, the computer informs the employee about the areas in which he needs help and returns him to the appropriate material.

A recent advance in programmed instruction known as **interactive video** adds a video machine to the computer. With interactive video, the employee sees a videotaped situation on a television screen. At the end of each situation, the employee chooses her response to the situation and the computer selects a video that shows what would happen based on the employee's response (Packer, 1988). In 1986, interactive video was being used by more than 15% of U.S. organizations, with another 20% indicating that they would use it within the next year (Gordon, 1986).

In general, programmed instruction has been a successful training method. Research has indicated that its greatest advantage is that it is quicker than many other methods and achieves higher levels of immediate learning (Nash, Muczyk, & Vettori, 1971). Furthermore, a meta-analysis by Manson (1989) concluded that programmed instruction can lead to improved performance at relatively low cost.

The training program used by Life of Virginia (Richmond, Virginia) is a good example. One problem encountered by the company was that more

Designing and
Evaluating Training
Systems

than 1,000 sales agents were spread over 140 offices throughout the country. Thus, to conduct a training program that would be both effective and practical, consultants Williams and Streit (1986) used sales experts to create seven training modules: marketing and asking for referrals, calling for appointments, interviews, preparing the insurance recommendation, presenting the recommendation, delivering the insurance policy, and periodic review. Each module contained a 5 to 10 page reading assignment, a written exercise on the reading, a videotape showing models performing the appropriate behaviors, a situational problem, and a series of questions to be answered by each insurance agent. Agents study at their own pace, taking between two and four weeks per module. This training program resulted in a 25% annual increase in sales and a 10% decrease in turnover.

Case Studies

Another type of classroom-training exercise, which is used by 42% of all U.S. organizations, is the **case study.** Case studies are similar to leader-less group discussions and situational interview problems (which were discussed in Chapters 4 and 5) and are the best training method for teaching problem-solving skills (Carroll et al., 1972; Newstrom, 1980). With this method, the members of a small group each read a case, which is either a real or hypothetical situation that is typical of those encountered on the job. The group then discusses the case, identifies possible solutions, evaluates the advantages and disadvantages of each solution, and arrives at what it thinks is the best solution to the problem.

For case studies to be most successful, the cases should be taken from actual situations. For example, to make their case study more realistic, Andrews and Noel (1986) had General Electric employees in New York use actual information about a problem within the company. Trainees not only discussed the problem, but interviewed employees to gather more information. This use of a **living case** was found to be superior to the typical case study: Not only was the problem relevant, but also the solution could actually be used, thus providing an incentive for the trainees to take the training program seriously.

Critical Incidents

Another useful but seldom-used training technique is that of critical incidents. In Chapter 2, of course, we discussed the Critical Incident Technique as a job-analysis method, and in Chapter 6 we discussed how these

The classroom type of training exercise known as the *case study* has been found to be the best training method for teaching problem-solving skills.

incidents could be used for performance-appraisal purposes. Critical incidents also can be used for training in two ways. In the simpler of the two methods, the critical incidents obtained from a job analysis are compiled in a notebook that is read by each employee, who is able to study actual examples of good and poor performance.

The second method of critical incidents use takes the first method a step further. The critical incidents are converted into situations, which is similar to the situational interview discussed in Chapter 3. The employee reads each situation and is given four possible responses. When the employee chooses a response, she is told whether the choice is correct and why the choice was or was not correct (O'Brien & Plooij, 1977). The

Bohdan Mrynewych/Stock Boston

289

Designing and
Evaluating Training
Systems

technique, of course, is ideally suited for use with computers, but it also can be used in booklet form.

Sample Job Performance

Simulation

Simulation exercises allow the trainee to work with equipment and in an environment that is similar to that found in the actual job. The exercises offer the advantage of allowing the trainee to work under actual working conditions without the consequences of mistakes.

For example, using a cash register or taking a customer's order is easy to learn. But they are much more difficult tasks with a long line of angry customers or irritable co-workers. Simulation exercises allow the trainee to feel such pressure but without actually affecting the organization's performance.

Like all training methods, simulation exercises come in many different forms. Some, such as airline simulators, are extremely expensive and complex to use, but others, such as a simulated restaurant counter, are relatively inexpensive. In fact, a good example of an inexpensive simulation exercise is that used by nurses to teach diabetics how to administer their insulin shots: The patients practice by injecting water into oranges.

Whatever the method used, a simulation exercise can only be effective if it physically and psychologically simulates actual job conditions. For example, dummy simulators are a standard part of CPR training as provided by the American Red Cross. People practice CPR on the dummies, which simulate the human body and also provide feedback on pressure and location of chest compressions. Although the use of these CPR simulators probably is better than lecture alone, there is some concern that the dummies do not adequately simulate the feel of the human chest. Even worse, practicing CPR on a dummy in front of fellow employees does not have the pressure or environment that often is encountered in an actual emergency.

Situational exercises from assessment centers also are commonly used in employee training and development. The majority of simulations involve training in oral communication, planning, and decision making (Keel, Cochran, Arnett, & Arnold, 1989).

Despite the fact that most simulators do not exactly replicate actual physical and psychological job conditions, they still are better than the single alternatives of either lecture or actual practice. That is, training a pilot is cheaper on a simulator than on a passenger jet, and it is safer for a medical student to practice on a pig rather than on a sick patient.

Role Play

The use of **role play** allows the trainee to perform necessary interpersonal skills by acting out simulated roles. For example, when conducting seminars in assertiveness training, psychologist Curt McKee has his seminar audience participate as actors in predetermined situations. The participants are given a problem situation and are told to use what they have learned about assertiveness to confront the individuals involved in each situation.

Role play is used in many types of training situations, from supervisors practicing performance-appraisal reviews to sales clerks taking customer orders. One interesting variation of the role play exercise has an employee play the role of "the other person." For example, a supervisor might play the role of an employee or a sales clerk might play the role of a customer who is frustrated with recently purchased merchandise. In this way, the employee can better understand the reasoning and feelings of the people with whom he works. This method is one of the best for learning interpersonal skills (Carroll et al., 1972; Newstrom, 1980).

Behavior Modeling

One of the most successful training methods has been behavior modeling. **Behavior modeling** is similar to role play—except the trainee role plays ideal behavior rather than the behavior he might normally perform. The behavior modeling procedure first begins with a discussion of a problem, why it occurred, and the employee behaviors necessary to correct the problem. Next the employee views a videotape of another employee who correctly solves a problem such as a customer who returns a jacket that he claims was torn when purchased. The trainee takes notes during the tape and is given an opportunity to ask questions.

After viewing the tape, the trainee rehearses the solution to the problem in the way that the employee solved it on the videotape; he then receives feedback on his performance (Mann & Decker, 1984). The employee also is given the opportunity to play the role of the "other" person so that he will gain the same insight that he would have by role-play training. By this procedure, the employee will already have had experience in dealing with the problem in the proper way when he encounters the same situation on the job. In other words, positive transfer of learning will have occurred.

Of course, for behavior modeling to be successful, the videotapes must represent commonly encountered problems and situations—thus the importance of a thorough job analysis. By observing and interviewing employees and by collecting critical incidents, the necessary problems and situations can be obtained.

An important and related issue is whether employees should be trained on specific situational skills or on generic skills that will cover any situation (Hultman, 1986). For example, a specific situational skill would be handling a bank customer who is angry about a bounced check. The related generic skill would be calming *any* angry customer. Obviously, generic skills are more difficult to teach and require the modeling of many different types of behavior in many different situations.

Another issue involves the number and types of models that are viewed in the training video. Russ-Eft and Zucchelli (1987) conducted a study at Zenger-Miller, Inc. (Cupertino, California), in which employees viewed either one or two models. If the employees saw two models, they saw either two models performing correct behaviors or one model performing correctly and the other performing incorrectly. The study results indicated that viewing two models increased training performance more than viewing one, but the addition of a negative model was no more effective in increasing training performance than two positive models. When the proper procedures are followed, behavior modeling can significantly increase employee performance (Meyer & Raich, 1983; Sorcher & Spence, 1982).

Job Rotation

Another excellent on-the-job training method is **job rotation.** In this method, an employee performs several different jobs within an organization. Job rotation is especially popular for managerial training because it allows a manager trainee to experience and understand most if not all of the jobs within the organization that her subordinates will perform.

Kroger and Wal-Mart train their managers by working them as clerks, stockers, and baggers during their jobs as assistant managers before promotion. Allstate trains its manager trainees in a similar fashion by having them spend a few months in sales, underwriting, personnel, cash control, and marketing. With job rotation, these organizations believe their managers will perform better by understanding more clearly how each employee performs his job.

Job rotation also is commonly used to train nonmanagerial employees. Aside from increasing employee awareness, the main advantage of job rotation is that it allows for both lateral transfers within an organization and greater flexibility in replacing absent workers. For example, if two bank tellers are ill, an employee who normally approves loans is thus able to temporarily take over the tellers' tasks.

Apprentice training provides an individual with the necessary knowledge and skills of a trade; after such training is complete, he or she can start his or her own business.

Another advantage, which will be discussed in greater detail in another chapter, is that job rotation also can improve job satisfaction by reducing the boredom that often comes with a task-repetitive job.

Informal Training

Apprentice Training

Apprentice training is used by more than 50,000 people annually and is typically found in craft and building trades such as carpentry and plumbing. With apprentice training, an individual usually takes 144 hours of formal classwork each year and works with an expert for several (usually four) years to learn a particular trade and perhaps become eligible to join a trade union. Although apprenticeships usually are formal agreements between labor and management and are regulated by the U.S. Department of Labor's Bureau of Apprenticeship and Training as well as by state agencies, apprenticeships also can be less formal.

For example, an apprentice working with a plumber will initially help the plumber by carrying supplies, picking up parts from suppliers, and holding tools. But with time, the apprentice is taught the necessary knowledges and skills for plumbing. When the apprenticeship is complete, the apprentice can start her own business.

Apprenticeships are good for both the apprentice and the expert. The apprentice learns a valuable trade and the expert or the organization gets inexpensive labor—usually one-half the cost of expert labor. This is why apprenticeships have become more popular over the last few decades. Despite this increased popularity, however, some researchers have criticized apprenticeship programs for two major reasons. First, the emphasis during the apprenticeship often is on the production of work as opposed to teaching new skills to the apprentice (Strauss, 1967). Second, unions use apprenticeships to restrict entry into their trades, which results both in inflated wages caused by high demand and a lower supply of workers and in unfair minority hiring practices (Strauss, 1971).

Coaching

Coaching is another popular method of training new employees. With coaching, a new employee is assigned to an experienced employee who is told to "show the kid the ropes." Coaching can be highly effective, allowing the new employee the chance to learn from a job expert. After all, who knows a job better than a person who has mastered it for several years? Furthermore, new employees report that such coaches are more empathic and knowledgeable than trainers who are assigned to orient new employees (Comer, 1989).

Coaching, however, has its own problems. First, good workers are not necessarily good trainers, and good trainers are not necessarily good workers. Being able to do a job is not the same as explaining it. Sports provide good examples of this point. The best coaches often have been terrible players. Charlie Lau was one of the most successful and best respected batting coaches of all time, yet as a player he hit just .255 over 11 seasons. Ted Williams, arguably the best hitter ever in baseball, was a bust as a manager. (Perhaps this explains the sports joke that "those who can't do—teach, and those who can't teach—teach P.E.")

This is not to say, of course, that excellent employees or players will never be good teachers or coaches. For example, in the world of sports we have seen such successful basketball players as Bill Russell and John Wooden become excellent coaches. In education, we see successful people leave industry to become fine educators. The key is finding a way to identify those workers who will be good coaches or trainers. One solution has been to establish "train the trainer" programs in which future trainers or coaches are taught the skills they will need to train other employees.

A second problem with coaching is that it diminishes the expert's productivity (Wexley & Latham, 1981). That is, while the expert shows the new employee how to do the job, his own production declines. If he is on a bonus system, he may lose money as his production declines, as will the organization if the experienced employee is an outstanding worker. As one solution to this problem, the organization can reward workers who do well in training new employees.

Many organizations such as Pitney-Bowes also have adopted **pass-through programs** in which experienced workers are temporarily assigned to the training department. These workers are taught training techniques and then spend several months training new employees before resuming their old jobs (Geber, 1987).

Mentoring is a form of coaching that has recently received much attention. A **mentor** is a veteran in the organization who takes a special interest in a new employee and helps her not only to adjust to the job, but also to advance in the organization. Typically, mentors are older and at least one level or position above the employee being mentored. As with coaching, not all employees make good mentors, thus both the mentor and the mentor–employee match must be carefully chosen (Mendleson, Barnes, & Horn, 1989).

Performance Appraisal

As discussed in the previous chapter, one of the major uses for employee-performance evaluation is in training. With one excellent method of on-the-job training, a supervisor meets with an employee to discuss his strengths and weaknesses on the job. Once the weaknesses have been identified, the supervisor and employee can determine what training methods would best help the employee to improve his job knowledge or skill.

But using performance appraisal for both training and determining raises and promotions can be difficult. As pointed out by Kirkpatrick (1986), three factors account for this difficulty. First, the focus on salary administration is on *past* behavior, while the focus for training is on *future* behavior. Second, performance appraisal for salary administration often is subjective and emotional, while such appraisal for training is objective and unemotional. Finally, salary administration looks at overall performance, while training looks at detailed performance. Because of these differences, Kirkpatrick (1986) suggests the use of two separate performance-appraisal systems in an organization, one for salary administration and the other for training.

Evaluation of Training Results

As discussed in Chapter 1, one important characteristic of industrial psychology is its reliance on research. Evaluating training results is a good example of this reliance. Because training programs can be costly in both time and money, it is essential to the I/O psychologist to know whether an employee-training program significantly increases performance or effects positive changes in behavior. A recent survey of training directors, however, found that 90% claimed that even though they believed the evaluation of training to be important, they did not conduct evaluations because their organizations did not require them (Bell & Kerr, 1987).

Research Designs for Evaluation

There are many ways to evaluate the effectiveness of a training program, and two factors differentiate the various methods. The first involves *practicality,* and the second is concerned with *experimental rigor.* Although scientifically rigorous research designs are preferred, their use is not always possible. And yet a practical research design without scientific rigor yields little confidence in research findings.

The most simple and most practical of research designs implements a training program and then determines whether significant change is seen in performance of job knowledge. To use this method, performance or job knowledge must be measured twice. The first measurement, a **pretest,** is taken before the implementation of training. The second measurement, a **posttest,** is taken after the training program is complete. A diagram of this simple design is as follows:

Pretest ⟶ Training ⟶ Posttest

Although this method is fairly simple, its findings are difficult to interpret for several reasons. First, there is no control group against which the results can be compared. That is, suppose a significant difference in performance is seen between the pretest and the posttest. If a training program has occurred between the two tests, it would be tempting to credit the training for the increase. The increase, however, may have resulted from other factors such as changes in machinery, changes in motivation caused by nontraining factors, or changes in managerial style or philosophy.

Likewise, suppose no significant increase in performance is observed between pretest and posttest. The natural inclination would be to conclude that the training program did not work. Again, without a control group that interpretation is not necessarily correct. The same changes noted above for an increase may have caused a decrease in performance in this second case. Thus, it is possible that the training program actually did increase performance but that other factors worked to reduce performance, which resulted in no net gain in performance resulting from training.

To overcome these problems, a **control group** thus should be used. In this case, a control group is a group of employees who will be tested and treated in the same manner as the experimental group except that it will not receive training. That is, the control group will be subject to the same policy, machinery, and economic conditions as the employees in the experimental group who receive training. The diagram for this design looks like this:

Experimental group: Pretest $\longrightarrow$ Training $\longrightarrow$ Posttest

Control group: Pretest $\longrightarrow$ Posttest

This second design has a big advantage over the first because the control group allows a researcher to look at the training effect after controlling for outside factors. But even though this design is an improvement on the first, it also has its drawbacks.

First, except for training manipulation, it is almost impossible to treat a control group in an identical manner to the experimental group. Control groups often consist of workers at other plants or in other shifts at the same plant. Such groups are used because often there is no alternative. But the fact that they are in different environments reduces confidence in the research findings.

Even if employees in the same plant on the same shift can be randomly split into control and experimental groups, problems will still exist. The most glaring of these involves the possibility that because the two groups are close to one another, the training effect for the experimental group will spill over to the control group. Employees in the control group also may resent that they were not chosen for training. This resentment alone may lead to a decrease in performance by employees in the control group. Finally, it is possible that the untrained employees will pressure the newly trained employees to revert to the "old way" of doing things (Spitzer, 1986).

With both of the above designs, the pretest itself presents a problem. That is, the mere taking of a test may itself lead to increases in performance. Because of this, a rather complicated method called the **Solomon Four Groups Design** can be used (Campbell & Stanley, 1963). With this design, one group will undergo training but will not take the pretest, a second group will undergo training but will take the pretest, a third group will neither undergo training nor take the pretest, and a fourth group will not undergo training but will take the pretest. The diagram for this design is as follows:

Group 1		Training $\longrightarrow$ Posttest
Group 2	Pretest $\longrightarrow$	Training $\longrightarrow$ Posttest
Group 3	Pretest $\longrightarrow$	Posttest
Group 4		Posttest

This design allows a researcher not only to control for outside effects, but also to control for any pretest effect. This is the most scientifically rigorous of the research designs used to evaluate training, but even it has a serious drawback: It is often not practical. That is, four groups of employees must be used, two of which do not receive training. Thus, to use this design at one organization or plant, a relatively large number of employees must be available, and these employees ideally should be kept from discussing the training with one another. Obviously, using this design is difficult.

Evaluation Criteria

Content Validity

Even though all of the designs suffer from problems with practicality or scientific rigor, training effects still should be evaluated in the best way possible given each particular situation. At times, the only way that training can be evaluated is by comparing training content with the knowledges, skills, and abilities required to perform a job. In other words, the **content validity** of the training can be examined.

For example, if a job analysis indicates that a knowledge of electronic circuitry is necessary to perform a job, then a seminar that is designed to teach this knowledge would have content validity. Although content analysis may ensure that a training program is job-related, it still does not indicate whether a particular training method is effective. But if a training program is content-valid and is conducted by a professional trainer who can *document* previous success in using a method with other organizations, then it may be a safe assumption that the training program will be successful. Keep in mind, however, that making such an assumption is only acceptable when actually evaluating the effect of training is not possible because there are too few employees.

Employee Reactions

Another way to evaluate training is by determining **employee reactions** to the training. Thus, when directly measuring training effects is not possible, trainee reactions can be used. Employee reactions to training are important because employees will not have confidence and thus will not be motivated to use training if they do not like the training process. Even though positive employee reactions are necessary for training to be successful, positive employee reactions do not necessarily mean that training will lead to changes in knowledge or performance (Alliger & Janak, 1989).

In fact, trainee reactions constitute the lowest level of training evaluation (Birnbrauer, 1987) and often can be misleading. For example, most seminars conducted by outside consultants are informative and well presented, so employee reactions are almost always positive, even though the training may not actually affect knowledge or future performance (Alliger & Janak, 1989).

Employee Learning

Instead of using employee reactions as the criterion in evaluating training performance, actual **employee learning** can usually be measured (Bell & Kerr, 1987). That is, if a training program is designed to increase employee knowledge of communication techniques, then creating a test to determine whether an employee actually learned is possible.

The measurements that will be used for the pretest and posttest, as with selection tests, must be both reliable and valid. Thus, if the purpose of a training program is to increase job knowledge, an appropriate job-knowledge test must be constructed or purchased. A trainer can spend a

Designing and
Evaluating Training
Systems

great deal of time creating a training program and evaluating its effectiveness, but the whole training effort will be wasted if the measure used to evaluate effectiveness is no good.

At times, reliable and valid measures of training effectiveness are difficult to obtain. Perhaps a good example of this is seen with the human relations seminars that are common to training programs (Buzzotta, 1986). Typically, an outside consultant conducts a seminar on a topic such as "better communication skills" or "calming irate customers." A seminar may run from two hours to two days in length. Once completed, however, it is important to measure the effectiveness of the seminar training. But how will it be measured?

Application of Training

Another criterion for evaluating the effectiveness of training is to determine the degree of **application of training,** or the extent to which employees actually can use the learned material (Del Gaizo, 1964), which can be done by testing. But even if an employee remembers the training, this does not mean he can or will use the information. Learning and memorizing new material is one thing, and applying it is another.

Bottom Line Measures

The final criterion that can be used to evaluate a training program's effectiveness is a **bottom line measure.** That is, did the organization actually save money following the training program? As an example, imagine that a bank trains its tellers to cross-sell Visa cards. The tellers rate the training session as being enjoyable, all of the employees pass a test on sales techniques, and sales attempts increase by 30%. The bottom-line approach would then ask the question, "If we spent $5,000 training the tellers, how much more revenue was brought in as a result of the training?" If the answer to the question is more than the amount spent on training, then the program would be considered a success.

Chapter Summary

In this chapter, we examined three major steps to training: conducting a needs assessment, developing training programs, and evaluating their effectiveness.

Needs analysis or assessment is the process of determining an organization's training needs. The most common needs-analysis methods are by performance-appraisal scores, task analyses, surveys, interviews with employees and supervisors, skill and knowledge tests, and critical incidents.

After needs analysis has identified areas that require attention, training programs are chosen to meet those needs. To be most effective, these training programs should account for several important principles of human learning. For example, operant-conditioning principles state that people will learn if they are rewarded for doing so. The learning is increased if the reward for learning follows soon after the training program and if the reward is one desired by the employee.

People also learn the behavior of others through modeling. We especially model the behavior of those who are similar to us, are successful in what they do, and who have status. Our ability to model the behavior of others is a consequence of our paying attention to the model, having the opportunity to retain the information that was modeled, and having the physical and mental ability to reproduce the modeled behavior.

Training also will be most effective if the training program is similar to the actual work that will be performed (transfer of training), if the training takes place over time (distributed practice), if we get feedback on our progress, and if there is an incentive for learning.

Training methods take many forms. Classroom learning techniques include seminars, audiovisual aids, programmed instruction, case studies, and critical incidents. Sample job-performance techniques include simulation, role play, behavior modeling, and job rotation. Informal training techniques include apprentice training, coaching, and performance appraisal.

Once the training programs have been designed and the actual training has been conducted, the training program's effectiveness must be evaluated. In addition to employees' reactions to the training, it is essential to measure actual changes in job performance.

Glossary

Application of training Measurement of the effectiveness of training by determining the extent to which employees apply the material taught in a training program

Apprentice training A training program, usually found in the craft and building trades, in which employees combine formal course work with formal on-the-job training

Association The idea that two events that occur at the same time are seen as belonging together

Behavior modeling A training technique in which employees observe correct behavior, practice that behavior, and then receive feedback about their performance

Behavior modification The application of learning principles for the purpose of improving human behavior (see also Operant conditioning)

Bottom line measure Evaluation of a training program by determining if the organization actually saved money as a result of the program

Case study A training technique in which employees, usually in a group, are presented with a real or hypothetical workplace problem and are asked to propose the best solution

Classical conditioning Learning through association, or the close occurrence of two events

Coaching A method of training in which a new employee receives on-the-job guidance from an experienced employee

Computer-Assisted Instruction (CAI) A type of programmed instruction presented through a computer

Content validity The extent to which the topics in a training program are consistent with the knowledge, skills, and abilities identified in a job analysis

Contingency of the consequence The extent to which a reward or punishment is based on the performance of a particular behavior

Control group A group of employees who do not receive a particular type of training so that their performance can be compared to that of employees who do receive training

Critical incidents Examples of good and bad employee behavior observed to have occurred on the job

Distributed practice Learning a few things at a time

Employee learning Evaluating the effectiveness of a training program by measuring how much employees learned from the training program

Employee reactions A method of evaluating training in which employees are asked their opinions of a training program

Feedback Providing employees with specific information about how well they are performing a task or series of tasks

Interactive video A training technique in which an employee is presented with a videotaped situation and is asked to respond to the situation and then receives feedback based on the response

Job rotation A method of training in which employees perform a variety of jobs within an organization

Knowledge test A test that measures the level of an employee's knowledge about a job-related topic

Living case A case study based on a real situation rather than a hypothetical one

Massed practice Learning many things at one time

Mentor An experienced employee who advises and looks out for a new employee

Modeling Learning through watching and imitating the behavior of others

Needs analysis The process of determining the training needs of an organization

Negative feedback Telling employees what they are doing incorrectly in order to improve their performance of a task

Operant conditioning A type of learning based on the idea that humans learn to behave in ways that will result in favorable outcomes and learn not to behave in ways that result in unfavorable outcomes

Organizational analysis The process of determining the organizational factors that will either facilitate or inhibit training effectiveness

Overlearning Practicing a task even after it has been mastered in order to retain learning

Pass-through programs A formal method of coaching in which excellent employees spend a period of time in the training department learning training techniques and training employees

Performance appraisal score A rating representing some aspect of an employee's work performance

Person analysis The process of identifying the employees who need training and determining the areas in which each individual employee needs to be trained

Posttest A measure of job performance or knowledge taken after a training program has been completed

Pretest A measure of job performance or knowledge taken before the implementation of a training program

Programmed instruction A training method in which employees learn information at their own pace

Role play A training technique in which employees act out simulated roles

Seminar A method of training in which a trainer using lectures or discussions trains several employees at one time

Simulation A training exercise in which employees practice job-related behavior under conditions similar to those actually found on the job

Skill-based pay Compensating an employee who participates in a training program designed to increase a particular job-related skill

Skill test A test that measures an employee's level of some job-related skill

Solomon Four Groups Design An extensive method of evaluating the effectiveness of training with the use of pretests, posttests, and control groups

Surveys Questionnaires asking employees about the areas in which they feel they need training

Task analysis The process of identifying the tasks for which employees need to be trained

Timing of the consequence The amount of time between the performance of a behavior and the reward or punishment that follows the behavior

Transfer of training The extent to which behavior learned in training will be performed on the job

8

Leadership

Theories of Leadership
Trait Theories
Leader Emergence
Leader Performance
  Needs
  Adaptability
  Unsuccessful Leaders
    Lack of Training
    Cognitive Deficiencies
    Personality
Leader Characteristics
Behavior Theories
Consideration and Initiating Structure
Theory X and Theory Y
Managerial Grid
  Impoverished Leadership
  Country Club Leadership
  Task-Centered Leadership
  Team Leadership
  Middle-of-the-Road Leadership
Situational Theories
Fiedler's Contingency Model
IMPACT Theory
  Informational Style
  Magnetic Style
  Position Style
  Affiliation Style
  Coercive Style
  Tactical Style
  Becoming an Effective Leader According
  to IMPACT Theory
Path–Goal Theory
Vertical Dyad Linkage Theory
Situational Leadership Theory

Specific Behavioral Theories
Leadership Through Decision Making
  The Vroom–Yetton Model
    Importance of Decision Quality
    Leader Knowledge of Problem Area
    Problem Structuredness
    Importance of Decision Acceptance
    Probability of Decision Acceptance
    Subordinate Trust and Motivation
    Probability of Subordinate Conflict
    Decision-Making Strategies Using the
    Vroom–Yetton Model
Leadership Through Contact
  Management by Walking Around
Leadership Through Power
  Expert Power
  Legitimate Power
  Reward and Coercive Power
  Referent Power
Leadership Through Persuasion
  Persuasion by Communication
    Expertise
    Trustworthiness
    Attractiveness
  The Message
    Message Discrepancy
    One-Sided Versus Two-Sided
    Arguments
    Threats
Leadership: Where Are We Today?
Chapter Summary
Glossary

Imagine a company with thousands of workers that has seen sales drop in each of the past five years. The president of the company steps down and a new president is installed. Several years later, the company makes a profit and everyone hails the new president as the reason for the improvement.

Also imagine a football team with a winning record in each of the last 10 years. The team's coach leaves for another school and the team loses the majority of its games in the next few years.

In both of these examples, a new leader took over. In the first example, the organization became more successful, while in the other it declined. How much of the organization's performance can be attributed to the leader? If the leader *was* the major cause of the changes in performance, why was one leader successful and the other a failure? These types of questions will be addressed in this chapter.

Theories of Leadership

Many different theories about leadership have been developed over the last few decades. Although none of the theories "tells the whole story" about leadership, each has received at least some empirical support. Understanding the theories and research behind leadership is important because the theory that company executives believe about leadership will, for the most part, determine how an organization selects or develops its managers.

For example, if we believe that certain people are "born to be leaders" because of what they possess (leadership trait theories), then managers should be selected based on their scores on certain tests. But if we believe that leadership consists of specific skills or behaviors (leader behavior theories), then we can take almost any employee and teach her how to become an outstanding leader. If we believe that good leadership is the result of an interaction between certain types of behaviors and particular aspects of the situation (situational leadership theory), then we might choose certain types of people to be leaders at any given time or we might teach a leader how to adapt her behavior to meet the situation.

The following pages provide brief explanations of the most popular leadership theories. When reading about each theory, think about what the theory would imply about the selection or development of leaders for an organization.

Personal Characteristics	Physical Characteristics	**Table 8.1** **Important** **Characteristics for** **Effective Leadership**
Adaptable	Athletic	
Assertive	Attractive	
Charismatic	Tall	
Creative		
Decisive		
Dominant		
Energetic		
Extraverted		
Friendly		
Honest		
Intelligent		
Masculine		
Outgoing		
Self-confident		
Wise		

Trait Theories

Trait theories are based on the idea that traits or characteristics of a
person play an important role in the leadership process. Trait theories
have concentrated on three aspects of leadership: leader emergence,
leader performance, and leader characteristics.

Leader Emergence

Leader emergence is the idea that leaders possess traits or characteristics different from nonleaders. That is, this theory would say that leaders such as Ronald Reagan, John Kennedy, Adolph Hitler, Martin Luther
King, Jr., and Elizabeth Dole share similar traits that your neighbor or a
cook at McDonald's do not. If you use your school as an example, this
theory would predict that the students in your student government would
be different than students who do not participate in leadership activities.

Almost 100 traits have been identified in studies as differentiating leaders from nonleaders, some of which are listed in Table 8.1. But only
three traits—intelligence, dominance, and masculinity—have been commonly found to relate to leader emergence. Even then, the relationship

between these traits and leader emergence is not especially strong (Kenny & Zaccaro, 1983; Lord, De Vader, & Alliger, 1986). Thus, the preponderance of research suggests that trait theories are not good predictors of leader emergence (Bird, 1940; Stogdill, 1948).

These findings are especially perplexing because anecdotal evidence suggests that leadership behavior has some stability. To illustrate this point, think of a friend whom you consider to be a leader. In all probability, that person is a leader in many situations. That is, she might influence a group of friends about what movie to see, she might make decisions about what time everyone should meet for dinner, and she might "take charge" when playing sports. Conversely, you probably have a friend or two who has never assumed a leadership role in his life. Thus, it appears that some people consistently emerge as leaders in a variety of situations, while others who share these characteristics nonetheless never emerge as leaders (Kenny & Zaccaro, 1983).

Leader Performance

Leader performance involves the idea that excellent leaders possess certain traits that poor leaders do not. For example, an excellent leader might be intelligent, assertive, friendly, and independent, while a poor leader might be shy, aloof, and calm. The idea behind trait theories certainly is appealing, but research indicates that only two traits—intelligence and interpersonal adjustment—have consistently been related to leadership performance (Heslin & Dunphy, 1964).

An interesting extension of the trait theory of leader performance suggests that certain traits are necessary requirements for leadership excellence but they do not guarantee it (Simonton, 1979). Instead, leadership excellence is a function of the right person being in the right place at the right time. The fact that one person with a certain set of traits becomes an excellent leader while another with the same traits flounders may be no more than the result of timing and chance.

As examples, consider Lyndon Johnson and Martin Luther King, Jr. Both were considered to be successful leaders because of their strong influence on improving civil rights. But other people prior to the 1960s had the same thoughts, ambitions, and skills as King and Johnson yet they did not become successful civil rights leaders because the "time was not right."

Needs

A specific trait theory that has received recent support concerns itself with the level of a leader's **need for power** and **need for affiliation.** These needs can be measured through various psychological tests. The most commonly used is the **Thematic Apperception Test (TAT).** The TAT is a projective test in which a person is shown a series of pictures and asked to tell a story about what is happening in each picture. The stories are then analyzed by a trained psychologist who identifies the needs themes that are contained in the stories. Obviously, this technique is time-consuming and requires a great deal of training.

Another commonly used measure is the **Job Choice Exercise (JCE)** developed by Stahl and Harrell (1982). With the JCE, a subject reads descriptions of jobs that entail varying degrees of power, achievement, and affiliation needs and then rates how desirable he finds each particular job. These ratings then are subjected to a complicated scoring procedure that uses regression analysis to reveal scores on the three need categories.

Research by McClelland and Burnham (1976) and McClelland and Boyatzis (1982) has demonstrated that high-performance managers have what is called a **leadership motive pattern.** A leader who has this pattern has a high need for power and a low need for affiliation. The need is not for personal power, but for organizational power.

This pattern of needs is thought to be important because it establishes that an effective leader should be more concerned with results rather than with being liked. A leader who needs to be liked by her subordinates will have a tough time making decisions. A decision to have employees work overtime, for example, may be necessary for the organization's survival, but it probably will be unpopular with employees. A leader with high affiliation needs may decide that being liked is more important than being successful, and so may be in conflict about her decision.

This theory also would explain why internal promotions often do not work. Consider, for example, a person who worked for six years as a loan officer. She and 10 co-workers often went drinking after work and away on weekends together. But one day she was promoted to manager and now had to lead the same people with whom she was friends. The friendships and her need to be liked hindered the new manager from giving orders and disciplining her employees. When she tried to separate herself from her friends, she was quickly thought of as "being too good for her friends"—a tough situation with no apparent solution according to this theory.

This does not mean that a leader should not be friendly and care about subordinates, but rather that the successful leader will not place being liked above the goals of the organization. Such conflict was thought to be the case with President Richard Nixon, who would make a tough decision and then apologize for it because he wanted to be liked by both the public and the press.

Adaptability

Another interesting trait theory was proposed by Foster (1989), who believes that good leaders need to possess only one stable trait: *adaptability*. Thus, good leaders will constantly change their behaviors to meet the demands of the situation or the person with whom the leader is dealing. (This thinking has also been echoed by Cohen and Bradford, 1990.) Support for this theory comes from a study by Caldwell and O'Reilly (1982), who found that field representatives who dealt with many different types of people were more effective if they were high self-monitors. High self-monitors are people who are sensitive to social cues and who are able and willing to adapt their behavior to fit a particular situation.

Unsuccessful Leaders

In a departure from research to identify characteristics of successful leaders, Hogan (1989) has attempted to identify traits of unsuccessful leaders. Hogan was interested in investigating poor leaders because both empirical research as well as anecdotal accounts indicate that most employees report that one of the greatest sources of stress in their jobs is their supervisors' poor performance, strange behavior, or both. This idea should come as no surprise: You probably can quickly recall many examples of poor performance or strange behavior with current or former supervisors.

Lack of Training Based on years of research, Hogan (1989) has concluded that poor leader behavior has three major causes. The first is a *lack of leadership training* given to supervisors. The armed forces are among the few organizations that require supervisors to complete leadership training before taking charge of groups of people. The norm for most organizations, however, is to either promote a current employee or hire a new employee and place her directly into a leadership role. The serious consequences of this lack of training can best be understood if we imagine allowing doctors to perform surgery without training or allowing truck drivers to drive the highways without first learning how to drive.

Cognitive Deficiencies The second cause of poor leadership stems from *cognitive deficiencies*. Hogan (1989) believes that poor leaders are those who have an inability to learn from experience and who are unable to think strategically (that is, to plan ahead). Thus, many poor leaders consistently make the same mistakes and do not plan ahead.

The manager of a local convenience store frequented by this author exemplified the problem of not learning from mistakes. The manager did not give employees their work schedules until one or two days before they were to work. The employees complained because the hours always changed and they could not schedule their social lives. But the manager continued to do it his way and most of the employees quit. Three years later, he still does it his way and his employees still leave at a high rate.

Personality The third, and perhaps most important source of poor leadership behavior involves the *personality* of the leader. Hogan (1989) believes that many poor leaders are insecure and that they express this insecurity by adopting one of three personality types: the paranoid/passive–aggressive, the high likability floater, and the narcissist.

The source of insecurity for leaders who are paranoid, passive–aggressive, or both is some incident in their lives in which they felt betrayed. This *paranoid/passive–aggressive* leader thus has deeply rooted, but perhaps unconscious, resentment and anger. On the surface, these leaders are charming, quiet people who often compliment their subordinates and fellow workers. But they resent the successes of others and are likely to act against subordinates in a passive–aggressive manner; that is, on the surface they appear to be supportive, but at the same time they will (figuratively) stab another person in the back.

The type of leader who is insecure and seldom rocks the boat or causes trouble is known as a *high likability floater*. This person goes along with the group, is friendly to everyone, and never challenges anyone's ideas. Thus, he or she travels through life with many friends and no enemies. But the reason that high likability floaters have no enemies is that they never do anything, challenge anyone, or stand up for the rights of their employees. These leaders will be promoted and never fired because even though they make no great performance advances, they are well liked. Their employees have high morale but show relatively low performance.

Narcissists are leaders who overcome their insecurity by overconfidence. They like to be the center of attention, promote their own accomplishments, and take most if not all of the credit for the successes of their group—but they avoid all blame for failure.

Leader Characteristics

The third aspect of leadership theory uses a **sociological approach** and is involved with identifying characteristics of leaders; it does not, however, involve comparing these characteristics to those of nonleaders. Although this line of research has little usefulness to human resource managers, it has had some interesting findings. For example, Presidents Franklin Roosevelt, Kennedy, and Reagan had high needs for power; Presidents Harding, Truman, and Nixon had high needs for affiliation; and Presidents Wilson, Hoover, and Carter had high needs for achievement (Winter, 1988).

Behavior Theories

Behavior theories focus on what a leader *does* as opposed to what she *is*. Trait and behavior theories first appear to be the same, but there is a subtle, yet very important, difference. For example, a leader may possess the trait of shyness and not truly want to communicate with other people. She knows, however, that talking to others is an important part of her job, so she says hello to her employees when she arrives at work, and at least once a day, she stops and talks with each employee. Thus, our leader has the trait of shyness although her behavior is not shy.

Consideration and Initiating Structure

The most well-known behavior theory of leadership resulted from a series of studies at Ohio State University in the early 1950s. After years of research, the investigators identified two main behavioral elements in leadership—consideration and initiating structure (Fleishman, Harris, & Burtt, 1955).

Consideration is the degree to which a leader acts in a warm and supportive manner and shows concern for her subordinates. Examples of such behavior would include consulting subordinates before making decisions, praising their work, asking about their families, and not looking over their shoulders.

Initiating structure is the degree to which a leader defines and structures her own role and those of her subordinates in attaining the group's formal goals. Examples of initiating-structure behaviors include setting goals, making decisions without consulting the group, rewarding and punishing subordinates based on their productivity, and giving orders.

Figure 8.1
Consequences of
Two Ohio State
Leadership Styles

Figure 8.1 content:

	Low performance Low turnover Low grievance rate	High performance Low turnover Low grievance rate
High		
Consideration		
Low	Low performance High turnover High grievance rate	High performance High turnover High grievance rate
	Low	High
	Initiating Structure	

A leader's tendency to use either consideration or initiating structure behaviors can be measured by several instruments, but the most popular are the **Leadership Opinion Questionnaire (LOQ)** and the **Leader Behavior Description Questionnaire (LBDQ).** The LOQ is filled out by a supervisor or leader who desires to know his own behavioral style. The LBDQ is completed by subordinates to provide a picture of how they perceive their leader's behavior.

Research on the effectiveness of consideration and initiating structure leadership styles has brought interesting findings. As shown in Figure 8.1, leaders who score high in consideration tend to have satisfied employees, while leaders who score high in initiating structure tend to have productive employees. Leaders scoring highly in both have satisfied and productive employees, while leaders scoring poorly in both tend to have unhappy and unproductive employees (Korman, 1966; Fleishman & Harris, 1962).

The above results certainly make sense, but other research indicates that the relationship between consideration and initiating structure is more complex than was first thought. Several studies have shown that variables such as leader experience and knowledge as well as external variables such as time pressures and work importance tend to moderate the relationship between consideration scores and satisfaction and between initiating structure scores and subordinate performance.

Theory X and Theory Y

A theory similar to that just described was developed by Douglas McGregor (1967). McGregor believes that leaders operate from one of two theories. **Theory X leaders** see their employees as lazy, extrinsi-

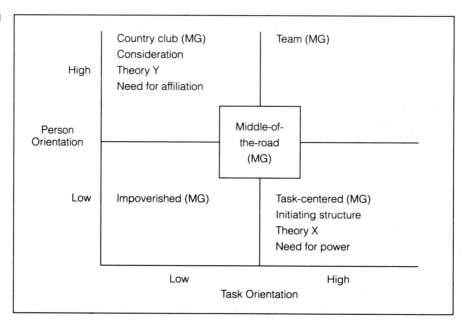

Figure 8.2
Relationship between Managerial Grid (MG) and Other Task/Person Behavior Theories

cally motivated, wanting security, undisciplined, and shirking responsibility. Because of these assumptions, Theory X leaders tend to manage or lead by giving directives, setting goals, and making decisions without consulting their subordinates.

Theory Y leaders, on the other hand, believe that employees are intrinsically motivated, seek responsibility, are self-controlled, and do not necessarily dislike work. Because of these assumptions, a Theory Y leader works with employees in making decisions and uses a more "hands-off" approach to leadership.

Managerial Grid

A third theory that essentially divides leaders into task or person orientations is the **managerial grid,** which was developed by Blake and Mouton (1984). In managerial grid theory, leadership style is measured through a leadership test. As can be seen in Figure 8.2, there are five main styles: impoverished, country club, task-centered, team, and middle-of-the-road.

Impoverished Leadership

The **impoverished** type of leader accepts almost any decision made by the group. She is concerned with neither production nor the feelings and well-being of her subordinates.

Country Club Leadership

The **country club**—type of leader has a high concern for the feeling of his subordinates but little concern for productivity. Such a leader will go out of his way to keep from making his subordinates unhappy.

Task-Centered Leadership

Task-centered leaders are concerned solely with production. The worth of a subordinate is measured according to how well she accomplishes an assigned task. Task-centered leaders give orders, do not ask for advice, and do not want discussion or subordinate input.

Team Leadership

Team leaders reflect the ideal of leadership styles, combining a concern with production with a concern for the welfare of subordinates. Such a leader makes decisions herself when she is able and asks for the advice of subordinates when necessary.

Middle-of-the-Road Leadership

Middle-of-the-road leaders have a balanced approach to task and people concerns. The difference between middle-of-the-road leaders and team leaders, however, is one of degree. Team leaders are high in both task and people orientation, while middle-of-the-road leaders are moderate in both orientations.

Situational Theories

As indicated above, the effectiveness of leader behavior often depends on the particular situation in which the leader finds himself. In the past few decades, several theories have emerged that have sought to explain the situational nature of leadership.

**Figure 8.3
Relationship Between
LPC Scores and
Group Success**

	Low	Moderate	High
High LPC Score	Low performance	High performance	Low performance
Low LPC Score	High performance	Low performance	High performance

Low   Moderate   High
Situation Favorability

Fiedler's Contingency Model

The most well-known and controversial of the situational theories was developed by Fred Fiedler in the mid-1960s (Fiedler, 1967). Fiedler believed that an individual's leadership style is the result of a lifetime of experiences and thus is extremely difficult to change. **Fiedler's Contingency Model** holds that any individual's leadership style is only effective in certain situations. The way to increase leader effectiveness, then, is to help a person understand her style of leadership and then how to manipulate a situation so that the two match. To help a person understand her leadership style, Fielder developed the **Least-Preferred Co-worker (LPC) Scale.**

To complete the LPC Scale, a leader identifies the subordinate or employee with whom she would least want to work. She then rates that person on several semantic differential scales that range from nice to nasty and friendly to unfriendly. The higher the leader rates her least-preferred co-worker, the higher the LPC score. This score then is compared to the favorableness of the situation to determine leader effectiveness. Low-scoring LPC leaders tend to be task-oriented, while high-scoring LPC leaders tend to be more concerned with interpersonal relations (Fiedler, 1978; Rice, 1978).

The favorableness of a situation is determined by three variables. The first is **task structuredness.** Structured tasks are those for which goals are clearly stated and known by group members, only a few correct solutions to a problem are possible, and the task can be completed in only a few ways. The more structured the task, the more favorable the situation.

The second variable is **leader position power.** That is, the greater the position or legitimate power of the leader, the more favorable the

IMPACT Style (Geier et al.)	Base of Power (French & Raven)
Informational	Expert
Magnetic	Referent
Position	Legitimate
Affiliation	
Coercive	Coercive/Reward
Tactical	

**Table 8.2
Comparison of
IMPACT Styles and
Bases of Power**

situation. Thus, a group or organizational setting in which there is no assigned leader is not considered to be a favorable leadership situation.

The third variable is **leader–member relations.** The more that subordinates like their leader, the more favorable the situation. The leader–member relationship is considered the most important of the three variables.

As shown in Figure 8.3, the relationship between LPC scores and group performance is complex. Basically, low-scoring LPC leaders (those who rate their least-preferred co-worker low) function best in situations that are either favorable or unfavorable, while high-scoring LPC leaders function best when the situation is only of moderate favorability.

Research generally has supported Fiedler's theory. Strube and Garcia (1981) conducted a meta-analysis of 145 independent studies that investigated Fiedler's model as well as 33 of Fiedler's own studies and concluded that the ideas were well supported by the research.

Fiedler's training program, called **Leader Match,** has also been supported by research (Strube & Garcia, 1981). This program is based on Fiedler's belief that an individual's leadership style is not easily changed. Thus, to improve their abilities, leaders learn through four-hour workshops how to diagnose situations and then change these situations to fit their particular leadership styles (Csoka & Bons, 1978).

IMPACT Theory

A more recent situational theory, known as **IMPACT theory,** was developed by Geier, Downey, and Johnson (1980), who believed that each leader is one of six behavioral types. Each type is only effective in a particular situation, or in what the researchers call an *organizational climate.* Shown in Table 8.2, the six styles are similar to the five bases of power suggested several years ago by French and Raven (1959; also Raven, 1965). The six IMPACT styles and their appropriate climates, according to Geier et al. are *i*nformational, *m*agnetic, *p*osition, *a*ffiliation, *c*oercive, and *t*actical.

Informational Style

The leader who has an **informational style** provides information in a climate of **ignorance.** Such a climate is one in which important information is missing from the group. For example, if a car containing four college professors and a mechanic broke down on the side of the road, who would become the leader? Almost certainly it would be the mechanic because she probably would be the one who had the most knowledge or information needed to solve the problem.

In recent years in the U.S. Senate, Sam Nunn (D–Ga.) has become one of the most powerful and respected congressional leaders. He became powerful by becoming an expert in defense matters, an area that was important and that few in congress knew as much about. Thus, Nunn used an informational style in a climate of ignorance to become a powerful leader.

Magnetic Style

A leader with a **magnetic style** leads through energy and optimism and is only effective in a climate of **despair,** which is characterized by low morale. Ronald Reagan is perhaps the best example of a magnetic leader. As president, he was optimistic and well liked, even by people who may not have agreed with him politically. He was elected at a time when the national mood was depressed because of high inflation, high unemployment, and the Iran hostage situation. The chances of successful leadership increase in a situation of general despair when a magnetic or charismatic individual assumes control (Latham, 1983).

Position Style

A person who uses the **position style** leads by virtue of the power inherent in that position. Such a person might lead through such statements as, "As your captain, I am ordering you to do it," or "Because I am your mother—that's why." Individuals who use a position style will only be effective in climates of **instability.** This style is especially effective during corporate mergers, particularly when people are not sure what actions to take. However, there are often questions about a leader's legitimate scope of power (Yukl, 1989).

Affiliation Style

A person who uses the **affiliation style** leads by liking and caring about others. This style is similar to that of consideration as defined by the Ohio State studies. A leader using affiliation will be most effective in a climate of **anxiety** or when worry predominates. Former president Jimmy Carter is an excellent example of the affiliation style. Carter was elected president shortly after the Watergate affair, when many voters were worried that they could not trust politicians or their government. Carter campaigned successfully with statements such as "I care" and "I'm not part of that Washington crowd."

Coercive Style

A person using the **coercive style** leads by controlling reward and punishment and is most effective in a climate of **crisis.** Such a leader often will use statements such as "Do it or you're fired," or "If you can get the package there on time, I will have a little something for you." This style is typical in war. If a soldier disobeys an order, an officer can have him shot. Conversely, if a soldier behaves with bravery and distinction, an officer can reward him with a medal or promotion.

Support for the situational appropriateness of coercive styles of leadership was found by Mulder, de Jong, Koppelaar, and Verhage (1986) when they studied the behavior of bankers whose leadership styles had been measured by the Influence Analysis Questionnaire. Mulder and his colleagues found that in crisis situations, bankers tend to use more formal and coercive types of power than in noncrisis situations.

Tactical Style

A leader with a **tactical style** leads through the use of strategy and is most effective in a climate of **disorganization.** A good example of this may be seen when a class breaks into small groups to complete an assignment. Ideally, every student knows the material well enough to complete the assignment, but normally there is a limited amount of time and too much work to do. The person who becomes the leader is the one who is best able to organize the group.

Becoming an Effective
Leader According to IMPACT Theory

If IMPACT theory is correct, then a person can become an effective leader by one of several methods. The first is by finding a climate that is consistent with her behavioral style. This method, however, involves either a great deal of luck or a lot of patience, requiring the leader to be in the right place at the right time.

In the second method, the leader changes her style to meet a particular climate (Suedfeld & Rank, 1976). That is, if the climate is one of ignorance, the individual changes her behavior and uses information to lead. On the other hand, if the climate is one of despair, then she becomes more outgoing and positive. Thus, a person who is willing to adapt her behavior and who has the ability to "play" each of the six leadership styles should be an effective leader.

A study by Manz and Sims (1986) suggests that leaders can indeed be taught different styles of leadership. Manz and Sims used a behavioral modeling approach to successfully teach 40 leaders how to use positive-reward behavior, reprimand behavior, and goal-setting behavior. Thus, those who are willing to use different leadership styles can learn the necessary skills and behaviors through training programs.

The third method by which a person can become an effective leader is to change followers' perception of the climate so that the perception matches the leader's behavioral style. This tactic is common in politics, in which each candidate tries to convince the voting public that he or she is the best person for an office.

The fourth method by which a leader can become effective is by actually changing the climate itself rather than simply followers' perceptions of the climate. Obviously, this is difficult to do, but it is the strategy advocated in Fiedler's Leader Match training. Such a strategy is difficult but can be successful.

Path–Goal Theory

House (1971) believes that a leader's behavior will only be accepted by subordinates to the extent to which the behavior helps them to achieve their goals. Thus, a leader will only be successful if his subordinates perceive him as working with them to meet certain goals and if those goals offer a favorable outcome for the subordinates.

Because the needs of subordinates change with each new situation, a supervisor must adjust his behavior to meet the needs of his subordinates. That is, in some situations subordinates need a leader to be directive and to set goals; in others, they already know what to do and only need emotional support.

According to House's **path–goal theory,** a leader can adopt one of four behavioral leadership styles to handle each situation: instrumental, supportive, participative, and achievement-oriented.

The **instrumental style** calls for planning, organizing, and controlling the activities of employees. The **supportive-style** leader shows concern for employees, the **participative-style** leader shares information with employees and lets them participate in decision making, and the leader who uses the **achievement-oriented style** sets challenging goals and rewards increases in performance.

Each style will only work in certain situations and depends on subordinates' abilities and the extent to which the task is structured. In general, the higher the level of subordinate ability, the less directive the leader should be. Likewise, the more unstructured the situation, the more directive the leader should be (Schriesheim & DeNisi, 1981).

House and Mitchell (1974) further advise that, to be effective, a leader should:

- recognize the needs of subordinates and work to satisfy those needs
- reward subordinates who reach their goals
- help subordinates identify the best paths to take in reaching particular goals
- clear those paths so that employees can reach their goals

Path–goal theory is intuitively appealing because it gives a manager direct advice about how to behave in certain situations. Furthermore, because it is behavior-based rather than trait-based, the theory could be used in training. Research thus far, however, has not supported application of this theory (Schriesheim & Schriesheim, 1980; Hammer & Dachler, 1975). Thus, if path–goal theory is to have real impact, it will need further revision.

Vertical Dyad Linkage Theory

Vertical dyad linkage (VDL) theory was developed by Dansereau, Graen, and Haga (1974) and is a unique situational theory that makes good intuitive sense. The situational theories discussed earlier concentrate on interactions between leaders and situations. VDL theory, however, concentrates on the interactions between leaders and subordinates.

The theory takes its name from the relationship between two people (a *dyad*), the position of the leader above the subordinate (*vertical*), and their interrelated behavior (*linkage*).

VDL theory holds that leaders develop different roles with different subordinates and thus act differently with different subordinates. Dansereau and his colleagues believed that subordinates fall into one of two groups—the *in-group* or *out-group*.

In-group subordinates are those who have developed trusting, friendly relationships with the leader. As a result, the leader deals with in-group members by allowing them to participate in decisions and by rarely disciplining them. Out-group subordinates are treated differently than those in the in-group, and are more likely to be given direct orders and have less say about how affairs are conducted.

In general, research on VDL theory has been supportive (Graen & Scheimann, 1978; Scandura, Graen, & Novak, 1986; Wakabayashi & Graen, 1984). There are, however, relationships between leaders and subordinates that probably can be categorized into types other than in-group and out-group. Thus, further research is needed into the relationship between leaders and subordinates.

Situational Leadership Theory

Another theory, which focuses on the relationship between leader and follower, is the **situational leadership theory** developed by Hersey and Blanchard (1988). Hersey and Blanchard postulate that a leader typically uses one of four behavioral styles: delegating, participating, selling, or telling. Although these styles are not much different from the styles of the previously mentioned theories, situational leadership theory does hold that a leader must adapt her behavior not only to situation and climate, but also to followers' characteristics.

Hersey and Blanchard termed the most important follower characteristic "follower readiness," or the ability and willingness to perform a particular task. The degree of follower readiness can be measured by either the manager's rating form or the self-rating form. Scores from these forms place followers into one of four categories, or readiness (R) levels:

R1: Unable and unwilling or insecure

R2: Unable but willing or confident

R3: Able but unwilling or insecure

R4: Able and willing or confident

For R1 followers, the most effective leader behavior is the *telling approach*. That is, the leader directs the follower by telling her what to do and how to do it.

A selling approach should be used with R2 followers because they are willing to do the work but are not sure *how* to do it. Leaders using this approach explain and clarify how work should be done.

R3 followers are given plenty of emotional support as well as opportunities for two-way communication. This approach is successful because these followers already know what to do but are not sure whether they *want* to do it.

R4 followers are most productive and happy when a delegating leadership style is used. These followers are both willing and able to perform the task. Thus, the only real job for the leader is to delegate specific tasks to subordinates and then let them complete those tasks with minimal supervision or guidance.

As with many theories of leadership, situational leadership theory has excellent intuitive appeal and has been successful in limited organizational applications (Gumpert & Hambleton, 1979). Unfortunately, however, until more research is available, it is difficult to determine how useful it will be in the long run.

Specific Behavioral Theories

Another way to think about leadership is that excellent leaders possess specific behaviors or skills that poor leaders do not. After observing thousands of leaders in a variety of situations, Yukl (1982), Carter (1952), Hemphill and Coons (1950), and Gibb (1969) have proposed a behavioral "theory." According to these researchers, leaders:

1. initiate ideas
2. informally interact with subordinates
3. stand up for and support subordinates
4. take responsibility
5. develop a group atmosphere
6. organize and structure work
7. communicate formally with subordinates
8. reward and punish subordinates
9. set goals

**Table 8.3
Specific Behaviors
Taught in Leadership
Training Programs**

Communication skills
Decision-making skills
Delegation
Discipline
Motivation
Persuasion
Public speaking
Reward and punishment
Running a meeting
Stress management
Team building
Time management
Training techniques
Understanding people
Writing

10. make decisions
11. train and develop employee skills
12. solve problems
13. generate enthusiasm

This theory is not particularly exciting and is the least described in textbooks—but it is the way that leadership is most often practiced in industry. If this theory is true, then leadership is something learned; if the specific behaviors and skills important for effective leadership can be identified, then almost anyone can be trained to become an effective leader. There are many examples of such training programs currently in use.

The city of San Diego has its own management academy that provides interested employees with the skills necessary to become managers. On weeknights and weekends, employees learn skills such as oral communication, report writing, decision making, conflict resolution, and performance appraisal. After an employee is trained and tested in each of these important skill areas, he or she receives a certificate of completion. Even though graduates of the management academy are not promised managerial positions, more often than not they are the employees who are promoted.

If you have ever attended a leadership conference, you probably have noticed that the training involved specific leadership skills such as time

Employment Profile

Jerri Frantzve, Ph.D.
Associate Professor
Radford University

I am an I/O psychologist with a Ph.D. from the University of Georgia. I have done consulting for about fifteen years and worked for one Fortune 10 company for five years and another for four (not that I'm that old, you understand; I consult in spurts and on a part-time basis).

The majority of my work with leadership has involved training managers to develop more effective leadership skills and assessing the leadership skills of candidates for promotion. In my consulting with a variety of organizations, I have found that the definitions of leadership are not consistent—they vary depending on the culture and values of the organization. Therefore, one of the first things I do is to define and clarify the behaviors considered to be associated with effective leadership. For instance, I once was observing six candidates interacting with one another in a leaderless group discussion when one became so frustrated with his inability to lead his peers toward his solution that he walked to the flipchart and ripped off the sheet the others were working on, crushed it into a ball, threw it in the trash, sat down and announced, "Now, this is what we need to do." This was evaluated as very ineffective behavior—for this particular organization. But when I related this instance to managers in a more traditional organization, they applauded his actions as an example of what they considered effective leadership.

One of the groups that has been the most fun to work with has been managers within the "oil business." The whole climate within this field seems to value "toughness," so it is a constant challenge to work within frameworks that involve anything other than strict authoritarian bases for leading others.

One group I trained with Managerial Grid approach—which involves a combination of focusing on the task at hand as well as a concern for the people involved—was especially challenging. These fellows had grown up in the oil field, where it was really rough and tumble and the styles of leadership to which they had been exposed, and for which they had been rewarded, were all very autocratic, abrupt, domineering, and almost power hungry. The week-long training involved an understanding of their current leadership approach, exposure to the concepts of the Managerial Grid, and numerous exercises and feedback to help them develop the skills to incorporate both concern for people and concern for the task. As you might suspect, all went well until it came time to put the theories into practice, then these fellows were not so sure they wanted to personally be associated with the "softer" side of leadership. A lot of macho swaggering and posturing suddenly started happening—almost the John Wayne syndrome. In anticipation of such resistance, I had scheduled the classic movie *Twelve Angry Men*. The movie deals with Henry Fonda's ability to "lead" a jury to reverse their opinion of the guilt of the accused. Fonda displays all of the combinations of concern for members of the jury involved in the decision, empathy for the victim as well as the accused, while focusing on the task of reaching a verdict. He confronts bullies, wimps, and all the other stereotypes one could imagine while maintaining a calm, rational, caring demeanor—many of the characteristics of true leadership. Once we critiqued his performance, it was much easier to go on and apply the theories and develop the skills. These managers just needed to be able to model their behavior on someone who was not only effective, but also very credible.

management, goal setting, persuasion, and communication. Such an agenda typifies the idea that leadership consists of specific and learnable skills and behaviors.

Although it is beyond the scope of this text to discuss each of the behaviors and skills listed in Table 8.3, we will discuss some of the best known specific behavioral theories as well as some specific leadership skills.

The employment profile of Jerri Frantzve demonstrates an interesting aspect of teaching these specific leadership skills.

Leadership Through Decision Making

The Vroom–Yetton Model

Decision making is a specific behavior or skill that is important for a leader to possess. Vroom and Yetton (1973), however, pointed out that previous research has shown that only in certain situations are decisions best made by the leader; in other situations, decisions are best made with the participation of a leader's subordinates, colleagues, or both. Because of this situational aspect to decision making, Vroom and Yetton believed that leadership performance can be improved by teaching leaders to become better decision makers. To aid this process, Vroom and Yetton developed a decision tree to help leaders decide when decisions should be made alone and when they should be made with the help of others.

Of course, developing a chart that would tell a leader what to do in every possible situation would be impossible. But the **Vroom–Yetton Model** does provide a flowchart that can tell a leader what process to go through to make a decision in a particular situation. As Figure 8.4 shows, the answers to seven important diagnostic questions will determine how such a decision should be made.

Importance of Decision Quality The first concern in making a decision is whether a particular decision will be better than another. For example, if a supervisor is trying to decide whether to sign a letter with blue ink or black ink, her decision probably will not make any difference to the company. Thus, the importance of the decision quality is low, and little time or effort should be spent making it.

Leader Knowledge of Problem Area The second concern of decision making involves the extent to which the leader has sufficient information to make the decision alone. If he does, then consultation with others is only desired if he wants his subordinates to feel involved.

Problem Structuredness The third concern involves the extent to which a leader knows what information is needed and how it can be obtained—that is, the problem's structure. If the leader does not know how to obtain this information, the decision-making process will require other people and the decision will take longer to reach.

Importance of Decision Acceptance The fourth concern of decision making involves the degree to which it is important that the decision is accepted by others. For example, if a supervisor is to decide what hours

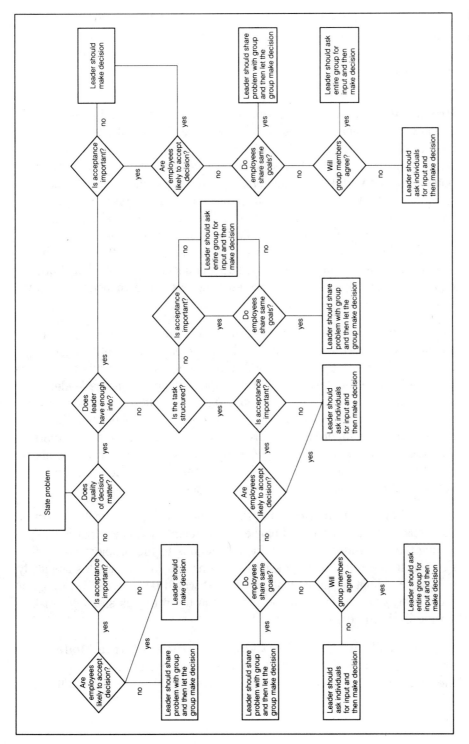

**Figure 8.4
The Vroom–Yetton
Decision-Making
Flowchart**

each employee will work, then it is important that the employees agree with and have input into the decision-making process. But if the supervisor is deciding what she wants for lunch, whether other people agree with or have input into the decision is not important (unless, of course, the choices involve onions or garlic).

Probability of Decision Acceptance The fifth concern in decision making is subordinate acceptance. If the leader feels that she can make the decision herself but that acceptance of the decision is important, she must determine whether her subordinates will accept it. If the leader is popular and powerful, they undoubtedly will accept and follow the decision. But if the leader is not popular, not powerful, or both, she probably will want help from her subordinates and colleagues in making the decision—even though she has the ability to make the decision herself. This is why leaders often ask subordinates and colleagues for their opinions. The leader may already know what she will decide, but "stroking" others' egos by eliciting opinions and comments increases the chances that they will support her decision when she announces it.

Subordinate Trust and Motivation The sixth concern of the decision-making process is the extent to which subordinates are motivated to achieve the organizational goals and thus can be trusted to make decisions that will help the organization. For example, suppose that the leader needs both information and acceptance from her subordinates. As shown in Figure 8.5, in such a situation she would need input from her subordinates. But if the subordinates were motivated to help themselves more than the organization (for example, with work schedules, salary, or affirmative action), then the leader must use their input when making the decision, although she still must make the decision herself.

Probability of Subordinate Conflict The seventh and final concern of the decision-making process involves the amount of conflict that is likely among the subordinates when various solutions to the problem are considered. If there are many possible solutions and the employees are likely to disagree about which is best, the leader would best be served by gathering information from them and then, as in the previous situation, making the decision herself.

Decision-Making Strategies Using the Vroom–Yetton Model
Answering the questions in the flowchart shown in Figure 8.4 results in one of five possible decision-making strategies, which are called autocratic

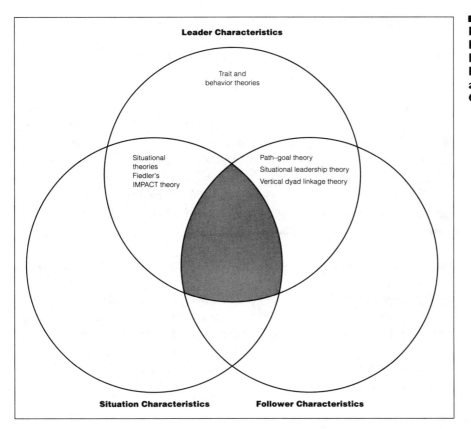

Figure 8.5
Effective Leadership:
Interaction of
Leader, Situation,
and Follower
Characteristics

Leader Characteristics

Trait and
behavior theories

Situational
theories
Fiedler's
IMPACT theory

Path–goal theory
Situational leadership theory
Vertical dyad linkage theory

Situation Characteristics   **Follower Characteristics**

I, autocratic II, consultative I, consultative II, and group I.

With the *autocratic I* decision-making strategy, the leader uses the available information to make the decision without consulting his subordinates. This is an effective strategy when the leader has the necessary information and acceptance by the group is either not important or is likely to occur regardless of the decision.

With the *autocratic II* strategy, the leader obtains the necessary information from his subordinates and then makes his own decision. The leader may or may not tell the subordinates about the nature of the problem. The purpose of this strategy is for the leader to obtain information he needs to make a decision even though acceptance of the solution by the group is not important.

The leader using the *consultative I* strategy shares the problem on an individual basis with some or all of his subordinates. After receiving their input, the leader makes a decision that may or may not be consistent with the thinking of the group. This strategy is especially useful in situations in which it is important for the group to accept the decision but the group members may not agree regarding the best decision.

The leader using the *consultative II* strategy shares the problem on a group basis with his subordinates. After receiving the group's input, the leader makes a decision that may or may not be acceptable to the group. This strategy is used when acceptance of the decision by the group is important and the individual group members are likely to agree with one another about the best solution.

With the *group I* strategy, the leader shares the problem with the group and lets the group reach a solution. The role of the leader is merely to help the decision-making process. This strategy is effective when group acceptance of the decision is important and when the group can be trusted to arrive at a decision that is consistent with the goals of the organization.

Although relatively little research has been conducted on the Vroom–Yetton model, the results of a few studies have been encouraging. For example, Jago and Vroom (1977) found that managers who used the decision strategy recommended by the model had better quality decisions than managers who used decision strategies that the model would not have recommended.

Leadership Through Contact

Management by Walking Around

Management by Walking Around (MBWA) is another popular specific behavioral theory. This one holds that leaders and managers are most effective when they are out of their offices, walking around and meeting with and talking to employees and customers. Many industry leaders such as Sam Walton of Wal-Mart have adopted this approach with great success.

In an interesting series of studies by Komaki and her associates (Komaki, 1986; Komaki, Zlotnick, & Jensen, 1986), the behavior of bank managers was observed to determine the differences between effective and ineffective managers. The results of the investigations indicated that the main difference between the two was that effective managers spent more time walking around and monitoring the behavior and performance of their employees. Empirical evidence thus seems to support the MBWA concept.

According to the theory of Management by Walking Around, effective leaders and managers get out of their offices to walk around and talk to employees and customers.

Leadership Through Power

Another strategy that leaders often adopt is the attainment of power. Power is important to a leader because as it increases, so does the leader's potential to influence others. Leaders who have power are able to obtain more resources, dictate policy, and advance farther in an organization than leaders who have little or no power.

Earlier in this chapter, French and Raven's bases of power were alluded to in terms of their relationships to Geier et al.'s IMPACT theory. French and Raven (1959) identified five basic types of power: expert, legitimate, reward, coercive, and referent.

Expert Power

As mentioned earlier in the chapter, in certain situations, leaders who know something useful—that is, have expert knowledge—will have power. But there are two requirements for **expert power.** First, the knowledge must be something that others in an organization need. In a university's psychology department, a researcher with an excellent grasp of statistics has power over those who do not. Similarly, a soldier who knows how to get around the military bureaucracy has more power than those who only know how to follow established channels and procedures.

Second, others must be aware that the leader knows something. Information is only powerful if other people know that the leader has it or if the leader uses it (Benzinger, 1982).

Legitimate Power

Leaders obtain **legitimate power** on the basis of their positions. For example, a sergeant has power over a corporal, a vice-president has power over a supervisor, and a coach has power over his football team.

Reward and Coercive Power

Leaders also have power to the extent that they can reward and punish others. **Reward power** involves having control over both the obvious—salary increases, bonuses, or promotions—and the subtle—praise or more favorable work assignments.

For a leader to have **coercive power,** it is important that others believe she is willing to use her ability to punish; she cannot maintain coercive power if employees believe she is bluffing. Punishment includes such actions as being fired or not being promoted and the more subtle actions of being given a "cold shoulder."

Referent Power

Another source of power for a leader may lie in the positive feelings that others hold for her. Leaders who are well liked can influence others even in the absence of reward and coercive power. Leaders can obtain such **referent power** by complimenting others, doing favors, and generally being friendly and supportive (Kipnis, Schmidt, & Wilkinson, 1980).

Leadership Through Persuasion

One skill that is commonly needed by leaders is the ability to persuade others. Supervisors often need to persuade upper-level managers that a new program will work; politicians need to persuade fellow politicians to vote a particular way; and public relations executives often want to persuade the public to change its perception of an organization or a product. We will only briefly discuss two important aspects of persuasion here—the communicator and the message.

Persuasion by Communication

Considerable research has indicated that people who have certain characteristics can communicate through persuasion more easily than people who lack these characteristics, which include expertise, trustworthiness, and attractiveness.

Expertise Research has found that, in general, a leader who either has or is perceived as having **expertise** about a topic will be more persuasive than a leader who does not (Maddux & Rogers, 1980). Thus, for a leader to be able to persuade his followers, he must be the most knowledgeable about their common interest. Thus, in many high-technology fields, technical knowledge is an essential characteristic for a leader. If, however, those who are to be persuaded also are knowledgeable about a topic, the leader's expertise plays a smaller role (Rhine & Severance, 1970).

Trustworthiness Another leader characteristic that is important in persuasion is **trustworthiness.** Used car salespeople, for example, have difficulties in persuading customers to buy cars because customers do not trust them. And in many corporations, management is distrusted by its employees and thus has trouble convincing union members, especially, that the organization does not have the money available to grant raises. When being persuaded, then, people look not only at the expertise of the persuader, but also at his motives.

To improve his trustworthiness, a leader can do several things. First, he occasionally can argue against what appears to be his own self-interest (Walster, Aronson, & Abrahams, 1966). For example, he can sometimes tell his employees not to work as hard or he can disagree with other managers. In doing so, he will not appear to be one-sided.

A leader also can communicate to those he hopes to persuade that not only is he similar to them (Dembroski, Lasater, & Ramirez, 1978) but also that his goals are the same as theirs (Cantor, Alfonso, & Zillman, 1976). For example, a manager trying to increase his department budget can explain to the vice-president that his goal includes saving the company money, but to do so he needs a larger recruiting budget so that better quality employees can be hired.

Attractiveness Chapter 4 briefly observed that attractive people tend to receive higher interview scores than do unattractive people. **Attractiveness** has the same effect with persuasion: Attractive people are more persuasive than are unattractive people (Chaiken, 1979). This is why television commercials generally use attractive people, and why attractive politicians are considered to be ideal candidates.

The Message

In addition to the leader's personal attributes, the type of message that is presented also has a role in persuasion.

Message Discrepancy Suppose that you are representing a group of employees in a labor negotiation. The employees currently are paid $8 per hour, but you think they deserve $10 per hour. What strategy would best achieve an increase to $10? Would it be to ask for $20 an hour and hope that management will actually give you more than $10? Or would the best strategy be honesty—that is, ask for exactly what you want—$10 per hour? Or would the best strategy be to ask for $13 an hour so that you appear reasonable but still have room to "give in" when management offers $8.50 per hour?

According to persuasion research, the third choice would be best. Ask for more than you want and then back down during negotiations (Jaccard, 1981; Cialindi, 1985). Asking for too much, or making an argument that is too far away from the other side's, will diminish your credibility. Asking for the amount you actually desire leaves no room for negotiation.

One-Sided Versus Two-Sided Arguments Another question that arises concerning the persuasive message is whether giving only one side of an argument is better than giving both sides. The answer is, "It depends." If the person being persuaded already is positive about an idea, it is usually better to argue only one side of an issue. If, however, the other person disagrees with the reasoning, it is better to argue both sides (Sawyer, 1973). When the other side is presented, the other person's perspective is acknowledged as legitimate and understood. But after the other side of the issue has been argued, it can be refuted and the favored side then can be reargued.

Threats The threat is another method of persuasion that a leader can choose to use when appropriate. For a threat to be effective, however, the person being persuaded must actually believe that it will be carried out—that is, that the consequences of not complying *are* undesirable and inevitable (Tedeschi, Bonoma, & Schlenker, 1972).

For example, a supervisor tells an employee that she will be fired if she does not work overtime. For the threat to be effective, the employee must believe that the supervisor has both the authority and the willingness to fire her. Even then, the threat will only be effective if the employee values her job.

Threats certainly can be effective in persuasion, but they also can have negative consequences. Few people like being threatened, and many will resent the person who makes the threat (Heilman, 1974; Rubin & Lewecki, 1973). Some may even so react against the threat that they do the opposite of what the leader wants (Brehm, 1966).

Leadership: Where Are We Today?

Most of this chapter has described leadership theories. Of course, when several theories address the same topic, the question comes to mind, "Which of the theories are true?" The answer probably is that each is somewhat true and that the best "theory" about leadership is some combination.

As Figure 8.5 shows, if we combine all of the theories discussed in this chapter, leadership emerges as a set of interactions: between a leader's traits and skills, between a situation's demands and characteristics, and between followers' needs and characteristics. Thus, certain people will be effective leaders in certain situations when particular types of people are followers. Unfortunately, we are not yet at the stage where we can determine the exact matches that result in the best leadership. But it is probably safe to make the following assumptions.

1. Because different situations require different leadership styles and skills, individuals who have a wide variety of relevant skills will be best able to be effective leaders in a larger variety of situations. That is, a person who only has excellent planning skills will only be an effective leader in situations that require planning. But a leader who has excellent skills in planning, persuasion, people, goal setting, and motivation will be able to lead in many different types of situations.

   The advice that follows from this assumption is obvious. As Table 8.4 shows, an individual interested in becoming an effective leader should obtain as many leadership skills as possible. By attending leadership conferences, taking college courses, and gaining a variety of experiences, a leader can gain most of these skills.

2. Because individuals have different needs and personalities, leaders who are able to adapt their interpersonal styles to fit the needs of followers will be better leaders than those who stick to just one behavioral style. It is much easier for a leader to adapt her style to fit the individual needs of her followers than for 30 people with different needs and styles to adapt their behavior to fit their leader's needs and style.

3. Because a leader must use different skills in different situations and act differently with different followers, it is important that she be able to understand the needs of the situation, the follower, or both

Leadership Skill	Requirements of the Situation/Follower				
	Information	Direction	Empathy/Support	Motivation	Persuasion
Decision making		X			
Goal setting		X			
Persuasion	X	X		X	X
Team building			X	X	
Stress management			X		
Friendliness			X	X	
Empathy			X		
Energy				X	
Time management		X			
Technical knowledge	X				
Intelligence	X	X			

Table 8.4
Effective Leadership Skills

and then behave accordingly. Thus, leaders who accurately recognize situational and follower needs will be more effective than those who are unable to distinguish one situation from another.

Chapter Summary

This chapter has discussed several leadership theories. The oldest theory, the trait theory, postulates that people who become leaders (leader emergence) and people who are effective leaders (leader performance) possess certain traits that nonleaders or unsuccessful leaders do not. Research, however, has not supported this theory well.

Behavior theories were discussed next. These theories state that certain leader behaviors are needed for effective leadership. The Ohio State studies suggest that leader behavior can be placed into the categories of consideration and initiating structure. McGregor categorizes leader behavior according to whether it conforms to Theory X or Theory Y. Theory X leaders are task-oriented, while Theory Y leaders are person-oriented. Managerial grid theory places leadership behavior into one of five categories: country club, impoverished, task-centered, team, and middle-of-the-road.

The third types of theory discussed were situational theories. These theories are based on the assumption that certain leader behaviors will only be effective in certain situations. Examples discussed were Fiedler's contingency theory, IMPACT theory, path–goal theory, and vertical dyad linkage theory.

The final types of leadership discussed were those from the specific behavioral and skill theories. This set of theories states that effective leaders possess specific skills such as persuasion, motivation, and decision making. Ineffective leaders do not. The skills discussed in this section included decision making, walking around, power, and persuasion.

Glossary

Achievement-oriented style In path–goal theory, a leadership style in which the leader sets challenging goals and rewards achievement

Affiliation style A leadership style in which the individual leads by caring about others and is most effective in a climate of anxiety

Anxiety An organizational climate in which worry predominates

Attractiveness The extent to which a leader is appealing to look at

Coercive power Leadership power that comes from the leader's capacity to punish others

Coercive style A leadership style in which the individual leads by controlling reward and punishment and is most effective in a climate of crisis

Consideration The degree to which a leader acts in a warm and supportive manner toward his or her subordinates

Country club leadership A style of leadership in which the leader is concerned about the well-being of employees but is not task oriented

Crisis A critical time for an organization in which the outcome to a decision has extreme consequences

Despair An organizational climate characterized by low morale

Disorganization A climate in which the organization has the necessary knowledge and resources but does not know how to efficiently use the knowledge or the resources

Expertise The amount of knowledge or skill possessed by a leader

Expert power The idea that a person who has knowledge also has power

Fiedler's Contingency Model A theory of leadership that states that leadership effectiveness is dependent on the interaction between the leader and the situation

Ignorance An organizational climate in which important information is not available

IMPACT Theory A theory of leadership that states that there are six styles of leadership (informational, magnetic, position, affiliation, coercive, and tactical) and that each style will only be effective in one of six organizational climates

Impoverished leadership A style of leadership in which the leader is concerned with neither productivity nor the well-being of employees

Informational style A style of leadership in which the leader leads through knowledge and information in a climate of ignorance

Initiating structure The extent to which a leader defines and structures his or her role and the roles of his or her subordinates

Instability An organizational climate in which people are not sure what to do

Instrumental style In path–goal theory, a leadership style in which the leader plans and organizes the activities of employees

Job Choice Exercise (JCE) An objective test that is used to measure various need levels

Leader Behavior Description Questionnaires (LBDQ) A test used to measure perceptions of a leader's style by his or her subordinates

Leader emergence A part of trait theory that postulates that certain types of people will become leaders and certain types will not

Leader Match A training program that teaches leaders how to change situations so that they are consistent with their leadership styles

Leader–member relations The variable in Fiedler's Contingency Model that refers to the extent to which subordinates like a leader

Leader performance A part of trait theory that postulates that certain types of people will be better leaders than will other types of people

Leader position power The variable in Fiedler's Contingency Model that refers to the extent to which a leader, by the nature of his or her position, has the power to reward and punish subordinates

Leadership motive pattern The name for a pattern of needs in which a leader has a high need for power and a low need for affiliation

Leadership Opinion Questionnaire (LOQ) A test used to measure a leader's self-perception of his or her leadership style

Least-Preferred Co-worker (LPC) Scale A test used in conjunction with Fiedler's Contingency Model to reveal leadership style and effectiveness

Legitimate power The power that an individual has because of his or her elected or appointed position

Magnetic style A style of leadership in which the leader has influence because of his or her charismatic personality, and is effective in a climate of despair

Managerial grid A measure of leadership that classifies a leader into one of five leadership styles

Middle-of-the-road leadership A leadership style reflecting an approach that balances people and task orientation

Need for affiliation According to trait theory, the extent to which a person desires to be around other people

Need for power According to trait theory, the extent to which a person desires to be in control of other people

Participative style In path–goal theory, a leadership style in which the leader allows employees to participate in decisions

Path–goal theory A theory of leadership that states that leaders will be effective if their behavior helps subordinates achieve relevant goals

Position style A leadership style in which the leader influences others by virtue of his or her appointed or elected authority, and is effective in a climate of instability

Referent power Leadership power that exists when followers can identify with a leader and the leader's goals

Reward power Leadership power that exists to the extent that the leader has the ability and authority to provide rewards

Situational leadership theory A theory of leadership that states that effective leaders must adapt their style of leadership to fit both the situation and the followers

Sociological approach A study of leadership that focuses on the identification of characteristics possessed by leaders

Supportive style In path–goal theory, a leadership style in which the leader shows concern for employees

Tactical style A leadership style in which a person leads through organization and strategy and is most effective in a climate of disorganization

Task-centered leadership A leadership style in which the leader is more concerned with productivity than with employee well-being

Task structuredness The variable in Fiedler's Contingency Model that refers to the extent to which tasks have clear goals and problems can be solved

Team leadership A leadership style in which the leader is concerned with both productivity and employee well-being

Thematic Apperception Test (TAT) A projective test that is used to measure various need levels

Theory X leaders Leaders who believe that employees are extrinsically motivated and thus lead by giving directives and setting goals

Theory Y leaders Leaders who believe that employees are intrinsically motivated and thus lead with a "hands-off" approach

Trait theory A type of leadership theory based on the idea that personal characteristics determine leader emergence and leader performance

Trustworthiness The extent to which a leader is believed and trusted by his or her followers

Vertical dyad linkage (VDL) theory A leadership theory that concentrates on the interaction between the leader and his or her subordinates

Vroom-Yetton Model A theory of leadership that concentrates on helping a leader choose how to make a decision

9

John R. Maher/Stock Boston

Group Behavior and Conflict

W ith few exceptions, most employee behavior takes place in groups. Firefighters work together when fighting a fire, managers make decisions in committee meetings, and bank tellers work together in dealing with customers. Because employees tend to work in groups, it is important for a manager or a leader to understand group dynamics.

Definition of a Group

Perhaps the first place to begin our discussion of group behavior is by deciding on what constitutes a group. For a collection of people to be called a group, the following four criteria must be met (Gordon, 1983): (1) The members of the group must see themselves as a unit; (2) the group must provide rewards to its members; (3) anything that happens to one member of the group affects every other member; and (4) the members of the group must share a common goal.

Multiple Membership

The first criterion is that the group must have multiple members. Obviously, one person does not constitute a group and two people are only considered a pair or a dyad. Thus, at least three people are necessary to form a group. But these three or more people also must see themselves as a unit. Thus, three individuals walking down the sidewalk would only be considered a group if they know one another and are together. Eight separate customers shopping at a store also would not be considered a group.

Group Rewards

The second group criterion is that membership must be rewarding for each individual in the group. We will shortly discuss the reasons that people join groups, but for now it is important to remember that people will only join or form a group if it provides some form of reward.

To demonstrate this point, imagine four students studying for an exam. If the four study in separate rooms and do not share information, they are not a group. But take the same four people and put them at one desk in the library. If each person studies the book separately and never communicates with the other three, then the four still will not be a group because none of the individuals is rewarded by the others. But if none of the four would have studied independently, then the four students would be considered a group because being together was rewarding. Even though they did not talk with one another during their time in the library, the fact that they were together provided the structure for each of them to study.

Corresponding Effects

The third group criterion is that if an event affects one group member, it affects all group members. That is, if something significant happens to one person and does not affect any of the other people gathered with her, then the collection of people cannot be considered a group. This criterion is called **corresponding effects.** For example, five bank tellers work side by side; one teller becomes ill and goes home. If the activities of the other four change as a result of the one teller leaving, the five might be considered a group. But if the activities of the four do not change after the one teller leaves, then the tellers cannot be considered a group.

Common Goals

The fourth and final criteria is that all members share a **common goal.** In the teller example, if the goal of one of the tellers is to meet only young, single customers, while the goal of another teller is to serve as many customers as possible, the tellers are not considered to be a group because they work in different ways and for different reasons.

Reasons for Joining Groups

Affiliation

Affiliation involves our need to be with other people. Thus, one of the reasons that people join groups is to be near and to talk with other people. Research has demonstrated that our need for affiliation is very strong. Mayo (1946), for example, found that employees at a textile plant who worked separately from other employees were not as satisfied with their jobs as were employees at the same plant who had the opportunity to work with others. Likewise, Burling, Lentz, and Wilson (1956) found that turnover in a hospital could be reduced by assigning maids to work in teams rather than work alone.

Perhaps the most interesting demonstrations of the strength of the human affiliation need come from the writings of Schein (1956) and Naughton (1975). These researchers were interested in the reasons why American prisoners of war (POWs) in World War II behaved so differently from those in the Korean and Vietnam Wars. More specifically, POWs in World War II made more escape attempts, suffered fewer deaths, and provided information less frequently to the enemy than did their counterparts in Korea and Vietnam.

Although the American public attributed the differences to a postwar decline in the American character (Hampton, Summer, & Webber, 1978), both Schein and Naughton pointed out the differences from a perspective of group dynamics. In World War II, the POWs were kept in groups that remained together for long periods of time. Thus, these men were able to receive emotional support from one another, they could work together to plan escapes, they were able to hear what each POW said to the enemy, and they knew about and supported a strong group norm about not talking to the enemy.

In the two Asian conflicts, the situations were entirely different than in World War II. Rather than living in groups, these POWs were isolated and not allowed to communicate with one another. Naughton (1975) reports that the men were so in need of contact and communication with others that they scraped their cell walls to make noise and establish contact and informal communication with one another. This behavior is similar to that reported by hostages held in Beirut and Syria.

These examples, as well as research studies, indicate that people often perform better and usually are more satisfied with their work when in groups. If people are not allowed the opportunity for affiliation, they make attempts to secure at least minimal contact. When even minimal contact is not possible, morale and perhaps even the will to live are lessened.

Of course, people are not equal in their desire or need to affiliate with others (Smart, 1965). For example, computer programmers have lower needs and desires to affiliate than do people in many other occupations. This point is especially interesting because a trend in the computer-programming industry is to place programmers and analysts into groups to debug programs and solve problems (Shneiderman, 1980). Although research is not yet available on the effects of such grouping, putting such strong individualists into groups does not sound like a promising idea.

Research indicates that people often perform better and are usually more satisfied with their work when they are placed in work groups.

Identification

Another reason why we join groups is our desire for **identification** with some group or cause. There are many examples of this need to identify with others. In the 1960s and 1970s, young men wore their hair long; although some thought it attractive and comfortable, many others grew long hair because it helped them to identify with other males of their generation as well as separate them from adult males of previous generations. Many of us still know someone who wears his hair long and refers to the 1960s and 1970s, thus identifying himself with an earlier period. In the 1980s, so-called punk styles of hair and clothes were worn by students in much the same way that long hair and tie-dyed shirts were worn by people in the 1960s. But each was separating himself from a more conservative majority and identifying with a more liberal or radical group.

Around your school you may notice that many students wear T-shirts with logos or messages. Students wearing "Twisted Sister," Los Angeles

Dodgers, or "Sail Florida" shirts are all identifying themselves with particular groups and thus making statements about themselves.

A study by Cialindi and his associates (Cialindi, Borden, Thorne, Walker, Freeman, & Sloane, 1976) investigated clothing as a means of identification. At several universities, Cialindi et al. observed the number of students who wore school-related clothing such as T-shirts and sweatshirts on the Monday following a school football game. They found that following a football victory, many more students wore school-related clothing than on Mondays following football losses. In a second study, Cialindi et al. also asked students who won the football game. As we might expect, when the football team won, the students answered by saying, "We won." When the team lost, the students answered by saying, "They lost." Based on these two studies, Cialindi called this identification process "basking in reflected glory."

Another example of the identification process comes from a major manufacturing plant in Virginia. Several months before union contract talks were to begin, the company gave each employee several nice shirts with the name of the company printed on the front. The company did this because it had noticed in the past that in the months before contract negotiations began, the employees began to wear more union caps and shirts. The company believed that this clothing helped increase the employees' level of identification with the union. To counter this effect, the company hoped that its shirts would influence the negotiation process. Although we cannot determine the exact effect of this strategy, that year was the only one in a decade that union members did not strike.

Emotional Support

We also join groups to obtain emotional support. Alcoholics Anonymous and Weight Watchers are good examples of groups that provide emotional support for their members.

Assistance or Help

People often join groups to obtain assistance or help, much as they form to satisfy emotional support needs. For example, students having problems with an algebra class might form a study group.

Common Interests

People often join groups because they share an interest in the same thing. At school, students joining a geology club share an interest in geology, students joining a fraternity share an interest in socializing, and students joining a service club such as Circle K or Alpha Phi Omega share an interest in helping people.

It is an interesting side note that most campus clubs that are based on common academic interests such as a psychology club or a Latin club usually are smaller and less active than other campus groups. Apparently, college students have many needs and common academic interests usually are not as strong as the social needs that are satisfied by the Greek organizations. For example, a service club on the Radford University campus was having difficulty attracting members, so several advisors suggested that it increase its number of social activities so as to attract people who had both community service and social needs. This slight change in activities increased membership from 15 to 45.

Common Goals

People who join political parties are examples of people joining groups in pursuit of a common goal. These people also may share common interests, but their primary purpose is to get a particular person or members of a particular party elected to office. The quality circles described in the employment profile of Corrinne Champion are also good examples of people joining groups because of a common goal.

Physical Proximity

One especially strong reason that people join groups, especially those that are informal in nature, is physical proximity. That is, people tend to form groups with people who either live or work nearby. For example, think of the intramural teams on your campus. Most teams consist of students who live in the same dorms or have classes together. At work, employees tend to form groups that consist of those who work in the same general area. And as we will discuss in greater detail in a later chapter, some employees seek close physical proximity to people in power in the hope that they will become part of an elite group.

Employment Profile

Corrinne Champion
Training Associate
AT&T Microelectronics

I began my career as a trainer in a rather unorthodox way. All of my past work experience had been in the clerical field, either as a secretary or an executive assistant. These positions included stints in a variety of business areas such as financial institutions, hospitals, and state and federal governments. After a period of time, I ended up in Virginia and sought work with my present employer, AT&T. This was previous to divestiture, when we were known as Western Electric.

I first accepted a clerical position in the training organization at AT&T. As I gradually became comfortable in my position, I became acutely aware that this was indeed my niche. I decided that I wanted to become a trainer and somehow needed to set goals and objectives to accomplish this career move.

I began with the secretarial/clerical universe by visiting employees in their work area and inquiring as to what they felt they needed in materials and training to perform their job more efficiently and effectively. From there, I outlined what I felt this universe of employees needed relative to training. I presented this to my supervisor, proposing that I design, develop, and conduct this training myself. To my delight, my supervisor not only approved the proposal, but also lent encouragement for my efforts and support for the program.

Becoming brave with my success, I designed, developed, and conducted orientation programs for our salaried and professional employees. From there I progressed to designing and conducting training programs for employees entering our supervisory universe. Included in the programs are sessions on effective communication, listening skills, company policies, attendance program, effective managing, problem solving, time management, production scheduling, and shop-floor training.

In addition to these responsibilities, I was requested to develop a program in participative management for our employees. Having no knowledge or background in this field, I researched the local library and developed a quality circle program designed for our facility and employees. I began with a secretarial/clerical circle and expanded to eight circles within a year's time to include several engineering circles and one supervisory circle. I initiated the formation of a quality-circle steering committee and served as a resource person to this committee, actively working to promote the concept and growth of the program throughout the plant.

My first circle, the "Quality Analysts," became my favorite group. We began by resembling a toddler beginning to walk: hesitating, wobbling, and progressing into a confident, assured group. My reward and biggest thrill was seeing the group evolve, particularly those members who at first felt too shy to offer an idea or participate, and then seeing these members become the strongest participants in the circle.

Upon completion of their circle training, and brainstorming for their first problems to work on, it was easy for them to reach a consensus as to what problem they wanted to tackle. Their project evolved out of a real concern. Due to the makeup or nature of our work environment, about the only way for our secretarial/clerical people to advance was to bid on a position in the shop, particularly, the position of "quality checker." Our secretarial/clerical employees became a "feeder" group for this job. Unfortunately, their background in office skills did not match the job description for this position. The lack of these necessary skills was acutely brought home to them as they stepped into this position. Their solution to the problem was to design a training program to help them obtain these skills.

The quality analysts designed a formal six-week, forty-five-hour training course. This training was to be accomplished on company time. Using their job description as a guideline, the group members included training sessions on communication skills, quality statistics, blueprint reading, electrical theory and testing, proper use of mechanical measuring devices, and instruction in completing required paperwork.

The group worked zealously in preparing their presentation to management, following the steps learned in circle training and adhering to company training guidelines. Each member took responsibility for a portion of the proposal. Armed with facts and utilizing graphs and charts, the group made its presentation to management. It was outstanding! They were granted immediate approval and support for this program.

Again, following quality-circle guidelines, the group needed a way to measure the effectiveness of this training for evaluation purposes. At the circle's recommendation, pretests and posttests were given for the segments on communication skills, blueprint reading, and electrical theory and testing. At the end of the training period, the circle evaluated the program and made recommendations for improvement. Pretest and posttest scores validated the effectiveness of the training. In some cases, knowledge was increased by as much as 100%. Feedback from the participants indicated that the employees felt a lot more confident in the performance of their jobs as a direct result of this training. Additionally, the group recommended that another eight hours be added to the blueprint reading session, utilizing actual blueprints from members' respective shops.

Factors Affecting Group Performance

Group Cohesiveness

Group cohesiveness involves the extent to which its members like and trust one another. In general, the more cohesive the group, the greater its productivity (Speroff & Kerr, 1952), member satisfaction (Exline, 1957), and member interaction (Shaw & Shaw, 1962). Research has demonstrated that cohesive work groups perform best in such areas as safety (Speroff & Kerr, 1952), turnover and absenteeism (Van Zelt, 1952), and job satisfaction (Zander, 1982). Furthermore, cohesive baseball and volleyball teams tend to win more games than do less cohesive teams (Bird, 1977; Long, 1972).

In its 1989 strike against Pittston Coal Co., the United Mine Workers union realized the importance of cohesiveness and identification needs by adopting a unique strategy. Each union member as well as his or her family members and supportive friends wore camouflage shirts and fatigues as a sign of unity. Every time a miner looked around him, he saw others dressed like him. The union members thus developed a sense of unity and cohesiveness that helped them last through a lengthy strike. Groups such as the Boy Scouts and the Guardian Angels also wear uniforms to increase group cohesiveness.

But cohesiveness also can lower group performance, especially in a work setting. When employees become too cohesive, they often lose sight of organizational goals. For example, it is common for restaurant employees to put the needs of other employees above those of their customers. Similarly, police departments tend to be highly cohesive—so much so that anyone who is not a police officer is considered an outsider, which can make community relations difficult.

Research also has demonstrated that with cohesive work groups, employees will conform to a norm of lower production even though they are capable of higher performance (Forsyth, 1983; Roethlisberger & Dickson, 1939). An excellent example of this conformity to a group norm involved the Hollywood Division of the Los Angeles Police Department in the early 1980s. Many of the division's officers and detectives were extensively involved in property crimes. Breaking into various retail stores, they would radio that they were responding to the ringing burglar alarms. They then placed the stolen goods in their car trunks and proceeded as if they were investigating the break-ins. The officers later met at specific locations to hide and sell the stolen goods. Officers who did not participate in the crimes saw the merchandise and knew what was going on, but they did not report the offenders. Instead, they put their loyalty to their fellow officers above their loyalty to the city or the police department.

Although the majority of research supports the conclusion that cohesiveness results in better group performance, it is not always necessary to have cohesion to have high group performance. For example, the Oakland A's in the early 1970s and the New York Yankees in the mid-1970s were baseball teams that won championships despite constant fighting among the players.

Group Homogeneity

The homogeneity of a group concerns the extent to which its members are similar. A homogeneous group contains members who are similar in some or most ways, while a heterogeneous group contains members who are more different than alike. An important question for a leader to consider when developing a group is, which composition, homogeneous or heterogeneous, will lead to the best group performance? Many research studies have sought to answer this question, but only mixed results have been found, with some studies finding homogeneous groups to be more effective and others finding heterogeneous groups more effective. For example, Hoffman (1959) found groups with homogeneous personalities to be superior in a laboratory task, while Aamodt and Kimbrough (1982) found groups with heterogeneous personalities to be superior for solving a laboratory problem. Likewise, Klein and Christiansen (1969) found heterogeneous basketball teams to be best, while Vander Velden (1971) found that homogeneous basketball teams performed better than heterogeneous teams.

Neufeldt, Kimbrough, and Stadelmaier (1983) sought to explain these mixed results by predicting that certain types of groups would do better with certain types of tasks. Neufeldt and his colleagues thus had homogeneous and heterogeneous groups each perform several different tasks. Though they expected the homogeneous groups to perform better on simple tasks and the heterogeneous groups to perform better on more complex tasks, Neufeldt et al. instead found that the type of task did not moderate the relationship between group composition and performance.

Aamodt, Kimbrough, and Alexander (1983) then hypothesized that previous research yielded mixed results because the compositions of the best-performing groups were actually somewhere between completely homogeneous and completely heterogeneous. These authors thus labeled them **slightly heterogeneous groups.**

To test their hypothesis, Aamodt and his colleagues separated 202 NCAA Division I basketball teams into three categories based on the racial composition of the starting five players. Heterogeneous groups were teams with three whites and two blacks or two blacks and three whites (3–2), homogeneous groups had five blacks or five whites (5–0), and slightly heterogeneous groups had either four blacks and one white or four whites and one black (4–1). The study results supported the notion that slightly heterogeneous groups were superior—they won 60% of their games. Both heterogeneous and homogeneous teams won about 53% of their games (all winning percentages are above 50% because Division I teams played and usually beat many non–Division I teams).

These results were later supported by a study that divided contestants on the television game show *Family Feud* into the same three groups as described above but with gender rather than race as the variable. The results indicated that the slightly heterogeneous teams won more money than the other two group types. The slightly heterogeneous families won an average of $330, heterogeneous families an average of $278, and homogeneous families an average of $254.

Thus this research appears to support the conclusion that the best working groups consist primarily of people who are similar but with a dissimilar person adding tension and a different vantage point. But it is not yet clear which variable is most important in terms of determining group composition. That is, variables in previous research have included race, gender, personality, intelligence, attitudes, and background. Thus, a group might be homogeneous in terms of race but heterogeneous in gender. More research is needed to clarify this issue.

Stability of Membership

The greater the **stability** of the group, the greater the cohesiveness. Thus, groups whose members remain in the group for long periods of time are more cohesive and perform better than groups that have high turnover. A good example again can be found on a college campus. At most colleges, fraternities and sororities usually are the most active organizations and have high levels of performance, while professional clubs and honorary societies such as Psi Chi and Lambda Alpha Beta tend to be the least active. Why is this? Certainly, it cannot be the abilities of the memberships—honorary societies have more intelligent members than most fraternities and sororities. Instead, the answer might be in the stabilities of the groups. Students tend to join Greek organizations in their freshman or sophomore years, while students tend to join professional clubs in their junior year and honorary societies in their senior year to help "pad" their résumés. The Greek organizations thus have more stable memberships than the other organizations.

Isolation

Physical **isolation** is another variable that tends to increase a group's cohesiveness. Groups that are isolated or located away from other groups tend to be highly cohesive. A good example is the New River Valley (Virginia) branch of the AT&T Credit Union. The credit union has 10 branches, most located within a few miles of one another and within a few miles of the main branch in Winston–Salem, North Carolina. The New River Valley branch is 100 miles from the next closest branch; physically and psychologically, the branch is isolated from the main part of the organization. The New River Valley branch, however, is the only one to have no turnover in five years. It also is the branch where the employees are most cohesive.

Outside Pressure

Groups who are pressured by outside forces also tend to become highly cohesive. To some degree, this response to **outside pressure** can be explained by the phenomenon of *psychological reactance* (Brehm, 1966). When we believe that someone is trying to intentionally influence us to take some particular action, we often react and do the opposite (Van Leeuwen, Frizzell, & Nail, 1987). Consider, for example, a teenaged dating couple. As the boy calls to pick up his date, the girl's father notices the young man's beard and Harley-Davidson motorcycle and forbids his daughter to go out. Before this order, the daughter may not have been especially interested in the boy, but after being told she cannot go on the date, she reacts by liking him more.

On a larger scale, such reactions are commonly seen in labor negotiations. Company managements and unions tend to disagree with and criticize one another. But often such criticism backfires—attacking another group may serve to strengthen that group. In fact, if a company or group wants to increase the cohesiveness of its membership, it can artificially create pressure and attribute it to another group. This tactic involves building a "straw man"—an opponent who does not actually exist but to whom negative statements about the group can be charged (Schweitzer, 1979).

Group Size

Groups are most cohesive and perform best when **group size** is small. Studies have shown that large groups have less coordination and lower morale (Frank & Anderson, 1971) and are less active (Indik, 1965) than

Task Type	Group Activity
Additive	Typing pool
	Relay race
	Bowling team
	Car washing
Disjunctive	Problem solving
	Brainstorming
	Golf tournament
Conjunctive	Assembly line
	Hiking

Table 9.1
Examples of Task Types

smaller groups. In fact, research suggests that groups perform best (Manners, 1975) and have greater member satisfaction (Hackman & Vidmar, 1970) when they consist of approximately five members. Thus, a large organization probably works best when it is divided into smaller groups and committees, and work groups are limited to approximately five people.

This does not mean, however, that small groups are always best. Although small groups usually increase cohesiveness, high performance is only seen with certain types of tasks. **Additive tasks** are those for which the group's performance is equal to the sum of the performances by each group member. **Conjunctive tasks** are tasks for which the group's performance depends on the least effective group member. **Disjunctive tasks** are those on which the group's performance is based on the most talented group member. Examples of the three task types are shown in Table 9.1. Large groups are thought to perform best on disjunctive and additive tasks, while small groups perform best on conjunctive tasks (Steiner, 1972; Frank & Anderson, 1971).

The addition of more members has its greatest effect when the group is small. This idea was first investigated by Latane (1981) when he formulated **social impact theory.** As an example, imagine a four-person committee studying safety problems at work. If the group is stable and cohesive, adding a fifth person may be disruptive. But in a factory of 3,000 employees, the hiring of one new employee is not likely to change the complexion of the company. That is why sport experts have observed that a single great player can turn around a poor basketball team—as occurred with Bill Walton and the Portland Trailblazers or Kareem Abdul-Jabbar and the Milwaukee Bucks—but not a football or baseball team.

Group Status

The higher the group's status, the greater its cohesiveness. This is an important point: A group can be made more cohesive by increasing **group status.** The group does not actually have to *have* high status, but it is more important that its members *believe* they have high status.

Again, look around campus and notice the methods used by various groups to artificially increase their status. On our campus, one fraternity advertises itself as the "Porsche of fraternities," while another claims to be the "fraternity of distinction." Of course, there is little difference between the actual status and performance of most organizations, so effective leaders try to increase the cohesiveness of group members by claiming high status—and it apparently works.

One way that leaders can increase their groups' status is by increasing the perception that the groups are difficult to join but that, once in, members will find that the groups' activities are special. In most high schools, "two-a-day" practices are typical during the week before football practice begins. During this period, each prospective team member is worked close to exhaustion. Coaches have such "hell weeks" to increase team status and thus its cohesion and performance. Obviously, a player cannot get into shape in a week, so the purpose of two-a-day practices is not conditioning—it is to build the status of the group members who survive the week. A similar approach is taken by the Marine Corps. By its tough basic training, the corps builds the status of its enlistees so that Marines and non-Marines alike will believe that the corps consists of just a "few good men."

Fraternities and sororities also are notorious for hazing during their pledge weeks. Aside from the illegality and cruelty of this behavior, hazing serves the purpose of increasing the effort required for a potential member to join, thus increasing the group's cohesiveness and status. Football players, Marines, and fraternity or sorority members are not likely to quit a group that they have worked so hard to join.

Communication Structure

Another variable that can affect a group's performance is its **communication structure** or network. For a group to perform successfully, it is essential that there be good communication among members. As shown in Figure 9.1, a variety of communication networks can be used by small groups alone; even more complex networks are possible with larger groups. Each network has its advantages and disadvantages, but the best networks depend on the situations and goals of their groups. For exam-

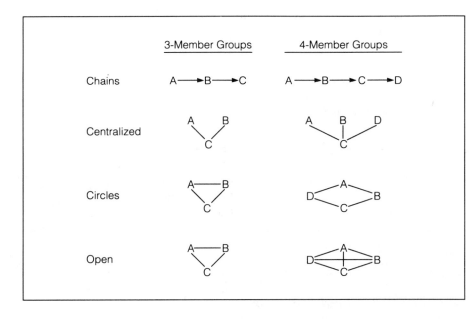

Figure 9.1
Possible
Communication
Networks for Small
Groups

ple, if the goals of fraternities and singles clubs are to allow the members to get to know one another, then a centralized structure is less conducive than a completely open one. Conversely, if the goal of a group is to solve a problem as quickly as possible, then the centralized network would be the best structure. A good leader thus carefully chooses the communication network that best facilitates the goals of his group.

Group Roles

Another factor that affects the performance of a group is the extent to which its members assume different roles. For a group to be successful, its members' roles must fall into one of three categories: task-oriented, maintenance-oriented, and individual (Benne & Sheets, 1948). Task-oriented roles involve behaviors such as offering new ideas, coordinating activities, and finding new information; maintenance-oriented roles involve encouraging cohesiveness and participation; and individual roles include blocking group activities, calling attention to one's self, and avoiding group interaction. Individual roles seldom result in higher group productivity.

Group members often will naturally assume these roles based on their individual personalities and experiences, although sometimes leaders must assign roles to certain individuals. For example, if a leader notices that every group member is filling a task-oriented role, she may either recruit a new group member or assign a current member to fill a maintenance role.

Skill Level	Facilitation: Increased Performance	Inhibition: Decreased Performance
Well-learned	Bicycle racing	—
	Pool shooting	—
	Simple mathematics	—
	Ant nest building	—
	Cockroaches running	—
Novice	—	Pool shooting
	—	Learning nonsense syllables
	—	Completing a maze
	—	Complex mathematics
	—	Cockroaches turning

**Table 9.2
Tasks Affected by
Social Facilitation
and Social Inhibition**

Presence of Others

Social Facilitation and Inhibition

In 1898, researcher N. Triplett noticed that cyclists rode faster when competing against other cyclists than when competing against a clock. Intrigued by this observation, Triplett conducted a study in which children completed a task either alone or while competing against other children. As expected, Triplett found that children who worked against others completed their tasks faster than did children who worked alone.

Since that first study, psychologists have studied what we now call *social facilitation* and *social inhibition*. **Social facilitation** involves the positive effects of the presence of others on an individual's behavior; **social inhibition** involves the negative effects of others' presence (research examples are listed in Table 9.2). Social facilitation and social inhibition can be further delineated by *audience effects* and *coaction*.

Audience Effects The phenomenon of **audience effects** takes place when a group of people passively watches an individual. An example would be a sporting event held in an arena.

The strength of the effect of having an audience present is a function of at least three factors. Latane (1981) hypothesized these factors to be an audience's size, its physical proximity to the person or group, and its status. Thus, groups are most likely to be affected by large audiences of experts who are physically close to the group (Jackson, 1986; Tanford & Penrod, 1984).

Social facilitation or social inhibition may occur when a manager looks over the shoulder of an employee who is working.

Coaction The effect on behavior when two or more people are performing the same task in the presence of one another is called **coaction**. Examples would be two runners competing against each other without a crowd present or two mail clerks sorting envelopes in the same room.

Explaining Social Facilitation Effects More than 200 studies of social facilitation have indicated that performance does not always increase in the presence of others. Performance will increase only when the task being performed is easy or well learned; performance will decrease when the task is difficult or not well learned (Bond & Titus, 1983; Zajonc, 1965). Social facilitation and coaction effects occur not only with humans, but also with cockroaches running a maze (Zajonc, Heingartner, & Herman, 1969), chickens eating food (Tolman, 1968), and ants building nests (Chen, 1937).

Job performance will increase in the presence of others when the task being performed is well learned or easy.

Although the exact reason for these findings has not been agreed upon by researchers, four explanations have each received some empirical support. The first explanation holds that the **mere presence** of others naturally produces arousal (Zajonc, 1980). This arousal or increase in energy helps an individual perform well-learned tasks but hinders him on poorly learned or unpracticed tasks.

The second explanation states that a coacting audience provides a means for **comparison.** If an individual is working on a task with another individual, she can directly compare her performance to the other person's (Seta, 1982). In some jobs, this comparison effect may increase competition and production quantity, while in other jobs, comparison effects may cause employees to slow down so as to be in line with the working norm.

The third explanation—that of **evaluation apprehension**—hypothesizes that judgment by others causes the differential effects of social facilitation (Cottrell, 1972). That is, individuals are aware that the presence of others can be rewarding (for example, when a crowd cheers) or punishing (when a crowd boos). Thus, on well-learned tasks, the individual knows that he normally performs well and thus expects a rewarding experience when in the presence of others. When the task is not well learned, however, the individual may believe that he will not perform well and will be embarrassed, and thus he performs even worse than if he were alone.

One example of this phenomenon was seen in an experiment by Michaels, Blommel, Brocato, Linkous, and Rowe (1982). Michaels and his colleagues observed students shooting pool and found that good players increased their shot accuracy from 71% to 80% when watched by an audience, while poor players' accuracy decreased from 36% to 25% when they were watched.

The evaluation-apprehension explanation has special application to industry and training settings. Imagine a waiter who must carry five plates of food to a table. For a new waiter, this is not a well learned task, and in the presence of others he is likely to be anxious. When the lack of practice in carrying plates is combined with a large restaurant crowd, the chance of an accident increases. So what is the solution? The waiter should practice carrying several plates before the restaurant opens.

The fourth explanation proposes that the presence of others is **distracting** to the individual who is trying to perform a task (Sanders, 1981). On well-learned tasks, the individual is able to perform despite the distraction because the behaviors are almost automatic. On a novel task, however, the distraction caused by other peoples' presence keeps the individual from concentrating and learning the task.

An example that demonstrates the effects emphasized by both the evaluation-apprehension and distraction theories is that of coaching children in sports. In a typical Little League practice, one coach must teach an 8-year old how to bat while 10 other children stand in the field and wait for a ball to be hit to them. Each time the child at the plate fails to hit the ball, the others tease him. After a while, the children in the field are bored and begin to throw rocks and talk with one another. What is the probability of success in teaching this child to hit under these circumstances? For the coach to be successful, he must teach the child alone and away from other children.

Social facilitation effects also have been examined in the sports world by investigating the advantage that a team might have by playing its game at home. In general, having a home crowd behind a team increases the probability of its winning; this is especially true with indoor sports (Schwartz & Barsky, 1977). The effect increases immediately after a crowd cheers a play or boos a referee's decision (Greer, 1983).

Social Loafing

While the social facilitation and social inhibition theory explains increases and decreases in performance when others are present and either watching the individual or working separately, the **social loafing** theory considers the effect on individual performance when people work together on a task. Social loafing was first investigated in a study by Ringleman (reported in Moede, 1927), whose subjects singly pulled as hard as possible on a rope while he measured their exerted force. Ringleman then had his subjects perform the task in pairs. He expected the force exerted by two subjects to be approximately twice that exerted by a single subject, but to his surprise he found that both subjects exerted less force than when they worked alone.

More recent research has supported the theory and has found that social loafing occurs with many tasks. For example, one study found that restaurant customers tipped about 19% of the bill when they dined alone, 16% of the bill when they dined with another person, and 13% when they dined with five others (Latane, 1981). This explains why tips, or gratuities, often are automatically added to a bill when six or more people dine at a table.

Although it is clear that social loafing occurs, it is not clear *why* it occurs. One theory is that because group members realize their individual efforts will not be noticed, there is little chance of individual reward. A second theory, called the *free-rider theory* (Kerr & Bruun, 1983), postulates that when things are going well, a group member realizes that his effort is not necessary and thus he does not work as hard as he would if he were alone. If this explanation is true, social loafing should only occur when a group project is going well.

The third theory, called the *sucker-effect theory* (Kerr, 1983), hypothesizes that social loafing occurs when a group member notices that other group members are not working hard and thus are "playing him for a sucker." To avoid this situation, the individual lowers his work performance to match those of the other members. This theory, however, does not explain the loafing of other members.

Social loafing is an important variable to keep in mind: Having employees work together on a project may not be as productive as having them work individually. Fortunately, social loafing can be reduced by identifying individual performance and providing feedback to each worker as to how hard he works when rated against some goal or standard (Williams, Harkins, & Latane, 1981).

Individual Dominance

Another variable that can affect group performance is **individual dominance** by a leader or single group member. If the leader or group member has an accurate solution to a problem the group is trying to solve then the group probably will perform at a high level. But if the leader or group member has an inaccurate solution, then he will lead the group astray and it will perform poorly.

Groupthink

The term **groupthink** was coined by Janis (1972) after studying the disastrous Bay of Pigs invasion of 1961. The Bay of Pigs was the Cuban landing site for 1,400 Cuban exiles who sought to overthrow the government of Fidel Castro. The plan called for the U.S. Navy and Air Force to covertly protect the invasion force and its supply ships. The invaders, however, were met unexpectedly by 20,000 Cuban troops and quickly killed or captured. The help promised by the U.S. government never developed. Janis (1972) proposed the concept of groupthink to explain how some of the nation's brightest men could hatch such an ill-conceived plan.

With groupthink, members become so cohesive and likeminded that they make poor decisions despite contrary information that might reasonably lead them to another decision. Groupthink most often occurs when the group:

- is cohesive
- is insulated from qualified outsiders
- has an illusion of invulnerability, infallibility, or both
- believes that it is morally superior to its adversaries
- is under great pressure to conform
- has a leader who promotes a favorite solution
- has gatekeepers who keep information from other group members

Groupthink can be reduced in several ways. First, the group leader should not state her own position or beliefs until late in the decision-making process. Second, the leader should promote open discussion and encourage group members to speak. Third, a group or committee can be separated into subgroups to increase the chance of disagreement. Fourth, one group member can be assigned the job of **devil's advocate**—that is, one who questions and disagrees with the group.

Individual versus Group Performance

One important decision that a leader must make is when to assign tasks to individuals and when to assign tasks to groups or committees. This decision should be based both on the type of task and the outcome desired. If the *quality* of the task is most important, it should be assigned to a group or committee. Research has shown that groups generally produce higher quality results than do individuals (Lorge, Fox, Davitz, & Brenner, 1958). Group superiority in performance probably is due to the fact that a group encourages its members to work on a task more seriously, provides emotional support, and provides a broader knowledge base (Maier, 1976).

If the task involves *creating* ideas, individuals should be asked to independently create ideas and then meet as a group. Although brainstorming is a commonly used technique, it is not an effective one. In **brainstorming,** group members are encouraged to say aloud any and all ideas that come to mind and are not allowed to comment on the ideas until all have been given. When research compares a brainstorming group's creativity with that of a single individual, the brainstorming group almost always will be more creative. The important comparison, however, would involve the same number of people who are in the brainstorming group independently creating ideas and then comparing the total number and quality of these ideas with the total number and quality of ideas created by the brainstorming group. When such a comparison is made, the sum of the individuals working independently are more creative than the group (Dunnette, Campbell, & Jaastad, 1963; Lamm & Trommsdorff, 1973; Diehl & Stroebe, 1987).

If the task involves *taking chances* or *being risky,* then the task should be assigned to a group or committee. Although showing somewhat mixed results, research generally has shown that groups make more decisions that require risk than do individuals (Clark, 1971; Johnson & Andrews, 1971). An example of this comes from a brokerage firm that was interested in getting its brokers to make riskier but higher yielding investments. A consulting firm was asked to develop a way to select such brokers. Using its knowledge of group dynamics, the consulting firm told the brokerage company that it could obtain better results by having its brokers make investment decisions in groups rather than individually. Implementing this suggestion, the company later reported that its brokers were indeed making riskier investments.

Group Conflict

As discussed early in this chapter, there are many reasons for joining groups and many factors that influence group performance. When individuals work together in groups, however, there is always potential for conflict.

Conflict can keep people from working together, lessen productivity, spread to other areas, and increase turnover. This does not mean that conflict is always bad. In fact, moderate conflict often produces higher group performance than either low or high levels of conflict (Brown, 1983). The energy resulting from moderate levels of conflict can stimulate new ideas and increase friendly competition (Litterer, 1966). Furthermore, moderate conflict can reduce the risk of much larger conflicts.

Types of Conflict

Interpersonal Conflict

Within an organization, employees can be in conflict with one another over many things. Two employees competing for a promotion, a new desk, or the opportunity to talk with the boss are all examples of opportunities for conflict. Although interpersonal conflict usually is the result of the factors that we will soon discuss, it also can result from an individual's play for power or need for conflict (Berne, 1964).

When a person is in conflict with another, she usually can respond with one of five styles (Thomas, 1970). With the **avoiding style,** she chooses to ignore the conflict and hopes that the conflict will resolve itself. When conflicts are minor and infrequent, this style may be fine, but obviously it is not the best way to handle every type of conflict.

When a person is so intent on settling a conflict that she gives in and risks hurting herself, she has adopted the **accommodating style.** People who use this style when the stakes are high usually are viewed as cooperative but weak. An example of this style was observed by this author at a self-serve gas station. Two drivers parked their cars next to the same pump at roughly the same time. Both drivers got out of their cars and simultaneously reached for the only pump. Obviously, one person had to give in to avoid conflict, and so would have to wait five minutes longer than the other. Yet one driver quickly told the other to "go ahead." Why did this person so quickly accede to the other? Probably because he has an accommodating reaction to potential conflict and, in this case, the stakes were low.

A person with a **forcing style** handles conflict in a win–lose fashion and does what it takes to win with little regard for the other person. This style can be effective in winning, but it also can damage relations so badly that other conflicts will result.

An individual with a **collaborative style** wants to win but also wants to see the other person win. These people seek win–win solutions—that is, ways in which both sides get what they want. This style is probably the best to use whenever possible (Burke, 1970).

The final strategy is the **compromising style**. The user of this type adopts give-and-take tactics that allow each side to get some of what it wants but not everything it wants.

Individual–Group Conflict

Conflict also can occur between an individual and a group just as easily as between two individuals. **Individual–group conflict** usually occurs when the individual's needs are different from the group's needs, goals, or norms. For example, a Marine might want more independence than the Corps will give him, a basketball player might want to shoot when the team needs him to set picks, a faculty member might be more interested in teaching when her university wants her to publish, and a store employee might be more interested in customer relations when the store wants him to concentrate on sales.

Group–Group Conflict

The third type of conflict is that which occurs between two or more groups. In academia, such **group–group conflict** occurs annually as departments fight for budget allocations and space. In industry, company divisions often conflict for the same reasons. A good example of group–group conflict occurred between two branches of the same bank located in the same town. The branches not only competed with other banks for customers, but also with each other. To make matters worse, the two branches were to be consolidated, so their staffs were involved in even more conflict as they tried to establish who would be in charge of the new and unified branch.

Causes of Conflict

Competition for Resources

In the marketplace, when customer demand exceeds product supply, prices increase. Similarly, in groups, when demand for a resource exceeds its supply, conflict occurs. This often occurs in organizations, especially when there is not enough money, space, personnel, or equipment to satisfy the needs of every person or every group.

A good example of this cause of conflict, **competition for resources,** annually occurs when Congress decides on the nation's budget. With only limited tax revenues and many worthy programs, tough choices must be made. But often instead of working together to solve the country's problems, our representatives come into conflict over whose favorite programs will be funded.

Another example of this competition occurs in colleges and universities across the country. There are probably few universities where parking and office spaces are not a problem. Faculty and students argue about who gets the parking places, and once that argument is settled, seniors and juniors argue over what is left.

This author once belonged to an organization that initially had no conflict over resources because there were none to fight over. There were no extra offices, no equipment, and no supplies. Organization members even had to supply their own paper! After several years, however, the organization received a large amount of money and a new building with plenty of space. But as expected, conflict increased. Everyone wanted more space, their own computers, and so on. What had once been a very cohesive group was now one characterized by conflict because of competition for new resources.

Task Interdependence

Another cause of conflict, **task interdependence,** comes when the performance of some group members depends on the performance of other group members (Pfeffer & Salancik, 1978). For example, a group is assigned to present a research report. The person who is assigned to type the report cannot do his job unless he can read what others have written, the person assigned to write the conclusion cannot do so until others have written their sections, and no member of the group is finished until every member has completed his or her assignment.

Conflict caused by task interdependence is especially likely when two groups who rely on each other have conflicting goals. For example, the production department in a factory wants to turn out a high volume of goods, while the quality control department wants the goods to be of high quality. Neither department can do its job without the help of the other, and yet a production department with high quantity goals probably will have lower quality standards than those desired by quality control. By insisting on high quality, the quality control department is forcing the production department to slow down. When this happens, conflict is likely to occur.

Jurisdictional Ambiguity

A third cause of conflict, **jurisdictional ambiguity,** is found when geographical boundaries or lines of authority are unclear. When lines of authority are not clear, conflict is most likely to result when new situations and relationships develop (Deutsch, 1973). A good example was seen in an organization that was changing from typewriters to computers that could use word-processing software. Before the change, the head of the secretarial department was in charge of selecting and purchasing all the secretarial equipment and the head of the data-processing department was responsible for selecting and purchasing all of the organization's computer equipment. Conflict came when it developed that the new machines were to be used by the secretaries but were to be considered computer equipment and thus under the purview of the data-processing department. The two department heads thus waged a "turf battle" to determine who would have authority for the word-processing equipment.

Communication Barriers

Communication barriers are the fourth cause of conflict. The barriers to interpersonal communication can be *physical,* such as separate locations on different floors or in different buildings; *cultural,* such as different languages or different customs; or *psychological,* such as different styles or personalities. An in-depth discussion of the communication process can be found in Chapter 11.

Personality

A fifth cause of conflict is **personality**—that is, the personalities of people involved in conflict. As we all have observed, certain people seem more inclined toward conflict than others. Research has revealed that people who are dogmatic and authoritarian and who have low self-esteem are involved in conflict more often than open-minded people who feel good about themselves.

Reactions to Conflict

When conflict does occur, people respond in several common ways (Blake, Shepard, & Mouton, 1964). While some are better responses than others, each of the following is appropriate in certain situations:

withdrawal, winning at all costs, persuasion, smoothing and conciliation, negotiation and bargaining, cooperative problem solving, and third-party intervention.

Withdrawal

When conflict occurs, **withdrawal** from the situation is one of the easiest ways to handle it. A person can leave a difficult marriage by divorce, an employee can avoid a work conflict by quitting the organization, or a manager can avoid a turf battle by letting another manager win. Even though withdrawal can make one feel better, often it only postpones conflict rather than prevents it.

Winning at All Costs

A second reaction to conflict is adopting what has been called a *win–lose mentality* in which the goal is to win a conflict and cause another person to lose (Johnson & Johnson, 1975). This strategy of **winning at all costs** occurs especially when a person regards his side as correct and the other person's side is viewed as incorrect or as the enemy.

This reaction often occurs when each side needs a victory to gain or retain status. Union–management conflicts provide good examples of this need for status. For a union to survive, its members must perceive it as being useful. Thus, during contract negotiations, union leadership must force management to "give in," or it runs the risk of losing status with its membership.

But the problem with putting status on the line is that it makes backing down to resolve a conflict very difficult. As a conflict escalates, each side "digs in" and becomes less willing to compromise. Unless one side has the resources to clearly win, the win-at-all-costs reaction is likely to prolong conflict. Thus, this strategy is only appropriate if the position holder actually is correct and if winning the conflict is more important than the probable damage to future relationships.

Persuasion

It is possible to resolve conflict without taking a win-at-all-costs strategy. If one side in a conflict is convinced that it is right, it can seek to "win" by solving the conflict through techniques of **persuasion.** This can be done by providing the other side with factual evidence on a position's correctness, discrediting the opponent's position, and pointing out how the proposal will benefit the other side.

Smoothing and Conciliation

An effective way to end conflict, or to at least limit its damage, is by using tactics of **smoothing and conciliation.** These tactics involve expressing a desire for cooperation, offering compliments, avoiding negative interaction, emphasizing the similarities of two groups, and pointing out common philosophies.

Osgood (1966) believes that one key to resolving conflict is to reduce tension and increase trust between two parties. This can be accomplished by stating an intention to reduce tension, publicly announcing what steps will be taken to reduce tension, inviting the other side also to take action to reduce tension, and making sure that each initiative offered is unambiguous. By taking these steps early on, minor conflict can be resolved quickly and serious conflict can be resolved through negotiation.

Negotiation and Bargaining

Most conflicts are resolved through some form of compromise so that a solution benefits both sides (Forsyth, 1983; Seitz & Modica, 1980). Thus, a good way to handle conflict is by **negotiation and bargaining.** That is, the most important points are negotiated and less important points are given up. This process usually begins with each side making an offer that asks for much more than it really wants. For example, union leaders might demand $10 an hour while management offers $5 an hour. Each side understands what the other is doing, so the union might lower its demand to $9 and management might raise its offer to $6. This process continues until an acceptable compromise has been reached.

An *acceptable compromise* is one that will fall within the settlement range for both sides (Schatzki, 1981). According to Schatzki, a settlement range is between the **least acceptable result (LAR)** and the **maximum supportable position (MSP)** for each side. The LAR is the lowest settlement that a person is willing to accept, one that must be realistic and satisfy the person's actual needs. The MSP is the best possible settlement that a person can ask for and still reasonably support with facts and logic. A short-order cook's proposal for $30 an hour would not be reasonably supportable and thus would not be a proper MSP.

As shown in Figure 9.2, negotiations usually begin with each side offering its MSP as an opening bid. The actual negotiating territory is the area between both sides' LARs. Each side then bargains for a settlement closest to its own MSP and the other's LAR. The final settlement will be a function of the skill of each negotiator as well as time pressures. Such

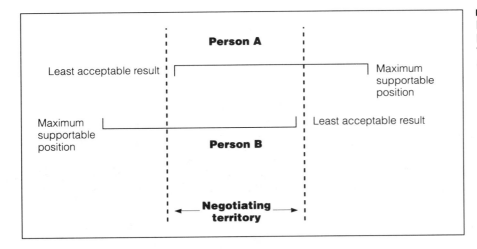

**Figure 9.2
Negotiating
Territory and
Conflict Resolution**

Person A

Least acceptable result

Maximum
supportable
position

Maximum
supportable
position

Least acceptable result

Person B

**Negotiating
territory**

pressures may be exerted by customers who cannot wait for a settlement or union members who cannot financially afford prolonged negotiations.

Seitz and Modica (1980) have suggested four indicators that tell when negotiations are coming to an end so that each side can prepare its final offer:

1. The number of counter-arguments are reduced.
2. The positions of the two sides appear closer together.
3. The other side talks about final arrangements.
4. The other side appears willing to begin putting things in writing.

Although this conflict-resolution strategy appears to be the best approach to take, it often is not. Sometimes, compromise results in a bad solution. For example, if Congress wants to include $100 million in the federal budget to construct a new nuclear-power plant and the President wants to budget only $50 million, then the two are likely to agree on a median figure such as $75 million. But if the project cannot be completed for less than $100 million, then the compromise may waste millions of dollars that could be spent elsewhere.

Cooperative Problem Solving

Another conflict-resolution strategy is for two sides to jointly arrive at a solution. A good example of **cooperative problem solving** is when the president of an organization forms a task force or committee with representatives from all of the departments or divisions that will be affected by the solution. Together these representatives work to define the problem, identify possible solutions, and arrive at the best solution.

Third-Party Intervention

If conflict cannot be resolved by the parties involved, it is often a good idea to bring in outside help—that is, ask for **third-party intervention.** This outside help usually is provided through arbitration or mediation.

Arbitration With **arbitration,** a neutral third party listens to both sides' arguments and then makes a decision. Within an organization, this neutral party often is the manager of the two employees in conflict (Katz & Kahn, 1978). Arbitration decisions can be either *binding* or *nonbinding.* If the decision is binding, the two sides have agreed to abide by the arbitrator's decision regardless of how displeased one or both sides may be with that decision. If the decision is nonbinding, then one or both sides can reject an unfavorable decision. Even though arbitration can end conflicts quickly, usually neither side is as satisfied with the outcome as they would be had they settled the conflict themselves (Stagner & Rosen, 1965).

Mediation With **mediation,** a neutral third party is asked to work with both sides to reach a mutually agreeable solution to the conflict. The job of a mediator usually is not to make a decision for the groups, but rather to facilitate the solution process. Mediators are most useful when two parties do not like one another (Kressel & Pruitt, 1985), and provide the best results when both sides consider them to be competent and trustworthy (Rubin & Brown, 1975).

Chapter Summary

Chapter 9 has provided an in-depth discussion of both group dynamics and group conflict. Groups were defined as consisting of multiple members who perceive themselves as a unit.

We also discussed the many reasons why people join groups. These reasons include a need for affiliation, a need to identify with success, a need for emotional support, and a need for assistance, common goals, and physical proximity. Groups can be successful in attracting members only if they satisfy important needs.

Not all groups are successful in terms of survival and performance. Some of the factors that influence a group's success include its level of cohesiveness, the composition of its membership, the stability of the membership, and the group's size, status, and communication structure. We saw, for example, how being in the presence of others in a group can increase performance through social facilitation or decrease performance through both social inhibition and social loafing.

Conflict also can occur when people work in groups. Such conflict can occur between two people, between a person and a group, or between two groups. Conflict usually results from factors such as competition for resources, task interdependence, jurisdictional ambiguity, communication barriers, and personality.

When conflict occurs, people or groups can react in several ways. They can ignore the conflict through withdrawal, try to win at all costs, try to persuade the other side to resolve the conflict in their favor, use smoothing and conciliation to end the conflict, bargain for an agreement, or ask for third-party help.

Glossary

Accommodating style The conflict style of a person who tends to respond to conflict by giving in to the other person

Additive tasks Tasks for which the group's performance is equal to the sum of the performances of each individual group member

Affiliation The need to be with other people

Arbitration A method of resolving conflicts in which a neutral third party is asked to choose which side is correct

Audience effects The effect on behavior when one or more people passively watch the behavior of another person

Avoiding style The conflict style of a person who reacts to conflict by pretending that it does not exist

Brainstorming A technique in which ideas are generated by people in a group setting

Coaction The effect on behavior when two or more people are performing the same task in the presence of each other

Collaborative style The conflict style of a person who wants a conflict resolved in such a way that both sides get what they want

Common goal An aim or purpose shared by members of a group

Communication barriers Physical, cultural, and psychological obstacles that interfere with successful communication and create a source of conflict

Communication structure The manner in which members of a group communicate with one another

Comparison The effect when an individual working on a task compares his performance with the performance of another person performing the same task

Competition for resources A cause of conflict that occurs when the demand for resources is greater than the resources available

Compromising style A style of resolving conflicts in which an individual allows each side to get some of what it wants

Conjunctive tasks Tasks for which the group's performance is dependent on the performance of the least effective group member

Cooperative problem solving A method of resolving conflict in which two sides get together to discuss a problem and arrive at a solution

Corresponding effects An event that affects one member of a group will affect the other group members

Devil's advocate A group member who intentionally provides an opposing opinion to that expressed by the leader or the majority of the group

Disjunctive tasks Tasks for which the performance of a group is based on the performance of its most talented member

Distracting The idea that social inhibition occurs because the presence of others provides a distraction that interferes with concentration

Evaluation apprehension The idea that a person performing a task becomes aroused because he or she is concerned that others are evaluating his or her performance

Forcing style The conflict style of a person who responds to conflict by always trying to win

Group cohesiveness The extent to which members of a group like and trust one another

Group-group conflict Conflict between two or more groups

Group homogeneity The extent to which members of a group are similar

Group size The number of members in a group

Group status The esteem in which the group is held by people not in the group

Groupthink A state of mind in which a group is so concerned about group cohesiveness that it ignores important information

Identification The need to associate ourselves with the image associated with other people, groups, or objects

Individual dominance When one member of a group dominates the group

Individual–group conflict Conflict between an individual and the other members of a group

Interpersonal conflict Conflict between two people

Isolation The degree of physical distance of a group from other groups

Jurisdictional ambiguity Conflict caused by a disagreement about geographical territory or lines of authority

Least acceptable result (LAR) The lowest settlement that a person is willing to accept in a negotiated agreement

Maximum supportable position (MSP) The highest possible settlement that a person could reasonably ask for and still maintain credibility in negotiating an agreement

Mediation A method of resolving conflict in which a neutral third party is asked to help the two sides reach an agreement

Mere presence The theory that states that the mere presence of others naturally produces arousal and thus may affect performance

Negotiation and bargaining A method of resolving conflict in which two sides use verbal skill and strategy to reach an agreement

Outside pressure The amount of psychological pressure placed on a group by people who are not members of the group

Personality Relatively stable traits possessed by an individual

Persuasion A method of resolving conflict in which one side uses facts to convince the other side that the first side's position is correct

Slightly heterogeneous group A group in which a few group members have different characteristics from the rest of the group

Smoothing and conciliation Resolving a conflict by cooperating with and praising the opponent

Social facilitation The positive effects that occur when a person performs a task in the presence of others

Social impact theory A theory that states that the addition of a group member has the greatest effect on group behavior when the size of the group is small

Social inhibition The negative effects that occur when a person performs a task in the presence of others

Social loafing The fact that individuals in a group often exert less individual effort than they would if they were not in a group

Stability The extent to which the membership of a group remains consistent over time

Task interdependence A potential source of conflict that arises when the completion of a task by one person affects the completion of a task by another person

Third-party intervention When a neutral party is asked to help resolve a conflict

Winning at all costs An approach to handling conflict in which one side seeks to win regardless of the damage to the other side

Withdrawal An approach to handling conflict in which one of the parties removes himself or herself from the situation in order to avoid the conflict

10

Employee Motivation
and Satisfaction

Needs Theories
Maslow's Needs Hierarchy
  Basic Biological Needs
  Safety Needs
  Social Needs
  Ego Needs
  Self-Actualization Needs
    Rotation, Enlargement, and Enrichment
  Evaluation of Maslow's Theory
ERG Theory
Two-Factor Theory
McClelland's Needs Theory
Cognitive Theories
Equity Theory
Expectancy Theory
Consistency Theory

Behavioral Theories
Operant Conditioning
  Premack Principle
  Goal Setting
  Feedback
Social Learning Theory
Individual Differences Theory
Measuring Job Satisfaction
Chapter Summary
Glossary

After an organization has selected and trained its employees, it must then ensure that the employees are both motivated by and satisfied with their jobs. Industrial psychologists generally define work **motivation** as the force that drives a worker to perform well. Ability and skill determine whether a worker *can* do the job, but motivation determines whether the worker *will* do it properly. Although actually testing the relationship between motivation and performance is difficult, researchers generally agree that increased worker motivation results in increased job performance.

But the same is not true of **job satisfaction,** which can be defined as the attitude an employee has toward his job. Research has shown that job satisfaction is related to an employee's attendance and tenure but not to his job performance (Iaffaldano & Muchinsky, 1985; Muchinsky & Tuttle, 1979). At first, this may seem surprising, but after some thought and an example it should make more sense.

Imagine taking a course that is required for graduation and in which you must make at least a B. Imagine that the topic is boring and the class instructor is terrible (obviously, this cannot be your industrial psychology class). It is doubtful that you will be satisfied with the class, but you still will perform well enough to earn the grade you need. That is, your level of satisfaction will not affect your performance. Instead, your dissatisfaction with the class and the teacher may motivate you to miss class, to withdraw and take another class, or to never again take a class from that instructor. In other words, your level of satisfaction will affect your class attendance and perhaps your tenure in that class, but it will not affect your performance.

The same is true in industry. Employees who are not satisfied with their jobs still will perform to earn money and job security, but they may frequently skip work, and they probably will change jobs if given the opportunity. Thus, even though increased job satisfaction probably will not result in higher performance, attendance and tenure are important enough variables to justify a concern for employee satisfaction. Furthermore, because it is believed that increased motivation will result in increased performance, it is essential to understand the reasons for and causes of worker motivation.

In this chapter, we will explore several theories that seek to explain why workers are satisfied with and motivated by their jobs. None of the theories completely and accurately explains job satisfaction and motivation, but each is valuable in that it suggests ways to increase employee performance and satisfaction. Thus, even though a theory itself may not be supported by research, the resulting suggestions generally have led to increased performance or longer tenure. This is an important point be-

Employment Profile

Devon Bryan, M.A.
Compensation Analyst
J. I. Case

Although I have recently changed jobs and am now a classification analyst for a major manufacturer of farm and construction equipment, located in Racine, Wisconsin, I would like to describe the work I performed while I was employed as a consultant.

This chapter in your text discusses several ways to increase job satisfaction for employees, and I would like to concentrate on one aspect of that process. One of the projects that I worked on involved testing employees to determine their abilities and interests, and then discussing with them potential careers that they might want to consider. One of the reasons that people leave their jobs is because either they do not enjoy the work they are performing or the job does not satisfy their needs. Thus, a nice way to make people more satisfied with their jobs is to find the perfect match between the person's interests and abilities and those required by a particular job. With this idea in mind, let me tell you about the project I was involved in.

We received a contract with an organization that is unique in that it is a joint venture between a union (Communication Workers of America) and a company (AT&T). The purpose of The Alliance is to promote employee growth and development.

For two years, we met with employees in groups of twenty. On the first day, each employee took a battery of tests that included eight short ability tests, an interest inventory, and a test of vocational values. This testing process lasted about three hours.

The following week, we met individually with each employee to discuss the results of the tests. The main idea behind the meetings was to show each employee the occupations for which his or her abilities, interests, and values were best suited and then to narrow these occupations to those in which each employee showed a special interest.

For example, the test results might show a strong match between the employee's abilities and interests and those needed for twenty different occupations. The employee would usually look at descriptions of each of these occupations and perhaps narrow the twenty down to four or five that seemed particularly appealing. Even though most of the employees performed identical jobs for AT&T, the range in their ideal occupations was astounding. Many wanted to enter careers in traditional areas such as computer programming, cosmetology, and clerical work. What made the job so interesting, however, were those who wanted to enter unusual jobs such as being a blacksmith, modeling, catering, and truck driving.

After the occupational choices had been narrowed, each employee took one or two weeks to further investigate his or her ideal occupation. This was accomplished by interviewing people already in the field and reading material about the jobs.

When the employee was through with his or her investigation, we talked about what he or she had found. Sometimes after investigating the occupations, they did not seem nearly as interested, and we developed new alternatives. Most of the time, however, the employee came back excited and anxious to pursue a new career. At this point, we discussed the steps that would be necessary to get a job in that field. Often the step involved taking courses at a local community college. Fortunately for the employee, The Alliance paid the tuition for these courses.

For many employees, we also discussed job search skills and helped them write résumés so that they would be better able to obtain their ideal jobs. Unquestionably, the best part of this project was when an employee would succeed in obtaining an ideal job and thus have a more satisfying life.

cause most textbooks have separate chapters for motivation and satisfaction. In this text, the two are combined—not because motivation and satisfaction are the same construct, but because the suggestions that result from these theories can be applied to increase both satisfaction and motivation.

An interesting way to increase job satisfaction can be found in the employment profile of Devon Bryan.

Needs Theories

Needs theories postulate that job satisfaction is determined by how well the job or the organization is able to satisfy certain employee needs such as safety and recognition. Although needs theories have brought beneficial ways of looking at employee behavior, they have generally been criticized as being untestable and involving wants rather than needs.

Maslow's Needs Hierarchy

Perhaps the most famous theory of satisfaction and motivation was developed by Abraham Maslow (1954). Maslow believed that an individual (and here we mean an employee) would be satisfied with her job at any given point in time if certain needs were met. As Figure 10.1 shows, Maslow believed that there are five major types of needs and that these needs are hierarchical—that is, lower-level needs must be satisfied before an employee will be concerned with the next level of needs. It is helpful to look at a **hierarchy** as if it were a staircase that is climbed one step at a time until the top is reached. The same is true of Maslow's hierarchy. Each level is taken one step at a time, and a higher level cannot be reached before a lower level.

Basic Biological Needs

Maslow thought that an individual first seeks to satisfy **basic biological needs** of food, air, water, and shelter. In our case, an individual who does not have a job, is homeless, and is on the verge of starvation will be satisfied with any job as long as it provides for these basic needs.

Safety Needs

After basic biological needs have been met, a job that merely provides food and shelter will no longer be satisfying. An employee then will become concerned about meeting his **safety needs.** That is, he may work in an unsafe coal mine to earn enough money to ensure his family's survival, but once his family has food and shelter, he will remain satisfied with his job only if the workplace is safe.

Social Needs

Once these first two need levels have been met, an employee will remain satisfied with his job only when his social needs have been met. **Social needs** involve working with others, developing friendships, and feeling

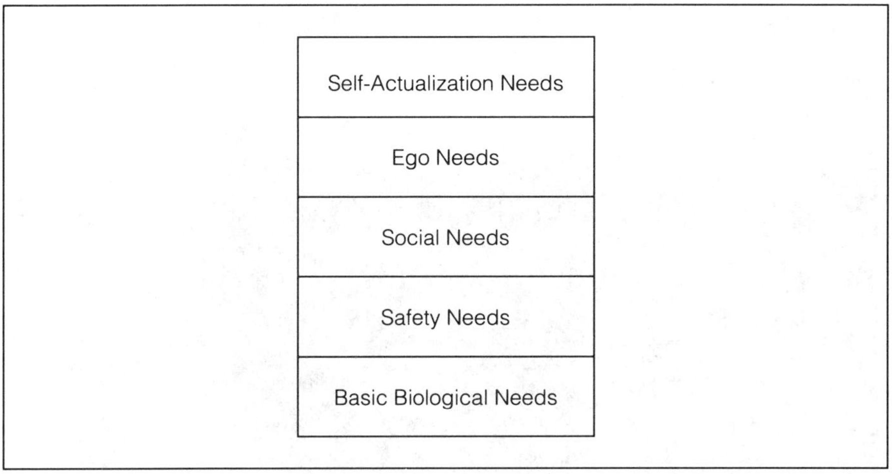

**Figure 10.1
Maslow's Hierarchy
of Needs**

Self-Actualization Needs
Ego Needs
Social Needs
Safety Needs
Basic Biological Needs

needed. Organizations attempt to satisfy their employees' social needs in a variety of ways. Company cafeterias provide workers the place and opportunity to socialize and meet other employees, company picnics allow families to meet one another, and company sports programs such as bowling teams and softball games provide opportunities for employees to play together in a neutral environment.

It is important that an organization make a conscious effort to satisfy these social needs when a job itself does not encourage social activity. For example, with a job such as that of a janitor or a night watchman, the employee will encounter few other people while working. Thus, the chance of making new friends is small.

Ego Needs

When social needs have been satisfied, the employee next concentrates on meeting his **ego needs.** These are needs for recognition and success, and an organization can help to satisfy them through praise, awards, promotions, salary increases, and publicity. Ego needs can be satisfied in many ways. For example, Johnny Carson has commented that the most prestigious sign at NBC is not the salary of the television star or producer, but rather whether the person has his or her own parking place. Likewise, many organizations use furniture to help satisfy ego needs. The higher the employee's position, the better her office furniture. Similarly, at one engineering firm in Louisville, Kentucky, engineers are not allowed to mount their diplomas or awards on the wall until they receive their professional certification.

A coal miner working in unsafe conditions might work enough to earn money to fill his family's survival needs, but after those needs are filled he will only be satisfied with the job if the workplace is made safe.

Jack Spratt/The Image Works

Michael J. Okoniewski/The Image Works

Assembly-line workers are likely to have difficulty satisfying their self-actualization needs on the job.

Self-Actualization Needs

Even when an employee has friends, has earned awards, and is making a relatively high salary, she may not be satisfied completely with her job: Her **self-actualization needs** might not have been satisfied yet. These needs are the fifth and final level of Maslow's needs hierarchy (the top level in Figure 10.1). Self-actualization might be best defined by the U.S. Army's recruiting slogan, "Be all that you can be." An employee striving for self-actualization wants to reach her potential in every task. Thus, an employee who has worked with the same machine for 20 years may become dissatisfied with her job. She has accomplished all that can be accomplished with that particular machine and now searches for a new challenge. If none is available, she may become dissatisfied.

With some jobs, satisfying self-actualization needs is easy. For example, a college professor always has new research to conduct, new classes to teach, new clients to consult. Thus, the variety of tasks and the new problems that are encountered provide a constant challenge that can lead to higher job satisfaction.

Other jobs, however, may not satisfy self-actualization needs. A good example is an employee who welds parts on an assembly line. For 8 hours a day, 40 hours a week, he performs only one task. Boredom and the realization that the job will never change begin to set in. It is no wonder that the employee becomes dissatisfied.

Rotation, Enlargement, and Enrichment To help satisfy self-actualization needs, several changes can be made. The easiest and most common are **job rotation, job enlargement,** and **job enrichment.** With job rotation and job enlargement, an employee learns how to use several different machines or conduct several different tasks within an organization. With job enlargement, an employee is given more tasks to do at one time. With job rotation, the employee is given the same number of tasks to do at one time, but the tasks change from time to time.

Job rotation and job enlargement accomplish two main objectives. First, they challenge the employee by requiring him to learn to operate several different machines or to perform several different tasks. Thus, once the employee has mastered one task or machine, he can then work toward mastering another.

Second, job rotation helps to alleviate boredom by allowing an employee to change tasks. Thus, if an employee welds parts one day, assembles bumpers on another, and tightens screws on a third, the boredom caused by performing the same task every day should be reduced.

But an even better way to satisfying self-actualization needs is through **job enrichment.** The main difference between job rotation and job enrichment is that with the former, an employee performs different tasks, and with job enrichment, the employee assumes more responsibility over the tasks (Ford, 1973).

If we look again at the job of college professor, job enrichment clearly is an inherent part of the job. That is, the professor decides what she will research and what she will teach in a particular course. This authority to make decisions about one's own work leads to higher job satisfaction.

With an assembly line worker, however, responsibility is something that must be added because the employee has minimal control over the way a job is done. After all, bumpers must be assembled in the same way each time and welded to the same place. So what can be done to enrich the typical factory worker's job?

One method is to give workers more responsibility over their jobs. For example, when an employee first begins working for a company, his work is checked by a quality control inspector. After the employee has been with the company long enough for the first four needs levels to be satisfied, the employee is given responsibility for checking his own quality. Likewise, more control can be given to the employee about where and when he will eat lunch, when he will take vacation time, or how fast he will accomplish his work. At one Kaiser Aluminum production plant, for example, time clocks were removed so that the workers could assume more responsibility for their performance by keeping track of their own hours.

It may seem strange to suggest that allowing an employee to make such trivial decisions as lunch times will result in higher job satisfaction. But research has shown that allowing residents in a nursing home to make such decisions resulted in lower death rates as did allowing them to own pets (Langer & Rodin, 1976; Schulz, 1976). Thus, it is not far-fetched to think that allowing control even in limited areas can increase one's level of job satisfaction.

Even when increased decision-making responsibilities are not possible, job-enrichment ideas still can be implemented. For example, many organizations have or work with credit unions whose credit committees and boards of directors consist of company employees. These committees and boards provide excellent opportunities to increase employees' decision-making powers even though the decisions are not related directly to their jobs.

Another method to increase the level of job enrichment is by showing employees that their jobs have meaning and that they are meeting some worthwhile goal through their work (Hackman & Oldham, 1975). At some automobile factories, for example, this is accomplished by having employees work in teams to build cars. Instead of an employee performing a single task all day, he does several tasks, as do the other employees in his group. Thus, at the end of the day, the employee can see a completed car that he has had a major role in building.

A plant that manufactured transformers provides another example. The training department realized that even though employees spent 8 hours a day manufacturing the product, few understood what it did, who used it, and what would happen if it were not manufactured correctly. To correct this problem, the employees participated in a training session in which they were shown how the transformer was used, who used it, and the consequences that resulted from poor manufacturing.

The final method for increasing employees' self-actualization needs that we will discuss here is the use of **quality circles.** With quality circles, employees meet as a group and make decisions about such quality-enhancing factors as the music played in the work area, the speed of the assembly line, and how to reduce waste. Quality circles are especially effective in increasing employees' job satisfaction when there is little or no chance for advancement. They allow employees to have more control and responsibility.

The concepts behind job enrichment were supported in a survey conducted by Hackman and Oldham (1975, 1976) that served as the basis for their **job characteristics theory.** This theory postulates that individuals differ in their need for growth. For those individuals who have a strong need for growth, jobs with high satisfaction levels allow the worker to use a variety of skills, allow independence, have a significant positive impact on society, and involve completing an entire project rather than just one part.

Evaluation of Maslow's Theory

Although Maslow's needs theory makes good intuitive sense and is popular with managers and marketing analysts, research generally has not supported it (Wahba & Bridwell, 1976). Perhaps the biggest problem with the theory concerns the number of levels. Although Maslow believed there are five needs levels, research has failed to support that number and suggests instead that there may only be two or three levels (Aldefer, 1972; Lawler & Suttle, 1972; Mitchell & Mougdill, 1976).

A second problem with the theory is that some people do not progress up the hierarchy as Maslow suggests they do. That is, most people move up from the basic biological needs level to safety needs to social needs and so on. Some people, however, have been known to skip levels. For example, Evel Knievil obviously skips the safety needs level and goes straight to satisfying his ego needs. Thus, when exceptions to the hierarchical structure occur, the theory loses support.

Another problem is that the theory predicts that once the needs at one level are satisfied, the next needs level should become most important. Research, however, has shown that this does not necessarily happen (Salancik & Pfeffer, 1977).

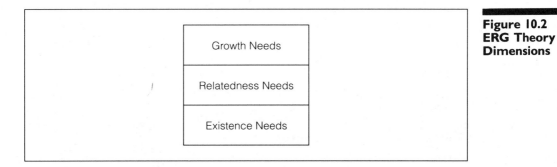

**Figure 10.2
ERG Theory
Dimensions**

Even if Maslow's theory has not been supported by research, it still may be useful. Some of the theory's specific assertions may not be true, but it still provides guidelines that organizations can follow to increase job satisfaction. Providing recognition, enrichment, and a safe workplace *do* increase employee satisfaction. The validity of these suggestions is probably why Maslow's theory still is widely used by industrial psychologists even though it is not popular with academicians and researchers.

ERG Theory

Because of the problems with Maslow's needs hierarchy, Aldefer (1972) developed a needs theory that has only three levels. As shown in Figure 10.2, the three levels are existence, relatedness, and growth—hence the name **ERG Theory**. Research by Wanous and Zwany (1977) has supported Aldefer's proposed number of levels.

Other than the number of levels, the major difference between Maslow's theory and ERG theory is that Aldefer views the three levels as being continuous rather than hierarchical. That is, a person can skip levels. By allowing for such movement, Aldefer has removed one of the biggest problems with Maslow's theory.

Furthermore, Aldefer has explained why a higher level sometimes does not become more important once a lower level need has been satisfied. Aldefer believes that for jobs in many organizations, advancement to the next level is not possible because of such factors as company policy or the nature of the job. Thus, the path to the next level is blocked, and the employee becomes frustrated and places more importance on the previous level. Perhaps that is why some unions demand more money and benefits for their members rather than job enrichment. They realize that the jobs always will be tedious and that little can be done to improve them. Thus, the previous needs level becomes more important. This idea has received at least some empirical support (Hall & Nougaim, 1968; Salancik & Pfeffer, 1977).

Hygiene Factors	Motivators
Pay	Responsibility
Security	Growth
Co-workers	Challenge
Working conditions	Stimulation
Company policy	Independence
Work schedule	Variety
Supervisors	Achievement
	Control
	Interesting work

**Table 10.1
Examples from
Herzberg's
Two-Factor Theory**

Two-Factor Theory

Still another needs theory was developed by Herzberg (1966), this one reducing the number of levels to two. As shown in Tables 10.1 and 10.2, Herzberg believes that job-related factors can be divided into two categories—motivators and hygiene factors—thus the name **two-factor theory. Hygiene factors** are those job-related elements that result from but do not involve the job itself. For example, pay and benefits are consequences of work but do not involve the work itself. Similarly, making new friends may result from going to work, but they also are not directly involved with the tasks and duties of the job.

Motivators are the elements of a job and *do* concern actual tasks and duties. Examples of motivators would be the level of responsibility, the amount of job control, and the interest that the work holds for the employee. Herzberg believes that hygiene factors are necessary but not sufficient for there to be job satisfaction and motivation. That is, if a hygiene factor is not present at an adequate level (for example, the pay is too low), the employee will be dissatisfied. But if all hygiene factors are represented adequately, the employee's level of satisfaction will only be neutral. Only the presence of both motivators and hygiene factors can bring job satisfaction and motivation.

Thus, an employee who is paid a lot of money but has no control or responsibility over her job probably will be neither satisfied nor dissatisfied. But an employee who is not paid enough *will* be dissatisfied even though she might have tremendous control and responsibility over her job. Finally, an employee who is paid well and has control and responsibility probably will be satisfied.

Again, Herzberg's is one of those theories that makes sense but has not received strong research support. In general, researchers have criticized the theory because of the methods used to develop the two factors

Maslow	ERG	Herzberg
Self-actualization	Growth	Motivators
Ego		
Social	Relatedness	Hygiene factors
Safety	Existence	
Physical		

Table 10.2
Comparison of the Herzberg, Maslow, and ERG Theories

as well as the fact that few research studies have replicated the findings obtained by Herzberg and his colleagues (Hinrichs & Mischkind, 1967; King, 1970).

McClelland's Needs Theory

The final needs theory that we will discuss was developed by McClelland (1961) and suggests that differences between individuals stem from the relationship between a job and each employee's level of satisfaction or motivation. McClelland believes that employees differ in their *needs for achievement, affiliation,* and *power.*

Employees who have a strong **need for achievement** desire jobs that are challenging and over which they have some control, while employees who have minimal achievement needs are more satisfied when jobs involve little challenge and have a high probability of success. In contrast, employees who have a strong **need for affiliation** prefer working with and helping other people. These types of employees are found more often in people-oriented service jobs than in management or administration (Smither & Lindgren, 1978). Finally, employees who have a strong **need for power** have a desire to influence others rather than simply be successful.

Research has shown that employees whose needs for power are very strong but who also have strong achievement needs often make the best managers (McClelland & Burnham, 1976; Stahl, 1983), and those employees who are motivated most by their affiliation needs probably make the worst managers.

These needs are measured by one of two tests. The first and most popular is the **Thematic Apperception Test (TAT)**, which was discussed briefly in Chapter 8. With the TAT, an employee is shown a series of pictures and then is asked to tell a story about each one. From the responses, a psychologist identifies the degree to which each theme of power, affiliation, and achievement is present in the stories.

The problem with the TAT is that it is time-consuming and must be administered by a psychologist trained in its use. To avoid these problems, Stahl (1983) developed a more objective and less expensive paper-and-pencil test that measures the same three needs. Although this test has not yet become popular, research seems to indicate that it is as reliable and valid a measure as the TAT (Stahl, 1983).

Cognitive Theories

Equity Theory

Equity theory was developed by Adams (1965) and is based on the premise that our levels of job satisfaction and motivation are related to how fairly we believe we are treated in comparison with others. If we believe we are treated unfairly, we attempt to change our beliefs or behaviors until the situation appears to be fair. Three components are involved in this perception of fairness: inputs, outputs, and input–output ratio.

Inputs are those personal elements that we put into our jobs. Obvious elements are time, effort, education, and experience. Less obvious elements include money spent on child care and distance driven to work.

Outputs are those elements that we receive from our jobs. A list of obvious outputs includes pay, benefits, challenge, and responsibility. Less obvious outputs are benefits such as friends and office furnishings.

According to the theory, each employee subconsciously lists all his outputs and inputs and then computes an **input–output ratio** by dividing output value by input value. By itself, this ratio is not especially useful. But each employee then computes the input–output ratios for other employees and then compares them to his own. If his ratio is lower than those of others, he becomes dissatisfied and thus is motivated to make the ratios equal in one or more ways.

First, the employee can seek greater outputs by such means as asking for a raise or for more responsibility. Second, the employee can make the ratio more equal by reducing his inputs. Thus, he might not work as hard or he might reduce his attendance.

A less practical way of equalizing the ratios would be changing the ratios of other employees. For example, an employee might try to get another employee to work harder and thus increase that employee's inputs.

Or he might try to reduce the outputs of another employee by withholding friendship or finding a way to reduce the other employee's bonuses. Fortunately, however, strategies to equalize input–output ratios seldom involve reducing others' outputs.

In general, research has supported the idea that our job satisfaction decreases when our input–output ratios are lower than others'. Research on this was conducted by Lord and Hohenfeld (1979) and Hauenstein and Lord (1989) with major league baseball players. Players who either had their salary cut during their first year of free agency or had lost an arbitration case performed at lower levels the following year. Thus, players who thought that their output (salary) was too low, responded by reducing their inputs (performance).

The degree of inequity that an employee feels when underpaid appears to be a function of whether the employee chose the actions that resulted in underpayment (Cropanzano & Folger, 1989). That is, if an employee chooses to work harder than others who are paid the same, he will not feel cheated, but if he is pressured into working harder for the same pay, he will be unhappy.

An interesting prediction from this theory is a situation in which an employee's input–output ratio is *higher* than the ratios of others. Because the theory is based on equity, the prediction would be that the employee still would strive for equal ratios by either increasing his inputs or decreasing his outputs. In other words, he would either work harder or ask to be paid less. In fact, research has indicated that employees often do respond to being "overpaid" by working harder (Adams & Rosenbaum, 1962; Pritchard, Dunnette, & Jorgenson, 1972). But feelings of inequity caused by being "overpaid" do not last long and probably do not produce long-term changes in behavior (Carrell & Dittrich, 1978).

One of the greatest problems with this theory is that despite its rational sense, it is difficult to implement. That is, based on this theory, the best way to keep employees satisfied is to treat them all fairly, which would entail paying the most to those employees who contributed the most. Although few of us would disagree with this approach, it is difficult to implement for several reasons.

The first is *practicality*. An organization certainly can control such variables as salary, hours worked, and benefits, but it cannot easily control other variables such as how far an employee lives from work or the number of friends an employee makes on the job.

The second reason that equity is difficult to achieve is that the employee's *perception* of inputs and outputs determines equity, not *actual* inputs and outputs. For example, two students of equal ability receive the same grade on an exam. One student knows that he studied 10 hours for the exam but never saw the other student in the library. He may feel that the scores are unfair because he studied harder than but received the same grade as the student whom he never saw study. Of course, the other student may have studied 20 hours while at work but the other student would not know that. In this case, the student's perception of input level may not match reality.

Thus, it is important that employees base their judgments on factual information. Of course, this may be easier said than done. Although one way to do this would be by open and public information on salaries, many organizations keep such information confidential and even include statements in their employee manuals that forbid employees from divulging their salaries to one another. Such policies, however, encourage employees to speculate about how much other people make. This speculation usually results in employees thinking the worst and believing that others make more than they do. Thus, it is probably in the best interests of an organization to make salaries and performance information available to all employees, although each employee's permission must be obtained before such information is released.

Even if an organization were able to maintain complete internal equity, employees would then compare their ratios with those for employees from other organizations. The problem with such comparisons is that an organization has little or no control over another's policies. Furthermore, perceptions of wages and benefits at other organizations most likely will be more distorted than internal perceptions. Thus, even if equity theory were completely accurate, maintaining a high level of employee satisfaction still would be difficult.

Expectancy Theory

The second cognitive theory that focuses on worker motivation is *expectancy theory,* which was first proposed by Vroom (1964) and then modified by others, including Porter and Lawler (1968). This theory has three components, the definitions of which vary with each modification of the theory. The following definitions, however, are combinations of those suggested by others and make the theory easier to understand:

- **expectancy (E):** the perceived relationship between the amount of effort an employee puts in and the resulting outcome
- **instrumentality (I):** the extent to which the outcome of a worker's performance, if noticed, results in a particular consequence

- **valence (V):** the extent to which an employee values a particular consequence

To understand or predict an employee's level of motivation, these components are used in the following formula:

$$\text{motivation} = E(I \times V)$$

Thus, all possible outcomes of a behavior are determined, the valence of each is multiplied by the probability that it occurs at a particular performance level, and then the sum of these products is multiplied by the expectancy of an employee putting in the effort to attain the necessary level of performance. As can be seen from this formula, the higher the score on each component, the greater the employee's motivation. To expound on this, let us examine each component in more detail.

In terms of *expectancy,* if an employee believes that no matter how hard she works, she will never reach the necessary level of performance, then her motivation probably will be low. For *instrumentality,* the employee will be motivated only if her behavior results in some specific consequence. That is, if the employee works extra hours, she expects to be rewarded, or if she is inexcusably absent from work, she expects to be punished. For a behavior to have a desired consequence, two events must occur. First, the employee's behavior must be noticed. If the employee believes that she is able to attain the necessary level of performance but that her performance will not be noticed, then her level of motivation will be low. Second, noticed behavior must be rewarded. If no rewards are available, then, again, motivation will be low. As will be discussed in greater detail later in this chapter, if appropriate behavior does not have positive consequences or if inappropriate behavior does not have negative consequences, then the probability that a worker will continue undesired behaviors increases and the probability that an employee will continue desired behaviors decreases.

For *valence,* if an employee is rewarded, then the reward must be something that the employee values. If good performance is rewarded by an award, then the employee will be motivated only if she values awards. Likewise, if we punish an employee by suspending her, then the punishment will be effective only if the employee needs the money. If she does not particularly like her job and would rather spend a few days at the lake, the suspension obviously will not be effective.

This theory can be used to analyze the situation experienced by one bank in Virginia. Concerned that the bank's tellers were averaging only three new Visa customers each month, the management sought to increase the number of Visa applications taken by each teller. To do so, the tellers were to ask each customer if he or she had a Visa card. If not, the tellers were to give them applications. The tellers would receive $5 extra per month each if they increased the number of new Visa customers per month to 25.

The program was a flop, much to management's surprise. Applying expectancy theory, however, would have led an I/O psychologist to predict the program's lack of success. First, let us look at the expectancy component. If the tellers currently averaged only three new Visa customers each month, they probably did not believe that, even working hard, they would be able to generate 25 new customers. Thus, the expectancy probability for the program was low.

Second, most tellers probably did not place much value on an extra $5 per month, so the valence component also was low. Thus, with two of three components having low values, the program was destined to fail from the start. The bank later reduced the monthly number of new Visa cards to 10 and increased the teller reward to $20. These simple changes brought the desired increase in new Visa customers.

In addition to predicting employee effort, expectancy theory has been applied successfully to predict speeding by drivers and cheating by students. To demonstrate this last behavior, imagine the typical examination in a typical college class.

First, look at the expectancy component. We might ask what the probability is for catching a cheater. Students who cheat most likely believe that it is very low. To determine the instrumentality component, we might ask what the probability is for some negative consequence if a cheater is caught. In many universities, this probability is low. Not only is it difficult to prove that a student cheated, but also if it is the first time a student is caught, punishment usually results in no more than a few days' suspension.

Finally, we examine the valence component. Even if a student *is* caught and suspended, how terrible would that be? For many students, a few days of vacation may not seem so terrible. Thus, combining the three components, we should not be surprised that cheating often occurs.

Expectancy theory also can be used to suggest ways to change employee motivation. As we saw with the bank, motivation was increased by making the performance standard more reasonable and increasing the value of the consequence. Similarly, if we wanted to apply the theory to decrease cheating, we would increase the probability of catching cheaters, make convicting a person who has cheated easier, and make the consequences for cheating more severe.

Although expectancy theory is an interesting and useful method of predicting and increasing employee motivation, some researchers also have criticized it. The major criticism involves the components equation. As it is now written, all of the components are multiplied. Some researchers have questioned whether the addition of some components would be more appropriate than their multiplication (Schmidt, 1973).

A second criticism involves the values that are assigned to each component (Ilgen, Nebeker, & Pritchard, 1981). Research has indicated that even though valence and instrumentality can be reliably measured (Mitchell, 1974), the theory is most predictive when people behave rationally (Stahl & Harrell, 1981), which they often do not, and have an internal locus of control (Lied & Pritchard, 1976), which may not always be the case. Despite problems with the equation, however, the theory still is one of the most useful for predicting employee behavior.

Consistency Theory

The third theory that explains job satisfaction and motivation was developed by Korman (1970, 1976) and concerns the relationship between an employee's level of **self-esteem** and job performance. According to this theory, there *is* a positive correlation between the two. Furthermore, employees with high self-esteem desire to perform at high levels, and employees with low self-esteem perform at low levels.

There are three types of self-esteem. **Chronic self-esteem** is a person's overall feeling about himself. **Situational self-esteem** is a person's feeling about himself in a particular situation such as operating a machine or talking to other people. **Socially influenced self-esteem** is how a person feels about himself based on the expectations of others. All three types of self-esteem are important to job performance.

If this theory is true, an employee's performance can be improved by increasing her self-esteem. But increasing self-esteem, especially chronic self-esteem, is difficult, although it is typically attempted in two ways. In the first, employees are given insights into their strengths, usually in workshops or sensitivity groups. These insights are thought to raise self-esteem by demonstrating to the employee that she has several strengths and is a good person.

In the second method, an employee is given a task so easy that she almost certainly will succeed. This success is thought to increase self-esteem, which should increase performance, then further increase self-esteem, then further increase performance, and so on. This method is based loosely on the principle of **self-fulfilling prophecy,** which states that an individual will perform as well or as poorly as she expects to perform. In other words, if she believes she is intelligent, she should do well on tests. If she thinks she is dumb, she should do poorly.

Research certainly has supported the concept of self-fulfilling prophecy. Rosenthal (1968) has demonstrated that our expectations of others' performance lead us to treat them differently. That is, if we think that someone will do a poor job, we probably will treat them in ways that bring that result. Thus, when an employee becomes aware of others' expectations and matches her own with them, she will perform in a manner that is consistent with those expectations.

Sandler (1986) believes that our expectations are communicated to employees through nonverbal cues such as head tilting or eyebrow raising and through more overt behaviors such as providing low-expectation employees with less feedback, worse facilities, and less praise than high-expectation employees. He also believes that employees are quick to pick up on these cues. Along with Korman (1970) and Rosenthal (1968), Sandler believes that employees then adjust their behaviors to be consistent with our expectations and in a way that is self-sustaining.

Research on consistency theory has brought mixed results. Laboratory studies generally have supported the theory: Subjects who were led to believe that they would perform well on a task did so, and subjects who were led to believe that they would do poorly on a task also did so (Greenhaus & Badin, 1974). The theory, however, has been criticized by Dipboye (1977), who believes that factors other than self-esteem, such as the need to achieve or the need to enhance oneself, can explain the same results.

But given that consistency theory does have some reasonable research support, the next concern is how it can be used to increase employee performance. If employees do indeed respond to their managers' expectations, then it becomes reasonable to predict that managers who communicate positive and optimistic feelings to their employees will lead them to perform at higher levels.

Behavioral Theories

Another set of theories hypothesizes that workers are only motivated when they are *rewarded* for excellent performance. *Behavioral theories* predict many of the same behaviors as do cognitive theories, but there is a difference in *how* these behaviors are predicted. Behavioral theories only focus on overt employee behavior, but cognitive theories focus on employees' decision-making processes.

Operant Conditioning

Perhaps the most influential behavioral theory is operant conditioning, which we briefly discussed in Chapter 6. Essentially, operant conditioning principles state that an employee will continue to do those behaviors for which he is reinforced. Thus, if an employee is rewarded for not making errors, he is more likely to produce high quality work. If the employee is rewarded for the amount of work done, he will place less emphasis on quality and try to increase his quantity. Finally, if an employee is not rewarded for any behavior, he will search for behaviors that will be rewarded. Unfortunately, these might include absenteeism (which is rewarded by going fishing) or carelessness (which is rewarded by spending more time with friends).

Obviously, it is important to reward employees for productive work behavior. But different employees like different types of rewards, which is why supervisors should have access to and be trained to administer different types of reinforcers. For example, some employees can be rewarded with praise, others with awards, some with interesting work, and still others with money.

The use of money to motivate better worker performance has again become popular and takes many forms. With a **pay-for-performance** plan, employees are paid according to how much they individually produce.

The first step in creating such a plan is to determine the average or standard amount of production. For example, the average number of envelopes sorted by mail clerks might be 300 per hour. The next step is to determine the desired average amount of pay. We might decide that, on average, our mail clerks should earn $9 an hour. We then compute the piece rate by dividing hourly wage by number of envelopes sorted ($9 \div 300$), which is .03. Thus, each correctly sorted envelope is worth three cents. If a mail clerk is good and sorts 400 envelopes per hour, she will make $12 per hour. If our clerk is not a good worker and can sort only 200 pieces per hour, she makes $6 per hour. To protect workers from the effects of external factors, minimum wage laws ensure that even the worst employee will make enough money to survive.

Union National Bank in Little Rock, Arkansas, has had tremendous success by paying its workers for the number of customers they service, the number of new customers gained, the amount of time taken to balance accounts at the end of the day, and so on. The bank's pay-for-performance program has resulted in the average employee making 25% more in take-home pay, and the bank itself has almost doubled its profits.

Nucor in Charlotte, North Carolina, is another company that has used a pay-for-performance plan. By paying its steelworkers for the amount of

Employee Motivation
and Satisfaction

work they do, Nucor has seen productivity more than double and its workers make more than $30,000 per year while the industry average is some $27,000.

A related plan, known as **gainsharing,** uses pay incentives based on group rather than individual performance. The typical gainsharing program works as follows. First, the company monitors performance measures over some period of time to derive a **baseline.** Then, productivity goals above the baseline are set, and the employees are told that they will receive bonuses for each period that the goal is reached. To make goal setting more effective, constant feedback is provided to employees on how current performance is in relation to the goal. At the end of each reporting period, bonuses are paid based on how well the group did.

An excellent example of a successful gainsharing program can be found at the Dana Spicer Heavy Axle Division facility in Ohio (Hatcher, Ross, & Ross, 1987). Employees at the Dana plant receive a financial bonus when productivity surpasses the baseline. The gainsharing program has dramatically increased the number of employee suggestions, quality, and productivity. Employees' bonuses average 14% above their normal pay each month, with year-end bonuses between 11% and 16%.

Another method of financially rewarding employees for excellent performance is through **merit pay.** The major distinction between merit pay and the two methods previously discussed is that merit-pay systems base their incentives on performance-appraisal scores rather than on objective performance measures. Thus, merit pay is a potentially good technique for jobs in which productivity is difficult to measure.

The actual link between performance-appraisal scores and the amount of merit pay received by an employee varies greatly around the United States. In the state of Virginia's merit-pay system, employees' performance-appraisal scores at each office are ranked and the top 30% of employees each receive a $1,000 annual bonus.

In the merit-pay system used by one nonprofit mental health agency, each employee's performance-appraisal rating is divided by the total number of performance points possible, and this percentage then is multiplied by the maximum 3% merit increase that can be received by an employee. With this system, an employee must receive a perfect rating to receive the full 3% increase. Most employees receive between 2% and 2.5%.

The merit-pay system used by a California public transit system is similar to that used by the mental health agency with the exception that the merit increase becomes part of an employee's base salary for the next pay period. Thus, increases are perpetuated each year, unlike the mental health system's one-time reward.

Research on merit pay has brought mixed reviews. Some research has shown that employees like the idea of merit pay, but other research has found that it is not popular with all employees and that many employees do not consider the merit ratings to be fair (Hills, Scott, Markham, & Vest, 1987; Wisdom & Patzig, 1987).

One of merit pay's biggest problems is that increases are based on subjective performance appraisals. Aware of this, some supervisors will inflate performance-appraisal scores to increase their employees' pay and thus more positive employee feelings about the supervisors. Managers also have been known to inflate performance-appraisal ratings when they believe the base salaries for certain positions are too low.

Another problem with merit pay is that its availability or amount often changes with each fiscal year. Thus, excellent performance one year might result in a large bonus, while the same performance another year might bring no bonus at all. This is especially true in the public sector. Thus, for merit pay to be successful, funding must be consistently available and information about its availability and amount should be shared with employees (Wisdom & Patzig, 1987).

Premack Principle

Another reinforcement technique stems from the **Premack Principle** (Premack, 1963), which states that reinforcement is relative and that a supervisor can reinforce an employee with something that on the surface does not appear to be a reinforcer. The best way to explain this principle is to construct a **reinforcement hierarchy** on which an employee lists her preferences for a variety of reinforcers. As Figure 10.3 shows, our hypothetical employee most desires money and time off from work and least desires typesetting and cleaning the press. Our employee can enjoy and do a better job of cleaning her press if we give her money for each time she properly completes the task, but such a reward system can become expensive. Thus, according to the Premack Principle, we can get our employee to properly clean her press by allowing her to do one of the activities she likes more than cleaning. From her reinforcement hierarchy, we can see that she ranked throwing out oily rags as more enjoyable because she can take a short break by walking outdoors to the disposal area. Thus, all we need for a reward is to let her dispose of the rags.

The Premack Principle may sound silly, but think of the reinforcers you have used to reward yourself for studying. After reading a certain number of pages, you might allow yourself a trip to the water fountain. Certainly, getting a drink of water is hardly anyone's idea of a good time,

**Figure 10.3
Example of a
Reinforcement
Hierarchy**

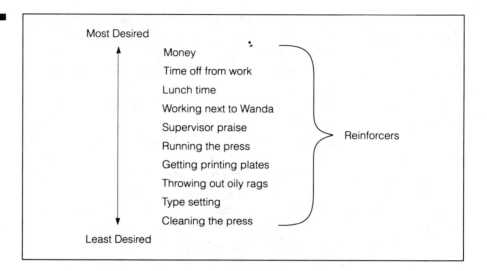

Most Desired

Money
Time off from work
Lunch time
Working next to Wanda
Supervisor praise
Running the press
Getting printing plates
Throwing out oily rags
Type setting
Cleaning the press

} Reinforcers

Least Desired

but it may be more interesting than studying and so can become a reinforcer to increase studying.

Even though operant conditioning has been successful in improving motivation and performance, a note of caution comes from Deci (1972), who believes that for some people and some jobs, work is intrinsically motivating. That is, people are motivated because they enjoy working, not because they are being rewarded. A reasonable body of research, much of it conducted by Deci himself, demonstrates that paying a person for the amount of work done will reduce the degree to which he enjoys performing the task. Thus, when financial incentives are no longer available, the employee will be less motivated to work than before rewards were used.

Goal Setting

To further increase the effectiveness of reinforcement, goal setting should be used. With **goal setting**, each employee is given a goal, which might be a particular quality level, a certain quantity of output, or a combination of the two. For goal setting to be most successful, the goals themselves should possess certain qualities.

First, they should be *concrete* and *specific* (Terborg, 1977; Wood, Mento, and Locke, 1987). A goal such as "I will produce as many as I can" will not be as effective as "I will print 5,000 pages in the next hour." The more specific the goal, the greater the productivity. To underscore this point, we will use an example involving push-ups. If a woman says that she will "do as many push-ups as I can," does that mean she will do as many as she can until she tires? Or does it mean she will do as many as she can before she begins to sweat? Or does it mean she will do as many as she did her last time? The problem with such a goal is its ambiguity and lack of specific guidelines. Setting more specific subgoals can also improve performance (Klawsky, 1990).

Second, a properly set goal is high but reasonable (Locke, 1968; Locke & Latham, 1990). If an employee regularly prints 5,000 pages an hour and sets a goal of 4,000 pages, performance certainly is not going to increase. Conversely, if the goal becomes 20,000 pages, it also will not be effective because the employee will quickly realize that he cannot meet the goal and will quit trying.

A good example of goals set too high comes from the academic retention program at Radford University. This program is designed to help special students who are having academic trouble and whose G.P.A.'s have fallen below that needed to stay in school. The program involves tutoring, study skills, and goal setting. Although it generally has been a success, many students' fail to improve their academic performances. A brief investigation revealed that the goal-setting process was one of the reasons for these failures. Students were allowed to set their own G.P.A. goals for the semester—and students with G.P.A.'s of 1.0 were setting goals of 4.0! Obviously, none of the students was able to reach this goal. The problem typically came when a student did poorly on his first test and his chance for an A in a class was gone, as was his chance for a 4.0 G.P.A. for the semester. Because their goals could not be attained, the students felt they had failed and quit trying.

Until fairly recently, it was generally thought that a goal will lead to the greatest increase in productivity if it is set at least in part by the employee. That is, although performance will increase if the supervisor sets the employee's goal, it will increase even more if the employee participates. However, several meta-analyses have indicated that participating in goal setting does not increase performance (Mento, Steel, & Karren, 1987; Tubbs, 1986).

The first goal-setting study that caught the interest of industrial psychologists was conducted by Latham and Blades (1975). Their study was brought about because truck drivers at a logging mill were not completely filling their trucks before making deliveries. Empty space in the trucks obviously cost the company money. To increase each delivery's load, the drivers were given specific weight goals and were told that they would be neither punished for missing the goal nor rewarded for reaching it. A significant increase in the average load per delivery resulted. Although this is the most celebrated study, goal setting has been shown to be effective in a wide variety of situations.

Feedback

To further increase the effectiveness of reinforcement and goal setting, feedback should be provided to the employee about his progress in reaching his goal (Locke & Latham, 1990). Feedback can include verbally telling an employee how he is doing, placing a chart on a wall, or displaying a certain color of light when the employee's work pace will result in goal attainment and a different color of light when the pace is too slow to reach the goal.

An excellent example of the use of feedback comes from Domino's Pizza. Each month, the average delivery and service times for each store are printed as "box scores" in *The Pepperoni Press,* the company's newsletter (Feuer, 1987c). These box scores provide each store with feedback on how it compares with other stores. This feedback is one reason why Domino's is the world's fastest growing fast food outlet.

Social Learning Theory

A second behavioral theory postulates that employees observe the levels of motivation and satisfaction of other employees and then model those levels. Thus, if an organization's older employees work hard and talk positively about their jobs and their employer, new employees will model this behavior and be both productive and satisfied. The reverse also is true: If veteran employees work slowly and complain about their jobs, so will new employees.

To test this theory, Weiss and Shaw (1979) had subjects view training videos in which assembly line workers made either positive or negative comments about their jobs. After viewing a videotape, each subject was given an opportunity to perform the job. The study found that those subjects who had seen the positive tape enjoyed the task more than did subjects who viewed the negative tape.

This theory has not yet been heavily researched, but it certainly makes intuitive sense. Think of courses you have taken in which one student participated more than anyone else. After a while, the student's level of participation probably decreased to be more in line with the rest of the class. In work as in school, social pressures force a person to behave in ways that are consistent with the norm, even though the person may privately believe something different (Nail, 1986).

Individual Differences Theory

A more recent theory of job satisfaction and motivation holds that certain types of people generally will be satisfied and motivated regardless of the type of job they hold (Weaver, 1978). This idea also makes intuitive sense. We all know people who constantly complain and whine about every job they have, and we also know people who are motivated and enthusiastic about their every job or task.

One such "personality" theory of work motivation was developed by Wherry and South (1977), who used a 70-item test to measure a person's general level of work motivation. The results of their investigation provided support for the notion that levels of work motivation may be fairly stable across people and jobs.

Similar results were obtained for job satisfaction measures in a study by Dubin and Champoux (1977). This study indicated that some people have a job-oriented focus of life and that these people are happier in their jobs than people without this focus. Orpen (1978) also found a small but positive correlation between satisfaction with work and satisfaction with life.

In more recent studies, Staw and Ross (1985) found a significant correlation ($r = .33$) between the job-satisfaction levels of employees in 1969 and in 1971. And Staw, Bell, and Clausen (1986) found a significant correlation between adolescent and adult levels of satisfaction. These studies have been interpreted as providing support for the hypothesis that job satisfaction might be at least partially affected by personality traits.

A recent study by Arvey, Bouchard, Segal, and Abraham (1989) suggested that job satisfaction not only may be fairly stable across jobs, but also may be genetically determined. Arvey and his colleagues arrived at this conclusion by comparing the levels of job satisfaction of 34 sets of identical twins who were separated from each other at an early age.

If job satisfaction is purely environmental, then there should be no significant correlation between levels of job satisfaction for identical twins who were raised in different environments and who were now working at different types of jobs. But if identical twins have similar levels of job satisfaction despite being reared apart and despite working at dissimilar jobs, then a genetic predisposition for job satisfaction would be likely.

Based on their analysis, Arvey and his colleagues found that approximately 30% of job satisfaction appears to be explainable by genetic factors. Thus, one way to increase the overall level of job satisfaction in an organization would be to hire only those applicants who show high levels of overall job and life satisfaction.

Measuring Job Satisfaction

This chapter has discussed several theories that seek to explain job satisfaction. But one important issue that remains is how an employee's level of job satisfaction is determined. Generally, it is measured by one of several different paper-and-pencil tests.

One of the first methods for measuring job satisfaction was developed by Kunin (1955) and is called the **Faces Scale** (a simulation is shown in Figure 10.4). Although the scale is easy to use, it no longer is commonly administered partly because it lacks sufficient detail.

The most commonly used scale today is the **Job Descriptive Index (JDI)** (see Figure 10.5). The JDI was developed by Smith, Kendall, and Hulin (1969) and consists of a series of job-related adjectives and statements that are rated by employees. The scales yield scores on five dimensions of job satisfaction: supervision, pay, promotional opportunities, co-workers, and the work itself.

A similar measure of job satisfaction is the **Minnesota Satisfaction Questionnaire (MSQ),** which was developed by Weiss, Dawis, England, and Lofquist (1967). The MSQ, the short form of which is shown in Figure 10.6, contains 100 items that yield scores on 20 scales.

The fact that the JDI has 5 scales and the MSQ 20 underscores the point that job satisfaction is not easy to measure. This is especially true when one considers that employees' responses on the JDI are not highly correlated with their responses on the MSQ (Gillet & Schwab, 1975).

Because both the JDI and the MSQ measure specific aspects of job satisfaction, Ironson, Smith, Brannick, Gibson, and Paul (1989) recently developed the **Job in General (JIG) Scale.** The JIG is useful when an organization wants to measure the overall level of job satisfaction rather than specific aspects of job satisfaction.

**Figure 10.4
Simulation of Faces
Scale of Job
Satisfaction**

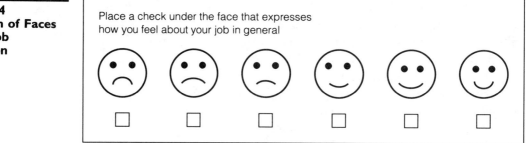

Place a check under the face that expresses
how you feel about your job in general

Figure 10.5
Sample Items from the Job Descriptive Index

Think of your present work. What is it like most of the time? In the blank beside each word given below, write

__Y__ for "Yes" if it describes your work

__N__ for "No" if it does NOT describe it

__?__ if you cannot decide

Work on Present Job

____ Routine

____ Satisfying

____ Good

____ On your feet

Think of the pay you get now. How well does each of the following words describe your present pay? In the blank beside each word, put

__Y__ if it describes your pay

__N__ for "No" if it does NOT describe it

__?__ if you cannot decide

Present Pay

____ Income adequate for normal expenses

____ Insecure

____ Less than I deserve

____ Highly paid

Think of the opportunities for promotion that you have now. How well does each of the following words describe these? In the blank beside each word put

__Y__ for "Yes" if it describes your opportunities for promotion

__N__ for "No" if it does NOT describe them

__?__ if you cannot decide

Opportunities for Promotion

____ Promotion on ability

____ Dead-end job

____ Unfair promotion policy

____ Regular promotions

Think of the kind of supervision that you get on your job. How well does each of the following words describe this supervision? In the blank beside each word below, put

__Y__ if it describes the supervision you get on your job

__N__ if it does NOT describe it

__?__ if you cannot decide

Supervision on Present Job

____ Impolite

____ Praises good work

____ Influential

____ Doesn't supervise enough

Think of the majority of the people that you work with now or the people you meet in connection with your work. How well does each of the following words describe these people? In the blank beside each word below, put

__Y__ if it describes the people you work with

__N__ if it does NOT describe them

__?__ if you cannot decide

People on Your Present Job

____ Boring

____ Responsible

____ Intelligent

____ Talk too much

Source: Smith, P. C., Kendall, L. M., & Hulin, C. L. (1969). *The measurement of satisfaction in work and retirement.* Chicago: Rand McNally. The Job Descriptive Index is copyrighted by Bowling Green State University. The complete forms, scoring key, instructions, and norms can be requested from Dr. Patricia C. Smith, Department of Psychology, Bowling Green State University, Bowling Green, Ohio 43403. Used by permission of the authors.

**Figure 10.6
Minnesota
Satisfaction
Questionnaire
Short Form**

Ask yourself: How **satisfied** am I with this aspect of my job?
Very Sat. means I am very satisfied with this aspect of my job.
Sat. means I am satisfied with this aspect of my job.
N means I can't decide whether I am satisfied or not with this aspect of my job.
Dissat. means I am dissatisfied with this aspect of my job.
Very Dissat. means I am very dissatisfied with this aspect of my job.

On my present job, this is how I feel about...	Very Dissat.	Dissat.	N	Sat.	Very Sat.
1. Being able to keep busy all the time	☐	☐	☐	☐	☐
2. The chance to work alone on the job	☐	☐	☐	☐	☐
3. The chance to do different things from time to time	☐	☐	☐	☐	☐
4. The chance to be "somebody" in the community	☐	☐	☐	☐	☐
5. The way my boss handles his men	☐	☐	☐	☐	☐
6. The competence of my supervisor in making decisions	☐	☐	☐	☐	☐
7. Being able to do things that don't go against my conscience	☐	☐	☐	☐	☐
8. The way my job provides for steady employment	☐	☐	☐	☐	☐
9. The chance to do things for other people	☐	☐	☐	☐	☐
10. The chance to tell people what to do	☐	☐	☐	☐	☐
11. The chance to do something that makes use of my abilities	☐	☐	☐	☐	☐
12. The way company policies are put into practice	☐	☐	☐	☐	☐
13. My pay and the amount of work I do	☐	☐	☐	☐	☐
14. The chances for advancement on this job	☐	☐	☐	☐	☐
15. The freedom to use my own judgement	☐	☐	☐	☐	☐
16. The chance to try my own methods of doing the job	☐	☐	☐	☐	☐
17. The working conditions	☐	☐	☐	☐	☐
18. The way my co-workers get along with each other	☐	☐	☐	☐	☐
19. The praise I get for doing a good job	☐	☐	☐	☐	☐
20. The feeling of accomplishment I get from the job	☐	☐	☐	☐	☐
	Very Dissat.	Dissat.	N	Sat.	Very Sat.

Source: *Minnesota Satisfaction Questionnaire* (short form), copyright 1967, Vocational Psychological Research, University of Minnesota. Used by permission.

Chapter Summary

In this chapter, we discussed several theories about and factors related to employee motivation and job satisfaction. The first set of theories, needs theories, postulates that job satisfaction is determined by how well an organization is able to satisfy its employees' needs. Maslow proposed that we have five needs (basic biological, safety, social, ego, and self-actualization), Aldefer proposed (in his ERG theory) that we have three needs (existence, relatedness, and growth), Herzberg proposed that we seek to satisfy two basic types of needs or factors (hygiene and motivators), and McClelland proposed that we have three important needs (achievement, power, and affiliation).

The second set of theories postulates that motivation and satisfaction are the result of cognitive factors. Equity theory states that our level of satisfaction and perhaps effort is based on a comparison of what we put into our jobs (inputs) and what we get from our jobs (outputs) with the inputs and outputs of others. If the input–output ratio does not match those of others, inequity results.

Expectancy theory states that our level of motivation is a function of three factors: expectancy, instrumentality, and valence. To be motivated to work hard, we must believe that we can perform a job, that we will be rewarded for our performance, and that the reward is something desirable.

Consistency theory states that our performance level is consistent with our level of self-esteem. If we have low self-esteem, we will perform at a low level, while if we have high self-esteem, we will perform at a high level.

The third set of theories, behavioral theories, postulates that we will exert effort if we are rewarded for doing so. The main theories in this category are operant conditioning and social learning theory.

The final type of theory discussed in this chapter was the individual difference theory, which postulates that certain types of people are born with a predisposition to be satisfied with their jobs while others are born predisposed to be dissatisfied.

The chapter also discussed ways in which job satisfaction can be measured. The most common method is by using job-satisfaction scales. These include the Faces Scale, the Job Descriptive Index (JDI), the Minnesota Satisfaction Questionnaire (MSQ), and the Job in General (JIG) Scale.

Glossary

Baseline The level of productivity before the implementation of a gainsharing plan

Basic biological needs The first step in Maslow's needs hierarchy, concerning survival needs such as the need for food, air, and water

Chronic self-esteem The positive or negative way in which a person views himself or herself as a whole

Ego needs The fourth step in Maslow's hierarchy, concerning the individual's need for recognition and success

ERG Theory Aldefer's needs theory that describes three levels of satisfaction: existence, relatedness, and growth

Expectancy In expectancy theory, the perceived probability that a particular amount of effort will result in a particular level of performance

Faces Scale A measure of job satisfaction in which raters place a mark under a facial expression that is most similar to the way they feel about their jobs

Gainsharing A group incentive system in which employees are paid a bonus based on improvements in group productivity

Goal setting A method of increasing performance in which employees are given specific performance goals to aim for

Hierarchy A system arranged by rank

Hygiene factors In Herzberg's two-factor theory, job-related elements that result from but do not involve the job itself

Input/output Ratio The ratio of how much employees believe they put into their jobs to how much they believe they get from their jobs

Inputs In equity theory, the elements that employees put into their jobs

Instrumentality In expectancy theory, the perceived probability that a particular level of performance will result in a particular consequence

Job characteristics theory The theory proposed by Hackman and Oldham that suggests that certain characteristics of a job will make the job more or less satisfying, depending on the particular needs of the worker

Job Descriptive Index (JDI) A measure of job satisfaction that yields scores on five dimensions

Job enlargement A system in which employees are given more tasks to perform at the same time

Job enrichment A system in which employees are given more responsibility over the tasks and decisions related to their jobs

Job in General (JIG) Scale A measure of the overall level of job satisfaction

Job rotation A system in which employees are given the opportunity to perform several different jobs in an organization

Job satisfaction The attitude employees have toward their jobs

Merit pay An incentive plan in which employees receive pay bonuses based on performance-appraisal scores

Minnesota Satisfaction Questionnaire (MSQ) A measure of job satisfaction that yields scores on 20 dimensions

Motivation The force that drives an employee to perform well

Motivators In Herzberg's two-factor theory, elements of a job that concern the actual duties performed by the employee

Need for achievement The extent to which a person desires to master a task

Need for affiliation The extent to which a person desires to be around other people

Need for power The extent to which a person desires to have influence over other people

Needs theory A theory based on the idea that employees will be satisfied with jobs that satisfy their needs

Outputs In equity theory, the things that employees get from their jobs

Pay for performance A system in which employees are paid based on how much they individually produce

Premack Principle The idea that reinforcement is relative both within an individual and between individuals

Quality circles Employee groups that meet to propose changes that will improve productivity and the quality of work life

Reinforcement hierarchy A rank-ordered list of reinforcers for an individual

Safety needs The second step in Maslow's hierarchy, concerning the need for security, stability, and physical safety

Self-actualization needs The fifth step in Maslow's hierarchy, concerning the need to realize one's potential

Self-esteem The positive or negative way in which a person views himself or herself

Self-fulfilling prophecy The idea that people behave in ways consistent with their self-image

Situational self-esteem The positive or negative way in which a person views himself or herself in a particular situation

Socially influenced self-esteem The positive or negative way in which a person views himself or herself based on the expectations of others

Social needs The third step in Maslow's hierarchy concerning the need to interact with other people

Thematic Apperception Test (TAT) A projective test that is designed to measure various need levels

Two-factor theory Herzberg's needs theory that postulates that there are two factors involved in job satisfaction: hygiene factors and motivators

Valence In expectancy theory, the perceived desirability of a consequence that results from a particular level of performance

11

Communication

In 1988, a U.S. Navy warship was unable to communicate with a plane that it believed might be hostile. Because of this lack of communication, the warship's crew shot down the plane, which turned out to be an Iranian airliner, killing all 295 people on board. Although certainly extreme, this example demonstrates the importance of communication. This importance is also demonstrated in the employment profile of consultant Nancy Abrams.

Management must communicate with employees to train and motivate them effectively. Thus, the effectiveness of company policy and the attainment of company goals is to a large extent determined by the way in which the policy and goals are communicated and the extent to which the organizational communication system meets each of the following four conditions (Neuner, Keeling, & Kallaus, 1972):

1. Information must be easy to access.

2. Information must be current.

3. Information must be sent economically.

4. Information must be accurate.

This chapter will look at the ways in which employees communicate within an organization, problems in the communication process, and ways in which communication can be improved. We begin our discussion of communication by examining the types of communication that occur within an organization.

Types of Organizational Communication

Intrapersonal

The first type of communication is **intrapersonal**—that is, the communication process that takes place within an individual. Although "talking to oneself" seems as if it belongs in an abnormal psychology textbook, intrapersonal communication concerns the transmission of information among the various senses. Here the most relevant aspect of this internal communication process is that of the thinking and encoding steps before *interpersonal* communication takes place. A person cannot communicate effectively, of course, unless she knows what she wants to say, how she wants to say it, and how the other person will receive and interpret the message.

Interpersonal

Once a person knows what she wants to say and how to say it, her next step is to actually communicate the message to either another person or a group of people. This process is called **interpersonal communication** and involves the exchange of a message across a communication channel from one person to another. Although this seems like a simple step, as in Figure 11.1, many things can go wrong and interfere with the message's accurate transmission or reception.

The first and often biggest problem in the communication process occurs at the encoding-and-transmission stage. As mentioned above, it is important that one person tell another person exactly what she wants rather than hope that the other person will correctly understand what she wants.

411

**Figure 11.1
The Interpersonal
Communication
Process**

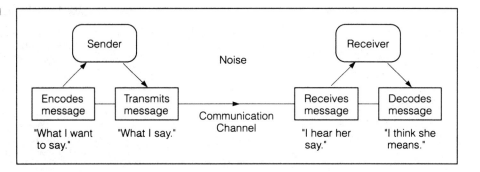

For example, you need a set of data by the end of the day, so you tell your assistant that you need the data immediately. At the end of the day, however, the data are not there. The next morning, the employee proudly brings you the data that she has compiled in "less than a day" and is confused about why you are angry. In this example, you encoded the message as "I need it by five o'clock," you transmitted the message as "I need it immediately," and the employee decoded it as "She needs it to-morrow."

The second point where problems in communication can occur is in the **channel** by which the message is transmitted. For example, a memo can be written and sent with one intended meaning but interpreted by the receiver as having an entirely different meaning.

To demonstrate this problem, consider the sentence "I didn't say Bill stole your car." At first reading, it does not seem unusual, but what does it actually mean? As Table 11.1 shows, if we emphasize the first word, *I*, the implication is that *someone else* said "Bill stole your car." But if we emphasize the word *Bill*, the meaning changes to "Someone else stole your car." And so on. Thus, a simple written message can be interpreted in seven different ways. As we can see, the message might have been better sent orally.

Another example of the channel's importance would be that of a super-visor criticizing an employee in front of other employees. The employee might be so embarrassed and angered that the criticism was made in front of others that she would not hear the message's content. Again, the transmission of a message through an inappropriate channel interferes with the message's meaning and accurate interpretation.

The third area in which problems can occur in interpersonal communi-cation involves the **noise** that surrounds the transmission channel. Noise can be defined as any interference that affects proper reception of a mes-sage. An obvious example is *actual* noise, such as the sound of a subway interfering with conversation. Other examples are the appropriateness of

Inflected Sentence	Meaning
I did not say Bill stole your car.	**Someone else** said Bill stole your car.
I **did not** say Bill stole your car.	I **deny** I said Bill stole your car.
I did not **say** Bill stole your car.	I **implied** that Bill stole your car.
I did not say **Bill** stole your car.	**Someone else** stole your car.
I did not say Bill **stole** your car.	He **borrowed** your car.
I did not say Bill stole **your** car.	Bill stole **someone else's** car.
I did not say Bill stole your **car**.	Bill stole **something else** of yours.

Table 11.1
**Inflection Changes
and Meaning**

the channel, the reputation of the person sending the message, and other information being received at the same time.

The fourth point at which problems in communication appear is at message *reception and decoding.* As we will discuss in greater detail later in the chapter, every person listens for certain types of information. That is, a person who is overly concerned about other peoples' feelings will decode a message based on nonverbal cues rather than on the message's actual verbal content. Thus, a message that is encoded and transmitted in one way may be received and decoded in another.

Intraorganizational

Intraorganizational communication is communication within an organization. This form of communication can be further divided into three communication directions: upward, downward, and horizontal.

Upward Communication

Upward communication is that of subordinate messages to superiors, or employees communicating to managers. Of course, in ideal upward communication employees speak directly to management in an environment that uses an "open door" policy. Such a policy, however, often is not practical for several reasons. Perhaps the most important of these involves the potential volume of communication if every employee were to communicate with a specific manager. Direct upward communication also may not be workable because employees often feel threatened by managers and may not be willing to openly communicate bad news or complaints. This is especially true of employees who have strong aspirations for promotion (Read, 1962) and for organizations that have distinct status levels (Hage, 1974).

Interpersonal communication involves the exchange of a message across a communication channel from one person to another.

Alan Carey/The Image Works

To minimize the number of different people communicating with the top executive, many organizations utilize **serial communication.** With serial communication, the message is relayed from an employee to her supervisor, who relays it to his supervisor, who relays it to her supervisor, and so on until the message reaches the top. Although this type of upward communication relieves the top executive of excessive demands, it suffers several serious drawbacks.

The first is that the message's content and tone change as it moves from person to person. The information becomes leveled, sharpened, and assimilated. For example, consider the following message:

> One of our new employees, John Atoms, came to work in an obviously intoxicated state. He arrived at 9 A.M., dressed in a red plaid shirt and blue pants, and went to his workplace over in the soldering lab. He was staggering all over the place until he finally passed out.

When such information is **leveled,** unimportant details are removed. For example, information about the color of the employee's shirt and pants probably would not be passed along to the next person. When information is **sharpened,** interesting and unusual information is kept. In the example here, the employee's drunkenness probably would be the story's main focus as it is passed from one employee to another. When information is

assimilated, it is modified to fit our existing beliefs and knowledge. Most of us have never heard the last name "Atoms," but we probably have known someone named "Adams." And most people use the word "drunk" rather than "intoxicated." Thus, in probable future tellings of this story, John Adams was the employee who went to work drunk.

The second drawback to serial communication is that bad news and complaints are seldom relayed. Rosen and Tesser (1970) have labeled this the **MUM (minimize unpleasant messages) effect.** The MUM effect negatively affects the organization by keeping important information from reaching the upper levels. But for an employee, the MUM effect is an excellent survival strategy—no one wants to be the bearer of bad news.

Serial communication's third drawback, especially when communication channels are informal, is that it is less effective the farther away two people are from one another. That is, a supervisor is more likely to pass along a message to another supervisor if the two are in close physical **proximity.** It is unlikely, therefore, that an informal message originating with an employee at a plant in Atlanta will reach another employee at the corporate office in Phoenix. The importance of physical proximity cannot be overstated. In fact, a major source of power often comes from being physically near an executive. Seasoned executives have been known to place rising executives in distant offices to reduce their potential power. And going to lunch "with the guys" has long been recognized as a means of obtaining new information and increased power.

Because of these problems with serial communication, organizations use several other methods to facilitate upward communication. One method, the **attitude survey,** usually is conducted on an annual basis by an outside consultant. The consultant administers a questionnaire that asks employees to rate their opinions on factors such as satisfaction with pay, working conditions, and supervisors. Employees also are given the opportunity to list complaints or suggestions that they want management to read. The consultant then tabulates the responses and reports the findings to management.

Although attitude surveys are commonly used, they are only useful if an organization takes the results seriously. If an organization finds that its employees are unhappy and does nothing to address the problem areas, the survey results will not be beneficial. Furthermore, it is also wise for the organization to share survey results with employees (Rosen, 1987).

If survey results are to be shared, then management must share *all* of them. While proposing a project to a local police department, this author encountered a great deal of hostility from many of the senior officers.

After a little probing, the officers revealed that several years earlier they had completed an attitude survey for the city. A few months later, the results were made public and the city cited five main complaints by the officers and promised that action would be taken to solve these problems. The officers were happy until they realized that none of their complaints about pay and working conditions were included in the report—the city was ignoring them. The officers became so resentful and mistrustful of consultants and management, that they vowed never again to participate in a project.

Another method for facilitating upward communication is the use of a **suggestion box** or a **complaint box.** Theoretically, these two boxes should be the same, but a box asking for suggestions is not as likely to get complaints as a box specifically labeled "complaints" and vice versa. The biggest advantage of these boxes is that they allow employees to immediately communicate their feelings. With attitude surveys, of course, employee thoughts are communicated only once or twice a year.

For these boxes to be beneficial, management must respond to the suggestions and complaints and in a timely manner. Management can respond to every suggestion or complaint by placing it on a bulletin board along with management's response. In this way, employees receive feedback about their ideas, which further encourages other employees to use the boxes to communicate.

Some organizations take employee suggestions quite seriously and reward employees who provide useful ideas. Hercules, Inc., for example, provides cash awards up to $10,000 for employees who suggest money-saving ideas, and Ingersoll-Rand gives plaques to employees who submit cost-saving ideas that are ultimately adopted by the company.

The use of a **liaison** or an **ombudsperson** is another method that can increase upward communication. Both of these types of employees are responsible for taking employee complaints and suggestions and personally working with management to find solutions. The advantage of this system is that the ombudsperson is neutral and works for a solution that is acceptable to both an employee and management. Furthermore, the ombudsperson typically is supervised at the vice-presidential level, so she is not concerned about being fired if she steps on a few toes while looking for a solution.

The ombudsperson method is a good one, but it often is not used because organizations do not want the expense of an employee who "does not produce." To overcome this problem, Moore Tool Company in Springdale, Arkansas, started its "Red Shirt" program in which selected senior employees wear red shirts that identify them as informal ombudspeople. If an employee has a problem, she can seek help from Red Shirt, who has authority to help find a solution. This system not only opens communication channels, but also provides job enrichment for an employee who works at an otherwise boring job.

In organizations that have their employees represented by unions, the job of the ombudsperson typically is handled by the **union steward.** But management–union relationships are often adversarial, so the union steward has a difficult time solving problems because she is perceived by neither management nor union members as being neutral.

Downward Communication

Downward communication is that of superior to subordinate or management to employees. Such communication can be accomplished in many ways. One of the most common methods, of course, is the memorandum or *memo.* Memos have the advantage of providing detailed information to a large number of people in a short period of time. With the widespread use of photocopy and ditto machines, however, employees (especially office workers) now receive so many memos that often they do not read them. In fact, the executive of a major company once stated that he never read a memo when it first came to him. Instead, his attitude was that if the message were really important, the person would talk to him about it later. Although such an attitude probably is not a good one, it does underscore the excessive use of memos and their diminishing effectiveness in communication.

Another method of downward communication is the use of the *telephone call.* In the past, this method was appropriate only when the message was short and when only a few people needed to receive the communication. But with the advent of conference calls, the number of people who can be reached by this method has certainly increased. Furthermore, telephone calls previously were appropriate only for messages that did not involve detail. But the facsimile, or Fax, machine now allows detailed sketches or numbers to be sent to other people in different locations in a matter of seconds, and these then can be discussed by telephone. It also has been shown that phone calls, even when long distance, can be less expensive than most memos or letters (Fulger, 1977).

One limitation of phone calls, of course, is that nonverbal cues are not available. Thus, a major portion of the message often is not communicated. For important calls, however, video-enhanced teleconferencing now can be used. In fact, many organizations save interview expenses by having job applicants across the company participate in such teleconferences, which allow both parties to see one another.

The **bulletin board** is yet another method of downward communication. The next time you visit a company, look around for bulletin boards. You will see them everywhere. Their main use, however, is to communicate nonwork-related opportunities such as scholarships, optional meetings, and items for sale. Important information seldom is seen because the bulletin board is not the appropriate place to post a change of policy or procedure. Still, bulletin boards have the advantage of low cost and wide exposure to both employees and visitors. This is especially true if the boards are placed in high traffic areas such as near time clocks or outside restrooms and cafeterias. Electronic bulletin boards allow the display of even more current information.

Instead of the bulletin board, the **company manual** is the place for posting important changes in policy or procedure. This manual contains all the rules under which employees must operate. Most manuals are written in highly technical language, although they should be written in a less technical style to encourage employees to read them as well as to make them easier to understand. Furthermore, the contents of these manuals are considered binding contracts by courts, so the manuals must be updated each time a policy changes. Usually this is done by sending updated pages to employees so that they can replace older material with newer. To make this process easier, many organizations punch binder holes in the pages to facilitate their replacement.

The typical company manual is hundreds of pages long, so it is not surprising that many employees do not want to read them. To thus reduce length problems, most organizations have two types of company manuals. The first, called a *policy manual,* is very specific and lengthy, containing all of the rules and policies under which the organization operates. The second type of manual, usually known as the *employee handbook,* is much shorter and contains only the most essential policies and rules as well as general summaries of the less important rules.

An example of this need for two manuals involved security guards at a manufacturing plant. The security guards were paid minimum wage and had an average tenure of about three months before quitting. The company became concerned for two reasons. First, three months was not enough time for the guards to learn all of the policies in the 300-page emergency procedures manual. Second, the manual was written by an engineer and none of the security guards was able to understand the writing. The organization thus had I/O graduate student interns develop a short, easy-to-read procedure manual that could be read and understood in a day or two. Tips for effective manual writing as developed by Reddout (1987) are shown in Table 11.2.

Avoid Using	Instead Use
Abstract and general words:	*Concrete and specific words:*
Office equipment	Typewriter
Vehicle	Truck
Several	Six
Writing implement	Pen
Formal words:	*Common words:*
Utilize	Use
Facilitate	Help
Optimal	Best
Remainder	Rest
Competencies	Skills
Phrases:	*Single words:*
Perform the calculation	Calculate
Until such time as	Until
For the reason that	Because
Should it prove to be true	If
For the purpose of	For

Table 11.2
Tips for Effective Manual Writing

Source: Adapted from Reddout, D. J. (1987). Manual writing made easier. *Training and Development Journal, 41*(4), 68, copyright 1987, American Society for Training and Development. Reprinted with permission.

Horizontal Communication

The third direction of organizational communication is **horizontal communication.** As the name implies, this is communication among employees at the same level. Often, horizontal communication is transmitted through what we know as the **grapevine,** a term that can be traced back to the Civil War when loosely hung telegraph wires resembled grapevines. The communication across these lines was often distorted, and because unofficial employee communication also is thought to be distorted, the term has become synonymous with an informal communication network (Davis, 1977).

Davis (1953) studied the grapevine and was able to establish the existence of four grapevine patterns: single strand, gossip, probability, and cluster. As Figure 11.2 shows, in the **single strand** grapevine, Jones passes a message to Smith who passes the message to Brown, and so on until the message is either received by everyone or someone "breaks the chain." This pattern is similar to the children's game of "telephone." In the **gossip** grapevine, Jones passes the message only to a select group of people. Notice that with this pattern, only one person passes the message along and not everyone has a chance to receive, or will receive, the

Figure 11.2
Grapevine Patterns

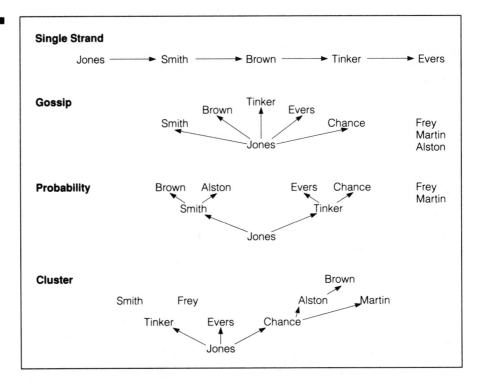

message. In the **probability** grapevine, Jones tells the message to a few other employees and they in turn randomly pass the message along to other employees. In the **cluster grapevine,** Jones tells only a few select employees who in turn tell a few select others.

Research on the grapevine has supported several of Davis' (1953) findings. Sutton and Porter (1968) studied 79 employees in a state tax office and reached several interesting conclusions. First, they found that employees could be placed into one of three categories. **Isolates** were employees who received less than half of the information, **liaisons** were employees who both received most of the information and passed it to others, and **dead-enders** were those who heard most of the information but seldom passed it on to other employees.

Managers tended to be liaisons because they had heard 97% of the grapevine information and most of the time passed this information on. Nonmanagerial employees heard 56% of the grapevine information but seldom passed it on. Only 10% of nonmanagerial employees were liaisons; 57% were dead-enders and 33% were isolates.

Although most people consider the grapevine to be inaccurate, research has shown that information in the grapevine often contains a great deal of truth (Zaremba, 1988). Walton (1961) found that 82% of the information transmitted across the grapevine in one company was accurate. Such a statistic, however, can be misleading. Consider the following hypothetical example: A message travels through the grapevine that "the personnel director will fire 25 people on Monday morning at 9 o'clock." The truth, however, is that the [personnel director] will [*hire*] [25 people] on [Monday] morning at [9 A.M.]. Thus, even though four out of five parts of the message, 80%, are correct, the grapevine message paints a picture quite different from reality.

Not to be confused with the grapevine, **rumor** is poorly substantiated information that is transmitted across the grapevine. Usually, rumor will occur when the available information is both interesting and ambiguous (Allport & Postman, 1947).

Communication Overload

With many jobs, communication overload can occur when an employee receives more communication than she can handle. When an employee is overloaded, she can adapt or adjust in one of several ways to reduce the stress (Miller, 1960): through omission, error, queuing, escape, using a gatekeeper, or using multiple channels.

Omission

One way to manage communication overload is **omission**: a conscious decision not to process certain types of information. For example, a busy supervisor may let the phone ring without answering it so that she can finish her paperwork. Although this technique can work if the overload is temporary, it will be ineffective if the employee misses an important communication.

Error

In the **error** type of response, the employee attempts to deal with every message he receives. But in so doing, each processed message includes reception error. The processing errors are not intentional, but result from processing more than can be handled.

Perhaps a good example of this would be a student who has two hours in which to study four chapters for a test. A student using the error

Figure 11.3
Example of a
Signature Memo

DATE: June 21, 1990

TO: All Department Managers
DS Donald Shula
TL Thomas Landry
___ Patrick Reilly
___ William Daly
___ William Walsh

FROM: William Walsh

Attached is a copy of last month's productivity
report. Please look it over carefully, initial
that you have read it, and then send it to the
next manager on the list.

method would attempt to read and memorize all four chapters in two hours. Obviously, her test score probably will indicate that even though she did all of her reading, much of it was not remembered or remembered correctly.

The probability of error occurring can be reduced in two ways. First, the message can be made *redundant*. That is, after communicating an important message over the telephone, it is a good idea to write a memo to the other person in which the major points of the conversation are summarized. Furthermore, after sending an important memo, it is wise to call its recipient to make sure that the memo was not only received but also read.

Second, error can be reduced by having the recipient *verify* the message. This can be done by asking the person to repeat the message or acknowledge that she has read and understood it. For example, after a customer has placed an order at the drive-through window of a fast food restaurant, the employee repeats the order to the customer to make sure that he has heard it correctly. (Of course, with the poor quality intercoms used by such places, most people still cannot understand the employee.) In a second example of verification, a single copy of a memo is sent to several different people. As shown in Figure 11.3, the person who heads the list reads the memo, puts his initials next to his name, and sends the memo to the next person on the list.

Queuing

Another method of dealing with communication overload is **queuing**—placing the work into a *queue,* or waiting line. The order of the queue can be based on such variables as the message's importance, timeliness, or sender. For example, a memo sent by the company president probably will be placed near or at the beginning of the queue, as would an emergency phone message. On the other hand, a message to return the phone call of a salesperson most likely would go at the end of the queue.

With this method of handling communication overload, all of the work usually will get done. Queues are only effective, however, if the communication overload is temporary. If the employee is constantly overloaded, she will never reach the work at the end of the queue.

Escape

If communication overload is prolonged, a common employee response is to **escape,** which usually takes the form of absenteeism and, ultimately, resignation. This response certainly is not beneficial to an organization, but it can be beneficial to an employee if it protects her mental and physical health by relieving stress.

An example of the escape response often is seen with students who withdraw from college courses. A student may enroll in six classes and realize after two months that he does not have enough time to do all of the reading and writing required for six classes. Rather than choosing the error or omission strategies, both of which would result in lower grades, the student withdraws from one of his classes to reduce his overload.

Use of a Gatekeeper

A response to communication overload used by many executives is the use of a **gatekeeper,** or a person who screens potential communication and allows only the most important to go through. Receptionists and secretaries are the most obvious examples of gatekeepers.

Use of Multiple Channels

The final coping response to communication overload is the use of **multiple channels.** With this strategy, an organization reduces the amount of communication going to one person by directing some of it to another. For example, in a small restaurant all of the problems that involve customers, employees, finances, and vendors are handled by the owner. But as the business grows, the owner may not be able to handle all of the communication and thus may hire others to deal with finances (a book-keeper) and vendors (an assistant manager).

Knowing and understanding this list of responses to communication overload is important. When communication overload occurs, employees will react in ways that reduce the increased stress. Some of these strategies (omission, error, escape) result in negative consequences for the organization. Thus, the organization must recognize when overload occurs and aggressively adopt an acceptable strategy to deal with it.

Listening

Listening probably is the most important communication skill that a supervisor should master. In a study of managers, Nichols and Stevens (1957) found that 70% of the white-collar workday is spent communicating. Of that, 9% is spent in writing, 16% is spent in reading, 30% is spent in speaking, and 45% is spent in listening. Thus, a manager spends more time in listening than in any other single activity. This is an important point for two reasons.

First, our formal education in high school and college does not prepare us for managerial communication. We are required to take English courses to improve our reading and writing and usually are required to take one speech course to improve our oral communication skills—but we spend little if any time learning how to listen. Thus, the amount of time spent in college on various types of communication is inversely related to the actual amount of time spent by managers on the job.

Second, listening effectiveness is poor. It has been estimated that, immediately after a meeting, we retain only 50% of the material we have heard and only 25% of the material 48 hours later (Nichols & Stevens, 1957). Although much of this loss can be attributed to poor memory practices, some is the result of poor listening habits.

Styles of Listening

What can be done to increase listening effectiveness? Perhaps the most important thing we can do is to recognize that every person has a particular "listening style" that serves as a communication filter. Geier and Downey (1980) have developed a test, the **Attitudinal Listening Profile System,** to measure an employee's listening style. Their theory postulates six main styles of listening: leisure, inclusive, stylistic, technical, empathic, and nonconforming.

Leisure

Leisure listening is the listening style that is practiced by "good-time" people who listen only for words that indicate pleasure. For example, as a student, a leisure listener will pay attention only when the teacher is interesting and tells jokes. As an employee, she is the last one to "hear" that employees are needed to work overtime.

Inclusive

Inclusive listening is the style of the person who listens for the main ideas behind any communication. In an hour-long meeting full of details and facts about a decline in sales, the only information that this type of listener will "hear" is the main point that sales are down and that things better improve. This listening style can be an advantage in allowing the listener to cut through a jungle of detail, but it can be a disadvantage when detail is important.

Stylistic

Stylistic listening is that practiced by the person who listens to the way in which communication is spoken. Stylistic listeners will not listen unless the speaker's style is appropriate, or the speaker "looks the part," or both. For example, when speaking to a stylistic listener, a lecturer on finance will find an attentive ear only if she wears a nice suit. After all, this listener reasons, if the lecturer cannot afford a nice suit, why listen to what she has to say about investing money? Similarly, if the speaker says that an event will be fun, she must *sound* as if she means it. And if an employee calls in sick to a manager who is a stylistic listener, she had better "sound" sick.

Technical

Technical listening is the style practiced by the "Jack Webb" of the listening world—he or she wants just the facts. The technical listener hears and retains large amounts of detail—but he does not hear the *meaning* of those details. Using the earlier example of the meeting in which employees are told that sales have decreased, the technical listener will hear and remember that sales last year were 12.3% higher than this year, that profits are down by 21%, and that six employees probably will be laid off—but he will miss the point that, unless sales improve, he could be one of those six.

Empathic

The user of **empathic listening** tunes in to the feelings of the speaker and, of the six listening types, is the most likely to pay attention to nonverbal cues. Thus, an empathic listener will listen to an employee complain about her boss, and is the only one of the six types of listeners who will not only pay attention, but also understand that the employee's complaints indicate true frustration and unhappiness.

Nonconforming

In **nonconforming listening,** the listener attends only to information that is consistent with her way of thinking. If the nonconforming listener does not agree with a speaker, she will not listen to what he says. Futhermore, the nonconforming listener will pay attention only to those people whom she consideres to be strong or to have authority.

How Listening Styles Affect Communication

The following example will demonstrate the importance of the six listening styles in a work setting. Suppose that an employee approaches a supervisor and tells him that she has a temperature of 106 degrees. How would each of the six listeners react?

The leisure listener would pay little attention to the employee because she does not like to hear about unpleasant things and illness certainly is not pleasant. The inclusive listener probably would tell a story about when he had a high temperature, thinking that the topic of conversation was fever. You may have friends who often say things that are not related to your conversation; as this example points out, they are probably inclusive listeners who mistake the main points of a conversation. In this case, the employee is communicating that she does not feel well; she is not discussing "temperatures I have had."

The stylistic listener would pay attention only if the employee sounded and looked ill. You may have also called a professor or a date and tried to sound ill in order to cancel an appointment or a date. Few people actually sound ill, even when they are, but we understand the importance of style in listening and behave accordingly.

The technical listener would hear every word but would not realize their meaning. That is, 10 minutes later when another employee asks whether Sue is sick, the supervisor would respond "She didn't say. She has a temperature of 106, but I'm not sure how she is feeling."

The nonconforming listener would pay little attention to the employee. After all, if she actually had a temperature of 106 degrees, she would be dead, and because she is not dead, she must be lying. Of course, the employee has exaggerated her temperature because she is emphasizing the point that she is sick. But the nonconforming listener would not "hear" anything once an initial statement is incorrect.

In this example, the empathic listener would be the only one who would understand the real point of the communication. The employee is mentioning her temperature because she does not feel well and wants to go home.

Understanding each of the six styles can make communication more effective in two ways. First, becoming aware of one's own style allows a person to understand the filter that he or she uses when listening to others. For example, a student who uses a leisure style may need to recognize that if she only listens to lectures that she finds interesting, she probably will miss a lot of important information. She might want to learn how to concentrate on lectures even when they are boring. Second, understanding the six styles can lead to better communication with others. For example, when speaking to an inclusive listener, we must either write down relevant details that we want her to remember or have her repeat the details. Otherwise, the inclusive listener will remember only the main point: "I know that there is a party tonight, but I'm not sure when or where." On the other hand, when we speak to a technical listener, it is important to tell her what the details mean. For example, if you tell a technical listener that there will be a party at your house on Thursday at 8 P.M., you also should add that she is invited, or she will understand only that there is a party and not that she has been invited.

Of course, the million dollar question is, How can we tell what style of listener is listening to us? The best way might be to test the listener on the Attitudinal Listening Profile mentioned earlier, but this is hardly practical. The most practical method is that of using the persons' speaking style as an indicator of listening style. If the person usually mentions how she feels about things, she probably is an empathic listener, but if she speaks with a lot of detail, she probably is a technical listener.

Someone speaking to a group, of course, must relate to all styles of listeners. The best communicators thus will have something for everyone. A good instructor will provide jokes and humorous stories for leisure listeners, use an outline format and provide main points for inclusive listeners, provide specific facts and details for technical listeners, discuss his feelings about the topic for empathic listeners, have good speaking skills and appropriate dress for stylistic listeners, and be confident and accurate for nonconforming listeners.

Table 11.3
Ten Keys to Effective Listening

Keys	The Bad Listener	The Good Listener
1. Find areas of interest.	Tunes out dry subjects.	Opportunitizes; asks "What's in it for me?"
2. Judge content, not delivery.	Tunes out if delivery is poor.	Judges content, skips over delivery errors.
3. Hold your fire.	Tends to enter into argument.	Doesn't judge until comprehension is complete.
4. Listen for ideas.	Listens for facts.	Listens for central themes.
5. Be flexible.	Takes intensive notes using only one system.	Takes fewer notes. Uses 4–5 different systems, depending on speaker.
6. Work at listening.	Shows no energy output. Attention is faked.	Works hard, exhibits active body state.
7. Resist distractions.	Is distracted easily.	Fights or avoids distractions, tolerates bad habits, knows how to concentrate.
8. Exercise your mind.	Resists difficult expository material; seeks light, recreational material.	Uses heavier material as exercise for the mind.
9. Keep your mind open.	Reacts to emotional words.	Interprets color words; does not get hung up on them.
10. Capitalize on fact that *thought* is faster than speech.	Tends to daydream with slow speakers.	Challenges, anticipates, mentally summarizes, weighs the evidence, listens between lines to tone of voice.

Source: Adapted from Steil, L. K. (1980). Prepared by Dr. Lyman K. Steil for the Sperry Corporation. Reprinted with permission of Dr. Steil and Unisys Corporation.

Tips for Effective Listening

In addition to understanding the way in which our listening style serves as a filter, we can improve our listening effectiveness in many other ways. The best tips that this author has seen are in a booklet prepared for the Sperry Corporation by Steil (1980). These tips are shown in Table 11.3.

Other authors also have offered tips for more effective listening. For example, Davis (1967) provides the following suggestions:

1. Stop talking.
2. Put the speaker at ease.
3. Show the speaker that you want to listen.
4. Remove distractions.
5. Empathize with the speaker.

6. Be patient.

7. Hold your temper.

8. Go easy on argument and criticism.

9. Ask questions.

10. Stop talking.

De Mare (1968) further suggests:

1. Establish an agreeable atmosphere (put the speaker at ease).

2. Be prepared to hear the other person through on his own terms.

3. Be prepared on the subject to be discussed.

4. Evaluate the speaker and make allowances for circumstances.

5. Avoid getting mentally sidetracked when subjects are not central to the issue or touch on sore points.

6. Listen for and summarize basic ideas.

7. Restate the substance of what you have heard to the speaker.

Golen (1990) found that bad listeners are lazy, closed minded, opinionated, insincere, bored, and inattentive.

Nonverbal Communication

Much of what we communicate is conveyed by nonverbal means. Our words often say one thing, while our actions say another. For example, a supervisor may tell an employee that she is interested in hearing his opinions, while at the same time she is frowning and looking out the window. The verbal message from the supervisor may be "I care," but the nonverbal message is "I'm bored." Which message will the employee pay attention to? Most likely, it will be the nonverbal, even though nonverbal cues often lead to incorrect impressions (Malandro & Barker, 1983). Nonverbal cues can be divided into five categories (Costley & Todd, 1987): body language, use of space, use of time, paralanguage, and artifacts.

Body Language

The ways in which we move and position our bodies—our *body language*—communicates much to other people. For example:

- When one's body faces another person, it often is interpreted as a sign of liking, while a person's body turned away from another often is interpreted as a sign of dislike or disinterest (Clore, Wiggins, & Itkin, 1975).

- Direct eye contact often is interpreted by others to indicate liking or interest (Kleinke, Meeker, & LaFong, 1974).

- A person who makes eye contact while speaking but not while listening often is perceived as being powerful or dominant.

- Raising or lowering the head or the shoulders may indicate superiority or inferiority, respectively.

- Touching someone usually indicates liking. In fact, one study has shown that a waitress who touches her customers will receive a larger tip than one who does not touch (Crusco & Wetzel, 1984). Another study found that library clerks who briefly touched patrons as they were being handed books were rated by the patrons as being better employees than clerks who did not touch (Fisher, Rytting, & Heslin, 1976).

- Fleeting facial expressions and changes in voice pitch and eye contact can indicate that a person is lying (DePaulo, Stone, & Lassiter, 1985; Frick, 1985; Knapp, 1978). In fact, voice cues are more accurate than facial expressions when determining deception (DePaulo, Zuckerman, & Rosenthal, 1980). Thus, at times it might be advantageous to interview a job applicant or an employee by telephone rather than in person.

Research has shown that body language can affect employee behavior. For example, Forbes and Jackson (1980) found that effective use of nonverbal cues resulted in a greater probability of being hired for a job. Similarly, Rasmussen (1984) found that the use of nonverbal cues during an interview will help if the applicant gives the correct answer to an interview question but will hurt the applicant if an incorrect answer is given.

Use of Space

The way in which people make use of space also can provide nonverbal cues about their feelings and personalities. Dominant people or those who have authority are given more space by others and at the same time take space from others. For example, people stand farther away from such status figures as executives and police officers (and even college professors) and stand in an office doorway rather than directly enter such a person's office. These same status figures, however, often move closer as a show of power. Police officers are taught that moving in close is one method of intimidating a person.

On the other hand, status figures also increase space to establish differences between themselves and the people with whom they are dealing. A common form of this use of distance is for an executive to place a desk between himself and another person. An interesting story is told by a sports agent who was negotiating a player's contract with George Steinbrenner, owner of the New York Yankees baseball club. When the agent arrived at Steinbrenner's office, he noticed that Steinbrenner sat at one end of a long desk. At the other end was a small chair in which the agent was to sit. Recognizing the spatial arrangement to be a power play, the agent moved his chair next to Steinbrenner's. As the story goes, the Yankee owner was so rattled by this ploy that the agent was able to negotiate an excellent contract for his player client.

Another example also illustrates how the use of space can enhance a person's status by adding an image of importance. Recently, the psychology building at Radford University was renovated, and with efficient use of attic space, every faculty member was given an office. Students who visited during office hours had been accustomed to faculty members sharing offices. Many of these students commented on how important a faculty member must be to receive his or her own office. (Of course, we never told them that we all had our own offices and that faculty members in other departments also would soon have their own.)

The way that an office is furnished also communicates a lot about that person. As mentioned earlier, certain desk placements indicate openness and power; visitors and subordinates prefer not to sit before a desk that serves as a barrier (Davis, 1984). People whose offices are untidy are perceived as being busy, while people whose offices contain plants are perceived as caring and concerned.

Four major spatial distance zones have been recognized and defined (Hall, 1963): intimacy, personal distance, social distance, and public distance.

The **intimacy zone** extends from physical contact to 18 inches away from a person and is usually reserved for close relationships such as dates, spouses, and family. When this zone is entered by strangers in such situations as crowded elevators, we generally feel uncomfortable and nervous. The **personal distance zone** ranges from 18 inches to 4 feet away from a person and is the distance usually reserved for friends and acquaintances. The **social distance zone** is from 4 to 12 feet away and is the distance typically observed when dealing with businesspeople and strangers. Finally, the **public distance zone** ranges from 12 to 25 feet away and is characteristic of such large group interactions as lectures and seminars.

Use of Time

The way in which people make use of time is another element of nonverbal communication. If an employee is supposed to meet with a supervisor at 1 P.M. and the supervisor shows up at 1:10, the supervisor is communicating an attitude about the employee, the importance of the meeting, or both. Tardiness is more readily accepted from a higher-status person than from a lower-status person. Dean Smith, the great basketball coach at the University of North Carolina, suspends any player who is even a minute late for a practice because he believes that tardiness is a sign of arrogance and works against the team concept.

In a similar fashion, before a meeting a supervisor sets aside 30 minutes and tells others that he is not to be disturbed because he is in conference. A definitive message thus is conveyed, one that is likely to prevent constant interruptions by telephone calls or people stopping by to say hello because they saw an open door.

Paralanguage

Paralanguage involves the way in which something is said and consists of variables such as tone, tempo, volume, number and duration of pauses, and rate of speech. A message that is spoken quickly will be perceived differently than if it is spoken slowly. In fact, research has shown that people with fast rates of speech are perceived to be more intelligent than people with slow rates of speech. People who use many "uh-hums," "ers," and "ahs" also are considered less intelligent. Men with high-pitched voices are considered to be weak, while females with high-pitched voices are considered to be petite.

Artifacts

A final element of nonverbal communication concerns the objects, or *artifacts,* a person wears or with which he or she surrounds himself or herself. A person who wears bright and colorful clothes is perceived differently than a person who wears conservative colors such as white or gray. Similarly, the manager who places all of her awards on her office wall, the executive with a large and expensive chair, and the student who carries a briefcase rather than a book bag are all making nonverbal statements about themselves.

Improving Employee Communication Skills

Organizations are always looking for employees who have excellent communication skills. The difficulty in finding such employees recently was exemplified by the experience of a national insurance company. The company was having difficulty with a position that required that employees respond to customer complaints. The company had hired expensive consultants to teach its employees how to write effective letters, but performance had not improved. The company then constructed sample letters so that an employee could read a customer complaint, find a standard response form, and add a few personal lines. This also did not work. Finally, the company tried using a standardized writing test before hiring its employees. Although the test showed significant prediction for the performance of black employees, it did not predict the performance of white employees. This case of single-group validity made the test risky to use. Thus, the question remains, How can an organization increase the communication skills of its employees?

Interpersonal Communication Skills

One of the most common methods used to increase interpersonal communication skills is the training workshop conducted by an outside consultant. Although a large number of consultants lead communication workshops, research has generally indicated that such workshops bring only short-term improvement in skills.

An exception to this general failure to produce long-term improvements was reported by Freston and Lease (1987) from their work with Questar Corporation in Salt Lake City. As the personnel manager at Questar, Freston believed that the organization's managers were not properly trained in communication. Questar thus hired Lease as a communications consultant and together Freston and Lease designed a new training program that included seminars on awareness, nonverbal communication, assertiveness, and listening. In addition to the seminars, Freston and Lease also utilized role play and group discussion. The revised training program brought more positive attitudes for supervisors as well as increased performance quality in tasks such as performance appraisal and training.

Written Communication Skills

Attempts to improve the quality of written communication have generally taken two paths. One approach concentrates on improving the writer's skills, and the other concentrates on making material easier to read.

Improving Writing

It is difficult for an organization to overcome an employee's lack of formal training in writing. Several consulting firms, however, specialize in the improvement of employee writing by teaching employees the most important concepts of writing. Dumaine (1987) and Fey (1987) believe that to improve writing, employees must learn certain basic concepts. For example, an employee needs to analyze his or her audience. If a written communication is intended for a blue-collar employee, then the readability must be kept simple. If the intended audience is a busy executive, the message must be kept short. A list of strategies for effective business writing can be found in Figure 11.4.

Readability

Written communication can break down when material is too difficult for many employees to read. For example, research has shown that Federal Aviation Administration (FAA) regulations and many airline company–pilots' association agreements are too difficult for pilots to read (Blumenfeld, 1985). The Position Analysis Questionnaire, the job-analysis instrument discussed earlier in this book, also is too difficult for most job incumbents to read (Ash & Edgell, 1975). Thus, providing employees with important material to read will be an effective communication form only if the employees can understand what is written.

To ensure that employees will be able to understand written material, several readability indices are available. When using such an index, an

☐ Impact	Did you state the bottom line at the beginning?	
☐ Ideas	Do your main ideas come first, followed by those less important?	
☐ Headlines	Did you use enough headlines, subheads, and sidelines?	
☐ Clear Expectations	Did you make a clear request for action if you need it?	
☐ Completeness	Did you say everything you needed to say?	
☐ Clarity	Did you use common language rather than jargon, formal words, and cliches?	
☐ Conciseness	Did you avoid using extra words or adding unnecessary information?	
☐ Positive Approach	Is your correspondence upbeat and confident?	
☐ Active Voice	Did you avoid the passive approach?	
☐ Paragraphing	Are your paragraphs short, with one idea in each?	
☐ Sentence Clarity	Are your sentences varied in strucure and length?	
☐ Proofreading	Did you reread carefully to correct facts, grammar, and punctuation?	
☐ Readability	Does the readability level suit your audience?	
☐ Consistency	Is your point of view clear throughout?	

**Figure 11.4
Checklist for
Effective Business
Writing**

Source: Dumaine, D. (1987). Strategic writing for trainers. *Training and Development Journal, 47*(1), 60. Used with permission.

organization analyzes the material to be read and then compares its readability level with the typical education of the employees who will read the document. For example, if most employees have high school degrees and have not been to college, the document should be written at less than a 12th-grade level.

Each index uses a slightly different formula or method. For example, the **Fry Readability Graph** (Fry, 1977) uses the average number of syllables per word and the average length of sentences to determine readability (see Figure 11.5). The Flesch Index (Flesch, 1948) uses the average sentence length and number of syllables per 100 words; the **FOG Index** (Gunning, 1964) uses the number of words per sentence and the number of 3-syllable words per 100; and the **Dale–Chall Index** (Dale & Chall, 1948) uses the number of words that are not included in a list of words known by 80% of fourth graders.

All of the readability indices show reasonable reliability and correlate highly with one another (Blumenfeld & Justice, 1975; Forbes & Cottle,

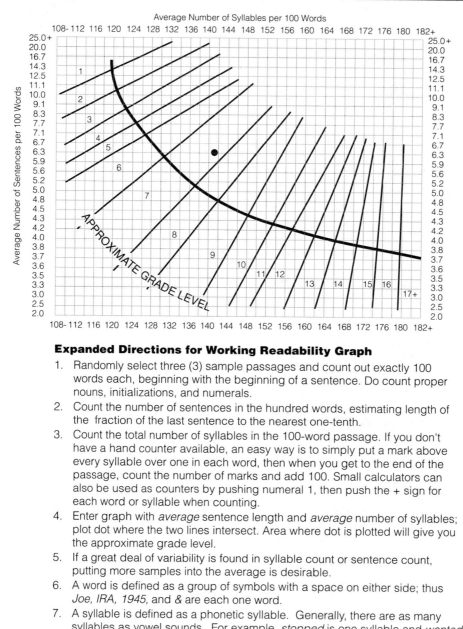

Average Number of Syllables per 100 Words

Expanded Directions for Working Readability Graph

1. Randomly select three (3) sample passages and count out exactly 100 words each, beginning with the beginning of a sentence. Do count proper nouns, initializations, and numerals.

2. Count the number of sentences in the hundred words, estimating length of the fraction of the last sentence to the nearest one-tenth.

3. Count the total number of syllables in the 100-word passage. If you don't have a hand counter available, an easy way is to simply put a mark above every syllable over one in each word, then when you get to the end of the passage, count the number of marks and add 100. Small calculators can also be used as counters by pushing numeral 1, then push the + sign for each word or syllable when counting.

4. Enter graph with *average* sentence length and *average* number of syllables; plot dot where the two lines intersect. Area where dot is plotted will give you the approximate grade level.

5. If a great deal of variability is found in syllable count or sentence count, putting more samples into the average is desirable.

6. A word is defined as a group of symbols with a space on either side; thus *Joe, IRA, 1945,* and *&* are each one word.

7. A syllable is defined as a phonetic syllable. Generally, there are as many syllables as vowel sounds. For example, *stopped* is one syllable and *wanted* is two syllables. When counting syllables for numerals and initializations, count one syllable for each symbol. For example, *1945* is four syllables, *IRA* is three syllables, and *&* is one syllable.

Figure 11.5
Graph for Estimating
Readability—Extended

Document	Readability Level
FAA regulations	Graduate Student
Position Analysis Questionnaire	College Graduate
Air Line Pilot magazine	College Student
Study of Values	12th Grade
Playboy magazine	11th Grade
Time magazine	11th Grade
Newsweek	11th Grade
Reader's Digest	10th Grade
Otis Employment Test	9th Grade
Ladies' Home Journal	8th Grade
Most comic books	6th Grade
Minnesota Multiple Personality Inventory	6th Grade

Table 11.4
Readability Levels of Selected Publications

1953). (The readability levels of selected publications are shown in Table 11.4.) As we can see from these indices, an easily read document has short sentences, uses simple rather than complicated words, and uses common rather than unusual words.

Specialized indices also have been introduced by both Flesch (1948), who measures the human-interest level of reading material, and Tysinger and Pitchford (1988), who developed a method for determining the readability of trait-based psychological tests.

Chapter Summary

This chapter has discussed the importance of organizational communication. We began by discussing three types of organizational communication: *Intrapersonal communication,* which involves knowing what one wants to communicate before it actually is communicated; *interpersonal communication,* or communication between two individuals; and *intraorganizational communication,* or communication within an organization.

Intraorganizational communication can take several directions. *Upward communication* is that which moves from employees to management and utilizes methods such as serial communication, attitude surveys, suggestion boxes, and ombudspeople. *Downward communication* is that which moves from management to employees and utilizes methods such as telephone calls, memos, bulletin boards, and company manuals. *Horizontal communication* is that communication between people at the same level of an organization and includes such types of communication as rumors and grapevines.

Although effective communication is essential, too much can cause *communication overload*. When such overload occurs, employees can react by using one or more of several strategies, including omission, error, queuing, escape, use of a gatekeeper, and use of multiple channels.

Organizational communication also can be improved with more effective *listening skills*. This can be done by explaining the six different styles of listening (leisure, inclusive, stylistic, technical, empathic, and nonconforming) and that a person needs to communicate in a different way to each of the six styles.

Effective communication also can be enhanced by understanding how we use *nonverbal communication*. This communication takes place through body language, use of space, use of time, paralanguage, and artifacts.

Communication skills can be improved as well by teaching interpersonal communication skills, by teaching writing skills, and by writing organizational documents at a reading level that matches the reading level of most employees.

Glossary

Assimilated A description of a message in which the information has been modified to fit the existing beliefs and knowledge of the person sending the message before it is passed on to another person

Attitude survey A form of upward communication in which a survey is conducted to determine employee attitudes about an organization

Attitudinal Listening Profile System A test developed by Geier and Downey that measures individual listening styles

Bulletin board A method of downward communication in which informal or relatively unimportant written information is posted in a public place

Channel The medium by which a communication is transmitted

Cluster A pattern of grapevine communication in which a message is passed to a select group of people who each in turn pass the message to a few select others

Company manual Also called a policy manual, a book containing formal company rules and regulations

Complaint box A form of upward communication in which employees are asked to place their complaints in a box

Dale–Chall Index A method of determining the readability level of written material

Dead-enders Employees who receive much grapevine information but who seldom pass it on to others

Downward communication Communication within an organization in which the direction of communication is from management to employees

Empathic listening The listening style of a person who listens for the feelings of the speaker

Error A type of response to communication overload that involves processing all information but processing some of it incorrectly

Escape A response to communication overload in which the employee leaves the organization to reduce the stress

Flesch Index A method of determining the readability level of written material

FOG Index A method of determining the readability level of written material

Fry Readability Graph A method of determining the readability level of written material

Gatekeeper A person who screens potential communication for someone else and allows only the most important information to pass through

Gossip A pattern of grapevine communication in which a message is passed to only a select group of individuals

Grapevine An unofficial, informal communication network

Horizontal communication Communication between employees at the same level in an organization

Inclusive listening The listening style of a person who listens only for the main points of a communication

Interpersonal communication Communication between two individuals

Intimacy zone A distance zone within 18 inches of a person into which only people with a close relationship to the person are allowed to enter

Intraorganizational communication Communication within an organization

Intrapersonal communication Communication that takes place within an individual

Isolate An employee who receives less than half of all grapevine information

Leisure listening The listening style of a person who listens only for interesting information

Leveled A description of a message from which unimportant information details have been removed before the message is passed from one person to another

Liaison A person who acts as an intermediary between employees and management; or the type of employee who both sends and receives most grapevine information

Multiple channels A strategy for coping with communication overload in which an organization reduces the amount of communication going to one person by directing some of it to another person

MUM (minimize unpleasant messages) effect The idea that people prefer not to pass on unpleasant information, with the result that important information is not always communicated

Noise Any variable concerning or affecting the channel that interferes with the proper reception of a message

Nonconforming listener The listening style of a person who listens only to information that is consistent with his or her way of thinking

Ombudsperson A person who investigates employees' complaints and solves problems

Omission A response to communication overload that involves the conscious decision not to process certain types of information

Personal distance zone A distance zone from 18 inches to four feet from a person that is usually reserved for friends and acquaintances

Probability A pattern of grapevine communication in which a message is passed randomly among all employees

Proximity Physical distance between people

Public distance zone A distance zone greater than 12 feet from a person that is typical of the interpersonal space allowed for social interactions such as large group lectures

Queuing A method of coping with communication overload that involves organizing work into an order in which it will be handled

Rumor Poorly substantiated information that is passed along the grapevine

Serial communication Communication passed consecutively from one person to another

Sharpened A description of a message in which interesting and unusual information has been kept in the message when it is passed from one person to another

Single strand A pattern of grapevine communication in which a message is passed in a chain-like fashion from one person to the next person until the chain is broken

Social distance zone An interpersonal distance zone from 4 to 12 feet from a person that is typically used for business and for interacting with strangers

Stylistic listening The listening style of a person who listens to the way in which words are spoken

Suggestion box A form of upward communication in which employees are asked to place their suggestions in a box

Technical listening The listening style of a person who listens for facts and details

Union steward An employee who serves as a liaison between unionized employees and management

Upward communication Communication within an organization in which the direction of communication is from employees up to management

12

Working Conditions
and Absenteeism

Work Schedules

Today, most employees work eight hours a day, five days a week. Usually, the workdays are Monday through Friday, and the work times are from 8 A.M. to 5 P.M. with an hour break for lunch. But these have not always been the typical work hours. In the late 18th century, it was common for employees to work 14 to 16 hours a day, 6 days per week. By the early to mid-19th century, there was a movement to reduce working hours to a maximum of 10 per day. This reduction was opposed by many religious organizations, which feared the trouble that supposedly would be caused by people with idle time. But by 1950, the 5-day, 40-hour work week was fairly standard.

Compressed Work Weeks

Although the vast majority of people still work 8 hours a day, 5 days a week, there is a trend toward working fewer days a week but more hours per day. These deviations from the typical 5-day work week are called **compressed work weeks** and usually involve an employee working either 10 hours a day for 4 days or 12 hours a day for 3 days.

The first formal use of a compressed work schedule was in 1940 when both the Mobil Oil and Gulf Oil companies had their truck drivers work 10 hours a day for 4 days and then take 3 days off. The "explosion" in organizations that used compressed schedules came in the early 1970s after Riva Poor (1970) published the first book on the topic. The number of organizations using such schedules jumped from 40 in 1970 to 3,000 by 1973 (Kopelman, 1986).

The potential advantages of compressed work schedules are obvious. From the employees' perspective, they get more vacation days, can spend more time with their families, have increased opportunities to moonlight, and have reduced commuting costs and times. Furthermore, if both parents work compressed schedules but on different days, child care costs also are greatly reduced.

Because it appears obvious that the employee's nonwork-related life will improve with a compressed schedule, the important question to be answered becomes, What is the effect of a compressed schedule on an employee's performance at work? When asked that question, most people answer that a worker will be more tired, make more mistakes, and be involved in more accidents.

The research thus far, however, does not support such speculation. Instead, research generally indicates that even though workers do feel more fatigued, their work behavior and work attitudes generally improve

Criterion	Number of Studies	Mean Effect Size
Absenteeism	5	−.44
Fatigue	1	.35
Productivity	8	.25
Satisfaction	5	.73

Source: Adapted with permission from Moores (1990).

**Table 12.1
Effect Sizes
for Compressed
Work Schedules**

once a compressed work schedule has been adopted. In a recent meta-analysis, Moores (1990) identified 186 different articles on compressed schedules; 51 were studies, but only 15 were empirically valid enough to be analyzed. Based on these 15 studies, Moores concluded that compressed schedules generally bring a moderate reduction in absenteeism, a small increase in productivity, a large increase in job satisfaction, and a moderate increase in fatigue. Furthermore, based on 3,800 employees in 6 studies, Moores (1990) concluded that almost 90% of employees who worked compressed schedules are satisfied with them. The effects of compressed work schedules are more pronounced with white-collar jobs than with blue-collar jobs.

The exact effect sizes for the above variables are shown in Table 12.1. From Chapter 1, remember that effect sizes are listed as d scores, which can be interpreted as being roughly twice the size of a correlation coefficient. Thus, a d of .25 is similar in size to a correlation of .13, neither of which is very large.

In addition to these empirically verified benefits to employees, an organization that adopts the use of compressed work schedules may realize other advantages. Perhaps the greatest of these is the reduction in start-up and cleanup times that are associated with many jobs. For example, a printer spends considerable time inking and setting up a press before beginning work. At the end of the day, the printer also must spend time cleaning the press and putting supplies away. If these beginning and ending activities together take an hour, then at least an hour a week can be saved if the printer works four days rather than five. Extended across a year and multiplied by the number of employees in a company, such savings can be substantial.

Flexible Work Hours

A second and increasingly popular alternative work schedule involves flexible work hours and is called **flextime.** Flextime originated in West Germany as a way to alleviate traffic problems by staggering the hours

Figure 12.1
Diagram of One
Bank's Flextime
Arrangement

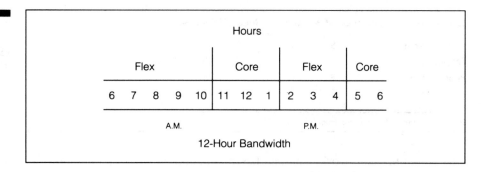

that people worked. The plan then spread to North America, where it was used first in Canada and then in the United States in the mid-1970s. Since 1977, the percentage of organizations using flextime has increased steadily from 15% to 29% by 1987. Flextime is most popular in the South and least popular in the West.

With flextime, employees are given greater control over the hours they work. This increase in control and flexibility is thought to have many advantages for employees. First, the schedule allows an employee to take care of personal tasks such as going to the doctor, picking up children from school, and even sleeping in after a rough night. Furthermore, as we discussed in an earlier chapter, the increased control given to the employee should enrich his job, thus resulting in increased job satisfaction, at least theoretically.

Flextime can be arranged in many ways, but all share the same three basic components: bandwidth, core hours, and flexible hours. As shown in Figure 12.1, the **bandwidth** is the total number of potential hours available for work each day. For example, an employee can work his 8 hours anytime in the 12-hour bandwidth between 6 A.M. and 6 P.M.

Core hours are those that everyone must work and typically consist of the hours during which an organization is busiest with its outside contacts. For example, a restaurant might have core hours between 11 A.M. and 1 P.M. to cover its lunchtime business, while a bank might have core hours from 12 noon to 1 P.M. and from 5 P.M. to 6 P.M. to cover the periods of highest customer volume.

Finally, **flexible hours** are those that remain in the bandwidth and in which the employee has a choice of working. For example, if the bandwidth is the 12-hour period from 6 A.M. to 6 P.M. and the core hours are from 9 A.M. to 12 noon, then the employee can schedule the remaining six hours (including her lunch hour) anywhere from 6 A.M. to 9 A.M. and from 12 noon to 6 P.M. The actual degree to which these hours are truly flexi-

Table 12.2
Meta-Analysis of
Flextime Studies

Variable	Effects Observed		
	Positive	None	Negative
Absenteeism	47	6	1
Leave usage	4	3	1
Family/leisure time	21	0	0
Organizational costs	6	5	5
Overtime pay	9	1	0
Productivity	51	8	2
Satisfaction	43	0	0
Transportation ease	23	0	0
Turnover	8	0	0

Source: Adapted with permission from Estes (1990).

ble depends on the specific flextime program that is used by the organization.

The most flexible of these schedules is called **gliding time.** With this system, an employee can choose his own hours without advance notice or scheduling. Employees can come and go as they please as long as they work 8 hours each day and 40 hours each week. Such a flexible schedule, however, will work only where it is not necessary to always have an employee working, such as in typing or accounting. In an organization such as a retail store or a restaurant, such a system would mean that at any given time, there may not be *any* employee present, which, of course, is probably not the best way to conduct a business.

Most flexible working schedules are categorized as **flexitour** or **modified flexitour**, with the employee enjoying greater flexibility in working hours although they must be scheduled in advance. With a flexitour system, the employee must submit a schedule on a weekly, biweekly, or monthly basis, depending on the organization. In a modified flexitour, the employee must schedule her hours in advance but can change these hours on a daily basis if so desired as long as she gives some advance notice.

Understandably, flexible working schedules are not only popular with employees, but also beneficial to organizations. Estes (1990) conducted a meta-analysis of more than 60 studies and found that flextime resulted in less absenteeism, less overtime, higher job satisfaction, less role conflict, and a slight increase in productivity (see Tables 12.2 and 12.3). These effects were strongest for smaller organizations and for those organizations in which employees shared limited physical resources such as space and equipment.

Table 12.3
Effect Sizes for
Flextime Programs

Variable	Number of Studies	Mean Effect Size
Absenteeism	10	−.59
Family/leisure time	3	.23
Leave usage	13	−.15
Productivity	29	.19
Role conflict	2	−.48
Satisfaction	9	.27

Source: Adapted with permission from Estes (1990).

Peak-Time Pay

A third alternative work schedule is **peak-time pay.** With peak-time pay, certain employees are encouraged to work only part-time but are paid at a higher hourly rate for those hours than employees who work full-time. Thus, an employee will make more per hour than his full-time counterpart, although he will make less money per day.

The concept of peak-time pay came from the banking and fast food industries, both of which face unique problems (Mahlin & Charles, 1984). Both types of organizations need to be open during the entire day yet only have approximately four hours that are busy. For example, a McDonald's restaurant might need 20 employees to cover its lunch-time crowd but need only 5 employees from 2 P.M. until 5 P.M., at which time the dinner crowd begins for another two-hour peak period. Rather than paying 20 employees to sit around for most of the day, it would be better to have 15 employees work for three hours a day during peak time and only 5 employees work the full eight hours.

Unfortunately, few people want to work only three hours a day at $4 per hour. And those who would be willing, such as students, often are not available during the hours that they are most needed. Thus, with peak-time pay, 15 people may be paid $6 or $7 per hour to work only the three peak hours. Thus, the employee makes a reasonable amount of money per day and the organization still saves money over what it would have spent had its employees worked the entire eight hours.

Job Sharing

A fourth alternative working schedule is called **job sharing,** and it involves two employees who share their work hours. Rather than one person working 40 hours each week, two employees combine their hours so that they total 40. At first glance, job sharing may seem to be little more than part-time work. There are, however, big psychological, if not administrative, differences.

First, part-time work usually involves lower-level jobs such as those found in the retail and restaurant industries. But job sharing allows those in complex occupations such as teaching and accounting also to enjoy the advantages of fewer work hours.

Second, with part-time work, the performance of one employee rarely affects the performance of the person who follows him. That is, the work completed by two part-time employees is considered to result from two separate jobs. But with job sharing, the work may be done by two different employees, and yet they share one job title and one position. Poor quality work by one employee must be corrected by the other.

From a psychological standpoint, the main difference between job sharing and part-time employment is the level of employee commitment, both to the organization and to the other employee. Job-sharing programs are targeted at attracting employees who have family responsibilities. Thus, an organization can attract a highly qualified employee who would not be able to work a full-time job.

Furthermore, an increasing trend is for husbands and wives who work in similar professions to share the same position. One such situation recently occurred with a high school teaching position, with the wife teaching three morning classes while her husband took care of their two children; the husband then taught three afternoon classes while his wife cared for their children.

Homework

The fifth and final alternative work schedule that we will discuss is **homework.** With this type of schedule, the employee works at home rather than at the workplace. Although homework has received much recent attention, it certainly is not a new concept. For more than a century, women have sewn garments at home and then sold them to factories for piece-rate prices. Today, with the increase in computers, other types of work also can be done in the home.

Homework has many advantages for both the employee and the employer. For the employee, it offers the opportunity to avoid or minimize child care and commuting costs, while allowing flexibility and comfort in working conditions. For the employer, money is saved on both office space and utilities.

Homework has the advantage of offering the employee the opportunity to avoid child care and commuting costs, while allowing flexible and comfortable working conditions.

But with the advantages come certain disadvantages, which is why most unions oppose homework. First, it is difficult for a union to organize workers when they are scattered around many locations. Second, it is difficult for the government to enforce safety and fair treatment standards when employees are not in a central location. Finally, employees cannot be easily supervised with homework. Unfortunately, the actual evaluation of the merits of homework will have to wait until more research has been conducted. Until then, homework sounds like a promising idea when used with controls and checks to ensure employee safety and fair treatment.

Shift Work

Even though most people work from 8 or 9 A.M. to 5 P.M., approximately 25% of all employees work evening or late night shifts. Working at these other times often is necessary because of economic and safety factors. Police officers and nurses must work around the clock because neither crime nor illness stops at 5 P.M., retail employees must work late hours because those are the times when most people are able to shop, and factory workers work these shifts because it allows one plant to be three times as productive if it can operate around the clock.

Because **shift work** is necessary and affects approximately 25% of all employees, research has attempted to identify its effects as well as ways to reduce any negative effects. As Table 12.4 shows, research clearly indicates that working evening ("swing") and late night ("graveyard") shifts has many physical, mental, and work-related effects.

These negative effects are thought to occur because of disruptions in the **circadian rhythm**, the 24-hour cycles of physiological functions that are maintained by every person. For example, most people sleep at night and eat in the morning, at noon, and in the evening. Although there are individual differences in the exact times for each function (such as eating or sleeping), people generally follow the same pattern. Working evening and late night shifts disrupts this pattern and often causes digestive, appetite, and sleeping problems.

Many of the psychological and social effects of shift work are caused by the incompatibility of an employees' schedule with the schedules of other people. That is, a person who works nights and sleeps mornings may be ready to socialize in the afternoon. Unfortunately, fewer people are around. And when the family is active, the employee is sleeping and thus requires quiet.

Factor	Effect		
	Improvement	No Change	Decrease
Physical health			Akerstedt & Torsvall (1978)
			Colligan, Frockt, & Tasto (1970)
			Dunham (1977)
			Frese & Semmer (1986)
			Meers, Maasen, & Veerhagen (1978)
			Mott, Mann, McLoughlin, & Warwick (1965)
			Wolinsky (1982)
Performance			Malaviya & Ganesh (1977)
			Mott et al. (1965)
			Wyatt & Mariott (1953)
Attendance		Gannon, Norland, & Robeson (1983)	Colligan et al. (1970)
			Jamal (1981)
			Nicholson, Jackson, & Howes (1978)
Fatigue			Wedderburn (1978)
Social and family life			Akerstedt & Torsvall (1978)
			Bast (1960)
			Dunham (1977)
			Jamal (1981)
			Ulrich (1957)
			Wedderburn (1978)
			Wyatt & Mariot (1953)
Mental health			Colligan et al. (1979)
			Jamal (1981)
			Wedderburn (1978)
Job satisfaction		Dunham (1977)	Frost & Jamal (1979)
			Jamal (1981)

**Table 12.4
Effects of Working
Evening and Late
Night Shifts**

As Figure 12.2 shows, many factors influence the degree to which shift work will affect an employee. For example, an employee who has a family is affected more than a single employee because the employee must adjust his sleeping schedule to those of others in the household. Other important factors are uniqueness of shift, whether a shift is fixed or rotating, frequency of rotation, and individual differences.

Uniqueness of Shift

The social effects of shift work can be greatly reduced if other organizations in the geographical area also use other shifts. The higher the per-

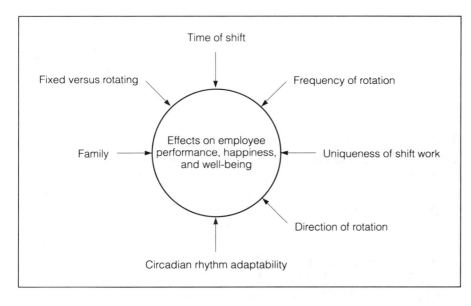

Time of shift

Fixed versus rotating

Frequency of rotation

Family

Effects on employee
performance, happiness,
and well-being

Uniqueness of shift work

Direction of rotation

Circadian rhythm adaptability

**Figure 12.2
Factors Influencing
Shift Work Effects**

centage of organizations with shifts, the greater the number of stores and restaurants that are open during the evening and the greater the number of other people available with whom to socialize. Shift work especially affects male workers; females tend to adjust their schedules to domestic concerns, while male shift workers pattern their schedule around leisure concerns (Chambers, 1986).

Fixed Versus Rotating Shifts

Shifts can be either fixed or rotated. With **fixed shifts,** separate groups of employees permanently work the day shift, swing shift, and night shift. **Rotating shifts** are those in which an employee rotates through all three shifts, working the day shift for a while, then switching to the swing shift, then working the night shift, and so on.

The rationale for rotating shifts is that because working swing and night shifts has negative effects on people, if each employee is allowed to work the day shift part of the time, the effects are lessened. On the other hand, with fixed shifts, even though two-thirds of all workers will have hours that are not compatible with their circadian rhythms, by staying permanently on the same shifts, they should be able to adjust better than if they change shifts, especially when considering that about two days are needed to adjust to each shift change.

Research on shift rotation has strongly suggested that fixed shifts result in fewer physical and psychological problems than do rotating shifts

(Frese & Okonek, 1984; Jamal & Jamal, 1982; Verhaegen, Cober, de Smedt, & Dirkx, 1987). For example, Jamal (1981) found that employees on fixed shifts had less absenteeism and tardiness, greater job satisfaction and social participation, and better mental health than did their counterparts working rotating shifts.

Frequency of Rotation

As the above discussion concludes, fixed shifts are better than rotating shifts. At times, however, shifts must be rotated because employees who feel stuck on swing and night shifts insist on having the opportunity to work days. In such situations, the frequency of the shift rotation must be decided upon. That is, should the rotation occur daily, weekly, monthly (and so on)?

Research on this point has been sparse and has not provided a clear and obvious solution. Both Williamson and Sanderson (1986) and Knauth and Kiesswetter (1987) studied changes from seven-day to three-day rotations and found the faster rotating shifts to result in fewer sleep and eating difficulties. Frese and Semmer (1986), however, found no such effect after controlling for the amount of on-the-job stress. Furthermore, the first two studies comparing the two had relatively fast rotations. Research still is needed that compares slower rotations of at least one month with the faster rotations before the effects of rotation frequency can be clarified.

Individual Differences

The final factor that we will discuss concerning the effects of shift work involves individual differences in employees. Obviously, not all employees will react to shift work in the same way because different employees have slightly different biological time clocks. In fact, we all probably have known people who claimed to be "night people" or those who "prefer the morning."

Several questionnaires have been developed to distinguish so-called morning people from evening people. Perhaps the best of these is that developed by Smith, Reilly, and Midkiff (1988), which contains the 13 most reliable and valid questions from 3 other available scales (Reilly & Smith, 1988). Such a questionnaire can be used to select and place employees into their optimal shifts.

Organization	Location
Abt Associates	Cambridge, MA
American West Airlines	Phoenix, AZ
Apple Computer	Cupertino, CA
Campbell Soup Co.	Camden, NJ
Corning	Corning, NY
Dominion Bankshares	Roanoke, VA
First National Bank of Atlanta	Atlanta, GA
Georgia Baptist Medical Center	Atlanta, Ga
Greenville News-Piedmont	Greenville, SC
Halmode Apparel	Roanoke, VA
Hill, Holliday, & Connors	Boston, MA
Hoffman–La Roche Pharmaceuticals	Nutley, NJ
Intermedics Int.	Freeport, TX
Merck & Co.	Rahway, NJ
Nyloncraft, Inc.	Mishawaka, IN
PCA International	Matthews, NC
Proctor and Gamble	Cincinnati, OH
Prudential	Woodbridge, NJ
Red Rope	Bristol, PA
Roanoke Memorial Hospital	Roanoke, VA
Roanoke Valley Community Hospital	Roanoke, VA
St. Albans Hospital	Radford, VA
Spartanburg General Hospital	Spartanburg, SC
Stride Rite	Boston, MA
Syntex	Palo Alto, CA
Zale Corp.	Dallas, TX

**Table 12.5
Organizations with
Progressive Child
Care Programs**

Issues Related to Work Schedules

Child Care

With the increasing number of dual-income families, the number of organizations that have involved themselves with child care also has increased. A small sample of these organizations is shown in Table 12.5. Organizational child care programs usually fall into one of three categories: on-site care, voucher systems, and referral services. In the first category, an organization such as Dominion Bankshares will build an **on-site child care facility.** Such a facility will allow a parent to save commuting time by avoiding a separate stop at a child care center; this also allows the parent to visit the child during breaks.

The number of organizations attempting to provide on-site child care has increased because of the growing number of dual-income families.

Some organizations fully fund the cost of child care, while others charge the employee the "going rate." There are advantages for both an organization that pays the full cost of child care and the employee whose child is enrolled in the facility. For example, the child care cost can be used as a benefit, meaning that neither the employee nor the organization will have to pay taxes on the amount. Of course, tax laws may eventually change the situation, but until that time, calculating child care as an employee benefit is financially rewarding for both the employee and the organization.

Although the employee response to such on-site programs has been overwhelmingly positive, on-site centers cost about $100,000 to start and more than $2,000 per child to maintain (Fooner, 1986). Because of such high costs, it is important to determine whether these centers "pay off" by reducing such phenomena as employee turnover and absenteeism. Unfortunately, there is little empirical research available to answer this question (Johnson, 1990).

Positive evidence has been provided from three sources: Intermedics, in Freeport, Texas, reported a 23% decrease in turnover and absenteeism, Scott and Markham (1982) reported an average decrease of 19% in absenteeism for organizations that established on-site centers, and Tioga Sportswear, in New Jersey, found a 50% decrease in turnover (LaMarre & Thompson, 1984). Negative evidence has been provided by Miller (1984), who reviewed published studies and concluded that day care may not have the impacts that they were initially thought to have. Still, child care centers probably will have their greatest impact on organizations with high percentages of young, married female workers.

A second avenue that can be taken with child care is to provide employees with *vouchers* to be used with private daycare centers. From the perspective of the organization, **voucher systems** alleviate both the high start-up costs and the high costs of liability insurance that are associated with on-site centers. From an employee's perspective, this approach reduces the cost of private child care.

Unfortunately, for several reasons this approach probably does not reduce employee turnover or absenteeism. First, an employee still must leave work to visit a sick child or to attend parent conferences. Second, most private child care centers operate from 7 A.M. until 6 P.M. Thus, employees who work swing or night shifts are not helped. Finally, there is often a shortage of quality child care in many areas.

The final avenue taken by organizations is to provide a **referral service** to quality child care centers. This approach has been taken by both IBM and Digital Corp. Although this is certainly a useful service, nothing about it would suggest that it would reduce either absenteeism or turnover.

Moonlighting

Another interesting problem involving work hours is seen with employees working more than one job, or **moonlighting.** For example, an employee might work the day shift as a machine operator for Ford Motor Co. and then work the night shift as a store clerk for a 7–11 convenience store. People moonlight for obvious reasons: they want or need to earn extra money, and they enjoy the second job (Jamal, 1988). Approximately 5% of American employees work more than one job (Jamal, 1988), and this rate goes as high as 30% in highly skilled fields such as data processing (Lasden, 1983). These high percentages of moonlighting employees raise concerns about the effects of extra work on performance and absenteeism for these employees' primary jobs.

As with child care, thus far few studies have investigated the effects of moonlighting. Jamal (1981) and Jamal and Crawford (1984) surveyed more than 400 workers at 6 organizations and found that moonlighters were no different than nonmoonlighters in terms of mental health, quality of life, job performance, and intention to leave their companies. But moonlighters did miss about one day more of work per year than did nonmoonlighters.

Neither Arcuri and Lester (1990), Miller and Sniderman (1974), nor Mott, Mann, McLoughlin, and Warwick (1965) found any negative effects for moonlighting. In fact, Mott et al. (1965) found that moonlighters were better adjusted and more active in the community than were their non-moonlighting counterparts.

Work Environment

Noise

If you have ever been upset when someone played their stereo too loudly while you were studying, then you can understand why psychologists would be interested in studying the effects of noise in the workplace. If the "obvious" were true, we could start and end our discussion of noise by stating that high levels of noise reduce performance and make workers unhappy. But as Figure 12.3 shows, the relationship between noise and worker behavior is much more complicated than we might first think.

To understand this relationship, we must first realize that not all noise is the same. Two sounds with the same level of loudness can have different frequencies. For example, the sound of a tug boat whistle is much lower in frequency than a train whistle. Lower frequencies do not affect employee performance as much as higher frequencies.

Furthermore, sounds that have the same frequency, intensity, and loudness can differ in their *pleasantness*. For example, noise levels at rock concerts and nightclubs are certainly loud, yet we enjoy the sound enough to pay money to hear it. We probably would not pay money to hear a jet engine producing the same sound levels as a rock concert.

This effect can be seen with an employee who listens to music through headphones at work. The noise level of the music often is greater than that of the machines in the environment, but it is considered to be more pleasant. Keep in mind, however, that even though the music may be

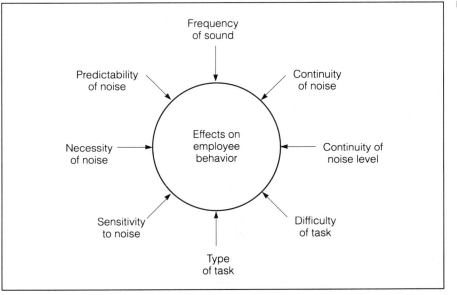

**Figure 12.3
Factors Determining
Possible Noise
Effects**

more interesting than the machine noise, the noise level has the same potential effects: Hearing loss can occur just as easily from music as it can from factory noise.

Noises also differ in whether they are continuous or intermittent. Constant noise has less effect on employee behavior, and so environments with steady noise levels are not as disrupting as those in which either noise frequency or intensity changes (Teichner, Arees, & Reilly, 1963; Vernon & Warner, 1932).

Another factor that affects the relationship between noise and employee behavior is the *type and difficulty of the task*. Noise affects difficult tasks, or those that involve cognitive and perceptual skills, more than it affects less difficult tasks or those that involve physical performance (Cohen & Weinstein, 1981).

Individual differences in people also determine the degree to which noise will affect performance. Weinstein (1978) examined individual differences in noise sensitivity in college students and found that noise-sensitive students had lower academic performance, were less comfortable in the presence of others, and became more disturbed than their less noise-sensitive peers.

The effect of noise also depends on the *reason* for and *familiarity* of the noise. When certain noises cannot be avoided—for example, the sound of an office typewriter—they are less irritating than unnecessary noises such as an employee talking too loudly or a roommate playing a stereo at full volume.

Likewise, familiar noise is less irritating than unfamiliar noise, probably for two reasons. First, a familiar noise is less distracting or meaningful than one that we hear for the first time. For example, the regular passing of a train outside an office produces less distracting noise than a suddenly dropped glass. Even though the train is louder, it is expected and familiar and thus not as distracting. Soldiers with war experience often have reported that they were able to sleep through artillery explosions but would awaken instantly at the sounds of snapped twigs or close footsteps.

Familiar sounds also may be less distracting because our hearing loses sensitivity to loud sounds. For example, on first entering a factory, the noise levels often are very high and distracting. After a few minutes, however, the noise is less noticeable because we have become temporarily less sensitive to it.

Finally, noise affects certain *types* of employee behaviors in different ways. Noise is more likely to decrease the quality of performance rather than its quantity (Broadbent & Little, 1960), it causes people to walk faster and make less eye contact (Korte & Grant, 1980), and it decreases performance on cognitive tasks (Cohen & Weinstein, 1981). But perhaps the greatest effects of noise are not on performance, but on employee health and morale.

As Table 12.6 shows, research indicates that in addition to hearing loss, continued exposure to high levels of noise (measured in decibels [db]) can raise blood pressure (Burns, 1979), increase worker illness (Cohen, 1972), cause people to be less helpful (Fisher, Bell, & Baum, 1984), and produce more aggression and irritability (Donnerstein & Wilson, 1976).

Noise also causes people to narrow their focus of attention so that they concentrate only on the most important stimuli. In one experiment, Korte and Grant (1980) placed unusual objects and people along the sidewalk of a busy shopping district, including a woman wearing a large pink hat and a bouquet of brightly colored balloons tied to a lamp post. Korte and Grant then asked shoppers if they had seen anything unusual and read them a list of the unusual people and things they could have seen.

The study results indicated that when traffic noise was high, only 35% of the shoppers noticed the items compared to more than 50% when the noise was low. Although such narrowing of attention may decrease the

Sample Noise	db	Effect
Rocket launch	180	
	170	
	160	
	150	
Gunshot blast	140	
Jet takeoff	130	Brief exposure can result in permanent deafness (Trahiotis & Robinson, 1979)
	125	
Disco	120	
Riveting machine	115	Maximum legal exposure to noise
Power lawn mower	110	A person cannot speak over a sound at this level
	105	
Textile-weaving plant	100	Blood pressure increases (Burns, 1979)
Food blender	95	Cognitive performance is reduced (Hockey, 1970)
		Employees report more illness and somatic complaints (Cohen, 1972)
	93	Angry people become more aggressive (Baron, 1977)
		Driving performance decreases (Finkleman, Zeitlin, Filippi, & Friend, 1977)
City traffic	90	Legal acceptable noise limit for eight-hour day
Computer card verifier	85	Helping behavior decreases (Mathews & Canon, 1975)
Train (100 feet away)	80	Reaction time decreases by 3% (Lahtela, Niemi, Kunsela, & Hypen, 1986)
Car	75	
Noisy restaurant	70	Telephone use is difficult
	68	Reduced detection of grammatical errors during proofreading (Weinstein, 1977)
	65	Hearing loss can occur in sensitive individuals
Normal speech	60	
	50	
Normal noise at home	40	
Soft whisper	30	
	20	
Breathing	10	
	0	

**Table 12.6
Effects of Noise at
Different Levels**

performance levels of employees for whom it is important to notice many stimuli (for example, police officers or safety inspectors), it may help the performance of employees who need only focus on a few different stimuli (Broadbent, 1971).

Time per Day (hours)	Maximum db
8	90
7	91
6	92
5	93
4	95
3	97
2	100
1.5	102
1	105
0.5	110
0.25	115

Table 12.7 Maximum Legal Exposures to Noise

Noise Reduction

Given that noise affects employee morale, health, and perhaps performance, employers have attempted to solve or minimize the problem of noise by several methods. One has been by setting legal time limits on the exposure to noise at different decibel levels. These are shown in Table 12.7. A second method has been by reducing the amount of unwanted noise that reaches an employee. Examples have included employees wearing protective ear plugs and muffs or working in soundproof areas away from the sources of noise. Although these methods may limit the effects on employee health, they also may decrease performance in jobs that require detection of or attention to certain types of noise (Mershon & Lin, 1987).

Another method used to limit the problem of noise has been through engineering technology—that is by reducing the actual amount of noise emitted. For example, rubber pads on typewriters reduce noise by reducing vibration, laser technology greatly reduces the noise from dot-matrix and thimble printers, and belt drives instead of gears reduce the noise made by many types of machines.

The above discussion has concentrated on the potential harmful effects of noise, but noise also can be beneficial in the working environment, especially as a warning method. For example, loud noises alert workers that a forklift is backing up, loud whistles tell workers when it is time to go home, and alarms tell workers when a machine has malfunctioned.

Music

One intriguing method for enhancing worker performance and morale has been the use of music during work. The rationale is that music will help reduce the periods of boredom and keep employees alert. More than 10,000 organizations have music played for their employees and customers by subscribing to Muzak.

Rather than playing any type of music, Muzak is highly specific, playing 486 soft instrumental songs per day, each selected so that it can be heard but not be distracting. Furthermore, the music is played in 15-minute programs, with the music at the beginning of the program less stimulating than that played toward the end of the program (is any of Muzak stimulating?).

Although use of music is popular, questions still remain about its effectiveness. In general, research has shown that employees enjoy listening to music at work and believe that they are more productive because of it (Newman, Hunt, & Rhodes, 1966). But little well-conducted research is available that has tested the actual effects of music on productivity. The little research that is available, however, generally has been favorable (Fox, 1971). For example, a Japanese study found that worker fatigue was reduced by 32% (Wokoun, 1980), and Muzak's own research shows a 17% increase in factory productivity, a 13% increase in clerical performance, and a 53% decrease in turnover by airline reservation agents. Furthermore, research has demonstrated that the presence of fast music causes customers in a restaurant to eat faster (Roballey & Gardner, 1986), while the presence of slow music causes supermarket customers to spend 38% more money (Milliman, 1986). Thus, music might indeed make working conditions better.

Much more research is necessary, however, because the relationship between music and performance probably depends on several factors. One is undoubtedly the type of music being played. Muzak uses a specific type and sequence of music that it believes is best. But employees often listen to classical, jazz, rock, and country music on their own headphones. What effects do these types of music have? And what if an employee does not like the music being played?

Another issue that needs further investigation is the relationship between music and task type. Music might increase performance in manual tasks that require little thinking, but it is doubtful that the same would hold true for complex tasks involving focused mental effort (Gilmer & Deci, 1977; Uhrbrock, 1961).

Many jobs, such as those in the steel and construction industry, involve working in intense heat, which can affect employee performance and health.

Temperature

Another important issue concerning the working environment is the effect of temperature on employee performance and health. This is an important issue because many jobs such as those in construction and in the steel

Humidity (%)	Air Temperature (°F)					
	41	50	59	68	77	86
100	39	52	64	78	96	120
80	39	52	63	75	90	111
60	40	51	62	73	86	102
40	40	51	61	72	83	96
20	41	50	60	70	81	91
0	41	50	59	68	77	86

**Table 12.8
Effective
Temperature as a
Function of Air
Temperature
and Humidity**

industry involve working in intense heat, while others such as rescue squads and meat-packing plants often involve working in extreme cold.

Perhaps the best place to begin a discussion of the effects of temperature is by describing how the human body tries to maintain an ideal temperature. When body temperature is above normal, we cool down in one of two ways. The first is through **radiation**, with the excess heat radiating away from the body. The second way is by **evaporation**, or by sweating away excess heat.

When body temperature is below normal, blood vessels constrict. Although this process helps protect against cold, it also produces numbness by reducing circulation. That is why our feet and hands are the first parts of the body to feel numb when we are cold. Police officers working a beat often can be seen stomping their feet in cold temperatures to stimulate circulation.

We must next understand how different factors affect what is called the **effective temperature**, or how hot or cold our environment feels to us. In theory, effective temperature has four components—air temperature, humidity, airflow, and temperature of objects in the environment—but it usually is computed by considering only air temperature and humidity. Note that effective temperature is more than simple air temperature. A 90-degree day in a Nevada desert feels cooler than a 90-degree day in a Georgia swamp. As Table 12.8 shows, the higher the humidity, the warmer the air temperature feels, and thus the higher the effective temperature.

In addition to humidity, airflow also is important. We all probably can recall the feeling of relief from a breeze coming off a lake or off the ocean. The air temperature probably did not change, but discomfort de-

Working Conditions
and Absenteeism

creased along with the effective temperature. Likewise, we might recall a "biting wind" that made a winter day seem so cold.

Finally, the effective temperature is affected by the heat that radiates from other objects in the environment. For example, the field-level temperature of outdoor sports stadiums that use artificial turf usually is much higher than the air temperature in the stands. The reason is that heat radiates from the artificial turf. Other examples of this radiation effect include how much hotter it feels when sitting with a group of people than when sitting alone or how much hotter it feels when lying on the sand at the beach than when sitting up.

This author can remember many summer days in Los Angeles when the air temperature was already more than 100 degrees but combined with heat radiating from a sidewalk to add 15 degrees and thus make walking uncomfortable. Similarly, a manager who thinks that his outdoor salespeople will be fine in an 85-degree temperature also must account for the effective temperature caused by radiating heat. An air temperature of 85 degrees above a concrete sidewalk is not the same as 85 degrees above a dirt road.

Both air temperature and humidity interact with the body's ability to cool down through radiation and evaporation. When air temperature is higher than body temperature, we are unable to radiate heat. When humidity is high, it is more difficult to lose body heat through evaporation. Thus, high air temperature and high humidity make the body's "natural cooling system" less effective.

The relevant question here, of course, is what happens when the effective temperature in the working environment is high or low? As shown in Figure 12.4, the answer is that performance usually deteriorates. The degree of deterioration, however, depends on several factors, including the type of task, the workload, and the number and frequency of rest periods that are allowed.

Effects on Tasks

Research indicates that high effective temperatures can affect performance on cognitive, physical, and perceptual tasks. For example, Fine and Kobrick (1978) found that after 7 hours of exposure to 95-degree temperatures with 88% humidity, employees made twice as many errors on a cognitive task than did a control group that worked in a moderate temperature of 75 degrees with 25% humidity.

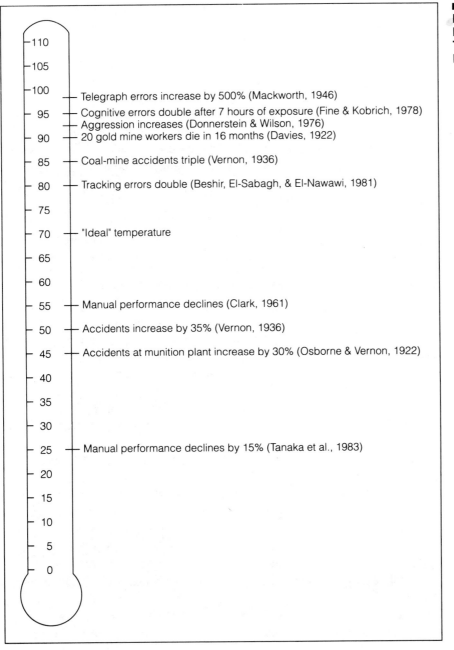

Figure 12.4
Effects of Various Temperatures (°F) on Employee Behavior

- 110
- 105
- 100 — Telegraph errors increase by 500% (Mackworth, 1946)
- 95 — Cognitive errors double after 7 hours of exposure (Fine & Kobrich, 1978)
  — Aggression increases (Donnerstein & Wilson, 1976)
- 90 — 20 gold mine workers die in 16 months (Davies, 1922)
- 85 — Coal-mine accidents triple (Vernon, 1936)
- 80 — Tracking errors double (Beshir, El-Sabagh, & El-Nawawi, 1981)
- 75
- 70 — "Ideal" temperature
- 65
- 60
- 55 — Manual performance declines (Clark, 1961)
- 50 — Accidents increase by 35% (Vernon, 1936)
- 45 — Accidents at munition plant increase by 30% (Osborne & Vernon, 1922)
- 40
- 35
- 30
- 25 — Manual performance declines by 15% (Tanaka et al., 1983)
- 20
- 15
- 10
- 5
- 0

Beshir, El-Sabagh, and El-Nawawi (1981) also investigated the effects of heat exposure on a perceptual tracking task. Beshir and his colleagues found that subjects' performance did not greatly decrease after working 90 minutes at 68 degrees. At 86 degrees, however, performance decreased significantly within 30 minutes.

While employee comfort and performance is important, heat also can affect the performance of machines and equipment. For example, a California printing and bookbinding company ran into interesting problems that involved airflow in one of its plants. The facility had many different types of printing presses as well as binders that required the melting of glue chips. As we can imagine, the heat from summer air, binding machines, and employees' bodies combined to make working conditions uncomfortable.

To solve this problem, the managers decided to increase the airflow by opening all of the plant's doors and windows and thus let ocean breezes cool the plant. Unfortunately, the increased airflow not only cooled the plant and made the employees more comfortable, but also caused the mechanical collating machines to malfunction.

The collating machines use sensors that warn their operators when too many or too few sheets of paper have been picked up. The breezes ruffled the sheets and thus set off the sensors. The increased airflow may have made the employees more comfortable and productive, but it reduced the equipment's productivity. Because the potential output of the collating machines was much greater than the outputs of the individual employees, the windows were closed. As a result, the employees became irritable, but overall productivity increased.

A similar case occurred at a knitting mill, whose owners discovered that yarn tended to snap when humidity was low. Therefore, they made no attempt to dehumidify the air. Unfortunately for the millworkers, the high humidity made working conditions uncomfortable. Thus, a decision had to be made as to the ideal humidity level that would keep the employees happy and productive without causing the yarn to snap. So, the humidity level was lowered slightly.

A final example of the differential effects of temperature comes from baseball. When temperatures are high, players are uncomfortable and pitchers tire more quickly than when temperatures are moderate. But the hotter air allows a baseball to travel farther and often there are more home runs. Thus, the higher temperatures negatively affect pitchers but positively affect batters.

Effects Related to Workload

High temperatures obviously most affect work performance when workloads are heavy. That is, an effective temperature of 95 degrees would quickly affect a person using a sledgehammer but take longer to affect a person pulling weeds.

Rest Periods

Temperature will have the greatest effect on performance when work activity is continuous. With rest breaks, the effects of either heat or cold can be greatly reduced. For example, most people can work for approximately 120 minutes at 90 degrees without impaired performance. At 100 degrees, however, the maximum time for continued performance is approximately 30 minutes; after that time, performance deteriorates (Wing, 1965). Thus, in temperatures of 90 degrees, rest breaks scheduled at a maximum of two hours apart will help keep performance (and the employee) from deteriorating. At 100 degrees, rest breaks must occur at intervals of less than 30 minutes.

An interesting problem developed at a large amusement park when its employees were exposed to summer heat. The park had several employees dress in theme costumes, which we will call gnomes here to protect the park's reputation. The thick and heavy gnome costumes were worn even during summer when temperatures were almost always in the 90s and 100s. The job of each costumed employee was to walk around the park and greet customers, especially children.

Problems, however, began when children punched the gnomes and knocked them over (a rolling gnome actually was a fairly funny sight). Normally, the gnomes kept their sense of humor and laughed, but after an hour in costume in 100 degree temperatures, they sometimes lost their humor and began punching back. And when they were not hitting children, the gnomes were passing out from the heat. Obviously, something had to be done.

The park's management decided to solve the problem by having the gnomes work shifts of four hours instead of eight. As we might expect from the above discussion, this solution was ineffective. Why? Because the outside temperature was 100 degrees and the effective temperature inside the costumes was at least 20 degrees higher. At such high temperatures, continuous activity brought decreased performance in less than 30 minutes. The solution that worked, of course, was to have the gnomes

Study	Finding
Mason (1984)	VDT users have 550% more vision-related complaints.
Rice (1983)	33% of VDT users are anxious; 5% show symptoms of nausea, high blood pressure, and dizziness.
DeGroot and Kamphois (1983)	VDT users report increased eye strain, migraine headaches, and back problems.
Dainoff, Happ, and Crane (1981)	VDT users complain about sore arms, sore backs, and headaches.
Harris (1981)	Increased eye strain, migraines, and back problems.
Smith, Cohen, and Stammerjohn (1981)	Increased strain, boredom, work load and back pains.
Savage (1988)	High percentages of miscarriages for women using VDTs.
Nussbaum (1980)	VDT typists report twice as much fatigue.
Gunnarson and Ostberg (1977)	Increased monotony and loss of control for VDT users.

**Table 12.9
Research Showing
Problems from
VDT Use**

work for 20 minutes and then take short breaks in an air-conditioned room, thus taking advantage of what we know about exposure limits to heat as well as frequency of breaks.

Computer Terminals

There is little doubt that the emergence of computers over the last two decades has greatly changed the work environment. Word-processing programs allow material to be typed faster and without spelling errors, statistical programs and spreadsheets make research and accounting duties easier, and desktop-publishing systems allow material to be attractively produced at a fraction of the cost of using a professional typesetter. But with the improvements in efficiency and quality have come certain problems. Perhaps the most publicized are the "dangers" of computer terminals and the "fear" of computers.

Video Display Terminals

In the last few years, employees who use **video display terminals (VDTs)** have complained about health problems from their use. These complaints even have been voiced by students, half of whom believe that VDTs are dangerous (Trinkaus, 1986). As listed in Table 12.9, these complaints have ranged from simple fatigue to increased numbers of miscarriages suffered by pregnant employees.

Even though employees may report such symptoms, it is unclear how accurate the reports are. For example, Dainoff, Happ, and Crain (1981) believe that the symptoms result from an increase in stress that is brought about by the lack of control an employee feels when using a computer as well as by the increased amount of work that can be done on the computer. Thus, the terminal or computer itself does not cause problems, but the loss of control and increased work load do.

Research by the National Research Council (1983) has indicated that while VDT use may cause eye strain, it does not result in permanent eye damage. Furthermore, eye strain can be reduced greatly by eliminating the glare from the terminal screens. This can be done in several ways, including changing the angle of the screen to limit light reflection, using hoods to screen the terminal from overhead light, using antiglare screens, and changing the lighting in the room in which the terminal is located.

Eye strain also can be reduced by using large screens with good resolution. Early computer screens tended to be small (for example, the first models of the Kaypro computer) and had print that was difficult to read (the early Apple monitors). Although many different screen colors are available, including amber, green, and white, research has shown no advantage of one color over another. The best color is simply a matter of individual preference, indicating that the employee who will use the screen should be the one to pick the color.

Many of the other physical symptoms reported by VDT users are caused by poorly designed workstations (Overman, 1990). Employees often use the same desk and chair for both their terminal and their typing, writing, and other work. Kroemer and Price (1982) and Grandjean, Hunting, and Pidermann (1983) have conducted extensive research on the optimal design of a computer workstation and how a VDT user should sit. For example, the optimal elbow angle when using a terminal is 99 degrees, with a 104-degree trunk incline. Obviously, few VDT users are going to measure their elbow angles, but they can be trained to sit in a particular way and be provided with equipment such as detachable keyboards and adjustable tables. These ergonomic changes probably will greatly reduce the symptoms of VDT use.

Fear of Computers

Another problem with the use of computers in the workplace is that many employees, especially older ones, are afraid of them (Martin, 1973). Again, however, it is not clear whether employees are actually frightened by the computers themselves or of some aspect of their required use.

Galagan (1983) believes that the fear reported by new users actually is a fear that they will damage the computer. This is analogous to a person who will not pick up an expensive piece of crystal in a store. The shopper obviously does not have a fear of crystal, but does fear dropping this particular piece.

After conducting hundreds of interviews, Zuboff (1982) believes that the "fear of computers" really is a "fear of change." Employees fear that computers will limit their control, make their jobs boring, and perhaps take away their job (Kalimo & Leppanen, 1985). This also might explain the increased reluctance of older employees who have used typewriters or accounting ledgers for decades and simply do not want to change. Finally, Brod (1985) believes that many people fear technology, not computers. That is, regardless of whether the new equipment is a computer, a photocopy machine, or a complicated washing machine, these people will be afraid.

To test these three hypotheses of fear, Reardon (1986) had students work on either a computer or a complicated tape recorder to test their fear of computers against their fear of technology. Furthermore, the subjects either had or did not have previous experience with the piece of equipment so that their fear of computers could be tested against their fear of change. Finally, the subjects were told either that they had to be careful because the computer or the tape recorder was sensitive and easily damaged or that it was indestructible—this tested their fear of computers against their fear of causing damage.

Reardon's study results supported the proposition that fear of computers really is fear of technology and that computers themselves do not necessarily produce fear or anxiety. Thus, the best way to introduce computers or new technology to employees is through training, which includes information not only on the use of new equipment, but also its consequences (Cirillo, 1983; Shneiderman, 1980).

Office Design

Landscaped Offices

In the past decade or so, many organizations have adopted what is called an "open" or "landscaped" office design (Martinez, 1990). Originally developed by furniture manufacturers in West Germany, the design uses large, open office areas without walls. Individual work units are separated by such items as plants, bookcases, and desks. The idea behind this de-

Table 12.10
Effects of Landscaped
Office Environments

Study	Employee Effects
Brookes and Kaplan (1972) Davis (1984)	Increased socialization
Allen and Gertsberger (1973)	Increased communication Decreased construction costs Decreased relocation costs Decreased lighting and electrical costs Decreased office attractiveness
Sundstrom, Burt, and Kamp (1980)	Decreased privacy Decreased productivity Decreased satisfaction
Oldham and Brass (1979)	Decreased motivation Decreased satisfaction Decreased concentration Increased noise

sign is that without the physical barriers of walls, employees will communicate better with one another and be easier to supervise and help.

There are three common designs for open or landscaped offices (Martinez, 1990). In a *freestanding design* (also called a bullpen design), all desks are placed in a large area that is completely open. With *uniform plans,* desks are placed at uniform distances and are separated by panels into cubicle areas. *Free-form work stations* use a combination of designs so that the different needs of each worker can be accommodated.

The landscaped office may be appealing, but as Table 12.10 shows, the research generally has not been especially supportive. Landscaped offices can increase contact and communication and are less expensive than regular offices, but they often lessen productivity and job satisfaction.

Office Furniture

Given that private offices are more common than, and probably superior to, open office environments, research has sought to determine the factors that affect the placement and perception of furniture within the private office. In particular, this research has concentrated on visitors' perceptions of certain office characteristics as well as on the personalities of office occupants.

Research on visitors' perceptions of certain office characteristics has brought several interesting but not necessarily surprising findings. One

**Figure 12.5
Open and Closed
Desk Placements**

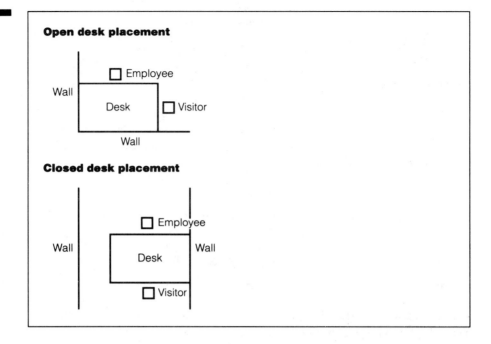

Open desk placement

Closed desk placement

line of research examined the perceptions of visitors to offices that used either open or closed desk arrangements. As shown in Figure 12.5, an **open desk arrangement** faces a desk against a wall so that a visitor can sit next to or adjacent to the person who sits behind the desk. A **closed desk arrangement** places a desk so that a visitor must sit across from the person behind the desk.

Visitors to offices that use open rather than closed desk arrangements perceive the offices to be more comfortable and their occupants as friendlier and more trustworthy, open, interested, and extraverted (Campbell, 1979; McElroy, Morrow, & Wall, 1983; Widgery & Stackpole, 1972). Conversely, visitors rate people with messy offices as being active and busy, those with clean offices as being organized and introverted, and those with organized offices (lots of papers placed in stacks) as being active and achievement-oriented (McElroy, Morrow, & Wall, 1983; Morrow & McElroy, 1981). Finally, visitors rate offices that have plants and posters as more comfortable, inviting, and hospitable than offices that do not have plants and posters (Campbell, 1979).

This line of research is not only interesting, but also important. A supervisor who has a messy office and a closed chair arrangement is sending out the message that she does not want to be bothered. This may not be her intended message, but it is the one that is perceived by her subordinates. Thus, a manager who wants to be more open and improve communication with her employees might want to start by changing the appearance of her office.

With the above research indicating that people make judgments about others based on their offices, the next logical step is to determine whether people with different types of offices actually have different types of personalities. Limited research, in fact, does seem to show that the appearance of an office provides insight into the personality of the occupant.

McElroy, Morrow, and Ackerman (1983) looked at the personalities of faculty members who had open desk arrangements and those who had closed desk arrangements, and found that those with open desk arrangements were more extraverted and "people-oriented" than their closed desk counterparts. Furthermore, faculty members who used open desk arrangements had lower external loci of control orientation and scored higher on the Least-Preferred Co-Worker (LPC) Scale, which we discussed in Chapter 8.

In another study, Zweigenhaft (1976) compared desk placement using several variables and found that older, higher-status faculty members used closed desk arrangements more than did younger members. Even more interesting was the finding that faculty members who used closed desk arrangements also were evaluated less favorably in the classroom. Thus, desk placement was able to partially predict the effectiveness of a faculty member, providing support for the idea that different types of people arrange their offices in different ways.

In a study of personnel managers, Cochran, Kopitzke, and Miller (1984) compared the office characteristics used by each manager with his or her personality. Cochran et al. found that dominant, achievement-oriented managers did not decorate their offices with anything other than standard furniture; outgoing managers had photographs of their vacations to remind them of good times and clocks to let them know when it was quitting time; introverted managers had plants and paintings so that their office would remind them of home; and organized managers had cartoons to show that even though they were neat and compulsive, they also had a sense of humor.

The presence of windows is another factor that seems to affect the way in which an office is decorated. Heerwagen and Orians (1986) examined the way in which people decorated both windowed and windowless offices and found that occupants of windowless offices used twice as many decorative items such as posters, pictures, and paintings. Not surprisingly, the posters in windowless offices contained more landscapes and fewer cityscapes than did offices with windows.

Absenteeism

A problem faced by many organizations is that of absenteeism, which is approximately 2% for most organizations. Although 2% may not seem like much, absenteeism costs employers billions of dollars a year in lost productivity. To solve the problem, we must first understand why people

	Attending Work	**Missing Work**
Advantages	Earning money	More sleep
	Enjoyment of work	Increased leisure activities
	Being with friends at work	More time with family and friends
	Recognition	No commuting time or costs
	Sick days saved for later use	
Disadvantages	Boredom	No pay
	Unsafe working conditions	Being suspended or fired
	Stress	Resentment from other employees
	Working with unfriendly employees	Fewer sick days left in event of real illness
	Poor relations with management	
	Commuting time and costs	

**Table 12.11
Considerations in the
Decision to Attend
or Miss Work**

miss work and what can be done to address these reasons. The employment profile of Kim Carr is a good example of how one professional attempts to deal with the problem of absenteeism.

Reasons for Missing Work

The **decision-making theory** about absenteeism essentially holds that employees make a decision each day as to whether they will or will not attend work. Although the decision-making process is not clearly understood, it probably includes weighing both the advantages and disadvantages of going to work against the advantages and disadvantages of not going to work. Examples of each are shown in Table 12.11.

If this theory is true, then absenteeism can be reduced by increasing the advantages of going to work, making not going to work even more disadvantageous, and decreasing the disadvantages of going to work. Obviously, it is difficult to alter the advantages of not going to work unless the organization changes its location to a place that offers no outside activities, no television, no good weather, and so on. Of course, with such a location, absenteeism probably will not be a problem because the organization probably will not be able to recruit employees in the first place.

Stimulating Attendance

Increasing the advantages of an employee going to work can be done in several ways. From previous chapters, we know that one way to do this is by making the work more interesting and challenging through such techniques as job rotation and job enrichment. Another way is through the use of incentives, which can take at least three forms.

The first of these forms, called **well pay,** involves paying employees for their unused sick leave. One variation gives unused sick time back to the employee for later use as vacation time. One of this author's neighbors works for a hospital and has not missed a day of work in five years. As a consequence, she how has three months' extra vacation time, which she plans to spend with her newborn son.

The second form provides a **financial bonus** to employees who attain a certain level of attendance. With this method, an employee with perfect attendance over a year might receive a $1,000 bonus and an employee who misses 5 days might receive $300, while an employee who misses 10 days receives nothing.

A meta-analysis conducted by Johnson (1990) found that well pay and financial incentives showed excellent results. But the effectiveness of incentive plans is based on several factors such as the size of the incentive, the nature of the incentive, and the time that elapses between attending and being rewarded.

The third form is to use **games** to reward employees who attend work. There are many examples. One company used poker as its game, giving a playing card each day to employees who attended. At the end of the week, employees with five cards compared the value of their hands, and the winning employee would be given a prize such as a dinner for two at the best restaurant in town or a gas barbecue grill. Although some studies have reported success in using such games, the meta-analysis conducted by Johnson (in press) found that the mean effect size for games was close to zero.

One other way that we can make work attendance more advantageous is through recognition and praise rather than financial incentives. In an award-winning study, Scott, Markham, and Robers (1985) directly compared recognition with other techniques such as incentives and discipline. The results of their investigation supported the effectiveness of recognition, as did Johnson's meta-analysis (also see Table 12.12).

Method	Number of Studies	Effect Size
Well pay	4	.86
Flextime	10	.59
Compressed work schedules	5	.44
Discipline	12	.36
Recognition	6	.30
Wellness programs	6	.18
Financial incentives	7	.17
Games	6	.08

Source: Adapted from Johnson (1990). Used with permission.

**Table 12.12
Reducing
Absenteeism:
Effect Sizes of
Various Methods**

Reducing Absenteeism

Absenteeism also can be reduced by punishing or disciplining an employee who misses work. Discipline can range from receiving a warning, to getting less popular work assignments, to being fired. As shown in Table 12.12, discipline works fairly well, especially when combined with some positive reinforcement for attending.

Another way to increase the negative consequences of missing work is through policy and record keeping. Most organizations measure absenteeism by counting the number of days missed, or *frequency,* but perhaps the best method records the number of *instances* of absenteeism rather than the number of days. For example, instead of giving employees 12 days of sick leave, they are given 3 or 4 instances of absenteeism. Missing 1 day or 3 consecutive days each count as one separate instance of absenteeism.

As shown in Figure 12.6, the number of days missed and the instances of absenteeism often yield different results. By decreasing the number of times that a person can miss, the odds increase that the employee will utilize sick leave only for actual illness.

Eliminating Causes of Absenteeism

Absenteeism also can be reduced by removing the negative factors that an employee associates with going to work and that might motivate that employee to avoid attending. One of the most important of these factors is *stress.* The greater the job stress, the greater the probability that most people will want to skip work. One form of stress is boredom, and it is easy to understand why a person would avoid attending a boring job or class.

**Figure 12.6
Frequency and
Instance Methods of
Measuring
Absenteeism**

Frequency Method

Patricia Austin

Days Missed:				
	March	4		
	April	9		
	May	2		
	May	30	Days Missed	= 8
	June	7	Instances	= 8
	July	3		
	Sept	2		
	Nov	24		

Instance Method

Christine Evert

Days Missed:				
	April	3		
	April	4		
	April	5		
	July	15	Days Missed	= 8
	July	16	Instances	= 3
	Dec	2		
	Dec	3		
	Dec	4		

Personal problems with other employees or with management constitute another reason for wanting to avoid work. If the employee feels that
he is not liked or will be verbally abused, it should come as no surprise
that he would want to avoid dealing with his fellow employees or his superiors. Finally, employees might miss work to avoid physical dangers
involved with work such as dealing with hazardous chemicals.

To increase attendance, then, the negative factors cited above must be
eliminated. The first step in this elimination, of course, is to become
aware of the negative factors that bother employees. These can be determined by asking supervisors or by employee questionnaires. After the
problems are known, it is important that management diligently work to
eliminate the identified problems from the workplace.

Illness and Personal Problems

Another obvious reason why employees miss work is illness. No data are
available to indicate the percentage of absenteeism in industry that results
from illness, but a study conducted with college students provides some

insight. Kovach, Surrette, and Whitcomb (1988) asked more than 500 general psychology students to anonymously provide the reason for each day of class they missed. Less than 30% of the missed days were the result of illness!

However strong its effect, illness is a leading cause of missed work. The question, of course, is whether illness-induced absenteeism can be reduced. The answer is not as clear as we would like, but most indications are that organizational wellness programs involving exercise, stress reduction, smoking cessation, and improved nutrition seem to help. In a meta-analysis of the small number of available studies, Bonner (in press) found that the mean effect size for wellness programs in reducing absenteeism was .18, a fairly small effect.

Other sources of absenteeism are personal problems such as divorce and alcoholism. Industry, however, can reduce their effects in two ways. First, the factors in the workplace that contribute to family problems and stress can be eliminated or reduced. These factors or variables include extensive employee travel, overtime, fatigue, and job-related stress. Second, some form of **Employee Assistance Program (EAP)** can be implemented. EAPs use professional counselors to deal with employee problems. An employee with a problem can either choose to see a counselor on her own or be recommended by her supervisor. Some large organizations have their own EAP counselors, but most use private agencies, which often are run through local hospitals.

The motivation for EAPs may be good, but little if any empirical evidence supports their effectiveness. Still, many organizations have used EAPs and have been quite pleased with them. Independently operated EAPs typically claim a 3-to-1 return on the dollars invested through increased productivity and reduced absenteeism and turnover.

Individual Traits

One interesting theory of absenteeism postulates that one reason that people miss work is the result of a particular set of personality traits they possess. That is, certain types of people are more likely to miss work than are other types.

Although little research has been conducted on this theory, Kovach, Surrette, and Whitcomb (1988) did find that the best predictor of student attendance in general psychology courses was the tendency of compulsive, rule-oriented behavior. If more research supports this theory, then a new strategy for increasing employee attendance might be to screen out people who have a tendency to miss work during the selection stage.

Unique Events

Many times an individual will miss work because of events or conditions that are beyond a management's control. For example, bad weather is one reason why absenteeism is higher in the Northeast than in the South. Although an organization can do little to control weather, the accessibility of the plant or office can be considered in the decision of where to locate. In fact, this is one reason why many organizations have started in or moved to the so-called Sunbelt in the last decade. An organization also may want to offer some type of shuttle service for its employees to avoid not only weather problems, but also any resulting mechanical failures of employees' automobiles.

Bad weather certainly can be a legitimate reason for an employee to miss work, but one study found that job satisfaction best predicted attendance on days with poor weather. That is, in good weather, most employees attended, but in inclement weather, only those employees with high job satisfaction attended. Thus, even in bad weather, the degree to which the employee likes his job will help to determine his attendance. As industrial psychologist Dan Johnson has asked: "How come we hear about employees not being able to get to work and students not being able to attend class because of bad weather, yet we don't ever hear about an employee or a student who can't get home because of bad weather?" It certainly makes one think!

Chapter Summary

Rather than working the traditional 8 hours per day, 5 days each week, an employee can work one of several alternative work schedules. Compressed work schedules involve working 40 hours over a 3- or 4-day period rather than the traditional 5-day period, while flextime schedules allow employees to select their own hours. Research indicates that both compressed work schedules and flextime increase job satisfaction and decrease absenteeism. Other alternative schedules include peak-time pay, job sharing, and homework.

Many employees work traditional 5-day, 40-hour work weeks but do so during swing and night shifts. Although these shifts often are economically necessary, research indicates that shift work has negative effects on physical health, performance, and leisure time. Factors that modify how shift work will affect an employee include family, the uniqueness of the shift, whether the shift is fixed or rotating, and the frequency of the rotation.

In addition to schedules, such influences as noise and temperature also can affect employee behavior. Noise can reduce job performance and satisfaction, depending on its frequency, pleasantness, purpose, familiarity, and continuity as well as the type of task being performed. Temperature will affect work behavior depending on the type of task being performed, the workload, and the number and length of rest periods that are allowed.

The effects of computer terminals also were discussed in this chapter. Computer terminals increase eye strain and levels of stress, although the latter probably results from the loss of control one feels when working with a computer as well as a fear of technology. Eye strain can be corrected through the proper design and construction of computer workstations.

The office environment is another factor that can affect work behavior. Private offices are superior to open or landscaped offices. An interesting finding is that the way in which a person decorates his office not only indicates his personality, but also affects the behavior of office visitors.

A major problem faced by most organizations is that of employee absenteeism. Decreases in absenteeism can be accomplished by increasing the reasons that an employee has for going to work (well pay, bonuses, games), increasing the negative consequences of missing work (discipline, better record keeping), and decreasing the negative consequences of attending work (reducing stress, boredom, and personal problems).

Glossary

Bandwidth The total number of potential work hours available each day

Circadian rhythm The 24-hour cycle of physiological functions that are maintained by every person

Closed desk arrangement An office arranged so that a visitor must sit across from the person behind the desk

Compressed work weeks Work schedules in which 40 hours are worked in less than the traditional five-day work week

Core hours The hours in a flextime schedule during which every employee must work

Decision-making theory A theory about absenteeism that holds that employees daily make a conscious decision about whether to attend work

Effective temperature The combination of air temperature, humidity, air flow, and heat radiation that determines how hot or cold the environment feels

Employee Assistance Program (EAP) A program designed to help employees overcome alcohol, drug, and psychological problems

Evaporation One way our bodies maintain a normal temperature, in which perspiration reduces excess heat

Financial bonus A method of absenteeism control in which employees who meet an attendance standard are given a cash reward

Fixed shift A shift schedule in which employees never change the shifts that they work

Flexible hours The part of a flextime schedule in which employees may choose which hours to work

Flexitour A flextime schedule in which employees have flexibility in scheduling but must schedule their work hours at least a week in advance

Flextime A work schedule that allows employees to choose their own work hours

Games An absenteeism control method in which games such as poker and bingo are used to reward employee attendance

Gliding time A flextime schedule in which employees can choose their own hours without any advance notice or scheduling

Homework A system in which employees work at home rather than in an organization's building

Job sharing A work schedule in which two employees share one job by splitting the work hours

Modified flexitour A flextime schedule in which employees have flexibility in scheduling but must schedule their work hours a day in advance

Moonlighting Working more than one job

On-site child care facility A child care center that is located on the site of the organization employing the parent

Open desk arrangement An office arranged so that a visitor can sit adjacent to rather than across from the person behind the desk

Peak-time pay A system in which part-time employees who work only during peak hours are paid at a higher hourly rate

Radiation One way our bodies maintain a normal temperature, by the emission of heat waves

Referral service A system of child care in which an employer maintains a list of certified child care centers that can be used by its employees

Rotating shift A shift schedule in which employees periodically change the shifts that they work

Video display terminals (VDTs) Computer screens

Voucher system A system of child care in which an organization pays its employees child care costs at private child care centers by providing the employees with vouchers

Well pay A method of absenteeism control in which employees are paid for their unused sick leave

References

Aamodt, M. G. (1986, June). *Validity of expert advice regarding the employment interview.* Paper presented at 10th Annual Meeting of International Personnel Management Association—Assessment Council, San Francisco, CA.

Aamodt, M. G., Bryan, D. A., & Whitcomb, A. J. (1989). Validity of the Peres and Garcia technique for predicting performance with letters of recommendation. *Proceedings of 13th Annual Meeting of International Personnel Management Association—Assessment Council,* pp. 151–154.

Aamodt, M. G., & Carr, K. (1988). Relationship between recruitment source and employee behavior. *Proceedings of 12th Annual Meeting of International Personnel Management Association,* pp. 143–146.

Aamodt, M. G., & Kimbrough, W. W. (1982). Validity considerations in acceptance of Personal Profile System interpretations. *Educational and Psychological Measurement, 42,* 625–628.

Aamodt, M. G., & Kimbrough, W. W. (1983). The Arkansas Index: An efficient system to match workers' personality dimensions with objective personality tests. *Psychological Reports, 53,* 231–246.

Aamodt, M. G., & Kimbrough, W. W. (1985). Comparison of four methods for weighing multiple predictors. *Educational and Psychological Measurement, 45,* 477–482.

Aamodt, M. G., Kimbrough, W. W., & Alexander, C. J. (1983). A preliminary investigation of the relationship between team racial heterogeneity and team performance in college basketball. *Journal of Sports Sciences, 1,* 131–133.

Aamodt, M. G., Kimbrough, W. W., Keller, R. J., & Crawford, K. (1982). Relationship between sex, race, and job performance level and the generation of critical incidents. *Educational and Psychological Research, 2,* 227–234.

Aamodt, M. G., & Peggans, D. (1988). Tactfully rejecting job applicants. *Personnel Administrator, 33,* 58–60.

Aamodt, M. G. & Pierce, W. L. (1987). Comparison of the rare response and vertical percent methods of scoring the biographical information blank. *Educational and Psychological Measurement, 47,* 505–511.

Aamodt, M. G., Reardon, C., & Kimbrough, W. W. (1986). The Critical Incident Technique revisited. *Journal of Police and Criminal Psychology, 2,* 48–59.

Adair, B., & Pollen, D. (1985, September 23). No! No! A thousand times no: The declining art of the rejection letter. *The Washington Post,* p. C-5.

Adams, J. S. (1965). Inequity in social change. In L. Berkowitz (Ed.), *Advances in experimental social psychology* (Vol. 2) (pp. 267–299). New York: Academic Press.

Adams, J. S., & Rosenbaum, W. B. (1962). The relationship of worker productivity to cognitive dissonance about wage inequities. *Journal of Applied Psychology, 46,* 161–164.

Adams, L., & DeLucca, J. (1987). Effect of confidentiality and likeability on performance evaluations. *Proceedings of 8th Annual Graduate Conference on Industrial/Organizational Psychology and Organizational Behavior,* 183–184.

Akerstedt, T., & Torsvall, L. (1978). Experimental changes in shift schedules: Their effects on well-being. *Ergonomics, 21,* 849–856.

Aldefer, C. P. (1972). *Existence, relatedness, and growth: Human needs in organizational settings.* New York: Free Press.

Allen, T. J., & Gertsberger, P. C. (1973). A field experiment to improve communications in a product engineering department: The nonterritorial office. *Human Factors, 15,* 487–498.

Alliger, G. M., & Janak, E. A. (1989). Kirkpatrick's levels of training criteria: Thirty years later. *Personnel Psychology, 42,* 331–342.

Allport, G. W., & Postman, L. (1947). *The psychology of rumor.* New York: Holt, Rinehart & Winston.

Amalfitano, J. G., & Kalt, N. C. (1977). Effects of eye contact on the evaluation of job applicants. *Journal of Employment Counseling, 14,* 46–48.

Ammerman, H. L. (1965). *A model of junior officer jobs for use in developing task inventories.* HumPRO Technical Report 65-10. Alexandria, VA: Human Resources Research Organization.

Anastasi, A. (1982). *Psychological testing.* New York: Macmillan.

Anderson, N. H. (1965). Adding versus averaging as a stimulus combination rule in impression formation. *Journal of Experimental Psychology, 70,* 394–400.

Andrews, E. S., & Noel, J. J. (1986). Adding life to the case study method. *Training and Development Journal, 40*(2), 28–33.

Arcuri, A. E., & Lester, D. (1990). Moonlighting and stress in police officers. *Psychological Reports, 66,* 350.

Arvey, R. D. (1979). *Fairness in selecting employees.* Reading, MA: Addison-Wesley.

Arvey, R. D., & Begalla, M. E. (1975). Analyzing the homemaker job using the PAQ. *Journal of Applied Psychology, 60,* 513–517.

Arvey, R. D., Bouchard, T. J., Segal, N. L., & Abraham, L. M. (1989). Job satisfaction: Environmental and genetic components. *Journal of Applied Psychology, 74,* 187–192.

Arvey, R. D., & Campion, J. E. (1982). The employment interview: A summary and review of recent research. *Personnel Psychology, 35,* 281–327.

Arvey, R. D., Davis, G. A., McGowen, S. L., & Dipboye, R. L. (1982). Potential sources of bias in job analytic processes. *Academy of Management Journal, 25,* 618–629.

Ash, R. A., & Edgell, S. A. (1975). A note on the readability of the Position Analysis Questionnaire (PAQ). *Journal of Applied Psychology, 60,* 765–766.

Ash, R. A., & Levine, E. L. (1980, November-December). A framework for evaluating job analysis methods. *Personnel, 57*(6), 53–59.

Asher, J. J., & Sciarrino, J. A. (1974). Realistic work sample tests: A review. *Personnel Psychology, 27,* 519–533.

Athey, T. R., & McIntyre, R. M. (1987). Effect of rater training on rater accuracy: Levels of processing theory and social facilitation perspectives. *Journal of Applied Psychology, 72,* 567–572.

Banks, M. H., Jackson, P. R., Stafford, E. M., & Warr, P. B. (1983). The Job Components Inventory and the analysis of jobs requiring limited skill. *Personnel Psychology, 36,* 57–66.

Banks, M. H., & Miller, R. L. (1984). Reliability and convergent validity of the Job Components Inventory. *Journal of Occupational Psychology, 57,* 181–184.

Bannister, B. D. (1986). Performance outcome feedback and attributional feedback: Interactive effects on recipient responses. *Journal of Applied Psychology, 71,* 203–210.

Baron, R. A. (1977). *Human aggression.* New York: Plenum.

Baron, R. A. (1983). Sweet smell of success: The impact of pleasant artificial scents on evaluations of job applicants. *Journal of Applied Psychology, 68,* 709–713.

Baron, R. A. (1988). Negative effects of destructive criticism: Impact on conflict, self-efficacy, and task performance. *Journal of Applied Psychology, 73,* 199–207.

Barr, S. H., & Hitt, M. A. (1986). A comparison of selection decision models in manager versus student samples. *Personnel Psychology, 39,* 599–617.

Bassett, G. A., & Meyer, H. H. (1968). Performance appraisal based upon self-review. *Personnel Psychology, 21,* 421–430.

Bast, G. H. (1960). *Ploegenarbeid in de industry.* Arnheim: Contract groepvuoering productivit eit Van Loghum Slaterus. Cited by P. E. Mott, *Shift work.* (1965). Ann Arbor, MI: University of Michigan Press.

Baxter, J. C., Brock, B., Hill, P. C., & Rozelle, R. M. (1981). Letters of recommendation: A question of value. *Journal of Applied Psychology, 66,* 296–301.

Beatty, L. K. (1989). Salaries: How does yours compare? *Personnel Administrator, 34*(7), 86–89.

Bell, J. D., & Kerr, D. L. (1987). Measuring training results: Key to managerial commitment. *Training and Development Journal, 41*(1), 70–73.

Bender, J. M. (1973). What is "typical" of assessment centers? *Personnel, 50*(6), 50–57.

Benge, E. J., Burk, S. L., & Hay, E. N. (1941). *Manual of job evaluation.* New York: Harper & Row.

Benne, K. D., & Sheets, P. (1948). Functional roles of group members. *Journal of Social Issues, 4*(2), 41–49.

Ben-Shakhar, G., Bar-Hillel, M., Bilu, Y., Ben-Abba, E., & Flug, A. (1986). Can graphology predict occupational success? Two empirical studies and some methodological ruminations. *Journal of Applied Psychology, 71,* 645–653.

Benzinger, K. (1982, May-June). The powerful woman. *Hospital Forum,* pp. 15–20.

Bernard Hodes Advertising. (1985). *Employee referral policies and programs.* New York: Doyle Dane Bernbach Advertising.

Bernardin, H. J., & Buckley, M. R. (1981). Strategies in rater training. *Academy of Management Review, 6,* 205–242.

Bernardin, H. J., & Kane, J. S. (1980). A second look at behavioral observation scales. *Personnel Psychology, 33,* 809–814.

Bernardin, H. J., LaShells, M. B., Smith, P. C., & Alvares, K. M. (1976). Behavioral expectation scales: Effects of developmental procedures and formats. *Journal of Applied Psychology, 61,* 75–79.

Bernardin, H. J., & Pence, E. C. (1980). Effects of rater training: Creating new response sets and decreasing accuracy. *Journal of Applied Psychology, 65,* 60–66.

Bernardin, H. J., & Walter, C. S. (1977). Effects of rater training and diary-keeping on psychometric error in ratings. *Journal of Applied Psychology, 62,* 64–69.

Berne, E. (1964). *Games people play.* New York: Grove Press.

Beshir, M. Y., El-Sabagh, A. S., & El-Nawawi, M. A. (1981). Time on task effect on tracking performance under heat stress. *Ergonomics, 24,* 95–102.

Bird, A. (1977). Team structure and success as related to cohesiveness and leadership. *Journal of Social Psychology, 103,* 217–223.

Bird, C. (1940). *Social psychology.* New York: Appleton-Century-Crofts.

Birnbrauer, H. (1987). Evaluation techniques that work. *Training and Development Journal, 41*(1), 53–55.

Blake, R. R., & Mouton, J. S. (1984). *The managerial grid III.* Houston: Gulf Publishing.

Blake, R. R., Shephard, H., & Mouton, J. S. (1964). *Managing intergroup conflict in industry.* Houston: Gulf Publishing.

Blanz, F., & Ghiselli, E. E. (1972). The mixed standard scale: A new rating system. *Personnel Psychology, 25,* 185–200.

Blum, M. L., & Naylor, J. C. (1968). *Industrial psychology.* New York: Harper & Row.

Blumenfeld, W. S. (1985). Appropriateness of readability of a Federal Aviation Agency regulation, a flight crew manual, and a company pilot labor agreement for an airline's pilots. *Perceptual and Motor Skills, 61,* 1189–1190.

Blumenfeld, W. S., & Justice, B. M. (1975). Six replicated investigations of the relationship between Flesch and Gunning readability indices. *Perceptual and Motor Skills, 40,* 110.

Bond, C. F., & Titus, L. J. (1983). Social facilitation: A meta-analysis of 241 studies. *Psychological Bulletin, 94,* 265–292.

Bonjean, C. M., Hill, R. J., & McLemore, S. D. (1967). *Sociological measurement: An inventory of scales and indices.* San Francisco: Chandler.

Bonner, D. (in press). Effectiveness of wellness programs in industry. *Applied H.R.M. Research.*

Borman, W. C. (1978). Exploring upper limits of reliability and validity in job performance ratings. *Journal of Applied Psychology, 63,* 135–144.

Boudreau, J. W. (1983). Economic considerations in estimating the utility of human resource productivity improvement programs. *Personnel Psychology, 36,* 551–576.

Breaugh, J. A. (1981). Relationships between recruitment sources and employee performance, absenteeism, and work attitudes. *Academy of Management Journal, 24,* 261–267.

Breaugh, J. A., & Mann, R. B. (1984). Recruiting source effects: A test of two alternative explanations. *Journal of Occupational Psychology, 57,* 261–267.

Brehm, J. W. (1966). *A theory of psychological reactance.* New York: Academic Press.

Bretz, R. D. (1989). College grade point average as a predictor of adult success: A meta-analytic review and some additional evidence. *Public Personnel Management, 18,* 11–22.

Brigham, T. A. (1989). On the importance of recognizing the difference between experiments and correlational studies. *American Psychologist, 44*(7), 1053–1061.

Brinkerhoff, R. O. (1986). Expanding needs analysis. *Training and Development Journal, 40*(2), 64–65.

Broadbent, D. E. (1971). *Decision and stress.* New York: Academic Press.

Broadbent, D. E. & Little, E. A. (1960). Effect of noise reduction in a work situation. *Occupational Psychology, 343,* 133–140.

Brod, C. (1985). How to deal with technostress. *Office Administration and Automation, 28*(8), 46–47.

Brookes, M. J., & Kaplan, A. (1972). The office environment: Space planning and effective behavior. *Human Factors, 14,* 373–391.

Broussard, R. D., & Brannen, D. E. (1986). Credential distortions: Personnel practitioners give their views. *Personnel Administrator, 31*(6), 129–145.

Brown, L. D. (1983). *Managing conflict at organizational interfaces.* Reading, MA: Addison-Wesley.

Brown, S. H. (1978). Long-term validity of a personal history item scoring procedure. *Journal of Applied Psychology, 63,* 673–676.

Browning, R. C. (1968). Validity of reference ratings from previous employers. *Personnel Psychology, 21,* 389–393.

Brumback, G. (1986, June). *Performance appraisal in a time capsule.* Address to 10th Annual Meeting of International Personnel Management Association—Assessment Council, San Francisco, CA.

Brumback, G. B. (1988). Some ideas, issues, and predictions about performance management. *Public Personnel Management, 17,* 387–402.

Bryan, D. A. (1989). Differences in trait interpretations between black and white professionals when evaluating letters of recommendation. *Proceedings of 10th Annual Graduate Conference in Industrial/Organizational Psychology and Organizational Behavior.*

Bucalo, J. P. (1983). Good advertising can be more effective than other recruitment tools. *Personnel Administrator, 28,* 73–79.

Buchner, L., Carr, K., & Manson, T. (1988). Interrater reliability of situational interviews as a function of the number of benchmark answers. *Proceedings of 9th Annual Graduate Conference in Industrial/Organizational Psychology and Organizational Behavior.*

Buckley, M. R., & Eder, R. W. (1989). The first impression. *Personnel Administrator, 34*(5), 72–74.

Burke, R. J. (1970). Methods of resolving superior–subordinate conflict: The constructive use of subordinate difference and disagreement. *Organizational Behavior and Human Performance, 5,* 393–411.

Burke, R. J., Weitzel, W., & Weir, T. (1978). Characteristics of effective employee performance review and development interviews. *Personnel Psychology, 31,* 903–919.

Burling, T., Lentz, E., & Wilson, R. (1956). *To give and take in hospitals.* New York: Putnam.

Burns, W. (1979). Physiological effects of noise. In C. M. Harris (Ed.), *Handbook of noise control* (pp. 15-1–15-23). New York: McGraw-Hill.

Buros, O. K. (1975a). *Personality tests and reviews II.* Highland Park, NJ: Gryphon Press.

Buros, O. K. (1975b). *Vocational tests and reviews.* Highland Park, NJ: Gryphon Press.

Buzzotta, V. R. (1986). Does "people skills" training really work? *Training, 23*(8), 59–60.

Byrne, D. (1971). *The attraction paradigm.* New York: Academic Press.

Caldwell, D. F., & O'Reilly, C. A. (1982). Boundary spanning and individual performance: The impact of self-monitoring. *Journal of Applied Psychology, 67,* 124–127.

Caldwell, D. F., & Spivey, W. A. (1983). The relationship between recruiting source and employee success: An analysis by race. *Personnel Psychology, 36,* 67–72.

Campbell, D. E. (1979). Interior office design and visitor response. *Journal of Applied Psychology, 64,* 648–653.

Campbell, D. T., & Stanley, J. C. (1963). *Experimental and quasi-experimental designs in research.* Chicago: Rand McNally.

Campbell, J. C. (1983). *Using job descriptions to increase job performance.* Nashville, TN: James C. Campbell & Associates.

Campion, J. E., Greener, J., & Wernli, S. (1973). Work observation versus recall in developing behavioral examples for rating scales. *Journal of Applied Psychology, 58,* 286–288.

Campion, M. A., Pursell, E. D., & Brown, B. K. (1988). Structured interviewing: Raising the psychometric properties of the employment interview. *Personnel Psychology, 41,* 25–42.

Cantor, J., Alfonso, H., & Zillman, D. (1976). The persuasive effectiveness of the peer appeal and a communicator's first-hand experience. *Communication Research, 3,* 293–310.

Cardy, R. L., & Dobbins, G. H. (1986). Affect and appraisal accuracy: Liking as an integral dimension in evaluating performance. *Journal of Applied Psychology, 71,* 672–678.

Carlson, R. E. (1970). Effects of applicant sample on ratings of valid information in an employment setting. *Journal of Applied Psychology, 54,* 217–222.

Carrell, M. R., & Dittrich, J. E. (1978). Equity theory: The recent literature, methodological considerations, and new directions. *Academy of Management Review, 3,* 202–210.

Carroll, S. J., & Nash, A. N. (1972). Effectiveness of a forced-choice reference check. *Personnel Administration, 35,* 42–146.

Carroll, S. J., Paine, F. T., & Ivancevich, J. J. (1972). The relative effectiveness of training methods: Expert opinion and research. *Personnel Psychology, 25,* 495–510.

Carter, J. H. (1952). Military leadership. *Military Review, 32,* 14–18.

Cascio, W. F. (1987, April). *Utility analysis and strategic management.* Paper presented at 8th Annual Conference in Industrial/Organizational Psychology and Organizational Behavior, Knoxville, TN.

Cascio, W. F., & Phillips, N. F. (1979). Performance testing: A rose among thorns. *Personnel Psychology, 32,* 751–756.

Cash, T. E., Gillen, B., & Burns, D. S. (1977). Sexism and "beautyism" in personnel consultants' decision making. *Journal of Applied Psychology, 62,* 361–370.

Ceci, S. J., & Peters, D. (1984). Letters of reference: A naturalistic study of the effects of confidentiality. *American Psychologist, 39,* 29–31.

Cedarbloom, D. (1982). The performance appraisal interview: A review, implications, and suggestions. *Academy of Management Review, 7,* 219–227.

Cedarbloom, D. (1989). Peer and supervisor evaluations: An underused promotion method used for law enforcement. *Proceedings of 13th Annual Meeting of International Personnel Management Association—Assessment Council.*

Cedarbloom, D., Pence, E. C., & Johnson, D. L. (1984). Making I/O psychology useful: The personnel administrator's view. *The Industrial/Organizational Psychologist, 21*(3), 9–17.

Chaiken, S. (1979). Communicator physical attractiveness and persuasion. *Journal of Personality and Social Psychology, 33,* 1387–1397.

Chambers, D. A. (1986). The constraints of work and domestic schedules on women's leisure. *Leisure Studies, 5,* 309–325.

Chauran, T. (1989). Taking Texas on the road. *Recruitment Today, 2*(2), 48–52.

Chen, S. C. (1937). Social modification of the activity of ants in nest-building. *Physiological Zoology, 10,* 420–436.

Cialindi, R. B. (1985). *Influence: Science and practice.* Glenview, IL: Scott, Foresman.

Cialindi, R. B., Borden, R., Thorne, A., Walker, M., Freeman, S., & Sloane, L. T. (1976). Basking in reflected glory: Three (football) field studies. *Journal of Personality and Social Psychology, 34,* 366–375.

Cirillo, C. J. (1983). Office ergonomics: Coping with causes of stress in the automated workplace. *Management Review, 25,* 38–39.

Clark, R. D. (1971). Group-induced shift toward risk: A critical appraisal. *Psychological Bulletin, 76,* 251–271.

Clark, R. E. (1961). *The limiting hand skin temperature for unaffected manual performance in the cold.* Natick, MA: Quartermaster Research and Engineering Command, Technical Report EP-147.

Cleveland, J. N., Murphy, K. R., & Williams, R. E. (1989). Multiple uses of performance appraisal: Prevalence and correlates. *Journal of Applied Psychology, 74,* 130–135.

Clore, G. L., Wiggins, N. H., & Itkin, S. (1975). Gain and loss in attraction: Attributions from nonverbal behavior. *Journal of Personality and Social Psychology, 31,* 706–712.

Cochran, A., Kopitzke, K., & Miller, D. (1984). Relationship between interviewer personality and interior office characteristics. *Proceedings of the 5th Annual Graduate Student Conference in Industrial/Organizational Psychology and Organizational Behavior.*

Cohen, A. (1972, September). *The role of psychology in improving worker safety and health under the Worker Safety and Health Act.* Paper presented at annual meeting of the American Psychological Association, Honolulu, HI.

Cohen, A. R., & Bradford, D. L. (1990). *Influence without authority.* New York: John Wiley & Sons.

Cohen, J. (1977). *Statistical power analysis for the behavioral sciences.* New York: Academic Press.

Cohen, S., & Weinstein, N. (1981). Nonauditory effects of noise on behavior and health. *Journal of Personality and Social Psychology, 37,* 36–70.

Cohen, S. L. (1980). Pre-packaged vs. tailor made: The assessment center debate. *Personnel Journal, 59*(12), 989–991.

Colligan, M. J., Frockt, I. J., & Tasto, D. L. (1970). Frequency of sickness absence and worksite clinic visits among nurses as a function of shift. *Applied Ergonomics, 10,* 79–85.

Comer, D. R. (1989). Peers as providers. *Personnel Administrator, 34*(5), 84–86.

Conoley, J. C., & Kramer, J. J. (1989). *The tenth mental measurements yearbook.* Lincoln, NB: University of Nebraska Press.

Cooper, W. H. (1981a). Ubiquitous halo. *Psychological Bulletin, 90,* 218–244.

Cooper, W. H. (1981b). Conceptual similarity as a source of illusory halo in job performance ratings. *Journal of Applied Psychology, 66,* 302–307.

Cornelius, E. T., Carron, T. J., & Collins, M. N. (1979). Job analysis models and job classification. *Personnel Psychology, 32,* 693–708.

Cornelius, E. T., & Hakel, M. D. (1978). *A study to develop an improved enlisted performance evaluation system for the U.S. Coast Guard.* Washington, DC: Department of Transportation.

Cornelius, E. T., Hakel, M. D., & Sackett, P. R. (1979). A methodological approach to job classification for performance appraisal purposes. *Personnel Psychology, 32,* 283–297.

Costley, D. L., & Todd, R. (1987). *Human relations in organizations.* St. Paul, MN: West Publishing.

Cottrell, N. B. (1972). Social facilitation. In C. G. McClintock (Ed.), *Experimental social psychology* (pp. 185–236). New York: Holt, Rinehart & Winston.

Cowan, G., & Kasen, J. H. (1984). Form of reference: Sex differences in letters of recommendation. *Journal of Personality and Social Psychology, 46,* 636–645.

Cronbach, L. J. (1951). Coefficient alpha and the internal structure of tests. *Psychometrika, 16,* 297–334.

Cropanzano, R., & Folger, R. (1989). Referent cognitions and task decision autonomy: Beyond equity theory. *Journal of Applied Psychology, 74,* 293–299.

Crusco, A. H., & Wetzel, C. G. (1984). The midas touch: The effects of interpersonal touch on restaurant tipping. *Personality and Social Psychology Bulletin, 10,* 512–517.

Csoka, L. S., & Bons, P. M. (1978). Manipulating the situation to fit the leader's style: Two validation studies of leader match. *Journal of Applied Psychology, 63,* 295–300.

Cureton, E. E. (1965). Reliability and validity: Basic assumptions and experimental designs. *Educational and Psychological Measurement, 25,* 327–346.

Currer-Briggs, N. (1971). *Handwriting analysis in business: The use of graphology in personnel selection.* New York: John Wiley & Sons.

Dainoff, M. J., Happ, A., & Crane, P. (1981). Visual fatigue and occupational stress in VDT operators. *Human Factors, 23,* 420–437.

Dale, E., & Chall, J. S. (1948). A formula for predicting readability. *Educational Research Bulletin, 27,* 37–54.

Daniel, M. V. (1989). The use of employee referral programs in the public sector. *Proceedings of 10th Annual Graduate Conference in Industrial/Organizational Psychology and Organizational Behavior.*

Daniel, S. (1987). Strength and endurance testing. *Personnel Journal, 66*(6), 112.

Dansereau, F., Graen, G., & Haga, W. J. (1974). *A vertical dyad linkage approach to leadership within the formal organization.* Unpublished report, State University of New York, Buffalo.

Davies, E. (1922). *Transactions of the Institute of Mining Engineering, 63,* 326.

Davis, K. (1953). Management communication and the grapevine. *Harvard Business Review, 31*(5), 43–59.

Davis, K. (1967). *The dynamics of organizational behavior.* New York: McGraw-Hill.

Davis, K. (1977). *Human behavior at work.* New York: McGraw-Hill.

Davis, T. R. (1984). The influence of the physical environment in offices. *Academy of Management Review, 9,* 271–283.

Day, D. V., & Silverman, S. B. (1989). Personality and job performance: Evidence of incremental validity. *Personnel Psychology, 42,* 25–36.

Deci, E. L. (1972). The effects of contingent and noncontingent rewards and controls on instrinsic motivation. *Organizational Behavior and Human Performance, 8,* 217–229.

Decker, P. J., & Cornelius, E. T. (1979). A note on recruiting sources and job survival rates. *Journal of Applied Psychology, 64,* 463–464.

DeGroot, J. P., & Kamphois, A. (1983). Eyestrain in VDT users: Physical correlates and long-term effects. *Human Factors, 25,* 409–413.

Del Gaizo, E. (1984). Proof that supervisory training works. *Training and Development Journal, 38*(3), 30–31.

de Mare, G. (1968). *Communicating for leadership—A guide for executives.* New York: Ronald Press.

Dembroski, T. M., Lasater, T. M., & Ramirex, A. (1978). Communicator similarity, fear arousing communications, and compliance with health care recommendations. *Journal of Applied Social Psychology 8,* 254–269.

DeNisi, A. S., Cornelius, E. T., & Blencoe, A. G. (1987). Further investigation of common knowledge effects of job analysis ratings. *Journal of Applied Psychology, 72,* 262–268.

DeNisi, A. S., Randolph, W. A., & Blencoe, A. G. (1983). Potential problems with peer ratings. *Academy of Management Journal, 26,* 457–464.

DeNisi, A. S., Robbins, T., & Cafferty, T. P. (1989). Organization of information used for performance appraisals: Role of diary-keeping. *Journal of Applied Psychology, 74,* 124–129.

DePaulo, B. M., Stone, J. L., & Lassiter, G. D. (1985). Deceiving and detecting deceit. In B. R. Schlenker (Ed.), *The self and social life* (pp. 323–370). New York: McGraw-Hill.

DePaulo, B. M., Zuckerman, M., & Rosenthal, A. R. (1980). Detecting deception: Modality effects. In L. Wheeler (Ed.), *The review of personality and social psychology.* Beverly Hills, CA: Sage Publications.

Dessler, G. (1984). *Personnel management.* Reston, VA: Reston Publishing.

Deutsch, M. (1973). *The resolution of conflict.* New Haven, CT: Yale University Press.

Dickenson, T. L., & Zellinger, P. M. (1980). A comparison of the behaviorally anchored rating and mixed standard scale format. *Journal of Applied Psychology, 65,* 147–154.

Dickson, D. H., & Kelly, I. W. (1985). The "Barnum Effect" in personality assessment: A review of the literature. *Psychological Reports, 57,* 367–382.

Diehl, M., & Stroebe, W. (1987). Productivity loss in brainstorming groups: Toward the solution of a riddle. *Journal of Personality and Social Psychology, 53,* 497–509.

Dipboye, R. L. (1977). A critical review of Korman's self-consistency theory of work motivation and occupational choice. *Organizational Behavior and Human Performance, 18,* 108–126.

Dipboye, R. L., & dePontbriad, R. (1981). Correlates of employee reactions to performance appraisals and appraisal systems. *Journal of Applied Psychology, 66,* 248–251.

Dipboye, R. L., Fromkin, H. L., & Wilback, K. (1975). Relative importance of applicant sex, attractiveness and scholastic standing in evaluation of job applicant résumés. *Journal of Applied Psychology, 60,* 39–43.

Dipboye, R. L., Stramler, C. S., & Fontenelle, G. A. (1984). The effects of the application on recall of information from the interview. *Academy of Management Journal, 27,* 561–575.

Donaldson, L., & Scannell, E. E. (Eds.). (1986). *Human resource development: The new trainer's guide.* Reading, MA: Addison-Wesley.

Donnerstein, E., & Wilson, D. W. (1976). Effects of noise and perceived control on ongoing and subsequent aggressive behavior. *Journal of Personality and Social Psychology, 34,* 774–781.

Donnoe, W. (1986, June). *Implications of validity generalization and utility analysis in job knowledge testing.* Presented at 10th Annual Meeting of International Personnel Management Association—Assessment Council, San Francisco, CA.

Dougherty, T. W., Ebert, R. J., & Callender, J. C. (1986). Policy capturing in the employment interview. *Journal of Applied Psychology, 71,* 9–15.

Douglas, J. A., Feld, D. E., & Asquith, N. (1989). *Employment testing manual.* Boston: Warren, Gorham & Lamont.

Dubin, R., & Champoux, J. E. (1977). Central life theory and job satisfaction. *Organizational Behavior and Human Performance, 18,* 366–377.

Dumaine, D. (1987). Strategic writing for trainers. *Training and Development Journal, 47*(1), 57–60.

Dunham, R. B. (1977). Shiftwork: A review and theoretical analysis. *Academy of Management Review, 2,* 626–634.

Dunnette, M. D., Campbell, J. D., & Jaastad, K. (1963). The effects of group participation on brainstorming effectiveness for two industrial samples. *Journal of Applied Psychology, 47,* 30–37.

Ellenburg, G., Kremen, M., Hicks, L., & Stewart, R. (1990). A meta-analysis of the validity of weighted application blanks. *Proceedings of the 11th Annual Graduate Conference in Industrial/Organizational Psychology and Organizational Behavior.*

Ellenburg, G., Stewart, R., Hicks, L., & Kremen, M. (1989). Employee referral programs as a source of recruitment in private industry. *Proceedings of 10th An-*

nual Graduate Conference in Industrial/Organizational Psychology and Organizational Behavior.

Ellis, R. A., & Taylor, S. M. (1983). Role of self-esteem within the job search process. *Journal of Applied Psychology, 68,* 632–640.

England, G. W. (1971). *Development and use of weighted application blanks.* Minneapolis: University of Minnesota Industrial Relations Center.

Estes, R. (in press). Effects of Flexi-time: A meta-analytic review. *Applied H.R.M. Research.*

Exline, R. V. (1957). Group climate as a factor in the relevance and accuracy of social perception. *Journal of Abnormal and Social Psychology, 55,* 382–388.

Faley, R. J., Kleiman, L. S., & Lengnick-Hall, M. L. (1984). Age discrimination and personnel psychology: A review and synthesis of the legal literature with implications for future research. *Personnel Psychology, 37,* 327–350.

Faloona, D., Henson, C., Jahn, M., & Snyder, A. (1985). Effect of paper type and color on personnel managers' evaluation of résumés. *Proceedings of 6th Annual Graduate Conference in Industrial/Organizational Psychology and Organizational Behavior,* pp. 97–98.

Farh, J. L., & Werbel, J. D. (1986). Effects of purpose of the appraisal and expectation of validation on self-appraisal leniency. *Journal of Applied Psychology, 71,* 527–529.

Farr, J. L. (1973). Response requirements and primacy–recency effects in a simulated selection interview. *Journal of Applied Psychology, 57,* 228–233.

Farr, J. L., & York, C. M. (1975). Amount of information and primacy–recency effects in recruitment decision. *Personnel Psychology, 28,* 233–238.

Fay, C. H., & Latham, G. P. (1982). Effects of training and rating scales on rating errors. *Personnel Psychology, 35,* 105–116.

Feldman, D. C. (1986). The MBA-ing of Ph.D. education. *The Industrial/Organizational Psychologist, 23*(4), 43–46.

Feldman, J. (1981). Beyond attribution theory: Cognitive processes in performance appraisal. *Journal of Applied Psychology, 66,* 127–148.

Feuer, D. (1987a). Training's 1987 salary survey. *Training, 24*(11), 27–38.

Feuer, D. (1987b). Paying for knowledge. *Training, 24*(5), 57–66.

Feuer, D. (1987c). Domino's Pizza: Training for fast times. *Training, 24,* 25–30.

Fey, C. (1987). Engineering good writing. *Training, 24*(3), 49–54.

Fiedler, F. E. (1967). *A theory of leadership effectiveness.* New York: McGraw-Hill.

Fiedler, F. H. (1978). Recent developments in research on the contingency model. In L. Berkowitz (Ed.), *Group processes* (pp. 207–223). New York: Academic Press.

Field, H. S., & Holley, W. H. (1982). The relationship of performance appraisal system characteristics to verdicts in selected employment discrimination cases. *Academy of Management Journal, 25,* 392–406.

Fine, B. J., & Kobrick, J. L. (1978). Effects of altitude and heat on complex cognitive tasks. *Human Factors, 20,* 115–122.

Fine, S. A. (1955). What is occupational information? *Personnel and Guidance Journal, 33,* 504–509.

Fine, S. A., & Wiley, W. W. (1971). *An introduction to functional job analysis.* Washington, DC: W. E. Upjohn Institute for Employment Research.

Finkelman, J. M., Zeitlin, L. R., Filippi, J. A., & Friend, M. A. (1977). Noise and driver performance. *Journal of Applied Psychology, 62,* 713–718.

Fisher, J. D., Bell, P. N., & Baum, A. (1984). *Environmental psychology.* New York: Holt, Rinehart & Winston.

Fisher, J. D., Rytting, M., & Heslin, R. (1976). Hands touching hands: Affective and evaluative effects of an interpersonal touch. *Sociometry, 39,* 416–421.

Flanagan, J. C. (1954). The critical incident technique. *Psychological Bulletin, 51,* 327–358.

Flanagan, J. C., & Burns, R. K. (1955). The employee performance record: A new appraisal and development tool. *Harvard Business Review, 33,* 95–102.

Fleishman, E. A. (1979). Evaluating physical abilities required by jobs. *Personnel Administrator, 23*(6), 82.

Fleishman, E. A., & Harris, E. F. (1962). Patterns of leadership behavior related to grievances and turnover. *Personnel Psychology, 15,* 43–56.

Fleishman, E. A., Harris, E. F., & Burtt, H. E. (1955). *Leadership and supervision in industry.* Columbus: Ohio State University Press.

Flesch, R. (1948). A new readability yardstick. *Journal of Applied Psychology, 32,* 221–233.

Fooner, A. (1986, October). Six good solutions for child care. *Working Woman,* p. 173.

Forbes, F. W., & Cottle, W. C. (1953). A new method for determining readability of standardized tests. *Journal of Applied Psychology, 37,* 185–190.

Forbes, R. J., & Jackson, P. R. (1980). Non-verbal behaviour and the outcome of selection interviews. *Journal of Occupational Psychology, 53,* 65–72.

Ford, R. (1973). Job enrichment lessons at AT&T. *Harvard Business Review, 73,* 96–106.

Forst, J. K. (1987). Factors affecting the evaluation of administrator competence. *Proceedings of 8th Annual Graduate Conference in Industrial/Organizational Psychology and Organizational Behavior,* pp. 165–166.

Forsyth, D. R. (1983). *An introduction to group dynamics.* Monterey, CA: Brooks/Cole.

Forsyth, S., & Galloway, S. (1988). Linking college credit with in-house training. *Personnel Administrator, 33*(11), 78–79.

Forsythe, S., Drake, M. F., & Cox, C. E. (1985). Influence of applicant's dress on interviewer's selection decisions. *Journal of Applied Psychology, 70,* 374–378.

Foster, M. (1986). Relationship between interviewer–interviewee personality similarity and employment interview scores. *Proceedings of 7th Annual Graduate Conference in Industrial/Organizational Psychology and Organizational Behavior.*

Foster, M. (1989). *Relationship between self-monitoring, personality and supervisor performance.* Unpublished master's thesis, University of Georgia.

Fox, J. G. (1971). Background music and industrial productivity: A review. *Applied Ergonomics, 2,* 70–73.

Frank, C. L., & Hackman, J. R. (1975). Effects of interviewer–interviewee similarity on interviewer objectivity in college admissions interviews. *Journal of Applied Psychology, 60,* 356–360.

Frank, F., & Anderson, L. R. (1971). Effects of task and group size upon group productivity and member satisfaction. *Sociometry, 34,* 135–149.

French, J. R. P., & Raven, B. H. (1959). The bases of social power. In D. Cartwright (Ed.), *Studies in social power* (pp. 150–167). Ann Arbor: University of Michigan Press.

Frese, M., & Okonek, K. (1984). Reasons to leave shiftwork and psychological and psychosomatic complaints of former shiftworkers. *Journal of Applied Psychology, 69,* 509–514.

Frese, M., & Semmer, N. (1986). Shiftwork, stress, and psychosomatic complaints: A comparison between workers in different shiftwork schedules, non-shiftworkers, and former shiftworkers. *Ergonomics, 29,* 99–114.

Freston, N. P., & Lease, J. E. (1987). Communication skills training for selected supervisors. *Training and Development Journal, 41*(7), 67–70.

Frick, R. W. (1985). Communicating emotion: The role of prosodic features. *Psychological Bulletin, 97,* 412–429.

Friedman, L., & Harvey, R. J. (1986). Can raters with reduced job descriptive information provide accurate Position Analysis Questionnaire (PAQ) ratings? *Personnel Psychology, 39,* 779–789.

Frizzell, M. L. (1989). The placement of I/O Master's degree graduates. *Proceedings of 10th Annual Graduate Conference in Industrial/Organizational Psychology and Organizational Behavior.*

Frost, P. J., & Jamal, M. (1979). Shift work, attitudes and reported behaviors: Some associations between individual characteristics and hours of work and leisure. *Journal of Applied Psychology, 64,* 77–81.

Fry, E. (1977). Fry's Readability Graph: Clarifications, validity, and extension to level 17. *Journal of Reading, 21,* 243–252.

Fulger, R. (1977). Which costs less—the phone or the letter? *Management World, 6,* 13–14.

Fyock, C. D. (1988). New ways to say "help wanted." *Personnel Administrator, 33,* 100.

Gabris, G. T., & Mitchell, K. (1988). The impact of merit raise scores on employee attitudes: The Matthew effect of performance appraisal. *Public Personnel Management, 17,* 369–386.

Gael, S. (1983). *Job analysis: A guide to assessing work activities.* San Francisco: Jossey-Bass.

Galagan, P. (1983). Treating computer anxiety with training. *Training and Development Journal, 37,* 57–60.

Gandy, J. A., & Dye, D. A. (1989). Development and initial validation of a biodata inventory in a merit system context. *Proceedings of 13th Annual Meeting of International Personnel Management Association—Assessment Council,* pp. 138–142.

Gannon, M. J., Norland, D. L., & Robeson, F. E. (1983). Shiftwork has complex effects on lifestyles and work habits. *Personnel Administrator, 28*(5), 93–97.

Gaugler, B. B., Rosenthal, D. B., Thornton, G. C., & Bentson, C. (1987). Meta-analysis of assessment center validity. *Journal of Applied Psychology, 72,* 493–511.

Geber, B. (1987). Who should do the sales training? *Training, 24*(5), 69–76.

Geier, J. G., & Downey, D. E. (1980). *Attitudinal Listening Profile System.* Minneapolis, MN: Performax Systems International.

Geier, J. G., Downey, D. E., & Johnson, J. B. (1980). *Climate impact profile.* Minneapolis, MN: Performax Systems International.

Gent, M. J., & Dell'Omo, G. G. (1989). The needs assessment solution. *Personnel Administrator, 34*(7), 82–84.

Ghiselli, E. E. (1966). *The validity of occupational tests.* New York: John Wiley & Sons.

Ghiselli, E. E. (1973). The validity of aptitude tests in personnel selection. *Personnel Psychology, 26,* 461–477.

Gibbs, C. A. (1969). Leadership. In G. Lindzey & E. Aronson (Eds.), *Handbook of Social Psychology* (pp. 205–282). Reading, MA: Addison-Wesley.

Giffin, M. E. (1989). Personnel research on testing, selection, and performance appraisal. *Public Personnel Management, 18,* 127–137.

Gillet, B., & Schwab, D. P. (1975). Convergent and discriminant validities of corresponding Job Descriptive Index and Minnesota Satisfaction Questionnaire scales. *Journal of Applied Psychology, 60,* 313–317.

Gilmer, B. V. H., & Deci, E. L. (1977). *Industrial and organizational psychology.* New York: McGraw-Hill.

Gilmore, D. C. (1989). Applicant perceptions of simulated behavior description interviews. *Journal of Business and Psychology, 3,* 279–288.

Gilmore, D. C., Beehr, T. A., & Love, K. G. (1986). Effects of applicant sex, applicant physical attractiveness, type of rater and type of job on interview decisions. *Journal of Occupational Psychology, 59,* 103–109.

Glickman, A. S., & Vallance, T. R. (1958). Curriculum assessment with critical incidents. *Journal of Applied Psychology, 42,* 329–335.

Goldman, B. A., & Busch, J. C. (1978). *Directory of unpublished experimental measures* (Vol. 2). New York: Human Sciences Press.

Goldman, B. A., & Busch, J. C. (1982). *Directory of unpublished experimental measures* (Vol. 3). New York: Human Sciences Press.

Goldman, B. A., & Osborne, W. L. (1985). *Directory of unpublished experimental measures* (Vol. 4). New York: Human Sciences Press.

Goldman, B. A., & Saunders, J. L. (1974). *Directory of unpublished experimental measures—Volume I*. New York: Behavioral Publishers.

Goldstein, I. L. (1971). The application blank: How honest are the responses? *Journal of Applied Psychology, 55,* 491–492.

Goldstein, I. L. (1986). *Training in organizations*. Monterey, CA: Brooks/Cole.

Golen, S. (1990). A factor analysis of barriers to effective listening. *Journal of Business Communication, 27,* 25–36.

Golightly, C., Huffman, D., & Byrne, D. (1972). Liking and loaning. *Journal of Applied Psychology, 56,* 521–523.

Gordon, J. (1986). Why CBT isn't just for training anymore. *Training, 23*(4), 42–50.

Gordon, J. R. (1983). *A diagnostic approach to organizational behavior*. Boston: Allyn & Bacon.

Gordon, M. E., Slade, L. A., & Schmitt, H. (1986). The "science of the sophomore" revisited: From conjecture to empiricism. *Academy of Management Review, 11,* 191–207.

Graen, G., & Scheimann, W. (1978). Leader member agreement: A vertical dyad linkage approach. *Journal of Applied Psychology, 63,* 206–212.

Graham, J. K., & Mihal, W. L. (1986). Can your management development needs surveys be trusted? *Training and Development Journal, 40*(3), 38–42.

Grandjean, E., Hunting, W., & Pidermann, M. (1983). VDT workstation design: Preferred settings and their effects. *Human Factors, 25,* 161–175.

Green, S. B., Sauser, W. I., Fagg, F. N., & Champion, C. H. (1981). Shortcut methods for deriving behaviorally anchored rating scales. *Educational and Psychological Measurement, 41,* 761–775.

Green, S. B., & Stutzman, T. (1986). An evaluation of methods to select respondents to structured job-analysis questionnaires. *Personnel Psychology, 39,* 543–564.

Greenhaus, J., & Baldin, I. (1974). Self-esteem, performance, and satisfaction: Some tests of a theory. *Journal of Applied Psychology, 59,* 722–726.

Greer, D. L. (1983). Spectator booing and the home advantage: A study of social influence in the basketball arena. *Social Psychology Quarterly, 46,* 252–261.

Guion, R. N., & Gibson, W. M. (1988). Personnel selection and placement. *Annual Review of Psychology, 39,* 349–374.

Gumpert, R. A., & Hambleton, R. K. (1979). Situational leadership: How Xerox managers fine-tune managerial styles to employee maturity and task needs. *Management review, 12,* 9.

Gunnarson, E., & Ostberg, O. (1977). *Physical and psychological working environment in a terminal-based data system*. Research Report No. 35. Stockholm: National Board of Occupational Safety and Health.

Gunning, R. (1964). *How to take the FOG out of writing*. Chicago: Dartnell Corp.

Guzzo, R. A., Jette, R. D., & Katzell, R. A. (1986). The effects of psychologically based intervention programs on worker productivity: A meta-analysis. *Personnel Psychology, 38,* 275–291.

Hackman, J. R., & Oldham, G. R. (1975). Development of the job diagnostic survey. *Journal of Applied Psychology, 60,* 159–170.

Hackman, J. R., & Oldham, G. R. (1976). Motivation through the design of work: Test of a theory. *Organizational Behavior and Human Performance, 16,* 250–279.

Hackman, R., & Vidmar, N. (1970). Effects of size and task type on group performance and member reactions. *Sociometry, 33,* 37–54.

Hage, J. (1974). *Communication and organizational control: Cybernetics in health and welfare settings.* New York: Wiley & Sons.

Hakel, M. D., Ohnesorge, J. P., & Dunnette, M. D. (1970). Interviewer evaluations of job applicants' résumés as a function of the qualifications of the immediately preceding applicant: An examination of contrast effects. *Journal of Applied Psychology, 54,* 27–30.

Halcrow, A. (1989). You're in good hands with direct mail. *Recruitment Today, 2*(1), 21–23.

Hall, D. T., & Nougaim, K. E. (1968). An examination of Maslow's need hierarchy in an organizational setting. *Organizational Behavior and Human Performance, 3,* 12–35.

Hall, E. T. A. (1963). A system for the notation of promemic behavior. *American Anthropologist, 65,* 1003–1026.

Hammer, T. H., & Dachler, H. P. (1975). A test of some assumptions underlying the path goal model of supervision: Some suggested conceptual modifications. *Organizational Behavior and Human Performance, 14,* 60–75.

Hampton, D. R., Summer, C. E., & Webber, R. A. (1978). *Organizational behavior and the practice of management.* Glenview, IL: Scott, Foresman.

Harper, D. C. (1988). An Rx for the RN shortage. *Recruitment Today, 1*(2), 18–26.

Harriman, T. S., & Kovach, R. (1987). The effects of job familiarity on the recall of performance information. *Proceedings of 8th Annual Graduate Conference in Industrial/Organizational Psychology and Organizational Behavior,* pp. 49–50.

Harris, M. (1981). *America now.* New York: Simon & Schuster.

Harris, M. M., & Schaubroeck, J. (1988). A meta-analysis of self-supervisor, self-peer, and peer-supervisor ratings. *Personnel Psychology, 41,* 43–62.

Harrison, K. (1986). Validity of a weighted application blank in predicting tenure of mental health counselors. *Proceedings of 7th Annual Graduate Conference in Industrial/Organizational Psychology and Organizational Behavior.*

Harvey, R. J., Friedman, L., Hakel, M. D., & Cornelius, E. J. (1988). Dimensionality of the Job Element Inventory, a simplified worker-oriented job analysis questionnaire. *Journal of Applied Psychology, 73,* 639–646.

Hatcher, L., Ross, T. L., & Ross, R. A. (1987). Gainsharing: Living up to its name. *Personnel Administrator, 32*(6), 154–164.

Hattie, J., & Cooksey, R. W. (1984). Procedures for assessing the validities of tests using the "known-groups" method. *Applied Psychological Measurement, 8,* 295–305.

Hauenstein, N. M. A. (1986). *A process approach to ratings: The effects of ability and level of processing on encoding, retrieval, and rating outcomes.* Unpublished doctoral dissertation, University of Akron, Akron, OH.

Hauenstein, N. M. A., & Foti, R. J. (1989). From laboratory to practice: Neglected issues in implementing frame-of-reference rater training. *Personnel Psychology, 42,* 359–378.

Hauenstein, N. M. A., & Lord, R. G. (1989). The effects of final-offer arbitration on the performance of major league baseball players: A test of equity theory. *Human Performance, 2,* 147–166.

Heerwagen, J. H., & Orians, G. H. (1986). Adaptations to windowlessness: A study of the use of visual decor in windowed and windowless offices. *Environment & Behavior, 18,* 604–622.

Heilman, M. E. (1974). Threats and promises: Reputational consequences and transfer of credibility. *Journal of Experimental Social Psychology, 10,* 310–324.

Heilman, M. S., & Saruwaturi, L. R. (1979). When beauty is beastly: The effect of appearance and sex on evaluations of job applicants for managerial and nonmanagerial jobs. *Organizational Behavior and Human Performance, 23,* 360–372.

Helmreich, R. L., Sawin, L. L., & Carsrud, A. L. (1986). The honeymoon effect in job performance: Temporal increases in the predictive power of achievement motivation. *Journal of Applied Psychology, 71,* 185–188.

Hemphill, J. K., & Coons, A. E. (1950). *Leader behavior description.* Columbus: Personnel Research Board, Ohio State University.

Hersey, P., & Blanchard, K. H. (1988). *Management of organizational behavior* (5th ed.). Englewood Cliffs, NJ: Prentice-Hall.

Herzberg, F. (1966). *Work and the nature of man.* Cleveland: World Publishing.

Heslin, R., & Dunphy, D. (1964). Three dimensions of member satisfaction in small groups. *Human Relations, 17,* 99–112.

Hills, F. S. (1987). *Compensation and decision making.* New York: Dryden Press.

Hills, F. S., Scott, K. D., Markham, S. E., & Vest, M. J. (1987). Merit pay: Just or unjust desserts. *Personnel Administrator, 32*(9), 53–59.

Hinrichs, J. R., & Mischkind, L. A. (1967). Empirical and theoretical limitations of the two-factor hypothesis of job satisfaction. *Journal of Applied Psychology, 51,* 191–200.

Hockey, G. R. (1970). Signal probability and spatial locations as possible bases for increased selectivity in noise. *Quarterly Journal of Experimental Psychology, 22,* 37–42.

Hodap, R. (1986, June). The State of Wyoming performance appraisal system. Paper presented at the 10th Annual Meeting of International Personnel Management Association—Assessment Council, San Francisco, CA.

Hoffman, L. R. (1959). Homogeneity of member personality and its effect on group problem solving. *Journal of Abnormal and Social Psychology, 58,* 27–32.

Hogan, R. (1989, June). *The darker side of charisma.* Paper presented at 13th Annual Meeting of International Personnel Management Association—Assessment Council, Orlando, FL.

Hollman, T. D. (1972). Employment interviewers' errors in processing positive and negative information. *Journal of Applied Psychology, 56,* 130–134.

Holzbach, R. L. (1978). Rater bias in performance ratings: Supervisor, self- and peer ratings. *Journal of Applied Psychology, 63,* 579–588.

Hom, P. W., DeNisi, A. S., Kinicki, A. J., & Bannister, B. D. (1982). Effectiveness of performance feedback from behaviorally anchored rating scales. *Journal of Applied Psychology, 67,* 568–576.

Hopkins, J. T. (1980). The top twelve questions for employment agency interviews. *Personnel Journal, 59*(5), 379–381.

House, R. J. (1971). A path–goal theory of leader effectiveness. *Administrative Science Quarterly, 9,* 321–332.

House, R. J., & Mitchell, T. R. (1974, Autumn). Path–goal theory of leadership. *Journal of Contemporary Business, 3,* 81–98.

Howard, G. S., & Dailey, P. R. (1979). Response-shift bias: A source of contamination of self-report measures. *Journal of Applied Psychology, 64,* 144–150.

Huegli, J. M., & Tschirgi, H. D. (1975). Monitoring the employment interview. *Journal of College Placement, 39,* 37–39.

Hughes, J. F., Dunn, J. F., & Baxter, B. (1956). The validity of selection instruments under operating conditions. *Personnel Psychology, 9,* 321–324.

Hultman, K. E. (1986). Behavior modeling for results. *Training and Development Journal, 40*(12), 60–63.

Hunter, J. E., & Hunter, R. F. (1984). Validity and utility of alternative predictors of job performance. *Psychological Bulletin, 96*(1), 72–98.

Hunter, J. E., & Schmidt, F. L. (1982). Fitting people to jobs: The impact of personnel selection on national productivity. In M. D. Dunnette & E. D. Fleishman (Eds.), *Human performance and productivity, Vol. 1: Human capacity assessment* (pp. 233–284). Hillsdale, NJ: Erlbaum.

Hunter, J. E., & Schmidt, F. L. (1983). Quantifying the effects of psychological interventions on employee job performance and work-force productivity. *American Psychologist, 38,* 473–478.

Iaffaldano, M. T., & Muchinsky, P. M. (1985). Job satisfaction and job performance: A meta-analysis. *Psychological Bulletin, 97,* 251–273.

Ilaw, M. (1985). Reading between the lines. *Black Enterprise, 15,* 95–96.

Ilgen, D. R., Fisher, C. D., & Taylor, M. S. (1979). Consequences of individual feedback on behavior in organizations. *Journal of Applied Psychology, 64,* 349–371.

Ilgen, D. R., Mitchell, T. R., & Frederickson, J. W. (1981). Poor performers: Supervisors' and subordinates' responses. *Organizational Behavior and Human Performance, 27,* 386–410.

Ilgen, D. R., Nebeker, D. M., & Pritchard, R. D. (1981). Expectancy theory measures: An empirical comparison in an experimental simulation. *Organizational Behavior and Human Performance, 28,* 189–223.

Indik, B. P. (1965). Organization size and member participation: Some empirical tests of alternate explanations. *Human Relations, 15,* 339–350.

Ironson, G. H., Smith, P. C., Brannick, M. T., Gibson, W. M., & Paul, K. B. (1989). Constitution of a Job in General Scale: A comparison of global, composite, and specific measures. *Journal of Applied Psychology, 74,* 193–200.

Ivancevich, J. M. (1982). Subordinates' reactions to performance appraisal interviews: A test of feedback and goal-setting techniques. *Journal of Applied Psychology, 67,* 581–587.

Jaccard, J. (1981). Toward theories of persuasion and belief change. *Journal of Personality and Social Psychology, 40,* 260–269.

Jackson, D. E., O'Dell, J. W., & Olson, D. (1982). Acceptance of bogus personality interpretations: Face validity reconsidered. *Journal of Clinical Psychology, 38,* 588–592.

Jackson, J. M. (1986). In search of social impact theory: Comment on Mullen. *Journal of Personality and Social Psychology, 50,* 511–513.

Jacobs, R., Kafry, D., & Zedeck, S. (1980). Expectations of behaviorally anchored rating scales. *Personnel Psychology, 33,* 595–640.

Jago, A. G., & Vroom, V. H. (1977). Hierarchical level and leadership style. *Organizational Behavior and Human Performance, 18,* 131–145.

Jamal, M. (1981). Shift work related to job attitudes, social participation, and withdrawal behavior: A study of nurses and industrial workers. *Personnel Psychology, 34,* 535–547.

Jamal, M. (1988). Is moonlighting mired in myth? *Personnel Journal, 67*(5), 48–53.

Jamal, M., & Crawford, R. L. (1981). Consequences of extended work hours: A comparison of moonlighters, overtimers, and modal employees. *Human Resource Management, 4,* 18–23.

Jamal, M., & Jamal, S. M. (1982). Work and nonwork experiences of employees on fixed and rotating shifts: An empirical assessment. *Journal of Vocational Behavior, 20,* 282–293.

Janis, I. L. (1972). *Victims of groupthink.* New York: Houghton Mifflin.

Jansen, A. (1973). *Validation of graphological judgments: An experimental study.* The Hague, Netherlands: Mouton.

Jaques, E. (1961). *Equitable payment.* New York: John Wiley & Sons.

Johnson, D. L., & Andrews, I. R. (1971). The risky-shift hypothesis tested with consumer products as stimuli. *Journal of Personality and Social Psychology, 30,* 382–385.

Johnson, D. L., & King, J. (1988, August). *Judgment of experts' decisions when using high technology.* Paper presented at annual meeting of American Psychological Association, Atlanta, GA.

Johnson, D. W., & Johnson, F. P. (1975). *Jointing together: Group theory and group skills*. Englewood Cliffs, NJ: Prentice-Hall.

Johnson, L. (1990). *Employer supported child care: What are the effects?* Unpublished master's thesis, Radford University, Radford, VA.

Johnson, T. L. (1990). A meta-analytic review of absenteeism control methods. *Applied H.R.M. Research, 1*(1), 23–26.

Jones, A. P., Main, D. S., Butler, M. C., & Johnson, L. A. (1982). Narrative job descriptions as potential sources of job analysis ratings. *Personnel Psychology, 35,* 813–828.

Jones, J. J., & DeCotiis, T. A. (1969). Job analysis: National survey findings. *Personnel Journal, 48,* 805–819.

Jones, J. W., & Terris, W. (1989). After the polygraph ban. *Recruitment Today, 2*(2), 24–31.

Kaiser, P., & Brull, H. (1987, June). I hate it when that happens. Paper presented at the 11th Annual Meeting of the International Personnel Management Association—Assessment Council, Philadelphia, PA.

Kalimo, R., & Leppanen, A. (1985). Feedback from video display terminals, performance control and stress in text preparation in the printing industry. *Journal of Occupational Psychology, 58,* 27–38.

Kaman, V. S., & Bentson, C. (1988). Roleplay simulations for employee selection: Design and implementation. *Public Personnel Management, 17,* 1–8.

Kane, J. S., & Lawler, E. E. (1979). Performance appraisal effectiveness: Its assessment and determinants. In B. M. Staw (Ed.), *Research in organizational behavior, Vol. 1* (pp. 425–478). Greenwich, CT: JAI Press.

Kaplan, A., & Wilk, D. (1989). Relationship between characteristics of recruitment advertisements and applicant pool quantity and quality. *Proceedings of 10th Annual Graduate Conference in Industrial/Organizational Psychology and Organizational Behavior.*

Katz, D., & Kahn, R. L. (1978). *The social psychology of organizations*. New York: John Wiley & Sons.

Katzell, R. A., & Dyer, F. J. (1977). Differential validity revived. *Journal of Applied Psychology, 62,* 137–145.

Kearney, R. C., & Whitaker, F. (1988). Behaviorally anchored disciplinary scales (BADS): A new approach to discipline. *Public Personnel Management, 17,* 341–350.

Keel, S. B., Cochran, D. S., & Arnett, K., & Arnold, D. R. (1989). AC's are not just for the big guys. *Personnel Administrator, 34*(5), 98–101.

Keenan, A. (1978). Selection interview outcomes in relation to interviewer training and experience. *Journal of Social Psychology, 106,* 249–260.

Keinan, G. A., & Barak, A. (1984). Reliability and validity of graphological assessment in the selection process of military officers. *Perceptual and Motor Skills, 58,* 811–821.

Kelly, C. M. (1984, January). Reasonable performance appraisals. *Training and Development Journal, 38,* 79–82.

Kenny, D. A., & Zaccaro, S. J. (1983). An estimate of variance due to traits in leadership. *Journal of Applied Psychology, 68,* 678–685.

Kerr, N. L. (1983). Motivation loss in small groups: A social dilemma analysis. *Journal of Personality and Social Psychology, 45,* 819–828.

Kerr, N. L., & Brunn, S. E. (1983). Dependability of member effort and group motivation loss: Free-rider effects. *Journal of Personality and Social Psychology, 44,* 78–94.

King, J. (1986). Computer based instruction. In L. Donaldson & E. E. Scannell (Eds.), *Human resource development: The new trainer's guide* (pp. 79–85). Reading, MA: Addison-Wesley.

King, N. (1970). Clarification and evaluation of the two-factor theory of job satisfaction. *Psychological Bulletin, 74,* 18–31.

King, P. (1984). *Performance planning and appraisal.* New York: McGraw-Hill.

Kingstrom, P. O., & Bass, A. R. (1981). A critical analysis of studies comparing behaviorally anchored rating scales (BARS) and other rating formats. *Personnel Psychology, 34,* 263–289.

Kipnis, D., Schmidt, S., & Wilkinson, I. (1980). Intraorganizational influence tactics: Exploration in getting one's way. *Journal of Applied Psychology, 65,* 440–452.

Kirkpatrick, D. L. (1986). Performance appraisal: When two jobs are too many. *Training, 23*(3), 65–68.

Klawsky, J. D. (1990). The effect of subgoals on commitment and task performance. *Proceedings of the 11th Annual Graduate Conference in Industrial/Organizational Psychology and Organizational Behavior.*

Kleiman, L. S., & Faley, R. H. (1978). Assessing content validity: Standards set by the court. *Personnel Psychology, 31,* 701–713.

Klein, M., & Christiansen, G. (1969). Group composition, group structure, and group effectiveness of basketball teams. In J. W. Loy & G. S. Kenyon (Eds.). *Sport, culture, and society* (pp. 397–428). Toronto: Macmillan.

Kleinke, C. L., Meeker, F. B., & LaFong, C. (1974). Effects of gaze, touch, and use of name in evaluation of "engaged" couples. *Journal of Research in Personality, 7,* 368–373.

Klimoski, R. J., & Rafaeli, A. (1983). Inferring personal qualities through handwriting analysis. *Journal of Occupational Psychology, 56,* 191–202.

Klimoski, R. J., & Strickland, W. J. (1977). Assessment centers—validity or merely prescient? *Personal Psychology, 30,* 353–361.

Knapp, M. L. (1978). *Nonverbal communication in human interaction.* New York: Holt, Rinehart & Winston.

Knauth, P., & Kiesswetter, E. (1987). A change from weekly to quicker shift rotations: A field study of discontinuous three-shift workers. *Ergonomics, 30,* 1311–1321.

Knouse, S. B. (1983). The letter of recommendation: Specificity and favorability of information. *Personnel Psychology, 36,* 331–341.

Knouse, S. B., Giacalone, R. A., & Pollard, H. (1988). Impression management in the résumé and the cover letter. *Journal of Business and Psychology, 3,* 242–249.

Komaki, J. L. (1986). Toward effective supervision: An operant analysis and comparison of managers at work. *Journal of Applied Psychology, 71,* 270–279.

Komaki, J. L., Zlotnick, S., & Jensen, M. (1986). Development of an operant-based taxonomy and observational index of supervisory behavior. *Journal of Applied Psychology, 71,* 260–269.

Kopelman, R. E. (1986). *Managing productivity in organizations.* New York: McGraw-Hill.

Korman, A. K. (1970). Toward a hypothesis of work behavior. *Journal of Applied Psychology, 54,* 31–41.

Korman, A. K. (1966). Consideration, initiating structure, and organizational criteria: A review. *Personnel Psychology, 19,* 349–361.

Korman, A. K. (1976). Hypothesis of work behavior revisited and an extension. *Academy of Management Review, 1,* 50–63.

Korte, C., & Grant, R. (1980). Traffic noise, environmental awareness, and pedestrian behavior. *Environment & Behavior, 12,* 408–420.

Kosidiak, J. G. (1987). DACUM: An alternative job analysis tool. *Personnel, 64*(3), 14–21.

Kovach, R., Surrette, M. A., & Whitcomb, A. J. (1988, January). *Contextual, student, and instructor factors involved in college student absenteeism.* Paper presented at 10th Annual National Institute on the Teaching of Psychology, St. Petersburg, FL.

Kozlowski, S. W., Kirsch, M. P., & Chao, G. T. (1986). Job knowledge, ratee familiarity, conceptual similarity and halo error: An exploration. *Journal of Applied Psychology, 71,* 45–49.

Kraiger, K., & Ford, J. K. (1985). A meta-analysis of ratee race effects. *Journal of Applied Psychology, 70,* 56–65.

Kramm, K. R., Kramm, D. A. (1988). Having the competitive edge. *Personnel Administrator, 33*(10), 88–92.

Kressel, K., & Pruitt, D. G. (1985). Themes on the mediation of social conflict. *Journal of Social Issues, 41,* 179–198.

Kroemer, K. H. E., & Price, D. L. (1982). Ergonomics in the office: Comfortable work stations allow maximum productivity. *Industrial Engineering, 14*(7), 24–32.

Kuder, G. F., & Richardson, M. W. (1937). The theory of estimation of test reliability. *Psychometrika, 2,* 151–160.

Kunin, T. (1955). The construction of a new type of attitude measure. *Personnel Psychology, 8,* 65–78.

Lacho, K. J., Stearns, G. K., & Villere, M. R. (1979). A study of employee appraisal systems of major cities in the United States. *Public Personnel Management, 8,* 111–125.

Lahtela, K., Niemi, P., Kuusela, V., & Hypen, K. (1986). Noise and visual choice reaction time. *Scandinavian Journal of Psychology, 27,* 52–57.

LeMarre, S. E., & Thompson, K. (1984). Industry sponsored day care. *Personnel Administrator, 29*(2), 53–65.

Lamm, H., & Trommsdorff, G. (1973). Group versus individual performance on tasks requiring ideational proficiency (brainstorming): A review. *European Journal of Social Psychology, 3,* 361–388.

Landy, F. J., & Bates, F. (1973). Another look at contrast effects in the employment interview. *Journal of Applied Psychology, 58,* 141–144.

Landy, F. J., & Guion, R. M. (1970). Development of scales for the measurement of work motivation. *Organizational Behavior and Human Performance, 5,* 93–103.

Langdale, J. A., & Weitz, J. (1973). Estimating the influence of job information on interviewer agreement. *Journal of Applied Psychology, 57,* 23–27.

Langer, E. J., & Rodin, J. (1976). The effects of choice and enhanced personal responsibility for the aged: A field experiment in an institutional setting. *Journal of Personality and Social Psychology, 34,* 191–198.

Larson, J. R. (1989). The dynamic interplay between employees' feedback seeking strategies and supervisors' delivery of performance feedback. *Academy of Management Review, 14,* 408–422.

Lasden, M. (1983). Moonlighting: A double standard? *Computer Decisions, 15*(3), 83–92.

Latane, B. (1981). The psychology of social impact. *American Psychologist, 36,* 343–356.

Latham, G. P., & Blades, J. J. (1975). The practical significance of Locke's theory of goal setting. *Journal of Applied Psychology, 60,* 122–124.

Latham, G. P., Fay, C. H., & Saari, L. M. (1979). The development of behavioral observation scales for appraising the performance of foremen. *Personnel Psychology, 32,* 299–311.

Latham, G. P., & Saari, L. M. (1984). Do people do what they say: Further studies on the situational interview. *Journal of Applied Psychology, 69,* 569–573.

Latham, G. P., Saari, L. M., Pursell, E. D., & Campion, M. A. (1980). The situational interview. *Journal of Applied Psychology, 65,* 422–427.

Latham, G. P., & Wexley, K. N. (1977). Behavioral observation scales for performance appraisal purposes. *Personnel Psychology, 30,* 225–268.

Latham, V. M. (1983). Charismatic leadership: A review and proposed model. *Proceedings of 4th Annual Graduate Conference in Industrial/Organizational Psychology and Organizational Behavior.*

Laumeyer, J., & Beebe, T. (1988). Employees and their appraisals. *Personnel Administrator, 33*(12), 76–80.

Lawler, E. E., & Suttle, J. L. (1972). A causal correlational test of the need hierarchy concept. *Organizational Behavior and Human Performance, 7,* 265–287.

Lawshe, C. H., Bolda, R. A., Brune, R. L., & Auclair G. (1958). Expectancy Charts II: Their theoretical development. *Personnel Psychology, 11,* 545–559.

509

Lazer, R. I., & Wikstrom, W. S. (1977). *Appraising managerial performance.* New York: The Conference Board.

Ledvinka, J., & Schoenfeldt, L. F. (1978). Legal developments in employment testing: Albemarle and beyond. *Personnel Psychology, 31,* 1–13.

Lee, J. A., Moreno, K. E., & Sympson, J. R. (1986). The effects of test administration on test performance. *Educational and Psychological Measurement, 46,* 467–474.

Levine, E. L. (1983). *Everything you always wanted to know about job analysis.* Tampa, FL: Mariner Publishing.

Levine, E. L., Ash, R. A., & Bennett, N. (1980). Exploratory comparison study of four job analysis methods. *Journal of Applied Psychology, 65,* 524–535.

Levine, E. L., Ash, R. A., Hall, H., & Sistrunk, F. (1983). Evaluation of job analysis methods by experienced job analysts. *Academy of Management Journal, 26,* 339–348.

Levin-Epstein, M. D. (1987). *Primer of equal employment opportunity.* Washington, DC: Bureau of National Affairs.

Lied, T. L., & Pritchard, R. D. (1976). Relationship between personality variables and components of the expectancy-valence model. *Journal of Applied Psychology, 61,* 463–467.

Lin, T. R., Petersen, B. C, & Manligas, C. L. (1987, June). Rater and ratee race effects in the structured selection interview: A field study. Paper presented at the 11th Annual Meeting of International Personnel Management Association—Assessment Council, Philadelphia, PA.

Litterer, J. A. (1966). Conflict in organizations: A re-examination. *Academy of Management Journal, 9,* 178–186.

Locke, E. A. (1968). Toward a theory of task motivation and incentives. *Organizational Behavior and Human Performance, 3,* 157–189.

Locke, E. A., & Latham, G. P. (1990). *A theory of goal setting and task performance.* Englewood Cliffs, NJ: Prentice-Hall.

Lockowandt, O. (1976). Present status of the investigation of handwriting psychology as a diagnostic method. *JSAS Catalog of Selected Documents, 6*(4), MS No. 11172.

Long, G. (1982). *Cohesiveness of high school baseball teams.* Unpublished master's thesis, Southern Illinois University, Carbondale, IL.

Lopez, F. E., Rockmore, B. W., & Kesselman, G. A. (1980). The development of an integrated career planning program at Gulf Power Company. *Personnel Administrator, 25*(10), 21–29.

Lopez, F. M., Kesselman, G. A., & Lopez, F. E. (1981). An empirical test of a trait-oriented job analysis technique. *Personnel Psychology, 34,* 479–502.

LoPresto, R. L. Mitcham, D. E., & Ripley, D. E. (1985). *Reference checking handbook.* Alexandria, VA: American Society for Personnel Administration.

Lorber, L. Z., Kirk, J. R., Samuels, S. L., & Spellman, D. J. (1985). *Sex and salary.* Alexandria, VA: ASPA Foundation.

Lord, R. G., De Vader, C. L., & Alliger, G. M. (1986). A meta-analysis of the relation between personality traits and leadership perceptions: An application of validity generalization procedures. *Journal of Applied Psychology, 71,* 402–410.

Lord, R. G., & Hohenfeld, J. A. (1979). Longitudinal field assessment of equity effects in the performance of major league baseball players. *Journal of Applied Psychology, 64,* 19–26.

Lorge, I., Fox, D., Davitz, J., & Brenner, M. (1958). A survey of studies contrasting the quality of group performance versus individual performance. *Psychological Bulletin, 55,* 337–372.

Mabe, P. A., & West, S. G. (1982). Validity of self-evaluation of ability: A review and meta-analysis. *Journal of Applied Psychology, 67,* 280–296.

Machungwa, P. D., & Schmitt, N. (1983). Work motivation in a developing country. *Journal of Applied Psychology, 68,* 31–42.

Mackworth, N. H. (1946). Effects of heat on wireless telegraphy operators hearing and receiving Morse messages. *British Journal of Industrial Medicine, 3,* 145.

Maddux, J. E., & Rogers, R. W. (1980). Effects of source expertness, physical attractiveness, and supporting arguments on persuasion: A case of brains over beauty. *Journal of Personality and Social Psychology, 39,* 235–244.

Mahlin, S. J., & Charles, J. (1984). Peak-time pay for part-time work. *Personnel, 63*(11), 60–65.

Maier, N. R. F. (1976). *The appraisal interview.* La Jolla, CA: University Associates.

Malandro, L. A., & Barker, L. L. (1983). *Nonverbal communication.* Reading, MA: Addison-Wesley.

Malaviya, P., & Ganesh, K. (1977). Individual differences in productivity across type of work shift. *Journal of Applied Psychology, 62,* 527–528.

Mann, K. O. (1965). Characteristics of job evaluation programs. *Personnel Administration, 28,* 45–57.

Mann, R. B., & Decker, P. J. (1984). The effect of key behavior distinctiveness on generation and recall in behavior modeling training. *Academy of Management Journal, 27,* 900–910.

Manners, G. E. (1975). Another look at group size, group problem solving, and member consensus. *Academy of Management Journal, 18,* 715–724.

Manson, T. (1989). The effectiveness of computer based training in organizational settings: A meta-analysis. *Proceedings of 10th Annual Meeting of Graduate Conference in Industrial/Organizational Psychology and Organizational Behavior.*

Manz, C. C., & Sims, H. P. (1986). Beyond limitation: Complex behavioral and affective linkages resulting from exposure to leadership training models. *Journal of Applied Psychology, 71,* 571–578.

Martin, C. L., & Nagao, D. H. (1989). Some effects of computerized interviewing on job applicant responses. *Journal of Applied Psychology, 74,* 72–80.

Martin, G. M. (1979, Spring). Getting chosen: The job interview and before. *Occupational Outlook Quarterly,* pp. 2–9.

Martin, J. (1983). *Design of man-computer dialogues*. New York: AMACOM.

Martinez, M. N. (1990). In search of a productive design. *HR Magazine, 35*(2), 36–39.

Maslow, A. H. (1954). *Motivation and personality*. New York: Harper & Row.

Maslow, A. H. (1970). *Motivation and personality* (2nd ed.). New York: Harper & Row.

Mason, N. A., & Belt, J. A. (1986). The costs and strategies of recruitment advertising. *Journal of Management, 12*(3), 425–432.

Mason, R. M. (1984). Ergonomics: The human and the machine. *Library Journal, 15,* 331–332.

Mathews, K. E., & Canon, L. K. (1975). Environmental noise level as a determinant of helping behavior. *Journal of Personality and Social Psychology, 32,* 571–577.

Maurer, S. D., & Fay, C. (1988). Effect of situational interviews, conventional structured interviews, and training on interview rating agreement: An experimental analysis. *Personnel Psychology, 41,* 329–344.

Mayfield, E. C. (1964). The selection interview: A reevaluation of published research. *Personnel Psychology, 17,* 239–260.

Mayfield, E. C., Brown, S. H., & Hamstra, B. W. (1980). Selection interviewing in the life insurance industry: An update of research and practice. *Personnel Psychology, 33,* 725–739.

Mayo, E. (1946). *The human problems of an industrial civilization*. Cambridge, MA: Harvard University Press.

McClelland, D. C. (1961). *The achieving society*. Princeton, NJ: Van Nostrand.

McClelland, D. C., & Boyatzis, R. E. (1982). Leadership motive pattern and long-term success in management. *Journal of Applied Psychology, 67,* 737–743.

McClelland, D. C., & Burnham, D. H. (1976). Power is the great motivator. *Harvard Business Review, 54*(2), 102–104.

McCormick, E. J. (1979). *Job analysis: Methods and applications*. New York: AMACOM.

McCormick, E. J., Jeanneret, P. R., & Mecham, R. C. (1969). *Position Analysis Questionnaire*. West Lafayette, IN: Purdue Research Foundation.

McCormick, E. J., Jeanneret, P. R., & Mecham, R. C. (1972). A study of job characteristics and job dimensions as based on the Position Analysis Questionnaire (PAQ). *Journal of Applied Psychology, 56,* 347–368.

McElroy, J. C., Morrow, P. C., & Ackerman, R. J. (1983). Personality and interior office design: Exploring the accuracy of visitor attributions. *Journal of Applied Psychology, 68,* 541–544.

McElroy, J. C., Morrow, P. C., & Wall, L. C. (1983). Generalizing impact of object language to other audiences: Peer response to office design. *Psychological Reports, 53,* 315–332.

McEvoy, G. M. (1988). Evaluating the boss. *Personnel Administrator, 33*(9), 115–120.

McGehee, W., & Thayer, P. W. (1961). *Training in business and industry*. New York: Wiley.

McGregor, D. (1957). An uneasy look at performance appraisal. *Harvard Business Review, 35,* 89–94.

McGregor, D. (1967). *The professional manager*. New York: McGraw-Hill.

McIntyre, R., Smith, D., & Hassett, C. (1984). Accuracy of performance ratings as affected by rater training and perceived purpose of training. *Journal of Applied Psychology, 69,* 147–156.

McMillan, J. D., & Walters, C. O. (1988). Dominating the dollars. *Personnel Administrator, 33*(8), 26–31.

McShane, T. D. (1990). Effect of nonverbal cues and primacy in unstructured and situational interview settings. *Proceedings of the 11th Annual Graduate Conference in Industrial/Organizational Psychology and Organizational Behavior.*

Meehl, P. E. (1965). See over sign: The first good example. *Journal of Experimental Research in Personality, 1,* 27–32.

Meers, A., Maasen, A., & Verhaagen, P. (1978). Subjective health after six months and after four years of shift work. *Ergonomics, 21,* 857–859.

Mehrabian, A. (1965). Communication length as an index of communicator attitude. *Psychological Reports, 17,* 519–522.

Mellor, E. F. (1984, June). Investigating the differences in weekly earnings of women and men. *Monthly Labor Review,* pp. 17–28.

Mendleson, J. L., Barnes, A. K., & Horn, G. (1989). The guiding light to corporate culture. *Personnel Administrator, 34*(7), 70–71.

Mento, A. J. (1980). *A review of assessment center research*. Washington, DC: U.S. Office of Personnel Management.

Mento, A. J., Steel, R. P., & Karren, R. J. (1987). A meta-analytic study of the effects of goal setting on task performance: 1966–1984. *Organizational Behavior and Human Decision Processes, 39,* 52–83.

Mershon, D. H., & Lin, L. (1987). Directional localization in high ambient noise with and without the use of hearing protectors. *Ergonomics, 30,* 1161–1173.

Meyer, H. H. (1980). Self-appraisal of job performance. *Personnel Psychology, 33,* 291–296.

Meyer, H. H., & Raich, M. S. (1983). An objective evaluation of a behavior modeling training program. *Personnel Psychology, 36,* 755–761.

Michaels, J. W., Blommel, J. M., Brocato, R. M., Linkous, R. A., & Rowe, J. S. (1982). Social facilitation and inhibition in a natural setting. *Replications in Social Psychology, 2,* 21–24.

Miller, G. W., & Sniderman, M. S. (1974). Multijobholding of Wichita public school teachers. *Public Personnel Management, 3,* 392–402.

Miller, J. G. (1960). Information input, overload, and psychopathology. *American Journal of Psychiatry, 116,* 695–704.

Miller, T. I. (1984). Effects of employee-sponsored day care on employee absenteeism, turnover, productivity, recruitment or job satisfaction: What is claimed and what is known. *Personnel Psychology, 37,* 277–289.

Milliman, R. E. (1986). The influence of background music on the behavior of restaurant patrons. *Journal of Consumer Research, 13,* 290–296.

Miner, J. B. (1963). Evidence regarding the value of a management course based on behavioral science subject matter. *The Journal of Business of the University of Chicago, 36,* 325–335.

Mitchell, J. V. (1983). *Tests in print III.* Lincoln, NB: University of Nebraska Press.

Mitchell, M. B. (1985). *Ninth mental measurements yearbook.* Lincoln, NB: University of Nebraska Press.

Mitchell, T. R. (1974). Expectancy models of job satisfaction, occupational preference, and effort: A theoretical, methodological, and empirical approach. *Psychological Bulletin, 81,* 1053–1077.

Mitchell, T. R. (1985). An evaluation of the validity of correlational research conducted in organizations. *Academy of Management Review, 10,* 192–205.

Mitchell, V. F., & Mougdill, P. (1976). Measurement of Maslow's need hierarchy. *Organizational Behavior and Human Performance, 16,* 334–349.

Moede, W. (1927). Die Richtlinien der Leistungs-Psycholgie. *Industrielle Pscyhotechnik, 4,* 193–207.

Molloy, J. T. (1975). *Dress for success.* New York: Warner Books.

Molloy, J. T. (1978). *The woman's dress for success book.* New York: Warner Books.

Moores, J. (1990). A meta-analytic review of the effects of compressed work schedules. *Applied H.R.M. Research, 1*(1), 12–18.

Morrow, P. C., & McElroy, J. C. (1981). Interior office design and visitor response: A constructive replication. *Journal of Applied Psychology, 66,* 646–650.

Morse, C. S. (1988). Employer liability for negligent hiring and retention of employees. *PAR Employment Law Update, 5*(1), 1–4.

Mosel, J. N., & Goheen, H. W. (1952). Agreement among replies to an employment recommendation questionnaire. *American Psychologist, 7,* 365–366.

Mosel, J. N., & Goheen, H. W. (1959). The validity of the Employment Recommendation Questionnaire in personnel selection: Skilled traders. *Personnel Psychology, 11,* 481–490.

Mott, P. E., Mann, F. C., McLoughlin, Q., & Warwick, D. P. (1965). *Shift work.* Ann Arbor: University of Michigan Press.

Mount, M. K. (1983). Comparisons of managerial and employee satisfaction with a performance appraisal system. *Personnel Psychology, 36,* 99–110.

Mount, M. K., & Thompson, D. E. (1987). Cognitive categorization and quality of performance ratings. *Journal of Applied Psychology, 72,* 240–246.

Muchinsky, P. M. (1979). The use of reference reports in personnel selection: A review and evaluation. *Journal of Occupational Psychology, 52,* 287–297.

Muchinsky, P. M., & Tuttle, M. L. (1979). Employee turnover: An empirical and methodological assessment. *Journal of Vocational Behavior, 14,* 43–77.

Mulder, M., de Jong, R. D., Koppelaar, L., & Verhage, J. (1986). Power, situation, and leaders' effectiveness: An organizational field study. *Journal of Applied Psychology, 71,* 566–570.

Mullins, W. C. (1986, October). *Cattle and crime: The inappropriate interpretation of correlation coefficients in criminal justice.* Paper presented at annual meeting of Society for Police and Criminal Psychology, Little Rock, AR.

Mullins, W. C., & Kimbrough, W. W. (1988). Group composition as a determinant of job analysis outcomes. *Journal of Applied Psychology, 73,* 657–664.

Mumford, M. D. (1983). Social comparison theory and the evaluation of peer evaluations: A review and some applied implications. *Personnel Psychology, 36,* 867–881.

Munsterberg, H. (1913). *Psychology of industrial efficiency.* Boston: Houghton Mifflin.

Murphy, K. R., & Blazer, W. K. (1986). Systematic distortions in memory-based behavior ratings and performance evaluations: Consequences for rating accuracy. *Journal of Applied Psychology, 71,* 39–44.

Murphy, K. R., & Constans, J. I. (1987). Behavioral anchors as a source of bias in rating. *Journal of Applied Psychology, 72,* 573–577.

Murphy, K. R., Gannett, B. A., Herr, B. M., & Chen, J. A. (1986). Effects of subsequent performance on evaluations of previous performance. *Journal of Applied Psychology, 71,* 427–431.

Murphy, K. R., Martin, C., & Garcia, M. (1982). Do behavioral observation scales measure observation? *Journal of Applied Psychology, 67,* 562–567.

Myers, J. H., & Errett, W. (1959). The problem of preselection in weighted application blank studies. *Journal of Applied Psychology, 43,* 94–95.

Nail, P. R. (1986). Toward an integration of some models and theories of social response. *Psychological Bulletin, 100*(2), 190–206.

Nanry, C. (1988). Performance linked training. *Public Personnel Management, 17,* 457–463.

Nash, A. N., & Carroll, S. J. (1970). A hard look at the reference check: Its modest worth can be improved. *Business Horizons, 13,* 43–49.

Nash, A. N., Muczyk, J. P., & Vettori, F. L. (1971). The relative practical effectiveness of programmed instruction. *Personnel Psychology, 24,* 397–418.

Nathan, B., & Lord, R. (1983). Cognitive categorization and dimensional schemata: A process approach to the study of halo in performance ratings. *Journal of Applied Psychology, 68,* 102–114.

National Research Council. (1983). *Video displays, work, and vision.* Washington, DC: National Academy Press.

Naughton, R. J. (1975). Motivational factors of American prisoners of war in Vietnam. *Naval War College Review, 27*(4), 2–14.

Neufeldt, D., Kimbrough, W. W., & Stadelmaier, M. F. (1983, April). *Relationship between group composition and task type on group problem solving ability.* Paper presented at 11th Annual Graduation Conference in Personality and Social Psychology, Norman, OK.

Neuner, J., Keeling, L., & Kallaus, N. (1972). *Administrative office management.* Cincinnati: Southwestern Publishing.

Newman, R. L., Hunt, D. L., & Rhodes, F. (1966). Effects of noise on productivity in a skateboard factory. *Journal of Applied Psychology, 50,* 493–496.

Newstrom, J. W. (1980). Evaluating the effectiveness of training methods. *Personnel Administrator, 25,* 55–60.

Nichols, R. G., & Stevens, L. A. (1957). *Are you listening?* New York: McGraw-Hill.

Nicholson, N., Jackson, P., & Howes, G. (1978). Shiftwork and absence: A study of temporal trends. *Journal of Occupational Psychology, 51,* 127–137.

Norton, T. W. *Personnel marketplace.* New York: Fidelifacts.

Nussbaum, K. (1980). *Race against time.* Cleveland, OH: National Association of Office Workers.

O'Brien, G. E., & Plooij, D. (1977). Comparison of programmed and prose culture training upon attitudes and knowledge. *Journal of Applied Psychology, 62,* 499–505.

O'Connor, E. J., Wexley, K. N., & Alexander, R. A. (1975). Single group validity: Fact or fallacy? *Journal of Applied Psychology, 60,* 352–355.

O'Grady, T., & Matthews, M. (1987). Video: Through the eyes of the trainee. *Training, 24*(7), 57–59.

Oldham, G. R., & Brass, D. J. (1979). Employee reactions to an open-plan office: A naturally occurring quasi-experiment. *Administrative Science Quarterly, 24,* 267–284.

Oliphant, V. N., & Alexander, E. R. (1982). Reactions to résumés as a function of résumé determinateness, applicant characteristics, and sex of raters. *Personnel Psychology, 35,* 829–842.

Orpen, C. (1978). Work and nonwork satisfaction: A causal-correlational analysis. *Journal of Applied Psychology, 63,* 530–532.

Osborne, E. E., & Vernon, H. M. (1972). The influence of temperature and other conditions on the frequency of industrial accidents. Cited in Harrell, T. W. (1958). *Industrial Psychology.* New York: Rinehart & Co.

Osgood, C. (1966). *Perspective in foreign policy.* Palo Alto, CA: Pacific Books.

Overman, S. (1990). Prescriptions for a healthier office. *HR Magazine, 35*(2), 30–34.

Pace, L. A., & Schoenfeldt, L. F. (1977). Legal concerns in use of weighted applications. *Personnel Psychology, 30,* 159–166.

Packer, A. (1988). America's new learning technology. *Personnel Administrator, 33*(9), 62–132.

Padgett, V. R. (1989). Empirical validation of firefighter vision standards. *Proceedings of 13th Annual Meeting of International Personnel Management Association—Assessment Council.*

Parsons, F. W. (1986). Inexpensive interactive video training. *Training and Development Journal, 40*(9), 38–39.

Patrick, J., & Moore, A. K. (1985). Development and reliability of a job analysis technique. *Journal of Occupational Psychology, 58,* 149–158.

Patterson, J. (1976). *Interpreting handwriting.* New York: McKay.

Pearce, J. L., & Porter, L. W. (1986). Employee responses to formal performance appraisal feedback. *Journal of Applied Psychology, 71,* 211–218.

Peggans, D., Chandra, L., & McAlarnis, C. (1986). Managers' perceptions of the appropriateness of I/O psychology and M.B.A. coursework. *Proceedings of 7th Annual Graduate Conference in Industrial/Organizational Psychology and Organizational Behavior.*

Pendleton, C. S. (1986). Drug abuse strategies for business. *Security Management, 8,* 75.

Peres, S. H., & Garcia, J. R. (1962). Validity and dimensions of descriptive adjectives used in reference letters for engineering applicants. *Personnel Psychology, 15,* 279–286.

Peter, L. J., & Hull, R. (1969). *The Peter principle: Why things go wrong.* New York: Morrow.

Petro, S., & Kelly, T. (1988). The Radford Index: A guide to employment tests. *Proceedings of 9th Annual Graduate Conference in Industrial/Organizational Psychology and Organizational Behavior.*

Pfeffer, J., & Salancik, G. (1978). *The external control of organizations.* New York: Harper & Row.

Phillips, A. P., & Dipboye, R. L. (1989). Correlational tests of predictions from a process model of the interview. *Journal of Applied Psychology, 74,* 41–52.

Pibal, D. C. (1985). Criteria for effective résumés as perceived by personnel directors. *Personnel Administrator, 30*(5), 119–123.

Pinneau, S. R. (1961). *Changes in intelligence quotients from infancy to maturity.* Boston: Houghton Mifflin.

Poor, R. (1970). *4 days, 40 hours.* Cambridge, MA: Bursk and Poor Publishing.

Porter, L. W., & Lawler, E. E. (1968). *Managerial attitudes and performance.* Homewood, IL: Dorsey.

Premack, D. (1963). Prediction of the comparative reinforcement values of running and drinking. *Science, 139,* 1062–1063.

Premack, S. L., & Wanous, J. P. (1985). A meta-analysis of realistic job preview experiments. *Journal of Applied Psychology, 70,* 706–719.

Prien, E. P. (1977). The function of job analysis in content validation. *Personnel Psychology, 30,* 167–174.

Primoff, E. S. (1975). *How to prepare and conduct job element examinations.* Washington, DC: U.S. Civil Service Commission.

Pritchard, R. D., Dunnette, M. D., & Jorgenson, D. O. (1972). Effects of perceptions of equity and inequity on worker performance and satisfaction. *Journal of Applied Psychology, 56,* 75–94.

Pulakos, E. D., White, L. A., Oppler, S. H., & Borman, W. C. (1989). Examination of race and sex effects on performance ratings. *Journal of Applied Psychology, 74,* 770–780.

Pursell, E. D., Campion, M. A., & Gaylord, S. R. (1980). Structured interviewing and avoiding selection problems. *Personnel Journal, 59*(11), 907–912.

Pursell, E. D., Dossett, D. L., & Latham, G. P. (1980). Obtaining valid predictors by minimizing rating errors in the criterion. *Personnel Psychology, 33, 91–96.*

Quaglierei, P. L. (1982). A note on variations in recruiting information obtained through different sources. *Journal of Occupational Psychology, 55,* 53–55.

Rafaeli, A., & Klimoski, R. J. (1983). Predicting sales success through handwriting analysis: An evaluation of the effects of training and handwriting sample content. *Journal of Applied Psychology, 68,* 212–217.

Rand, T., & Wexley, K. N. (1975). Demonstration of the effect "similar to me" in simulated employment interviews. *Psychological Reports, 26,* 535–544.

Rapp, B. (1978, May). You asked for it—but did you get it? *Public Management,* pp. 8–11.

Rasmussen, K. G. (1984). Nonverbal behavior, verbal behavior, résumé credentials, and selection interview outcomes. *Journal of Applied Psychology, 69,* 551–556.

Rassenfoss, S. E., & Kraut, A. I. (1988). Survey of personnel research departments. *The Industrial/Organizational Psychologist, 25*(4), 31–37.

Raven, B. H. (1965). Social influence and power. In I. D. Steiner & M. Fishbein (Eds.), *Current studies in social psychology* (pp. 371–382). New York: Holt, Rinehart & Winston.

Rawlinson, H. (1988). What do your classified ads say about you? *Recruitment Today, 1,* 47–52.

Raza, S. M., & Carpenter, B. N. (1987). A model of hiring decisions in real employment interviews. *Journal of Applied Psychology, 72,* 596–603.

Read, W. (1962). Upward communication in industrial hierarchies. *Human Relations, 15,* 3–16.

Reardon, C. E. (1986). *Effect of equipment type, fear of damaging equipment, and novelty of equipment on anxiety of computer terminal users.* Unpublished master's thesis, Radford University, Radford, VA.

Reddout, D. J. (1987). Manual writing made easier. *Training and Development Journal, 41*(4), 66–68.

Reilly, C. E., & Smith, C. (1988). Effects of shiftwork and psychometric evaluation of shiftworker selection instruments. *Proceedings of 9th Annual Graduate Conference in Industrial/Organizational Psychology and Organizational Behavior.*

Reilly, R. R., & Chao, G. T. (1983). Validity and fairness of some alternative employee selection procedures. *Personnel Psychology, 35,* 1–62.

Reynolds, A. H. (1979). The reliability of a scored oral interview for police officers. *Public Personnel Management, 8,* 324–328.

Rhine, R. J., & Severance, L. J. (1970). Ego-involvement, discrepancy, source credibility, and attitude change. *Journal of Personality and Social Psychology, 16,* 175–190.

Rice, B. (1983). Curbing cyberphobia. *Psychology Today, 8,* 79.

Rice, R. W. (1978). Psychometric properties of the esteem for least preferred co-worker (LPC) scale. *Academy of Management Review, 3,* 106–118.

Roballey, T. C., & Gardner, E. (1986). Eat to the beat. *Psychology Today, 20*(2), 16.

Robertson, I. T., & Kandola, R. S. (1982). Work sample tests: Validity, adverse impact, and applicant reaction. *Journal of Occupational Psychology, 55,* 171–183.

Robinson, D. D. (1981). Content-oriented personnel selection in a small business setting. *Personnel Psychology, 34,* 77–87.

Robinson, J. P., Athanasious, R., & Head, K. B. (1969). *Measurements of occupational attitudes and occupational characteristics.* Ann Arbor, MI: Institute for Social Research.

Roethlisberger, F., & Dickson, W. (1939). *Management and the worker.* Cambridge, MA: Harvard University Press.

Rohmert, W., & Landau, K. (1983). *A new technique for job analysis.* New York: Taylor & Francis.

Rose, G. L., & Andiappan, P. (1978). Sex effects on managerial hiring decisions. *Academy of Management Journal, 21,* 104–112.

Rosen, N. (1987). Employee attitude surveys: What managers should know. *Training and Development Journal, 41*(11), 50–52.

Rosen, S., & Tesser, A. (1970). Reluctance to communicate undesirable information: The MUM effect. *Sociometry, 33,* 253–263.

Rosen, T. H. (1987). Identification of substance abusers in the workplace. *Public Personnel Management, 16*(3), 197–208.

Rosenthal, R. (1968). *Pygmalion in the classroom.* New York: Holt, Rinehart & Winston.

Ross, J. D. (1979). A current review of public sector assessment centers: Cause for concern. *Public Personnel Management, 8,* 41–46.

Rothstein, H. R., Schmidt, F. L., Erwin, F. W., Owens, W. A., & Sparks, C. P. Biographical data in employment selection: Can validities be made generalizable? *Journal of Applied Psychology, 75,* 175–184.

Rouleau, E. J., & Krain, B. F. (1975). Using job analysis to design selection procedures. *Public Personnel Management, 4,* 300–304.

Rowe, P. M. (1989). Unfavorable information and interview decisions. In R. W. Eder, & G. R. Ferris (Eds.), *The employment interview* (pp. 77–89). Newbury Park, CA: Sage Publications.

Rubin, J. Z., & Brown, B. R. (1975). *The social psychology of bargaining and negotiation.* New York: Academic Press.

Rubin, J. Z., & Lewecki, R. J. (1973). A three-factor experimental analysis of promises and threats. *Journal of Applied Social Psychology, 3,* 240–257.

Rupert, G. (1989). Employee referrals as a source of recruitment and job performance. *Proceedings of 10th Annual Graduate Conference in Industrial/Organizational Psychology and Organizational Behavior.*

Russ-eft, D., & Zucchelli, L. (1987). When wrong is all right. *Training and Development Journal, 41*(11), 78–79.

Rynes, S. L., & Miller, H. E. (1983). Recruiter and job influences on candidates for employment. *Journal of Applied Psychology, 68,* 147–154.

Saal, F. E. (1979). Mixed standard rating scale: A consistent system for numerically coding inconsistent response combinations. *Journal of Applied Psychology, 64,* 422–428.

Sackett, P. R., Burris, L. R., & Callahan, C. (1989). Integrity testing for personnel selection: An update. *Personnel Psychology, 42,* 491–528.

Salancik, G., & Pfeffer, J. (1977). An examination of need-satisfaction models of job satisfaction and job attitudes. *Administrative Science Quarterly, 22,* 427–456.

Sanders, G. S. (1981). Driven by distraction: An integrative review of social facilitation theory and research. *Journal of Experimental Social Psychology, 17,* 227–251.

Sandler, L. (1986). Self-fulfilling prophecy: Better management by magic. *Training, 23,* 60–64.

Savage, J. I. (1988). Study refires VDT safety debate: Shows link between heavy use and miscarriages. *Computerworld, 22*(6), 1–2.

Sawyer, A. (1973). The effects of repetition or refutational and supportive advertising appeals. *Journal of Marketing Research, 10,* 23–33.

Scandura, T. A., Graen, G. B., & Novak, M. A. (1986). When managers decide not to decide autocratically: An investigation of leader–member exchange and decision influence. *Journal of Applied Psychology, 71,* 579–584.

Schatzki, M. (1981). *Negotiation.* New York: Signet.

Schein, E. (1956). The Chinese indoctrination program for prisoners of war. *Psychiatry, 19,* 149–177.

Schmidt, F. L. (1971). The relative efficiency of regression and simple unit predictor weights in applied differential psychology. *Educational and Psychological Measurement, 31,* 699–714.

Schmidt, F. L. (1973). Implications of a measurement problem for expectancy theory research. *Organizational Behavior and Human Performance, 10,* 243–251.

Schmidt, F. L., Gast-Rosenberg, I., & Hunter, J. E. (1980). Validity generalization results for computer programmers. *Journal of Applied Psychology, 65,* 643–661.

Schmidt, F. L., Greenthal, A. L., Hunter, J. E., Berner, J. G., & Seaton, F. W. (1977). Job sample vs. paper and pencil trades and technical tests: Adverse impact and examinee attitudes. *Personnel Psychology, 30,* 187–197.

Schmidt, F. L., & Hunter, J. E. (1978). Moderator research and the law of small numbers. *Personnel Psychology, 31,* 215–232.

Schmidt, F. L., & Hunter, J. E. (1981). Employment testing: Old theories and new research. *American Psychologist, 36,* 1128–1137.

Schmidt, F. L., Hunter, J. E., Pearlman, K., & Hirsh, H. R. (1985). Forty questions about validity generalization and meta-analysis. *Personnel Psychology, 38,* 697–798.

Schmitt, N., & Cohen, S. A. (1989). Internal analyses of task ratings by job incumbents. *Journal of Applied Psychology, 74,* 96–104.

Schmitt, N., Coyle, B. W., & Rauschenberger, J. (1977). A Monte Carlo evaluation of three formula estimates of cross-validated multiple correlation. *Psychological Bulletin, 84,* 751–758.

Schmitt, N., & DeGregorio, M. (1986). Results of society survey. *The Industrial/ Organizational Psychologist, 23*(4), 27–34.

Schmitt, N., Gooding, R. Z., Noe, R. A., & Kirsch, M. (1984). Meta-analysis of validity studies published between 1964 and 1982 and the investigation of study characteristics. *Personnel Psychology, 37,* 407–421.

Schneier, C. E., Guthrie, J. P., & Olian, J. D. (1988). A practical approach to conducting and using the training needs assessment. *Public Personnel Management, 17,* 191–205.

Schramm, W. (1962). Learning from instructional television. *Review of Educational Research, 32,* 156–157.

Schriesheim, C. A., & DeNisi, A. S. (1981). Task dimensions as moderators of the effects of instrumental leadership: A two-sample replicated test of path–goal leadership theory. *Journal of Applied Psychology, 66,* 589–597.

Schriesheim, J. F., & Schriesheim, C. A. (1980). A test of the path–goal theory of leadership and some suggested directions for future research. *Personnel Psychology, 33,* 349–370.

Schultz, R. (1976). Effects of control and predictability on the physical and psychological well-being of the institutionalized aged. *Journal of Personality and Social Psychology, 33,* 563–573.

Schwab, D. P. & Heneman, H., G. (1969). Relationship between interview structure and inter-interviewer reliability in an employment situation. *Journal of Applied Psychology, 53,* 214–217.

Schwab, D. P., Heneman, H. G., & DeCotiis, T. A. (1975). Behaviorally anchored rating scales: A review of the literature. *Personnel Psychology, 28,* 549–562.

Schwartz, B., & Barsky, S. (1977). The home advantage. *Social Forces, 55,* 641–666.

Schweitzer, S. C. (1979). *Winning with deception and bluff.* Englewood Cliffs, NJ: Prentice-Hall.

Scott, D., & Markham, S. (1982). Absenteeism control methods: A survey of practice and results. *Personnel Administrator, 27*(6), 73–84.

Scott, K. D., Markham, S. E., & Roberts, R. W. (1985). Rewarding good attendance: A comparative study of positive ways to reduce absenteeism. *Personnel Administrator, 30,* 72–75.

Scott, W. D. (1903). *The theory of advertising.* Boston: Small Maynard.

Seitz, D. D., & Modica, A. J. (1980). *Negotiating your way to success.* New York: Mentor.

Serlin, R. C., & Lapsley, D. K. (1985). Rationality in psychological research: The good-enough principle. *American Psychologist, 40,* 73–83.

Seta, J. J. (1982). The impact of comparison processes on coactor's task performance. *Journal of Personality and Social Psychology, 42,* 281–291.

Shaffer, D. R., & Tomarelli, M. (1981). Bias in the ivory tower: An unintended consequence of the Buckley Amendment for graduate admissions. *Journal of Applied Psychology, 66,* 7–11.

Shapira, Z., & Shirom, A. (1980). New issues in the use of behaviorally anchored rating scales: Level of analysis, the effects of incident frequency, and external validation. *Journal of Applied Psychology, 65,* 517–523.

Shaw, M. E., & Shaw, I. M. (1962). Some effects of social grouping upon learning in a second grade classroom. *Journal of Social Psychology, 57,* 453–458.

Shneiderman, B. (1980). *Software psychology: Human factors in computer and information systems.* Cambridge, MA: Winthrop Publishing.

Sieber, J. E., & Saks, M. J. (1989). A census of subject pool characteristics and policies. *American Psychologist, 44*(7), 1053–1061.

Sieling, M. S. (1984). Staffing patterns prominent in female–male earnings gap. *Monthly Labor Review, 107*(6), 29–30.

Simonton, D. K. (1979). Multiple discovery and invention: Zeitgeist, genius, or chance? *Journal of Personality and Social Psychology, 37,* 1603–1616.

Sims, R. R., Veres, J. G., & Heninger, S. M. (1987). Training appraisers: An orientation program for improving supervisory performance ratings. *Public Personnel Management, 16,* 37–46.

Sims, R. R., Veres, J. G., & Heninger, S. M. (1989). Training for competence. *Public Personnel Management, 18,* 101–107.

Skinner, B. F. (1938). *The behavior of organizations.* New York: Appleton.

Skinner, B. F. (1969). *Contingencies of reinforcement.* New York: Appleton-Century-Crofts.

Smart, R. (1965). Social group membership, leadership, and birth order. *Journal of Social Psychology, 67,* 221–225.

Smith, C., Reilly, C., & Midkiff, K. (1988, August). *Psychometric evaluation of circadian rhythm questionnaires with suggestions for improvement.* Paper presented at annual meeting of American Psychological Association, Atlanta, GA.

Smith, D. E. (1986). Training programs for performance appraisal: A review. *Academy of Management Review, 11,* 22–40.

Smith, J. E., & Hakel, M. D. (1979). Covergence among data sources, response bias, and reliability and validity of a structured job analysis questionnaire. *Personnel Psychology, 32,* 677–692.

Smith, M. J., Cohen, B. G., & Stammerjohn, L. W. (1981). An investigation of health complaints and job stress in video display operations. *Human Factors, 23*(4), 387–400.

Smith, P. C., & Kendall, L. M. (1963). Retranslating expectations: An approach to the construction of unambiguous anchors for rating scales. *Journal of Applied Psychology, 47,* 149–155.

Smith, P. C., Kendall, L. M., & Hulin, C. L. (1969). *The measurement of satisfaction in work and retirement.* Chicago: Rand McNally.

Smither, J. W., Barry, S. R., & Reilly, R. R. (1989). An investigation of the validity of expert true score estimates in appraisal research. *Journal of Applied Psychology, 74,* 143–151.

Smither, J. W., Reilly, R. R., & Buda, R. (1988). Effect of prior performance information on ratings of recent performance: Contrast versus assimilation revisited. *Journal of Applied Psychology, 73,* 487–496.

Smither, R., & Lindgren, H. C. (1978). Salary, age, sex, and need for achievement in bank employees. *Psychological Reports, 42,* 334.

Snyman, J. (1990). *The fakeability of honesty tests.* Unpublished master's thesis, Radford University, Radford, VA.

Society for Industrial and Organizational Psychology. (1986). *Graduate training programs in I/O psychology and organizational behavior.* College Park, MD: Author.

Sonnemann, U., & Kernan, J. (1962). Handwriting analysis—a valid selection tool? *Personnel, 39,* 8–14.

Sorcher, M., & Spence, R. (1982). The Interface Project: Behavior modeling as social technology in South Africa. *Personnel Psychology, 35,* 557–581.

Speroff, B., & Kerr, W. (1952). Steel mill "hot strip" accidents and interpersonal desirability values. *Journal of Clinical Psychology, 8,* 89–91.

Spitzer, D. (1986). Five keys to successful training. *Training, 23*(6), 37–39.

Spock, G., & Stevens, S. (1985). A test of Anderson's averaging versus adding model on résumé evaluations. *Proceedings of 6th Annual Graduate Conference in Industrial/Organizational Psychology and Organizational Behavior,* pp. 95–96.

Spool, M. D. (1978). Training programs for observers of behavior: A review. *Personnel Psychology, 31,* 853–888.

Springbett, B. M. (1958). Factors affecting the final decision in the employment interview. *Canadian Journal of Psychology, 12,* 13–22.

Srinivas, S., & Motowidlo, S. J. (1987). Effects of rater's stress on the dispersion and favorability of performance ratings. *Journal of Applied Psychology, 72,* 247–251.

Stafford, E. M., Jackson, P. R., & Banks, M. H. (1984). An empirical study of occupational families in the youth labor market. *Journal of Occupational Psychology, 57,* 141–155.

Stagner, R. (1958). The gullibility of personnel managers. *Personnel Psychology, 11,* 347–352.

Stagner, R., & Rosen, H. (1965). *Psychology of union–management relations.* Monterey, CA: Brooks/Cole.

Stahl, M. J. (1983). Achievement, power, and managerial motivation: Selecting managerial talent with the job choice exercise. *Personnel Psychology, 36,* 775–789.

Stahl, M. J., & Harrell, A. M. (1981). Modeling effort decisions with behavioral decision theory: Toward an individual differences model of expectancy theory. *Organizational Behavior and Human Performance, 27,* 303–325.

Stahl, M. J., & Harrell, A. M. (1982). Evolution and validation of a behavioral decision theory measurement approach to achievement, power, and affiliation. *Journal of Applied Psychology, 67,* 744–751.

Staw, B. M., Bell, N. E., & Clausen, J. A. (1986). The dispositional approach to job attitudes: A lifetime longitudinal test. *Administrative Science Quarterly, 31,* 56–77.

Staw, B. M., & Ross, J. (1985). Stability in the midst of change: A dispositional approach to job attitudes. *Journal of Applied Psychology, 70,* 469–480.

Stead, W. H., & Shartle, C. L. (1940). *Occupational counseling techniques.* New York: American Book Co.

Steadham, S. V. (1980). Learning to select a needs assessment strategy. *Training and Development Journal, 30*(1), 56–61.

Steil, L. K. (1980). *Your personal listening profile.* Great Neck, NY: Sperry Corp.

Steiner, I. D. (1972). *Group process and productivity.* New York: Academic Press.

Stogdill, R. M. (1948). Personal factors associated with leadership. *Journal of Psychology, 23,* 36–71.

Stone, D. L., Gueutal, H. G., & McIntosh, B. (1984). The effects of feedback sequence and expertise of the rater on performance feedback accuracy. *Personnel Psychology, 37,* 487–506.

Storer, T. S. (1986). Technical training by videotape. *Training, 23*(7), 27–30.

Strauss, G. (1967). Related instruction: Basic problems and issues. In *Research in apprentice training.* Madison: University of Wisconsin, Center for Vocational and Technical Education.

Strauss, G. (1971). *Union policies and the admission of apprenticeships.* Reprint No. 357. Berkeley: University of California Press.

Strube, M. J., & Garcia, J. E. (1981). A meta-analytic investigation of Fiedler's contingency model of leadership effectiveness. *Psychological Bulletin, 90,* 307–321.

Suedfeld, P., & Rank, A. D. (1976). Revolutionary leaders: Long-term success as a function of changes in conceptual complexity. *Journal of Personality and Social Psychology, 34,* 169–178.

Sundstrom, E., Burt, R. E., & Kamp, D. (1980). Privacy at work: Architectural correlates of job satisfaction and job performance. *Academy of Management Journal, 23,* 101–117.

Surrette, M. A. (1988). *Effect of amount of information and job analysis experience on the reliability and convergent validity of job analysis ratings.* Unpublished master's thesis, Radford University, Radford, VA.

Surrette, M. A. (1989). Ranking I/O graduate programs on the basis of student research presentations. *The Industrial/Organizational Psychologist, 26*(3), 41–44.

Sutton, H. W., & Porter, L. W. (1968). A study of the grapevine in a governmental organization. *Personnel Psychology, 21,* 223–230.

Swaroff, P. G., Bass, A. R., & Barclay, L. A. (1985). Recruiting sources: Another look. *Journal of Applied Psychology, 70,* 720–728.

Sweetland, R. C., & Keyser, D. J. (1983). *Tests.* Kansas City, MO: Test Corp. of America.

Tanaka, M., Tochihara, Y., Yamazaki, S., Ohnaka, T., & Yoshida, K. (1983). Thermal reaction and manual performance during cold exposure while wearing cold-protective clothing. *Ergonomics, 26,* 141–149.

Tanford, S., & Penrod, S. (1984). Social influence model: A formal integration of research on majority and minority influence processes. *Psychological Bulletin, 95,* 189–225.

Taylor, H. C., & Russell, J. T. (1939). The relationship of validity coefficients to the practical effectiveness of tests in selection: Discussion and tables. *Journal of Applied Psychology, 23,* 565–578.

Taylor, L. R. (1978). Empirically derived job families as a foundation for the study of validity generalization. Study 1. The construction of job families based on the component and overall dimensions of the PAQ. *Personnel Psychology, 31,* 325–340.

Taylor, M. S., & Schmidt, D. W. (1983). A process-oriented investigation of recruitment source effectiveness. *Personnel Psychology, 36,* 343–354.

Tedeschi, J. T., Bonoma, T. V., & Schlenker, B. R. (1972). Influence, decision, and compliance. In J. T. Tedeschi (Ed.), *The social influence process* (pp. 346–418). Chicago: Aldine-Atherton.

Teichner, W. H., Arees, E., & Reilly, R. (1963). Noise and human performance. *Ergonomics, 6,* 83–97.

Telenson, P. A., Alexander, R. A., & Barrett, G. V. (1983). Scoring the biographical information blank: A comparison of three weighting techniques. *Applied Psychological Measurement, 7,* 73–80.

Terborg, J. R. (1977). Validation and extension of an individual differences model of work performance. *Organizational Behavior and Human Performance, 18,* 188–216.

Thayer, P. W. (1988). Some things non–I/O psychologists should know about I/O psychology. *The Industrial/Organizational Psychologist, 26*(1), 55–65.

Thomas, K. W. (1970). Conflict and conflict management. In M. D. Dunnette (Ed.), *Handbook of Industrial and Organizational Psychology.* Chicago: Rand McNally.

Thompson, D. E., & Thompson, T. A. (1982). Court standards for job analysis in test validation. *Personnel Psychology, 35,* 865–874.

Tolman, C. W. (1968). The role of the companion in social facilitation of animal behavior. In E. C. Simmel, R. A. Hoppe, & G. A. Milton (Eds.), *Social facilitation and initiative behavior* (pp. 33–54). Boston: Allyn & Bacon.

Trahiotis, C., & Robinson, D. E. (1979). Auditory psychophysics. *Annual Review of Psychology, 30,* 31–61.

Trinkaus, J. W. (1986). Perceived hazard of video display terminals: An informal look. *Perceptual and Motor Skills, 62,* 118.

Triplett, N. (1898). The dynamogenic factors in pacemaking and competition. *American Journal of Psychology, 9,* 507–533.

Tubbs, M. E. (1986). Goal setting: A meta-analytic examination of the empirical evidence. *Journal of Applied Psychology, 71,* 474–483.

Twomey, D. P. (1986). *A concise guide to employment law.* Cincinnati, OH: Southwestern Publishing.

Tysinger, A., & Pitchford, L. (1988, April). *A readability index for trait based psychological tests.* Paper presented at 9th Annual Graduate Conference in Industrial/Organizational Psychology and Organizational Behavior, Toledo, OH.

Uhrbrock, R. S. (1961). Music on the job: Its influence on worker morale and production. *Personnel Psychology, 14,* 9–38.

Ulrich, E. (1957). Zur frage der belastung des arbeitenden menschen durch nacht-und shicktarbeit. *Psychologische Rundschar, 8,* 42–61.

Ulrich, L., & Trumbo, D. (1965). The selection interview since 1949. *Psycholocigal Bulletin, 63,* 100–116.

U.S. Department of Labor (April, 1989). *News.* Washington, D.C.: Author.

Vander Velden, L. (1971). *Relationships among member, team, and situational variables and basketball team success.* Unpublished doctoral dissertation, University of Wisconsin, Madison, WI.

Van Leeuwen, M., Frizzell, M. D., & Nail, P. R. (1987, April). *An examination of gender differences in response to threatening communications.* Paper presented at annual meeting of Oklahoma Psychological Association, Oklahoma City, OK.

Van Zelt, R. H. (1952). Sociometrically selected work teams increase production. *Personnel Psychology, 5,* 175–186.

Veglahn, P. A. (1989). Drug testing that clears the arbitration hurdle. *Personnel Administrator, 34*(2), 62–64.

Verhaegen, P., Cober, R., de Smedt, M., & Dirkx, J. (1987). The adaptation of night nurses to different work schedules. *Ergonomics, 30,* 1301–1309.

Vernon, H. M. (1936). *Accidents and their prevention.* London: Cambridge University Press.

Vernon, H. M., & Warner, C. G. (1932). Objective and subjective tests for noise. *Personnel Journal, 11,* 141–149.

Vroom, V., & Yetton, P. W. (1973). *Leadership and decision making.* Pittsburgh, PA: University of Pittsburgh Press.

Vroom, V. H. (1964). *Work and motivation.* New York: John Wiley & Sons.

Wahba, M. A., & Bridwell, L. T. (1976). Maslow reconsidered: A review of research on the need of hierarchy theory. *Organizational Behavior and Human Performance, 15,* 212–240.

Wainer, H. (1976). Estimating coefficients in linear models: It don't make no nevermind. *Psychological Bulletin, 83,* 213–217.

Wakabayashi, M., & Graen, G. B. (1984). The Japanese career progress study: A seven-year follow-up. *Journal of Applied Psychology, 69,* 603–614.

Waldman, D. A., & Avolio, B. J. (1986). A meta-analysis of age differences in job performance. *Journal of Applied Psychology, 71,* 33–38.

Walster, E., Aronson, E., & Abrahams, D. (1966). On increasing the persuasiveness of a low prestige communicator. *Journal of Experimental Social Psychology, 2,* 325–342.

Walton, E. (1961). How efficient is the grapevine? *Personnel, 28,* 45–49.

Wanous, J. P. (1980). *Organizational entry: Recruitment, selection, and socialization of newcomers.* Reading, MA: Addison-Wesley.

Wanous, J. P., & Zwany, A. (1977). A cross-sectional test of need hierarchy theory. *Organizational Behavior and Human Performance, 18,* 78–97.

Ward, E. A. (1989). Field study of job knowledge, job satisfaction, intention to turnover, and ratings of simulated performance. *Psychological Reports, 64,* 179–188.

Weaver, C. N. (1978). Job satisfaction as a component of happiness among males and females. *Personnel Psychology, 31,* 831–840.

Webster, E. D. (1964). *Decision making in the employment interview.* Montreal: Eagle.

Wedderburn, A. A. (1978). Some suggestions for increasing the usefulness of psychological and sociological studies of shiftwork. *Ergonomics, 21,* 827–833.

Weekley, J. A., & Geier, J. A. (1987). Reliability and validity of the situational interview for a sales position. *Journal of Applied Psychology, 72,* 484–487.

Weins, A. N., Jackson, R. H., Manaugh, T. S., & Matarazzo, J. D. (1969). Communication length as an index of communicator attitude: A replication. *Journal of Applied Psychology, 53,* 264–266.

Weinstein, N. D. (1977). Noise and intellectual performance: A confirmation and extension. *Journal of Applied Psychology, 62,* 104–107.

Weinstein, N. D. (1978). A longitudinal study in a college dormitory. *Journal of Applied Psychology, 63,* 458–466.

Weiss, H. M., Dawis, R. V., England, G. W., & Lofquist, L. H. (1967). *Manual for the Minnesota Satisfaction Questionnaire.* Minneapolis, MN: University of Minnesota, Industrial Relations Center.

Weiss, H. M., & Shaw, J. B. (1979). Social influences on judgments about tasks. *Organizational Behavior and Human Performance, 24,* 126–140.

Wernimont, P. F. (1962). Re-evaluation of a weighted application blank for office personnel. *Journal of Applied Psychology, 46,* 417–419.

Wernimont, P. F., & Campbell, J. P. (1968). Signs, samples and criteria. *Journal of Applied Psychology, 52,* 372–376.

Wexley, K. N., & Latham, G. A. (1981). *Developing and training human resources in organizations.* Glenview, IL: Scott, Foresman.

Wexley, K. N., Sanders, R. E., & Yukl, G. A. (1973). Training interviewers to eliminate contrast effects in employment interviews. *Journal of Applied Psychology, 57,* 233–236.

Wexley, K. N., Yukl, G. A., Kovacs, S. Z., & Sanders, R. E. (1972). Importance of contrast effects in employment interviews. *Journal of Applied Psychology, 56,* 45–48.

Whelchel, B. D. (1985). Use of performance tests to select craft apprentices. *Personnel Journal, 65*(7), 65–69.

Wherry, R. J., & South, J. C. (1977). A worker motivation scale. *Personnel Psychology, 30,* 613–636.

Whisler, T. L. (1958). Performance appraisal and the organization man. *Journal of Business, 31,* 19–27.

Whitcomb, A., & Bryan, D. (1988). Validity of the Peres and Garcia method of scoring letters of recommendation. *Proceedings of 9th Annual Graduate Conference in Industrial/Organizational Psychology and Organizational Behavior.*

Widgery, R., & Stackpole, C. (1972). Desk position, interviewee anxiety, and interviewer credibility: An example of cognitive balance in a dyad. *Journal of Counseling Psychology, 19,* 173–177.

Wiesner, W. H., & Cronshaw, S. F. (1988). A meta-analytic investigation of the impact of interview format and degree of structure on the validity of the employment interview. *Journal of Occupational Psychology, 61,* 275–290.

Williams, K., Harkins, S., & Latane, B. (1981). Identifiability as a deterrent to social loafing: Two cheering experiments. *Journal of Personality and Social Psychology, 40,* 303–311.

Williams, S. W., & Streit, T. (1986). Learner-driven sales training at Life of Virginia. *Training, 23*(2), 65–68.

Williamson, A. M., & Sanderson, J. W. (1986). Changing the speed of shift rotation: A field study. *Ergonomics, 29,* 1085–1089.

Willis, S. C., & Miller, T. A. (1987). Effectiveness of situation wanted advertisements as a means for obtaining job inquiries and offers. *Proceedings of 8th Annual Graduate Conference in Industrial/Organizational Psychology and Organizational Behavior,* pp. 177–178.

Wing, J. F. (1965). Upper tolerance limits for unimpaired mental performance. *Aerospace Medicine, 36,* 960–964.

Winter, D. G. (1988). What makes Jesse run? *Psychology Today, 22*(6), 20–24.

Wisdom, B., & Patzig, D. (1987). Does your organization have the right climate for merit? *Public Personnel Management, 16,* 127–133.

Wokoun, W. (1980). *A study of fatigue in industry.* New York: Muzak Board of Scientific Advisors.

Wolinsky, J. (1982). Beat the clock. *APA Monitor, 13,* 12.

Wood, R. F., Mento, A. J., & Locke, E. A. (1987). Task complexity as a moderator of goal effects: A meta-analysis. *Journal of Applied Psychology, 72,* 416–425.

Wyatt, S., & Marriot, R. (1953). Night work and shift changes. *British Journal of Industrial Medicine, 10,* 164–177.

Yager, E. (1980). When new hires don't make the grade: The case for assessment centers. *Personnel Journal, 59*(5), 387–390.

Yoder, D. (1962). *Personnel management and industrial relations* (5th ed.). Englewood Cliffs, NJ: Prentice-Hall.

Yoder, D., & Heneman, H. G. (1979). *Motivation and commitment: Wage and salary administration.* Washington, DC: American Society for Personnel Administration.

Young, D. M., & Beier, E. G. (1977). The role of applicant nonverbal communication in the employment interview. *Journal of Employment Counseling, 14,* 154–165.

Yukl, G. (1982, April). *Innovations in research on leader behavior.* Paper presented at annual meeting of Eastern Academy of Management, Baltimore, MD.

Yukl, G. A. (1989). *Leadership in organizations.* Englewood Cliffs, NJ: Prentice-Hall.

Zajonc, R. B. (1965). Social facilitation. *Science, 149,* 269–274.

Zajonc, R. B. (1980). Compressence. In P. B. Paulus (Ed.), *Psychology of group influence.* Hillsdale, NJ: Erlbaum.

Zajonc, R. B., Heingartner, A., & Herman, E. M. (1969). Social enhancement and impairment of performance in the cockroach. *Journal of Personality and Social Psychology, 13,* 83–92.

Zander, A. (1982). *Making groups effective.* San Francisco: Jossey-Bass.

Zaremba, A. (1988). Working with the organizational grapevine. *Personnel Journal, 67*(6), 38–42.

Zdep, S. M., & Weaver, H., B. (1967). The graphoanalytic approach to selecting life insurance salesman. *Journal of Applied Psychology, 51,* 295–299.

Zuboff, S. (1982). New worlds of computer-mediated work. *Harvard Business Review, 60*(5), 142–152.

Zweigenhaft, R. L. (1976). Personal space in the faculty office: Desk placement and the student–faculty interaction. *Journal of Applied Psychology, 61,* 529–532.

Name Index

Subject Index